1995
The Supreme Court Review

1995
The

"Judges as persons, or courts as institutions, are entitled to
no greater immunity from criticism than other persons
or institutions . . . [J]udges must be kept mindful of their limitations and
of their ultimate public responsibility by a vigorous
stream of criticism expressed with candor however blunt."
—*Felix Frankfurter*

". . . while it is proper that people should find fault when
their judges fail, it is only reasonable that they should recognize the
difficulties. . . . Let them be severely brought to book,
when they go wrong, but by those who will take the trouble
to understand them."
—*Learned Hand*

THE LAW SCHOOL

THE UNIVERSITY OF CHICAGO

Supreme Court Review

EDITED BY

DENNIS J. HUTCHINSON

DAVID A. STRAUSS

AND GEOFFREY R. STONE

 THE UNIVERSITY OF CHICAGO PRESS

CHICAGO AND LONDON

INTERNATIONAL STANDARD BOOK NUMBER: 0-226-36312-0

LIBRARY OF CONGRESS CATALOG CARD NUMBER: 60-14353

THE UNIVERSITY OF CHICAGO PRESS, CHICAGO 60637

THE UNIVERSITY OF CHICAGO PRESS, LTD., LONDON

© 1996 BY THE UNIVERSITY OF CHICAGO, ALL RIGHTS RESERVED, PUBLISHED 1996

PRINTED IN THE UNITED STATES OF AMERICA

The paper used in this publication meets the minimum requirements of American National Standard for Information Sciences–Permanence of Paper for Printed Library Materials, ANSI Z39.48-1984. ♾

FOR

MIKE

*"They helped every one his
neighbor, and every one said to
his brother, Be of good courage"*

CONTENTS

DAVID A. STRAUSS

AFFIRMATIVE ACTION AND
THE PUBLIC INTEREST

The first affirmative action case came before the Supreme Court more than twenty years ago.[1] In that time, several basic issues have been resolved. Some early intimations that affirmative action might sometimes be required by the Constitution have been firmly rejected and have not reappeared.[2] The opposite view, that affirmative action is essentially always unconstitutional, has been rejected

David A. Strauss is Harry N. Wyatt Professor of Law, The University of Chicago.

AUTHOR'S NOTE: I thank Elizabeth Garrett, Tracey Meares, Lawrence Rosenthal, Louis Michael Seidman, Cass Sunstein, and the participants in a workshop at the University of Chicago Law School for their comments on an earlier draft, and Peter Rutledge, Zoe Milak, and Carol Harper for both research assistance and helpful comments. The Russell Baker Scholars Fund and the Lee and Brena Freeman Faculty Fund at the University of Chicago Law School provided financial support. To discount for possible bias, the reader should know that I participated as counsel for parties supporting affirmative action in some of the cases mentioned in this article.

[1] *DeFunis v Odegaard*, 416 US 312 (1974), was the first case to come to the Court that was generally regarded as an "affirmative action" case, so-called. Earlier cases presented similar issues, however. See note 2, text at notes and notes 54–57.

[2] For example, in a separate opinion in *Keyes v School Dist No 1*, 413 US 189, 217–53 (1973), Justice Powell called for abandoning the distinction between de facto and de jure segregation and suggested that any school district in which there was substantial segregation had an obligation to "pursu[e] an affirmative policy of desegregation" whether or not the segregation was traceable to intentional government actions. Id at 236. This amounts to saying that school districts have an obligation to adopt race-conscious policies to aid minorities. Also, before *Washington v Davis*, 426 US 229 (1976), several Supreme Court cases had suggested, and some lower courts had ruled, that the Constitution forbade measures, however properly motivated, that imposed disproportionate burdens on minorities. See id at 242–43, 244 n 12. This is equivalent to saying that in some circumstances the Constitution requires the government to take racially conscious actions to aid minorities. See John Hart Ely, *Legislative and Administrative Motivation in Constitutional Law*, 79 Yale L J 1205, 1259–61 (1970). *Washington v Davis* of course rejected this view. See 426 US at 244–45. See also the discussion of the school desegregation cases, text at notes and notes 54–57.

many times, although it continues to have adherents among the Justices.[3] And the Court has not accepted the position that affirmative action should be routinely upheld whenever governments choose to engage in it.[4]

Last Term's decision in *Adarand Constructors, Inc. v Pena*,[5] together with *City of Richmond v J.A. Croson Co.*,[6] decided in 1989, was viewed by many as resolving, for now at least, perhaps the last important unanswered question about government affirmative action programs. Those cases held that affirmative action measures will be constitutional only if they satisfy "strict scrutiny," that is, only if they "promote a compelling state interest" and are "necessary" or "narrowly tailored" to that objective.[7] *Croson* adopted that standard for laws enacted by state and local governments; *Adarand* extended it to federal affirmative action measures.

"Strict scrutiny" applies to laws discriminating against minorities as well. In fact the Court, last Term in particular, was emphatic that the same standard should apply to all laws that differentiate on the basis of race, whether or not they purport to favor minorities. But laws discriminating against minorities are essentially always unconstitutional. None has ever been upheld, except by cases that are now discredited. And the Court has made clear, not least in last Term's case, that affirmative action measures will be upheld more often than that.[8] So the equivalence in standards seems, to some degree at least, nominal.

There are more difficulties. If "strict scrutiny" isn't a euphemism for automatic unconstitutionality, then the crucial questions are how precisely "tailored" the law must be, and what will count as a "compelling interest." At times the Court has suggested (although it has never held) that the only compelling interest that can justify affirmative action is remedying discrimination in a specific

---

[3] See *Adarand Constructors, Inc. v Pena*, 115 S Ct 2097, 2119 (1995) (Thomas concurring); *City of Richmond v J.A. Croson Co.*, 488 US 469, 524–28 (Scalia concurring).

[4] This position is urged in, for example, John Hart Ely, *The Constitutionality of Reverse Racial Discrimination*, 41 U Chi L Rev 723 (1974).

[5] 115 S Ct 2097 (1995).

[6] 488 US 469 (1989).

[7] *Adarand*, 115 S Ct at 2112–13; *Croson*, 488 US at 498–508; id at 493–98 (plurality opinion).

[8] See, for example, 115 S Ct at 2117 ("[W]e wish to dispel the notion that strict scrutiny is 'strict in theory, but fatal in fact.' "). See also *Croson*, 488 US at 509.

context, such as a particular employment market. Remedying more general "societal" discrimination is not sufficient.[9] But why aren't nonremedial interests—having a diverse academic setting or work-force, or an effective police force, or a minority population that is more integrated into the economic mainstream, for example—sufficiently compelling? For that matter, if "compelling" is really the standard, why isn't remedying society-wide discrimination at least as important as remedying more localized discrimination? On the other hand, in just what sense is affirmative action ever really a "remedy," when it usually takes the form of broad-based measures that benefit members of a minority group generally, with little or no effort to identify those who have been the victims of specific acts of discrimination?

Despite all these difficulties, the Court's resolution of the affirmative action issue may actually be more definitive and coherent than it appears. That is not to say that it is the right resolution, or that it will survive. But what the Court has done is to revive, in the area of affirmative action, one of the noble dreams of American public law—that courts should try to ensure that legislation does not just benefit narrow interest groups but instead serves a public interest. This dream has at times turned into what would generally be thought a nightmare, as in the *Lochner* era. The Court's selectivity, in dealing only with affirmative action laws (and perhaps a few others) in this way, is hard to defend. There are enormous theoretical and practical problems in trying to define a public interest, as distinguished from special interests. But however questionable, the Court's approach to affirmative action should be

---

[9] See, for example, *Croson*, 488 US at 497–98 (plurality opinion), quoting *Wygant v Jackson Bd. of Educ.*, 476 US 267, 276 (1986) (plurality opinion); *Croson*, 488 US at 499. *Croson* held that the government is not limited to remedying its own discrimination. 488 US at 492 (plurality opinion); id at 536 (Marshall, Brennan, and Blackmun dissenting). The prevailing opinion in *Croson* states that a government may use affirmative action if necessary to remedy a condition in which it "ha[s] essentially become a 'passive participant' in a system of racial exclusion practiced" by private parties. 488 US at 492. Beyond that, however, it appears that under *Croson* a unit of government may remedy any private "discriminatory practices within local commerce under its jurisdiction," id at 492, even if the unit of government is not implicated, even passively, in the discriminatory practices. See, for example, id at 509, citing *New York State Club Assn v New York City*, 487 US 1 (1988) (a case in which the unit of government was not in any obvious way a "passive participant"); *Roberts v United States Jaycees*, 468 US 609, 623 (1984) (referring to a state's "compelling interest in eradicating discrimination against its female citizens"); *Croson*, 488 US at 518 (Kennedy concurring) ("the State has the power to eradicate racial discrimination and its effects in both the public and private sectors").

understood, and evaluated, as the latest display of this undeniably attractive leitmotif of American law.

I. Strict Scrutiny for Affirmative Action?

A. THE ADARAND DECISION

Adarand Constructors, last Term's decision, involved a complex federal program that gave some federal contractors a financial incentive to let subcontracts to small businesses "owned and controlled by socially and economically disadvantaged individuals."[10] Certain minority groups, including African Americans and Hispanic Americans, were "presume[d]" to be socially and economically disadvantaged; the presumption could be overcome in a particular case.[11] *Adarand* was a suit by a firm that had lost a subcontract to a minority firm, allegedly because of the federal program. The Court treated the program as establishing a classification based on race.

The Court did not, however, reach any conclusion about the constitutionality of the program, a question it left for the lower courts on remand. Instead the opinions just addressed the abstract question of the standard that should apply to federal programs, and the Court concluded that federal affirmative action measures would have to satisfy strict scrutiny. The Court relied on *Croson* and overruled another decision, *Metro Broadcasting, Inc. v FCC*,[12] which had differentiated federal and state affirmative action and applied "intermediate scrutiny," a more lenient standard, to the former.

Whatever the merits of its conclusion, the *Adarand* opinion seems curiously deficient.[13] Justice O'Connor's opinion for the

---

[10] 115 S Ct at 2103 (internal quotations omitted).

[11] Id at 2103.

[12] 497 US 547 (1990).

[13] Even the designation of the opinions is odd. The bulk of Justice O'Connor's opinion is said to be "for the Court except insofar as it might be inconsistent with the views expressed in Justice Scalia's concurrence." 115 S Ct at 2101. (Justice Scalia stated that he "join[ed] the opinion of the Court . . . except insofar as it may be inconsistent with the following." Id at 2118.) An opinion like this does not provide litigants and lower courts with any more guidance than a plurality opinion does. But by calling it an opinion of the Court, the Court avoids acknowledging that it has been unable to agree on what the law is. Also, the concurring Justice is relieved from having to decide whether the prevailing opinion, even if not perfect in his view, is acceptable—or even in which particular respects it is acceptable.

Court details a series of cases holding that the standards of the Equal Protection Clause, which of course mentions only the states, apply equally to the federal government. *Metro Broadcasting*, accordingly, was "a surprising turn,"[14] and fit for overruling.

It is true that, since *Bolling v Sharpe*,[15] the Supreme Court has said in many cases that Equal Protection Clause standards apply to the federal government as well. But none of those cases involved affirmative action. In the area of affirmative action, *Metro Broadcasting*—far from being surprising—had been anticipated by Justice O'Connor's own prevailing opinion in *Croson*.[16] That opinion explained why in affirmative action cases, unlike other areas to which the Equal Protection Clause applies, the federal government should have more latitude than the states. *Croson* had to do this in order to distinguish *Fullilove v Klutznick*.[17] *Fullilove* upheld a federal affirmative action program without prescribing any particular standard of review. The Richmond, Virginia, affirmative action program that was invalidated in *Croson* had been patterned on the federal plan upheld in *Fullilove*, and Richmond urged that *Fullilove* controlled the case. Justice O'Connor's answer in *Croson* was that *Fullilove* did not control because it involved a federal program.

By treating the precedents this way, the Court was able to make its task easier than it should have been, in at least two respects. It deprived *Fullilove* of precedential significance without ever fully admitting that it was doing so.[18] And the Court was able to treat *Metro Broadcasting* as an outlier—"[b]y refusing to follow *Metro Broadcasting* . . . we do not depart from the fabric of the law; we restore it"[19]—when in fact *Metro Broadcasting* was not inconsistent with *Fullilove* (the only other case involving a federal affirmative action program) and was affirmatively supported by *Croson*'s treatment of *Fullilove*. The conclusion that federal and state affirmative action programs should be treated in the same way may be correct;

---

[14] Id at 2111.

[15] 347 US 497 (1954).

[16] See 488 US at 490–91.

[17] 448 US 448 (1980).

[18] The Court in *Adarand*, after discussing at length how *Metro Broadcasting* supposedly departed from established law, simply remarked: "Of course, it follows that to the extent (if any) that *Fullilove* held federal racial classifications to be subject to a less rigorous standard, it is no longer controlling." 115 S Ct at 2117.

[19] Id at 2116.

Justice O'Connor's suggestions to the contrary in *Croson* are not entirely convincing.[20] But that conclusion represents much more of a departure from previous decisions than the Court admits.

B. TWO KINDS OF "STRICT SCRUTINY"

The notion that racial classifications are subject to "strict scrutiny" derives from a case involving not affirmative action but discrimination against a minority group. *Korematsu v United States*,[21] which upheld the internment of Japanese Americans during World War II, proceeded from the ostensible premise that "all legal restrictions which curtail the civil rights of a single racial group are immediately suspect" and that "courts must subject [such laws] to the most rigid scrutiny."[22] Many of the landmarks in the development of the constitutional prohibition against discrimination, such as *Strauder v West Virginia*[23] and *Brown v Board of Education*,[24] did not use the language of strict scrutiny. But beginning in 1964, when *McLaughlin v Florida*[25] struck down a Jim Crow–era law forbidding interracial cohabitation, the Court came to use this standard in cases involving discrimination against minorities; in *McLaughlin* the Court formulated this standard as requiring that a racial classification be "necessary, and not merely rationally related" to an "overriding" government purpose.[26]

The problem is that this standard has been used in essentially two different ways in the cases. "Necessary" (or "narrowly tailored") to "promote a compelling state interest" might be given what could be called a "means-ends" interpretation: the law will

---

[20] Justice O'Connor's principal argument was that the Equal Protection Clause reflects "a distrust of state legislative enactments based on race." 488 US at 491 (plurality opinion); see id at 490–92. It is uncontroversial that the Equal Protection Clause reflected a concern that states would discriminate against African Americans, but to generalize that concern to a distrust of laws "based on race"—including laws favoring African Americans—requires additional argument of the kind that (as I argue below) the Court has not provided and does not really accept. See Part IC.

[21] 323 US 214 (1944).

[22] Id at 216.

[23] 100 US 303 (1879).

[24] 347 US 483 (1954).

[25] 379 US 184 (1964).

[26] Id at 196, 192. See also *Palmore v Sidoti*, 466 US 429, 432 (1984); *Crawford v Bd of Educ*, 458 US 527, 536 (1982); *Hunter v Erickson*, 393 US 385, 391–92 (1969); cf *Personnel Administrator v Feeney*, 442 US 256, 272 (1979).

be upheld if the government can show that the racial classification is an especially appropriate means to an important objective. If the same objective can be achieved nearly as well without using a racial classification, and at only slightly greater cost, then the classification will not be upheld; but otherwise it will be.

In several areas not involving racial discrimination, the Court has applied strict scrutiny in this way. For example, the Court sometimes uses a means-ends version of strict scrutiny in determining whether content-based restrictions on speech violate the First Amendment.[27] The Court has applied strict scrutiny, or a standard like it, in rejecting First Amendment challenges to restrictions on campaign expenditures and contributions, to disclosure requirements applied to contributors to political campaigns, to restrictions on access to the ballot, and to limits on the freedom of association.[28] Under the Free Exercise Clause, before *Employment Division v Smith*,[29] the Court sometimes applied strict scrutiny in evaluating neutral measures that restricted religious practices, and

---

[27] In *Simon & Schuster, Inc. v Members of New York State Crime Victims Bd.*, 502 US 105, 118–23 (1991), the Court applied strict scrutiny to invalidate a law on First Amendment grounds. But instead of treating the law as automatically invalid, the Court undertook a careful analysis of the ends (concluding that some were "compelling"; see id at 118–21) and the connection between means and ends (see id at 121–23). Significantly, Justice Kennedy, concurring only in the judgment, urged that the Court should not have applied strict scrutiny in this way but instead should have used a rule of automatic invalidity. Id at 124–28. In *Burson v Freeman*, 504 US 191, 198–211 (1992), a plurality of the Court, applying strict scrutiny, upheld a state law prohibiting certain campaign activities within 100 feet of a polling place. Finally, in *RAV v City of St. Paul*, 505 US 377, 393–96 (1992), the Court again appeared to apply a means-ends version of strict scrutiny while invalidating a measure that forbade certain forms of so-called hate speech.

[28] See, for example, *Austin v Michigan Chamber of Commerce*, 494 US 652, 657–61 (1990) (holding that a restriction on corporate campaign expenditures was "narrowly tailored to serve a compelling state interest" (id at 657; see id at 660, 661)); *Buckley v Valeo*, 424 US 1, 24–29 (1976) (holding that a restriction on campaign contributions satisfied a "rigorous standard of review" (id at 29) because the government "demonstrate[d] a sufficiently important interest and employ[ed] means closely drawn to avoid unnecessary abridgment of associational freedoms" (id at 25)); *Buckley*, 424 US at 64–69 (upholding compelled disclosure requirement under a "strict test" (id at 66) that requires not just "some legitimate governmental interest" but "subordinating interests" that "survive exacting scrutiny" and have a " 'relevant correlation' or 'substantial relation' " to the information disclosed (id at 64; footnotes omitted)); *American Party of Texas v White*, 415 US 767, 779–88 (1974) (upholding certain ballot access restrictions whose "validity depends upon whether they are necessary to further compelling state interests" (id at 780)); *Roberts v United States Jaycees*, 468 US 609, 623 (1984) (citing cases) ("Infringements on" the "right to associate for expressive purposes" are "justified by regulations adopted to serve compelling state interests, unrelated to the suppression of ideas, that cannot be achieved through means significantly less restrictive of associational freedoms.").

[29] 494 US 872 (1990).

it often upheld such measures.[30] After *Smith*, Congress enacted the Religious Freedom Restoration Act, which required that strict scrutiny, apparently as defined in "prior Federal court rulings," be applied to such measures;[31] and the lower courts have sometimes upheld them.[32] There are other instances, as well, in which the Supreme Court has applied something like a means-ends version of strict scrutiny and has upheld measures on the ground that they were sufficiently well suited to promoting important objectives.[33]

This is not the way strict scrutiny has been applied in cases involving discrimination against racial minorities, however. In those cases, the standard "necessary to promote a compelling state interest" seems better described as a rule of automatic invalidity with an escape clause. Racial classifications will be invalid except in a truly extraordinary

[30] See, for example, *United States v Lee*, 455 US 252 (1982) (applying a standard that required a "showing that [a measure] is essential to accomplish an overriding governmental interest" (id at 257–58) to uphold a law requiring the collection of social security taxes from the Old Order Amish); *Bob Jones University v United States*, 461 US 574, 603–04 (1983) (upholding government's denial of a tax exemption to a racially discriminatory private school on the ground that "[t]he governmental interest at stake here is compelling" and "no 'less restrictive means' . . . are available to achieve the governmental interest" (id at 604; citation and footnote omitted)). See also *Hernandez v Commissioner*, 490 US 680, 699–700 (1989).

[31] Specifically, the RFRA reports a congressional "find[ing]" that "the compelling interest test set forth in prior Federal court rulings is a workable test for striking sensible balances between religious liberty and competing prior governmental interests" (42 USC 2000bb(a)(5) (Supp V 1993)). The Act then generally prohibits the government from "substantially burden[ing] a person's exercise of religion even if the burden results from a rule of general applicability" (42 USC 2000bb-1(a) (Supp V 1993)). A substantial burden is permitted, however, if the government demonstrates that the burden "(1) is in furtherance of a compelling governmental interest; and (2) is the least restrictive means for furthering that compelling governmental interest." 42 USC 20000bb-1(b) (Supp V 1993). See generally Sanford Levinson, *Identifying the Compelling State Interest: On "Due Process of Lawmaking" and the Professional Responsibility of the Public Lawyer*, 45 Hastings L J 1035 (1994).

[32] See, for example, *Fleischfresser v Directors of School Dist. 200*, 15 F3d 680, 692 (7th Cir 1994); *Council for Life Coalition v Reno*, 856 F Supp 1422, 1430 (S D Cal 1994).

[33] *Roe v Wade*, 410 US 113 (1973), applied strict scrutiny (see id at 155) to restrictions on abortion and held that certain such restrictions could be upheld in the second and third trimesters of pregnancy. See id at 162–64. The Court has also applied a standard resembling strict scrutiny in upholding measures challenged under the Fourth Amendment. See *Vernonia School Dist. 47J v Acton*, 115 S Ct 2386, 2395 ("That the nature of the [government's] concern is important—indeed, perhaps compelling—can hardly be doubted."); id ("[T]he efficacy of this means for addressing the problem . . . seems to us self-evident."); id at 2395–96 (concluding that no less intrusive means would be adequate). See also *National Treasury Employees Union v Von Raab*, 489 US 656, 672 (1989) (upholding certain warrantless searches on the ground that the government interest is "compelling"); *Skinner v Railway Labor Executives' Assn.*, 489 US 602, 628 (1989) (same). The Fourth Amendment cases do, however, involve an assessment of the significance of the intrusion, and therefore a more explicit balancing of the government's objectives against the invasion of constitutionally protected interests. See, for example, *Vernonia School Dist.*, 115 S Ct at 2394–95.

situation in which it is obviously imperative to classify by race. The only classification discriminating against minorities that has ever been upheld under "strict scrutiny" was the one in *Korematsu*.[34] And *Korematsu* now has the status—vigorously confirmed by *Adarand*—of an anti-precedent.[35] In any event, on the government's factual premises, which the Court accepted, *Korematsu* would qualify as a case in which the need for a racial classification was truly overwhelming and the escape clause could legitimately be invoked.

Ever since *Brown*, for measures discriminating against minorities, strict scrutiny has been, in a familiar phrase, " 'strict' in theory [but] fatal in fact."[36] There are occasional suggestions in the opinions that racial classifications discriminating against minorities might be permissible in certain extraordinary circumstances.[37] But the Court does not seriously inquire into the means-ends connection in cases involving discrimination against minorities.[38]

The constitutional law of race discrimination would look very different if the courts consistently used the means-ends version of strict scrutiny, instead of the "automatic invalidity" version. Racial

---

[34] In *Swain v Alabama*, 380 US 202, 227–28 (1965), the Court ruled that peremptory challenges based on race are not unconstitutional. But the ruling was carefully qualified; the Court did not explicitly apply strict scrutiny; and the case was later overruled by *Batson v Kentucky*, 476 US 79, 92–93 (1986). See also note 38 (discussing *United States v Brignoni-Ponce*, 422 US 873 (1975)).

[35] See Bruce Ackerman, *Constitutional Politics/Constitutional Law*, 99 Yale L J 453, 514 (1989) (using this term).

[36] Gerald Gunther, *The Supreme Court, 1971 Term—Foreword: In Search of Evolving Doctrine on a Changing Court: A Model for a Newer Equal Protection*, 86 Harv L Rev 1, 8 (1972).

[37] See, for example, *Lee v Washington*, 390 US 333, 334 (1968) (Black, Harlan, and Stewart concurring).

[38] The one clear instance of the Supreme Court's allowing race (or national origin) to be used as a basis for classifying people (since *Brown*) is *United States v Brignoni-Ponce*, 422 US 873, 886–87 (1975). *Brignoni-Ponce* ruled that law enforcement officers may use Mexican-American ancestry as a "relevant factor" (id at 887) in determining whether there is reasonable suspicion that a person is an undocumented alien.

The result in *Brignoni-Ponce* is consistent with the discussion in the text in the sense that the Court did not consider any Equal Protection issue in *Brignoni-Ponce* and so did not apply strict scrutiny. But it seems reasonably clear that *Brignoni-Ponce* represents a category of cases in which the courts would allow race or national origin to be used as a basis for classification—for example, if police officers seeking a suspect concentrate on individuals whose race matches the description given by a witness. Thus the prohibition on the use of racial generalizations is not as absolute as the cases suggest. But whatever accounts for the (presumed) willingness to allow the use of racial criteria in cases like this—perhaps the perceived importance of the interests on the other side, perhaps a sense that the underlying generalization is less likely to be the result of prejudice, perhaps the belief that the use of relatively unarticulated generalizations of this kind is less stigmatizing to minority groups— the Supreme Court shows no inclination to apply a means-ends version of strict scrutiny to racial classifications generally.

classifications discriminating against minorities might sometimes be, in the means-ends sense, necessary to promote a compelling state interest. This could happen in cases of rational statistical discrimination—if a racial generalization unfavorable to minorities is true enough so that it is the only way to achieve an important end at less-than-prohibitive costs. Suppose, for example, that minority teenagers who drive are, as a statistical matter, more likely to have accidents than nonminorities; and there is no test that can identify the specific drivers who will have accidents. A law raising the driving age from 17 to 21 for minorities only (leaving it at 17 for nonminorities) might be, in the means-ends sense, narrowly tailored to promoting a compelling state interest. The interest is avoiding either more accidents or the great costs and inconvenience of raising the driving age for everyone; the law is narrowly tailored because there is no other way of accomplishing these objectives.[39]

There is no reason to doubt that statistical racial generalizations of this kind will sometimes be true. The long history of racial discrimination alone practically ensures that some such generalizations will be true; they have been forced, as it were, on the minority population. But there is also no doubt that such a law would be unconstitutional. Oddly, it is hard to find a case squarely holding this. The cases forbidding the use of peremptory challenges on the basis of race repeatedly and vehemently disapprove the use of racial generalizations, without suggesting at all that their use might be allowed if they are accurate.[40] And in *Palmore v Sidoti*,[41]

---

[39] On the compelling nature of this interest, see, for example, *Skinner v Railway Labor Executives' Assn.*, 489 US 602, 628 (1989) (holding that the interest in preventing railway accidents is compelling); *Mackey v Montrym*, 443 US 1, 19 (1979) ("compelling interest in highway safety"); *South Dakota v Neville*, 459 US 553, 558–59 (1983) (same). The degree of "narrow tailoring" seems roughly comparable to that held sufficient in *Austin v Michigan Chamber of Commerce*, 494 US 652, 657–61 (1990); *United States v Lee*, 455 US 252, 257 (1982); and *Buckley v Valeo*, 424 US 1, 24–29 (1976).

[40] See, for example, *Georgia v McCollum*, 112 S Ct 2348, 2359 (1992); *Edmonson v Leesville Concrete Co.*, 500 US 614, 630 (1991); *Powers v Ohio*, 499 US 400, 410 (1991). See also *Hernandez v United States*, 500 US 352, 361 (1991) (plurality opinion). In *J.E.B. v Alabama ex rel T.B.*, 114 S Ct 1419 (1994), which forbade the use of gender-based peremptory challenges, the Court stated explicitly that generalizations about gender could not be used as the basis for peremptory challenges even if they were true to a degree. See id at 1427 n 11. For an account of why apparently accurate racial generalizations might not be trustworthy, see Linda Hamilton Krieger, *The Content of Our Categories: A Cognitive Bias Approach to Discrimination and Equal Employment Opportunity*, 47 Stan L Rev 1161 (1995). For an argument that the refusal to use accurate generalizations is justifiable as a form of affirmative action, see David A. Strauss, *The Myth of Colorblindness*, 1986 Supreme Court Review 99.

[41] 466 US 429, 433–34 (1984).

the Court unanimously disapproved the use of a generalization that it conceded might be accurate—that the children of an interracial couple might suffer a social stigma in their community—as a basis for a child custody determination, even though the interest in protecting the child's well-being surely qualifies as compelling, and there was no other way to do it. But in fact the very absence of cases might be the best indication. It is simply understood that racial generalizations, however accurate and however indispensable in achieving important ends, cannot be used as a basis for measures disadvantaging minorities.

In *Adarand* particularly, and in *Croson* as well, the Court made much of what it characterized as a principle of "consistency"— " 'the standard of review under the Equal Protection Clause is not dependent on the race of those burdened or benefited by a particular classification' . . . all racial classifications . . . must be strictly scrutinized."[42] But *Adarand* was almost as emphatic in saying that affirmative action is not always unconstitutional. The Court specifically denied that strict scrutiny, as it envisioned it, would be "strict in theory, but fatal in fact."[43] And a majority of the Court has repeatedly rejected invitations from separate opinions to declare affirmative action unconstitutional in all circumstances.[44] So while the nominal standards are the same, the actual standards are not. The actual standard for measures that discriminate against minorities is absolute invalidity, subject to an exception for truly extraordinary circumstances. The standard for affirmative action is not so restrictive.

C. THE PERILS OF "CONSISTENCY"

This should not be surprising. Notwithstanding the rhetoric of "consistency"—a question-begging term, since it is not inconsistent to treat things differently if they are materially different—and notwithstanding whatever questions might legitimately be raised about affirmative action, surely few people really believe that affirmative action is morally or constitutionally equivalent to discrimination against minority groups. The arguments are familiar

---

[42] *Adarand*, 115 S Ct at 2111, quoting *Croson*, 488 US at 494 (plurality opinion).

[43] *Adarand*, 115 S Ct at 2117.

[44] See id; *Croson*, 488 US at 509 (plurality opinion).

ones and were powerfully presented by Justice Stevens in his dissent in *Adarand*.[45] Racial discrimination against African Americans, of the kind that the original "strict scrutiny" standard was intended to uproot, inflicts harms that are qualitatively different from those inflicted on nonminorities by affirmative action. Discrimination against African Americans, not discrimination in their favor, was historically the central concern of the Civil War Amendments.

In other areas the point is clear enough: No one believes that providing the extra tax exemption for blind people is morally equivalent to deliberately imposing an extra tax burden on blind people. There is an argument, which I have not yet considered, that affirmative action, despite its pretensions, inflicts harms on minority groups and should be regarded as just a disguised form of old-fashioned discrimination against them.[46] But that is an argument that affirmative action should be disapproved because it is actually a form of discrimination against minorities. The "consistency" idea is that discrimination in favor of minorities is equally troublesome as old-fashioned discrimination against minorities. That idea is implausible.

In general the notion of "consistency" used in *Adarand* and *Croson* would lead to implausible, even bizarre, conclusions. Legislation is subject to strict scrutiny if it classifies on the basis of membership in a "suspect class." The usual reasons for concluding that a group is a suspect class are that the group has historically been discriminated against; that the group is the victim of widespread prejudice, so that legislation against it is more likely to reflect prejudice than legitimate concerns; and that the group has dispropor-

---

[45] See 115 S Ct at 2120–31.

[46] This may be the best way to understand several of the cases in which the Supreme Court has invalidated classifications that discriminate on the basis of gender. In many of those cases, the immediate effect of the classification was to injure men, not women. See, for example, *Orr v Orr*, 440 US 268 (1979); *Craig v Boren*, 429 US 190 (1976). The Court has occasionally allowed such classifications on the ground that they compensate for past discrimination against women. See, for example, *Califano v Webster*, 430 US 313 (1977); *Schlesinger v Ballard*, 419 US 498 (1975). But the Court has not permitted such classifications when they, for example, "tend[] to perpetuate the stereotyped view of nursing as an exclusively woman's job." *Mississippi University for Women v Hogan*, 458 US 718, 729 (1982) (footnote omitted). See also *Orr*, 440 US at 283; *Craig*, 429 US at 220 & n 2 (Rehnquist dissenting). That is, laws that superficially confer concrete advantages on women (as affirmative action measures do for minorities) are unconstitutional if (and, perhaps, only if) they actually reinforce unfavorable stereotypes of women or otherwise redound to their long-term disadvantage.

tionately little power in the political process.[47] But under the "consistency" logic of *Adarand* and *Croson*, the conclusion that a group has suffered from these disabilities means that the government's power to *help* that group is restricted—far more restricted than its power to enact legislation favoring groups who suffer none of these disadvantages.

The Court has never ruled, for example, that homosexuals are a suspect class. Today, therefore, affirmative action legislation favoring homosexuals would be treated the same as legislation favoring, say, optometrists, or any other group: all such legislation is almost automatically constitutional under the rational basis standard.[48] But suppose the Court were to decide that the extent of prejudice against homosexuals is sufficiently great, and their political power is sufficiently limited, to warrant declaring homosexuality a suspect classification. Under *Adarand* and *Croson*, that decision would automatically make it much more difficult to enact legislation favoring homosexuals than to favor optometrists or tobacco farmers. In other words, under the "consistency" principle, the decision that homosexuals have historically been discriminated against, are currently the victims of prejudice, and lack political power would yield the conclusion that legislation seeking to *aid* homosexuals is subject to strict scrutiny and generally unconstitutional. This cannot possibly be the right approach.

The underlying problem with the Court's "consistency" principle is that it confuses two different reasons for opposing racial (or ethnic, or religious) classifications.[49] One is that those classifications are a means by which a dominant group oppresses a subordinate group. That is of course the setting in which the American

---

[47] These reasons derive from *United States v Carolene Products Co.*, 304 US 144, 152–53 n 4 (1938), and are applied in, for example, *Cleburne v Cleburne Living Center*, 473 US 432, 443–46 (1985); *Massachusetts v Murgia*, 427 US 307, 313–14 (1976); *San Antonio Ind School Dist. v Rodriguez*, 411 US 1, 28 (1973); *Graham v Richardson*, 403 US 365, 373 (1971); *Frontiero v Richardson*, 411 US 677, 684–87 (1973) (plurality opinion). See generally John Hart Ely, *Democracy and Distrust* ch 4 (Harvard University Press, 1980).

[48] See *Williamson v Lee Optical*, 348 US 483, 489 (1955), quoted in *FCC v Beach Communications, Inc.*, 113 S Ct 2096, 2102–03 (1993); see also, for example, *Nordlinger v Hahn*, 505 US 1 (1992); *Burlington Northern Railroad v Ford*, 504 US 648 (1992).

[49] These correspond to the two different patterns of ethnic relations identified in, for example, Max Weber, *"Ethnic" Segregation and "Caste,"* in H. H. Gerth and C. Wright Mills, eds, *From Max Weber: Essays in Sociology* 188–90 (Routledge & Kegan Paul, 1948). See the discussion in Donald L. Horowitz, *Ethnic Groups in Conflict* 22–24 (University of California Press, 1985) and sources cited therein.

law of race relations developed. The other is that, although there is no dominant group or subordinate group—if there are, for example, a number of ethnic or religious groups, all of roughly equal power—such classifications might still be unacceptable because they are too divisive, or because ethnicity or religion is a morally offensive criterion, or for some similar reason. What the Court called "consistency"—perhaps better termed "symmetry"—assumes that the American law of race relations, specifically strict scrutiny, has been developed according to the latter model. Manifestly it has not; the roots of that law are in a period of unmistakable one-sided oppression. Divisiveness, the blanket moral unacceptability of racial criteria, and kindred concerns, may be part of the story, but they are not remotely the whole story.

That is why, for all the rhetoric of "consistency," the Court cannot bring itself to apply the same standard to affirmative action that it has applied to discrimination against minorities, and properly so. The law governing discrimination against minorities was developed to dismantle a system of subordination—"White Supremacy," as the Court put it in a pivotal case.[50] Whatever the supposed vices of affirmative action, maintaining a system of racial supremacy is not among them. Accordingly, the doctrine developed in the earlier cases cannot be carried over bag and baggage to affirmative action, and the Court, on some level, understands that.

II. Is Affirmative Action Really a Remedy?

If affirmative action is not automatically invalid, but is to be judged by a means-ends version of strict scrutiny, then the questions are which interests are sufficiently compelling, and what degree of "tailoring" will be required. The Court's answers to these questions often (although not always) assume that affirmative action is a remedy. But the remedy must be for what the Court calls "identified" discrimination, not "societal" discrimination. "Identified" discrimination apparently means discrimination in a particular context—in a specific employment market, or in the purchase

---

[50] *Loving v Virginia*, 388 US 1, 7 (1967).

of certain kinds of goods or services by the government, or in admissions by a state university.[51] The Court has been adamant that remedying "societal" discrimination cannot be the basis for affirmative action.[52]

There are several puzzles. Why the preoccupation with remedies to the exclusion of other potential interests? Why only "identified" and not "societal" discrimination? After all, if the premise is that racial classifications are generally harmful, one would want them employed only to remedy the greatest evils, and offhand societal discrimination seems like a greater evil than discrimination in a specific area. But why—to come at the question from the other side—are we justified in treating affirmative action as a "remedy" at all? Even affirmative action that remedies "identified" discrimination characteristically provides benefits to a large, undifferentiated group of minority citizens, without requiring any showing that those particular beneficiaries were injured by discrimination.[53] In fact, because affirmative action programs generally rely on market mechanisms to some degree—contractors are allowed to choose the best minority subcontractors they can find; universities choose the best minority students, and so on—they might seem perversely designed to benefit the minority group members who are the least wounded by discrimination. In what sense, then, is affirmative action a remedy?

---

[51] The contrast between "identified" discrimination (for which affirmative action is an acceptable remedy) and "societal" discrimination (for which it is not) was first drawn in Justice Powell's opinion in *Regents of the University of California v Bakke*, 438 US 265, 307, 309 (1978). Justice Powell then used the term repeatedly in his concurring opinion in *Fullilove*, making clear that "identified" discrimination, while narrower than "societal" discrimination, could be ascertained by legislative "findings" (not just by judicial or quasi-judicial determinations) and would justify a remedy that swept more broadly than the specifically identified victims of discrimination. See 448 US at 515 ("When Congress acts to remedy identified discrimination, it may exercise discretion in choosing a remedy that is reasonably necessary to accomplish its purpose."); id at 496, 497, 507, 510; see also id at 486 (opinion of Burger, White, and Powell). "Identified discrimination" became a central focus of the prevailing opinion in *Croson*, which again did not define the term precisely but emphasized that it had to be conceived in a way that would impose some enforceable limits on a government's power to engage in remedial affirmative action. See 488 US at 496–97, 499–501, 509 (plurality opinion of O'Connor); id at 505, 507 (opinion of the Court).

[52] See *Croson*, 488 US at 497, 499; *Wygant*, 476 US at 276 (plurality opinion).

[53] *Wygant*, 476 US at 286 (plurality opinion), rejected the argument that race-conscious measures could be used only to benefit individuals who could show that they were victims of specific acts of discrimination.

A. THE REMEDIAL ORIGINS OF AFFIRMATIVE ACTION

History answers these questions to a degree. In the courts, the first uses of race-conscious action to try to aid African Americans were remedial in a clear sense. Race-conscious actions were upheld in two settings in particular: school desegregation and employment. In the school cases, after *Brown v Board of Education*, many districts whose schools had been officially segregated declared that they would instead assign pupils on a discretionary, but supposedly race-neutral, basis. Other school districts adopted "freedom of choice" plans that ostensibly allowed all parents to enroll their children in any school. In both cases, the typical result was continuing segregation of a form no less pernicious than had existed before. The white school remained unmistakably the white school, and the black school remained unmistakably the black school, with all the connotations of the Jim Crow regime.[54]

The Supreme Court considered this state of affairs unacceptable and insisted that school boards take steps to make sure that the pattern of segregation was broken. Often these steps were, of necessity, race-conscious. Sometimes the only way to break up the entrenched pattern of segregation was for the courts to order school boards to enroll a certain number of African American children in formerly white schools.[55] The most explicit recognition of the need for race-conscious measures occurred in 1971, when the Supreme Court unanimously upheld a lower court order requiring an ambitious program of race-conscious busing to accomplish desegregation.[56] The precise justification for these race-

---

[54] See, on these points, Mark Tushnet, *Making Civil Rights Law: Thurgood Marshall and the Supreme Court, 1936–61* at 241–56 (Oxford University Press, 1994); L. A. Powe, Jr., *The Road to Swann: Mobile County Crawls to the Bus*, 51 Tex L Rev 505 (1973). Indeed, the degree of desegregation was minuscule until the Civil Rights Act of 1964 gave enforcement powers to the executive branch. See Gerald Rosenberg, *The Hollow Hope: Can Courts Bring About Social Change?* 51–52 (University of Chicago Press, 1991).

[55] *Green v County School Board*, 391 US 430 (1968), was "the first major step" in this direction. See Mark V. Tushnet, *The Supreme Court and Race Discrimination, 1967–1991: The View from the Marshall Papers*, 36 Wm & Mary L Rev 473, 477 (1995).

[56] *Swann v Charlotte-Mecklenburg Bd. of Ed.*, 402 US 1. See also *Davis v School Comm'rs*, 402 US 33 (1971); *McDaniel v Barresi*, 402 US 39 (1971) (upholding the constitutionality of pupil assignments explicitly based on race). Notably, this was not just permissible but constitutionally compelled affirmative action. In *North Carolina State Bd. of Ed. v Swann*, 402 US 43 (1971), for example, the Court invalidated a state statute that forbade school assignments on the basis of race or for the purpose of maintaining a racial balance—that is, the Court held that it was unconstitutional for a state *not* to engage in race-conscious affirmative action.

conscious measures is a matter of some complexity and controversy: Were they really just correcting actions that had already been determined to be violations of the Constitution? Or did these supposedly remedial decisions actually redefine what constituted a violation?[57] But what is important for present purposes is that race-conscious measures of this sort were seen as remedies for de jure school segregation.

In employment, race-conscious government action occurred primarily under Title VII of the Civil Rights Act of 1964, although there were some important constitutional cases as well, involving public employers. Here the typical pattern was that an employer was repeatedly found, or suspected, to have engaged in discrimination despite court orders to stop. Courts in some cases ordered such employers to hire specified numbers of minority employees or be held in contempt, unless they could show good reasons for their inability to hire the prescribed numbers. The justification for this remedy was that it would bring about an end to discrimination sooner than either a back-pay remedy or an injunction that simply forbade discrimination: the former would require individual claimants, and both would require potentially protracted proceedings to prove acts of discrimination. But a numerical requirement would, without more, force an employer to stop discriminating.[58]

The first cases involving voluntary race-conscious action by governments or private employers—what we now think of as the core affirmative action issue—began coming before the courts in the mid-1970s. By that time, the school desegregation and employment cases were familiar to the courts, and the lawfulness of race-

---

[57] See the discussions in Geoffrey Stone, et al, eds, *Constitutional Law* 510, 512, 516–17 (Little Brown, 2d ed 1991); Tushnet, 36 Wm & Mary L Rev at 477–78 (cited in note 55); Paul Gewirtz, *Choice In the Transition: School Desegregation and the Corrective Ideal*, 86 Colum L Rev 728 (1986).

[58] A plurality of the Supreme Court explained this in 1986, when it ratified the many lower court decisions that had imposed race-conscious remedies for this reason:

Where an employer has engaged in particularly longstanding or egregious discrimination, an injunction simply reiterating Title VII's prohibition against discrimination will often prove useless and will only result in endless enforcement litigation. In such cases, requiring recalcitrant employers or unions to hire and to admit qualified minorities roughly in proportion to the number of qualified minorities in the work force may be the only effective way to ensure the full enjoyment of rights protected by Title VII.

Local 28, Sheet Metal Workers v EEOC, 478 US 421, 448–49 (1986) (citing numerous cases). See also *United States v Paradise*, 480 US 149, 166–85 (1987) (plurality opinion).

conscious action had been litigated in that setting. Affirmative action was known elsewhere in the society by the mid-1970s—such as in Executive Order 11,246, applicable to government contractors[59]—but the remedial uses in school desegregation and employment cases were the ones that had generated the case law.

Not surprisingly, lawyers trying to justify affirmative action by, for example, state universities, put their case in remedial terms. That was the framework that was available, and it seemed more promising than breaking new ground. In addition, in the case of many private employers, affirmative action was a self-imposed remedy. They engaged in race-conscious recruitment, hiring, and promotion in order to settle or forestall discrimination claims that might have been brought against them.[60] The Supreme Court accordingly thought of voluntary affirmative action, like court-ordered affirmative action, as a remedy and analyzed it as such. The law took shape around that principle. As more cases were decided in which affirmative action was analyzed as a remedy, it became more risky for lawyers to try to break out of the remedial mold in defending affirmative action measures.

B. HOW AFFIRMATIVE ACTION FUNCTIONS AS A REMEDY

This historical background also helps explain the sense in which an affirmative action measure might be a remedy for discrimination, even though it benefits a broad class and does not attempt to identify victims of particular acts of discrimination. There are at least three ways in which affirmative action can be said to be remedial in a specific sense—not to deal with societal discrimination generally, but to address what the Court calls "identified" discrimination.

1. First, when there has been discrimination in a particular set-

---

[59] 3 CFR 339 (1965).

[60] See, for example, *United Steelworkers v Weber*, 443 US 193, 208, 209 n 9 (1979); id at 209–11 (Blackmun concurring). This was particularly true because Title VII of the Civil Rights Act of 1964, 42 USC § 2000e et seq (1988), was interpreted to forbid not just intentional discrimination but employment practices that had a disproportionate adverse effect on minorities and were not justified by a business necessity. See *Griggs v Duke Power Co.*, 401 US 424 (1971); see also 42 USC § 2000e-2(k)(1) (Supp III 1992) (codifying the disparate impact standard). Employers faced with a potential "disparate impact" claim (if they could not show a business necessity) could be sure to protect themselves only if they engaged in some form of affirmative action; even scrupulously race-neutral employment practices would not always be enough.

ting in the past, imposing a race-conscious goal can be an effective way of preventing further discrimination; this is why affirmative action was used as a remedy in the employment discrimination cases. Suppose a senior corporate official feared that her managers had been discriminating in personnel decisions and wanted them to stop. She might just threaten to discipline anyone who was shown to have discriminated. But she might also think that, given the costs (material and otherwise) of proving discrimination, and the ease of escaping detection, that approach would be wasteful and ineffective. Instead of case-by-case review of specific employment decisions, she might instruct her subordinates to fill a certain number of positions with minority applicants, unless they could show good reasons for their failure to do so. Then she could be reasonably assured that there was little discrimination. There would be costs, because some of the minority applicants might be less qualified than nonminorities to whom they were preferred. But a rational personnel director might easily think that this was the best way to root out discrimination.

This rationale supports the use of affirmative action not just in employment but in programs like the one at issue in *Adarand*. Affirmative action is, on this understanding, not a compensatory remedy for past discrimination but an effort to prevent future discrimination; the past discrimination functions as evidence that discrimination is likely to be a problem in the future. Suppose the government thought there was a danger of discrimination by general contractors: it might decide that, instead of (or in addition to) a relatively clumsy antidiscrimination regime that provided for compensatory and punitive remedies when a contractor was shown to have discriminated, it would order contractors to maintain a certain number of minority subcontractors.[61] Of course, isolated instances of discrimination wouldn't justify an affirmative action remedy (unless there were some reason to think the danger of discrimination would be much greater in the future); that is because affirmative action, if it is seen simply as a way of preventing future discrimination, is fairly costly. But if there is reason to think that

---

[61] Compare *Croson*, 488 US at 509 (plurality opinion) (suggesting that affirmative action might be constitutional if used "to dismantle [a] closed business system"); *Associated Gen'l Contractors v Coalition for Economic Equity*, 950 F2d 1401, 1415 (9th Cir 1991) (affirmative action plan justified in part on ground that government determined "that an 'old boy network' still exists").

widespread discrimination is likely in the future, affirmative action, despite its costs, may be a much more sensible remedy than the case-by-case adjudication characteristic of a conventional antidiscrimination regime.

This remedial use of affirmative action is especially appropriate when the potential future discrimination is of a kind that will be especially difficult to prove through the usual adjudicatory means. People might, for example, act on the basis of stereotypes that are unconsciously held; or an unconscious belief in the inferiority of a minority group might be reflected in the design of apparently neutral standards. In such cases, there is likely to be no way at all of preventing discrimination in the future, except to insist on affirmative action of some sort. In other cases, people might develop highly sophisticated means of covering up the evidence of discriminatory actions. For these reasons—again from the point of view of, for example, a rational personnel manager or contracting officer who wanted to prevent discrimination—affirmative action remedies might be especially appropriate; indeed, even more appropriate now, when racial discrimination is almost never openly avowed, than they were a generation ago, when discrimination was often overt.[62]

2. Second, affirmative action might be remedial in a sense that is roughly analogous to the school desegregation cases. The perception that a particular industry or occupation is the preserve of a certain group can operate as a barrier to entry.[63] Minority or women applicants might be unwilling to seek certain jobs if they think they will be rejected, or will be unwelcome in the jobs even if hired. Over time, an antidiscrimination regime will tend to bring these barriers down, but only over time. The way to remove the barriers quickly is to insist that employers hire women and minorities in certain numbers. Then employers have an incentive to break down the barriers, and they are often in the best position to do so. On this theory, affirmative action is a remedy for discrimination that would be undetectable through the usual means because

---

[62] See generally John J. Donohue III and Peter Siegelman, *The Changing Nature of Employment Discrimination Litigation*, 43 Stan L Rev 983 (1991); David A. Strauss, *The Law and Economics of Racial Discrimination in Employment*, 79 Geo L J 1619, 1644–48 (1991).

[63] See generally Harry T. Edwards and Barry L. Zaretsky, *Preferential Remedies for Employment Discrimination*, 74 U Mich L Rev 1, 31–46 (1975); *Local 28, Sheet Metal Workers*, 478 US at 449–50; *Morrow v Crisler*, 491 F2d 1053, 1056 (5th Cir 1974) (en banc).

it is attributable not to any individual, but to the combined actions of many people, over generations, that created the psychological barriers.

3. Third, affirmative action might be used to remedy discrimination in the sense of compensating for its effects. Indeed, neither the Supreme Court nor the lower courts have drawn a sharp line between remedying discrimination and remedying "the continuing effects of past discrimination."[64] A person might be subject to the effects of past discrimination even if he himself has never been the victim of a specific act of discrimination, or has not been discriminated against for decades. Discrimination at an earlier time (or even discrimination against earlier generations) can leave people without the resources, particularly human capital resources, needed to compete—education, experience, reputation, contacts. The notorious discrimination in craft unions, for example, undoubtedly left a dearth of African Americans in a position to become construction subcontractors. A program like that in *Adarand* might help remedy the effects of this discrimination. It forces the general contractor, and ultimately the government, to absorb some of the costs of the human capital deficiencies caused by discrimination.

This form of remedy is at least as imprecise as the others, maybe more so. The subcontracting affirmative action program might in fact benefit people who suffered least from discrimination, since they will be in the best position to take advantage of it. In any event, as discrimination becomes less extensive, the likelihood that the benefits of a program go to a victim of discrimination will diminish. Moreover, determining the extent to which any human capital or other deficiencies are the result of past discrimination, as opposed to other factors, will often be an intractable and divisive inquiry.

Nonetheless, despite all these difficulties, in some settings, affirmative action may be a relatively effective way of remedying the effects of discrimination. It is likely to be less costly than trying to give the victims of discrimination directly the educational and other advantages of which they were wrongfully deprived. If there is a clear history of discrimination, and if it is relatively easy to

---

[64] See the discussion in *Adarand*, 115 S Ct 2133–34 (Souter dissenting).

identify the kinds of deficiencies that discrimination will have produced—such as a lack of the experience and informal contacts needed to succeed in certain businesses—affirmative action may be an entirely appropriate compensatory remedy.

C. STRICT SCRUTINY AND THE REMEDIAL USES
OF AFFIRMATIVE ACTION

The Supreme Court in *Adarand* gave few indications about exactly how strict scrutiny was to operate. The *Croson* opinion was a little clearer, however, and by now the lower courts have been applying *Croson* for several years. In most of the lower court cases, governments have tried to justify affirmative action as a remedy, not surprisingly in view of the Supreme Court's emphasis on the remedial nature of affirmative action. In that context, "narrow tailoring" generally seems to require four things: (i) good evidence that discrimination existed in the past;[65] (ii) some form of quasi-judicial investigation—for example, by the government body that enacted the affirmative action measure, by an outside consultant or commission, or by a court in litigation that prompted the affirmative action plan—into the existence of discrimination and the likelihood that affirmative action would remedy it; (iii) a careful choice of any numerical standard used as part of the affirmative action measure, including flexibility in applying the numerical standard; and (iv) a basis for thinking that conventional remedies will be ineffective and affirmative action is needed, including a provision for terminating affirmative action at a specified time when it will no longer be needed.[66]

This approach is reasonably well suited to using affirmative action in the remedial senses I mentioned above. It could be further refined: usually the different remedial rationales are not clearly distinguished, and the courts (and proponents of affirmative action)

---

[65] See *Croson*, 488 US at 500, quoting *Wygant*, 476 US at 277 (requiring a " 'strong basis in evidence for [the] conclusion that remedial action was necessary' ").

[66] For these requirements, see, for example, *Concrete Works v City and County of Denver*, 36 F3d 1513 (10th Cir 1994), cert denied, 115 S Ct 1315 (1995); *Peightal v Metropolitan Dade County*, 26 F3d 1545 (11th Cir 1994); *Stuart v Roache*, 951 F2d 446 (1st Cir 1991), cert denied, 504 US 913 (1992); *Coral Constr Co. v King County*, 941 F2d 190 (9th Cir 1991), cert denied, 502 US 1033 (1992); *Associated Gen'l Contractors v Coalition for Economic Equity*, 940 F2d 1401 (9th Cir 1991); *Donagy v City of Omaha*, 933 F2d 1448 (8th Cir), cert denied, 502 US 1059 (1991).

are not clear on whether they are trying to aid people who were victims in the past or to ensure that there will be no discrimination in the future. But if the goal is to allow affirmative action to be used as a remedy in one of these ways, then strict scrutiny, as it has evolved, is a plausible way of doing that. The questions that the courts are asking are not too different from what a personnel manager might ask if she were considering using affirmative action to deal with discrimination in a firm: Are we sure there's a problem? How do we know it's not just a misperception? Is this really the best way to fix it? How will we know when it's been fixed?

The question is why affirmative action should be so limited. There are three issues in particular. First, even if a rational manager would consider whether an affirmative action plan was "narrowly tailored" before adopting it, why should the courts play that role? Why can't the government be relied upon to manage its own remedies? If the affirmative action plan is badly designed, the government's own interests will suffer; it will have poorer employees, or its contractors will produce inferior work. Why is the government less able to internalize the cost of a poorly designed remedial affirmative action program than it is to internalize the cost of any other poorly designed program?

Second, why is the Supreme Court so hostile to the argument that "societal discrimination" justifies affirmative action? The idea would be that affirmative action is a rough form of reparations. Chances are that most African Americans are worse off in some important respects than they would have been if they, or their ancestors, had not been discriminated against—or at least so the government might reasonably conclude. Affirmative action is an effort to compensate for this. It is inevitably crude, but at this point nothing better is possible. Since racial discrimination had many sources and manifestations, and occurred in many areas of social and economic life, one would ordinarily think that addressing the effects of "societal" discrimination is at least as compelling a goal as remedying "identified" discrimination in, for example, a particular industry. In addition, when affirmative action is used to remedy "identified" discrimination, there will usually be a significant divergence between the class of people who were actual or potential victims of that discrimination and the class of beneficiaries; the generalization that all African Americans have been, to some degree, the victims, proximate or remote, of discrimination of some kind, may well be more sound than the generalizations used in many cases of "identified" discrimination.

Finally, there remains the question why affirmative action should be seen only in remedial terms. There is a historical explanation for why the law has developed in this way, but there does not seem to be any good reason for the law to continue to have an exclusively remedial focus. In fact, the Supreme Court has never squarely held that affirmative action is to serve only remedial purposes, and there are suggestions in the opinions that it can serve other purposes.[67] Many of the government institutions (and private firms) that engage in affirmative action hiring probably do not see it as a remedy but rather see it as a way to promote diversity and similar goals. Why should the law retain its remedial focus?

One cannot answer these questions by saying that affirmative action should be kept to a minimum because it is generally harmful to society and unfair to the nonminorities who lose out. That view doesn't explain why affirmative action should be allowed to remedy "identified" discrimination and nothing else. This remedial interest, after all, is not an overwhelmingly strong one. Preventing discrimination is undoubtedly important, and affirmative action can be, as I have suggested, an indispensable means of accomplishing this aim; but it is hard to see that the marginal gains in prevention are on the same order as, say, a national security emergency. Indeed, it is hard to see that they are on the same order as the national interest in improving race relations generally, an interest that apparently would be too "amorphous" to justify affirmative action under the Court's current doctrine. And while the law generally tries to compensate victims of wrongdoing, there are many instances in which it fails (owing to immunity doctrines, limits on consequential damages, and the like); in any event, the justification

---

[67] See, for example, *Regents of University of California v Bakke*, 438 US 265, 311–14 (1978) (opinion of Powell); *Wygant*, 476 US at 286, 288 n * (opinion of O'Connor). See also *O'Donnell Constr. Co. v District of Columbia*, 963 F2d 420, 429 (DC Cir 1992) (R.B. Ginsburg concurring). Justice Stevens has repeatedly urged that affirmative action can serve nonremedial purposes. See, for example, *Adarand*, 115 S Ct at 2127–28 (Stevens dissenting); *Wygant*, 476 US at 314–15 (Stevens dissenting). *Metro Broadcasting* upheld the use of a nonremedial justification. See *Adarand*, 115 S Ct at 2127–28 (Stevens dissenting) (asserting that this aspect of *Metro Broadcasting* survives *Adarand*). For criticism of the remedial focus of the affirmative action cases, see, for example, Kathleen M. Sullivan, *Comment: Sins of Discrimination: Last Term's Affirmative Action Cases*, 100 Harv L Rev 78 (1986).

for compensatory justice has never been fully worked out.[68] So the puzzle about the Court's doctrine remains: why do the gains from affirmative action outweigh the costs when affirmative action is used as a remedy, but nowhere else? If the goal is simply to restrict affirmative action because it is generally a harmful thing, then limiting its use to remedying identified discrimination seems arbitrary.

III. Affirmative Action and Interest Groups

A. CONFINING, NOT COMPELLING, STATE INTERESTS

What best explains the affirmative action decisions is that the Supreme Court is trying—as it has before, sporadically—to control the power of interest groups and to ensure that legislation promotes a genuine public interest. The Court is, in general, not hostile to affirmative action measures that are genuine efforts to promote some legitimate public interest. What the Court is concerned about is the risk that affirmative action plans will be enacted simply because groups that favor them have gained sufficient power.

There are several intimations of this in the opinions. The controlling opinion in *Croson* referred repeatedly to the possibility that affirmative action was the result of "racial politics." For example, *Croson* gave the following explanation for adopting strict scrutiny:[69]

> Absent searching judicial inquiry into the justification for . . . race-based measures, there is simply no way of determining what classifications are "benign" or "remedial" and what classifications are in fact motivated by illegitimate notions of racial inferiority or simple racial politics. Indeed, the purpose of strict scrutiny is to "smoke out" illegitimate uses of race by assuring that the legislative body is pursuing a goal important enough to warrant use of a highly suspect tool. The test also ensures that the means chosen "fit" this compelling goal so closely that there is little or no possibility that the motive for the classification was illegitimate racial prejudice or stereotype.

---

[68] See, for discussion, Robert Goodin, *Compensation and Redistribution*, in John W. Chapman, ed, *Nomos XXXIII: Compensatory Justice* 143 (New York University Press, 1991); Richard A. Epstein, *Nuisance Law: Corrective Justice and Its Utilitarian Constraints*, 8 J Legal Stud 49 (1979).

[69] 488 US at 493 (plurality opinion).

This passage envisions that strict scrutiny will be applied in a means-ends fashion, rather than as a rule of automatic invalidity; some affirmative action measures will have sufficiently "legitimate" justifications. More specifically, "the purpose of strict scrutiny" is to "smoke out" impermissible "motivat[ions]"; and a principal impermissible motivation is "racial politics." The references to "notions of racial inferiority," "racial prejudice" and "stereotyping" can be understood in the same way—as bases for affirmative action that are impermissible because they amount to simple favoritism toward minorities, or animosity toward nonminorities, rather than legitimate public interests.[70]

The opinion in *Croson* repeatedly returns to what the Court viewed as the sinister possibility that "racial politics" or "politics of racial hostility" produced the set-aside that the Court struck down in that case.[71] Many members of the Court are aware of the view that government contracting set-asides are the product of interest group action and do not really serve a legitimate public purpose. (Justice Stevens, who is otherwise disposed to allow governments broad latitude to adopt affirmative action measures, is skeptical about set-asides, explicitly for this reason.[72]) The facts in

---

[70] See *McDonald v Santa Fe Trail Transportation Co.*, 427 US 273 (1976) (discrimination based on simple prejudice against a nonminority group is actionable under both Title VII and 42 USC § 1981). The references to "racial inferiority" and stereotyping in the *Croson* opinion, as well as the opinion's subsequent reference to "a danger of stigmatic harm" and "promot[ing] notions of racial inferiority" (488 US at 493) can also be seen in a different way: as addressing the concern that affirmative action measures may harm rather than help minorities. See text at note and note 46; *Adarand*, 115 S Ct at 2119 (Thomas concurring). But the stigmatizing harm to minorities is generally seen as an *effect* of affirmative action, rather than the motivation for it. Particularly in *Croson*, it would have been implausible to say that the motivation of the affirmative action measure—adopted by an African American majority of the city council as one of its first acts—was to "promote notions of [the] racial inferiority" of African Americans. In addition, it is unclear how strict scrutiny, at least of the means-ends variety, can help avert this risk: the stigmatizing effects of affirmative action, if any, are likely to be greatest when the generalization on which it rests—that the benefited minority group is especially in need of assistance in order to succeed—is most clearly true.

[71] See 488 US at 493; id at 505–06, 510: "To accept Richmond's claim that past societal discrimination alone can serve as the basis for rigid racial preferences would be to open the door to competing claims for 'remedial relief' for every disadvantaged group. The dream of a Nation of equal citizens . . . would be lost in a mosaic of shifting preferences based on inherently unmeasurable claims of past wrongs. . . . The random inclusion of racial groups that, as a practical matter, may never have suffered from discrimination in the construction industry in Richmond suggests that perhaps the city's purpose was not in fact to remedy past discrimination. . . . Absent [proper] findings, there is a danger that a racial classification is merely the product of unthinking stereotypes or a form of racial politics." See generally Daniel A. Farber, *Richmond and Republicanism*, 41 Fla L Rev 623 (1989).

[72] See *Croson*, 488 US at 516 n 9 (concurring); *Fullilove*, 488 US at 541–42 (dissenting).

Croson, which was the pivotal case in determining that strict scrutiny would apply to affirmative action, did little to allay the concern with interest group politics; the record in that case could be read to suggest that when African American members of the Richmond City Council gained a majority, they adopted a set-aside ordinance as a matter of routine, with virtually no consideration, except for some hastily created legislative history by a member of the Council who realized that the ordinance was legally vulnerable.[73]

The selectivity of the Court's approach is not easy to defend. If the new African American majority on the Richmond City Council thought that giving public contracts to its supporters was a matter of routine, that is probably because giving public benefits to one's supporters—defined not just by political affiliation or personal connection but by ethnicity as well—*is* a matter of routine, and has been for generations, in cities and states throughout the nation.[74] In partial defense of the Court, there are, as I will discuss, a few other areas, unrelated to race or affirmative action, where the Court may be, again without fully realizing it, also acting on the basis of a concern with interest groups. But whatever one thinks about the selectivity, the Court's approach to affirmative action can be seen as growing out of the concern with interest group power. The Court is no doubt concerned that affirmative action is generally unhealthy and divisive. But the way the Court has expressed its concern is to establish a doctrine that is designed to "smoke out" interest group legislation—measures that are solely the product of "racial politics."

The clearest evidence of this is not just the language of the opinions but the doctrine itself. The various anomalies and puzzles in the doctrine begin to make sense if one sees them as a way to

---

[73] See 488 US at 480.

[74] See, for example, Nathan Glazer and Daniel Patrick Moynihan, *Beyond the Melting Pot: The Negroes, Puerto Ricans, Jews, Italians, and Irish of New York City* 223–29 (M.I.T. Press, 1963). See also Justice Scalia's dissenting opinion in *Rutan v Republican Party,* 497 US 62, 108 (1990), defending the constitutionality of patronage systems partly on the precise ground that they have served as a means by which ethnic minorities advanced, and condemning the majority in that case for restricting patronage just when African Americans are able to take advantage of it. This opinion was written in the Term after Justice Scalia excoriated the Richmond set-aside in *Croson.* (Justice Scalia did insist that patronage was used by ethnic groups "on the basis of their politics rather than their race or ethnicity" (497 US at 108).)

enable the courts to separate truly public-interested affirmative action from affirmative action that is just a response to interest group pressure. Why does the Court use a "means-ends" version of strict scrutiny in dealing with affirmative action, as opposed to the "automatic invalidity" version? In applying strict scrutiny, why has the Court concluded that the interest in remedying "identified discrimination" is sufficiently "compelling" to justify affirmative action, but the interest in remedying societal discrimination is not, and nonremedial interests may not be? It is certainly not obvious that these interests would rank this way on any commonly accepted scale of values. If the Court just wants to reduce the overall quantity of affirmative action in society, this is an arbitrary way to do it.

But if the Court's concern is with interest groups, these aspects of the doctrine begin to make sense. One way to ensure that a measure does not just promote the interests of a narrow group is, straightforwardly, to insist that the measure have a strong means-ends connection to some genuine public interest. Under the "means-ends" form of strict scrutiny—as opposed to the form historically used in cases of discrimination against minorities—a measure will be upheld if there is such a connection.

If the concern is interest groups, however, then the public interest need not be unusually strong or compelling.[75] It need only be a genuine public interest, genuinely promoted by the statute. In the Court's own words, the government interest need only be "important enough" to " 'smoke out' illegitimate uses of race." That is why the Court has shown so little interest in explaining why the interest in remedying "identified" discrimination is "compelling" in the sense of being extraordinarily important.

What this approach does require, though, is that the state not be allowed to advance interests that can justify every affirmative action measure. Otherwise the supposed public interest can serve as a pretext for interest group legislation. The government interests needn't be compelling, in the sense of especially important, but they must be *confining*: the claim that a measure promotes that particular government interest must be falsifiable. This is why the

---

[75] See *Wygant*, 476 US at 286 (O'Connor concurring): "[A]s regards certain state interests commonly relied upon in formulating affirmative action programs, the distinction between a 'compelling' and an 'important' governmental purpose may be a negligible one."

Court ruled out "societal discrimination": it is the kind of government interest that can be use to justify essentially any affirmative action measure. Therefore that government interest cannot be used to "smoke out" measures that are the product of "simple racial politics."

The Court has been explicit about this, too. The Court does not disparage the importance of societal discrimination as a concern; on the contrary, it repeatedly acknowledges the "sorry history of racial discrimination" and its effects.[76] But the Court repeats, time and again, that societal discrimination cannot be used to justify affirmative action because it would authorize virtually any affirmative action measure[77]—including those that, in the Court's view, are in fact the product of interest group pressures and do not further a genuine public interest. By contrast, there are specific questions that a court can ask to determine if a measure really does help remedy, in one or more of the senses described above, "identified" discrimination. The claim that affirmative action remedies "identified" discrimination is falsifiable.

This is how the means-ends version of strict scrutiny operates in other areas as well. The requirement that an interest be "compelling" is seldom what defeats a statute; over the years, the Supreme Court has found an enormous range of government interests to be "compelling."[78] It is the requirement that a measure

---

[76] *Croson*, 488 US at 499; see, for example, *Adarand*, 115 S Ct at 2117 (plurality opinion); *Wygant*, 476 US at 276 (plurality opinion).

[77] See, for example, *Croson*, 488 US at 505, 507; id at 496–97, 499–501, 509 (plurality opinion of O'Connor); *Wygant*, 476 US at 276 (plurality opinion of Powell); *Bakke*, 438 US 265, 310 (1978) (opinion of Powell).

[78] See, for example, *Waters v Churchill*, 114 S Ct 1878, 1885 (1994) ("[W]e have never set forth a general test to determine what constitutes a compelling state interest."); *In re Griffiths*, 413 US 717, 722 n 9 (1973) ("We attribute no particular significance to the [ ] variations in diction" among the terms "overriding," "compelling," "important," and "substantial."). For examples of the many interests that the Court has found compelling, see *Vernonia School District 47J v Acton*, 115 S Ct 2386, 2395 (1995) (deterring drug use by schoolchildren); *Gregory v Ashcroft*, 501 US 452, 472 (1991) ("The people of Missouri have a legitimate, indeed compelling, interest in maintaining a judiciary fully capable of performing the demanding tasks that judges must perform."); *Boos v Barry*, 485 US 312, 329 (1988) (leaving open the possibility that dignitary interest of foreign embassies may be compelling); *Department of the Navy v Egan*, 484 US 518, 527 (1988) (compelling interest "in withholding national security information from unauthorized persons in the course of executive business"); *Moran v Burbine*, 475 US 412, 426 (1986) (compelling interest "in finding, convicting, and punishing those who violate the law"); *Roberts v United States Jaycees*, 468 US 609, 623 (1984) ("eradicating discrimination against . . . female citizens"); *Bill Johnson's Restaurants, Inc. v NLRB*, 461 US 731, 741 (1983) ("maintenance of domestic peace"); *South Dakota v Neville*, 459 US 553, 558–59 (1983) (highway safety); *Larson v*

be "necessary" or "narrowly tailored" that has proved difficult to satisfy.[79] States seldom have a difficult time advancing some obviously important interest that is arguably or plausibly promoted by a challenged law. What makes strict scrutiny effective is that it is difficult to show that the measure is an especially good way of promoting that objective. In order to maintain the effectiveness of strict scrutiny, then, what is needed is not so much a requirement that the state interest be especially important as a requirement that the state interest be precisely enough specified so that the claim of a means-ends connection can be falsified.

It follows that, in the affirmative action cases, the nearly exclusive focus on remedy is an overreaction. Nonremedial interests should also be able to justify an affirmative action measure, so long as they are confining in the necessary way. Suppose, for example, that a city with a large minority population justifies affirmative action in hiring by asserting that it needs to have a certain number of minority police officers in minority neighborhoods or to serve minority citizens. It seems likely that a court could assess the plausibility of this means-ends connection.[80] It could consider the de-

---

Valente, 456 US 228, 248 (1982) ("protecting its citizens from abusive practices in the solicitation of funds for charity"); *Brown v Hartlage*, 456 US 45, 58 (1982) (avoiding appearance of "corrupt arrangement"); *Lefkowitz v Cunningham*, 431 US 801, 808 (1977) ("maintaining an honest police force and civil service"); *Goldfarb v Virginia State Bar*, 421 US 773, 792 (1975) ("States have a compelling interest in the practice of professions within their boundaries, and . . . as part of their power to protect the public health, safety, and other valid interests they have broad power to establish standards for licensing practitioners and regulating the practice of their profession."); *Storer v Brown*, 415 US 724, 736 (1974) (preventing "splintered parties and unrestrained factionalism"); *Memorial Hospital v Maricopa County*, 415 US 250, 268 (1974) ("preventing fraud by an applicant for medical care"); *Rosario v Rockefeller*, 410 US 752, 760–61 (1973) (preventing "raiding" by rival political parties).

[79] See, for example, Ely, 41 U Chi L Rev at 727 n 26 (cited in note 4): "[S]pecial scrutiny in the suspect classification context has in fact consisted not in weighing ends but rather in insisting that the classification in issue fit a constitutionally permissible state goal with greater precision than any available alternative."

[80] Compare, for example, *Detroit Police Officers' Assn v Young*, 608 F2d 671, 695–96 (6th Cir 1979), cert denied 452 U S 938 (1981) (accepting such a justification), with *Hayes v North State Law Enforcement Officers Assn*, 10 F3d 207, 213–15 (4th Cir 1993) (rejecting such a justification). Compare *Bakke*, 438 US at 310–11 (opinion of Powell).

Notably, the Supreme Court has consistently upheld affirmative action measures designed and implemented not by politically responsive bodies but by courts. See, for example, *Local 28, Sheet Metal Workers*, 478 US 421 (1986); *United States v Paradise*, 480 US 149 (1987); *Swann v Charlotte-Mecklenburg Bd. of Ed.*, 402 US 1 (1971). This is the setting in which one would least fear interest group domination, so the Court's willingness to approve these affirmative action measures is consistent with the hypothesis that its principal concern is interest group politics.

mographic character of the city's neighborhoods, the history of relationships between the police force and minority citizens, the duties that the city assigns to police officers, and so on. There is no reason to disqualify government interests such as these just because they are not remedial.

The Court's decisions do not foreclose nonremedial objectives. In fact, there are suggestions that the interests in diversity in state university admissions and public school faculty hiring can justify affirmative action.[81] There is a danger, though, that the momentum toward thinking of affirmative action entirely as a remedy for "identified" discrimination will become too great. That would be an arbitrary limit on affirmative action. Once the current doctrine is seen in interest-group terms, it becomes clear that the list of acceptable interests can include nonremedial objectives, such as diversity in educational institutions and government bureaucracies. The only requirement is that those objectives be specified in a way that allows for a meaningful review of the claim that affirmative action is an especially good means to the end, and that the objective not serve as an open-ended justification for every affirmative action measure.

B. CAN THE PUBLIC INTEREST BE IDENTIFIED?

The idea that government action should promote the public interest, instead of the narrow interests of well-organized groups, is familiar. Many people have urged the courts to take such an approach, either in establishing constitutional limits on legislation or in interpreting statutes.[82] The attention to this issue in the last two decades was no doubt spurred by the increased study of interest groups in the political process by public choice economists and political scientists. But as long ago as *Lochner v New York*,[83] the

---

[81] See *Bakke*, 438 US at 311–14 (opinion of Powell); *Wygant*, 476 US at 286, 288 n * (opinion of O'Connor).

[82] See, for example, Cass R. Sunstein, *The Partial Constitution* 24–39 (Harvard University Press, 1993); Frank H. Easterbrook, *The Supreme Court, 1983 Term—Foreword: The Court and the Economic System*, 98 Harv L Rev 4, 15–18 (1984); William N. Eskridge, Jr., *Politics Without Romance: The Implications of Public Choice Theory for Statutory Interpretation*, 74 Va L Rev 275 (1988); Jerry L. Mashaw, *Constitutional Deregulation: Notes Toward a Public, Public Law*, 54 Tulane L Rev 849 (1980); Frank I. Michelman, *Politics and Values, or What's Really Wrong with Rationality Review?* 13 Creighton L Rev 487 (1979).

[83] 198 US 45 (1905).

Court followed an approach similar to the one it appears to be using in the affirmative action cases.

The *Lochner* Court, in considering the argument that a maximum-hours law could be justified as a regulation of health, insisted that the government interest in promoting health be conceived narrowly. Otherwise, the Court said, that objective could justify any law. And when the connection between this objective and the law became too attenuated, in the Court's view, the Court concluded that the law was in fact the product of what we today would call interest group politics: "[When] assertions [of this kind] . . . become necessary in order to give . . . a plausible foundation for the contention that the law is a 'health law,' it gives rise to at least a suspicion that there was some other motive dominating the legislature than the purpose to subserve the public health or welfare."[84] This anticipates the *Croson* Court's conclusion that the poor design of the set-aside in that case, and the difficulty of connecting it to a remedial objective, gave rise to the suspicion that "racial politics" was involved.

As the connection to *Lochner* suggests, there is a great danger in any effort to structure judicial review to limit interest group influence. The danger is that "interest group legislation" will come to mean, simply, what the court considers bad legislation. Sometimes interest group influence is not good, but sometimes interest group influence is good: sometimes an intensely interested minority should be able to prevail over the majority. Civil rights legislation, veterans' legislation, farm subsidies, legislation requiring that landowners be compensated for certain forms of regulation, rent control, the *repeal* of rent control—all of these are examples of legislation that is, in general, crucially supported by well-organized, intensely interested minorities. But nearly everyone will think some of this is good legislation and some not. That suggests that people actually make judgments on the basis of their substantive normative theories about what kinds of legislation are good, rather than on the basis of opposition to interest group influence.[85]

These dangers are obviously present in dealing with affirmative action. Suppose a local government defends a set-aside program as

---

[84] Id at 62–63.

[85] For a sustained argument to this effect, see Einer Elhauge, *Does Interest Group Theory Justify More Intrusive Judicial Review?* 101 Yale L J 31, 48–59 (1991).

a way to increase the financial stability and the social and economic integration of the African American middle class. Some will see that as a legitimate interest; others will see it as just redescribing obvious interest group legislation. The same might even be true of diversity in university student bodies and faculties. Some will see that as a legitimate educational objective; others will believe it is a cover for capitulating to interest groups.

There are other areas, more reputable than *Lochner*, where the Court's decisions are best understood as an effort to separate public-interested legislation from legislation that merely promotes interest group concerns. Rational basis review—the requirement, under the Due Process Clause, that all legislation be rationally related to some legitimate government purpose—can perhaps be understood only in this way. There are few measures that do not promote some purpose, desired by someone (and judicial review is unlikely to be needed to deal with those few). If rational basis review is to work at all, the Court must have in mind a distinction between public-regarding objectives and objectives that, while sought by groups influential enough to get the law passed, are not sufficiently connected to the public interest to be "legitimate."[86] If there were no such thing as a public interest, separate from interest group interests, rational basis review would make no sense.[87] On occasion, the Court has used rational basis review to invalidate measures that it thought were generated by a pernicious form of popular self-interest.[88] But few people would say that rational basis review has been successful in weeding out interest group legislation. For the most part, rational basis review has been, notoriously, toothless.[89]

Other areas may be more promising. The antitrust state action

---

[86] See the discussions in Cass R. Sunstein, *Naked Preferences and the Constitution*, 84 Colum L Rev 1689 (1984); Note, *Legislative Purpose, Rationality, and Equal Protection*, 82 Yale L J 123, 128 (1972).

[87] See, for this criticism of rational basis review, Alexander M. Bickel, *The Least Dangerous Branch* 225–27 (Bobbs-Merrill, 1962).

[88] This has occurred principally in cases where the laws discriminated against persons who were living, or recently had lived, outside the state. See, for example, *Attorney General v Soto-Lopez*, 476 US 898 (1986); *Hooper v Bernalillo County Assessor*, 472 US 612, 624 (1985); *Metropolitan Life Ins. Co. v Ward*, 470 US 869 (1985); *Zobel v Williams*, 457 US 55, 65 (1982).

[89] See, for recent examples of highly deferential opinions, *FCC v Beach Communications, Inc.*, 113 S Ct 2096 (1993); *Nordlinger v Hahn*, 505 US 1 (1992); *Burlington Northern Railroad v Ford*, 504 US 648 (1992).

doctrine seems to try in part to distinguish anticompetitive government actions that are the result of public-interested decisions from instances in which the government is simply being used by interested private groups that want to stifle competition.[90] Opinions differ on whether the state action doctrine has succeeded in this respect.[91] Some First Amendment decisions concerning commercial speech try to separate measures that promote a legitimate public objective, such as preventing deception or overbearing, from measures that just insulate firms from competitors' advertising.[92] Decisions under the Takings Clause and Contract Clause also can be seen as resting on a distinction between the public interest and private interests;[93] indeed, the requirement of a "public use" in the Takings Clause seems to direct courts to prohibit even compensated takings of private property, if they benefit only a self-interested group. But the Supreme Court has not made a serious effort to enforce that requirement, perhaps believing that the distinction cannot be drawn.[94]

The affirmative action decisions make sense if they are seen as responding to this same concern. The question is how the courts might go about trying to distinguish affirmative action that promotes a public interest from affirmative action that reflects only interest group concerns. Of course, the fact that interest groups are active in bringing about a measure does not mean that it should be invalidated. Interest group activity is inevitable in a democracy, and sometimes interest groups support measures that, by nearly anyone's lights, promote a legitimate public purpose—laws against drunk driving, for example, or (an example more closely related to affirmative action) laws like the Civil Rights Act of 1964. The

---

[90] See John S. Wiley, Jr., *A Capture Theory of Antitrust Federalism*, 99 Harv L Rev 713 (1986).

[91] Compare id with Einer R. Elhauge, *The Scope of Antitrust Process*, 104 Harv L Rev 667 (1991).

[92] For an argument to this effect, see David A. Strauss, *Constitutional Protection for Commercial Speech: Some Lessons from the American Experience*, 17 Can Bus L J 45 (1990). See also *Florida Bar v Went For It, Inc.*, 115 S Ct 2371, 2386 (1995) (Kennedy dissenting).

[93] See Sunstein, *Partial Constitution* 35–37 (cited in note 82).

[94] Instead the Court has treated the "public use" requirement in a way that parallels rational basis review under the Due Process Clause. See, for example, *Hawaii Housing Authority v Midkiff*, 465 US 229, 239–45 (1984); *Berman v Parker*, 348 US 26, 31–33 (1954); see the discussion in Gerald Gunther, *Constitutional Law* 477–78 (Foundation Press, 12th ed 1991); Richard A. Epstein, *Takings: Private Property and the Law of Eminent Domain* ch 12 (Harvard University Press, 1985).

question must be not who supported a law, or who was instrumental in getting it enacted, but what it actually does: whether it promotes a public interest or merely promotes the interests of well-organized groups.

In trying to implement this approach in affirmative action cases, the courts can use at least three guideposts. First, they can insist on the articulation of a public interest and on a reasonably detailed showing that the measure actually promotes that interest. This is essentially the "narrow tailoring" aspect of the current law. Second—as a sufficient but not necessary condition (that is, a principle of inclusion only)—they can look to parallel conduct by private entities subject to the market. Third, they can try, through common law methods of elaboration, to work out a catalogue of permissible, public objectives. All of these options are highly imperfect. No way of identifying interest group legislation, in the affirmative action context or elsewhere, is going to overcome all of the practical and theoretical difficulties of distinguishing between the public interest and narrow special interests. The task is to identify some approaches that the courts might use to make them more likely to succeed than they otherwise would be.

1. *Narrow tailoring, or a hard look.* One way to try to ensure that legislation promotes a genuine public interest is to insist that its defenders articulate a public interest and show that that interest is actually furthered by the legislation. Of course, there is disagreement about what constitutes a public interest. And self-interest often masquerades as public-spiritedness. But this requirement at least weeds out the most egregiously self-interested measures: those that cannot be shown to promote any objective that anyone could, without embarrassment, characterize as a public interest.

This is essentially what the Supreme Court has done in requiring "narrow tailoring." The Court, and the lower courts following *Croson*, have insisted that governments defend affirmative action measures by identifying the objective they claim to be promoting and by showing good reasons to believe that that objective is actually promoted by the measure in question.

Metro Broadcasting, the case overruled by *Adarand*, illustrates how this inquiry might work. *Metro Broadcasting* upheld the constitutionality of certain preferences that the Federal Communications Commission gave to minority firms seeking broadcast licenses. The government claimed, and the Court agreed, that the preferences promoted an interest in providing diverse programming content, and that preferences were the only way to do this because the First Amendment limits the government's ability to control content directly. The dissenters in *Metro Broadcasting* attacked this interest as "too amorphous, too insubstantial, and too unrelated to any legitimate basis for employing racial classifications."[95] But this criticism is misdirected: the interest in content diversity is not amorphous at all, at least not in the sense that remedying societal discrimination is amorphous. The claim that minority ownership promotes content diversity is readily falsifiable.

The more telling criticism of the *Metro Broadcasting* preferences is that they may be an example of an interest group giveaway that does not serve a public purpose. The potential beneficiaries of a minority preference in broadcast licensing are likely to be a relatively small group of wealthy individuals who stand to gain a great deal if preferences are authorized, and who therefore (under the standard public choice assumptions) are likely to be unduly influential in the political process. But a careful examination of the connection between minority ownership and content diversity, the professed objective, can determine whether the preferences actually promote that objective; if they do not, then one can assume that they just promote the self-interest of the potential beneficiaries.

When the courts examine the means-ends connection in this way, they are doing something parallel to what courts reviewing administrative agency actions do under the "hard look" doctrine— a doctrine that is sometimes seen as a way to reduce the danger of interest group "capture" of administrative agencies.[96] That doctrine requires that an agency articulate its objectives, show that it had a basis for believing that its action would promote those objectives, and show that it has considered the alternatives and had reasons for rejecting them—the kinds of things the lower courts have

---

[95] 497 US at 612 (O'Connor dissenting).

[96] On the "hard look" doctrine, see, for example, *Motor Vehicle Manufacturers' Assn. v State Farm Mutual Automobile Ins. Co.*, 463 US 29 (1983). For discussion, see, for example, Cass R. Sunstein, *Deregulation and the Hard-Look Doctrine*, 1983 Supreme Court Review 177; Harold Leventhal, *Environmental Decisionmaking and the Role of the Courts*, 122 U Pa L Rev 509 (1974). On the connection between the hard look doctrine and interest groups, see, for example, Cass R. Sunstein, *Factions, Self-Interest and the APA: Four Lessons Since 1946*, 72 Va L Rev 271 (1986).

been requiring under *Croson*.[97] Of course requirements of this kind are ordinarily not applied, as a matter of constitutional law, to legislation. But if the Supreme Court is especially concerned about interest group influence in an area, it makes sense to pursue this approach. And *Metro Broadcasting* suggests that this approach might succeed, in a significant number of cases, in determining whether an affirmative action measure actually promoted the professed, public-interested objective.

The problem arises not when measures like the FCC preferences are justified by reference to programming diversity, but rather if they were defended as simply an effort to create an established, visible, wealthy minority elite. On the one hand, this alleged public interest could be seen as just redescribing an interest group benefit. On the other hand, defenders of the legislation might ask: what warrant do the courts have to decide that creating a visible minority elite is not an appropriate way to address some of the problems of race relations—and therefore a legitimate public interest?[98] There is no good answer to this question; it is parallel to the problems that have defeated courts' efforts in other areas to identify interest group legislation. This problem is in general not as acute in administrative law, because the statute under which the agency is acting will often limit the kinds of ends it can pursue. But if a court's charter is not to promote the objectives specified by a statute, but simply to invalidate interest group legislation, the court will have a difficult time limiting the category of permissible ends without simply imposing a judgment about what kinds of legislation are a good idea.

Still, a "hard look" to ensure "narrow tailoring," as the Court calls it, can go a long way toward reducing interest group influence. Some objectives might be such obvious cover for interest group politics that the statute's defenders will be unwilling to avow them; it seems unlikely that a government would defend an affirmative action measure simply on the ground that it will enrich a minority elite. If a statute's defenders are unwilling even to avow an objective, then the courts are justified in not regarding that objective as a legitimate public interest; and if a statute cannot be

---

[97] See text at notes and notes 65–66 above.

[98] Cf David B. Wilkins, *Two Paths to the Mountaintop? The Role of Legal Education in Shaping the Values of Black Corporate Lawyers*, 45 Stan L Rev 1981, 2011–12 (1993).

shown to promote any legitimate public interest, then the courts can be confident that it just benefits interest groups.

These gains in identifying interest group legislation will, of course, come at a cost. Many of the costs are familiar from criticisms of the hard look doctrine.[99] Needed, legitimate government action might be blocked because of fear that the courts will find it inadequately considered and invalidate it. Governments may concentrate more on papering the record, and otherwise protecting themselves from judicial review, and less on the substance of policy. Courts may substitute their own assessment of the wisdom of a measure. Even if they do not, they will often have a difficult time determining whether a measure in fact furthers the objectives it is said to promote; if the proponents of a measure are determined to create a record that supports it, they will often be able to do so, even if the measure is in fact very dubious. Notwithstanding these costs, however, the lower courts generally appear to have settled on something roughly like hard look review in evaluating affirmative action measures under *Croson*, and their decision to do so fits well with the concern with interest group politics that seems to animate the Supreme Court's decisions.

2. *Parallel private conduct.* Today affirmative action is common in at least parts of the private sector.[100] If a certain form of affirmative action is engaged in by a private firm, which is subject to the discipline of the market, then it is harder to say that a government decision to engage in a parallel form of affirmative action is just a capitulation to interest groups. If most major private universities engage in affirmative action to promote diversity in their faculties and student bodies, then public universities should be able to do so. If most major corporations with large minority representation in their workforces deliberately seek minority supervisors, governments should be able to act the same way; similarly for corporations that hire minority employees in response to what they per-

---

[99] See, for example, Jerry L. Mashaw and David L. Harfst, *The Struggle for Auto Safety* (Harvard University Press, 1990); Stephen G. Breyer, *Judicial Review of Questions of Law and Policy*, 38 Admin L Rev 363 (1986).

[100] See, for example, Note, *Rethinking Weber: The Business Response to Affirmative Action*, 102 Harv L Rev 658 (1989); Anne B. Fisher, *Businessmen Like to Hire by the Numbers*, Fortune (Sept 16, 1985), at 26; *Race in the Workplace: Is Affirmative Action Working?* Business Week (July 8, 1991), at 50.

ceive as the needs of their business. If, however, there is no private sector counterpart to contractor set-asides, then that is evidence— not necessarily conclusive—that this form of affirmative action is the result of interest group politics.

This is a principle of inclusion, not exclusion. The fact that there is a private counterpart to a certain form of government affirmative action helps defend the government program against the charge that it benefits only interest groups. But the fact that comparable private entities do not engage in affirmative action should not disqualify the government from doing so. Governments pursue objectives that market-directed private entities do not. Public universities might have different self-conception from private universities; they might legitimately have a greater interest in providing a means for minority groups to advance in society. Government agencies might properly be more concerned with responding to minority groups that are generally too poor to attract much attention from private firms. More generally, public institutions may seek to engage in the redistribution of resources. A private firm that must answer to the market cannot do that.

There are several possible objections to using private parallels even as a principle of inclusion. To some extent it will be difficult to identify comparable enterprises. Some public employers (police departments, for example) may have no obvious private sector counterparts. In addition, some private affirmative action may be a response to government requirements. But these points only suggest that private parallels cannot be relied upon in any mechanical way. A judge trying to get a sense of whether government affirmative action genuinely promotes a public interest will still be able to get some enlightenment from evidence of the practices of private firms. This will particularly be true if the pattern in private industry is clear—if, for example, nearly all the major private universities engage in affirmative action in admissions, or most large employers engage in affirmative action in hiring.

A more fundamental objection is that private conduct is itself influenced by interest groups. Groups advance their interests not just through politics but in the way they spend their money; private sector parallels to government actions may show only that the same interest groups have been active in both arenas. For example, a well-funded trade association might, through the way it spends its money, influence both private sector actions (such as the content of television programs[101]) and the government. But this does not seem to describe the reason that private firms engage in affirmative action. Affirmative action in the private sector does not seem to be the product of the concerted exercise of market power by small self-interested groups, perhaps because the groups benefited by private sector affirmative action are usually not wealthy. Indeed, even vociferous critics of affirmative action by universities and other private institutions do not blame financial pressures so much as what might be called moral pressures—public relations concerns, managers' or administrators' beliefs about their moral obligations, or relatively broad-based market forces, such as the demands of employees or consumers.[102]

To the extent that pressures of this kind are involved, the fact that a private institution must compete in a market will limit its willingness to respond to interest groups and increase the likelihood that its actions reflect legitimate institutional needs. In fact, if a group is successfully using nonfinancial, moral pressure, it is problematic to say that its actions reflect solely the group's self-interest and not some public interest: if a firm believes that the failure to adopt an affirmative action measure would hurt its standing in the public at large, then it is difficult to see how that measure can be said to be the product of narrow group interests.

Finally, to the extent the Court is concerned about the particular pathologies of interest group *politics*—that affirmative action will spawn a "racial spoils system," as is sometimes said—the existence of private sector parallels provides some reassurance. It shows that the group benefited by the affirmative action measure has some broader strength, some ability to succeed in a nonpolitical arena, and has not just exploited the political advantages that well-organized groups possess. If both private sector and government institutions are engaged in similar behavior, then probably something other than a spoils system—that is, the leveraging of political power into economic benefits—is at work.

3. *Common law evolution.* If the effort to combat interest group

---

[101] See generally C. Edwin Baker, *Advertising and a Democratic Press* (Princeton University Press, 1994).

[102] See, for example, Dinesh D'Souza, *Illiberal Education: The Politics of Race and Sex on Campus* (Free Press, 1991).

politics is to succeed in this area, it will, in all likelihood, have to proceed case by case, in response to specific explanations of the need for affirmative action in a particular setting. In this way, the courts might be able to work out a catalogue of interests that can justify affirmative action. The interests will have to be sufficiently confining so that the courts can decide whether a measure actually promotes them. At the same time, the courts will have to give the elected branches sufficient latitude by accepting objectives that the judges themselves might find unappealing. Otherwise, judicial review in this area, supposedly concerned with interest group pressures, may just collapse into review based on the courts' notions of what constitutes good affirmative action. The actions of private entities can be one guide; traditional conceptions of the purposes of the government can be another. It is possible for people who disagree with a policy to recognize, nonetheless, that the policy is a good-faith effort to promote some public purpose and not simply a capitulation to interest groups.

To some degree this case-by-case development has already begun. Opinions in the Supreme Court and the lower courts have identified a few possible interests: remedying identified discrimination, of course; diversity in student bodies, in higher education; diversity in public bureaucracies that must deal with minority populations; possibly faculty diversity in secondary education, where it is not justified simply as a way to mirror the student population.[103]

This case-by-case approach seems best, if the project of limiting interest group influence is to be pursued. The courts are unlikely to succeed if they try to define in the abstract a line between legitimate public purposes and ostensible purposes that are only a cover for interest group activity. The experience in other areas suggests that that line is very hard to identify. But evidence in a particular case about the need for minority representation on a big city police force, or about the need for diversity in public school faculties or social service bureaucracies, or about the need for state universities to educate students from minority groups who do not meet conventional admissions criteria—evidence of this kind may persuade judges that specific affirmative action measures reflect a genuine

---

[103] See *Bakke*, 438 US at 311–14 (opinion of Powell); *Wygant*, 476 US at 275–76 (plurality opinion); id at 286, 288 n * (opinion of O'Connor); *Detroit Police Officers' Assn. v Young*, 608 F2d 671, 695–96 (6th Cir 1979), cert denied 452 U S 938 (1981).

effort to solve a social problem, even if the solution is one that the judges themselves would not choose.

IV. Conclusion

The Supreme Court's affirmative action cases seem, at first glance, to present several anomalies. But the doctrine makes sense if one understands it as a response, not to the kinds of concerns that led to outlawing discrimination against minorities, but to a more ubiquitous problem in democratic politics. The Court's concern in these cases, only partially articulated but implicit in the doctrine, is to ensure that affirmative action measures genuinely promote a public interest and do not simply award benefits to powerful interest groups.

Inevitably, strict scrutiny of affirmative action, even strict scrutiny of the means-ends variety, will cause some worthwhile, legitimate affirmative action measures to be lost. They may be erroneously invalidated by a court that is unable to perform the difficult, perhaps impossible, task of separating its own ideas about when affirmative action is appropriate from an account of the legitimate public interests that might be served by affirmative action. Or legitimate affirmative action measures may be deterred by the fear of invalidation (which can lead to personal damages liability for the officials involved) or by the administrative costs of establishing a program in a way that will enable it to survive judicial review.

The question that the Court has not yet fully answered is why these costs should be incurred in this area but in so few others. Interest group politics is a general problem in a democracy. In other areas we accept interest group measures, wasteful as they are. Affirmative action tends to be, politically, an unusually salient issue; that should, if anything, mitigate the danger of interest group domination. And of course affirmative action, unlike other measures, at least makes a feint at addressing what has historically been the nation's gravest domestic problem.

The explanations the Court offers for treating affirmative action differently from ordinary legislation echo the reasons why discrimination against minorities is objectionable. But the notion that affirmative action is like discrimination against minorities is unconvincing in the abstract and, not surprisingly, the Supreme Court has not followed through on it in the design of the doctrine. The

Court's effort to raise affirmative action above the level of ordinary politics—to insist that the adoption of an affirmative action measure be attended by a quasi-judicial solemnity—is more coherent than it might appear to be at first, and it responds to legitimate concerns. But it still awaits a full justification.

SAMUEL ISSACHAROFF

THE CONSTITUTIONAL CONTOURS
OF RACE AND POLITICS

In *Shaw v Reno*,[1] Justice O'Connor announced a new, "analytically distinct"[2] cause of action to assess the constitutionality of race-conscious redistricting. The precise contours of this new standard were well concealed, but clearly they involved some notions of excessive reliance on race as manifested through grotesquely configured district line-drawing. Justice O'Connor's refusal either to condemn all reliance on race as unconstitutional or to impose a constitutional template of compactness on redistricting left the opinion without an operational core. As commentators and lower courts scrambled to divine the requirements of this "analytically distinct" constitutional command, challenges to the 1990 round of redistricting continued to mount. The unresolved issues of race and politics appeared likely to condemn the decennial redistricting process to a decade's worth of litigation. Worse yet, given the rather persistent four-one-four division on the Supreme Court, the battles over redistricting seemed doomed to be fought under the terms of Justice O'Connor's enigmatic and idiosyncratically fact-based views of how any particular cartographical arrangement might strike her fancy. As Professor Pamela Karlan has evocatively

Samuel Issacharoff is the Charles Tilford McCormick Professor of Law at the University of Texas School of Law.

AUTHOR'S NOTE: This article benefitted from the comments of Cynthia Estlund, Daniel Farber, Pamela Karlan, Douglas Laycock, Sanford Levinson, Richard Pildes, William Powers, Scot Powe, and from the research assistance of Karen Mendenhall.

[1] 113 S Ct 2816 (1993).

[2] Id at 2830, 2838–39.

conjectured,[3] constitutional law seemed headed for a period of political *"Redrupping"*[4]—the unseemly practice by which the Justices of the Supreme Court once gathered in the inner sanctums of the Court to determine whether any particular pornography was indeed obscene.

With a mild amount of hindsight, Justice O'Connor emerges as straddling two distinct approaches to race-conscious state action. On the one hand stands what may be termed the principle of historical remediation. At its simplest, this is a recognition of societal responsibility for the continued badges of inferiority borne prototypically by black Americans. As expressed aphoristically by Justice Blackmun a decade ago, "[i]n order to get beyond racism, we must first take account of race."[5] The difficulty with the historic remediation principle is that it knows no natural limits. Since the record of past discrimination is ever-present, claims of redressing past wrongs border onto an ahistoric historicism—claims made upon state actors that show no obvious connection between past wrongs and present desires.

This then leads to the second prong of O'Connor's concern, the potential for race-based capture in the political process. While O'Connor repeatedly cites with evident approval Justice Powell's efforts at a cautiously tolerant view of race-conscious remediation,[6] she sees a different world than that under review by Powell. Most notably in *City of Richmond v J.A. Croson Co.*,[7] O'Connor has clearly focused on the danger that principles of remediation would slide ominously into simple racial factionalism in the distribution of societal goods, such as city contracts.[8] Most critically, O'Connor has

---

[3] Pamela S. Karlan, *Still Hazy After All These Years: Voting Rights in the Post-Shaw Era*, 26 Cumb L Rev 287 (1996).

[4] This was the period inaugurated by *Redrup v New York*, 386 US 767 (1967), and lasted until the determination of obscenity was handed over to community standards by *Miller v California*, 413 US 15 (1973). See Lucas A. Powe, Jr., *The Fourth Estate and the Constitution* 95 (California, 1991) (defining *Redrupping* as the reversal of an obscenity conviction without providing any reasons).

[5] *Regents of the Univ. of California v Bakke*, 438 US 265, 407 (1978).

[6] *Miller v Johnson*, 115 S Ct 2475 at 2482, 2488, 2491 (1995); *Shaw v Reno*, 113 S Ct 2816 at 2836, 2837, 2838, 2846, 2847 (1993); *Metro Broadcasting, Inc., v FCC*, 497 US 547 at 579, 596 (1990); *City of Richmond v J. A. Croson Co.*, 488 US 469 at 494, 497, 506 (1989); *Wygant v Jackson Bd. of Education*, 476 US 267 at 285, 286, 288 (1986).

[7] 488 US 469 (1988).

[8] "If a 30% set-aside was 'narrowly tailored' to compensate black contractors for past discrimination, one may legitimately ask why they are forced to share this 'remedial relief' with an Aleut citizen who moves to Richmond tomorrow? The gross overinclusiveness of

looked to the emergence of real minority political power as a potential source for the claims of historical injustice serving as a
screen for interest group demands of the present.[9] From this van-
tage point, there is a distinction, albeit of imprecise dimensions,
between race-conscious steps to dismantle complete exclusion and
the fact of a majority-black Richmond city council voting rather
extravagant minority set-asides in municipal contracting.[10]

If this is indeed the source of O'Connor's constitutional tension,
then it is not altogether surprising to find the Court's equal protection angst being played out squarely in the domain of politics.
Equal protection law as applied after the Warren Court reforms
of the 1960s always carried a potential for redistributionist claims,
whether in the form of direct entitlements to state benefits or indirectly in the form of challenges to governmental regulation. A
properly functioning pluralist politics holds out the prospect of
an equitable distribution of societal benefits through the political
process and thereby insulates the judiciary from having to scruti-
nize the distributionist consequences of governmental decisions.
At the same time, the emergence of politically powerful racial and
ethnic minorities raises a separate concern that a renewed factionalism will infect the political process. The presence of well-
organized minority political actors introduces the prospect of the
superordinate influence predicted by public choice theory for any
given (or all) cohesive, well-disciplined minorities.

For those who sought resolution of this tension, most notably
for state actors desperately seeking a safe harbor from suit, the
Court's 1994 Term brought no relief. In the first part of this article, I will briefly discuss last Term's two decisions. In one, *Miller
v Johnson*,[11] the Court reviewed Georgia's post-1990 congressional
redistricting and reiterated that statutory inroads through the Vot-

---

Richmond's racial preference strongly impugns the city's claim of remedial motivation."
488 US at 506.

[9] See Daniel A. Farber, *Richmond and Republicanism*, 41 Fla L Rev 623, 623–24 (1989)
(interpreting O'Connor as emphasizing the importance of keeping open the prospect of
political deliberation as opposed to strategic politics).

[10] 488 US at 495–96 ("In this case, blacks constitute approximately 50 percent of the
population of the city of Richmond. Five of the nine seats on the city council are held by
blacks. The concern that a political majority will more easily act to the disadvantage of a
minority based on unwarranted assumptions or incomplete facts would seem to militate
for, not against, the application of heightened judicial scrutiny in this case").

[11] 115 S Ct 2475 (1995).

ing Rights Act will not insulate racial classifications from constitutional review. In the second, *Hays v Louisiana*,[12] the Court chose to trivialize the best developed fact record for elucidating a clearer constitutional command—that concerning Louisiana's congressional redistricting—and instead issued a rather inconsequential standing opinion whose only effect was to dispose of the case at bar. In the second part of the article, I will focus on *Miller* and the Court's curious affirmance of a California redistricting case, *DeWitt v Wilson*,[13] to explore the possible political equilibrium for which the Court is searching. Unfortunately, what emerges from the 1994 Term is an inconclusive search for a means to downplay the evident racial divide in American politics. To the extent that the Court, largely through Justice O'Connor, is searching for a means to obscure the still critical role that race plays in defining the American political arena, that search remains at its formative stages.

I. SHAW V RENO: CHAPTER II

The constitutionalization of voting rights law following *Shaw* exposed the uneasy application of vote dilution law to the process of redistricting. With the 1982 Amendments to the Voting Rights Act, Congress ushered in a decade-long period in which multimember and at-large electoral arrangements ceded to minority-controlled single-member districts. The result, as superbly chronicled by Chandler Davidson and Bernard Grofman,[14] transformed the political institutions of the country, most notably by creating a significant pool of minority elected officials who were emerging at the state and local level as significant political players. As a result, the 1990 round of redistricting featured a markedly different political and legal landscape than prior decennial battles. Minority political actors could leverage not only their political power but the enforcement provisions of Section 5 of the Voting Rights Act, and the threat of suit under Section 2 of the Act against adverse districting decisions.

---

[12] 115 S Ct 2431 (1995).

[13] 115 S Ct 2637 (1995), summarily aff'g, 856 F Supp 1409 (E D Cal 1994).

[14] Chandler Davidson and Bernard Grofman, eds, *Quiet Revolution in the South: The Impact of the Voting Rights Act 1965–1990* (Princeton, 1994).

How this new configuration of enhanced minority political power and the statutory protections of minority electoral opportunity would play out in the redistricting context was entirely unclear. Prior to *Shaw*, two decades of voting rights law had turned on the question of electoral systems that threatened to dilute minority voting strength by subsuming minority voting blocs within larger multimember electoral configurations. As against the claim of diminished electoral opportunity, conservatives on the Court and off argued that the idea of vote dilution was meaningless absent some benchmark of proper electoral outcomes.[15] While this argument failed in challenges to the dismantlement of multimember local electoral units, the tide shifted with the application to redistricting. The application to the more publicly obvious distributive process of districting sharpened the debates over the normative baselines for defining adequate levels of minority representation.[16]

In particular, *Shaw* drew attention to the more elaborate manipulations of district lines that could result from claims for majority-minority districts. *Shaw* attempted to limit such claims for minority representation by drawing a constitutional line at cartographic departures from "traditional districting principles."[17] In doing so,

---

[15] See Abigail M. Thernstrom, *Whose Votes Count?: Affirmative Action and Minority Voting Rights* (Harvard, 1987). Perhaps the most forceful articulation of this point comes in Justice Thomas's dissent in *Holder v Hall*, 114 S Ct 2581, 2584 (1994), in which he charges that all vote-dilution caselaw is based on competing visions of a proper political theory of representation for which the courts have no aptitude. Id at 2592. See also Lani Guinier, *The Supreme Court, 1993 Term Comment: [E]racing Democracy: The Voting Rights Cases*, 108 Harv L Rev 109, 124–28 (1994) (accepting Thomas's challenge that the legitimacy of the Voting Rights Act must be found within "a broader theory concerning the democratic representation of groups").

[16] While the principal terrain for the Supreme Court (and for this article) has shifted to the constitutional plane, the issue of the distributive baseline for minority representation continues to play a major role in statutory voting rights claims. The Supreme Court has recently rejected a claim of Cuban-Americans to superrepresentation under Section 2 of the Act. *Johnson v De Grandy*, 114 S Ct 2647 (1994). Most recently, the Court summarily affirmed a three-judge court in Tennessee that had allowed the presence of minority "influence" districts (districts with significant minority populations that did not constitute an electoral majority) to defeat a claim for additional majority-minority districts. *Rural West Tennessee African-American Council, Inc. v McWherter*, 877 F Supp 1096 (W D Tenn 1995) (three-judge court), aff'd sub nom *Rural Tennessee African-American Council v Sundquist*, 116 S Ct 42 (1995).

[17] For discussions of the greater contortions of district lines following the 1990 reapportionment, see Richard H. Pildes and Richard G. Niemi, *Expressive Harms, "Bizarre Districts," and Voting Rights: Evaluating Election District Appearances After Shaw v Reno*, 92 Mich L Rev 483, 570–75 (1993) (providing quantitative data on greater dispersion of congressional districts after 1990); Timothy G. O'Rourke, *Shaw v Reno: The Shape of Things to*

Shaw shifted the terms of the debate by putting the conservative wing of the Court in the precarious position of defining a legal violation in terms of a departure from an unspecified baseline. If anything, "traditional districting principles" appeared more difficult for the conservative wing of the Court to clarify than the notion of "undiluted" voting strength had been for the liberal wing.

The most significant case of the 1994 Term is *Miller v Johnson*, in which the Court struck down Georgia's post-1990 congressional redistricting. In facts strongly reminiscent of *Shaw*, the state's first efforts at redistricting created two black-majority congressional districts for its eleven-member congressional delegation. Because Georgia is a covered jurisdiction under Section 5 of the Voting Rights Act, the state needed prior approval of the Department of Justice before implementing its redistricting plan. That preclearance was twice denied by the Department, which instead demanded that Georgia, a state that was 27 percent black, create three black-majority districts. The Justice Department relied on a "max-black" plan drafted by the American Civil Liberties Union on behalf of the state general assembly's black caucus[18] to demand the creation of a third black-majority district as a condition for preclearance. Although the resulting third black congressional district was not as aberrantly drawn as the district under challenge in *Shaw*, it was nonetheless characterized by the *Almanac of American Politics* as a geographical "monstrosity."[19] In the first instance, therefore, *Miller* must be evaluated in terms of its clarification of how "traditional districting principles" would forestall the descent into a politics of "balkanization" against which O'Connor warned in *Shaw*.

A. THE FEDS AND RACIAL POLITICS

Perhaps the most notable feature of *Miller*, and of the equal protection cases of the 1995 Term, was the Court's repudiation of expansive congressional enforcement powers through Section 5 of the Fourteenth Amendment and Section 2 of the Fifteenth Amendment. The Court's caustic rejection of extraordinary minority-

---

Come, 26 Rutgers L J 723, 762–64 (1995) (giving county and city level data for congressional districting in four states).

[18] 115 S Ct at 2483.

[19] Quoted in *Miller*, 115 S Ct 2484.

controlled districts in *Shaw* anticipated a direct confrontation with congressional authority to expand minority representation through the Voting Rights Act. The Court had previously advertised its willingness to entertain a frontal challenge to Section 2 of the Voting Rights Act,[20] and *Shaw* itself cautioned that any construction of the Voting Rights Act that required the creation of contorted minority districts would be unconstitutional.[21] The district court's extensive fact findings of the indispensable role of the Justice Department in forcing the creation of the challenged districts in *Miller*[22] made the confrontation with federal power inescapable.

The Court in *Miller* squarely held that "compliance with federal antidiscrimination laws cannot justify race-based districting where the challenged district was not reasonably necessary under a constitutional reading and application of those laws."[23] This put state authorities in an impossible bind since refusal of Justice Department preclearance imposed a tortuous path of litigation to secure litigated preclearance in the District of Columbia district court, but concessions made to the Justice Department would provide no safe harbor from suit. The Court, however, was more attentive to the flip side of this argument. If Justice Department preclearance served as a self-executing compelling state interest for using racial classifications, then the effect of Section 5 of the Voting Rights Act would be to entrust the Justice Department in particular, and the federal government in general, with the power to determine the constitutionality of local governmental conduct. This in turn would give a constitutional aura to whatever policy objectives the federal government might pursue in the name of the enforcement clauses of the Reconstruction Amendments.

While such extraordinary federal power was decisively (and derisively) rejected in *Miller*, such an expansive view of federal power held sway not so long ago. In *Croson*, for example, Justice Scalia opined that, "[a] sound distinction between federal and state (or

---

[20] See *Voinovich v Quilter*, 113 S Ct 1149, 1157 (1993) (holding open the constitutionality of the Act); *Chisom v Roemer*, 111 S Ct 2354, 2376 (1991) (Kennedy, J, dissenting) (questioning the constitutionality of the Act).

[21] *Shaw*, 113 S Ct at 2816 ("if § 2 did require adoption of North Carolina's revised plan, § 2 is to that extent unconstitutional").

[22] *Johnson v Miller*, 864 F Supp 1354 at 1364–65, 1368, 1378, 1382 (SD Ga 1994).

[23] 115 S Ct at 2499.

local) action based on race rests not only upon the substance of the
Civil War Amendments, but upon social reality and governmental
theory."[24] The basis for federal authority lay in a combination of
presumed "dispassionate objectivity"[25] and in the relative immunity of large institutions to political capture by self-interested factions. Thus, James Madison writes in the *Federalist Papers* of the
great capacity for factional interests acting in concert in small lo-
cales; yet,

> Extend the sphere and you take in a greater variety of parties
> and interests; you make it less probable that a majority of the
> whole will have a common motive to invade the rights of other
> citizens; or if such a common motive exists, it will be more
> difficult for all who feel it to discover their own strength and
> to act in unison with each other.[26]

The understanding of the federal government has clearly shifted
in the Court's eyes since the time of Madison. In the first instance,
the Court is much more sensitive to the application of federal policy through federal administrative oversight, as opposed to first-
order articulation of statutory objectives by Congress. The "commands" of the Voting Rights Act that figured so prominently in
the 1990 round of redistricting can hardly be described as the literal application of the Act as last amended by Congress in 1982.
Rather, a combination of judicial decisions, most notably *Thorn-
burg v Gingles*,[27] and regulatory guidelines under Sections 2 and 5
of the Act, guided the application of the Voting Rights Act to a
redistricting context largely unexplored by Congress.

The undisputed loser in *Miller*, therefore, is the federal government, and especially the Justice Department. The direct association between the preclearance powers under Section 5 of the Voting Rights Act, the "max-black" plan of the ACLU, and the black
caucus of the Georgia legislature served to turn the Justice Department into a suspect interest group advocate no different from the

---

[24] *Croson*, 488 US at 522.

[25] *Fullilove v Klutznick*, 448 US at 527 (1980) (Stewart, J, dissenting).

[26] *The Federalist* No 10, at 127 (Penguin, Isaac Kramnick ed 1987).

[27] 478 US 40 (1986) (streamlining the Act to strike down multimember electoral districts
where minorities are sufficiently numerous to form a majority in a single district, where
minority voters are politically cohesive, and where racially polarized voting results in the
usual defeat of minority-supported candidates).

Richmond City Council in *Croson*. While there is more than a touch of irony in the Justice Department under President Bush being depicted as a "captured" agent of the ACLU,[28] *Miller* is an integral part of the Court's reevaluation of the role of the federal government's presumed immunity from faction-dominated politics.

The permissibility of race-conscious state action is an area where the realignment of the Supreme Court is most directly evident, and extends not just to federal administrative power, but to Congress as well. Not only are Justices Brennan and Marshall no longer on the Court to argue the broad principle of benign uses of racial classifications to overcome past discrimination, but the Court is missing the strong pro-federal government views of Justice White.[29] *Miller* is therefore the perfect parallel case to *Adarand v Pena*,[30] in which the Court held federally enacted minority set-asides to the same standard of review as those imposed at the state and local level. The overriding theme of the 1995 Term was that, in the Court's view, the federal government is as capable of succumbing to racial interest group politics as any other organ of government, and will accordingly be subject to the Court's vigilance on that basis. Government, it turns out, is a suspect enterprise that is susceptible to rent-seeking political behavior in all its permutations.[31]

B. RACIAL PREDOMINANCE

Once the standard of review is set forth, the question still remained of clarifying the operational definitions of improper racial considerations left open by *Shaw*. *Miller* echoes *Shaw* in identifying the harm caused by the state's use of race as an "essentializing" classification:

---

[28] Bill Peterson, *Bush Depicts Dukakis as Out of Sync with Partner*, Wash Post (July 23, 1988) at A15 (chronicling Bush attack on Dukakis for association of latter with ACLU).

[29] Although not writing on this subject, Justice White consistently voted for greater latitude for the federal government. See *Fullilove v Klutznick*, 448 US 448 (1980); *Metro Broadcasting, Inc. v FCC*, 497 US 547 (1990).

[30] 115 S Ct 2097 (1995).

[31] In the Court's view of the world, the notable exception is the judiciary. Unfortunately, one of the alarming trends of current voting rights law is the ease with which judicial review has emerged as a substitute forum for political factionalism. See Pamela S. Karlan, *The Rights to Vote: Some Pessimism About Formalism*, 71 Tex L Rev 1705 (1993) (describing political jockeying in reapportionment litigation).

> When the State assigns voters on the basis of race, it engages
> in the offensive and demeaning assumption that voters of a
> particular race, because of their race, "think alike, share the
> same political interests, and will prefer the same candidates at
> the polls."[32]

If, indeed, race has as little explanatory value as is argued in *Miller*,
it may be that there is no basis for judicial intervention under any
circumstances since there is no predictable alteration of the political process that would ensue from gerrymandering.[33] The evidence, however, is still to the contrary, as can be gleaned not only
from the enormous energy expended by political parties on redistricting battles, but by every systematic chronicling of studies of
voter behavior.[34] The redistricting battles leading up to *Shaw* and
Miller were the product of complex political dynamics that included the desire of minority incumbents and aspirants for solidly
minority electoral districts and the corresponding aim of the Republican Party to pack minority voters into districts that would
leech traditional Democratic votes from some vulnerable incumbent Democrats.[35] The maximization of minority districts policy
was in turn actively pursued by the Department of Justice in those
jurisdictions under the preclearance requirements of Section 5 of
the Voting Rights Act.[36] Ironically, this policy remained essentially

---

[32] 115 S Ct at 2486, quoting *Shaw v Reno*, 113 S Ct at 2827.

[33] This is a variant of the no-baseline argument advocated by Professor Alexander. See
Larry Alexander, *Lost in the Political Thicket*, 41 Fla L Rev 563 (1989).

[34] See, e.g., Richard H. Pildes, Book Review: *The Politics of Race*, 108 Harv L Rev 1359
(1995) (summarizing empirical findings of Davidson and Grofman (cited in note 14)).

[35] A particularly instructive lesson is provided by Ohio, the site of *Voinovich v Quilter*,
113 S Ct 1149 (1993). *Voinivich* illustrates the Republican Party strategy of packing minority
voters into a few black-majority districts. This acts to deprive "white Democrats of a critical
element of their base of support and thereby allow Republicans to win elections in predominantly white districts." Karlan (cited in note 31), 71 Tex L Rev at 1733. Moreover, Republicans have financially supported minority-generated challenges to redistricting alignments.
Id. In Ohio, the redistricting plan which came out of the Republican-controlled Apportionment Board created, to be sure, black-majority voting districts but also "promised substantial partisan benefits to the Republican Party." Id at 1734. Democrats challenged the plan,
claiming it violated minority voting strength. The District Court agreed, and additionally
held that Ohio violated the Fifteenth Amendment by using the majority-minority remedy
to create a political advantage. Subsequently, the Supreme Court stayed the District Court.
116 S Ct 42 (1995).

[36] This is the fact pattern described at length in the lower court opinion in *Miller*. While
the Justice Department has denied ever formally pursuing this strategy, the record in litigation is to the contrary. See, e.g., *DeGrandy v Wetherell*, 815 F Supp 1550, 1574–76, 1580
(ND Fla 1992), rev'd sub nom, *Johnson v DeGrandy*, 114 S Ct 2647 (1994) (describing
Justice Department litigation on behalf of maximization strategy in Florida redistricting
litigation).

unchanged under the Bush and Clinton Justice Departments; the first in response to the Republican National Committee,[37] the second seeking to protect the newly incumbent minority elected officials who appeared on the scene after the 1990 round of redistricting.[38]

The claim in *Miller* that the racial dimensions of politics are unknown runs counter to the practical wisdom of political observers both inside and outside electoral politics.[39] If voter preferences were indeed as unknown as the majority in *Miller* makes out, this would legitimately raise the issue, argued strenuously by the dissents in both *Shaw* and *Miller*,[40] of what is the precise nature of the harm in redistricting. Even the *Miller* majority backs off the more extreme implications of its pure color-irrelevancy views by admitting that "[r]edistricting legislatures will, for example, almost always be aware of racial demographics . . . in the redistricting process."[41] Instead, the majority is searching for a "distinction between being aware of racial considerations and being motivated by them."[42] That distinction is provided by proscribing only the use of race that rises to the level of serving as the "predominant" factor in redistricting.

What then is the properly motivated state legislature to do with

---

[37] The Republican National Committee had a change of heart in 1992 as a result of a Democratic electoral upswing triggered by the presidential election. Despite the fact that Republicans actively sought the creation of minority-dominated districts, the Republican National Committee filed an amicus brief in *Shaw* urging the position ultimately advanced by Justice O'Connor. Brief Amicus Curiae of the Republican National Committee in Support of Appellants, *Shaw v Reno*, 113 S Ct 2816 (1993) (No 92–357). In the aftermath of the 1994 election, however, there is strong evidence that the concentration of black voters in particular did provide assistance to the dramatic advances of the Republican Party. See David I. Lublin, *Racial Redistricting and the New Republican Majority: A Critique of the NAACP Legal Defense Fund Report on the 1994 Congressional Elections*, (1995 Manuscript, on file with author); Charles S. Bullock III, *Winners and Losers in the Latest Round of Redistricting*, 44 Emory L J 944 (1995).

[38] In 1992 an additional 19 minority members of Congress were elected. Paul M. Barrett, *High Court Rules Racial Redistricting Could Violate Rights of White Voters*, Wall St J (June 29, 1993), A20.

[39] See, e.g., Edward G. Carmines and James A. Stimson, *Issue Evolution: Race and the Transformation of American Politics* (Princeton, 1989); Jennifer L. Hochschild, *Facing Up to the American Dream: Race, Class, and the Soul of the Nation* (Princeton, 1995); Thomas Byrne Edsall and Mary D. Edsall, *Chain Reaction: The Impact of Race, Rights and Taxes on American Politics* (Norton, 1991).

[40] 113 S Ct 2816, 2834 (1993); 115 S Ct 2475, 2498 (1995).

[41] 115 S Ct 2488.

[42] Id.

the Court's new admonition not to allow race to serve as the "predominant" factor in redistricting? Unfortunately, the fact pattern of *Miller* makes such a determination perplexing if not utterly futile. In *Miller*, Justice Kennedy clearly intimates that the trigger for unconstitutionality was the creation of a third majority-black congressional district. The infirmity of the suspect plan stemmed from the fact that "the social, political, economic makeup of the Eleventh District tells a tale of disparity, not community."[43] This heterogeneity of the district is significant not because there is a constitutional command toward truly homogeneous districts (this would indeed come close to O'Connor's invocation of apartheid in *Shaw*), but because the heterogeneity is evidence of the insidious predominance of racial considerations.

Yet, under this standard, there is no principled distinction between two and three majority-black congressional districts. The constitutional proscription under *Miller* is formulated so that "the essence of the equal protection claim recognized in *Shaw* is that the State has used race as a basis for separating voters into districts."[44] Perhaps *Shaw* could have offered some basis for distinguishing the first two black congressional districts in Georgia from the one struck down in *Miller*. Such a distinction would be available based on the degree of geographical contortions required to create three but not two congressional districts. But *Miller* is rather categorical in its refusal to limit the application of the equal protection clause to bizarre districts alone. Bizarreness, apparently like district heterogeneity, is at best one of a number of possible evidentiary routes to the ultimate issue of racial classifications:

> Our circumspect approach and narrow ruling in *Shaw* did not erect an artificial rule barring accepted equal protection analysis in other redistricting cases. Shape is relevant not because bizarreness is a necessary element of the constitutional wrong or a threshold requirement of proof, but because it may be persuasive circumstantial evidence that race for its own sake, and not other districting principles, was the legislature's dominant and controlling rationale in drawing its district lines.[45]

---

[43] 115 S Ct 2484.

[44] 115 S Ct 2485–86.

[45] 115 S Ct 2486.

Under this view, there are apparently no mediating principles inherited from *Shaw* or elsewhere that would protect districts created for minority representation. If indeed shape is only a concern as a proxy for a process in which race played a "dominant and controlling" role, then even the most natural of black-majority districts could be vulnerable. Take, for example, Charles Rangel's 15th Congressional District covering Harlem and other parts of upper Manhattan. While a 92 percent minority-dominated district might seem entirely appropriate in one of the cradles of the urban black experience, the district nonetheless abuts the 80 percent white 16th Congressional District.[46] Is there any question that the sharp divide into a minority and a white congressional district was anything but the product of "dominant and controlling" racial considerations?[47] In the final analysis, Charles Rangel's district may not advertise the racial considerations that went into its creation, largely because of the lack of extensive distortions of district lines, but its preordained racial base cannot be doubted.

As a result, the use of the term "predominant" to draw a new constitutional line in *Miller* leaves unresolved the level of causation required for a redistricting plan to fall. Contributing to the puzzle is the fact that the Court's "predominant factor" standard has no direct antecedents in either constitutional law or, perhaps more relevantly, in the common law of causation. Whereas *Shaw* turned its analysis outwardly to the impression on the body politic created by contorted districts—"[this] is one area in which appearances do matter"[48]— *Miller* redirects the inquiry inwardly to the role that race played in the chain of causation. But the use of "predominant" to demarcate the measure of unconstitutionality does little to elucidate the exact notion of causation that triggers constitutional infirmity.

Unfortunately, by turning to tort-like concepts of causation, the Court is taking a difficult and unresolved area of constitutional law and saddling it with a segment of the common law that has been caustically termed the "last refuge of muddy thinkers."[49] Clearly,

---

[46] *National Journal, Almanac of American Politics* 942, 944 (1995).

[47] For a history of this district, which provided the Court's first encounter with the intentional creation of minority-controlled electoral districts, see *Wright v Rockefeller*, 376 US 52 (1964).

[48] 113 S Ct 2816, 2827 (1993).

[49] Kenneth Vinson, *Proximate Cause Should Be Barred from Wandering Outside Negligence Law*, 13 Fla St U L Rev 215 (1985).

the Court in *Miller* is not imposing a simple but/for standard of causation under which all that would be required is proof that the event in question was not capable of occurring absent the challenged conduct.[50] Such a but/for standard does not seal off the point in the causal chain at which the relation between two factors becomes too attenuated to serve as the basis for liability. Professors Hart and Honoré give as a classic example the statement that, "If she had never married she would not have been a widow."[51] In such a sense, the connection may be descriptively accurate, but it would hardly serve as the basis for ascribing a cause of widowhood. Given the palpability of racial concerns in the political arena, such a broad standard of "cause" would either doom all attempts to distribute political power in multiethnic communities or would fail to provide a basis for distinguishing proper from improper considerations in redistricting.[52]

At the other extreme, holding racial considerations unconstitutional only when they are the sole proximate cause of the redistricting would accomplish nothing. In the multifactored calculations that go on in the redistricting context, there are rarely "sole" causes of anything. Rather, each decision, most centrally where ultimately to draw the actual district lines, is the product of innumerable political compromises such as to make impossible any determination of a unique causal factor.[53]

---

[50] "The defendant's conduct is not a cause of the event, if the event would have occurred without it . . . . the event would not have occurred 'but for' the defendant's negligence." William L. Prosser, *The Law of Torts* § 41 at 239 (4th ed 1971).

[51] H. L. A. Hart and Tony Honoré, *Causation in the Law* 114 (Oxford, 2d ed 1985).

[52] The problem with relying solely on a but/for test is that the inquiry is too broad and does not provide a means of limitation. "In a philosophic sense, the consequences of an act go forward to eternity, and the causes of an event go back to the dawn of human events, and beyond." W. Page Keeton, et al, *Prosser and Keeton on the Law of Torts* § 41, at 264 (5th ed 1984). Therefore, legal responsibility must be "limited to those causes which are so closely connected with the result and of such significance that the law is justified in imposing liability." Id. The inescapability of racial awareness in American politics gives particular salience to the observation that "we do not have a choice between colorblindness and race-consciousness; we have only a choice between different forms of race-consciousness." David A. Strauss, *The Myth of Colorblindness*, 1986 Supreme Court Review 99, 114.

[53] This is the defense taken by Texas in its appeal of an adverse ruling in a *Shaw*-based challenge to its congressional districting. *Vera v Richards*, 861 F Supp 1304 (W D Tex 1994) (three-judge court) prob jur noted sub nom, *Vera v Bush*, 115 S Ct 2639 (1995). The state argues that since the actual drawing of the district lines was heavily conditioned by partisan and incumbent considerations, race could not have played a uniquely causal role. Appellant's Brief, *Vera v Bush*, 115 S Ct 2639 (1995) (Nos 94-805, 94-806, 94-988).

Even the more moderate renditions of the "hopeless riddle"[54] of the common law of causation are unlikely to advance the inquiry. The only invocation of the concept of a "predominant factor" that I have located dates back more than half a century to the writings of Leon Green: "The only manner in which a cause issue could have become pertinent was by considering whether the defendant's negligence, as a factor in comparison with the other operative factors, really contributed appreciably to the injury."[55] Professor Green's approach then takes the inquiry directly into the concept of proximate cause which, under the RESTATEMENT definition of proximate cause, would allow for an actor's conduct to result in liability if (*a*) his conduct is a substantial factor in bringing about the harm, and (*b*) there is no rule of law relieving the actor from liability because of the manner in which his negligence has resulted in the harm.[56] This in turn raises the two critical questions obscured by *Miller*: What constitutes a substantial factor? and What intervening grounds may justify the use of race or negate the significance of having used race? In the first instance, the search for what is a "substantial factor," as developed in tort law, immediately turns on itself:

> The word "substantial" is used to denote the fact that the defendant's conduct has such an effect in producing the harm as to lead reasonable men to regard it as a cause, using that word in the popular sense, in which there always lurks the idea of responsibility, rather than in the so-called "philosophic sense," which includes every one of the great number of events without which any happening would not have occurred.[57]

Second, the *Miller* court gives no guidance to the inquiry as to when intervening factors, such as the desire to create only two black districts in Georgia, might relieve a redistricting authority of the consequences of using an otherwise forbidden racial classi-

---

[54] Patrick J. Kelley, *Proximate Cause in Negligence Law: History, Theory, and the Present Darkness*, 69 Wash U L Q 49 (1991).

[55] Leon Green, *Rationale of Proximate Cause* 33 (Vernon, 1927).

[56] *Restatement (Second) of Torts* § 431 (1965).

[57] *Restatement (Second) of Torts* § 431 at 429, cmt a (1965). Thus, once again pointing back to Justice O'Connor, context makes all the difference. As expressed by my colleague William Powers, consider the problem of an actor who tosses a lit match into a raging forest fire. While both the match and the fire could cause a house to burn, the law must have some principle for decreeing the act of negligently tossing a lit match to be inconsequential in light of extrinsic and overwhelming causal factors.

fication. The Court offers that, "[a] State is free to recognize communities that have a particular racial makeup, provided its action is directed toward some common thread of relevant interests."[58] But how, and under what circumstances, remain hopelessly obscure. Ultimately, the Court's facile reliance on standards of causation vaguely reminiscent of tort law does nothing to defer confronting the hard issue of acceptable standards of conduct. As expressed by Justice Andrews in the classic *Palsgraf* case: "What we do mean by the word 'proximate' is that, because of convenience, of public policy, of a rough sense of justice, the law arbitrarily declines to trace a series of event beyond a certain point."[59]

Contributing to the puzzle is the ever enigmatic Justice O'Connor. In creating what Professor Eric Schnapper termed a five-five split on the Court,[60] O'Connor not only provided the indispensable fifth vote for Justice Kennedy's majority opinion, but also concurred on wholly different grounds. For O'Connor, nothing in the Court's opinion should call into question "the vast majority of the Nation's 435 congressional districts . . . even though race may well have been considered in the redistricting process."[61] O'Connor does not reconcile this limited reading of *Miller* with Kennedy's broader indictments of race-based districting. Nor does she show how *Miller* may be limited to instances where "the State has relied on race *in substantial disregard* of customary and traditional districting practices."[62] Instead, under O'Connor's view, *Shaw* and *Miller* somehow combine to achieve only the limited objective of "making extreme instances of gerrymandering subject to meaningful judicial review."[63]

C. STANDING AND PUNTING

In light of *Miller*, the Court's resolution of *Hays* emerges as a wasted opportunity to provide some concrete guidance to lower courts and besieged state officials. *Hays* provided the Court an op-

---

[58] 115 S Ct at 2480.

[59] *Palsgraf v Long Island Railroad Co.*, 248 NY 339, 352, 162 NE 99 (NY 1928) (Andrews, J, dissenting).

[60] Linda Greenhouse, *On Voting Rights, Court Faces a Tangled Web*, NY Times (July 14, 1995) at A1.

[61] 115 S Ct at 2497 (O'Connor, J, concurring).

[62] 115 S Ct at 2497.

[63] Id.

portunity to assess race-conscious line-drawing in the concrete circumstances of a not-particularly-odd district that more or less followed the contours of previous white-dominated congressional
districts.[64] While *Hays* also featured heavy-handed intervention by
the Justice Department, the resulting districting plan was not so
wildly contorted as to announce its departure from "traditional
districting principles" to the casual observer. *Hays* therefore could
have offered some guidance as to the extent to which compactness was an independently controlling factor in the Court's constitutional analysis, as well as some indication of the extent to
which political boundaries such as precincts or parishes could be
breached in order to provide representation to historically excluded minority communities.

Instead, the Court put off its confrontation with the application
of its new constitutional principles by holding that since none of
the plaintiffs lived within the challenged majority-black congressional district, none met the injury-in-fact requirement for standing. For a Court seemingly so attentive to geometric precision,
Justice O'Connor's opinion for the majority was itself rather bizarre. As every child sitting attentively at the dinner table knows,
when a pie is to be divided into seven pieces for dessert, the dimensions and contours of each slice affect each other. However
the injury is defined—whether it comes through the state's essentializing citizens into their racial characteristics, or through the
"apartheid"-like[65] concentration of minority voters into the
"political homelands"[66] of one electoral district, or through the
state's excessive reliance on race to the complete subordination of

---

[64] Originally, the state legislature passed Act 42 in 1992, which created a district colloqui-
ally known as the "Zorro" district for its "Z"-like shape running across the northern and
eastern borders of Louisiana. This district ran through 28 parishes and five of Louisiana's
largest cities. See *U.S. v Hays*, 115 S Ct 2431, 2434 (1995). That district was struck down
by a district court in 1993. *Hays v Louisiana*, 839 F Supp 1188 (W D La 1993). After *Shaw*,
the Legislature substituted Act 1, which created the new district under challenge, the 4th
Congressional District. This new district to a large extent followed the boundaries of the
prior 8th Congressional District, which had been "crafted for the purpose of ensuring the
reelection of Congressman Gillis Long." *Hays v Louisiana*, 862 F Supp 119, 122 (WD La
1994). Despite the overlap, the district court concluded that the "*fundamental factor driving
[redistricting] Act 1 was race*." Id (emphasis in original).

[65] The unfortunate comparison of electoral districts to apartheid is from Justice O'Connor's opinion in *Shaw*, 113 S Ct 2816, 2827 (1993).

[66] This is the formulation used by Justice Thomas in his broadside attack on what he
termed the racial presumptions underlying two decades of vote-dilution caselaw. See *Holder
v Hall*, 114 S Ct 2581, 2598 (1994) (Thomas, J, concurring).

all other relevant public policies, or simply through the distortive effects of predictable groups not having electoral influence across a variety of districts—the injury appears common to all citizens of the state, and not simply those found residing within the allegedly malformed district.[67]

The Court's sudden concern for standing generally took commentators and, one suspects, the parties to the case, by surprise.[68] Only two Terms prior, the Court had written expansively on standing in *Northeastern Florida Contractors v Jacksonville*[69] to allow suit against a minority set-aside in municipal contracting to be brought by any potential bidder, regardless whether the set-aside actually resulted in the denial of a contract to the plaintiff. More immediately, the sudden interest in standing brought *Hays* into direct conflict with *Shaw* in which the Court entertained a challenge to a district in which no plaintiff resided.[70]

While doctrines such as standing and ripeness have an independent constitutional component stemming from the case or controversy requirement of Article III, they also serve important prudential aims as gatekeepers to the federal courts. Unfortunately, the standing requirement in *Hays* is unlikely to serve as a significant deterrent to litigation. In highly charged, highly visible cases affecting the distribution of real political power, the Court should expect plaintiffs to be readily available and readily recruitable. Indeed, this is what has already happened in *Hays*. Despite the Court's instructions on remand to dismiss the complaint, the district court permitted a simple amendment reinstituting the action with some different named plaintiffs. In light of *Miller*, the three-judge district court in *Hays* can be expected to reinstitute its prior

---

[67] Interestingly, Professor Karlan goes at the standing requirement after *Hays* in the opposite direction. She raises the issue whether each citizen within the allegedly contorted district has been *"personally* . . . subjected to a racial classification." *Hays*, 115 S Ct at 2433 (emphasis added). Professor Karlan makes two distinct arguments. First, she takes the category of "filler" persons (individuals who need to be added to a district to meet the numerical requirements of equipopulational districts) as being a group whose racial identity is really not of interest to the state. Second, and more centrally, she argues that the conception of harm is itself misplaced when the end result is districts that are heavily integrated. Karlan, *Still Hazy* (cited in note 3).

[68] Although the issue was raised, appellants devoted only three pages to the issue in their brief. Brief for Appellant, *Louisiana v Hays*, 115 S Ct 1311 (1995).

[69] 113 S Ct 2297 (1993).

[70] Pamela S. Karlan, *All Over the Map: The Supreme Court's Voting Rights Trilogy*, 1993 Supreme Court Review 245, 278.

opinion,[71] thereby putting off until next Term the Supreme Court's confrontation with the constitutional interplay of race and politics in Louisiana. Meanwhile, the *Supreme Court Review* appears poised for a Dickensian descent into installment tribulations in the halls of justice.

II. MODELS OF POLITICS

There is no escaping the fact that the Supreme Court's equal protection law is being driven by Justice O'Connor. Not since *Metro Broadcasting*[72] has she cast her vote in dissent, despite the numerous five-to-four opinions in this area. What emerges from the Court's unsatisfying confrontation with the racial gerrymandering cases, then, is three distinct views of the role of race in politics that correspond to the divided four-member blocs and to Justice O'Connor alone.

1. *Racial neutrality.* Four members of the Court (Chief Justice Rehnquist and Justices Kennedy, Scalia, and Thomas) seem clearly inclined to hold all state race-based decision making unconstitutional absent truly extraordinary, compelling state interests. This wing of the Court has now articulated two distinct arguments for race neutrality. The first draws from cases under either the Constitution[73] or antidiscrimination statutes such as Title VII[74] in which a formal reading of equality denies to state authorities any capacity to rely on racial classifications except in the narrowest remedial circumstances. Of late, this wing of the Court has added a stigmatic harm argument to its demand for formal equality. The source of the stigmatic harm is the "essentialized" treatment of individuals as nothing more than a constituent component of a homogeneous, racially defined group.[75] While present in both

---

[71] While this article was in press, the challenged *Hays* district was again struck down. *Cleofields' District Rejected*, Times-Picayune (Jan 6, 1996), at A2.

[72] 497 US 547 (1990).

[73] *Regents of the Univ. of California v Bakke*, 438 US 265, 289–90 (1978); *Wygant v Jackson Bd. of Educ.*, 476 US 267, 279–82 (1986).

[74] *Johnson v Transportation Agency, Santa Clara County, Cal.*, 480 US 616, 664–66 (1987) (Scalia, J, dissenting); *Firefighter Local Union No. 1784 v Stotts*, 467 US 561, 581 (1984) (Scalia, J, dissenting).

[75] For a fuller account of the strengths and limitations of the anti-essentialism principle, see T. Alexander Aleinikoff and Samuel Issacharoff, *Race and Redistricting: Drawing Constitutional Lines After Shaw v Reno*, 92 Mich L Rev 588, 615–18 (1993).

Shaw and *Miller*, the strongest articulation has come from Justice Thomas's advocation of the repeal of all vote-dilution law:

> The dabbling in political theory that dilution cases have prompted, however, is hardly the worst aspect of our vote dilution jurisprudence. Far more pernicious has been the Court's willingness to accept the one underlying premise that must inform every minority vote dilution claim: the assumption that the group asserting dilution is not merely a racial or ethnic group, but a group having distinct political interests as well. Of necessity, in resolving vote dilution actions we have given credence to the view that race defines political interest.[76]

This wing of the Court has not yet held a solid majority for its equal protection jurisprudence.[77] More significantly, there has been no hint in the cases to date whether this equal protection approach could extricate the exquisite knowledge of local demographics from the process of redistricting.

2. *Racial opacity.* This has emerged as the heart of Justice O'Connor's equal protection jurisprudence. Unwilling to call a halt to all beneficial uses of racial classifications to remediate societal inequities, but also deeply troubled by the increasing evidence of racial factionalism, O'Connor demands primarily that the use of race not be excessive.[78] Where race or racialism is visible to the casual eye, it is constitutionally infirm. Given the intensity of all interest group demands during the redistricting process, obscuring the racial dynamic of political systems is no mean feat. Seemingly, Justice O'Connor is willing to consider the racial dimensions of majority-minority districts to be sufficiently opaque when such districts appear either as the product of natural configurations (e.g., Maxine Waters's 35th Congressional District in south-central Los Angeles, or Charles Rangel's 15th Congressional District in Harlem), or as I shall return to, when such districts emerge as the product of a system at some remove from naked racial demands.

---

[76] *Holder v Hall,* 114 S Ct 2581, 1597 (1994) (Thomas, J, dissenting).

[77] In those cases in which these Justices have been in the majority, the opinion of the Court was either written by Justice O'Connor (e.g., *Croson, Shaw*) or else one may speculate that the need to secure O'Connor's indispensable fifth vote tempered the final majority opinion (e.g., *Miller*).

[78] In this regard, O'Connor clearly harkens back to Justice Powell. See John C. Jefferies, Jr., *Justice Lewis F. Powell, Jr.* 472–500 (Scribner, 1994) (describing the impetus toward nonobvious racial considerations as motivating Powell's opinion in *Bakke*).

3. *Racial pluralism.* At the opposite pole of the Court are Justices Breyer, Ginsburg, Souter, and Stevens. While lacking a fully formed version of what Professor Lani Guinier would term a "concept of group representation as a universal remedial principle of democratic accountability and legitimacy,"[79] these Justices nonetheless share a strong pluralist commitment to representative bodies. In other words, these Justices seem less concerned with the decision-making processes by which political actors achieve a redistricting plan as with the output in terms of representational opportunity. In Justice Souter's dissent in *Shaw* and again in the dissenting opinions of Justices Stevens and Ginsburg in *Miller*, the focus is exclusively on the integrated quality of the governmental bodies that result from the redistricting process. Accordingly, in the absence of distortion of the opportunity for roughly equal group-based representation, no one may claim to have "suffered any legally cognizable injury."[80] Rather than abjure group-based allocative decisions, as advocated by Justice Thomas, this pole of the Court accepts them as both inescapable in the political context and as indispensable in conferring legitimacy to governmental decision makers.

Either the first or last model could be operationalized. The first would condemn any redistricting activity in which race played a role. Under this view, courts would be expected to play an active role in checking the inevitable propensity of savvy political actors to peek at the demographic consequences of redistricting. Whether redistricting as we know it could survive this standard of judicial review has not yet been tested. The last Court approach,

---

[79] Guinier (cited in note 15) at 137.

[80] *Miller*, 115 S Ct at 2497 (Stevens, J, dissenting). The flip side of this argument was articulated by Justice Souter in rejecting a claim by Dade County Cuban-Americans that the Voting Rights Act entitled them to superordinate representation simply because the state could have drawn more beneficial district lines:

> [The district court's reading of] § 2 to define dilution as any failure to maximize tends to obscure the very object of the statute and to run counter to its textually stated purpose. One may suspect vote dilution from political famine, but one is not entitled to suspect (much less infer) dilution from mere failure to guarantee a political feast. However prejudiced a society might be, it would be absurd to suggest that the failure of a districting scheme to provide a minority group with effective political power 75 percent above its numerical strength indicates a denial of equal participation in the political process. Failure to maximize cannot be the measure of § 2.

Johnson v DeGrandy, 114 S Ct 2647, 2659–60 (1994) (footnote omitted).

by contrast, would license an extremely robust process of political jockeying in which interest-group factionalism would likely and perhaps necessarily emerge as a dominant force. Under this view, judicial review would return to the less thicket-bound role of insuring that no group is denied a roughly adequate place at the table.

The unresolved issue after *Miller* is how either of these approaches to race and politics can combine with the O'Connor approach to yield a stable doctrinal basis for judicial oversight of the redistricting process. O'Connor's views through *Shaw* and *Miller* allow for a balanced and nuanced use of race that requires almost a precise rendering of the individual factors taken into account in the redistricting process and a balance sheet of how they were weighted. This type of procedural balancing of different factors is difficult to reconcile with the rough-and-tumble world of political deals. Indeed, O'Connor, the one former state legislator on the Court, should know this better than any of her brethren. But, perhaps, it is precisely because of O'Connor's familiarity with the tenacity of interest group factionalism once unleashed in the political process that she emerges as the spokesperson for the appearance of disinterestedness in the districting process. In the final analysis, the consequence of her demand for opacity may well be to doom the efforts of legislative redistricting altogether.

It is here that *DeWitt v Wilson* may offer some insight. As made clear in the dissenting opinion of Justice Mosk in the California Supreme Court, the redistricting process in California was driven to an overwhelming extent by the desire to accommodate claims for minority representation and avoid even the possibility of challenge under Section 2 of the Voting Rights Act.[81] Indeed, the Special Masters who oversaw redistricting were charged with giving the Voting Rights Act "the highest possible consideration in order to minimize the risk of challenge and resulting delay."[82] While this may appear an invitation to the same process of maximizing minority voting strength that doomed redistricting in Georgia, there is a critical difference.

---

[81] The *Wilson* court adopted the report of the Special Masters, *Wilson v Eu*, 1 Cal 4th 707, 715 (1992), with its express emphasis on "minimiz[ing] Voting Rights Act challenges based on failure to acknowledge a particular geographically compact minority group . . . ."

[82] *Wilson v Eu*, 1 Cal 4th 707, 742 (1992).

California interposed a buffer between direct political demands and the outcomes of the redistricting process. Pursuant to state law, the failure of the legislature to redistrict transferred the reapportionment process to a three-member tribunal comprised of retired Justices of the state Supreme Court. The role of the Special Masters in mediating the demands of minority constituents, incumbent officials, and other interested parties allowed the Court to accept a characterization of the redistricting process in California as not driven exclusively or even "predominantly" by racial and ethnic considerations. Only by redistricting at one remove from interested political officials could the Masters claim that they only "attempted to reasonably accommodate the interests of every 'functionally, geographically compact' minority group of sufficient voting strength to constitute a majority in a single-member district."[83] Only such a buffer could allow the California Supreme Court to describe the clear awareness of the racial and ethnic consequences of redistricting as nonetheless properly circumscribed: "the functional aspect of geographical compactness takes into account the presence or absence of a sense of community made possible by open lines of access and communication."[84] And only this process of imposing a filter on clear interest group demands allowed the three-judge federal reviewing court to likewise conclude that

> The Masters did not draw district lines based deliberately and solely on race, with arbitrary distortions of district boundaries. The Masters, in formulating the redistricting plan, properly looked at race, not as the sole criteria in drawing lines but as one of many factors to be considered.[85]

Thus, California stands in contrast to the process under review in *Miller* where the Justice Department played the role of a direct political heavy with no intermediary to filter its "max-black" strategy. This augurs poorly for the fate of North Carolina's redistricting in the return engagement of *Shaw*.[86] Presumably, this

---

[83] Id at 714–15 (quoting the Report of the Special Masters, pp 399–400 of 4 Cal Rptr 2d 565–66).

[84] 1 Cal 4th at 715.

[85] *DeWitt v Wilson*, 856 F Supp 1409, 1413 (E D Cal 1994).

[86] The Supreme Court remanded *Shaw* with instructions for the district court to review the claims under strict scrutiny. Subsequently, the district court found that the challenged districting plan was narrowly tailored to meet a compelling state interest in providing for minority representation. *Shaw v Hunt*, 861 F Supp 408 (E D N C 1994) (three-judge court).

augurs poorly as well for districts such as the 13th in Texas where the direct beneficiary of the extravagant line-drawing, Congresswoman Eddie Bernice Johnson, was a central player in the state senate in devising the post-1990 congressional districts.[87]

I have previously addressed the effect of litigation-generating imprecise rules on the capacity of political bodies to redistrict.[88] A number of factors have come together to make redistricting increasingly complex. Computer technology has made ever greater manipulations of district lines not only possible but readily accessible to a vast array of interested parties. Political players, not only parties but interested factions, are more attentive to the spoils of redistricting. But the imprecision of legal constraints and the absence of any appreciable safe haven from litigation have brought the process to the brink of collapse. Since 1980 there has been a marked increase in the number of state and local bodies unable to discharge their redistricting obligations and instead leaving the battles to be fought out in the courts or settled before nonpartisan commissions. Now that the Court has decisively added equal protection uncertainty, redistricting begins to appear as only the initial step in a decade's worth of expensive and caustic litigation.

If one bright spot emerges from the Court's 1994 Term it is the prospect that nonpartisan commissions may provide the same protection from equal protection challenge as they appear to have from charges of partisan gerrymandering.[89] Perhaps the Court is adding one more signal that the time has come to remove redistricting entirely from the hands of political actors who are most susceptive to capture.

The Supreme Court accepted a second appeal in this case, which has been argued this Term. *Shaw v Hunt*, prob jur noted, 115 S Ct 2639 (1995).

[87] See the specially concurring opinion of Judge Hittner at the district court level detailing the pitched battles of insiders for defined racial and ethnic constituents. *Vera v Richards*, 861 F Supp 2639, 1346–51 (SD Tex 1994).

[88] See Samuel Issacharoff, *Judging Politics: The Elusive Quest for Judicial Review of Political Fairness*, 71 Tex L Rev 1643 (1993) (describing the imprecise demands of the constitutional prohibition on the "consistent degradation" of partisan political influence through gerrymandering); Samuel Issacharoff, *Supreme Court Destabilization of Single-Member Districts*, XX Univ Chicago Legal Forum XX (forthcoming 1995) (describing the inconsistency between the positive demands made on political systems under Supreme Court caselaw and that which single-member districts can be expected to meet).

[89] Samuel Issacharoff, *Supreme Court Destabilization of Single-Member Districts*, 1995 U Chi Legal F 205.

III. Conclusion

Taken in combination, *Miller* and *Hays* serve primarily to underscore that the current fault line in the Court's equal protection law runs smack through the constitutive steps of the political process. *Miller* is no doubt the more significant case in that for the first time the Court brought the force of the Constitution to bear directly against a districting arrangement that had been created under the compulsion of the Voting Rights Act.[90] The Court's assertion of a muscular standard of constitutional scrutiny sent tremors through the emerging minority political establishment. It also seemed to foreshadow repeated confrontations between a recalcitrant Court and the most important legacy of the voting rights revolution: a political system increasingly accessible to minority political actors. *Miller*, however, served only to heighten the tension between formal equal protection law and the rough-and-tumble of interest group politics. Like its direct predecessor *Shaw*, *Miller* left the hard issues clouded behind harsh rhetoric and a cautious definition of actual legal standards.

The Court's repeated yet indecisive entry into the tangled world of redistricting exacts real institutional costs. If ever there was doubt, the experience since *Shaw* has demonstrated that redistricting is not an arena in which the Court can provide "a cue to a fellow constitutional actor" through a broad articulation of constitutional principle.[91] The stakes in the redistricting battles are too great and the number of interested potential litigants too many to allow the Court such an elegant exit from this difficult terrain. Narrowly construed in terms of doctrinal law, the Court's opinions in *Shaw*, *Miller*, and *Hays* already carry the imprint of a jurisprudence formed by what Judge Augustus Hand once termed a "judicial hunch."[92] The absence of identifiable, guiding constitutional

---

[90] In *Shaw*, the Court had held only that redistricting decisions based on racial considerations were actionable and were subject to strict scrutiny. 113 S Ct 2816, 2828 (1993).

[91] See Philip Bobbitt, *Constitutional Fate: Theory of the Constitution* 194 (Oxford, 1982), who describes this function as "not the threat of invalidating legislation *per se* so much as the argument for a different construction of the Constitution."

[92] Letter from Augustus N. Hand to Louis D. Brandeis (Nov 21, 1931), quoted in Alexander M. Bickel and Harry H. Wellington, *Legislative Process and the Judicial Process: The Lincoln Mills Case*, 71 Harv L Rev 1, 16 (1957).

principles threatens the integrity of judicial review over the political process. As Justice Frankfurter warned at the commencement of the reapportionment revolution,

> The Court's authority—possessed of neither the purse nor the sword—ultimately rests on sustained public confidence in its moral sanction. Such feeling must be nourished by the Court's complete detachment, in fact and in appearance, from political entanglements and by abstention from injecting itself into the clash of political forces in political settlement.[93]

The doctrinal morass is in turn made all the more impenetrable by the persistence of the constitutional redistricting question on the Court's docket. *Shaw* begets *Miller*, which in turn will yield in short order to the latest pronouncements concerning North Carolina,[94] Texas,[95] and perhaps Ohio and Louisiana once again. What appears fairly settled is that at mid-decade the Court is more squarely entwined in the political thicket than at any point since it entered the world of reapportionment thirty years ago.

---

[93] *Baker v Carr*, 369 US 186, 267 (1962) (Frankfurter, J, dissenting).

[94] *Shaw v Hunt*, 115 S Ct 2639 (1995).

[95] *Vera v Bush*, 115 S Ct 2639 (1995).

FREDERICK SCHAUER

ASHWANDER REVISITED

It is a fixed point of American constitutionalism that judicial review is an exceptional event. The judicial invalidation of an Act of Congress, and to a lesser extent the invalidation on constitutional grounds of state legislation or the acts of federal and state executive officials, is disfavored, a route to be taken only when it is "unavoidable."[1] We accept the authority of the courts to invalidate the decisions of other bodies, but just barely. The background of judicial review in the United States appears to be a social contract that grants the power of judicial review to the judiciary on the understanding that that power will be exercised only with the greatest reluctance. In part this reluctance stems from what is routinely labeled the "countermajoritarian difficulty,"[2] the tension between the powers exercised by an unelected judiciary and the political primacy of legislative and executive bodies substantially more responsive to the short-term popular will. And in part the reluctance to exercise the power of judicial review is driven, or at least heightened, by the absence of any specific authorization in the constitutional text for the courts to exercise the power of judicial review at all.[3]

Frederick Schauer is Frank Stanton Professor of the First Amendment, John F. Kennedy School of Government, Harvard University.

AUTHOR'S NOTE: I have profited greatly from the discussions of the *X-Citement Video* case at a seminar on Law and Linguistics organized by Professors Clark Cunningham and Judith Levi, and sponsored by the School of Law of Washington University and the Department of Linguistics of Northwestern University.

[1] *Specter Motor Service, Inc. v McLaughlin*, 323 US 101, 105 (1944).

[2] Alexander Bickel, *The Least Dangerous Branch* 16 (1962).

[3] See Learned Hand, *The Bill of Rights* (1958); David Currie, *The Constitution in the Supreme Court, 1801–1835*, 49 U Chi L Rev 646, 660 (1982); William W. Van Alstyne, *A Critical Guide to Marbury v Madison*, 1969 Duke L J 1, 17.

The disfavor of judicial invalidation on constitutional grounds of the actions of more popularly responsive bodies is operationalized by numerous theories, doctrines, rules, principles, maxims, and standards. Of all of these, few have been as enduring as the collection of principles set forth by Justice Louis Brandeis in his concurring opinion in *Ashwander v Tennessee Valley Authority*.[4] Here Brandeis restated seven principles for the avoidance of constitutional questions, at least three of which involved the discretionary refusal of jurisdiction,[5] with the balance setting forth ways in which constitutional decisions can and should be avoided by deciding a case on narrower or nonconstitutional grounds. And of these principles for avoiding constitutional questions in preference for decision on other grounds, none has been as important as the one directing courts to construe a statute to avoid reaching a constitutional question if such a construction is at all possible.

Indeed, the principle of avoiding constitutional questions by statutory construction appears in two different versions in Brandeis's list. First, he says that "[t]he Court will not pass upon a constitutional question although properly presented by the record, if there is also present some other ground upon which the case may be disposed of. This rule has found most varied application. Thus, if a case can be decided on either of two grounds, one involving a constitutional question, the other a question of statutory construction or general law, the Court will decide only the latter."[6] Brandeis then added what he presented as a separate principle—" '[w]hen the validity of an act of the Congress is drawn in question, and even if a serious doubt of constitutionality is raised, it is a cardinal principle that this Court will first ascertain whether a construction of the statute is fairly possible by which the question may be avoided' "[7]—even though this principle is plainly very closely related to the previously quoted one. Under both of these principles, therefore, constitutional adjudication is to be treated as a "last resort."[8]

---

[4] 297 US 288, 347–48 (1936) (Brandeis concurring).

[5] See *Rescue Army v Municipal Court of Los Angeles*, 331 US 549 (1947); Bickel at 115–32 (cited in note 2). Compare Gerald Gunther, *The Subtle Vices of the Passive Virtues*, 64 Colum L Rev 1 (1964).

[6] 297 US at 347.

[7] Id at 348, citing *Crowell v Benson*, 285 US 22, 62 n 8 (1932).

[8] *Ashwander*, 297 US at 346 (Brandeis concurring), citing *Chicago & Grand Trunk Ry. v Wellman*, 143 US 339, 345 (1892). For an important description and analysis of the last

Although the strategy of construing a statute so as to avoid having to make a constitutional decision did not originate with Brandeis's *Ashwander* opinion,[9] it was *Ashwander* that gave the principle
so much of its enduring importance.[10] Today, as disputes centered
on the interpretation of federal statutes occupy an increasingly
larger percentage of the Supreme Court's workload,[11] this last of
the *Ashwander* principles has become ever more important. Although the standard citation to the Brandeis opinion in *Ashwander*
has been supplanted by an equally standard citation to *Edward J.
DeBartolo Corp. v Florida Gulf Coast Building and Construction Trades
Council,*[12] the Court still routinely interprets statutes in order to
immunize them from constitutional objection, and in so doing

---

resort principle generally, see Lisa A. Kloppenberg, *Avoiding Constitutional Questions,* 35 BC
L Rev 1003 (1994).

[9] The earliest emergence of the principle is traceable to Chief Justice Marshall. "[I]f the
case may be determined on other grounds, a just respect for the legislature requires, that
the obligation of its laws should not be unnecessarily and wantonly assailed." *Ex parte Ran-
dolph,* 20 F Cas 242, 254 (CCD Va 1833) (No 11, 538) (Marshall). See also *Murray v The
Schooner Charming Betty,* 6 US (2 Cranch) 64, 118 (1804) (Marshall); *Hooper v California,*
155 US 648. 657 (1895).

[10] For important applications, see *Jean v Nelson,* 472 US 846, 854 (1985); *Heckler v Ma-
thews,* 465 US 728, 741–42 (1984); *United States v Clark,* 445 US 23, 27 (1980); *NLRB v
Catholic Bishop,* 440 US 490, 499–501 (1979); *United States v Bass,* 404 US 336 (1971); *Int'l
Ass'n of Machinists v Street,* 367 US 740, 749 (1961).

[11] To support my general impression I have informally consulted the section entitled
"The Statistics" in the annual Supreme Court issue of the *Harvard Law Review.* The category "Civil Actions from Inferior Federal Courts" is a good if imperfect guide to the trends
in the Court's involvement with statutory interpretation issues because the editors distinguish the grounds of decision into "Constitutional" and "Other." In the 1972 Term there
were 40 Constitutional and 58 Other, for a percentage of Other of 59%. In the 1973 Term
there were 34 Constitutional and 59 Other, for a percentage of Other of 63%. In the 1977
Term there were 33 Constitutional and 53 Other, for a percentage of Other of 61%. In
the 1981 Term there were 41 Constitutional and 72 Other, for a percentage of Other of
64%. In the 1985 Term there were 36 Constitutional and 66 Other, the percentage of
Other being 65%. Since the 1987 Term, however, the percentages of Other have risen
significantly. In the 1987 Term there were 20 Constitutional and 72 Other, for a percentage
of Other of 75%. In the 1990 Term there were 16 Constitutional and 58 Other, a percentage of Other of 79%. In the 1991 Term there were 17 Constitutional and 51 Other, for
a percentage of Other of 75%. In the 1992 Term there were 23 Constitutional and 54
Other, for an Other percentage of 70%. In the 1994 Term there were 13 Constitutional and
36 Other, the percentage of Other being 75%. The 1987 figure is the highest percentage of
Other in any of the past 25 years, and 1990 is second. The lowest was the 1976 Term
with 48%.

[12] 485 US 568 (1988). For examples of recent reliance on *Ashwander* as filtered through
DeBartolo, see *Concrete Pipe and Products of California, Inc. v Construction Laborers Pension
Trust for Southern California,* 113 S Ct 2264 (1993); *Burns v United States,* 501 US 129, 138
(1991); *Cheek v United States,* 498 US 192, 203 (1991); *Public Citizen v United States Depart-
ment of Justice,* 491 US 440 (1989); and the disputes in *Zobrest v Catalina Foothills School
Dist.,* 113 S Ct 2462 (1993), and *Rust v Sullivan,* 500 US 173 (1991).

diminishes the number of decisions on overtly constitutional grounds that it and the lower federal courts must make.

Yet in interpreting statutes so as to avoid "unnecessary" constitutional decisions, the Court frequently interprets a statute in ways that its drafters did not anticipate, and, constitutional questions aside,[13] in ways that its drafters may not have preferred. Accordingly, it is by no means clear that a strained interpretation of a federal statute that avoids a constitutional question is any less a judicial intrusion than the judicial invalidation on constitutional grounds of a less strained interpretation of the same statute. At the very least, such practices make clear that it is too quick to take the avoidance of constitutional questions as a principle having a lexical priority over all other principles of judicial behavior. Rather, the increasingly common practice of interpreting statutes so as to avoid constitutional questions involves paying a price for the benefits thought to come from judicial reticence in the exercise of its constitutional authority. Yet as the arguments for such judicial reticence become more attenuated—*Marbury v Madison*[14] is, after all, 193 years old, and a clear majority of the current Court accepts without embarrassment the concept of substantive due process[15]—it may be time to revisit this most important of the *Ashwander* principles, and at the same time to examine more carefully the relationship between the *Ashwander* principle of constitutional avoidance and the various other rules and principles that guide the process of statutory interpretation. In doing this we will discover that the costs of *Ashwander* are greater than are commonly appreciated, and that its benefits are becoming increasingly remote.

I. United States v X-Citement Video, Inc.

Although numerous recent cases illustrate the persistence of the *Ashwander* principle of avoidance of constitutional ques-

---

[13] The phrase in the text indulges in the harmless but often false assumption that legislators would sacrifice some of their political or policy preferences in order to produce constitutionally sound (in the opinion of the courts) legislation.

[14] 5 US (1 Cranch) 137 (1803).

[15] See *United States v Carlton*, 114 S Ct 2018 (1994). I would trace the era of nonembarrassment about explicitly relying on substantive due process to *Moore v City of East Cleveland*, 431 US 494 (1977).

tions,[16] and although a substantial proportion of these cases pose the conflict between the avoidance of constitutional questions and the other goals of statutory interpretation, no case does so with the clarity of *United States v X-Citement Video, Inc.*[17] This decision thus provides a timely vehicle for exploring the conflict among the multiple goals of statutory interpretation, and also for putting on the table the central question—whether the *Ashwander* principle of constitutional avoidance by statutory construction should be scrapped in its entirety.

X-Citement Video was a child pornography case, before the Supreme Court on certiorari from a Ninth Circuit decision overturning a criminal conviction under the amended version of the Protection of Children Against Sexual Exploitation Act of 1977.[18] That act, as described in Chief Justice Rehnquist's opinion for the Court, "prohibits the interstate transportation, shipping, receipt, distribution or reproduction of depictions of minors engaged in sexually explicit conduct."[19] After *New York v Ferber*,[20] it is clear that the sexually explicit material involved in a child pornography prosecution need not satisfy the three-part obscenity test of *Miller v California*[21] in order to provide the basis for a constitutionally permissible criminal conviction. As long as the material depicts "sexual conduct" or "lewd exhibition of the genitals" by minors, it is not constitutionally necessary for the material, taken as a whole, to "appeal to the prurient interest," to be "patently offensive," or to be lacking in "serious literary, artistic, political, or scientific value," these being the primary components of the *Miller* test for obscenity. Yet although *Ferber* departs from the *Miller* standards when the issue is child pornography, even after *Ferber* the concerns of the First Amendment are not absent from child pornography doctrine. In particular, *X-Citement Video* raised the issue of what kind of knowledge and intent a defendant in a child

---

[16] See citations in note 12. For ease of exposition I will abbreviate to "*Ashwander* principle" the two specific and related principles quoted above.

[17] 115 S Ct 464 (1994).

[18] 18 USC § 2252 (1988 and Supp V).

[19] 115 S Ct at 468.

[20] 458 US 747 (1982). For a contemporaneous analysis of the decision, see Frederick Schauer, *Codifying the First Amendment: New York v Ferber*, 1982 Supreme Court Review 285.

[21] 413 US 15 (1973).

pornography case must be shown to have had in order that the conviction be consistent with the First Amendment.

In a standard (not child pornography) obscenity case, it has been settled since *Smith v California*[22] in 1959 that criminal obscenity convictions require proof of *scienter*, a showing that the defendant not only knowingly sold materials later found to be legally obscene, but at the time of sale (or transportation, distribution, or whatever) was in fact aware of the sexual explicitness of the materials. It is not necessary under *Smith* that the prosecution prove that the defendant knew that the materials were in fact legally obscene, but it is necessary to show that the defendant knew of the "nature and character" of the materials, as the Court subsequently made clear in *Hamling v United States*.[23]

In the context of a child pornography prosecution, *Ferber* explicitly held that the *scienter* requirement of *Smith* and *Hamling* persists, and thus even in a child pornography case it is necessary for the prosecution to establish that the defendant was aware of the sexually explicit nature of the materials providing the basis for the charge.[24] But *Ferber* did not address the precise issue before the Court in *X-Citement Video*: whether the defendant must be shown not only to have had knowledge of the sexually explicit nature of the materials, but also to have had knowledge that the materials portrayed people who were, or at least likely were (or appeared to be), under the age of sixteen. The argument in favor of a *scienter* requirement directed specifically to the likely age of the participants is a straightforward extension of the argument that prevailed in *Smith* itself: The principal concern of *Smith* was that the distribution of constitutionally protected materials not be chilled by the excess caution of a distributor legally responsible for scrutinizing an entire inventory, much of it not even plausibly unlawful. Since the child pornography laws make criminal the distribution of materials less sexually explicit than the degree of explicitness required for an obscenity conviction, the danger of self-censorship by excess caution is even greater for child pornography than it was in *Smith* itself. Yet since *Ferber* is based precisely on the fact that the concern for protecting children from sexual ex-

---

[22] 361 US 147 (1959).

[23] 418 US 87 (1974).

[24] *Ferber*, 458 US at 764.

ploitation is a sufficiently compelling interest to justify relaxing what would otherwise have been the requirements of the First Amendment, there is also a strong argument to the contrary—that imposing the obligation of prior scrutiny on the shipper, transporter, receiver, exhibitor, seller, or distributor, even if that imposition does produce some excess self-censorship, is a price worth paying for the social benefits achieved by lessening the incentive to produce, distribute, transport, or sell child pornography.

Against this background of doctrinal silence, coupled with plausible constitutional and policy arguments both for and against imposing an age-focused *scienter* requirement, the Supreme Court confronted a statute that on its miserably drafted face did not appear to impose such a requirement. As amended, the statute provides that

> (a) Any person who—
> (1) knowingly transports or ships in interstate or foreign commerce by any means including by computer or mails, any visual depiction, if—
>> (A) the producing of such visual depiction involves the use of a minor engaging in sexually explicit conduct; and
>> (B) such visual depiction is of such conduct;
>> . . .
> shall be punished as provided in subsection (b) of this section.[25]

The key issue is the referent of the adverb "knowingly." If "knowingly" is interpreted to modify "the use of a minor engaging in sexually explicit conduct" as well as to "transports or ships in interstate or foreign commerce . . . ," then there can be no possible First Amendment *scienter* objection, since the statute itself would then include a requirement of knowledge as to every element of the offense, including the age of the performers. But if "knowingly" is interpreted to refer only to knowledge of the transportation or shipping, and not to the possibility that minors were depicted in the materials transported or shipped, then it is not an element of the offense, at least on the face of the statute, that the defendant have had any knowledge about the actual, likely, or ap-

---

[25] 18 USC §h 2252(a)(1) (1988 and Supp V). The ellipsis in the text pertains to an essentially identical subsection (a)(2), which refers to receipt, distribution, and reproduction.

parent age of the individuals depicted in the sexually explicit materials.

Given the *scienter* requirement in obscenity law, and given the explicit determination in *Ferber* that some *scienter* requirement definitely applied to child pornography law as well, constitutional questions plainly lurked in the vicinity.[26] Yet the particular statute at issue in *X-Citement Video* is a prime example of the way in which the constitutional problem necessarily presented by one reading of the statute could be eliminated by another. And this is exactly the approach taken by Chief Justice Rehnquist for the *X-Citement Video* majority. If the Protection of Children Against Sexual Exploitation Act were to be interpreted such that "knowingly" did not apply to the age of the performer, then the statute might have been unconstitutional on its face under a plausible extension of *Smith, Hamling,* and *Ferber*. Citing *DeBartolo* and maintaining that "[i]t is incumbent upon us to read a statute to eliminate [constitutional] doubts so long as such a reading is not plainly contrary to the intent of Congress,"[27] the Chief Justice accordingly concluded that the constitutional problem suggested by *Smith, Hamling,* and *Ferber* should be avoided by interpreting the statute so that "knowingly" applied to age as well as to transportation. Because the *scienter* requirement consequently became an element of the offense under the statute, the constitutional *scienter* objection was eliminated and the statute emerged facially constitutional. And since there had been proof at trial directed to what was now an element of the offense, and the jury had been appropriately charged, interpreting the statute to include an age-focused *scienter* requirement so as to make it facially constitutional also resulted in the Supreme Court's reversing the Ninth Circuit and reinstating the conviction at trial.

Chief Justice Rehnquist acknowledged that the constitutionally guided interpretation was a less natural reading than one that would have had "knowingly" apply only to the transportation element, and not to the words that came after "if" in the statute.[28]

---

[26] The issue had in fact appeared in quite a large number of lower court cases. See, for example, *United States v Burian,* 19 F3d 188 (1994); *United States v Cochran,* 17 F3d 56 (1994); *United States v Gifford,* 17 F3d 462 (1994); *United States v Colavito,* 19 F3d 69 (1994); *United States v Gendron,* 18 F3d 955 (1994).

[27] 115 S Ct at 478.

[28] At one point the Chief Justice acknowledged that "[t]he most natural grammatical reading, adopted by the Ninth Circuit, suggests that the term 'knowingly' modifies only the

But for the majority, the cost of abandoning the most natural and most grammatical reading of the statute was worth the gain of avoiding the constitutional problem.[29] Indeed, for Justice Stevens, who issued a brief concurring opinion, the sacrifice was even less. Relying not so much on rules of syntax that applied across all occurrences of the English language but more on how he read *this* criminal statute in *this* particular context, Justice Stevens argued that "[i]n my opinion, the normal, commonsense reading of a subsection of a criminal statute introduced by the word 'knowingly' is to treat the adverb as modifying each of the elements of the offense identified in the remainder of the subsection."[30] Although Justice Stevens acknowledged that this reading was different from "the most grammatically correct reading,"[31] for him the majority's interpretation was hardly strained at all, since "reading this provision to require proof of scienter for each fact that must be proved is far more reasonable than adding such a requirement to a statutory offense that contains no scienter requirement whatsoever."[32]

In marked contrast to the views of Justice Stevens, Justice Scalia, joined in his dissent by Justice Thomas, found the majority's reading simply too hostile to the plain grammatical construction to permit what he saw as a blatant rewriting of the statute. For Justice Scalia, the majority's construction was a construction of the statute "that its language simply will not bear."[33] No precedent of the Court, he maintained, allowed the Court to add a *scienter* require-

---

surrounding verbs: transports, ships, receives, distributes, or reproduces. Under this construction, the word 'knowingly' would not modify the elements of the minority of the performers, or the sexually explicit nature of the material, because they are set forth in independent clauses separated by interruptive punctuation." 115 S Ct at 475. Accord, Brief Amicus Curiae of the Law and Linguistics Consortium in Support of Respondents, *United States of America v X-Citement Video, Inc., & Rubin Gottesman*, at 3–7. And at another point Chief Justice Rehnquist described this as "the most grammatical reading of the statute." 115 S Ct at 476.

[29] It is interesting to speculate about just what it is to have a "natural" reading of a statute with sections, subsections, parts, and subparts, and which nowhere contains anything that resembles an English sentence. This suggests the possibility—and I do no more here than suggest the possibility—that standard *legal* English contains not only individual terms otherwise absent from (or at least rare in) the English language (*trover*, for example, or *interrogatory* as a noun), but that it contains grammatical structures and syntactical rules designed to serve the distinctive functions of the legal system.

[30] Id at 478 (Stevens concurring).

[31] Id (Stevens concurring).

[32] Id (Stevens concurring).

[33] 115 S Ct at 479 (Scalia dissenting).

ment *"even when the plain text of the statute says otherwise."*[34] Justice Scalia's opinion, however, was guided not only by his view of the inexorable grammatical structure of the statute, but also, and likely more, by his view of the underlying substantive constitutional issue. To him the First Amendment did not compel attaching a requirement of knowledge to the age element of the offense at all, and the urgency of action against child pornography and its victims demanded that *Smith* not be extended in this way. He thus accused the majority of "rewrit[ing]" the statute "more radically than its survival demands," and of "rais[ing] baseless constitutional doubts that will impede congressional enactment of a law providing greater protection for the child-victims of the pornography industry."[35] Justice Scalia, therefore, saw the majority as having not only misinterpreted the plain language of the statute, but also as having done so in the service of the wrong constitutional result.

Assuming that the majority's construction of the statutory language was at the very least strained, as even Chief Justice Rehnquist admitted, or a total rewrite, as Justice Scalia argued, the conflict between competing goals is plainly presented. To be modest in rewriting the statute, as Justice Scalia urged, would have required the Court to confront a constitutional issue—application of the *scienter* requirement to age as a matter of the dictates of the First Amendment—that might otherwise have been avoided. But to avoid the constitutional question, and thus to avoid calling into question the validity of an Act of Congress, required the Court to undertake a moderately aggressive judicial redrafting of the statute, and that action would have been avoided were the Court to have been less reluctant to take on the constitutional question. Thus, *X-Citement Video* makes clear that the choice presented by the *Ash-*

---

[34] Id (Scalia dissenting) (emphasis in original). "I have been willing, in the case of civil statutes, to acknowledge a doctrine of 'scrivener's error' that permits a court to give an unusual (though not unheard-of) meaning to a word which, if given its normal meaning, would produce an absurd and arguably unconstitutional result. Even if I were willing to stretch that doctrine so as to give the problematic text a meaning it cannot possibly bear; and even if I were willing to extend the doctrine to criminal cases in which its application would produce conviction rather than acquittal; it would still have no proper bearing here. For the sine qua non of any 'scrivener's error' doctrine, it seems to me, is that the meaning genuinely intended but inadequately expressed must be absolutely clear; otherwise we might be rewriting the statute rather than correcting a technical mistake. That condition is not met here." Id at 480 (Scalia dissenting) (citation omitted).

[35] Id at 481 (Scalia dissenting).

wander principle is not a choice between judicial deference and judicial aggressiveness. Rather, it is a choice between two different types of judicial aggressiveness. Implicit in the *Ashwander* principle is the view that judicial aggressiveness in statutory interpretation is less politically and systemically troublesome than judicial aggressiveness in taking on constitutional questions, and even in declaring Acts of Congress unconstitutional. But why is that so?

II. The Cost of Ashwander

In the absence of the constitutional consideration, the interpretive question presented by *X-Citement Video* is not especially close. Unguided by substantive legal principles, whether from the Constitution or from the general principles of criminal law, the most natural reading of the language in the statute would suggest that "knowingly" attaches to transportation, shipping, receipt, distribution, and reproduction, but not to the age of the performers. Even Justice Stevens, for whom the Court's conclusion is least inconsistent with the most natural reading of the statutory language, does not go so far as to say that the reading he finds comfortably permissible in the context of this criminal statute is the one he would have reached unguided by substantive principles external to the bare language of the statute. So although the opinions of the Justices represent a range of views about whether the majority's interpretation is simply impermissible as a matter of the syntactical and grammatical rules of standard English (Scalia and Thomas), permissible even though difficult (Rehnquist, O'Connor, Kennedy, Souter, Ginsberg, and Breyer), and permissible and not especially difficult (Stevens), it is clear that the majority's reading is different from the conclusion that would have been reached in the absence of the constitutional concern. If the *scienter* requirement existed nowhere in the law, or did not inform (whether as a matter of constitutional law or as a matter of the "general part" of the criminal law) the interpretation of this statute, we would hardly have expected a court on this language to conclude that the defendant must be shown to have had knowledge of the actual, likely, or apparent age of the performers.

Moreover, this conclusion is not just a matter of a literal or acontextual reading of the words and grammatical structure of the statute.[36] If we look instead to the likely intentions of Congress, or if we consider what we might expect Congress to have answered if asked the specific question about the application of the *scienter* requirement to the age of the performers, there is little in history or politics that would suggest a congressional eagerness, or even willingness, to add elements to the prosecution's burden in child pornography cases other than those elements plainly required by the applicable cases and principles of constitutional law. That the most recent child pornography bill before Congress passed in the Senate on a voice vote, and in the House by a vote of 417–0,[37] speaks volumes about the congressional proclivity to add elements to the offense whose effect would be to decrease the likelihood of a conviction in a child pornography case. Congress certainly has a desire, we can assume, not to have its statutes declared unconstitutional. But it is fair to surmise that any inference about congressional intent to include a *scienter* requirement would be inspired solely by congressional views about surviving a court challenge, and not at all about Congress's views about sound policy. Nothing other than the substantive principles of constitutional law would have given an interpreting court warrant to assume that uncertainties in the statutory language should be resolved in favor of a defendant in a child pornography case.

The nature of the substantive issue, therefore, ought to leave little doubt that the interpretation chosen by the *X-Citement Video* majority is a less comfortable interpretation of the statutory language standing alone than the opposite interpretation would have been, and is as well a less comfortable interpretation of the statutory language in light of the legislative intent than the opposite interpretation would have been. This discomfort makes it apparent, even without the exclamation point added by Justice Scalia's

---

[36] Unlike most modern American students of statutory interpretation, I do not take the references to a "literal" or "acontextual" reading as necessarily pejorative. See Frederick Schauer, *Playing by the Rules: A Philosophical Examination of Rule-Based Decision-Making in Law and in Life* 92–97 (1991); Frederick Schauer, *The Practice and Problems of Plain Meaning*, 45 Vand L Rev 715 (1992); Frederick Schauer, *Statutory Construction and the Coordinating Function of Plain Meaning*, 1990 Supreme Court Review 231. Compare William N. Eskridge, Jr., *The New Textualism*, 37 UCLA L Rev 621 (1990); Cass R. Sunstein, *Interpreting Statutes in the Regulatory State*, 103 Harv L Rev 405 (1989).

[37] HR 1240, the Sexual Crimes Against Children Protection Act of 1995, passed in the House on March 15, 1995, and in the Senate on April 6, 1995. The two versions are slightly different, and the bill is now before a conference committee to reconcile the differences.

dissent, that the *Ashwander* principle of constitutional avoidance is not without cost to whatever systemic values lead a constitutionally unimpeded interpreter to interpret a statute in one way rather than another. Nor is there any reason to suppose that it ever would be. It is hard to imagine a case in which, constitutional considerations aside, there would be two identically plausible interpretations, such that, constitutional considerations again aside, the rational judge would be reduced to something akin to tossing a coin. In almost any case we can imagine, the constitution-free principles of statutory interpretation will likely favor one result over another. And thus in almost any case likely to arise, a constitutional or prudential principle directing courts to reach conclusions other than the ones they would have reached absent that principle involves a cost measured in the value of those considerations of policy and principle that generated what would otherwise have been the result. As Justice Marshall articulated the point, the *Ashwander* principle requires the Court to "select less plausible candidates from within the range of permissible constructions."[38] To select what would otherwise be a suboptimal (from the perspective of Congress, or from the perspective of the otherwise-applicable principles of statutory construction) alternative is thus to incur some cost, a point highlighted by the particular nature of the substantive issue in *X-Citement Video* but present in less substantively charged cases as well.

This conclusion about the cost of the *Ashwander* principle is agnostic as to most of the contemporary controversies about interpretive methodology or legal theory. Some would interpret statutes according to the standard English meaning of their texts.[39] Others would rely more heavily on trying to determine or reconstruct what the enactors intended.[40] Still others would encourage the interpreters to fold into the mix their own views of desirable

---

[38] *EEOC v Arabian American Oil Co.*, 499 US 244, 263 (1991) (Marshall dissenting).

[39] Justice Scalia is the obligatory contemporary citation here. See, for example, *Pierce v Underwood*, 487 US 552 (1988); *Immigration and Naturalization Service v Cardozo-Fonseca*, 480 US 421, 452–53 (1987) (Scalia, concurring in the judgment). For analysis and critique, see Nicholas S. Zeppos, *Justice Scalia's Textualism: The "New" New Legal Process*, 12 Cardozo L Rev 1597 (1991).

[40] See, for example, Richard A. Posner, *The Problems of Jurisprudence* 262–79 (1990); Richard A Posner, *The Federal Courts: Crisis and Reform* 286–93 (1985); Earl M. Maltz, *Statutory Interpretation and Legislative Power: The Case for a Modified Intentionalist Approach*, 63 Tulane L Rev 1 (1988).

public policy, their own views of public and political morality, their own views about what the enactors would have done when faced with this situation at this time, their own views about how a statute enacted in the past should be made applicable to current circumstances, or their own views about which interpretations should be rejected as unreasonable.[41] Yet whichever of these approaches (or any of numerous others) is selected, the interpreter will necessarily come up with *some* interpretation of the statute before facing the constitutional question, or will have some view about what, the Constitution aside, the best interpretation would have been. In only the rarest of cases, if that, will an interpreter see the Constitution-independent interpretive alternatives as being so much in equipoise that she will welcome a constitutionally inspired opportunity to break the tie.

In all but a very few instances, therefore, the interpreter will have a preconstitutional preference for one interpretation over another. Yet the strength of these constitutionally antecedent preferences may vary. In some they may be so firm that a constitutional intrusion will seem interpretively unbearable, while in others these interpretive preferences will seem only slightly strained. In this sense the references of Brandeis in his *Ashwander* opinion to interpretive options that are "present" or are "fairly possible" are potentially highly misleading. Brandeis appears to suppose that there are interpretations that are simply not possible (and this is what Justice Scalia thought in *X-Citement Video*) under whatever the interpretive methodology employed, and on this point few would argue with Brandeis's conclusion. If there were no preconstitutionally impermissible interpretations, then the *Ashwander* principles would swallow up the entire process of constitutional adjudication.[42] Without there being unbearable interpretive alternatives,

---

[41] For contemporary American theorists, the *loci classici* for the kinds of more creative approaches I refer to here are Guido Calabresi, *A Common Law for an Age of Statutes* (1982); William N. Eskridge, Jr., *Dynamic Statutory Interpretation* (1994); Cass R. Sunstein (cited in note 36). For a critique, see John C. Nagle, *Newt Gingrich, Dynamic Statutory Interpreter*, 143 U Pa L Rev 2209 (1995).

[42] There are points of contact here between what I argue and works in the tradition of, for example, Henry Monaghan, *Our Perfect Constitution*, 56 NYU L Rev 353 (1981). Just as written constitutions seem pointless if they never indicate results other than what some interpreter would do without them, so too does constitutional adjudication seem pointless if it always generates the same result that would have been generated by prevailing interpretive methodologies outside the constitution, and similarly interpretive methodologies are close to pointless if we could always engage in constitutional adjudication to achieve the same result.

the Court in *Marbury* itself could simply have interpreted the Judiciary Act of 1789 as not giving the Supreme Court original jurisdiction in cases like Marbury's, and the Court in *Immigration and Naturalization Service v Chadha*[43] could have interpreted the one-house veto as requiring the concurrence of both houses and presentment to and agreement by the President. Only because these alternatives would have excessively strained[44] the statutory language or the legislative intent—or whatever the best theory of statutory interpretation would have generated—was it necessary to declare the statutes unconstitutional.

But although Brandeis was correct in supposing that some interpretive alternatives are simply impossible, he was on shakier ground in appearing to suggest that for all other cases there is an undifferentiated domain of the "fairly possible" in which constitutional considerations could relatively costlessly be brought to the fore. In reality, "fairly possible" is a matter of degree, even assuming some interpretations are not fairly possible. Extending "no vehicles in the park" to bicycles is more possible—less of a reach—than extending it to sleds, even though neither extension is compelled and neither is prohibited. Similarly, we can imagine versions of the statute at issue in *X-Citement Video* that would make the rewriting even more acceptable than it was to Justice Stevens (for whom the rewriting was easiest). For example, if the statute had made reference to "knowingly producing" rather than simply to "producing" in subpart 2252(a)(1)(A), the presence of "knowingly" both closer to the contested clause (which is in the same subpart), and in reference to production as well as to transportation and shipping, would have made the rewriting easier, even though it would again not be compelled, as it would have been if the statute had explicitly said something like "involving the use of one known by the transporter or shipper to be a minor." And, in the other direction, we can imagine versions of the statute that would have made the rewriting even more intolerable for Justice Scalia (for whom it was already intolerable). For example, if the statute had made reference after "knowingly transports" also to "knowingly

---

[43] 462 US 919 (1983).

[44] The claim that the statutory language is or is not being "strained" recurs repeatedly in *Ashwander*-variety cases. See, for example, *Aptheker v Secretary of State*, 378 US 500, 515 (1964).

ships," the repetition of the "knowingly" would have made it even less possible, although still probably not impossible even to the majority, to add judicially a "knowingly" to refer to the age requirement as well.

Yet once we see that "impossible" and "fairly possible" mark the extremes of a scale rather than simply polar alternatives, we see as well that we cannot avoid asking how strong the *Ashwander* principle should be. If the *Ashwander* principle of constitutional avoidance is quite strong, analogous in weight to a compelling interest standard or proof beyond a reasonable doubt, then the principle ought to be applied even when the "fairly possible" reading verges on, but does not quite reach, impossible. But if the principle of interpretation for constitutional avoidance is weak, little more than a *ceteris paribus* principle or a tie-breaker, then it ought to be employed only when the preconstitutional alternatives verge on, but do not quite reach, a state of complete equipoise. And so for weights in between as well. Given that use of the *Ashwander* principle necessarily displaces what would otherwise have been a different interpretation, and given that the *Ashwander*-independent interpretation is presumably based on substantive, methodological, and institutional values that themselves are worth something, the displacement is desirable only insofar as the values underlying the *Ashwander* principle are more substantial than the values they displace. The entire *Ashwander* tradition seems to suppose that the constitutionally inspired substitution of one interpretation for another sacrifices nothing. But unless the rejected interpretation was preferred for no reason at all, the assumption of nonsacrifice is simply wrong.

Although in the following section I will focus on the weight that the *Ashwander* principle ought to have, a weight we must consider in determining whether the sacrifice is worth making, it is important to explore at this point the possibility that the principle is simply illusory. For although the *Ashwander* principle is a principle for the avoidance of constitutional questions, using the principle is anything but avoidance. Continuing the line of argument I suggested just above, and again assuming that in almost no cases will the preconstitutional interpretive alternatives be in genuine equipoise, then application of the *Ashwander* principle will occur in two kinds of cases. In one the interpreter's preferred preconstitutional and pre-*Ashwander* interpretive alternative is the same as the

Ashwander-guided interpretation that allegedly "avoids" the constitutional issue. In the other the interpreter's otherwise preferred alternative is different from the interpretation that leans on *Ashwander* in order to avoid the constitutional issue. In the first, however, the principle is superfluous. If the principle of constitutional avoidance leads only to the same result that the interpreter would have reached without even considering the relevance of the Constitution, then it is hardly worth thinking about. In all other cases, the cases that are worth worrying about in this context, the *Ashwander* principle supplants what would otherwise have been the result, and does so in the service of the value of avoiding the constitutional question and so avoiding unnecessary constitutional adjudication.

Yet in these cases, the ones in which what would otherwise have been the interpretive preference is supplanted, the constitutional question is not avoided at all. As in *X-Citement Video*, the Court will supplant the otherwise-best result only when it believes that there is a serious or substantial constitutional question involved. Yet this determination is itself a confrontation with the very issue that *Ashwander* seeks to avoid. Even while claiming not to be dealing with constitutional matters, Chief Justice Rehnquist talks in the language of "absurdity" about why Congress could not have intended there to be strict liability in child pornography cases for retail druggists, successor tenants, or Federal Express couriers.[45] Yet given that there are strict liability crimes for the manufacture and distribution of adulterated foods,[46] given the degree of public and legislative concern about child pornography, and given that strict liability crimes are not *eo ipso* unconstitutional, it is not nearly so clear as the Chief Justice seems to suppose that Congress would not have selected the strict liability alternative. The Chief Justice does rely on *Morissette v United States*[47] to imply a mens rea requirement unless Congress clearly states otherwise, but this is little more than *Ashwander* in different clothing. Like the *Ashwander* principle, plain statement rules[48] sneak constitutional considerations in the back door, and thus again are instances not of avoid-

---

[45] 115 S Ct at 468–69.

[46] See 21 USC § 333 (1995).

[47] 342 US 246 (1952).

[48] See, for example, *Gregory v Ashcroft*, 501 US 452 (1991).

ing constitutional questions but of deciding them. This is not to say that that alternative would have been a good idea, or even that it would have been constitutional. It is to say that the Chief Justice reaches his conclusion by bringing in the First Amendment in a whisper rather than with a shout, for it is First Amendment-ish concerns that produce the conclusion. The notion that the Court is avoiding addressing the constitutional question just does not stand up. Moreover, when the majority does get around to citing *DeBartolo* and explaining why it chooses the interpretive alternative as opposed to declaring the statute unconstitutional (or upholding its natural reading as constitutional), it says that it wants to "eliminate" the constitutional "doubts" that are prompted by *Smith*, *Hamling*, and *Osborne v Ohio*.[49] Yet in doing so it does not avoid the constitutional question.[50] It decides it.

As a practical matter, the issue is even more serious. Although it would be possible for Congress to amend the statute after the interpretation in order both to reaffirm (what might have been) its original view and to force the Court to confront unmistakably the constitutional question that it thought it at least partially avoided, the use of *Ashwander* is a sufficiently strong signal that it would be quite silly for Congress to engage in this effort only to face a highly likely invalidation. Take again the situation presented in *X-Citement Video*. In theory it would now be possible for Congress to amend the federal child pornography laws to make clear *its* view that the prosecution in a child pornography case need show only knowledge of transportation in interstate commerce, and not

---

[49] 495 US 103, 115 (1990).

[50] This appears also to be the view of Judge Easterbrook. "The canon about avoiding constitutional decisions, in particular, must be used with case, for it is closer cousin to invalidation than to interpretation. It is a way to enforce the constitutional penumbra, and therefore an aspect of constitutional law proper." *United States v Marshall*, 908 F2d 1312, 1318 (7th Cir 1990). See also *Marozsan v United States*, 852 F2d 1469, 1495 (7th Cir 1988) (Easterbrook dissenting). This sounds right (although, as I shall maintain below, it does not go far enough), although the language of the "penumbra" is curious in this context. Judge Easterbrook believes that there is a "penumbra between elaboration and novation," *Artistic Carton v Paper Industry Union-Management Pension Fund*, 971 F2d 1346, 1354 (7th Cir 1992), but this may confuse the location of a norm with the confidence that a decision maker has in its existence or soundness. What the Court is doing in *X-Citement Video* is not enforcing a penumbra of the variety that we see in *Griswold v Connecticut*, 381 US 479 (1965), or *NAACP v Alabama*, 357 US 449 (1958). Rather, it is tentatively (or so it thinks) deciding an issue at the center of the right involved. *Smith v California* was never treated by the Court as penumbral, and nothing about the nature of the Court's application of *Smith* in *X-Citement Video* makes it so.

knowledge of the likely age of the performers, such that the prosecution would prevail by showing only that the defendant knew about the transportation or shipping in interstate commerce, that the defendant knew about the sexually explicit nature of the materials (*Smith* presumably still applies, largely because *Ferber* says it does), and that the materials were in fact, whether the defendant knew it or not, child pornography. But why Congress would take this action knowing that seven members of the Supreme Court think such a statute probably unconstitutional is a mystery.[51]

Ashwander avoidance is in fact triply problematic. First, *Ashwander* avoidance is only important in those cases in which the result is different from what the result would have been by application of a judge's or court's preconstitutional views about how a statute should be interpreted. But because the identification of the "potential" constitutional problem turns out for this set of cases necessarily to be dispositive, the idea that the court is avoiding a constitutional decision is illusory. It is in fact making one. Second, the identification of a constitutional problem is sufficiently probative of the nontentative views of the identifiers that the act of identifying a problem will be treated by rational legislative actors as conclusive, and they will act accordingly. As a result, there is only negligible difference between the effect of the tentative decision in an *Ashwander* case and the effect of a final decision in a case that actually decides the constitutional question. And, third, all of this takes place without the necessity of the full statement of reasons supporting the constitutional decision.

It may be an open question whether the necessity of giving reasons to support a decision improves the quality of the decision, and whether the cost of reason-giving is as low compared to its benefits as is commonly supposed.[52] Nevertheless, it is widely accepted that giving reasons for a decision is a good thing.[53] But if

---

[51] Subsequent to *X-Citement Video*, the House and Senate have passed the Sexual Crimes Against Children Protection Act of 1995, HR 1240. See note 37. The Act makes several modifications to the existing federal child pornography law, but, not surprisingly, does not attempt to overrule the Supreme Court's interpretation of the *scienter* requirement. Three other child pornography bills are now pending in Congress—the Sex Crimes Against Children Prevention Act of 1995, S 705; the Prevention of Sexual Exploitation of Children Act, S 241; and the Child Pornography Prevention Act of 1995, S 1237—and none of them attempts to overturn the result in *X-Citement Video*.

[52] Frederick Schauer, *Giving Reasons*, 47 Stan L Rev 633 (1995).

[53] See, for example, Henry M. Hart, Jr. and Albert M. Sacks, *The Legal Process: Basic Problems in the Making and Application of Law* 143–52 (William N. Eskridge, Jr. and Philip

a court persists in the illusion that it is not making a decision even when it is doing something that has the effect of a decision, then the decision it actually makes will be unsupported by the kinds of public reasons that we have come to expect in constitutional cases. If the Court in *X-Citement Video* had expressly said that it was going to consider in this case declaring unconstitutional a child pornography statute that did not contain an age-specific *scienter* requirement, we would have expected to see more in the way of constitutional rationales than the simple citation to *Smith, Hamling,* and *Osborne,* yet this is, in effect, all the Court gives us. Indeed, the comparison between the majority's scanty discussion of the constitutional question with the lengthy one in the dissent of Justice Scalia illustrates the way in which a consequence of the *Ashwander* strategy is to produce in reality the supposedly disfavored outcome of constitutional adjudication without the safeguard of reasoned elaboration that we associate with the exercise of that power.[54]

Thus, when these three considerations—actual confrontation with and not the alleged avoidance of the constitutional question, strong signals to Congress about likely constitutional outcomes, and the absence of reasons—are joined, it is clear that the *Ashwander* strategy exacts a high price for the benefits of the announced deference to legislative prerogatives. To identify the existence of a price is not to say that it is not worth paying. Still, it would be wise to conduct a closer examination of the benefits that deployment of the *Ashwander* principle supposedly brings.

III. The Case Against Ashwander

The rationale underlying the *Ashwander* principle is that the not inconsiderable costs I have just discussed are worth incurring because of the even higher costs of the alternative. These latter costs, the ones we think it important to avoid, are the costs associ-

---

P. Frickey, eds, 1994); Ernest J. Brown, *The Supreme Court, 1957 Term—Foreword: Process of Law,* 72 Harv L Rev 77 (1958); Michael Wells, *French and American Judicial Opinions,* 19 Yale J Int'l L 81, 92–103 (1994).

[54] In reality the situation is even worse. Not only does reliance on *Ashwander* lead the Court to ignore the desirability of giving reasons to support its constitutional conclusions, but the citation of *Ashwander* or *DeBartolo* also appears to allow the Court to avoid giving the kinds of reasons it would give in a "pure" statutory interpretation case.

ated with the power of judicial review itself, especially the costs of ignoring the "fundamental rule of judicial restraint"[55] and thus allowing an unelected judiciary unnecessarily to exercise the power to invalidate the acts of coordinate branches of the federal government.[56] The rationale of *Ashwander*, so it is said, is that "[t]he Court should avoid constitutional confrontations with Congress."[57] And although some of what lies behind *this* might be the kinds of concerns that motivate the "confrontations" strand of political question doctrine,[58] this rationale seems inapt in this context. Courts should be sensitive to the political ramifications of disobedience of their rulings, but this is especially a problem in the context of the executive branch, which, after all, has a unique ability actually to *do* things. Congress, on the other hand, legislates rather than executes, and there is little to suggest that Congress can or would do anything in response to a Supreme Court decision that would rise to the level of what we might call "disobedience." With respect to the flag desecration controversy, for example, congressional reaction to *United States v Eichman*[59] was not to pass the same law again, nor was it to try to have enforced the law that the Supreme Court declared unconstitutional. It was only to attempt to initiate the process of constitutional amendment, clearly not the kind of embarrassing confrontation that we think of in the context of the political question doctrine.

So if the federal judiciary is not (or should not be) concerned about congressional defiance of its authority, the worry seems more plausibly a slightly less prudential (in the institution-protective sense of prudence) one about respect for Congress and its closer attachment to popular wishes than we find in the judiciary. It is not my wish to rehearse or add variations to familiar themes about the exceptionality of judicial review, the countermajoritarian difficulty, and the legitimacy of an institutional design pursuant to which important policy decisions are made by an unelected judi-

---

[55] *Three Affiliated Tribes of Fort Berthold Reservation v Wold Engineering, P.C.*, 467 US 138, 157 (1984).

[56] See Geoffrey P. Miller, *Pragmatics and the Maxims of Interpretation*, 1990 Wis L Rev 1197, 1217.

[57] William N. Eskridge, Jr., *Public Values in Constitutional Interpretation*, 137 U Pa L Rev 1007, 1020 (1989).

[58] See *Powell v McCormack*, 395 US 486 (1969); *Baker v Carr*, 369 US 186 (1962).

[59] 496 US 310 (1990).

ciary rather than being left in the hands of more popularly responsive governmental institutions. But there are aspects of the nonmajoritarian character of judicial authority that are worth exploring further in this context. If it is assumed that one way of respecting the majoritarian provenance of Congress is by deferring to its judgments, then perhaps engaging in *Ashwander*-inspired avoidance of constitutional questions is a way of expressing this respect.

This respect, however, can take two forms. One is the assumption that Congress actually prefers the Court to do what it does when it goes out of its way to interpret a statute to avoid a potential constitutional problem. "The Court should assume that Congress is sensitive to constitutional concerns and presumably would not pass an unconstitutional statute."[60] This statement, which is quite typical of both judicial and extrajudicial statements in support of the *Ashwander* principle, could be read descriptively or prescriptively. As a descriptive statement, the most important thing to say about it is that it is false. Although it is perhaps extravagant to maintain that Congress passes unconstitutional statutes all the time, it is less extravagant to suspect that Congress is rarely concerned with the fact of unconstitutionality independent of the likelihood that an Act of Congress will be overturned by the courts. Even assuming that Congress is concerned about the latter, a question whose intrinsic importance dominates the amount of research devoted to answering it,[61] there is no evidence whatsoever that members of Congress are risk-averse about the possibility that legislation they believe to be wise policy will be invalidated by the courts. On the contrary, given the essentially political nature of the job of legislating, and given that the American political system does not penalize legislators for voting for good (in the eyes of the voters) policies that are determined by the courts to be unconstitutional, one would expect members of Congress to be anything but risk-averse. One would expect them to err on the side of as-

---

[60] Eskridge (cited in note 57), at 1020.

[61] I know of no serious research directed to determining the extent to which members of Congress (or legislators in general) take their understanding of constitutional norms, or their understanding of the (nonpredictive) import of Supreme Court decisions, as providing reasons for decision independent of the reasons for decision provided by their own best policy judgment, their own best political judgment, and their own estimate of the likelihood that what they do will be invalidated by the courts. For my own pessimistic speculations on the subject, see Frederick Schauer, *The Questions of Authority*, 81 Geo L J 95 (1992).

suming constitutionality under conditions of uncertainty about what the courts are likely to do. And if this is so, then it seems simply false to assume that members of Congress want the courts to assume unconstitutionality rather than constitutionality when courts are identifying constitutional issues as to which there is yet to be an authoritative decision.

But if the assumption that members of Congress desire to have the courts resolve doubts in favor of eliminating potential constitutional problems is false, it may, as a descriptive matter, be less false (although still an open question) that members of Congress would rather have courts announce their constitutional views sooner than later. *If* a court believes a congressional action unconstitutional— *if* a court believes that a child pornography law without an age-focused *scienter* requirement founders on the rocks of *Smith* and *Hamling*—then it may be true that Congress would just as soon get it over with, and have the courts do what they have to do so that Congress can get on with the business of making policy. Under these circumstances, it may be true that "Congress is sensitive to constitutional concerns" and wants the courts to intervene, but now it is only in the interest of having the courts do sooner what would otherwise be done later. But in this case, the courts are not avoiding constitutional decisions. They are revising the statutes, by implicit permission of Congress, in accordance with the courts' view of what the Constitution requires.

Alternatively, the assumption of congressional acquiescence may simply be prescriptive rather than descriptive. Congress may not be sensitive at all to constitutional concerns, and Congress may be quite happy to pass as many unconstitutional statutes as it can get away with, subject only to Constitution-free concerns of policy and politics.[62] But if this is so, then the assumption of congressional desire not to pass unconstitutional laws is in fact an imposition *on* Congress of the view that it should be the job of the courts to interpret statutes so as to *make* them constitutional. This is a plausible view about what the courts should be doing. Indeed, I think

---

[62] I want to underscore the reference to "policy." I do not claim that members of Congress are concerned only about their own personal political fortunes. I claim only that most members of Congress have deeply held views about what they think is good policy, and that they appear to be relatively unconcerned about the possible unconstitutionality of their own sincere policy judgments.

it is the correct view. It is not, however, an avoidance of constitutional decision making.

Even if I am wrong about the epiphenomenal nature of constitutional considerations in congressional decision making, it is hardly unreasonable to assume that Congress is substantially motivated by its view about what the best policy would be. At times, of course, the legislation it produces may ill serve that end, and a respectable body of scholarly commentary would have the courts serve a proactive function in ensuring that the legislation that Congress produces serves the ends that Congress desires.[63] But the issue here is not the role of the courts in making sure that what Congress does coincides with what Congress wants to do. So if the courts in reliance on the *Ashwander* principle interpret a statute in what is (as a matter of policy) a suboptimal way, they are doing nothing other than using constitutional norms to supplant what would otherwise be the outcome. This is not a bad thing to do. In fact it is a very good thing to do. Again, however, it is not an avoidance of constitutional decision making out of respect for Congress. It is an exercise of constitutional decision making out of respect for the Constitution.

Even if it is accepted that use of the *Ashwander* principle entails more judicial intrusion into legislative activities than the standard defense of *Ashwander* supposes, there is still the argument that this intrusion is a lesser intrusion than the explicit wholesale invalidation of a statute. To rely on *Ashwander* might thus be to make the assumption that declaring an Act of Congress unconstitutional is a particular affront to a coordinate branch of government, and a particularly intrusive action for a nonelected judiciary in an allegedly democratic and primarily majoritarian society. Yet consider again the alternative. In all but the most miraculous of cases, the *Ashwander* alternative displaces either the judgment of Congress, to put it most strongly, or, to put it less strongly, displaces a view about statutory interpretation that presumably takes into account the primacy of the legislature in the legislative process. Even under the latter way of putting it, the act of *Ashwander*-inspired judicial displacement is itself the very kind of intrusion that we think that *Ashwander* is designed to avoid. The Court is doing something to

---

[63] See sources cited in note 41.

the product of Congress, something Congress presumably did not want done or else it would have done it itself, and the Court is doing it without popular approval. To reach interpretation *A* of a statute under circumstances in which the Court would otherwise have reached interpretation *B* is to rewrite the statute, or at least that part of the statute that is at issue. And to rewrite a statute is to repeal, or invalidate, or render a nullity, or whatever, the statute or part of it in its unrewritten form.

So even if we think it a bad idea for courts to intrude on Congress, it is hardly clear that the intrusion of judicial rewriting is any less than the intrusion of judicial invalidation.[64] Judicial invalidation gives Congress the opportunity to decide what *it* wants to do next, in light of the enforced constitutional constraint. And of course one of those options is to reenact the statute in constitutionally acceptable form. This, generally speaking, produces the same outcome as judicial modification in light of the Supreme Court's view about the "likely" constitutional infirmity of the statute. And if the Court instead modifies the statute to conform to its views about the constitutional constraints, Congress would still have the power to repeal the statute, perhaps believing that nothing, or something quite different, was superior to the so-interpreted statute. Again, the conclusion is that the supposed difference between a constitutionally inspired rewriting and an invalidation turns out to be illusory.

Even apart from recognizing that a court that interprets a statute according to the *Ashwader* principle is engaging in rather than avoiding constitutional adjudication, it may also be inappropriate to continue to maintain the *Ashwander* presumption against judicial review. Although the relevant part of the text of the Constitution has not changed since *Ashwander* was decided, 58 years of a quite prominent Supreme Court have intervened. During these 58 years there have been continuing debates about the role of the Court, but nothing to suggest strong popular desire to curb its powers. And insofar as there have been such movements or outcries about judicial activism, they have surrounded issues such as desegregation, abortion, school prayer, criminal procedure, and reapportion-

---

[64] See Richard A. Posner, *The Federal Courts: Crisis and Reform* 285 (1985); Richard A. Posner, *Statutory Interpretation—In the Classroom and in the Courtroom*, 50 U Chi L Rev 800, 815–16 (1983).

ment, none of which centrally involved declaring an Act of Congress unconstitutional. The most prominent recent cases in which the Court has declared an Act of Congress unconstitutional— *United States v Lopez*[65] this Term, *United States v Eichman*[66] in the 1989 Term, *Bowsher v Synar*[67] in the 1985 Term, and *Immigration and Naturalization Service v Chadha*[68] in the 1982 Term—have generated virtually nothing in the way of broad-scale suggestions for cutting back the role of the Supreme Court.

All of this is only to suggest that the legitimacy of judicial review is, plausibly, a less controversial and less socially contested matter than it was several generations ago, and certainly less than it was in the previous century. To the extent this is so, then even a Court sensitive to its own legitimacy,[69] and sensitive to the countermajoritarian difficulty, might appropriately think of judicial invalidation of an Act of Congress as less exceptional than it did in the past, as less unauthorized by the people than it did in the past, as less illegitimate than it did in the past, and as less outside of "the Constitution" than it did in the past. And if this is so, then the supposed imbalance, to the extent that it ever existed, between the judicial intrusion of rewriting an Act of Congress and the judicial intrusion of invalidating an Act of Congress is far less. It thus appears that the use of the *Ashwander* principle implicates the countermajoritarian difficulty more than Brandeis and others supposed, and that the non-use of the principle—the avoidance of *Ashwander* avoidance, if you will—implicates the countermajoritarian difficulty less than has been the case in the past.

The modest consequence of all of this is that the Court could consider weakening the force of the *Ashwander* principle in ways that might be scarcely discernible. The use of *Ashwander* against the background of scalar rather than polar views about what the language (or the language as best interpreted apart from constitutional considerations) of a statute will bear means that the Court

---

[65] 115 S Ct 1624 (1995).

[66] 496 US 310 (1990).

[67] 478 US 714 (1986).

[68] 462 US 919 (1983).

[69] Nowhere is this more explicit than in the plurality opinion in *Planned Parenthood of Southeastern Pennsylvania v Casey*, 112 S Ct 2791 (1992) (joint opinion of O'Connor, Kennedy, and Souter).

is regularly deciding how much to stretch a statute in order to avoid invalidating it. If at the margin the Court were to decide that the line beyond which it would invalidate rather than stretch was somewhat closer to "home" than it had been in the past, little harm would be done; some of the more extreme forms of judicial rewriting might be eliminated (although I am far less convinced than Justice Scalia that *X-Citement Video* is one of them); and the Court could evaluate more plausibly the extent of judicial intrusion rather than rely excessively on the form that the intrusion happened to take.

The less modest consequence, of course, is to scrap the *Ashwander/DeBartolo* principle in its entirety. This would add the advantage of judicial candor, insofar as we think that a good thing, because *X-Citement Video* is hardly the only case in which pretensions of merely identifying a potential constitutional problem mask what is in fact and in effect a real constitutional decision with the same import as a full-scale invalidation. If the principle of constitutional avoidance were to be abandoned, the only thing that would be lost would be the pretense, since it is clear that whatever is going on when the Court relies on the *Ashwander* principle, avoidance is not it.

IV. Conclusion

In urging the rejection of *Ashwander*, I do not want to be understood as urging the rejection of the view that courts should be reluctant to intrude onto the prerogatives of the elected branches of government. It *is* possible that even that reluctance is misplaced; in a rights-based culture it is hardly self-evident that a principle of judicial modesty is advisable. But that question is for another day. My argument here is simpler. It is only that the *Ashwander* principle is based on the premise that an act of statutory interpretation is a less aggressive judicial performance than an act of judicial invalidation. On closer inspection, that seems not to be the case. As the Court itself acknowledged in *New York v United States*,[70] the *Ashwander* "rule of statutory construction pushes us away from"[71] what would otherwise have been the preferred result.

---

[70] 505 US 144 (1992).

[71] Id at 170.

The distance between the location before and after the "push" is not without consequence, and must be considered in evaluating the importance of and the price of the *Ashwander* principle. And in any event it is a mistake not to recognize that this "push" is itself, measured against a baseline of what the Court would otherwise have done based on principles of statutory construction that take account of legislative primacy, an incursion into this legislative primacy. Of course judicial invalidation may at times be more of an incursion into legislative prerogatives, but at times it may be less. Most often, as in *X-Citement Video*, the two will be roughly the same, with the interpretive act being neither more nor less invasive than an invalidating one. Consequently, the continued adherence to *Ashwander*, adding the metric of statutory versus constitutional to the metric or noninvasive versus invasive, is likely to be counterproductive. Little would be lost by abandoning *Ashwander* entirely. If that were to happen, courts could then focus directly on whether, in any particular case, judges should substitute their judgment for that of Congress, instead of invoking the unwarranted assumption that by "merely" interpreting a statute they have been respectful of the prerogatives and the status of a coordinate branch of government. The standard picture has been for many years that the *Ashwander* principle is an important vehicle of judicial restraint.[72] Perhaps it is anything but.

---

[72] See Lea Brilmayer, *The Jurisprudence of Article III: Perspectives on the "Case or Controversy" Requirement*, 93 Harv L Rev 297, 302–06 (1979).

EDMUND W. KITCH

GUSTAFSON v ALLOYD CO.:
AN OPINION THAT DID NOT WRITE

I. Introduction

The belief of lawyers like me that authoritative legal texts significantly limit the positions that a lawyer can plausibly advance, whether as a counselor, advocate, or judge, is based on the experience of finding that positions that I wish to take will not write. The opinion of the United States Supreme Court in *Gustafson v Alloyd*[1] provides an example of this phenomenon. The case involved the construction of § 12(2) of the Securities Act of 1933, which provides in part that:

> Any person who offers or sells a security . . . by means of a prospectus or oral communication, which includes an untrue statement of a material fact shall be liable to the person purchasing such security from him . . . .[2]

Edmund W. Kitch is Joseph M. Hartfield Professor of Law, the University of Virginia; Visiting Professor, the Brooklyn Law School (Fall 1995); and Jack N. Pritzker Distinguished Visiting Professor, Northwestern University (Spring 1996).

Author's note: An earlier version of this essay was given to a faculty workshop at the University of Virginia in June 1995. Comments of the participants at the workshop and the comments of George Cohen, Andrew Kull, Paul Mahoney, Anthony Sebok, and Norman Poser have greatly assisted in its completion.

[1] 115 S Ct 1061 (1995).

[2] Securities Act of 1933 § 12(2), 15 USC § 77l(2). The section provides a defense for a defendant who can sustain the burden of proof that "he did not know, and in the exercise of reasonable care could not have known, of such untruth or omission." The text of § 12 in full is:

> Sec. 12. Any person who—
> (1) offers or sells a security in violation of section 5, or
> (2) offers or sells a security (whether or not exempted by the provisions of 77c of this title [Section 3], other than paragraph (2) of subsection (a) of said section), by the use of any means or instruments of transportation or communication in

The term prospectus is defined in § 2(10) of the Act:

> The term "prospectus" means any prospectus, notice, circular, advertisement, letter, or communication, written or by radio or television, which offers any security for sale . . . .[3]

The "general understanding of the bar"[4] has long been that the definition of prospectus in § 2(10) should be read into the use of the term in § 12(2), so that the section reads:

---

interstate commerce or of the mails, by means of a prospectus or oral communication, which includes an untrue statement of a material fact or omits to state a material fact necessary in order to make the statements, in the light of the circumstances under which they were made, not misleading (the purchaser not knowing of such untruth or omission), and who shall not sustain the burden of proof that he did not know, and in the exercise of reasonable care could not have known, of such untruth or omission, shall be liable to the person purchasing such security from him, who may sue either at law or in equity in any court of competent jurisdiction, to recover the consideration paid for such security with interest thereon, less the amount of any income received thereon, upon the tender of such security, or for damages if he no longer owns the security.

[3] Securities Act of 1933 § 2(10), 15 USC § 77b(10). Section 2(10) provides in full:

(10) The term "prospectus" means any prospectus, notice, circular, advertisement, letter, or communication, written or by radio or television, which offers any security for sale or confirms the sale of any security; except that (a) a communication sent or given after the effective date of the registration statement (other than a prospectus permitted under subsection (b) of section 10) shall not be deemed a prospectus if it is proved that prior to or at the same time with such communication a written prospectus meeting the requirements of subsection (a) of section 10 at the time of such communication was sent or given to the person to whom the communication was made, and (b) a notice, circular, advertisement, letter, or communication in respect of a security shall not be deemed to be a prospectus if it states from whom a written prospectus meeting the requirements of section 10 may be obtained and, in addition, does no more than identify the security, state the price thereof, state by whom orders will be executed, and contain such other information as the Commission, by rules or regulations deemed necessary or appropriate in the public interest and for the protection of investors, and subject to such terms and conditions as may be prescribed therein, may permit.

[4] Richard W. Jennings, *Securities Regulation: Cases and Materials* 785 (5th ed 1992). *Wilko v Swan*, 346 US 427 (1953), which held that an agreement to arbitrate under the 1933 Securities Act was unenforceable, was a case brought by the customer of a brokerage house who had purchased stock on the open market under § 12(2) alleging that the purchase has been induced by misrepresentations of the brokerage house. This is the same transaction pattern as in the subsequent decision of *Ballay v Legg Mason Wood Walker, Inc.*, 925 F2d 682 (3d Cir 1991) (rejecting application of § 12(2) to transaction in the "aftermarket"), discussed in the text at note 13. The Court in *Wilko* did not discuss the scope of § 12(2) in the opinion, focusing only on the issue of the effect of the arbitration clause in the customer's account agreement. A § 12(2) cause of action arising out of a private placement was before the Court in *Randall v Loftsgaarden*, 478 US 647 (1986), which held that damages under both § 10(b)-5 and § 12(2) causes of action should not be offset by tax benefits accruing to the purchaser. Under the decision in *Gustafson*, neither of these claims was properly brought. The Dean of securities law scholarship, Louis Loss, called rejection of the long-accepted reading of § 12(2) a "flawed reading" and concluded that "*Ballay* must not become gospel." Louis Loss, *The Assault on Securities Act Section 12(2)*, 105 Harv L Rev

> Any person who offers or sells a security . . . by means of a communication, which includes an untrue statement of a material fact shall be liable to the person purchasing such security from him . . . .

In *Gustafson* the Court held, 5 to 4, that this reading is in error and that the scope of § 12(2) is limited to misrepresentations made in connection with offerings which are required to be registered under the statute.[5]

The best argument that can be made for the Court's result is the following. (1) It is desirable to limit the scope of § 12(2). (2) It is desirable that the line between what is and what is not within § 12(2) should be clear. (3) The line between what is and what is not an offering that must be registered under the 1933 Securities Act is clear. (4) Therefore, the line between what is and what is not an offering that must be registered under the 1933 Securities Act should be used to limit the scope of § 12(2). In its opinion, the Court addresses only point (1), and then only briefly and incompletely. Whatever the merits of this argument, and it is not entirely without merit, the text of the statute will not support it.

The interpretative strategy the opinion used to limit the scope of § 12(2) to those offerings required to be registered was to link

---

908, 908, 917 (1992). In *Gustafson*, *Ballay* and a good deal more became gospel, or at least as close to gospel as legal documents can get.

There has been a surprising amount of writing on § 12(2), none of which contemplated the possibility of the approach that the Court took in *Gustafson*. In addition to the Loss article cited in the previous paragraph, there has been: Therese Maynard, *The Future of Securities Act Section 12(2)*, 45 Ala L Rev 817, 857 (1994); Harold S. Bloomenthal, *Securities Law Handbook § 14.05(4)* (1993); Steven W. Hansen, et al, *Developments in Broker-Customer Litigation*, 25 Rev Sec & Commodities Reg 193 (1992); Louis Loss, *Securities Act Section 12(2): A Rebuttal*, 48 Bus Law 47 (1992); Maynard, *Liability Under Section 12(2) of the Securities Act of 1933 for Fraudulent Trading in Postdistribution Markets*, 32 Wm & Mary L Rev 847 (1991); Robert A. Prentice, *Section 12(2): A Remedy for Wrongs in the Secondary Market?* 55 Albany L Rev 97 (1991); Robert N. Rapp, *The Proper Role of Securities Act Section 12(2) as an Aftermarket Remedy for Disclosure Violations*, 47 Bus Law 711 (1992); Steve Thel, *Section 12(2) of the Securities Act: Does Old Legislation Matter?* 63 Fordham L Rev 1183 (1995); Elliott J. Weiss, *The Courts Have It Right: Securities Act Section 12(2) Applies Only to Public Offerings*, 48 Bus Law 1 (1992); Note, *Applying Section 12(2) of the 1933 Securities Act to the Aftermarket*, 57 U Chi L Rev 955 (1990); Note, *Does Section 12(2) of the Securities Act of 1933 Apply to Secondary Trading? Ballay v Legg Mason Wood Walker, Inc.*, 65 St John's L Rev 1179 (1991).

The analysis of § 12(2) developed in the text makes no use of legislative history. This is not because of an implicit assumption about the utility of legislative history, but because there is no legislative history that illuminates the scope of § 12(2).

[5] It is necessary to add: except for those offerings exempted only by reason of § 3, other than those exempted by reason of § 3(a)(2). This additional complexity is explained in the text at note 27.

the use of the term "prospectus" in § 12(2) not to the definition of prospectus in § 2(10), but to § 10, a section which describes what a prospectus used in an offering required to be registered must contain. The opinion did not write because the statute clearly contemplates that there are prospectuses that are used in offerings that need not be registered and need not comply with the requirements of § 10.

The *Gustafson* litigation arose out of the purchase of all of the stock in Alloyd, Inc., a closely held company, from its three shareholders. The contract to purchase was entered into on October 17, 1989, and closed December 20, 1989. The purchase price was $18,709,000, with an upward adjustment based on the book value of the firm as of December 31, 1989, a date after the planned closing. A critical number in the computation of the adjustment amount was the inventory. Alloyd regularly conducted a physical audit of its inventory in connection with its annual audits. The inventory had last been audited as of December 31, 1988, and would be audited again as of December 31, 1989.

The parties discussed conducting a separate, additional audit in order to precisely determine the amount of the adjustment. Instead, they negotiated a complex set of provisions in which the sellers would estimate the inventory and the resulting adjustment amount, the buyers would pay 90 percent of the estimated adjustment amount, and there would be an after-closing settling up when the accountants determined the exact amount of the adjustment amount based on their completion of the regular annual audit. The agreement contained detailed warranty and remedy provisions, including a provision in which the buyer waived the right to rescission.

At the closing the buyers paid the $18,709,000 plus $2,122,219 to reflect the estimated adjustment amount.

The year-end audit disclosed an inventory that was significantly less than the sellers had estimated. Under the contract, a return of a portion of the adjustment amount, $815,000, was due to the buyer, which the sellers paid. Instead of settling for the corrected adjustment amount, however, the buyers sued under § 12(2) seeking rescission of the transaction. Their theory was that the documents used to compute the adjusted amounts and other representations about the financial condition of the business contained untrue statements of material fact which entitled the buyers to rescission under § 12(2).

The transaction in *Alloyd* was the sale of a business which came within § 12(2) only because it was carried out not in the form of a sale of the business assets but in the form of the sale of all of the stock in the corporation which owned the business. In *Landreth Timber Co. v Landreth*,[6] the Court rejected the argument, which had been accepted by some circuit courts,[7] that such a transaction should be treated not as the sale of a security but as the sale of a business. The poor fit between the securities acts and such a face-to-face transaction as that in *Alloyd* had led some circuits to adopt a "sale of business" doctrine which treated such transactions not as the sale of a security but simply the sale of a business. In *Landreth* the Court relied on the definition of security in the statute to hold that form should prevail over substance. Ironically, in *Alloyd*, § 12(2) could have been applied to the transaction easily enough, but the Court was moved to hold that it did not apply because of concerns about the application of § 12(2) in public securities markets.

The buyers in *Alloyd* had explicitly waived their right of rescission in the contract. There are perfectly sensible reasons why the parties to a contract for the sale of an ongoing business such as the sale of Alloyd would choose to provide a waiver of the right of rescission. Assertion of a right to rescind the contract of purchase after closing creates uncertainty about the ownership of the business. Yet the purchaser is responsible, after closing, for making continuing decisions, including investment decisions, for the business. If the purchaser, who after the closing is the only one who can make these decisions, is uncertain about its future ownership, it will have incentives to operate the business in a way that maximizes short-run returns to the detriment of the long-term health of the business. This may cause the value of the business to decline, to the detriment of both of the parties. If, on the other hand, the purchaser after closing has clear ownership of the business subject only to a damage claim against the seller, the purchaser continues to have the incentive to maximize the value of the business. It

---

[6] 471 US 681 (1985).

[7] The circuit courts relied on the Court's decision in *United Housing Foundation, Inc. v Foreman*, 421 US 837 (1975), which held that shares of stock in a housing cooperative which entitled the purchaser to lease an apartment in the cooperative building were not securities even though they were stock.

seems unlikely that a court would in a case based on the common law cause of action for misrepresentation grant rescission for a representation whose uncertainty was the subject of express bargaining between the parties, and where the parties agreed upon a specific procedure for allocating the risk.[8]

An advantage for the plaintiff-seller of suing under § 12(2) was the possibility of avoiding the effect of the waiver-of-rescission clause in the sale contract under § 14 of the Securities Act. That section provides that "Any condition, stipulation, or provision binding any person acquiring any security to waive compliance with any provision of this title or of the rules and regulations of the Commission shall be void."[9] Although it can be persuasively argued that a clause waiving a remedy does not "waive compliance with any provision of this title," but simply modifies a remedy, the Supreme Court had held in *Wilko v Swan*,[10] a case based on § 12(2), that an agreement to arbitrate was in violation of § 14, reading § 14 to encompass not only the substantive provisions of the act but also an agreement which affected the remedies provided by

---

[8] A clause waiving the remedy of rescission amounts to a consensual (and ex ante) election of remedies. As such it would probably be judged by analogy to a liquidated-damage provision: enforceable if intended as a negotiated allocation of risks, void if intended as a penalty. A term that excludes the remedy of rescission for innocent misrepresentation by a seller allocates to the buyer some part of the risk that the terms of the exchange are the product of a mutual mistake, in that the misrepresentation that would otherwise have justified avoidance of the contract will instead be actionable only as a warranty. This is a form of risk allocation in which the parties are normally free to engage. See *Restatement (Second) of Contracts* § 154: "A party bears the risk of a mistake when (a) the risk is allocated to him by agreement of the parties, or (b) he is aware, at the time the contract is made, that he has only limited knowledge with respect to the facts to which the mistake relates but treats his limited knowledge as sufficient . . . ." *Deans v Layton*, 366 SE 2d 560 (NC App 1988); Dan B. Dobbs, *Dobbs Law of Remedies* § 11.2 (1993). Different problems are presented if the seller was aware of the misrepresentation. Under § 12(2) the plaintiff needs only to allege (and the plaintiff in *Alloyd* only alleged) that the misrepresentation was made.

[9] 15 USC § 77(n). This is not necessarily the case. It can be argued that waiving an available remedy is not the same as waiving "compliance with any provision of this title." However, in *Wilko v Swann*, 346 US 427 (1953), the Court held that a 12(2) claim arising in a dispute between parties who had signed an arbitration agreement would not be sent to arbitration because the arbitration clause was in conflict with § 14. *Wilko* was a claim by a brokerage house customer against the brokerage house for untrue statements of fact in a recommendation to purchase a security, just like *Ballay*. The arbitration clause was in the plaintiff's account agreement. The issue of the scope of 12(2) was not before the Court. *Wilko* was overruled in *Rodriguez de Quijas v Shearson/American Express, Inc.*, 490 US 477 (1989). However, the opinion in *Rodriguez* focuses on the conflict between the *Wilko* holding and policies favoring arbitration. Whether or not the reasoning of *Wilko* would now be applied to a waiver of rescission clause is unclear.

[10] 346 US 427 (1953).

the act. *Wilko* was overruled as to arbitration agreements in *Rodri-guez de Quijas v Shearson/American Express, Inc.*[11] The opinion in *Rodriguez de Quijas* suggests, but did not clearly adopt, a narrower reading of § 14. The decision accepted the argument that arbitra-tion is a fully adequate substitute for court proceedings, relying in part on the statement in § 2 of the Arbitration Act that arbitration agreements "shall be valid, irrevocable, and enforceable, save upon such grounds as exist at law or in equity for the revocation of any contract."[12] The plaintiff in *Gustafson* could argue that a clause that waives a remedy expressly conferred by the act rather than simply provide for an alternative forum for resolution of disputes is in violation of § 14. This is a weak, although possible argument, espe-cially given that the clause did not waive a right to rescissionary damages, a remedy also contemplated by § 12(2) and one which a court might well view as equivalent to rescission itself. Although the issue of the validity of the waiver-of-rescission clause under § 14 was not before the Court in *Gustafson*, the sense that the plaintiff was using § 12(2) to avoid the consequences of what was a sensible contractual provision may have affected the attitude of at least some Justices about the appropriate scope of § 12(2).

The District Court in *Gustafson* dismissed the complaint, relying on the construction of § 12(2) by the Third Circuit in *Ballay v Legg Mason Wood Walker, Inc.*[13] In *Ballay* the Third Circuit had held that § 12(2) did not protect buyers in the "aftermarket," but only buyers in the "initial distribution."[14] The Seventh Circuit re-versed, rejecting *Ballay*, and the Supreme Court granted certiorari to resolve the conflict with *Ballay*.[15]

In *Ballay*, purchasers of Wickes Company stock on the New York Stock Exchange sued their broker, Legg Mason, under § 12(2). Legg Mason had recommended purchase of the stock, and

---

[11] 490 US 477 (1989).

[12] 9 USC § 2.

[13] 925 F2d 682, cert denied, 112 US 79 (1991).

[14] 925 F2d 684.

[15] The route of *Gustafson* to the Supreme Court was actually more convoluted. The Sev-enth Circuit first rejected *Ballay* in another case, *Pacific Dunlop Holdings Inc. v Allen & Co.*, 993 F2d 578 (7th Cir 1993), cert granted, 114 S Ct 907 (1994), cert dismissed, 114 S Ct 1146 (1994). *Gustafson* was decided in the Seventh Circuit in light of *Pacific Dunlop* without further opinion. Certiorari was dismissed in *Pacific Dunlop* because the case was settled. After *Pacific Dunlop* was dismissed, the Court granted the petition for certiorari in *Gustafson*.

had made these recommendations both orally and in a number of documents sent to clients. The recommendations had erroneously stated the book value of Wickes, claiming that the stated figure "excluded goodwill" when it in fact included "goodwill." The § 12(2) theory was that these recommendations were both a prospectus and an oral statement under § 12(2), that Legg Mason had sold the stock by use of these prospectuses and oral statements, and that therefore § 12(2) was applicable. Under § 12(2) the plaintiffs could seek not just recovery of damages caused by the misrepresentation—which at least under some theories would be zero[16]—but rescission of their purchases. They could return their shares of Wickes (which had declined in value) and get their money back.

The Third Circuit held that there was no claim under § 12(2) on the grounds that the section did not apply to an "aftermarket" transaction. Courts following *Ballay* and commentators have understood this holding to mean that § 12(2) does not apply to "post-distribution" transactions.

II. The Transactions and Their Classification

The literal reading of § 12(2) makes the section applicable to a number of different transactions. As a basis for analysis it is useful to define the different types of transactions. The sections of the Securities Act dealing with when registration is required provide one system of classification. Section 5 of the Act requires that all sales of securities be registered. Section 4 then provides that several different transactions are exempt. The two key sections are 4(1) and 4(2).[17] Because of the consequences that attach to a

---

[16] Since it would have been difficult to prove that the *Legg Mason* recommendation had any impact on the price they paid for the stock, or that it had a role in the subsequent decline in price.

[17] They provide:

Sec. 4. The provisions of section 5 shall not apply to—
(1) transactions by any person other than an issuer, underwriter, or dealer.
(2) transactions by an issuer not involving any public offering.

The analysis of these sections that leads to the summary in the text is as follows (ignoring the dealer exemption). Any transaction involving an issuer must be registered unless exempt under § 4(2). Any transaction not involving an issuer must still be registered if it involves an underwriter. Section 2(10) defines underwriter as "any person who has purchased from an issuer with a view to or offers or sells for an issuer in connection with, the distribution of any security. . . ." The definition concludes: "As used in this . . . [definition] the term 'issuer' shall include in addition to an issuer, any person directly or indirectly controlling or controlled by the issuer." The term "distribution" is not defined in the statute.

sale of securities that is unregistered when it should have been registered,[18] the meaning of these Delphic sections has been the subject of extensive litigation, SEC interpretation, and commentary. Over time there has emerged a widely understood and well-defined set of distinctions. Ignoring the complications of the dealer's exemption, and of the step transaction doctrine,[19] they are three. First, transactions involving an issuer. Second, transactions involving a control person. And third, transactions involving neither. Transactions involving an issuer must be registered unless they do not involve a public offering, that is, unless they are a nonpublic or private offering. Transactions involving a control person must be registered unless they do not involve a distribution. All other transactions need not be registered. Although the statutory test for issuer and control person offerings is different—in the one case whether or not the offering is public, in the other whether or not the offering is a distribution—the case law and commentary make it clear that the test in both cases is the same.[20] The inquiry is focused on whether the transaction is one by which the securities move from the owner, either the issuer or a control person, to the public.

---

[18] The most important consequence is that § 12(1) provides that the purchaser of securities that were sold without the required registration has the right to the return of the purchase price upon tender of the securities for a period of one year from the sale. This gives the purchaser the right to recover the investment if the security performs poorly, but to keep the security if it performs well.

[19] By step transaction doctrine I mean the doctrine that allows the SEC or a court to characterize a transaction based on subsequent transactions. Thus an exempt transaction by either an issuer or control person is at risk of becoming nonexempt because of a subsequent transaction by the purchaser. This problem has often been discussed as the problem of identifying when a distribution ends and the securities have "come to rest." Much ink has been spilled on this subject, and the application of the statute in many situations remains unclear. The problem has been ameliorated by the SEC in practice by bright line regulations. An argument that Theresa Maynard made against the *Ballay* decision is that it required a determination as to whether a given transaction was part of a distribution or was after the distribution had ended under the statute, a issue that can be very unclear. To avoid the ambiguity, she argued that § 12(2) should apply to all sales. Therese Maynard, *The Future of Securities Act Section 12(2)*, 45 Ala L Rev 817 (1994).

The analysis in the text does not include analysis of transactions involving dealers, who are included in § 4(1) as persons whose presence will destroy the § 4(1) exemption. A further exemption of transactions involving dealers is provided in § 4(3) of the statute, an opaque provision which basically makes transactions involving dealers exempt except transactions that occur during or shortly after a public offering.

[20] Or nearly the same. The Second Circuit said they were equivalent in *Gilligan, Will & Co. v SEC*, 267 F2d 461, 466 (2d Cir 1959). "Since § 2(11) . . . defines an 'underwriter' as 'any person who has purchased from an issuer with a view to . . . the distribution of any security' and since a 'distribution' requires a 'public offering,' . . . the question is whether there was a 'public offering.' "

TABLE 1

Types of Transactions Under the Securities Act[21]

Seller and Nature of Offering	Registration Required?	Does § 12(2) Apply? Gustafson CA 7	Does § 12(2) Apply? Gustafson Supreme Court	Does § 12(2) Apply Under Ballay?
1. Issuer, not private placement under 4(2)	YES	YES	YES	YES
2. Issuer, private placement under 4(2)	NO	YES	NO	YES
3. Control person, distribution under 2(11)	YES	YES	YES	YES
4. Control person, not distribution under 2(10) [Gustafson]	NO	YES	NO	YES[22]
5. Anyone else [Ballay]	NO	YES	NO	NO

Table 1 summarizes these distinctions, relates the *Gustafson* and *Ballay* cases to the distinctions, and shows the application of § 12(2) both under the Court's analysis and under the analysis in *Ballay*.

III. The Opinion of the Court

The opinion attempts to tie the scope of § 12(2) to those offerings required to be registered through § 10. Section 10 contains provisions of the following form:

---

[21] The analysis reflected in the table does not consider the application of the dealer's exemption nor the step transaction doctrine. See note 19.

[22] Because this transaction was not actually before the court in *Ballay*, this categorization is not based on the holding. Rather, it is based on the analysis used in the opinion and the interpretation of the decision by other courts, most notably in *Hedden v Marinelli*, 796 F Supp 432 (ND Cal 1992). The *Ballay* opinion is quite careful not to say "§ 12(2) applies only to public offerings." Instead it says that § 12(2) applies to "initial distributions" or to "batch offerings." The Third Circuit did not mean by "initial distribution," "first distribution." A private placement by an issuer under § 4(2) or a nondistribution by a control person is part of a transaction which will become a distribution if the purchaser resells before the securities have "come to rest" (at least two years under present Rule 144(d)(1)). Therese Maynard, who has written in depth on this subject, reports that "The dominant approach in these decisions relies on the rule of *Ballay* and concludes that section 12(2) relief is not available to postdistribution buyers." Therese Maynard, *The Future of Securities Act Section 12(2)*, 45 Ala L Rev 817, 857 (1994). See also Therese Maynard, *Liability Under Section 12(2) of the Securities Act of 1933 for Fraudulent Trading in Postdistribution Markets*, 32 Wm & Mary L Rev 847 (1991). The *Ballay* doctrine began in decisions of judges in the Southern District of New York, who after *Shearson/American Express Inc. v McMahon*, 482 US 220 (1987) (claims under the Securities and Exchange Act subject to arbitration) but before *Rodriguez de Quijas v Shearson/American Express, Inc.*, 490 US 477 (1989) (claims under the Securities Act subject to arbitration), were faced with actions against brokers which were subject to arbitration on all counts except the § 12(2) claim. See the cases cited in *Mix v E.F. Hutton*, 720 F Supp 8, 10–11 (SDNY 1989). As of 1992, the Second Circuit was comfortable asserting that "The section has, however, consistently been applied to

[A] prospectus relating to a security . . . shall contain the information contained in the registration statement . . . .[23]

The Court reasons from this provision as follows:

In seeking to interpret the term "prospectus," we adopt the premise that the term should be construed, if possible, to give it a consistent meaning throughout the Act. That principle follows from our duty to construe statues, not isolated provisions. . . .
    We begin with § 10. . . . [quote].
    Although § 10 does not define what a prospectus is, it does instruct us what a prospectus cannot be if the Act is to be interpreted as a symmetrical and coherent regulatory scheme, one in which the operative words have a consistent meaning throughout. There is no dispute that the contract in this case was not required to contain the information contained in a registration statement and that no statutory exemption was required to take the document out of § 10's coverage. It follows that the contract is not a prospectus under § 10.[24]

This is a misreading of the "shall" in § 10. Section 10 of itself does not require anything. Section 10 is important only because of § 5(b). For instance, § 5(b)(1) requires that any prospectus relating to a security with respect to which a registration statement has been filed is unlawful "unless such prospectus meets the requirements of section 10." The "shall" in § 10 is used to designate what different types of prospectuses must contain—for instance, a prospectus relating to a security issued by a foreign government (§ 10(a)(2)), or a prospectus more than nine months old (§ 10(a)(3)), or a prospectus relating to a security issued by other than a foreign government (§ 10(a)(1)). Indeed, it would render §§ 5(b) and § 10 circular to define a prospectus as a document that contains what § 10 requires, for then the only documents that § 5(b) would require conform to § 10 would be documents that already conform to § 10. The Court immediately sees this point, for it shifts ground slightly to assert

That [the observation that the contract is not a prospectus] does not mean that a document ceases to be a prospectus when-

---

private as well as public offerings of securities." *Metromedia Co. v Fugazy*, 983 F2d 350, 360 (1992).

[23] Securities Act of 1933 § 10, 15 USC § 77j.

[24] 115 S Ct 1066–67.

ever it omits a required piece of information. It does mean that a document is not a prospectus within the meaning of that section, if absent an exemption, it need not comply with § 10's requirements in the first place.[25]

This still leaves the Court with a problem, however. What is the status of the written documents that can be used by an offeror to sell securities to a person who has received the final prospectus? Although in the classic fixed-price offering the selling effort occurs prior to the final prospectus, the statute contemplates selling efforts after the final prospectus is effective, and permits the use of selling documents (called in the jargon "free writing"), directed to persons who have already been sent the prospectus. This is done, for instance, in connection with the continuous offerings of open-ended mutual funds. Suppose there is a misrepresentation in these documents? Would § 12(2) be available? One answer easily could be that it is not, because the free writing privilege is a consequence of a caveat to the definition of prospectus in § 2(10). This caveat provides that "a communication sent or given after the effective date of the registration statement . . . shall not be deemed a prospectus if it is proved that prior to or at the same time with such communication a written prospectus meeting the requirements of subsection (a) of section 10 at the time of such communication was sent or given to the person to whom the communication was made." If something is not to be "deemed a prospectus," then why would it be a prospectus within § 12(2)? This result would be very odd, however, for § 12(2) explicitly includes oral statements. Why would Congress create an action for misrepresentations in oral statements but not in a written document, when a written document can have far greater capacity for harm? So the Court, apparently sensing that this cannot be right, subtly shifts ground again.

> An examination of § 10 reveals that, whatever else "prospectus" may mean, the term is confined to a document that, absent an overriding exemption, must include the "information contained in the registration statement." By and large, only public offerings by an issuer of a security, or by controlling shareholders of an issuer, require the preparation and filing of registration statements. See 15 USC §§ 77d, 77e, 77b(11). It follows, we conclude, that a prospectus under § 10 is confined to *docu-*

---

[25] 115 S Ct 1067.

> *ments related to public offerings* by an issuer or its controlling
> shareholders.[26]

That is, the document that is a prospectus must not itself be required to contain the information specified in § 10; the document
must only "relate" to an offering in which the use of a registration
statement is required, that is, an offering subject to the requirements of § 5.

A major problem with the implicit argumentation of the opinion
is obscured by the exception which the Court repeatedly acknowledges for exempt offerings, not subject to § 5. This exception is
acknowledged because the Court chooses not to ignore the fact
that § 12(2) explicitly provides that it is applicable "whether or not
[the security being sold is] exempted by the provisions of section 3,
other than paragraph (2) of subsection (a) thereof."[27] Section 3,
entitled "Exempted Securities," provides a number of different exemptions—for instance for securities issued by a religious, educational, benevolent, fraternal, or charitable issuer, for interests in a
railroad equipment trust, and for securities which are part of an
issue offered and sold in only a single state. Section 3 begins: "Except as hereinafter expressly provided, the provisions of this title
shall not apply to any of the following classes of securities . . . ."
Section 12(2) is one of the sections that "hereinafter expressly provides." Section 5, the section which forces registration before sale
and the use of a prospectus meeting the requirements of § 10, is
one of the sections that does not so expressly provide. Thus offerings of securities exempt under § 3 are clearly subject to § 12, but
not subject to § 10. The strategy that the Court adopts to deal
with this problem is to distinguish between offerings of securities
that would be subject to § 10 except for an exemption, and offerings of securities that are not subject to § 10 at all. Ah, ah, says
the Court, this contract of sale (in *Gustafson*) is not subject to §
10 because it is the sale of an offering exempt from § 10, § 10
simply did not apply.[28]

---

[26] Id (emphasis added).

[27] The full text of § 12(2) is set forth in note 2.

[28] The Court notes that "There is no dispute that the contract in this case was not required to contain the information contained in a registration statement and that no statutory
exemption was required to take the document out of § 10's coverage." Id at 1067. The
reason is that there was no dispute "that no statutory exemption was required to take the
document out of § 10's coverage" is that the lawyers on both sides could never have imagined the application of § 10 would be an issue in the case.

The problem is that the Court is wrong about the distinction it attempts to make. The offering in *Gustafson* was exempt from § 5, and hence from § 10, only because it was an offering exempt under § 4(1), it was not part of a distribution by a control person. A statutory exemption was in fact required to take the contract of sale out of § 10's coverage, exactly contrary to what the court asserts. And § 4, titled "Exempted Transactions," begins: "The provisions of section 5 shall not apply to— . . . . [enumerating the transactions exempt from § 5]. Thus the exemption that takes the sale by a control person in *Gustafson* out of § 5, and thus out of the requirements of § 10, expressly does not take the transaction out of § 12.

The Court implicitly attempts to distinguish between the § 3 and the § 4 exemptions by the use of the descriptor "overriding." "An examination of § 10 reveals that whatever else 'prospectus' may mean, the term is confined to documents that, absent an *overriding exemption*, must include the 'information contained in the registration statement.' "[29] It is of course true that the § 3 exemptions are "overriding" in the sense that the exemption "overrides" all other sections unless the section explicitly provides that it does not (as in § 12(2)), while the § 4 exemptions limit only § 5, but the Court provides no explanation what this distinction has to do with the issue of the scope of § 12(2), except to provide a spurious distinction between the impact of § 3 exemptions on § 12(2) and the impact of the § 4 exemptions on § 12(2).

The Court makes an attempt to shore up this distinction by an argument based on the fact that § 12, which expressly applies to securities offered in transactions exempt under § 3, expressly does not apply to transactions exempt under § 3(a)(2), a subsection that exempts government and bank securities. The Court reasons as follows:

> Our interpretation is further confirmed by a reexamination of § 12 itself. The section contains an *important guide* to the correct resolution of the case. By its terms, § 12(2) exempts from its coverage prospectuses relating to the sales of government-issued securities. . . . If Congress intended § 12(2) to create liability for misstatements contained in any written communication relating to the sale of a security—including second-

---

[29] 115 S Ct 1061 (emphasis added).

ary market transactions—there is no ready explanation for ex-
empting government-issued securities from the reach of the
right to rescind granted by § 12(2). Why would Congress grant
immunity to a private seller from liability in a rescission suit
for no reason other than that the seller's misstatements happen
to relate to securities issued by a governmental entity? No reason is apparent. The anomaly disappears, however, when the
term "prospectus" relates only to documents that offer securities sold to the public by an issuer. The exemption for government-issued securities makes perfect sense on that view, for it
then becomes a precise and appropriate means of giving immunity to governmental authorities.[30]

It does not occur to the Court that the reason for giving immunity
to securities of governmental authorities might be to reduce their
costs of selling those securities because the governmental issuers,
relieved of a cause of action for misstatements, can save the cost
of the precautions needed to avoid misstatements. But if the objective is to lower the government's cost of selling securities, this objective is also served if the costs of reselling government securities
are also reduced. An underwriter or dealer reselling government
securities that was subject to the § 12(2) action would want to insist
that the selling government take the same precautions that it
would take if it were subject to § 12(2), if the reseller faced that
liability. Thus to fully shield the government issuer from the costs
imposed by § 12(2) liability, it would be necessary to shield both
the government and the private resellers.

Having first turned to § 10 for guidance as to the meaning of
prospectus, the Court finally turns, almost as an afterthought, to
the section that defines prospectus, § 2(10). It asserts: "From the
terms 'prospectus, notice, circular, advertisement, or letter,' it is
apparent that the list [in the definition] refers to documents of
wide dissemination."[31] That would be true enough of circular and
advertisement, but there is nothing about a notice or letter that
requires that they be documents of wide dissemination. The Court
then relies on the 1910 edition of *Black's Law Dictionary*.

> When the 1933 Act was drawn and adopted, the term "pro-
> spectus" was well understood to refer to a document soliciting
> the public to acquire securities from the issuer. See Black's Law

---

[30] 115 S Ct 1067–68.
[31] 115 S Ct 1070.

Dictionary 959 (2d ed. 1910) (defining "prospectus" as a "document published by a company . . . or by persons acting as its agents or assignees, setting forth the nature and objects of an issue of shares . . . and inviting the public to subscribe to the issue"). In this respect, the word prospectus is a term of art, which accounts for Congressional confidence in employing what might otherwise be regarded as a partial circularity in the formal, statutory definition. See [§ 2(10)] . . . ("The term 'prospectus' means any prospectus. . . . ").[32]

This reference is anachronistic. In 1910 there was no definition of prospectus in American law. The term was, however, defined in an English statute in 1900. The Companies Act, 1900, provided that "The expression 'prospectus' means any prospectus, notice, circular, advertisement, or other invitation, offering to the public for subscription or purchase any shares or debentures of a company."[33] It is this definition that *Black's Law Dictionary* of 1910 appears to have used. What is notable about the statutory definition is that the drafters felt that it was necessary to add the qualifier "public" to the definition, implying that the term prospectus by itself did not imply an offering to the public. This is consistent with the definition of prospectus in *The Oxford English Dictionary*, which defines prospectus as "A description or account of the chief features of a forthcoming work or proposed enterprise, circulated for the purpose of obtaining support or subscriptions,"[34] without regard to the nature and extent of that circulation, and provides a number of pre-1933 examples which need not have involved a circulation to the public.[35]

That is not the end of the story. The definition in the Companies Act, 1900, remained in the English statutes,[36] and it is the definition that was the source of the definition in the securities act.[37] Both the securities act definition and the Companies Act

[32] Id.

[33] Companies Act, 1900, ch 48 § 30 (1900).

[34] *Oxford English Dictionary* (2d ed 1989), Vol 12 at 670.

[35] The first edition of the *OED* (1933) includes this example: "'A design for executing an universal dictionary of arts and sciences, the prospectus of which he actually printed and distributed among his acquaintance.' 1777, Life Goldsmith G.'s Wks." "'Prospectus of a school to be established at Round Hill, Northampton, Massachusetts.' 1823 Cogswell & Bancroft (title)." is added in the 2d ed.

[36] The definition in effect as of 1933, when the Securities Act was drafted, was 19 & 20 Geo 5, ch 23 § 380(1), and was the same as the definition in the Companies Act, 1900.

[37] Landis, *The Legislative History of the Securities Act of 1933*, 28 Geo Wash L Rev 29, 34 (1959).

definition have the same curious feature of including the term prospectus in the definition. But when the definition was adapted to the securities act, the qualifier public was omitted from the definition, which clearly indicates that the term was to include documents that do not make an offer to the "public."[38]

IV. THE BALLAY OPINION: WOULD IT WRITE?

Does the fact that the text of the 1933 Securities Act does not support the result the Court reached in *Gustafson* mean that the opinion of the Third Circuit in *Ballay* was also inconsistent with the statute? Would it have been possible for the Court to write a persuasive opinion that would have accepted the *Ballay* result while also holding that § 12(2) applies to a nondistribution sale by a control person?

A central assumption of the Court's *Gustafson* opinion is that *Gustafson* and *Ballay* present the same issue. This assumption, of course, is necessary to the existence of the conflict between the circuits that the Court undertook to resolve in the first place. This assumption was shared by the Seventh Circuit and the district court that dismissed the complaint in *Gustafson*, but not by other courts that have applied *Ballay*.

The importance of the assumption that the two cases present the same issue appears at the end of the opinion, when the Court turns from arguments ostensibly based on the language of the statute to an argument based on the relationship between the statute and the transactions to which it applies. The Court says:

> It is understandable that Congress would provide buyers with a right to rescind, without proof of fraud or reliance, as to misstatements contained in a document prepared with care, following well established procedures relating to investigations with due diligence and in the context of a public offering by an issuer or its controlling shareholders. It is not plausible to infer that Congress created this extensive liability for every casual communication between buyer and seller in the secondary market. It is often difficult, if not altogether impractical, for those engaged in casual communications not to omit some fact that would, if included, qualify the accuracy of a statement. Under Alloyd's view any casual communication between buyer

---

[38] This point is made in a dissent at 115 S Ct 1081.

and seller in the aftermarket could give rise to an action for rescission, with no evidence of fraud on the part of the seller or reliance on the part of the buyer. In many instances buyers in practical effect would have an option to rescind, impairing the stability of past transactions where neither fraud nor detrimental reliance on misstatements or omissions occurred. We find no basis for interpreting the statute to reach so far.[39]

What is notable about this passage is that it only gives arguments as to why 12(2) should not apply to nondistribution transactions, category 3—the *Ballay* category—in Table 1. A private offering, just like a public offering, will be prepared with "care," and follow "established procedures." Indeed, the Court's jurisprudence, which has stressed the availability of equivalent protections for purchasers in private offerings,[40] mandates that that is the case. Yet the Court discusses these arguments as if they apply to both *Ballay* and to *Gustafson*.

The Court's insistence that *Gustafson* and *Ballay* presented the same issue was not conceded by Alloyd in its briefs. Alloyd, whose attorneys could apparently see quite clearly that it was not going to help their case to argue against *Ballay*, were emphatic that it should be distinguished.[41] Their argument was the § 12(2) applied to public and private offerings, and that that had been the law both before and after *Ballay*.[42] The Court ignores their argument and attributes to *Alloyd* a position that requires overruling *Ballay*.

The plausibility of the Court's rhetoric treating the two different transactional settings as if they are the same was assisted by

---

[39] 115 S Ct 1071.

[40] *SEC v Ralston Purina Co.*, 346 US 119 (1953).

[41] Brief for Respondents, *Alloyd v Gustafson*, 115 S Ct 1061 (1995), p 18: "Sellers do not cite any case holding that section 12(2) is inapplicable to private transactions exempt under section 4 of the Act. Instead, the decisions cited by Sellers (Pet. Br. 12–14) address a different issue: whether section 12(2) applies only to 'initial' offerings of stock, as opposed to 'secondary market trading.'" The same point was made in the brief of the respondent in opposition to the petition for a writ of certiorari in *Allen & Co. v Pacific Dunlop Holdings Inc.*, Case No 93–201, pp 4–9. The United States did file a brief *amicus curiae* which obscured the point, apparently because the United States desired that the Court overrule *Ballay*.

[42] "Sellers erroneously state that the courts of appeal 'are in conflict on th[e] issue' in this case. (Pet. Br. 11) The appellate courts are not divided on the question whether the civil remedies in section 12(2) of the 1933 Act apply to 'private' sales exempt from registration by section 4 of the Act. To the contrary, as the Seventh Circuit stated in Pacific Dunlop, '[t]he courts have consistently held that the section 4 exemptions do not apply to section 12(2).' 993 F.2d at 587. *Accord Metromedia Co. v Fugazy*, 983 F.2d 350, 361 (2d Cir. 1992) (stating that section 12(2) has 'consistently been applied to private as well as public offerings of securities') . . . ." Id at 17.

the fact that the term secondary can be used to apply to both a sale by a control person and to a sale by neither an issuer nor a control person. In the first usage, a secondary offering or distribution is "secondary" because the sale is by a person other than the issuer, and the term distinguishes it from an offering by the issuer itself, which would be "primary."[43] *Gustafson* involved a secondary in this sense. In the second usage, a transactions occurs in the "secondary market" to distinguish the market for resales in shares from the "primary" market or the market in which shares are sold directly by an issuer or control person to the public.[44] *Ballay* involved a transaction in the secondary market, in this sense. This confusion appears in the second sentence of the opinion: "The question presented is whether this right of rescission extends to a private, secondary transaction, on the theory that recitations in the purchase agreement are part of a 'prospectus.'" The transaction in *Gustafson* was private, but the transaction in *Ballay* was not. Because *Gustafson* and *Ballay* were both secondary, although in different senses of the term, the Court appears comfortable using concerns about transactions in the resale market to decide a question about a sale by control persons.

The *Ballay* opinion itself was structured so that it applied only to what the Third Circuit called aftermarket or nonbatch transactions, category 3 in Table 1. Later courts, asked to apply *Ballay* to either categories 1 or 2 in Table 1, declined.[45] Would it have been possible for the Court to write an opinion affirming *Ballay* and affirming *Gustafson?*[46]

The best argument for *Ballay*'s refusal to apply § 12(2) to transactions in the trading market is that the structure of § 12(2), which

---

[43] *Black's Law Dictionary* (6th ed 1990) at 1351, definition of secondary distribution: "In securities, the new distribution of stock has been initially sold by the issuing corporation. It is not a new issue, but rather a public sale of stock which has previously been issued and held by large corporations and investors. Also, the sale of a large block of stock after the close of business of the exchange."

[44] Id, definition of secondary market: "Securities exchanges and over-the-counter markets where securities are bought and sold after their original issue (which took place in the primary market). Proceeds of secondary market sales accrue to selling investors not to the company that originally issued the securities."

[45] See note 22.

[46] If the Court had accepted this analysis, it might have decided to simply dismiss *Gustafson* on grounds that certiorari had been improvidently granted. Such a move, however, would have been awkward since the Court had already granted certiorari twice over the protest of respondents that *Gustafson* and *Ballay* were not the same case.

provides a remedy only for buyers against sellers, does not fit the structure of the resale markets. In the case of offerings by issuers or control persons, the seller has a relationship to information about the issuer that can be thought to give the seller a systematic advantage over buyers. But in the resale market, where the seller is simply an owner of the security with no special relationship with the issuer, there is no reason to provide a special remedy only for buyers. Sellers, too, can be injured by misinformation which causes them to sell their securities at too low a price.

The inferences from the one-way structure of § 12(2) is reinforced by the fact that it is placed in the statute next to sections dealing with misrepresentations in registered offerings (§ 11) and with unregistered offerings (§ 12(1)).

The Third Circuit opinion in *Ballay*, like the Supreme Court opinion, principally relied on the term prospectus in § 12(2) to narrow the scope of the section. It, however, read the term as meaning a document used in any offering, whether or not exempt from registration, a meaning of the term prospectus that is more consistent with accepted usage. But given the expansive definition of prospectus in § 2(10), it is heroic to infer restrictive meaning simply from the fact that the definition repeats the term being defined. This is particularly true in § 12(2), where the term prospectus is paired with the alternative but quite broad "oral communication."

The Third Circuit in *Ballay* did mention the rescission remedy of § 12(2) as a reason why the section should not apply to transactions in an impersonal exchange market. In such a market, the seller is anonymous, and the only misrepresentations will come from the buyer's broker. The rescission remedy is appropriate against someone who has sold stock and received the proceeds, reasoned the Court, but it is draconian when applied against someone who has only received a brokerage commission.[47]

These arguments, which narrow the scope of § 12(2) based on its remedial structure, run counter to the thrust of two Supreme

---

[47] 925 F2d at 693: "There is good reason why sellers in initial distributions should be liable for rescissionary damages. These sellers receive the full purchase price from the investors and are the investors' sole source of information concerning the value of the security. The same is not true of sellers in the aftermarket, such as Legg Mason, who receive only a commission and who are not the investors' sole source of information concerning the value of the stock."

Court precedents. *United States v Naftalin*,[48] construing the scope of § 17(a), and *Pinter v Dahl*,[49] construing the term "seller" in § 12. Both precedents can be distinguished, but only with some difficulty.

An argument that the sale-side-only structure of § 12(2) supports the inference that it does not apply to transactions in the postdistribution resale market must address the decision in *United States v Naftalin*. That case involved a criminal prosecution under § 17(a) of the 1933 Securities Act, which prohibits fraud in the offer or sale of a security. Section 17(a), like § 12(2), applies only to "the offer or sale of any securities," not to fraud in their purchase. In that case the defendant had sold shares that he did not own through brokerage houses without disclosing to them that he did not have the shares, nor the means to pay for the shares necessary to close out what was in fact a short position. He was hoping that the shares would fall in value and that he could quickly cover his position at a profit. The scheme did not work and he was prosecuted. Although his conduct was also a violation of Rule 10b-5, he was charged only with a violation of § 17(a).

Naftalin was able to convince a court of appeals that his conviction should be reversed because § 17(a) and the Securities Act in general were directed only to the protection of investors, not brokerage houses. The Supreme Court granted certiorari and rejected this argument, correctly observing that protection of investors and protection of brokerage houses are interrelated objectives, both consistent with the purposes of the securities acts. Naftalin also argued to the Supreme Court that his conviction should be reversed because the "Securities Act of 1933 was 'preoccupied with' the regulation of initial public offerings of securities, and that Congress waited until the Securities Exchange Act of 1934 to regulate abuses in the trading of securities in the 'aftermarket.'"[50] The court gave this argument, which was raised only in the Supreme Court, short shrift. "[T]he antifraud prohibition of § 17(a) was meant as a major departure from that limitation."[51]

A brokerage customer can, of course, pursue Naftalin's strategy

---

[48] 441 US 768 (1979).

[49] 486 US 622 (1988).

[50] Id at 777.

[51] Id at 778.

on the buying side. A customer can place orders to buy stocks in the hope that they will quickly rise in value and be resold before it is necessary to pay for them. Although this strategy presents the same risk of loss to the brokerage house, it would not violate § 17 because it would not be a "device, scheme, or artifice to defraud" in "the offer or sale of any security." The Court did not consider how odd it is for a statute to prohibit a swindle on the sale side, but not on the buy side.

Since the Court was not concerned about the application of the sell-side-only structure of § 17(a) to the aftermarket in *Naftalin*, it is difficult to argue that that feature of § 12(2) should be important in determining its scope. Of course, it would have been possible for the Court to overrule *Naftalin* as wrongly decided, or at least to hold that it was an insufficiently persuasive authority to preclude limiting the scope of § 12(2) based on its one-sided remedial structure. After all, *Naftalin* involved a clearly guilty defendant trying to escape conviction on a technicality—that he had been charged with a violation of § 17(a) rather than Rule 10b-5—with an argument that was raised very late in the litigation.

In *Pinter v Dahl*, the Court held that the term "anyone who sells" in § 12(1)—the companion section to 12(2) that provides a rescission remedy for purchasers of securities that were unregistered when they should have been registered—is not limited to persons who pass title or receive the proceeds, but includes persons who successfully solicit the purchase.

> The solicitation of a buyer is perhaps the most critical stage of the selling transaction. It is the first stage of a traditional securities sale to involve the buyer, and it is directed at producing the sale. In addition, brokers and other solicitors are well positioned to control the flow of information to a potential purchaser, and, in fact, such persons are the participants in the selling transaction who most often disseminate material information to investors. Thus, solicitation is the stage at which an investor is most likely to be injured, that is, by being persuaded to purchase securities without full and fair information. Given Congress' overriding goal of preventing this injury, we may infer that Congress intended solicitation to fall under the mantle of § 12(1).[52]

---

[52] 486 US 646–47.

The same reasoning would extend to § 12(2). In the offering context, § 12(2) extends liability for misrepresentations to those involved in the selling effort. Without § 12(2), so construed, the Securities Act would provide a remedy only for untrue statements in the registration statement, and by the seller of the securities, but would provide no remedy for false statements by salesmen in the course of soliciting purchases. Since it is far more likely that investors will be influenced by the assertions of the salesman than by the prospectus—which many purchasers do no read—it would be odd for the statute to provide a remedy for the one but not the other. As a result, it is unpersuasive to argue, as the Third Circuit did, that § 12(2) should not apply to persons whose only involvement in a sale is the receipt of a commission.

If the Court had been willing to overrule or at least to limit *Naftalin*, it would have been possible for it to write an opinion upholding the *Ballay* limitation to § 12(2) on the ground that a section that provides a remedy only for buyers does not fit the realities of the postdistribution, resale market.

V. Conclusion

In spite of the fact that the opinion in *Gustafson* displays a breathtaking disregard for the language and structure of the statute, when all is said and done the statute remains standing. If this is attributable to the Court, it is not apparent from the opinion. Although the Court provides a new and jarring definition of prospectus, the structure of § 5 continues to operate as it always has. The *Ballay* restriction on the scope of § 12(2) is affirmed, a restriction that can be plausibly justified by the one-sided remedial structure of the section. Surprisingly, the scope of § 12(2) was further restricted, so that private placements by control persons are also excluded from its coverage. But these transactions involve a relatively small number of parties, and if buyers in fact value the protection that § 12(2) formerly provided, the purchase agreements can be redrafted to provide for more stringent warranties. In most, if not all cases, there will a sufficiently plausible Rule 10b-5 claim to enable them to obtain federal court jurisdiction if they desire it.

What suffers in *Gustafson* is not the statute, but the Court as an institution. The Court's own authority centrally depends on the willingness of both legal professionals and citizens in general to accept that the language of legal authorities—including the Court's own opinions—have meaning. For the Court itself to read a statute in a manner inconsistent with the text is to give credence to the view that legal authorities have no meaning, that they are simply empty vessels into which those with the power to do so can pour whatever meaning they wish.

It seems very unlikely that the Court sought such a result. It seems more likely that the opinion in *Gustafson* simply reflects a failure in the Court's own internal procedures of quality control. If I as a teacher or scholar had prepared a draft with the flaws of the *Gustafson* opinion, I would have expected them to have been pointed out by my students, colleagues, or publication editors. If a partner at a law firm had prepared such a document, I would expect his partners or his associates to have told him, "Look, this just won't do." Apparently, no one was in a position to deliver that message to the author of the *Gustafson* opinion. The two dissenting opinions certainly did not perform that function. Although they point out at length the flaws in the Court's analysis, they were not taken as occasions for reconsideration and revision. Indeed, their only impact on the Court's opinion seems to be to provide an occasion for mocking.[53] The Justices are able lawyers, assisted by able if inexperienced clerks. Given the complexity and diversity of subject matter with which the Court is confronted, no Justice, working alone, can expect his or her work to be always free from error, even major error. The Court should explore ways to better bring its resources to bear on its work.

It is particularly important for the Court to be careful where, as it did in *Gustafson*, the Court chooses not to adopt an approach to a problem which has been embraced by others. Often, the Court chooses between alternative approaches which have been adopted by different courts after their own reflection and research. In *Gustafson*, the Court decided to adopt an approach that had never been endorsed by anyone else, whether by one of the parties in their briefs, in a lower court opinion, or in the secondary literature.

---

[53] "In the name of a plain meaning approach to statutory interpretation, the dissents discover in the Act two different species of prospectuses: formal (also called § 10) prospectuses, subject to both §§ 10 and 12, and informal prospectuses, subject only to § 12 but not to § 10. . . . Nowhere in the statute, however, do the terms 'formal prospectus' or 'informal prospectus' appear." 115 S Ct 1068. The dissents, of course, never claimed that these terms appeared in the statute.

There may be occasions when it is best for the Court to craft an approach that is uniquely its own, but it needs to be aware that when it does so it casts off the safeguards provided when it is adopting a position that has already been considered and analyzed by other informed and thoughtful people.

Although the immediate impact of the opinion in *Gustafson* on the securities laws is small, it may auger more, and perhaps more dramatic, changes to come. It is striking that five members of the Court were willing to join such an unpersuasive opinion in order to cut back the scope of a private cause of action for misrepresentation in the sale of securities. Not only that, but there is reason to think that two of the dissenters are inclined to give the statutes a nonexpansive reading. They dissented in *Gustafson* because the Court's reading of the statute was unsupported by the statutory text. And the kind of private securities litigation involved in *Gustafson* and *Ballay*—actions by disappointed purchasers in unregistered offerings and actions by purchasers against their brokers in the postdistribution resale markets—is not the kind of private securities litigation that has been controversial. The kind of securities litigation which has been the subject of controversy is the Rule 10b-5 action brought by buyers or sellers on the postdistribution resale markets against the issuer on the ground that the issuer has made statements that did not provide complete and accurate information to the market. These actions may benefit particular buyers or sellers, but they do nothing for the long-term shareholder who holds throughout the period of the alleged misrepresentation, and they require that all shareholders pay indirectly the continuing expense of director's and officer's liability coverage for the resulting liability risk.

Section 12(2) has always stood in the background of the debate over the scope of the Rule 10b-5 implied cause of action. One of the basic arguments for implying a private action under Rule 10b-5 was that it was necessary to cure the asymmetry of 12(2). Given the universally shared assumption that § 12(2) created a cause of action for any material misrepresentation for any buyer against the seller, the implied cause of action under Rule 10b-5 was necessary, it was argued, to provide a comparable right for sellers. Now that the Court has limited § 12(2) to registered offerings, where the remedial asymmetry makes sense, does that mean it can now reconsider the need for the implied right of action under Rule 10b-5?

The fact that rule 10b-5 requires proof of *scienter* by sellers, while § 12(2) required only proof of a misrepresentation by buyers, played an important role in the arguments over the scope of § 12(2). Now, will the limited scope of § 12(2) play a role in arguments about the implied right of action under Rule 10b-5?

There is an odd symmetry about all of this. Until 1975 the Court was an important force in the expansion of civil liability, on the theory, widely shared by experts in the field, that "more liability" inevitably furthered the purposes of the securities acts. This expansion took place without regard for the language and structure of the statutes themselves.[54] Most notably, the Court encouraged and ultimately ratified the private right of action under Rule 10b-5 in spite of the clear evidence that the Congress had clearly delineated those sections that were and were not to be enforceable by a private right of action.[55] In both periods, the Court's analysis of why either expansion or contraction of private remedies was a good idea has been unsophisticated, fragmentary, and unconvincing. In neither period, however, has the Court previously managed to issue an opinion as unpersuasive as the opinion in *Gustafson*.

---

[54] Which led Steven Thel to suggest in *Section 12(2) of the Securities Act: Does Old Legislation Matter?* 63 Fordham L Rev 1183 (1995), that the court should follow the implications of its own nonstatutory law rather than the statutory language. "If the courts are going to change the law by making section 12(2) recovery available to buyers who have been denied recovery under rule 10b-5, then the Supreme Court should decide whether this change is wise before it settles the question. Conventional conceptions of the proper role of the courts in applying legislation are especially strained when it comes to applying section 12(2), because the courts radically changed the federal law of private recovery for securities fraud when they created the private remedy for violations of rule 10b-5. It is simply too late to say that law-making in this area is for Congress alone and not for the courts. The courts made law when they created the private right of action for violations of rule 10b-5, and they have been making it ever since. The private right of action for violations of rule 10b-5 is firmly established and is now more central to the regime of federal securities regulation than section 12(2) ever was. The courts are not going to abandon the private remedy for violations of rule 10b-5. Given this history, when the Supreme Court decides the scope of section 12(2), it should not just focus on what Congress and the President intended in 1933. It should focus also on the implications of section 12(2) for the private-liability regime it has adopted under rule 10b-5. The Court should give section 12(2) the scope that it believes best serves a wise and coherent scheme of private liability." Id at 1193 and passim.

[55] David S. Ruder, *Civil Liability Under Rule 10b-5: Judicial Revision of the Legislation Intent?* 57 Nw U L Rev 627 (1963).

LAWRENCE LESSIG

TRANSLATING FEDERALISM:
UNITED STATES v LOPEZ

In 1835, two years after roaming through America, almost fifty years after the Constitution's founding, Alexis de Tocqueville wrote this about constitutionalism in America:

> I have hardly ever met one of the common people in America who did not surprisingly and easily perceive which obligations derived from a law of Congress and which were based on the laws of his state and who, having distinguished the matters falling within the general prerogatives of the Union from those suitable to the local legislature, could not indicate the point where the competence of the federal courts commences and that of the state courts ends.[1]

One cannot understand constitutionalism in America without considering just what this quotation from Tocqueville means. The American Constitution is in part a text; it "called into life"[2] a system of government constituted by this text. But the idea, for us, that the text called into life a system of government so well understood by "the common people" is unimaginable. It would be surprising enough to find a law professor who could "easily perceive which obligations derived from a law of Congress and which were based on the laws of his state," let alone the average citizen. The

Lawrence Lessig is Professor of Law at the University of Chicago.

AUTHOR'S NOTE: Thanks to David Currie and Dan Kahan for helpful comments on earlier drafts, and to David Sobelsohn for earlier help with this argument. Funding provided by the Russell Baker Scholars Fund. Excellent research assistance was provided by Anna Praschma, and especially Harold Reeves.

[1] Alexis de Tocqueville, *Democracy in America* 165 (Anchor, 1966).

[2] *Missouri v Holland*, 252 US 416, 433 (1920) (Holmes).

world Tocqueville describes is alien to us, even if it is the world from which we come.

Why is this so? Why can't we see the lines of federalism as easily as they could? Tocqueville had a sense of the answer:

> when one examines the Constitution of the United States, . . . it is frightening to see how much diverse knowledge and discernment it assumes on the part of the governed. *The government of the Union rests almost entirely on legal fictions. The Union is an ideal nation which exists, so to say, only in men's minds and whose extent and limits can only be discerned by the understanding.* When the general theory is well understood, there remain difficulties of application; these are innumerable, for the sovereignty of the Union is so involved with that of the states that it is impossible at first glance to see their limits. Everything in such a government depends on artificially contrived conventions, and it is only suited to a people long accustomed to manage its affairs, and one in which even the lowest ranks of society have an appreciation of political science.[3]

The constitutionalism that Tocqueville describes in the first passage presupposes the knowledge described in the second. It has life only because of the "fictions" and "conventions" that underlie it. So long as these fictions and conventions are understood, the system can function reasonably well. Lines are rarely crossed since the lines are well known; practices are seen to conform since supported by understandings that make them cohere. The system is not fundamentally different, in this sense, from baseball: For no one would say that baseball is just the rules of the game; more than the rules, it is the understandings of those rules, and the practices that they envision, that constitute the knowledge necessary to play the game.

But what happens when this "diverse knowledge and discernment" disappear? When these "artificially contrived conventions" lapse, how does a constitutional regime respond? More particu-

---

[3] Id at 164–65 (emphasis added). The sense of "fictions" here is of course different from our modern sense. See, for example, *Hodel v Virginia Surface Mining & Reclamation Assc., Inc.,* 452 US 264, 307 (1981) (Rehnquist concurring) ("one of the greatest 'fictions' of our federal system is that the Congress exercises only those powers delegated to it"). Compare Charles F. Amidon, *The Nation and the Constitution,* in Sydney R. Wrightington, ed, 10 *The Green Bag* 595 (Boston Book, 1907) (quoting Cooley) ("No instrument can be the same in meaning today and forever and in all men's minds. As the people change so does their written constitution change also. They see it in new lights and with different eyes: events may have given unexpected illumination to some of its provisions, and what they read one way before they read a very different way now.").

larly, how does a *written* constitution survive when the "fictions" upon which it rested indeed become fiction?

This is the distinctive feature of constitutionalism in America. For it is not that conventions and understandings behind the constitutional text disappear; it is that they change. They change both in their substance, and in their location: They not only direct different readings of the constitutional text, but they are possessed, or understood, no longer by "the common people," instead by a constitutional elite—lawyers, law professors, and members of government. The distinctive problem of American constitutionalism is how to read this constitutional text, when these understandings are fundamentally different from what they were.

We can sketch two very different responses. The first is a technique of interpretive fidelity, by far the dominant rhetoric in constitutional interpretation, and the one most directly tied to a theory of constitutional democracy. According to this technique, the proper way to read the Constitution is first, to read it against the framing background—fully excavating the presuppositions about which Tocqueville speaks so as to find its meaning in that original context—and then second, to apply it today in a way that preserves that original meaning. Thus, if conventions in the original context were understood, but not said, and if they today are neither understood, nor said, then the response of fidelity is to articulate these previously understood conventions, and apply them today to assure that the constitutional structure original established is, so far as possible, preserved.[4] The effort, we could say, is to *translate* that original structure into the context of today,[5] one version of a technique we can call *originalism.*

The second technique is less focused on fidelity. Its method is more direct. It simply reads a text according to relatively simple rules of interpretation, finding that understanding of the text that

---

[4] This is a practice well understood within the German tradition. See David P. Currie, *The Constitution of the Federal Republic of Germany* 117–18 (Chicago, 1995) ("As a codification grows older, the judge's 'freedom to develop the law creatively' increases.").

[5] Fidelity describes that approach to constitutional law concerned with linking today's applications to something the framers did. Within the terms John Ely sketched, fidelity theory is interpretive. John H. Ely, *Democracy and Distrust: A Theory of Judicial Review*, chs 1–2 (1980). But within this general class of interpretive theories, the class I am concerned with are theories of translation. Paul Brest, *The Misconceived Quest for the Original Understanding*, 60 BU L Rev 204, 218 (1980). See generally Lawrence Lessig, *Fidelity in Translation*, 71 Tex L Rev 1165 (1993).

is most compelling in the current context. It doesn't worry whether that current reading is the original reading. It aims simply at finding a reading that coheres best with what is now understood to be the case. This technique, for convenience, we can call *textualism*.[6]

Constitutionalism in America cycles between these two techniques.[7] It follows one for a bit, and then the other—one with one part of the constitutional text while the other with another part; or one with one part, and then later, the other with the same part. It is a cycle that is apparently unending; a cycle that any theory of American constitutionalism must help to explain.

My aim in this essay is to track one such cycle between originalism and textualism, and to use this story to build an account that might just explain, and justify, this cycling more generally. The story is the story of American federalism, as viewed through the narrow prism of the judiciary. At different times with the same text, and at the same time with different texts, judicial treatment of the Constitution's federalism clauses has followed these different responses. At times, that is, the Court has let the Constitution's text speak for itself—enforcing or allowing the full range of powers that the text, in the current context, might seem to allow. But at other times, the Court has cabined federal or state powers, in the name of a founding balance thought inconsistent with a plain reading.

The opportunity for this account is presented by federalism's latest twist, *United States v Lopez*.[8] In *Lopez*, for the first time in almost sixty years,[9] the Court struck, as beyond Congress's "commerce power,"

---

[6] All I mean to imply by invoking this "ism" is an interpretive practice focused primarily on text. See generally Mark V. Tushnet, *A Note on the Revival of Textualism in Constitutional Theory*, 58 S Cal L Rev 683, 683 (1985), commenting on the "sophisticated versions of textualism" offered in Robert F. Nagel, *Interpretation and Importance in Constitutional Law: A Re-assessment of Judicial Restraint*, 25 Nomos 181 (1983), and Douglas Laycock, *Taking Constitutions Seriously: A Theory of Judicial Review*, 59 Tex L Rev 343 (1981) (Book Review). See also Frank H. Easterbrook, *Statutes' Domains*, 50 U Chi L Rev 533 (1983); William Nichol Eskridge, Jr. and Philip P. Frickey, *Statutory Interpretation as Practical Reasoning*, 42 Stan L Rev 321 (1988); Richard S. Kay, *Adherence to the Original Intentions in Constitutional Adjudication: Three Objections and Responses*, 82 Nw U L Rev 226 (1988), distinguishing originalism and textualism.

[7] It should be clear from my usage here that I am thinking of these two techniques as ideal types, and not as complete descriptions of any particular practice or the full range of practices. For a wonderful account of this far wider range, see Philip Bobbitt, *Constitutional Interpretation* 1–43 (Blackwell, 1991). My aim here is to understand a pattern of movement, no so much the particulars of any point along that path.

[8] 115 S Ct 1624 (1995).

[9] The last time was *Carter v Carter Coal Co.*, 298 US 238, 297–310 (1936).

an act of Congress that aimed at regulating citizens (rather than states). In the shock after the decision, commentators attacked it[10] as either political, or activist, or fundamentally flawed. Flawed it may be, and activist it certainly is. But it is a mistake to see *Lopez* as mere politics. *Lopez* is an act of interpretive fidelity. It is an effort to reconstruct something from the framing balance to be preserved in the current interpretive context. It also marks a shift, from (what I will argue is) a textualist account to an originalist account. The question is whether this shift is justified, a question for which I hazard an answer here.

The argument that *Lopez* is a reading of fidelity begins with what all take as obvious: There is little doubt that the scope of the powers now exercised by Congress far exceeds that imagined by the framers. They struggled over whether the commerce power included the power to build roads; they wouldn't have struggled over its power to reach the possession of guns near schools.

But against this there is a second obviousness: That in the current interpretive context, the language of the Constitution's power clauses, read according to the formula given us by founding federal powers opinions,[11] plainly supports this expanse of federal power. This is the textualist account: That the Constitution gives Congress the power to regulate "commerce" "among the several states," and the power to pass laws "necessary and proper" to effect this regulation of commerce among the several states. Chief Justice Marshall's way of reading these words was quite expansive: So long as some activity could be said to "affect" the commerce of more than one state, that activity was within either the com-

---

[10] Not all commentators. Laurence Tribe said the decision might act as a useful corrective on Congress's exercise of its power. See Stuart Taylor, Jr., *Looking Right at the Justices*, Am Lawyer 37, 38 (Nov 1995) (reporting Tribe's view: "*Lopez* might well be a useful corrective to the tendency of Congress casually to assume that it can do anything it wants.").

[11] One could well question whether the founding powers opinions—*McCulloch v Maryland*, 17 US (4 Wheat) 316 (1819) and *Gibbons v Ogden*, 22 US (9 Wheat) 1 (1824)—truly represent the framers' view of the federal government's power. James Boyd White, for example, sees *McCulloch* as a plain amendment to the constitutional design of the framers. See James Boyd White, *When Words Lose Their Meaning: Constitutions and Reconstitutions of Language, Character, and Community* 247–63 (Chicago, 1984). That the chartering of a national bank was more than a hiccup is suggested by Jefferson's reaction, see Willard Sterne Randall, *Thomas Jefferson: A Life* 506 (HarperPerennial, 1993) ("To take a single step beyond the boundaries thus specially drawn around the powers of Congress is to take possession of a boundless field of power."). Marshall did not take kindly to the suggestion that he was extending the scope of the Constitution's power "by construction." For a description of his pseudonymous defense of *McCulloch*, see Raoul Berger, *Federalism: The Founder's Design* 90–91 (Oklahoma, 1987).

merce power, or the necessary and proper power. As commerce today seems plainly to reach practically every activity of social life, it would seem to follow that Congress has the power to reach, through regulation, practically every activity of social life. Put another way: If America were to adopt a constitution today that had this grant of authority within it, it would be perfectly reasonable to read this grant to give Congress the power to regulate the full range of economic (and hence social) life in America.

The textualist account conflicts with the originalist account. Yet for much of the past half-century, the Court has followed this textualism. It has allowed Congress a power that reaches to the extreme of what the words of the power clauses allow. And in so doing, it has ignored conventions and understandings, presupposed by the framers, and inconsistent with this broad reach of federal power.

Lopez reverses all that. It rejects this textualist reading of the power clauses, in the name of fidelity to a founding understanding about how far these powers of Congress were to reach. It finds implied in the constitutional structure limits on the federal government's power, limits that before may have been supported either by the understandings Tocqueville spoke of, or by the limits entailed by a diffuse national economy, but which today can be supported only by affirmative limits constructed by the Court. And so does the Court impose these limits, by artificial and incomplete readings of Congress's power clauses, rendered in the name of restoring a balance envisioned in the framing generation.

In this way is *Lopez* an act of fidelity, or what I would call an act of translation: Like the very best of the Warren Court, it limits an otherwise apparently unlimited grant of governmental power in the name of a framing conception of autonomy. *Lopez* limits federal power in the name of state autonomy; the Warren Court limited state and federal power in the name of individual autonomy. But both limit governmental power in the name of implied limits given us by the framers. Both, that is, translate this framing vision into the current interpretive context.

This is praise, not criticism, of the *Lopez* Court's work. For in my view, this effort at translation is essential if the American Constitution is to be something more than an ancient, dead text. This effort to breathe life into the structures originally established links *Lopez* with a long tradition of similar constructivism. Establishing this link will be my first aim in this essay—to offer a way to understand this recent revival of federalism jurisprudence not as some political anomaly from the right, but as part of a tradition that draws together much in our constitutional past. Justices might not like the pairings this understanding suggests, but that is of no matter. Their practices are the same, and the justification for their practices will stand or fall together.

But why then the switch? What explains the revival of translation after a half-century of plain reading? This again is the question about cycling, for the practice of textualism rejected by *Lopez* was itself born in the rejection of an earlier practice of translation. This was the switch that ratified the New Deal. If a theory is to explain the latest swing of *Lopez*, then it must explain just what justified the practice that *Lopez* rejects.

This is my aim in the second section of the paper. My strategy is just this: Fidelity is the dominant modality of constitutional interpretation. But sometimes, as I will argue, the interpreter is constrained not to follow this first-best strategy. Sometimes, that is, the interpreter must follow a second-best strategy. This is the strategy of textualism, and it will obtain so long as this constraint on fidelity exists. When, and if, the constraint is weakened, then the Court should (and does) return to the first-best strategy of fidelity. Thus this cycle of techniques should, if the theory is correct, track the presence of this constraint.

Once we have sketched this structure, we will be in a position better to evaluate the success of *Lopez*, and the promise for reform that it might offer. Here I am less optimistic. While *Lopez* properly stands within an important tradition of interpretive fidelity, my argument in the end will be that the techniques it has selected to this end of fidelity are poorly chosen. I do not believe the change *Lopez* announces will be significant. As it stands, the case is little more than an invitation. But if *Lopez* were to take on this larger role, my view is that it is not well equipped. Ironically, the techniques are too conservative to achieve this conservative end. What fidelity requires is a kind of radicalism in interpretation—a radicalism that this Court is unlikely to embrace.

CHANGED CIRCUMSTANCES AND TRANSLATION

I begin with a short introduction to the notion of fidelity that I argue is central to our interpretive tradition. This is not meant as a general theory of the practice that I am calling transla-tion; rather it is a particular application of that practice to a com-mon problem in interpreting the scope of government power.

Its general form is this: Distinguish between power clauses in the Constitution, and rights clauses. A power clause (such as the Commerce Clause) grants to the federal government certain pow-ers. A rights clause (such as the Free Speech Clause of the First Amendment) protects certain individual rights against federal (at least) interference. As originally understood, there is no reason to expect that the rights clauses and the power clauses would neces-sarily conflict—indeed, Madison originally thought the Bill of Rights unnecessary, since the power of Congress would not reach the domain of the Bill of Rights.[12] Nonetheless, these power and rights clauses are now seen to conflict. Now, because of changed circumstances, there is a change in the reach of the power clause, and in response, the Court finds reason in the rights clause to limit the scope of the power clause.[13] The list here is legion: the exclu-sionary rule, *Miranda*, contraception, *National League of Cities*.

What gives rise to the conflict is changed circumstances. The scope of the power clause is seen to turn upon facts in the world, and as these facts change, the scope of the power too is seen to change. Translation is the response. Changed circumstances de-scribe what the world does to the legal system; translation de-scribes what the legal system does in response—to neutralize the effects of these changes in the world.

A simple example should draw out the point. At the founding, the rule protecting domestic privacy was relatively simple. It was the rule of trespass. If the state entered my land and searched my belongings, then it trespassed, and to defend against this trespass, it needed good reasons. A trespass not authorized by a judicial warrant, or a trespass not supported by probable cause, rendered the officer liable for his violation of my rights.[14]

One consequence of this original rule was that searches that could be conducted without a trespass were not unlawful. Eaves-

---

[12] Cass R. Sunstein, *The Partial Constitution* 9 (Harvard, 1993).

[13] A similar argument is made by Bruce Ackerman, *Liberating Abstraction*, 59 U Chi L Rev 317 (1992).

[14] I do not mean to imply that a warrant was required. See Telford Taylor, *Two Studies in Constitutional Interpretation* 24–29, 57 (Ohio, 1969); Akhil Reed Amar, *Fourth Amendment First Principles*, 107 Harv L Rev 757, 764–66 (1994).

dropping, for example: If the state stood outside my window, on a public street, and listened to my conversations within, then so long as it had not trespassed on my property, it had not violated my Fourth Amendment rights.[15]

No doubt this rule about eavesdropping might be thought in principle inconsistent with important privacy interests. But law functions at the level of the pragmatic, and the regime was a pragmatic response to the existing technologies of privacy and invasion. It may well have marked, for the time, the most practical way to protect these rights. And if, for the most part, this regime of property adequately protected privacy, then adequacy was enough.

But adequacy depends upon the context. In particular, it depends upon the technology of that context. When wiretapping, for example, became a technological possibility, and when much of human life moved from the parlors of one's home to the first stages of cyberspace, then this rule about trespass began to fail. Whereas before this change in technology a very high proportion of one's private conversations had been protected from government's view, now, after the change, an increasingly small proportion was so protected.

This change in technology is what I am calling the changed circumstance. And by applying the original rule of privacy, this change had a severe effect on the substantive protections. If one continued to apply the old rule in the new context—as, for example, Chief Justice Taft did in *Olmstead v United States*[16]—then an increasingly small percentage of private life would continue to be private. The old rule applied to this changed context yielded a different constitutional regime.

This led some to suggest,[17] and the Court eventually to adopt, a response of translation. Because the old rule in this new context yielded a regime whose meaning and effect was fundamentally different from the meaning and effect of the old rule in the original context, these Justices suggested a new rule, which in the new context would yield roughly the same balance between public and private. Their aim was to restore the privacy that the changed circumstances had erased. Their technique was to find a new reading of

---

[15] See *Berger v New York*, 388 US 41, 45 (1967).

[16] 277 US 438 (1928).

[17] Id at 438, 471 (1928) (Brandeis dissenting).

the Fourth Amendment that would compensate for these changes in technology.

This is the practice that I call translation.[18] It presents really two distinct questions. The first asks what rights would, in this context, be equivalent to the rights in the original context. Any number of predicates could be used to describe this "sameness," and it is not my point here to select one that works best. One could ask, for example, which preserves the meaning from the original context, or which preserves the effect of the original structure, or which is more consistent with the purpose of the original context, etc. Whichever is selected, the first question of translation is what an equivalent structure would be today.

The second question is the more difficult. Since often the translation will be a translation of a constitutional right, often the translation will have to limit governmental power. (Not always—for example, the best translation of the President's power increases his power[19]—but often.) For a court, within a democracy, this act of limitation can be quite difficult. For the Court must devise tools that will function with a minimum of institutional cost, to effect the changes to restore an original balance. What these tools can be is the focus of much that follows below. My point here is simply to raise this issue as distinct from the question of what structure is equivalent.

Thus a question of translation gets raised in response to a change in context—changed circumstances—and it gets answered by specifying the tools that will be used to neutralize the effect of these changes. In the example just given (*Olmstead*), it gets raised about an individual right. In the essay that follows, it gets raised about what could be considered states' rights. But whether individual rights or states' rights, the issue is the same: How best to neutralize increased governmental power in the name of preserving an original conception of individual or states' rights.

---

[18] The translators in constitutional theory are many. For an excellent recent application, see William Michael Treanor, *The Original Understanding of the Takings Clause and the Political Process*, 95 Colum L Rev 782, 855–87 (1995). The origin of the argument is well traced to Brest, 60 BU L Rev 204 (cited in note 5). For a discussion of statutory interpretation, see generally William N. Eskridge, Jr., *Dynamic Statutory Interpretation* (Harvard, 1994).

[19] For a discussion of translation and the powers of the executive branch, see Lawrence Lessig and Cass R. Sunstein, *The President and the Administration*, 94 Colum L Rev 1, 85–118 (1994). Compare Abner S. Greene, *Checks and Balances in an Era of Presidential Lawmaking*, 61 U Chi L Rev 123, 125–26 (1993).

This is *Lopez*'s problem of translation. Changes no less significant than the changes of technology in *Olmstead* give rise to a
vastly increased reach of federal power;[20] as the emergence of wiretapping effectively destroyed much of an individual's private space,
this increased scope of federal power effectively destroys much of
the original space for state legislative autonomy; this suggests to
some the need to find, or imply, or construct, affirmative limitations on government's power, to restore a balance from the founding regime. In both cases, the nature of these limits is difficult to
specify—and the nature of the limits in federalism will consume
the balance of this essay—but in both cases, the function of the
limits is the same. They are to reestablish something ratifiers of
the Constitution chose, eroded by changes that no one chose, to
assure that something of the original structure survives these un-
chosen changes.

The Balance of Federalism

"There are," as Larry Kramer writes, "two sides to Federalism: not just preserving state authority where appropriate, but
also enabling the federal government to act where national action
is desirable."[21] The first side is about protecting states; it addresses
limits on federal power, and gets litigated in the context of the
positive commerce power, both over citizens directly, and over
sovereigns. The second side is about protecting federal interests;[22] it addresses limits on state power, and gets litigated directly
in the context of preemption, and less directly in the context of
the negative commerce power. The first side has been the focus
of most of the federalism disputes in the twentieth century; the
second side was the focus of disputes in the nineteenth century.

---

[20] Why technology increases the scope of Congress's power I discuss below. See the text
below at notes 26–41.

[21] Larry Kramer, *Understanding Federalism*, 47 Vand L Rev 1485, 1502 (1994). Justice
Kennedy has made the same point. As Kathleen Sullivan puts it, "Justice Kennedy alone
sees the Court's role in federalism disputes as a two-way ratchet, stopping the states from
'invad[ing]' the sphere of federal sovereignty' but also holding the federal government
'within the boundaries of its own power when it intrudes upon matters reserved to the
States.'" Kathleen M. Sullivan, *Dueling Sovereignties: U.S. Term Limits, Inc. v Thornton*, 109
Harv L Rev 78, 103 (1995).

[22] I'm understanding this second half more broadly than Kramer's language suggests. The
second half is about protecting federal interests generally, both by enabling federal legislation, and by disabling state legislation that is inconsistent with national interests.

My hope is to understand these two sides to federalism together—to see them as evolving in response to the same influences, and to look for a theory that can explain these separate evolutions. My argument is that both sides present the same
interpretive problem (the second just a century before the first),
and that both react to this problem with the same interpretive response. The interpretive problem is the problem of changed circumstances; the response is translation. Both are the focus of continued interpretive struggle, in large part because the nature of
each turns on social and economic factors which are, over the two
centuries since the Constitution was penned, in radical transformation. In both contexts, what the Court does in response to these
changing contexts is to devise tools that, in the particular context,
help recreate the initial balance of federalism. Not uniformly, and
not with uniform fidelity, but in the main this is how we can understand the progression of tests that can be collected from the
histories of both.

My aim is to collect these tests, and then map their evolutions.
But we should be clear up front about terms. If federalism has
"two sides," then we must locate two pair of rights, and powers.
The mapping of the first side—preserving state authority by limiting federal power—is the most direct, subject to an important
objection.[23] Here, the relevant power is all the power of Congress;
the relevant right is the right expressed in the Tenth Amendment,
reserving the balance of power to the "states, and to the people,
respectively."[24] The mapping of the second side—preserving federal interests—is more artificial, but salient nonetheless. Here the
relevant power is the power of the states to regulate within their
own domain, and the relevant right is the right of the federal government not to have its regulative authority interfered with by
these state regulations. The interpretive problem for both sides of

---

[23] The objection is that the Amendment "states but a truism that all is retained which
has not been surrendered." *United States v Darby*, 312 US 100, 124 (1941). For a complete
account of these and related views, see Laurence H. Tribe, *American Constitutional Law*
378–85 (Foundation Press, 2d ed 1988). See also Edward Corwin, *Constitutional Revolution,
Ltd.* 14–15 (1941) (describing Marshall's view). But in what follows, I assume the Amendment was to do more than state a truism.

[24] US Const, Amend 10. For other conceptions of the rights of the people, see Akhil
Reed Amar, *The Bill of Rights as a Constitution*, 100 Yale L J 1131, 1157–58 (1991).

the federalism problem then is just this—how to preserve the relevant right in light the expanding scope of the relevant power.[25]

THE PROBLEMS WITH INTEGRATION

The problem of federalism is to maintain two distinct balances over time. It is only an interpretive problem because one part of each balance is linked to a fact that, over the period in question, changes. The change that I claim is relevant here is the relative integration of social and economic forces; and the claim is that changes in this integration result in changes in the scope of both federal and state power.

This we can call the *integration thesis.* The intuition behind it is easy enough, though moving beyond an intuition is somewhat more difficult. The intuition is this: There is a sense in which economic and social forces are always linked—in some sense the price of rice in China does affect (and has always affected) the price of rice in New York. In this sense, local economic activity has never been just local. It has always been connected to economic activity more distant, within other jurisdictions.[26]

But from this certainly true premise, we should not conclude that the economy has always and everywhere been integrated to the same extent. Or in the same sense. There may always have been an international market for cotton, or gold; but it took the technologies of cold-car transport and pasteurization before there was a significant interstate market for milk. While in some sense the market for milk has always been integrated,[27] the extent to

---

[25] Here again there are objections. The strongest is that there is no need to conceive of this as a conflict of rights, since here, the holder of the right (the federal government) by virtue of the Supremacy Clause has all the power it needs to defend its rights without intervention by the courts. If the interests of the federal government are interfered with by the regulations of the states, the federal government can simply pass a law nullifying those interfering state regulations. But this objection is not so much an objection to the question of limits on state power as it is a particular solution to the problem of the proper limits on state power. It acknowledges, that is, that changed circumstances generate an interpretive problem; it simply offers the Supremacy Clause as the only remedy needed for that problem.

[26] I am making a claim here about what was or was not integrated. This is distinct from whether people at the time, given the contemporary economic theory, would have understood the same to be integrated.

[27] For example, even if you couldn't always ship the milk, it was always possible to move to set up a farm, so the price of milk in New York affected the price of milk in California in 1870 in just the sense that if it was too high in California and too low in New York, one might expect milk farmers to move from New York to California.

which it was integrated in 1789 is different from the extent it was integrated in 1989.

There is no simple way to describe this difference in the extent of integration, and no handy way to quantify it.[28] But I don't believe we need data to make the point that I want to make here: That integration in the sense I suggest has increased; that more operates in a national rather than local market; and that this change in the extent of the market properly has consequences for the scope of federal and state power.[29]

The consequences are these: As integration increases, the "effect" that local action will have beyond its own local border increases. It increases because as national markets increase, the influence of local effects is felt more broadly than before. Thus, in ways I will describe below, increasing integration both (a) increases the scope of federal power (since the effects of a local action are more consistently felt beyond state borders)[30] and (b) makes more

---

[28] One possibility would be to measure the extent of the market affecting various commodities. The intuition would be that increased integration would track an expanding geographical market, such that if the geographic market for, say, milk expanded, we could say that the integration of a national market with respect to milk had increased. See Kenneth G. Elzinga and Thomas F. Hogarty, *The Problem of Geographic Market Delineation in Anti-merger Suits*, 18 Antitrust Bull 45, 47 (1973), citing Alfred Marshall, 5 *Principles of Economics* 324 (Macmillan, 1920), quoting Cournot ("Alfred Marshall emphasized that the delineation of a geographic market did not involve looking for a place or geographic location, but rather for the buyers and sellers who were 'in such free intercourse with one another that the prices of the same goods tend to equality easily and quickly.' ").

As geographic markets then increased, integration in the sense that I am offering here would increase. This increase in turn might be quantified through a technique suggested by George Stigler and Robert A. Sherwin. They, for example, provide a simple formula for measuring whether two commodities compete within the same market. See George J. Stigler and Robert A. Sherwin, *The Extent of the Market*, 28 J L & Econ 555, 585 (1985).

Using this technique, one might imagine, for example, constructing an index listing the commodities comprising 80 percent of the GNP, and then calculating the percentage of that index for which the geographical market was wider than a single state. The change in that percentage, then, would be a measure of changing integration in the national market.

One might think interstate movement would be a good proxy for commerce that might affect interstate commerce, but if the question is whether goods are in the same market, then "neither the physical shipment of goods nor its absence always gives a reliable proof that the two areas are or are not in the same market." Id at 581.

[29] Justice Fried points to changing conceptions of economics as a reason why more was seen to fit within the "Commerce Clause" definition. See Charles Fried, *Foreword: Revolutions?* 109 Harv L Rev 13, 37–40 (1995). A full account would rely both on changing conceptions in economics, changing facts about the world, and changing understandings of an appropriate judicial role. I discuss all three in *Understanding Changed Readings: Fidelity and Theory*, 47 Stan L Rev 395, 454–72 (1995).

[30] Compare Justice O'Connor's view in *Garcia*:

In the decades since ratification of the Constitution, interstate economic activity has steadily expanded. Industrialization, coupled with advances in transportation

significant (for federal purposes) the power of the state governments (since regulations of the states more consistently influence
federal matters). Both changes then give rise to the need for an
interpretive response.[31]

Consider the federal side first: Since the start, or shortly after
the start,[32] the scope of Congress's commerce power has been defined by negative implication from what Chief Justice Marshall
said it was not. In *Gibbons v Ogden*, said Marshall, the power did
not reach objects:

> [1] completely within a particular State, [2] which do not affect
> other States, and [3] with which it is not necessary to interfere,
> for the purpose of executing some of the general powers of
> the government.[33]

From this, the power was understood to reach (1) objects passing

---

and communications, has created a national economy in which virtually every activity occurring within the borders of a State plays a part. The expansion and
integration of the national economy brought with it a coordinate expansion in the
scope of national problems.

Garcia v San Antonio Metro. Transit Auth., 469 US 528, 583 (1985) (O'Connor dissenting).
The Court has expressed the same view at times. See *New York v United States*, 112 S Ct
2408, 2418–19 (1992) (*New York II*); *Heart of Atlanta Motel, Inc. v United States*, 379 US
241, 251 (1964); *Stafford v Wallace*, 258 US 495, 520–21 (1922); see also Felix Frankfurter,
The Commerce Clause: Under Marshall, Taney and Waite 8 (Quadrangle, 1937) ("[N]ot until after the Reconstruction period . . . did those powerful economic forces emerge which
bring into play the affirmative possibilities of the authority over commerce granted to Congress . . . ."); John T. Ganoe, *The Roosevelt Court and the Commerce Clause*, 24 Or L Rev
71, 142 (1945); Louis Maier, *Federal Regulation of Manufacturing under the Interstate Commerce Power*, 24 Marq L Rev 175, 177–78 (1940).

[31] See also Joseph Roper, *The Constitution: Discovered or Discarded*, 16 Notre Dame Lawyer
97, 115 (1941) (describing "economic and social system, until about the year 1875 . . . [as]
relatively simple"); Frankfurter, *The Commerce Clause* at 63 (cited in note 30) ("New economic forces were bringing new issues to the Court.").

[32] On whether Marshall's view was the founders' view, see note and text accompanying
note 11.

[33] *Gibbons*, 22 US (9 Wheat) at 195 (bracketed numbers added). The same point is made
later in the opinion:

> No direct general power over these objects is granted to Congress; and, conse-
> quently, they remain subject to State legislation. If the legislative power of the
> Union can reach them, it must be for national purposes; it must be where the
> power is expressly given for a special purpose, or is clearly incidental to some
> power which is expressly given.

Id at 203–04. See also *Katzenbach v McClung*, 379 US 294, 302 (1964), quoting *Gibbons*,
22 US (9 Wheat) at 195 ("[t]he activities that are beyond the reach of Congress are 'those
which are completely within a particular State, which do not affect other States, and with
which it is not necessary to interfere, for the purposes of executing some of the general
powers of government.'").

between two or more states ("in" interstate commerce), (2) objects "affecting" interstate commerce, and (3) objects neither in nor affecting interstate commerce, but the regulation of which was "necessary . . . for the purpose of executing" the commerce power or some other power. As Marshall made clear there, and later courts followed, the source of the power in parts (1) and (2) is the Commerce Clause itself. The source of the power in part (3) is the Necessary and Proper Clause.[34]

What is important about this definition is that it makes the scope of federal power turn upon facts in the world. For the scope of Congress's power turns either upon a simple, or not so simple, factual question. Congress's power depends either upon how much commerce is "in" interstate commerce (the simple question), or upon how much power "affects" interstate commerce (the not so simple question). However they are answered, both questions make the scope of Congress's power contingent upon some fact in the world—either upon the extent of interstate commerce, or upon the *integration* of the national economy. The greater the integration, the greater the congressional power.

At the founding, or more precisely, at the time of *Gibbons*, this test would have left a large sphere of concerns that states could regulate without federal interference. Some markets, but relatively few, functioned on a national scale. But internal commerce was slight,[35] and a power that turned upon its extent would be slight as well.

Over time, of course, all this changed. Therefore did the predicate for federal power grow as well. The same would be true of

---

[34] See Forrest Revere Black, *The Commerce Clause and the New Deal*, 20 Cornell L Q 169, 179 (1935); *Garcia*, 469 US at 584–85 (O'Connor dissenting).

[35] See Bureau of Statistics, Treasury Department, *First Annual Report on the Internal Commerce of the United States* 8 (US GPO, 1877) (most "commerce" at founding was foreign commerce, with the result that little attention was paid to "comparatively small *internal commerce.*") (emphasis in original); id at 9 (describing growth in internal commerce). While no comprehensive account of the internal commerce is available, some comparative data points are interesting to collect. See Amidon, *The Nation and the Constitution* at 600 (cited in note 3) ("Actual statistics are wanting, but persons in a position to know, are of the opinion that the local business of the railroads does not exceed fifteen percent of their entire traffic" in 1907); R. V. Fletcher, *Some Aspects of the Commerce Clause*, 3 Miss L J 136, 141 (1930) (describing 80 percent of commerce as interstate); William Z. Ripley, *Railroads: Rates and Regulations* 442 (Longmans, Green, 1913) (75 percent "of the railway traffic . . . interstate" in 1886).

any test tied to the "extent" of interstate commerce.[36] For even if the test were limited just to commerce that traveled in interstate commerce, it is certain that the scope of Congress's power would be far greater than the framers imagined.[37] Given the structure of Marshall's test, this increase in federal power was a necessary consequence of economic integration.

In response to this increasing integration, the Court was at first willing to extend the reach of Congress's power quite generously. The changing economy meant both that the extent of federal regulation must increase, and that the commerce power would reach further than the objects touched originally. Chief Justice Waite, in *Pensacola*, provides a common account:

The powers thus granted are not confined to the instrumentali-

---

[36] See Edward Corwin, *Constitutional Revolution, Ltd.* 19 (1941) (describing the "inevitable tendency of Marshall's doctrines"). Of course, this nominalist understanding is not the only way to understand the reach of the commerce power. If we understood the reach of the clause more in line with its purpose, then there is a way to make sense of its scope without imagining it to reach all commerce whatsoever. If the clause was meant to assign to Congress regulation of matters that cannot effectively be regulated at the state level, then a better understanding of the "in" interstate commerce and "affects" interstate commerce categories would be to limit the power to objects operating within a national, or multistate economic market. An approach along these general lines is suggested by Donald Regan, *How to Think About the Federal Commerce Power (and Incidentally Rewrite United States v Lopez)* 94 Mich L Rev 554 (1995). The only problem with this approach, as I suggest below, is the difficulty in specifying a judicial test that could draw this conceptual line.

[37] So how much commerce is "in interstate commerce"? As a first step, this depends upon what one understands as "commerce." For the framers, the scope of items "in" interstate commerce was relatively small. Trade across state boundaries was primarily foreign commerce, as the facility with which items could move in interstate commerce was slight. But the scope of items actually in interstate commerce would not define the reach of what the framers imagined interstate commerce to be. Indeed, there is evidence that the notion "commerce," rather than having the strictly commercial sense that we give it today, reached much more broadly. As a legal term, the word had little significance prior to its inclusion in the Constitution; as a nonlegal term, it reached much more broadly than just business-related matters. As one commentator put it, its primary meaning at the time of the founding was the "interchange of ideas, sentiments, etc., as between man and man, formally also communication, channel or intercourse," while its secondary meaning was business related. See Bernard Gavit, *The Commerce Clause of the United States Constitution* 84 (Principia Press, 1932) ("This sense, of personal intercourse, was the most widely developed in the early use of the word *commerce*.").

Now, of course, nothing yet would suggest why the clause could be used for reasons other than the regulation of commerce—why, for example, it should be used as a jurisdictional basis, for example, for the regulation of immoral commerce (not in an economic sense) in women. The account of this extension comes later. But what this account does do is help distinguish between what really is an unlimited claim about the "affects" test and a more limited, and sensible, claim. Compare *Caminetti v United States*, 242 US 470, 491 (1917).

ties of commerce, or the postal service known or in use when
the Constitution was adopted, but they keep pace with the
progress of the country, and adapt themselves to the new developments of time and circumstances. They extend from the
horse with its rider to the stage-coach, from the sailing-vessel
to the steamboat, from the coach and the steamboat to the
railroad, and from the railroad to the telegraph, as these new
agencies are successively brought into use to meet the demands
of increasing population and wealth. They were intended for
the government of the business to which they relate, at all
times and under all circumstances.[38]

Quite unreflectively, the Court simply applied the test of Marshall
to these new circumstances of commerce, with the obvious implication that the scope of federal power would increase. As the Court
said (in an otherwise infamous case):

Up to a recent date commerce, both interstate and international, was mainly by water, and it is not strange that both the
legislation of Congress and the cases in the courts have been
principally concerned therewith. The fact that in recent years
interstate commerce has come mainly to be carried on by railroads and over artificial highways has in no manner narrowed
the scope of the constitutional provision, or abridged the power
of Congress over such commerce. On the contrary, the same
fullness of control exists in the one case as in the other, and
the same power to remove obstructions from the one as from
the other.[39]

The power of Congress extends further than before, the Court
says, not because the power has changed, but because the predicate
to the power's reach has changed. As one commentator put it near
the turn of the century, "if the power of Congress has a wider
incidence in 1918 than it could have had in 1789, this is merely
because production is more dependent now than then on extra-
state markets. No state liveth to itself alone to any such extent as
was true a century ago. What is changing is not our system of
government, but our economic organization."[40]

[38] *Pensacola Tel. Co. v Western Union Tel. Co.*, 96 US 1, 9 (1877).

[39] *In re Debs*, 158 US 564, 590–91 (1895). See also Maurice M. Feuerlicht, *The Interstate Commerce Clause and NRA*, 9 Ind L J 434, 435–41 (1934).

[40] Thomas Reed Powell, *The Child Labor Law, the Tenth Amendment and the Commerce Clause*, 3 Southern L Q 175, 200 (1918). See also David P. Currie, *The Constitution in the Supreme Court: The First Hundred Years, 1789–1888* 429 (Chicago, 1985), discussing view of *Pensacola Telegraph*, 96 US 1.

This increasing integration put great pressure then on the first side of federalism—that side concerned with preserving state authority against increasing encroachment by the federal government. For the more that was within the federal sphere, the less that would be left to the states. Increasing integration here meant that a great scope of what was before purely intrastate activity would affect interstate commerce, and therefore, a greater scope of what was before intrastate commerce would now be within the federal power.[41]

But more interesting, and less noted, is the effect of integration on the second half of federalism—that half concerned with preserving federal interests against interference from state regulation. For the more integrated the national economy, the more significant would be the effects of state regulation on federal interests as well. When the economy is less integrated, the significance of any action by an individual state on the national economy as a whole is small. For integration here is just a proxy for communication: When the economy is not significantly integrated, the effect of a state's action does not communicate efficiently to the economy as a whole. But as integration increases, the significance of state regulation increases. When the economy was not integrated, state regulation would have a relatively small effect on the national market; but when the economy was closely integrated, its effect would be much greater.

For both sides of federalism, increased economic integration put pressure on the balance struck by the framers. If this changed circumstance was not to undermine the original balance, accommodation would be needed. By the second half of the nineteenth century, this accommodation began, at first in the context of protecting national interests, and then in the context of preserving state interests. Through subtle shifts in the tests defining the reach of both the positive and negative commerce power, the Court at-

---

[41] The increase of federal regulation during the late nineteenth century here links as well to the growth of progressivism during the same period. Using "the territorial power, the treaty power, the postal power, the taxing power, and the commerce power," these reformers used the power of the federal government to achieve progressive ends. Richard F. Hamm, *Shaping the Eighteenth Amendment: Temperance Reform, Legal Culture, and the Polity, 1880–1920* 9 (North Carolina, 1995). Eventually, the form of this regulation shifted from abolition to regulation, id at 152, and as "shifting moral and spiritual values" of the early twentieth century became more laissez-faire, the push to progressivism shifted as well. Id at 269.

tempted to restore something of the framing balance. It is to those efforts at translation, then, that I want now to turn.

TRANSLATING FEDERALISM

In both halves of the federalism balance, in response to increasing economic integration, the Court adopted tools for limiting a "power" (whether state or federal) in the name of a relevant "right." In this section, I want to outline the tools constructed in the name of preserving state authority; in the next I sketch the tools constructed in the name of protecting federal interests. And finally, I map the first set of tools onto the second.

Both sketches will be incomplete, and not just because sketches. For partway into both stories, there is a break in the vigor with which the Court enforces limits on Congress in the name of fidelity. It is that shift that will be the most important to explain.

TRANSLATING FEDERALISM: LIMITS ON FEDERAL POWER

By the turn of the century, the Court couldn't help but worry about the increase in federal power. For by unreflectively expanding Congress's power through continual extension of the Commerce Clause, the Court was in effect decreasing the power of the states. Formally, of course, no change was occurring: The Tenth Amendment reserved to the states "powers" not granted the federal government, and the power that was increasing was plainly a federal power. But substantively, something more was happening. As the Court noted late in this history of recognition,

> [E]very addition to the national legislative power to some extent detracts from or invades the power of the states. . . . [42]

The question was whether the Court would sit by passively as real world changes, incorporated into the Constitution through the application of old world tests,[43] rendered the Constitution fundamen-

---

[42] *Carter Coal*, 298 US at 294–95.

[43] For the point is not that Marshall would have done what the New Deal Court did, but rather that the words of the Marshall tests, applied outside of their original context, extended federal power much more broadly than before.

tally different from the Constitution of the framers. The question was the same as in *Olmstead*: a change in technology threatened to change the meaning of the constitutional balance, and the question was what change the Court could adopt in response.

What it did—though not at all as consistently as modern accounts suggest[44]—was to search for affirmative limits on federal power, in the name of preserving state autonomy. As the limits that were before grounded in the relative sparseness of the economic context, and in the understandings of limited federal power, faded, these limits were replaced by affirmatively asserted judicial constraints. Limits before supplied by the context were now constructed by the Court.

An example will make the point more clearly. Madison believed the Bill of Rights unnecessary, in part because he didn't believe the powers of Congress extended into the domains protected by the Bill of Rights. He didn't believe, for example, that Congress had the power to regulate the press, and therefore he didn't see any need to state a limitation on Congress's power to protect the press.

Let's assume Madison was right in 1791. In 1991, however, circumstances have changed. Applying Marshall's formula for determining the scope of Congress's power, the power of Congress might well now include the power to regulate the press (as, for example, an aspect of commerce). If so, then the First Amendment would now be read as an affirmative limitation on Congress's power, where as before (under Madison's view) it was not.

It is in this sense that we could imagine the limits of federalism becoming an affirmative limitation on Congress's power. Originally there was a balance between the federal and state powers—this is the "original balance." But as federal power increases, federalism now (from this perspective) becomes an affirmative constraint on the scope of federal power. The implied balance is now made an express barrier, through the practice of deriving limits on the scope of federal power.

This practice—of implying limits on the growth of federal power—is the practice of translating federalism. Again, it is an act

---

[44] See the excellent account of Barry Cushman, in *Rethinking the New Deal Court*, 80 Va L Rev 201 (1994).

of translation because it is construction aimed at fidelity to an original value rendered helpless by changed circumstances. It functions just as the translation hinted at in *Olmstead*, and it is justified with a similar argument. Just as Brandeis threatened (what we would call) Orwellian consequences if translation was not engaged,[45] arguments for translating federalism threaten an analogous *reductio:* a move that says, "if we allow this, then everything can be regulated."[46] Some limit must be found.

Or better, constructed. For again, the limits that translation offers are not found in the text of the Constitution; they are implied from its original structure, and constructed by the Court in the form of rules limiting federal power. The practice begins with the rhetorical material at hand. And at hand at the time this construction began were a set of precedents interpreting not the scope of the positive Commerce Clause, but rather the scope of the *negative* Commerce Clause. In these negative Commerce Clause cases, in an effort to preserve the power of states to regulate though their regulation "affected" interstate commerce, the Court had built a set of formal categories to separate interstate from intrastate. Those state regulations deemed intrastate regulations would be permitted; those interstate, denied.[47]

It is these same categories then that were used for making the division the other way round. The Court stole these categories from the negative commerce jurisprudence to fashion a limit on the positive Commerce Clause. The regime for testing whether state regulation reached too far would now be used to test whether federal regulation reached to far. And because the tests had been

---

[45] *Olmstead*, 277 US at 472 (Brandeis dissenting).

[46] The examples of this *reductio* argument in the federalism context are endless, both in the Court, see, for example, *South Dakota v Dole*, 483 US 203, 215 (1987) (O'Connor dissenting); *Maryland v Wirtz*, 392 US 183, 204–05 (1968) (Douglas dissenting); *United States v Butler*, 297 US 1, 78 (1936); *Carter Coal*, 298 US at 302, discussing *Heisler v Thomas Colliery Co.*, 260 US 245, 259, 260 (1922); *Hammer v Dagenhart*, 247 US 251, 276 (1918); *Lottery Case*, 188 US 321, 372 (1903) (Fuller dissenting) ("An invitation to dine, or to take a drive, or a note of introduction, all become articles of commerce under the ruling in this case . . ."); *United States v E.C. Knight Co.*, 156 US 1, 16 (1895); *Kidd v Pearson*, 128 US 1, 21 (1888); and the academy, see, for example, Bruce Ackerman, 1 *We The People: Foundations* 103–04 (Belknap, 1991); David P. Currie, *The Constitution in the Supreme Court: The Second Century, 1888–1986* 222–23 (Chicago, 1990); Lindsay Rogers, *The Postal Power of Congress: A Study in Constitutional Expansion* 180 (Johns Hopkins, 1916); Ira Jewell Williams, *Does the Commerce Clause Give Power to Dominate All Industry?* 83 U Pa L Rev 23, 36 (1934).

[47] The story is of course more complex. I detail it below at text accompanying notes 94–125.

used for some time, their appearance in this context would not appear to be an innovation, so much as a continuation of the old regime with new questions.

This was interpretive opportunism. For there is nothing in the logic of the two halves of the commerce power that compels that the tests that limit one side should, or even can, limit the other. The purpose or function of the two sides of the Commerce Clause question are really quite different. And given this difference, there is no reason to believe that limits designed for one purpose would serve the second purpose as well.

This point of logic was well understood; it was also successfully ignored. Instead the Court simply borrowed with abandon. The first of these borrowings was in *Knight*. There, for the first time, the Court limited the scope of Congress's affirmative commerce power, using the negative commerce distinction between "manufacturing" and "commerce."[48] Echoing the opinion in the negative Commerce Clause case of *Kidd*, the Court held,

> Commerce succeeds to manufacture, and is not a part of it. The power to regulate commerce is the power to prescribe the rule by which commerce shall be governed, and is a power independent of the power to suppress monopoly.[49]

Given this origin, it is quite odd that *Knight* is seen to stand today for a principle of restraint, or authentic interpretation.[50] Its origin was plainly not that.[51] More importantly, it is not even clear that *Knight* is about the constitutional limitations on Congress's commerce power at all. For the case concerned the scope of the Sherman Act, not the Commerce Clause, and unlike the Constitution, the Sherman Act has no Necessary and Proper Clause. Thus, any limitation on the scope of "commerce" in the Sherman Act would not necessarily translate into a limit on Congress's power under the Constitution, for again, Congress's power under the

---

[48] *Knight*, 156 US at 12.

[49] Id.

[50] Compare Justice Thomas's concurring opinion in *Lopez*, 115 S Ct at 1648–49.

[51] See, for example, Augustine L. Humes, *The Power of Congress Over Combinations Affecting Interstate Commerce*, 17 Harv L Rev 83, 99 (1903) ("In regard to the regulation of such a monopoly of manufacture, it cannot be doubted that the power of Congress extends further than does that act.").

Constitution includes the power under the Necessary and Proper Clause.[52]

The suggestion that the significance of the opinion should be limited is even stronger when one considers that even as an interpretation of the Sherman Act, the case was soon effectively overruled.[53] And when one considers that the case was a criminal case, and that the limits the Court found may have had more to do with *mens rea* requirements of a criminal statute than the power of Congress under the Commerce Clause, the significance of the case from a constitutional standpoint becomes even more questionable.[54]

These points notwithstanding, *Knight* gave birth to a new industry in litigation—an industry challenging Congress's power by using the negative Commerce Clause categories to cabin the reach of the positive Commerce Clause. Once the link to the negative Commerce Clause was made, there was a treasure chest of ready-made justifications for cabining Congress's power—limitations that reflected the legal culture of the time: formal, absolute, and insensitive to matters of degree.[55]

[52] Others, though surprisingly few, have noted that this opinion may best be understood as an interpretation of a statute rather than the Constitution. See id at 90 ("In this case, nothing more is decided than that a monopoly of manufacture was not within the statute and, therefore, was not void."); id at 91 ("In none of these cases was the court called upon to define, and it did not declare, the limits of the Power of Congress to legislate."); Currie, *The Constitution in the Supreme Court, 1888–1986* at 23 (cited in note 46).

[53] See Currie, *The Constitution in the Supreme Court, 1888–1986* at 23 (cited in note 46), citing *Addyston Pipe & Steel Co. v United States*, 175 US 211, 240 (1899).

[54] What was central to Chief Justice Fuller's opinion was that there was no necessary connection between the monopoly of manufacturing and the interference in interstate commerce. However likely, the interference was neither shown, nor was the intent to interfere shown. Since the essence of the Sherman Act violation was an intent to obstruct interstate commerce, what the opinion says is simply that this level of intent had not been demonstrated. It could neither be presumed, that is, and it certainly had not been shown. See *Knight*, 156 US at 17 ("Nevertheless it does not follow that an attempt to monopolize, or the actual monopoly of, the manufacture was an attempt, whether executory or consummated, to monopolize commerce, even though, in order to dispose of the product, the instrumentality of commerce was necessarily invoked. There was nothing in the proofs to indicate any intention to put a restraint upon trade or commerce, and the fact, as we have seen, that trade or commerce might be indirectly affected was not enough to entitle complainants to a decree.").

[55] For a collection of how these distinctions get applied, see F. D. G. Ribble, *State and National Power Over Commerce* 120–21, n 72 (Columbia, 1937) ("Examples of exclusion in cases of particular activities may prove useful. 'Bookkeeping, it is said, is not interstate commerce. True it is not.' *Interstate Commerce Commission v. Goodrich Transit Co.*, 224 U.S. 194, 216 (1912). The making of contracts for the insertion of advertising matter in *The Saturday Evening Post*, *The Ladies' Home Journal*, and *The Country Gentleman* was declared not to be interstate commerce. *Blumenstock Bros. v. Curtis Publishing Co.*, 252 U.S. 436

But the limits of *Knight* were not applied generally to commerce cases through the early twentieth century. Indeed, *Knight* at first seemed an anomaly. For the quarter century after *Knight*, the Court continued, in the main, to take an organic view of the economy[56] ("[p]rimitive conditions have passed; business is now transacted on a national scale"[57]), and expanded Congress's power. As well as upholding bans on any interstate commerce, regardless of the motive of Congress,[58] and whether or not the communication was commercial,[59] the Court through this period took an essentially realist view about the effect of intrastate transaction on interstate commerce.

Swift & Co. v United States[60] was perhaps the signal case among these.[61] Said the Court, again interpreting the Sherman Act (and effectively overruling *Knight*,[62]) "commerce among the states is not a technical legal conception, but a practical one drawn from the course of business."[63] So too in *Southern Railway*,[64] where the

---

(1920). Notable recent cases have presented concepts of certain activities as not being interstate commerce. See *A. L. A. Schechter Poultry Corp. v. United States*, 295 U.S. 495 (1935); *United States v. Butler*, 297 U.S. 1 (1936); *Carter v. Carter Coal Co.*, 298 U.S. 238 (1936). Cf. *Ramsey Co. v. Associated Bill Posters of the United States and Canada*, 260 U.S. 501 (1922); *Indiana Farmer's Guide Publishing Co. v. Prairie Farmer Publishing Co.*, 293 U.S. 268 (1934). An exhibition of baseball, 'although made for money would not be called trade or commerce in the commonly accepted use of those words.' *Federal Baseball Club of Baltimore v. National League of Professional Baseball Clubs*, 259 U.S. 200, 209 (1922). See 19 Mich. L. Rev. 867 (1921). For other instances of activities declared not to be interstate commerce, see *Metropolitan Opera Co. v. Hammerstein*, 147 N.Y. Supp. 535 (1914); *American Baseball Club of Chicago v. Chase*, 149 N.Y. Supp. 6 (1914); *In re Oriental Society*, Bankrupt, 104 Fed. 975 (E.D. Pa. 1900); *National League of Professional Baseball Clubs v. Federal Baseball Club of Baltimore*, 269 Fed. 681 (Ct. of App. D.C. 1920) (affirmed in *Federal Baseball Club of Baltimore v. National League of Professional Baseball Clubs*, *supra*)." See also Edward Corwin, *Constitutional Revolution, Ltd.* 24 (1941) (describing limits on "commerce").

[56] William H. Nicholls, *Constitutional Aspects of Public Regulation of Business Price Policies*, 25 J Farm Econ 560, 564–65 (1943).

[57] Edward S. Corwin, *Congress's Power to Prohibit Commerce: A Crucial Constitutional Issue*, 18 Cornell L Q 477, 503 (1933), quoting *Farmers' Loan & T. Co. v Minnesota*, 280 US 204, 211 (1930).

[58] *Lottery Case*, 188 US at 356; *Hipolite Egg Co. v United States*, 220 US 45, 57–58 (1911).

[59] *Caminetti*, 242 US at 491–92 (White Slave Traffic Act).

[60] *Swift & Co. v United States*, 196 US 375 (1905).

[61] Black, 20 Cornell L Q at 179 (cited in note 34) (Chief Justice Taft characterized the *Swift* case as " 'a milestone in the interpretation of the commerce clause of the Constitution.' ").

[62] *Swift*, 196 US at 397.

[63] Black, 20 Cornell L Q at 179 (cited in note 34).

[64] *Southern Railway Company v United States*, 222 US 20, 26–27 (1911).

Court held that the power reached the regulation of intrastate rail-road cars; and a year later in *Interstate Commerce Commission v Goodrich Transit*,[65] where it wrote that the power included the power to regulate accounting practices; and in the following Term, when it held the power reached wholly internal railroad rates;[66] and five years after that, when the power was held to reach the regulation of bills of lading;[67] and then most expansively, in 1922, that it included the power to regulate "[w]hatever amounts to more or less constant practice, and threatens to obstruct or unduly to burden the freedom of interstate commerce" whether wholly internal or not.[68] On the whole, this was not a framers-focused Court.

It was *Hammer v Dagenhart*[69] that gave *Knight* its second wind. Before *Hammer*, the Court's actual limitations on Congress's power were quite thin.[70] But with *Hammer*, the Court began its last real run at building implied constraints on the scope of Congress's power.

The case concerned Congress's efforts to limit the interstate transportation of products made with child labor. The opinion began with the *reductio* argument: If the Court didn't draw the line here, then there would be no line left to draw.[71] And thus the Court sought to draw a line, again using as tools the tools that were lying around.

Two are familiar: the first, the manufacturing/commerce distinction of *Knight:*

> Over interstate transportation, or its incidents, the regulatory
> power of Congress is ample, but the production of articles,

---

[65] *Interstate Commerce Commission v Goodrich Transit Co.*, 224 US 194, 211 (1912).

[66] *Houston, E. & W. Texas Ry. Co. v United States*, 234 US 342, 353–54 (1914).

[67] *United States v Ferger*, 250 US 199, 204 (1919).

[68] *Stafford*, 258 US at 521.

[69] 247 US 251 (1918).

[70] Currie, *The Constitution in the Supreme Court, 1888–1986* at 27–29 (cited in note 46).

[71] As the Court wrote,

> To sustain this statute would not be in our judgment a recognition of the lawful exertion of congressional authority over interstate commerce, but would sanction an invasion by the federal power of the control of a matter purely local in its character, and over which no authority has been delegated to Congress in conferring the power to regulate commerce among the States.

Hammer, 247 US at 276.

intended for interstate commerce, is a matter of local regulation.[72]

And the second, the pretext analysis, suggested in *McCulloch*, but repackaged here for the occasion: The aim, said the Court, of this regulation of Congress was to invade the state regulatory domain, and it was this improper intent that made the statute invalid.[73] As the Court said:

> The act in its effect does not regulate transportation among the States, but aims to standardize the ages at which children may be employed in mining and manufacturing within the States.[74]

Hammer is in many respects the most extreme of the Court's cases limiting the commerce power. For this is a limit on Congress's direct interstate commerce power, rather than a limit on Congress's indirect, intrastate commerce power.[75] If it marked any great shift in the Court's view, it was not evident even one term later.[76] Again, *Hammer*'s primary role in the crisis that would follow it by fifteen years was as a handy precedent, which, like *Knight* before it, was remembered perhaps because it stood out so, and useful, because it stood out so clearly.

The limited effect of *Hammer* notwithstanding, the 1918 Term did represent a turning point when one looks beyond the Commerce Clause.[77] Prior to that time, it was primarily within the area

---

[72] Id at 272.

[73] See Henry Wolf Biklé, *The Commerce Power and Hammer v. Dagenhart*, 67 U Pa L Rev 21, 29 (1919); *Kentucky Whip and Collar Co. v Illinois Cent. R.R. Co.*, 299 US 334, 350 (1937) ("In the Hammer case, the Court concluded that the Act of Congress there under consideration had as its aim the placing of local production under federal control") (citations omitted).

[74] *Hammer*, 247 US at 272.

[75] The decision is contrary as well to the First Congress's decision to impose protective tariffs on foreign commerce—not only to raise revenues but to regulate and promote commerce. See David P. Currie, *The Constitution in Congress: Substantive Issues in the First Congress, 1789–1791*, 61 U Chi L Rev 775, 781 (1994).

[76] As David Currie writes,

> Any hopes that *Hammer* portended an era of increased protection of state prerogatives, however, were chilled by later decisions. In the very next term, for example, in *United States v. Doremus*, the Court permitted Congress effectively to regulate narcotics sales under the cloak of the federal tax power.

Currie, *The Constitution in the Supreme Court, 1888–1986* at 98 (cited in note 46).

[77] William O. Douglas, *Recent Trends in Constitutional Law*, 30 Or L Rev 279, 283 (1951) (noting that the "ebb" that occurred during the 1920s was "clear and distinct.").

of taxation that the Court had been most active in limiting the scope of government's power;[78] but after 1920, the Court's energy began to wander more broadly. In the first six years of that decade, the Court declared "social and economic legislation unconstitutional under the due process clauses . . . in more cases than in the entire fifty-two previous years."[79] And this activism only increased after the (first) New Deal legislation reached the Supreme Court. First on delegation grounds,[80] and then on Commerce Clause grounds as well,[81] the Court struck a string of Congress's statutes, all in the name of a founding vision of federal power.

The techniques were common. Once again the distinction between manufacture and commerce arose,[82] as did its sister distinction, between the effects of direct and indirect interstate commerce regulation,[83] as well as the pretext limitations of *Hammer*.[84] In addition to these limits, there was a forgetting of the Necessary and Proper Clause, most prominently in the *Carter Coal* case: For throughout these opinions about the Commerce power, the Court fails to explain how Congress's necessary and proper power might interact with its commerce power. Even if manufacturing was not commerce, what was there to show that regulating manufacturing was not a necessary and proper way to regulate commerce?

Drawing these tools together, the Court struck at the nationalizing instinct in Congress's legislation. It struck in the name of a vision of federalism that had long been eroded by increasing federal power; it struck, then, in the name of one conception of fidel-

---

[78] Vincent M. Barnett, Jr., *The Supreme Court, the Commerce Clause, and State Legislation*, 40 Mich L Rev 49, 53–57 (1941).

[79] Ray A. Brown, *Due Process of Law, Police Power, and the Supreme Court*, 40 Harv L Rev 943, 944 (1927), cited in Currie, *The Constitution in the Supreme Court, 1888–1986* at 133, n 1 (cited in note 46).

[80] *Panama Refining Co. v Ryan*, 293 US 388 (1935).

[81] See *Railroad Retirement Board v Alton R. Co.*, 295 US 330 (1935); *A. L. A. Schechter Poultry v United States*, 295 US 495 (1935); *Butler*, 297 US 1; *Carter Coal*, 298 US 238.

[82] *Carter Coal*, 298 US at 303.

[83] Id at 307. This test too, of course, was a test developed in the context of the negative Commerce Clause. See D. J. Farage, *That Which "Directly" Affects Interstate Commerce*, 42 Dickinson L Rev 1, 2–3 (1937). Local effects could become interstate if tied to the proper intent. See *Carter Coal*, 298 US at 304, distinguishing *Coronado Coal Co. v United Mineworkers*, 268 US 295 (1925).

[84] *Railroad Retirement Board*, 295 US at 368.

ity. Its attack was not simply blind formalism—for the Court was quite self-conscious at times, some member of the Court more than others, about the nature of these limitations. As Cardozo explained, some limit had to be drawn, and the question was just what.[85]

One could quibble with the strategy, one could question the ultimate motivation, but the best way to understand the effort is as an attempt to reclaim a lost reality of federalism. As Frankfurter put it, what was "submerged" in these distinctions was the view that "local affairs are subject to national control when that affect interstate commerce."[86] But they were submerged by the Court just because essentially all local affairs were now subject to national control. The Court was attempting to reconstruct an "initial fact of division,"[87] an effort not made any easier by the fact that these were two fields that were now "overlapping" in their reach.[88]

The battle to undo this limited vision of Congress's power, culminating in the switch in time in 1937, is well known. It is not a battle that need be relitigated here. Beginning with *NLRB v Jones & Laughlin*,[89] and ending with *U.S. v Darby*,[90] the Court deliberately withdrew the full range of limits on federal power to regulate that its earlier judgments had constructed. Limitations that just the year before had been declared limits in kind, not just degree, were now said to be "instances in which [a] metaphor has

---

[85] As Cardozo explained in *Carter Coal:*

> The underlying thought is merely this, that "the law is not indifferent to considerations of degree." . . . It cannot be indifferent to them without an expansion of the commerce clause that would absorb or imperil the reserved powers of the States. At times, as in the case cited, the waves of causation will have radiated so far that their undulatory motion, if discernible at all, will be too faint or obscure, too broken by cross-currents, to be heeded by the law. In such circumstances the holding is not directed at prices or wages considered in the abstract, but at prices or wages in particular conditions. The relation may be tenuous or the opposite according to the facts. Always the setting of the facts is to be viewed if one would know the closeness of the tie.

Carter Coal, 298 US at 327–28 (Cardozo dissenting) (citations omitted).

[86] Frankfurter, *The Commerce Clause* at 115–16 (cited in note 30).

[87] F. D. G. Ribble, *National and State Cooperation Under the Commerce Clause*, 37 Colum L Rev 43, 47 (1937).

[88] Ganoe, 24 Or L Rev at 74 (cited in note 30).

[89] 301 US 1 (1937).

[90] 312 US 100 (1941).

been used," "but particular, and not exclusive, illustrations of [Congress's] power."[91] These were all now matters of degree.[92]

The flip essentially ended judicially enforceable limits in the most important federalism domains; it represents a collapse of judicial restraints, not directly tracking any real change in the real world. And whether in one year, or five,[93] by the end of this effort at federalism, this fidelity had fallen dormant. For twenty years in Commerce Clause history, the Court had enforced limits on Congress's power. Now the question of how far Congress could go was no longer to be decided by the Court. The shift of the New Deal represents the end of affirmative judicial efforts to translate federalism—for the time being.

What explains the shift of the New Deal cannot be anything about the changed circumstances themselves, or at least not anything about changed circumstances alone. There was no radical shift in economic integration in 1937 through 1941, and the Court didn't pretend to the contrary. Nor can it be explained by anything internal to the idea of translation, for if the constitutional foundations remained constant, then the command of fidelity to translate federalism was the same. If anything changed, it was the ability of the Court to continue this effort of translation. What changed was something about the constraints on the Court's ability to translate. These constraints will be crucial to the analysis that follows, not so much to understand the extraordinary case of the New Deal shift, but to understand the ordinary case of ordinary shift in the tools used to translate.

Before we turn to examine these constraints, consider first the parallel steps of translation under the negative Commerce Clause, protecting the second half of federalism—federal interests.

TRANSLATING FEDERALISM: LIMITS ON STATE POWER

Before there were these (modest) efforts by the Court to translate federalism's first side (protecting state power), there were ef-

---

[91] *Jones & Laughlin*, 301 US at 36.

[92] As the Court said, the criterion was "necessarily one of degree and must be so defined. This does not satisfy those who seek for mathematical or rigid formulas. But such formulas are not provided by the great concepts of the Constitution. . . ." *Santa Cruz Fruit Packing Co. v NLRB*, 303 US 453, 467 (1938).

[93] That no clear flip had been made, or yet acknowledged in 1937, is suggested by the opinion of Justice Butler in *Santa Cruz Fruit Packing*, 303 US at 469 (Butler dissenting); see generally Cushman, 80 Va L Rev 201, 204–38 (cited in note 44).

forts to translate federalism's second side (protecting federal interests), responding, again, to the changing integration of the national economy. As the economy became more integrated, the significance of state regulation became more marked. In response, the Court increased its police over state regulation, to try to assure that the effect of local actions didn't propagate too broadly. Integration had now amplified the effect of state regulation; the Court's job was selectively to dampen those effects.

The limits designed to translate federalism's second side are of two kinds. The first is what we now call the negative Commerce Clause, which operates, without the action of Congress, to constrain the states in the exercise of their own power to regulate.[94] The second is the preemption doctrine, which has evolved as a device for protecting federal legislation from interfering or disabling state legislation. Both doctrines have undergone radical shifts. My aim in this section is to map these shifts with the heuristic of translation.

I begin with the negative Commerce Clause. The life of the negative Commerce Clause can be told in three stages; in this section, my focus is on the first two. The first is relatively passive. Like the positive Commerce Clause, it begins with *Gibbons,* and the boundary that *Gibbons* drew (though in dicta) for proper state regulation. At issue was the validity of a New York law granting a monopoly to Ogden's steamboat company. The Court held the law invalid under the Supremacy Clause, because it conflicted, the Court said, with a federal licensing law.

On his way to this conclusion, Marshall sketched tools for determining whether the state law was a regulation beyond the state power, and while *Gibbons* does not fully articulate their structure, together with *McCulloch,* their outline is clear. At the core is a means/ends test. Laws will be understood as means to some end; the question the Court must address is to what end is a particular law a means. It determines this by determining what purpose the legislature had in enacting this law—whether it was with a purpose to, for example, regulate commerce, or with some other police power purpose. If its purpose was to regulate commerce, then the

---

[94] For an extraordinary account of the development of this doctrine, see Donald Regan, *The Supreme Court and State Protectionism: Making Sense of the Dormant Commerce Clause,* 84 Mich L Rev 1091, 1206–68 (1986).

law was unconstitutional. This first part of the first stage of the negative Commerce Clause evolution we can call the *purpose test*.[95]

One important implication of the purpose test was that the very same statute could be passed by the federal and a state government, and both be constitutional; or, as a corollary, the very same statute could be passed by two different states, but only one be constitutional (since the other was passed with an improper purpose). The fact that the means used to the police power ends were the same as the means used to a commerce regulation end was not determinative. What mattered was the end; to two different ends, the same means could be used.[96]

Willson is a good example of this purpose test applied.[97] At issue in *Willson* was the constitutionality of a set of dams, constructed by the state of Delaware, that blocked parts of the navigable waterways of the United States. If what determined constitutionality was the effect of a given law, then *Willson* should have been no different from *Gibbons*. In *Gibbons*, a law of the State of New York made it legally impossible for Gibbons to use the waterways linking New

---

[95] See Louis M. Greeley, *What Is the Test of a Regulation of Foreign or Interstate Commerce?* 1 Harv L Rev 159, 163 (1887) (to determine "whether a given law is to be regarded as a regulation of foreign or interstate commerce, we must examine the object of the Legislature in passing the law.").

[96] As the Court said in *Miln*,

> In Gibbons v. Ogden, . . . the court say [*sic*], if a state, in passing laws on a subject acknowledged to be within its control and with a view to those subjects, shall adopt a measure of the same character with one which congress may adopt; it does not derive its authority from the particular power which has been granted, but from some other which remains with the state, and may be executed by the same means. All experience shows that the same measures, or measures scarcely distinguishable from each other, may flow from distinct powers; but this does not prove that the powers are identical.

New York v Miln, 36 US (11 Pet) 102, 137 (1837). The same point is made in *Gibbons* itself:

> All experience shows, that the same measures, or measures scarcely distinguishable from each other, may flow from distinct powers; but this does not prove that the powers themselves are identical.

Gibbons, 22 US (9 Wheat) at 204. Justice Johnson took the same view.

> Wherever the powers of the respective governments are frankly exercised, with a distinct view to the ends of such powers, they may act upon the same object, or use the same means, and yet the powers be kept perfectly distinct. A resort to the same means, therefore, is no argument to prove the identity of their respective powers.

Id at 239 (Johnson concurring).

[97] *Willson v Black Bird Creek Marsh Company*, 27 US (2 Pet) 245 (1829).

York and New Jersey. In *Willson*, a dam of the state of Delaware had the very same effect (indeed, no doubt more effective). In both cases, the person challenging the regulation was licensed to ride the waters of the United States,[98] but in *Gibbons* this license was held to trump the state regulation, while in *Willson*, it was not.[99]

What distinguished the cases in Marshall's view was the aim of the Delaware regulation. As Marshall saw it, the dams increased "[t]he value of the property on its banks" by "excluding the water from the marsh," and thereby the "health of the inhabitants probably [would be] improved."[100] In short, the aim was to advance the power of police.

> Measures calculated to produce these objects, provided they do not come into collision with the powers of the general government, are undoubtedly within those which are reserved to the states.[101]

The same is true in *Miln*, decided eight years later. Again, the question was simply what was the purpose of the state in passing the laws at issue. Citing *Gibbons*, the Court said,

> If we turn our attention to the purpose to be attained, it is to secure that very protection, and to provide for that very welfare. If we examine the means . . . , they bear a just, natural and appropriate relation to those ends.[102]

What determined the nature of a regulation, then, was its purpose. Something was not a regulation of commerce because of what it did; it was a regulation of commerce because of *why* it did it.

What is striking about the test is the interpretive facility it presumes on the part of the Court—the ability to divine from a statute, and scatterings of evidence about it, just what the aim of the legislature was in passing it. But precisely because the showing necessary to invalidate a statute was so severe, the test operated in effect simply to validate most state regulation. No state statute

---

[98] See Currie, *The Constitution in the Supreme Court, 1789–1888* at 175 (cited in note 46).

[99] This is not to say that every dam would have been so protected. Part of what must have motivated the Court was the idea that this was such a small stream that was being dammed.

[100] *Willson*, 27 US (2 Pet) at 250.

[101] Id. See also Greeley, 1 Harv L Rev at 163–65 (cited in note 95).

[102] *Miln*, 36 US (11 Pet) at 133.

was struck under this test alone; indeed, as we will see later, no state statute was struck solely on negative Commerce Clause grounds until 1873.[103] What the test did was to direct inquiry by forcing the Court to ask whether there was a legitimate state police power reason for the statute, and if there was, then there was an effective presumption that this was the reason for the statute.

Thus while the purpose test demanded a relatively high interpretive burden before a statute could be struck—in the sense that the Court would have to make an extremely contestable judgment about legislative purpose before striking a state statute—this burden was never actually borne by the court through the life of the test. As I argue more below, this link is not accidental. It is also revealed in the second of the two tests of this first stage of the negative Commerce Clause evolution.[104]

Eventually, this first cut at dividing state from federal authority came apart. Though there are echoes of the purpose test late into the nineteenth century,[105] by the middle of the century, its dominance began to wane. The first clear flip came in *The License Cases*,[106] where Chief Justice Taney took the position that the Commerce Clause did not, by its own force, operate to limit state power at all; only if Congress legislated could federal law limit state action.[107]

Then four years later the rebellion of Taney led to a compro-

---

[103] The case was *State Tax on Railway Gross Receipts*, 82 US (15 Wall) 284 (1873). See the discussion in Currie, *The Constitution in the Supreme Court, 1789–1888* at 338 (cited in note 46).

[104] Of course, by sketching the purpose test as I have, I do not mean to suggest that everyone viewed the matter in just this way. Story, in particular, thought a "regulation of Commerce" was determined by the nature of the regulation, not by the nature of its purpose. Hence in *Miln*, because the regulation was of the import of persons into the state, he thought this a regulation of commerce. That its purpose may have been to advance police power concerns was immaterial; what mattered were the means, not the ends. *Miln*, 36 US (11 Pet) at 156 (Story dissenting). Justice Thompson too may have shared this view, but he thought states had a concurrent power to regulate commerce until Congress took it up. Id at 148, 152–53 (Thompson concurring).

[105] See, for example, *Hennington v Georgia*, 163 US 299, 304 (1896). See also Greeley, 1 Harv L Rev at 184 (cited in note 95) ("In the opinion of the writer, according to the law as it stands to-day, the purpose or intention of the State Legislature in passing a law operating upon . . . interstate commerce is the only criterion of whether it is or is not a regulation of . . . interstate commerce.").

[106] *License Cases*, 46 US (5 How) 504 (1847). Taney's was one of six separate opinions.

[107] See Currie, *The Constitution in the Supreme Court, 1789–1888* at 226 (cited in note 46).

mise. In *Cooley v Board of Wardens of Port of Philadelphia*,[108] Justice Curtis sketched a second test for dividing federal from state authority. At issue was a set of state regulations of pilotage services. Curtis concluded that these were "regulations of commerce." Under Marshall's test, that should have been the end of the case. But Curtis's analysis was not so simple. Instead, the Court held that states have a concurrent power to regulate commerce, so long as they do not regulate subjects the "nature of [which] requires [ ] exclusive legislation" at the federal level.[109] Where subjects "in their nature" required federal regulation, then states were barred from regulating those subjects; but where subjects did not require federal regulation, then states could regulate commerce with respect to those subjects, at least so long as Congress does not. Looking at the first Congress's regulations of pilotage laws, Curtis then concluded that these were not subjects which in their nature required national legislation.[110]

The *Cooley* test was destined to become one of the most significant readings of the dormant Commerce Clause.[111] One reason it dominated the purpose test was its relative ease of administration. In a world where the appropriate objects of federal regulation are relatively uncontested, it would be easier simply to check the particular regulation against an understood list than to inquire into whether a particular statute was passed with an appropriate purpose.

Easier, but not yet easy. For its simplicity when striking a statute depended upon the relative uncontestedness of viewing a regulation as inherently national. Thus while relative to the purpose test, the *Cooley* test may have imposed a lesser rhetorical burden, it still required the Court to embrace something of a normative conception about the proper division of authority between states and the national government. To strike a state statute based upon this normative conception would still be relatively difficult. And consistent with this difficulty, again we find that the test alone served to strike

---

[108] 53 US (12 How) 299 (1851).

[109] Id at 319.

[110] See Currie, *The Constitution in the Supreme Court, 1789–1888* at 230–33 (cited in note 46).

[111] Id at 230. See also Douglas, 30 Or L Rev at 285 (1951); Ribble, 37 Colum L Rev at 50–53 (cited in note 87).

no state statutes. It was a less difficult test to administer to the end of upholding state statutes.

These two tests then constitute the first stage of the dormant Commerce Clause development. They both yield no statute that was unconstitutional. They reign during a period of relative economic isolation; they serve to sustain state statutes that actually have little effect on interstate commerce. They define boundaries that states cannot cross, but for the most part, when the economy is as unintegrated as this, states do not cross these boundaries.

The second stage of the dormant Commerce Clause evolution is more activist. It occurs roughly during the period of time when the national economy is becoming highly integrated (1875–1912).[112] And it responds, as Frankfurter put it, to this integration.

> As economic relationships became more interdependent, and the interaction between state legislation of every kind and interstate commerce became closer, the central inquiry necessarily shifted from the purpose of state legislation to its effect upon national commerce.[113]

The response was to reformulate the tests for limiting state power in a way that will be quite revealing. For what marks the tools of this period is that they are, within their context, rhetorically less burdensome; they avoid *Cooley*'s necessity of a thick conception of the proper role for national legislation, and they are easier to administer than the divining necessary in the purpose test. Instead, they make constitutionality turn on more formal, and neutral, conceptions of regulations effect. As we will see, and as one would expect, the reduction in this rhetorical burden yields an increase in the number of statutes struck.

Again, there are two tests. The first, given us by Justice Field, was the more formal: It asked whether the state regulation directly or indirectly regulates commerce.[114] Under this test, regulation having a direct effect on interstate commerce was a matter of exclusive congressional power, but "where the effect on interstate commerce was merely indirect, state power to regulate was at least

---

[112] Stephen A. Gardbaum, *The Nature of Preemption*, 79 Cornell L Rev 767, 795 (1994).

[113] Frankfurter, *The Commerce Clause* at 30–31 (cited in note 30).

[114] Gardbaum, 79 Cornell L Rev at 795 (cited in note 112). See, for example, *Sherlock v Alling*, 93 US 99, 103 (1876).

concurrent with that of Congress."[115] If regulating interstate commerce was an unnecessary consequence of the state regulation, even if it was quite likely to occur, the state regulation was deemed an indirect regulation of commerce, and hence not a violation of the Commerce Clause. If, however, the regulation only succeeded to the extent that it regulated interstate commerce, or if that was its direct object, then the state regulation failed.

What this tool didn't demand was any strong consensus on the appropriate objects of inter- and intrastate regulation. What it did demand was a capacity for making judgments of a formal kind, between direct and indirect. While at some level we can all understand a line between direct and indirect effects, we should not take for granted this ability of a legal system effectively, or consistently, to draw such a line. Such would be very difficult for us. But the legal culture of the late nineteenth century was different. For what marks it as distinct was its ability to draw, and sustain, formal categories of law generally. This was the age of formalism in legal thought; a time when the legal system generally practiced a kind of legal reasoning that insisted where possible on categorical resolutions rather than balancing; that sought and sustained ways to make legal reasoning mechanical and simple.[116]

Now what makes possible this way of reasoning is a complex question. It is a way of legal reasoning still dominant in parts of continental Europe. It is also a way of reasoning against which progressives in America rallied at the turn of this century. But however it is constructed, and sustained, what is important is to see how it makes possible a kind of regime that to us would not seem possible or effective. A categorical test for carving up direct from indirect regulations is an effective test in a legal culture that well supports such tests; it is not an effective test where the legal culture doesn't.

When this formal method became contestable, a second, more realist method took its place. This was a test that looked directly at the economic effect of a particular kind of state regulation,

---

[115] Id.

[116] See Hamm, *Shaping the Eighteenth Amendment* at 8 (cited in note 41); Morton J. Horwitz, *The Transformation of American Law, 1870–1960: The Crisis of Legal Orthodoxy* 199–200 (Oxford, 1992); John Henry Schlegel, *American Legal Realism and Empirical Social Science* 31–32 (North Carolina, 1995) (describing "classical legal thought").

rather than fitting the regulation into some category of direct or indirect effects. The question became how significant this effect was. This position had been advanced for some time, by Justice Miller in particular.[117] And "[a]s economic relationships became more interdependent, and the interaction between state legislation of every kind and interstate commerce became closer,"[118] the need for this focus increased as well. Thus, in many cases where it was clear that under Marshall's purpose test the state regulation was adequate, under this emerging effects test, state laws "operating upon foreign or interstate commerce . . . [were] nevertheless . . . held to be a regulation of such commerce."[119]

What pressed the need for an effects test was both a kind of judicial economy, and the increase in, and therefore increased effect of, state regulation on interstate commerce. The increasing effect made it necessary to construct more tools to limit state regulation; but the increasing conflict about the proper role for state and federal regulation made it necessary to construct tools that could limit state regulation without a contested normative conception of propriety behind it. Thus, rather than attempting to discover the undiscoverable through an intent or purpose test, or rather than arguing about appropriate objects of federal and state regulation, what becomes the most salient feature of the conflict between federal and state regulation is the actual economic effect of such state regulation on interstate commerce. And once this effect is identified, the easiest way to resolve it is simply on the facts of the effect.

Both tests together mark the first real use of the Commerce Clause alone to strike state legislation. For it is really only in the chief justiceship of Waite that the Court began to use the Commerce Clause to strike down state legislation. Eighteen seventy-three saw the first such case,[120] beginning a period during which the Court would decide "over fifty cases in which it was alleged that state action offended the Commerce Clause."[121]

But rather than mere activism, what is important is to under-

---

[117] Currie, *The Constitution in the Supreme Court, 1789–1888* at 406 (cited in note 46).

[118] Frankfurter, *The Commerce Clause* at 31 (cited in note 30).

[119] Greeley, 1 Harv L Rev at 177 (cited in note 90).

[120] Currie, *The Constitution in the Supreme Court, 1789–1888* at 403–04 (cited in note 46).

[121] Id at 404. See also Frankfurter, *The Commerce Clause* at 7 (cited in note 30).

stand the link between this activism, the framing balance, and a context where state economic regulation is more significant nationally. As integration increased, it made sense of the original balance for the Court to police more actively state regulation. And this increased policing yielded the increase in federal restriction on state regulation.

Now again, I do not means to suggest by this neat ordering of tests that these tools evolved serially, or separately, or regularly, or consistently. The were developed sporadically, often together. The 1888 case of *Smith v Alabama*[122] is a good example of these four approaches rolled into one. In upholding a state regulation of railroads, the *Smith* court first applied the *Cooley* test ("we find, [ ] [f]irst, that the statute . . . is not, considered in its own nature, a regulation of interstate commerce"), and then the *purpose* test ("that it is properly an act of legislation within the scope of the admitted power reserved to the states to regulate the relative rights and duties of persons being and acting within its territorial jurisdiction"), and then the *direct/indirect* test ("and, thirdly, that, so far as it affects transactions of commerce among the states, it does so only indirectly, incidentally, and remotely,"), and then the *effects* test ("and [affects interstate transactions] not so as to burden or impede them.").[123]

But regardless of the relative tidiness of these shifts, what is significant is how the rhetorical ground must move—how it becomes necessary to rely upon a less and less normative conception of what federal regulation ought to be (which the move to effects measures) and how the rhetorical burdens of an earlier test facilitate these moves. From *purpose* to *"in its nature national"* to *direct/indirect* to *effects:* As the legal culture becomes more diverse, this affects the test that can be applied.

The most activist period for policing state policies occurs then during just that period where we could expect that the rhetorical burden, in context, of the dominant tests is at a minimum. Rather than rely upon relatively normative conceptions of proper federal and state power, the activism peaks when the tools used rely upon formal, or categorical, distinctions not themselves explicitly normative. And as we have seen, these tests too gained support in this

---

[122] *Smith v Alabama*, 124 US 465 (1888).

[123] Id at 482.

legal context because of a general facility, within this legal culture, to think and treat law as a formalist technique. These two features combine to facilitate activism just at the period when the need for activism is high. While my interest is not in showing a causal relationship, we can say that if the objective of the Court was to translate federalism, the tools selected in this second stage were among the least expensive available, and, in context, extremely effective.

The activism of this second stage eventually comes to an end, again, for reasons we explore later. But we can note that the timing of this activism is not accidental; it links with the general retreat adverted to above, after the New Deal. For after a period of relative quiescence after the New Deal, the negative Commerce Clause entered a third stage of its evolution. Rather than implicitly balance the values of state regulation against the burden on interstate commerce, in this stage the primary focus is on discrimination, with a secondary focus on whether any nondiscriminatory state regulation might nonetheless too severely burden interstate commerce.[124]

Now the virtue of a discrimination rule is its simplicity: It selects a core value protected by the negative Commerce Clause, and limits its reach to just that value. Consistent with this simplicity is a relatively active docket of cases striking state laws falling afoul of this minimal requirement. But the vice of the discrimination rule is its underinclusiveness. For there are plenty of examples of state regulations that would burden interstate commerce without being

---

[124] The history of this third stage is admittedly more complex than discrimination alone. Throughout this stage, there are two themes that on the surface of the opinions, one pulling in the direction of discrimination alone, and the second, in a direction that would more carefully balance national and state interests. *Southern Pacific Co. v Arizona*, 325 US 761 (1945), is an example. There Justices Douglas and Black both implied that discrimination was a necessary condition to a finding of unconstitutionality; but Chief Justice Stone "took the occasion to entrench for the majority his original position that the validity of nondiscriminatory state regulations affecting commerce turned on 'accommodation of the competing demands of the state and national interests involved.'" Currie, *The Constitution in the Supreme Court, 1888–1986* at 327 (cited in note 46). The clearest counterexample to this nondiscrimination interpretation is *Pike v Bruce Church, Inc.*, 397 US 137 (1970), which, though focused primarily on discrimination, makes it seem as if even where there is no discrimination, a federal court must weigh the benefit of the state regulation against the burden on interstate commerce. But I follow Regan, 84 Mich L Rev 1091 (cited in note 94), here in arguing that the essence of the test, *Pike* notwithstanding, is discrimination. For a recent account far more explicit on this, see *National Paint & Coatings Association v City of Chicago*, 45 F3d 1124 (7th Cir 1995) (Easterbrook).

discriminatory.[125] By focusing on discrimination alone, the test fails to capture this category of burden.

What it does, however, is provide a minimal limitation that courts can carry into effect. For reasons I suggest more extensively below, this minimum may also be the maximum. For anything more than discrimination would require the courts to weigh values that they could not do without the appearance of acting politically. Thus here too there is a retreat from the more active limitation on state power because the burden of that more active test was too great.

TRANSLATING FEDERALISM: PREEMPTION

The timing of this retreat in the negative Commerce Clause links with a second retreat yet to be described. This is the retreat of the preemption doctrine. But before we can describe the retreat, we must establish its advance.

Though modern constitutional law tends to obscure the distinction,[126] as Stephen Gardbaum has argued, both conceptually, and historically, the doctrine of preemption is distinct from the doctrine of supremacy. Supremacy says that when two otherwise valid laws conflict, federal law will prevail; preemption determines the scope of that conflict. One could well have a doctrine of supremacy without a doctrine of preemption—indeed, as Gardbaum argued, this has been the case for most of the Constitution's history. Without preemption, the question is simply whether two laws conflict. What preemption adds to this is a tool for determining how far any such conflict will be said to extend. At its broadest, a preemption doctrine might say that the existence of a federal law within a certain field of regulation would operate to negate any state legislation within that field; at its narrowest, a preemption doctrine might say that a federal law conflicts with a state law only if it is impossible for someone to obey the commands of both.[127]

Throughout its history, the preemption doctrine moves between these two extremes. And this movement maps well onto the story

---

[125] Posner describes the simplest example in his discussion of a state tax. See Richard A. Posner, *Economic Analysis of Law* 638–43 (Little, Brown, 4th ed 1992).

[126] See, for example, Gardbaum, 79 Cornell L Rev at 787 (cited in note 112).

[127] Id at 770–73.

of translation that we have seen so far. For it is just at the point where the vigor to effect limits on federal and state power is at its highest that we see the preemption doctrine operate most broadly; and just at the point that we see the efforts at translation erode generally that we see the preemption doctrine too interpreted more narrowly.

Though hints of a doctrine like preemption pepper the U.S. Reports of the nineteenth century, it is not until 1912 that the doctrine is really born. Before that time, federal law trumped state law when the two laws conflicted.[128] But in 1912, in the case of *Southern Railway Co. v Reid*,[129] the Court began a short experiment with what was really quite a radical doctrine. Under this newly born preemption doctrine, once the Court noted that Congress had passed "some" regulation within "some" field of law, concurrent state legislation within that same field was annulled. What we would today call "field" preemption followed automatically from the fact of any federal regulation at all; no reference to congressional intent was necessary to invoke this doctrine; no indication of a balance of state and federal interests either. All that was required was the presence of a federal law to wipe away state laws within that field.[130]

The effect of this doctrine on the balance between federal and state authority was quite dramatic. As federal authority was exercised within concurrent domains of authority, preemption cleared the underbrush of related state regulation. And as more federal authority was exercised, the doctrine wiped away an ever greater scope of state power. This automatic field preemption thus oper-

---

[128] Id at 783.

[129] 222 US 424 (1912).

[130] See, for example, cases cited in discussion at 264–76 in Alexander M. Bickel and Benno C. Schmidt, Jr., 9 *History of the Supreme Court of the United States: The Judicial and Responsible Government*, 1910–21 264–76 (Macmillan, 1984). See also Gardbaum, 79 Cornell L Rev at 797 (cited in note 112) ("The difference between preemption and supremacy is precisely the difference between the sufficiency of 'some' federal regulation and the necessity of 'conflicting' regulation for the non-application of state law."); id at 801 ("The effect of congressional action is to end the concurrent power of the states and thereby to create exclusive power at the federal level from that time on."). The German Constitution expressly provides for "field preemption," such that if the Bund taxes something, the Länder may not. See Federal Republic of Germany Const, Art 72(1) ("In matters within the concurrent legislative power, the Länder shall have the power to legislate so long as and to the extent that the Federation does not exercise its right to legislate."). See also Currie, *Constitution of the Federal Republic of Germany* at 49, 53–54 (cited in note 46).

ated strongly to empower the nationalization of domains of law, at just the time that the federal government was actively increasing its regulatory role.[131]

But this tool of federal power carried with it a relatively high rhetorical burden. For to make the rule effective, it fell to the Court to determine what a particular "field" of regulation was, and it was upon that determination that state legislation was displaced. This judgment, however, is of course not obvious. The overlap and differences between state and federal legislation left many questions about how far a field could be said to run. These questions placed the Court then in a position reminiscent of the *Cooley* test, where the Court was in the business of deciding the nature and scope of a wide range of regulatory domains.

This burden was lifted after the switch in time that marked the triumph of the New Deal. Just at the time the Court recognized the authority of Congress to reach far more than before, it also transformed the significance of the statutes that Congress had passed by radically cutting back on this automatic preemption.

---

[131] A crude empiricism supports the suggesting that this change was significant. In the history of the Supreme Court's invalidation of state laws, the second major cycle of activism coincides precisely with this shift in the preemption doctrine. A raw count of Supreme Court opinions striking state and federal laws by decade is not inconsistent with this pattern of change. The table below was derived from the Senate's The Constitution of the United States of America: Analysis and Interpretation, S Doc No 99–16, 99th Cong, 1st Sess 1883, 1913 (1982), and its supplement.

Decade	State	Federal
1800	1	1
1810	7	0
1820	7	0
1830	3	0
1840	9	0
1850	7	1
1860	25	4
1870	29	8
1880	42	5
1890	32	6
1900	30	11
1910	107	6
1920	135	16
1930	85	16
1940	45	3
1950	51	6
1960	140	14
1970	180	17
1980	144	16

After the New Deal, the focus in preemption cases was not on whether a law was within a particular field in some way regulated by Congress; instead, what mattered was the judgment that Congress *intended* to preempt a particular state law. The presumption was against preemption; and the burden was to demonstrate the intent of Congress to preempt.[132] Thus, when preemption functioned to wipe away state regulation, the Court could shift responsibility for this preemption to Congress and away from itself.

How one measures the net effect of these two changes at once is a difficult question. The switch of the New Deal certainly increased the scope for permissible federal regulation; but the retreat of this field preemption doctrine also reduced the extent to which federal regulation would, by necessity, displace state regulation. Thus, rather than a zero-sum game between federal and state authority, what both shifts mark is an increase in governmental power, at both the federal and state level. All that we can note for certain is that the shift of the New Deal reduced the extent to which courts would limit the exercise of governmental power, whether federal or state.

This then is the second retreat in the second half of the federalism domain. For here again, the Court shifts the tools it was using to defend the interests of the national government, giving greater deference to state regulation. And as with the negative Commerce Clause cases, the substance of this shift is to focus upon a congressional judgment, rather than upon any formula for striking state laws embraced by the Court.[133] The judgment, then, was said to be Congress's, not the Court's.

THE LIMITS COMPARED

My argument so far has been quite simple: We can in part understand the effort of the Court to be the attempt to preserve, or restore, something of the framing balance between federal and state authority; that this balance has two sides; and that the collection of devices—what Frankfurter called "legal levers of con-

---

[132] See, for example, *Rice v Santa Fe Elevator Corp.*, 331 US 218, 230–31 (1947).

[133] See, for example, Currie, *The Constitution in the Supreme Court, 1888–1986* at 35 (cited in note 46), discussing *In re Rahrer*, 140 US 545 (1891).

trol"[134]—has evolved as the pressure on various aspects of this original balance has changed.

In the survey so far, we have seen three such levers—the first, the formal limits on the commerce power imposed in the name of preserving a sphere of state regulatory authority; the second, the similarly formal limits of the negative Commerce Clause, acting at first to sustain, and then to constrain, state regulation in areas that interfered with federal interests; and, finally, the third, the doctrine of preemption, used as a supplement to the negative Commerce Clause as a way to further protect federal interests from interfering state regulation. All three of these doctrines grow in their power through the nineteenth and early twentieth centuries; all three peak in their power just at the New Deal.

I have swept as broadly as I have here for two reasons: The first is to collect a sufficiently large sample of tools used to effect limits on governmental power, in the name of federalism, so as to make comparison meaningful; but the second is to make a bit more contestable what seems an organizing idea in our modern understanding of the transformation around the New Deal. For what the complexity here should suggest is that the effect of the New Deal on the federalism balance is more complex than the ordinary account suggests. No doubt the (partial[135]) collapse of the first lever of control, allowing Congress to regulate in areas not open to it before, yielded an increase in federal regulatory authority. But balancing this significant transformation are the relative retreats in both the negative Commerce Clause power and preemption doctrine. Congress could regulate more, but the effects of its regulations on competing state regulatory regimes were not as strong; nor would the Court automatically recognize federal dominance without the exercise of express congressional power. Therefore too could states regulate more. That there was a shift at the New Deal cannot be doubted; but its net effect on state authority is far more contestable.

Nonetheless, one aspect of the shift in these three areas cannot be denied: The shift here is a shift away from limitations on government *generally* rather than a shift away from limitation on federal power in particular. In a fairly dramatic manner, the Court's

---

[134] Frankfurter, *The Commerce Clause* at 26 (cited in note 30).

[135] The collapse is not total, and the timing is not perfect. See above note 124.

ability to enforce affirmative limits on state and federal power withered. Federal power may have increased, but it was not a federal power that the Court would be responsible for; it was instead power that had its pedigree in the action of Congress; and likewise, the effectiveness of competing state regimes would increase, again, not because of anything the Court did, but because now Congress would have the power, in the main, to trump competing state regimes. In all three areas, what we observe is a retreat from judicial control. And the question I want to raise now is just what explains this general retreat.

The Constraints on Translation

"The history of the commerce clause," Frankfurter wrote, "is the history of imposing artificial patterns upon the play of economic life."[136] The history of this "imposing," however, is not at all consistent. While against both state and federal governments the Court was increasingly active during the first third of this century, just after the first third, these interventions were in retreat. What explains the early activism may be something about increasing economic integration, and a need, grounded in fidelity, to restore a framing balance between federal and state authority. But no such convenient fact explains the retreat. What then does? To what are these changes responding?

If translation is a response to changes in the interpretive context—changes in the integration of the social and economic context of the Constitution—then my argument is that we understand limits on translation too as responses to changes in the interpretive context. But this time the changes are not in the social or economic context of interpretation. This time the change is in the legal culture of the context of interpretation. It is these changes that will matter by affecting the ability of a court to construct tools of translation. In some contexts, constructing such tools will be easier than constructing such tools in other contexts. This difference we can call a difference in *capacity*, and my aim in this section is to explain how such difference can be understood.

Whatever else defines a successful judicial system, one dimen-

---

[136] Frankfurter, *The Commerce Clause* at 21 (cited in note 30).

sion of its success is its ability to deliver consistent rulings in cases that appear to be the same. I want to pick out two features of a judicial system that might affect this ability.

One feature is the *determinateness* of the rules that the system produces.[137] The more determinate the rules (assuming good faith on the part of the judges) the more consistent the application. Determinacy is in part a function of the rules themselves—how well they are structured, whether internally consistent, whether vague, etc.—but it is also in part, and for our purposes, more importantly, a function of the rule appliers themselves, or more generally, the legal culture within which the rules are applied.[138] The very same rule, applied by two different rule appliers, or applied in two different legal cultures, can be differently determinate. For example, the rule against perpetuities is more determinately applied by a graduating class of Chicago law students than by a graduating class of Yale law students, or more certainly, by a class of Berkeley English grad students. This is not to say anything about the relative intelligence, or commitment, of these different classes of rule appliers. It is instead to say something about the consistency and rigor of the training of each. Likewise with legal cultures: For the class of lawyers generally, the rule against perpetuities is more determinate in late nineteenth-century America than late twentieth-century America, if only because the diversity and specialty of law in the twentieth century is so much greater than law in the nineteenth.

The difference is not only in consistency or rigor of training, however. The difference is also in the heterogeneity of the rule appliers. A law faculty composed of thirty-five white males will more consistently and determinately agree on "excellent candidates" for teaching positions than a law faculty of mixed gender and ethnicity. Likewise, a committee of citizens in Los Angeles will less consistently and determinately agree on what is "good for the community" than a committee of citizens in Minot, North

---

[137] This is the focus, or function, of formalism as Fred Schauer develops it in *Formalism*, 97 Yale L J 509, 538–48 (1988), and his question there is whether a legal system can use formalism as a technique to achieve a certain kind of determinateness. See, for example, id at 540–41. Cass Sunstein makes a related point in Cass R. Sunstein, *Problems with Rules*, 83 Cal L Rev 101, 132–33 (1995).

[138] For a related argument, see Frederick Schauer, *Plyaing by the Rules* 112–35 (Oxford, 1991), and William Twining and David Miers, *How to Do Things with Rules* 184–98 (Weidenfeld and Nicolson, 3d ed 1991).

Dakota. In both cases, the judgment in part turns on things taken for granted by those judging. Differences in background will mean differences in these things taken for granted, and hence differences in the outcomes of judgment. The point is to understand the relationship between the rules and the rule appliers, so as to understand the degree of determinateness, and consistency, that can be expected.[139]

The second feature of the legal system's ability to deliver consistency in judgment is the structure of the system for applying rules. For when considered together with the first feature, this second feature will exacerbate the problems in determinateness underlined by the first.

We can distinguish two systems of judicial review, one centralized, the other decentralized.[140] Constitutional courts in the European legal tradition are centralized—only one court gets to strike a law as unconstitutional. Constitutional courts in the American legal system are decentralized—any "court" in the American system gets to decide constitutional questions.[141] The difference here is crucial when considered along with the point about determinacy just made. For the cost of indeterminacy is magnified by decentralized judicial review: The more decentralized the system for applying rules, the more costly is any amount of indeterminacy. Costly, in just the sense that multiplying the rule appliers within a relatively indeterminate legal culture will increase the incidence of inconsistency. And while for some issues, inconsistency will not much matter—for example, the inconsistency between two Fourth Amendment judgments of "reasonableness"—for some matters, inconsistency will be quite significant. In particular, when determining whether a law of Congress is constitutional, inconsistency among federal courts can be quite significant.

We can draw these two points together then like this: The judicial capacity, in the limited sense I am considering here, of a given legal system can be understood along two dimensions. The one looks at the nature of the legal culture within which the judiciary

---

[139] Posner makes a similar point in Richard A. Posner, *Overcoming Law* 101–02 (Harvard, 1995).

[140] See Mauro Cappelletti, *The Judicial Process in Comparative Perspective* 132–48 (Oxford, 1989).

[141] Well, possibly not. See *Freytag v Commissioner*, 501 US 868, 888–92 (1991).

functions, and examines how determinate rules within that context can be. This is an account of the heterogeneity of the rule appliers, and we might say, the thickness of the legal culture within which they apply their rules. The second dimension looks at the structure of the judiciary, asking whether review is centralized or decentralized. The focus from this perspective will reveal the extent to which indeterminacy will matter in a given legal culture.

What both dimensions of determinacy suggest is that as a legal culture changes, its capacity for applying rules changes as well. As the legal culture changes, the rule appliers might be less able determinately to apply a given set of rules; and with a decentralized system of judicial review, this change in determinacy gets magnified by the multiplicity of rule appliers.

What follows then is an odd paradox of judicial power. To the extent that a legal system becomes less capable of applying a rule determinately, dispersing judicial review may actually reduce the power of judicial review. For in response to the relative lack of facility possessed by lower courts consistently to apply a given rule, the higher court will make the rule more determinate. One technique for making the rule more determinate will be to make it more simple, or crude; another would be to increase the deference to nonjudicial actors. But in either case, the reduction in the ability of the lower courts determinately to follow the higher court's rule will result in a less subtle control exercised by the higher court. Because each difficult rule produces a wide range of errors, the court would be pushed to find a rule that systematically produced fewer errors. In such a legal culture, then, centralized judicial review may actually increase the power of judicial review, since if centralized, the cost of indeterminacy decreases, and hence the ability of the legal system to construct subtle rules increases. Centralizing judicial review in a system of uncertain lower court fidelity may increase the power of judicial review; and likewise, diffusing judicial review in the same sense reduces the power of judicial review.

But why does indeterminacy matter? What is its cost? And in what sense does inconsistency decrease the capacity of a court?

What makes inconsistency important in understanding the vigor with which the Court pursues strategies of translation is not anything about the efficiency with which these rules can be implemented. Inconsistency does reduce efficiency, but that is not its most significant cost. Instead, the cost of inconsistency ties to an important institutional feature of judicial review in America. This is the sense that inconsistent application indicates that the judges might by guided by something other than law—that their decision, that is, might be political.

The point is just this: To the extent that results of a particular rule appear consistent, it is easier for the legal culture to view this rule as properly judicial, and its results as properly judicial, in just the sense determined by this rule. To the extent, however, that the results appear inconsistent, this pedigree gets questioned; it becomes easier for observers to view these results as determined, or influenced, by factors external to the rule—in particular, factors considered political. The appearance of inconsistency here breeds the flavor of politics.

What is critical is appearance; the question is what the Court credibly can say. I am making no claim about whether the results are actually political—they may or may not be. All that is important to the account that I am offering is how the results appear.

For this appearance points to what I want to assert is a constraint on judicial review in America, a constraint I want to call the *Frankfurter constraint*. The essence of the Frankfurter constraint is this: That a rule is an inferior rule if, in its application, it appears to be political, in the sense of appearing to allow extra-legal factors to control its application. And as a corollary to this rule, to the extent that a rule appears political, we can observe that the Court will trade away from that rule. A sense of institutional cost will guide the Court to select rules that minimize the political cost of the rules it selects, which means that as the legal culture renders a rule political, this sense of institutional cost will guide the Court to trade away from that rule.[142]

---

[142] Frankfurter discussed just this constraint in his explication of the history of the Commerce Clause, emphasizing the desire to minimize perceived "judicial policy-making" as a constant guiding force. See, for example, Frankfurter, *The Commerce Clause* at 54 (cited in note 30). At times he located the source of this constraint in the nature of the Court's fact-finding ability, see, for example, id at 72 (cited in note 30); *Lopez*, 115 S Ct at 1658 (Breyer dissenting) ("Courts must give Congress a degree of leeway in determining the existence of a significant factual connection between the regulated activity and interstate commerce."), but the more salient dimension of the concern is that the choices made by the Court would, in context, appear political. See Frankfurter, *The Commerce Clause* at 70–71 (cited in note 30). See also *Wickard v Filburn*, 317 US 111, 129 (1942) ("the conflicts of economic interest between the regulated and those who are advantaged by it are wisely left under our system to resolution by the Congress . . ."). Robert Bork's work in antitrust

What the Frankfurter constraint entails is a constant pressure on the Court to avoid rules that, in context, in their application, appear political. And because rules will appear political when applied inconsistently, and because rules can become inconsistent because the legal culture renders them less determinate, what this means is that over time the Frankfurter constraint will render some rules unusable that before were quite effective. Or again, a rule that at one time does not fall afoul of the Frankfurter constraint can at another time become inconsistent with it. And the same the other way round.[143]

The capacity of a court to effect translations turns then in part upon its ability, within a particular legal culture, to construct rules of translation that will survive the Frankfurter constraint. Rules that at one time survive it may, as the legal culture changes, no longer survive the constraint. *Why* the legal culture changes is beyond the scope of this essay. No doubt part of the reason it changes is because of actions of the Court itself. But only part. It

---

especially continues this concern, perhaps obsession, with the political costs of the rules the Court embraces. See, for example, Robert H. Bork, *The Antitrust Paradox: A Policy at War with Itself* 87–88 (Free Press, 1978).

[143] The argument that constitutional law tracks "prevailing morality and predominant public opinion" is of course quite familiar. See, for example, William Howard Taft, *The Anti-Trust Act and the Supreme Court* 47–48 (Harper and Brothers, 1914). Frankfurter went so far as to say, "[m]ore than any other branch of law, the judicial application of the Constitution is a function of the dominant forces of our society," Frankfurter, *The Commerce Clause* at 3 (cited in note 30), though what he means here, I believe, is less that political forces control as much as dominant ideas and attitudes affect how judges see constitutional questions. Professor Corwin puts the point better: "An act that is 'clearly' unconstitutional to a judge who is convinced that Mr. Herbert Spencer's Social Statistics was a second book of Revelations may appear to be 'clearly' constitutional to one who thinks that Mr. John L. Lewis introduced true democracy into the United States for the first time." Edward Corwin, *Constitutional Revolution, Ltd.* 33 (1941). What is distinctive about this relatively uncontested set of views is not that they triumph in some sort of battle of ideas in the mind of the judges. Rather, as Frankfurter describes it, what makes it possible for them to have the effect they have is that when a decision "harmonize[s] with public feeling," understanding the support of these underlying ideas becomes less pressing. Frankfurter, *The Commerce Clause* at 22–23 (cited in note 30). The phenomenon is not limited to constitutional law. Bork identifies the same in antitrust law, see Bork, *The Antitrust Paradox* at 425 (cited in note 142), and Gilmore in Contract law, see Grant Gilmore, *The Death of Contract* 95 (Ohio, 1974).

What I am adding is the case where there is no relatively uncontested set of views which, because of their uncontestedness, a Court can rely upon almost invisibly. My claim is just that when the views upon which a judgment would rest are rendered fundamentally contested, the response of the Court is to avoid taking sides in this conflict. The response is much like a summary judgment motion: where facts are not reasonably contested, the Court may rely upon them to resolve the question before it; when they are contested, the Court avoids a decision relying upon a resolution of the contested facts one way or the other.

is neither the case that the Court fully constructs the legal culture it functions within, nor the case that it has no effect on that legal culture. All my argument relies upon is that to some extent, the Court must take the legal culture as it finds it, and to that extent, how it finds the legal culture will constrain its ability to translate.

THE LIMITS OF TRANSLATION: THE NEW DEAL

The historical account I have provided so far stops with the New Deal. For some time late in the 1930s, or early 1940s, the constraints that I have described as the product of tools for translating federalism change. In each of the three contexts within which translation may be said to have been advancing federalism interests, the activism of the Court in enforcing these limits wanes. The question is how this change can be understood. My objective here is to use the Frankfurter constraint to explain some of this change.[144]

All three tools for translating federalism before the switch of the New Deal depended upon a relatively thick legal culture that sustained the lines drawn. In the positive Commerce Clause context, the rule depended upon being able credibly to distinguish "direct" from "indirect" regulation of commerce, "manufacturing" from "commerce," "intended" from "unintended" effects. In the negative Commerce Clause context too, the tools depended upon the same distinctions, plus the ability to measure the economic effects as a reason to strike a state statute. And in the preemption context, the rules depended upon being able credibly to say that a certain federal regulation was within a given "field" of regulation, thereby striking state legislation within that field.

All three tools thus depended upon the ability to make formal distinctions that divide proper from improper regulation, formal distinctions that themselves depended upon, as Tocqueville put it, "fictions" extant within the legal culture. All three tools could succeed in sustaining these distinctions, making them "credible" within each legal culture, only so long as the legal culture could

---

[144] My aim here is only to understand, not to justify, the changes of the New Deal. I have elsewhere tried to use a similar analysis to show how we can see these New Deal changes as justified by simply focusing on this dimension of what can be said, consistent with the Frankfurter constraint. See Lessig, *Understanding Changed Readings*, 47 Stan L Rev 453–72 (cited in note 29).

continue to support them. And a legal system can support them only so long as they can be drawn without producing a large number of apparently inconsistent results. So long, that is, as the culture allowed them to be made without them appearing "political."

But this, midway through the Depression, is just what the legal culture would no longer support.[145] While a story far too involved for this essay, the argument can be summarized like this: That the retreat of the "Old Court" tracks the collapse of what made it rhetorically possible for the Court to sustain these formalisms in the name of translating federalism. The formalisms themselves had been rendered political. They now seemed more the result of extra-judicial judgments than entailed by the legal material. The limits they imposed were now seen not as efforts at translation; they were seen as efforts at preserving a conservative status quo. Imposing these formalisms would violate the Frankfurter constraint.[146]

Why the old categories were rendered political is a complicated story.[147] In part it was because part of what these old limits rested upon had itself been drawn into doubt—had been rendered contestable. Not only the ideas of a passive government in the face of crisis, and the ideas of laissez-faire, but also some of the very premises of federalism itself. What the Depression had done was render these ideas fundamentally contestable, with the result that decisions resting on one side or the other of this contest were rendered political. To draw these artificial lines to limit governmental power became artificial; the effort, political.

Ordinarily, when a founding constitutional commitment is challenged, it is the duty of the Court to stand up to the challenge, and defend the founding commitment until changed by amend-

---

[145] Id.

[146] See id. See also Frank R. Strong, *John Marshall—Hero or Villain*, 6 Ohio St L J 42, 46 (1939); Nicholls, 25 J Farm Econ at 581–82 (cited in note 56) (summarizing attitudes about governmental regulation).

[147] Just as the opposite—categories at first deemed political, but then rendered nonpolitical—is a complicated story. An example of this might be the change in First Amendment doctrine. No doubt part of the impetus for this change comes from the efforts of the Court itself. But nonetheless, the Amendment takes on a status in the American legal culture by the late 1960s that gets its great strength in part from the solidity of the presuppositions that underlie it. Compare Jack M. Balkin, *Frontiers of Legal Thought II. The New First Amendment: Some Realism about Pluralism: Legal Realist Approaches to the First Amendment*, 1990 Duke L J 375.

ment. This minimum of courage is essential to a system of judicial review. But what the New Deal represents, I suggest, is an important exception to this principle. When the very act of defending this founding commitment has been rendered political, then the obligations of the Frankfurter constraint may trump the obligations of fidelity. When the act of defending principles of fidelity appears more likely to be an act of politics than principle, the Frankfurter constraint may counsel concession on principle, to preserve the institution of judicial review first.

This is what I believe best excuses the Court's retreat in the face of the New Deal.[148] A faithful translation of the framers' conception of federalism would have required that the Court continue to do something to assure that something from the original balance was preserved. The Court did not do that. But what would excuse the Court in this context (and, by implication, not necessarily in others) was the Frankfurter constraint: Where the effort at translation itself has been rendered political, the Court is excused from effecting that translation.

A better example is more recent. Consider the Court's refusal in *Planned Parenthood v Casey*[149] to overturn *Roe v Wade*.[150] *Roe* had extended the right to abortion in a context where the issue was not fundamentally contested in constitutional law, and in a context where extending rights under the Due Process Clause was not such an odd practice. By the mid-1980s, however, the issue of a constitutional right to abortion had become fundamentally contested. Whether rightly or wrongly, clearly at least five Justices on the Court believed that *Roe* was not a faithful reading of the Due Process Clause of the Fourteenth Amendment—that as an original matter, *Roe* was wrong. But not all of these five agreed that the decision should be overturned. For what apparently swung some of the anti-*Roe* Justices was just the fact that the issue—getting the Court to overturn *Roe*—had become so fundamentally politi-

---

[148] To say that this "excuses" the Court's retreat is not to say that this is the "reason" the Court made the retreat. The reason no doubt was a certain loss of will on the part of Hughes and Roberts, the only Justices who changed their vote during this period. But the question of justification looks beyond the subjective reason why judges vote as they vote. The question is whether there is an account of their votes that accords well with a conception of the judicial role, and fidelity.

[149] 505 US 833 (1992).

[150] 410 US 113 (1973).

cal. Two presidents had made it their political objective to appoint justices to the Court who would overturn *Roe*, thus turning the reversal of *Roe* into a political act. The success of this political act made it impossible for the Court believably to assert that it was reversing *Roe* for reasons of fidelity. It would have appeared the result of politics, not constitutional law. This was true even for justices who believed their primary motive was constitutional law. The context had rendered their actions political, even though their motives may well have been nonpolitical.

The switch at the New Deal was one level more complex than *Casey*. One might think the analog to *Casey* would be for the New Deal Court to have written an opinion about the significance of precedent, and, as in *Casey*, stuck firm. But the differences here are significant. First, the democratic pedigree of the challenge in *Casey* was not as solid as the pedigree in the "switch in time." This is the insight in Ackerman's very different account about the political change of the New Deal.[151] For with the "switch in time," and unlike *Casey*, there was a clearly democratic wish to give up the effort at translation; and when translation itself appeared political, the better answer was to yield to the democratic branches.

Second, in both cases what gave credibility to the resolution of the conflict was that the swing Justices appeared to be acting against interest. None of the Justices who penned the Joint Opinion could say that it was correct as an original matter, yet they nonetheless would affirm it in the name of avoiding an appearance of politics.

I do not mean to minimize the institutional cost suffered by the Court after the New Deal. After *Casey*, it is at least plausible to believe that the Court was a stronger institution; that is not true after the New Deal. But faced with the alternatives, the action taken by the Justices may well have been the action minimizing the political costs of the judicial action. Where limits in the name of federalism could no longer be imposed with relatively slight rhetorical cost, the limits fell away. When the Court could no longer sustain them without appearing political, it fell to the political bodies to impose them as an act of self-restraint.

What *Casey* and the New Deal switch suggest is something more

---

[151] See Ackerman, 1 *We the People* at 105–30 (cited in note 46).

about the contours of the Frankfurter constraint. However strong is the commitment to constitutional fidelity, at times the act of pursuing fidelity can appear an act of politics. And when it does, then it, no less than any other act that appears political, becomes costly for the Court to execute. When fidelity appears political, the Frankfurter constraint may trump.

LIMITING THE FEDERAL GOVERNMENT: IMMUNITY AND SOVEREIGNTY

What is common throughout these examples at the New Deal is the limit of the Frankfurter constraint. When the social meaning of the judicial act of translation has been rendered political, there is an institutional pressure to avoid taking that act.

But the principle is not limited to the New Deal. Instead, I suggest, the force of the Frankfurter constraint continues today. Two more examples will make the account complete. In each example, the pattern is the same: Each involves an effort to set limits on federal power to preserve regulatory space for the states; in each these limits self-destruct when they are rendered, in context, political. In each case, the response is to avoid this now political act.

The first is the example of intergovernmental tax immunity, though I will consider the example only from the perspective of state immunity from federal taxation. State immunity from federal taxation began as a reaction to the federal immunity from state taxation first announced in *McCulloch*. It was an expression of equality between two sovereigns, neither compelled by the framing conception of state sovereignty, nor by the logic that seemed to drive *McCulloch*.[152] Nonetheless, for a short time the doctrine flourished without apparent limit. But the combination of an increase in federal taxation and state activity combined to force again the question of the doctrine's justification.

All seemed to agree that every activity of the states was not immune from federal tax; all also seemed to agree that not every

---

[152] At least if the logic of *McCulloch* is grounded in the collective action problem that faces the federal government when the states act to tax it. That same problem would not exist the other way around. If, however, the logic of *McCulloch* is simply the notion that "the power to tax is the power to destroy," then it would seem that the same logic could support both immunities. I consider this latter justification, however, to be a less compelling account of the case than the former.

activity of the state was subject to federal tax. The question then was where to draw the line.

The first efforts looked to the traditional activities of state government. Where the activity of the state was a "traditional" function of the state, there was immunity; when not, there was no immunity. But as with any test that turns on tradition, this distinction was not stable. For as the state entered more and more activities, and as the technology of state activities changed, it became harder to decide which activities were traditional, and which not.[153]

The struggle came to a head in *New York v United States*.[154] New York ran a mineral water business; it claimed that this was a collective good that required state regulation optimally to exploit the wells. The court split on how to think of the matter. Four opinions sketched three distinct approaches to the question, two, in essence, the same approach.

The judgment in the case was announced by Justice Frankfurter, in an opinion joined only by Justice Black. Frankfurter recounted this history of the tax immunity doctrine, and worried the difficulty that the Court had had in finding any useful line to draw. In the end, Frankfurter concluded, there was no useful line for courts to draw. As he wrote,

> The whole tendency of recent cases reveals a shift in emphasis to that of limitation upon immunity. They also indicate an awareness of the limited role of courts in assessing the relative weight of the factors upon which immunity is based. Any implied limitation upon the supremacy of the federal power to levy a tax like that now before us, in the absence of discrimination against State activities, brings fiscal and political factors into play. The problem cannot escape issues that do not lend themselves to judgment by criteria and methods of reasoning that are within the professional training and special competence of judges. Indeed the claim of implied immunity by States from federal taxation raises questions not wholly unlike provisions of the Constitution, such as that of Art. IV, Sec. 4, guaranteeing States a republican form of government, see Pacific States Tel. & Tel. Co. v. Oregon, 223 U.S. 118, which this Court has deemed not within its duty to adjudicate.[155]

---

[153] This problem did not arise before the present century, partly because state trading did not actively emerge until relatively recently, and partly because of the narrow scope of federal taxation. *New York v United States*, 326 US 572, 579 (1946) (*New York I*).

[154] Id.

[155] Id at 581–82.

Rather than draw an impossibly costly line, Frankfurter opted for the simpler, if underinclusive line: discrimination. So long as the federal tax is not discriminatory against states, the federal tax would be deemed constitutional.

At the other extreme, though I suggest for the same reason, was the opinion of Justice Douglas. Douglas too agreed that there was no principled line for the Court to draw between places where immunity was proper, and places where it was not. But what followed from this, Douglas said, was that there should be immunity everywhere. Rather than all federal taxes to quash state innovation, Douglas said, states should be given free space within which to experiment.[156]

Both opinions (admittedly for only three Justices) turn on the same inability to discern. And in an opinion for four of the Court, Chief Justice Stone agreed the judgments were difficult, but declined to abjure all such judgments. There would be some federal taxes not on their face discriminatory which the Court would not uphold. However, how one drew that line would be difficult in the future to say.[157]

But, again, what unites all three opinions is an understanding that this act of drawing affirmative limits on the scope of federal taxing power, in the name of preserving traditional, or essential, state functions, could not help but make the Court, in context, look political. Even if one believed that in the abstract such lines could be manageable, the process of drawing them would render them political. Limits of this sort failed, in the view of these Justices, for just the reason that limits confronting the New Deal failed.

The second example was, before *Lopez*, the last great struggle in the Court to protect federalism interests. This is the battle that began with *National League of Cities*,[158] and ended, in a sense, with *Garcia*,[159] concerning the extent to which the federal government can regulate states.

The pattern of this cycle should be quite familiar. Indeed it is precisely the pattern just observed in the tax immunity cases. What

---

[156] Id at 590–98 (Douglas dissenting).

[157] Id at 586–90 (Stone concurring).

[158] *National League of Cities v Usery*, 426 US 833 (1976).

[159] 469 US 528.

gives rise to the conflict—the problem, in the terms used above—is the increasing scope of federal regulations and state regulatory activity, leading, as in the tax immunity cases, to the unavoidable conflict between the two. The solution, as the Court sees it, is again a move of translation; some limits to federal power must be implied to preserve to the states a domain of autonomy to allow them to regulate themselves. The question then is what tools will be implied—what kind of tools will be used to effect the limits that the Court believes the original balance requires.

The test announced in *National League*—limiting the federal government's power to regulate "states qua states"—was implemented with a set of tools. The tools were strikingly similar to those first selected in the tax immunity cases. Where the federal government regulated within traditional domains of state functions, *National League* invalidated such laws; where it regulated in an area not traditionally within the domain of state functions, the regulation was permissible.[160]

As one might have predicted, these tools were not destined to be especially useful. As lower courts began to implement the mandate of *National League*, the very same problems that had plagued the analogous test in the tax immunity cases plagued the courts here. How one determined which functions were "traditional," given the radical change in technologies over 200 years, was not clear. And because not clear, conflicting interpretations of various federal laws emerged. As these conflicts worked their way to the Court, it became more and more plain that this regime for translating federalism was not going to succeed. For it was generating an extraordinary amount of insecurity without any clear sense about how this uncertainty could be reduced.[161]

The uncertainty was ended, for the time being it appears, in *Garcia*. In an opinion written by Justice Blackmun, the Justice who had given *National League of Cities* its fifth vote, the Court gave

---

[160] *National League*, 426 US at 852.

[161] As the Court later recognized,

> Although *National League of Cities* supplied some examples of "traditional governmental functions," it did not offer a general explanation of how a "traditional" function is to be distinguished from a "nontraditional" one. Since then, federal and state courts have struggled with the task, thus imposed, of identifying a traditional function for purposes of state immunity under the Commerce Clause.

Garcia, 469 US at 530.

up the *National League* tools for translating federalism. The reasons, again, will be familiar. As in the tax immunity cases, what plagued the Court here was that there could be no firm line that would divide proper from improper federal regulation; the line instead was constantly shifting.[162] And if the line was constantly shifting, then the Court couldn't help but appear political in its shifting resolution of these federalism cases. As the list of cases on both sides of the test began to look more and more arbitrary, the arbitrariness of this test became an insurmountable burden for the Court. It gave up the search that *National League* began, because the institutional costs of the search had become too much.[163]

What the examples should suggest is the particular unavailability, in this legal culture, of a particular kind of tool for limiting the scope of federal or state power. This is any tool that attempts to draw categorical limitations that turn on the "nature" of the subject being regulated. Repeatedly, tools like this have failed.[164] They have failed because this is not a legal culture that can well

---

[162] In the words of Justice Black:

> There is not, and there cannot be, any unchanging line of demarcation between essential and non-essential governmental functions. Many governmental functions of today have at some time in the past been nongovernmental. The genius of our government provides that, within the sphere of constitutional action, the people— acting not through the courts but through their elected legislative representatives—have the power to determine as conditions demand, what services and functions the public welfare requires.

Garcia, 469 US at 546, quoting *Helvering v Gerhardt*, 304 US 405, 427 (1938) (Black concurring).

[163] As the Court held,

> We therefore now reject, as unsound in principle and unworkable in practice, a rule of state immunity from federal regulation that turns on a judicial appraisal of whether a particular governmental function is "integral" or "traditional." Any such rule leads to inconsistent results at the same time that it disserves principles of democratic self-governance, and it breeds inconsistency precisely because it is divorced from those principles.

Garcia, 469 US at 546–47.

[164] Again, the failures have been in the tax immunity context, see *Garcia*, 469 US 528, 541–42 (1985), and the "states qua states" context, see, for example, id at 538–39 ("Just how troublesome the task has been is revealed by the results reached in other federal cases. Thus, courts have held that regulating ambulance services, . . . licensing automobile drivers, . . . operating a municipal airport, . . . performing solid waste disposal, . . . and operating a highway authority, . . . are functions protected under National League of Cities. At the same time, courts have held that issuance of industrial development bonds, . . . regulation of intrastate natural gas sales, . . . regulation of traffic on public roads, . . . regulation of air transportation, . . . operation of a telephone system, . . . leasing and sale of natural gas, . . . operation of a mental health facility, . . . and provision of in-house domestic services for the aged and handicapped . . . are not entitled to immunity.") (citations omitted).

sustain these efforts at casuistry: not because there is anything in particular bad about casuistry, but because there is just nothing particularly good about our facility with these.

What this does not mean, however, is that there are no tools for limiting federal or state power—that there are no tools, that is, for translating federalism. Indeed, I believe there are such tools, and that we have seen the Court, whether knowingly or not, often follow a strategy that does embrace this kind of tool. These tools we can call second-best limits on governmental power. They are prophylactic, in just the way much of the Warren Court's rules for criminal procedure were prophylactic. They are tools that have the effect of advancing the interests of federalism, though they don't directly seem to do this. But what is important about them is that they are tools that can, meaningfully, be applied by a Court in the current legal context.

Translation's Second-Best Tools

The trick to translating limits on governmental power is to find limits that a court—or better, our Court—can impose, and sustain, over the run of cases that any such limit will produce. Translation is subject to these institutional constraints. The constraint that I have identified here is the Frankfurter constraint— that a tool that in its operation makes the Court appear political is a weaker tool for just that reason. The trick is to find tools that do not violate this constraint.

My aim in this section is to sketch three examples of rules for translating federalism that do not violate the Frankfurter constraint—or at least do not do so now, since again whether a tool violates the constraint is a function of the interpretive context. The primary author of these tools has been federalism's most avid translator, Justice O'Connor. Just about without exception,[165] O'Connor has offered rules for translating federalism that would do so consistent with the Frankfurter constraint. These rules succeed in imposing limits on federal interference with state activities

---

[165] But exceptions there have been. Justice O'Connor's proposed test in *Garcia*, 469 US at 580, 585–86 (Necessary and Proper Clause) as well as *South Carolina v Baker*, 485 US 505, 533–34 (1988) (O'Connor dissenting) (Republican Guarantee Clause) both would have violated the Frankfurter constraint.

without directly pursuing federalism values. Their motive is the protection of federalism values, and their effect will be the protection of federalism values. But their means is something different.

CLEAR STATEMENT

The first of these techniques was used as a supplement to *Garcia* in *Gregory v Ashcroft*.[166] At issue was the application of the Age Discrimination Act to state judges who, under the state constitution, were required to retire at age seventy. Under the rule that *Garcia* replaced, the rule of *National League of Cities*, the Court might have had to determine whether regulating the age at which states may force their judges to retire was a regulation of "states as states." *Garcia* disposed of that rule,[167] and replaced it with a rule that relied upon the political process.

The Court in *Gregory* sought to improve this political process through the use of a clear statement rule. Said the Court, affirming the rule of *Garcia*, "Congress may legislate in areas traditionally regulated by the States," but the Court will not assume that Congress exercises this power "lightly."[168] Therefore, before assuming that Congress has exercised this power, "it is incumbent upon the federal courts to be certain of Congress's intent. . . ."[169] To be certain, then, the Court requires that Congress speak with particular clarity when it attempts so to regulate. Citing a clear statement case from the Eleventh Amendment context, the Court said,

> If Congress intends to alter the "usual constitutional balance between the States and the Federal Government," it must make its intention to do so unmistakably clear in the language of the statute.[170]

This is the rule of clear statement. With this device, the Court measures Congress's statute against an implied standard of cer-

---

[166] 501 US 452 (1991).

[167] Subject, at least, to the limitations later imposed by *New York II*. See text accompanying notes 183–87.

[168] *Gregory*, 501 US at 460. This language notwithstanding, the focus is not field preemption, but rather clear statement.

[169] Id (internal citations omitted).

[170] Id, citing *Atascadero State Hospital v Scanlon*, 473 US 234, 242 (1985).

tainty, to measure whether the Court believes that Congress really intended to reach as far as it apparently did. Where a statute is ambiguous, or where a particularly strong state interest or individual right is being overridden by governmental action, then the Court will require of Congress that it make its intent more clear. The Court will not presume, from simple ambiguity, that Congress intended to invade a domain of state regulatory interest.

Now the contexts within which the Court has applied the clear statement rule are many. They range from individual rights cases,[171] to Eleventh Amendment cases,[172] to cases where the fear is Congress's invasion of traditional state functions.[173] In each case, the notion is simply that any intent to change the constitutionally preferred status quo must be demonstrated by clear language in the statute.[174] But it should be plain that in setting out such a rule, the Court is setting out a constitutionally preferred status quo. And by increasing the costs for deviating from that status quo, it is reducing the number of deviations.

The advantage of the clear statement rule is twofold. First, it functions primarily as a channeling device. It requires simply that Congress be certain of an intent to alter a presumed constitutional balance. Second, it can achieve this function without requiring of the Court some impossible interpretive task. Determining whether a statute is sufficiently clear is an activity within the ordinary ken of the Court. We can expect, then, that the Court's adjudication of these cases will yield a fairly consistent line of authority.

What application of the clear statement rule does require, however, is a plain articulation of the values underlying the selective application of this special rule of clarity on Congress's statutes.[175] This articulation itself may expose the Court to some political cost. But so long as the values articulated do not appear arbitrary, or do not change radically over the life of the Court, they are unlikely

---

[171] See, for example, *Kent v Dulles*, 357 US 116, 129 (1958).

[172] See, for example, *Atascadero*, 473 US at 242.

[173] *Gregory*, 501 US at 464.

[174] Id at 460.

[175] It is of course true that the rule applies only to Congress's statutes, but it is unclear what Justice Souter means by saying they are "merely rules of statutory interpretation." *Lopez*, 115 S Ct at 1655 (Souter dissenting). What informs these rules are constitutional values, and to the extent that these values undercut, or redefine the scope of Congress's statute, they are, to that extent, constitutional rules.

to cause any great political cost to the Court. If the values can instead reflect what at a minimum all can agree upon about the federalist origins of the constitutional design, the fact that the rule expresses these values would not render it political. Again, what renders a rule political is contestability, not values.

Finally, one should be candid about the role for the Court that such a rule presumes. If the Court's job were simply to find Congress's meaning, then it would have no right to impose on Congress anything like a clear statement rule. But the Court is not simply the handmaiden of Congress. Its duty is also to the Constitution. The question is how best it can satisfy that duty. In my view, there is nothing wrong with the Court asserting its own rules for reading Congress's statutes, so long as those rules are designed better to effect the values of the Constitution. Such is the nature of a clear statement rule.

SPENDING

The clear statement rule has relatively general application. The next two rules are more targeted. The first is a rule suggested by Justice O'Connor for policing the federal spending power. As a practical matter, there are no real federalism limits on the federal power to spend. While other federalist regimes have worried well about the danger that federal spending has on the autonomy of state authority, and have therefore imposed substantial limitations on federal power to spend,[176] our Court has done very little to limit federal spending in the name of state autonomy.

South Dakota v Dole[177] states the Court's most recent test.[178] In it, Chief Justice Rehnquist outlined a four-part test for limiting federal power to spend, and hinted at a fifth. The four limits on spending are as follows:

> The first of these limitations is derived from the language of the Constitution itself; the exercise of the spending power must be in pursuit of "the general welfare." [. . .] In considering

---

[176] Germany, for example, has very strict federalism limitations on federal spending authority. See Currie, *The Constitution of the Federal Republic of Germany* at 210 (cited in note 4).

[177] 483 US 203.

[178] For an excellent recent account of the evolution and theory of the spending power doctrine, see David E. Engdahl, *The Spending Power*, 44 Duke L J 1 (1994).

whether a particular expenditure is intended to serve general public purposes, courts should defer substantially to the judgment of Congress. [. . .] Second, we have required that if Congress desires to condition the States' receipt of federal funds, it "must do so unambiguously. . . , enabl[ing] the States to exercise their choice knowingly, cognizant of the consequences of their participation." [. . .] Third, our cases have suggested (without significant elaboration) that conditions on federal grants might be illegitimate if they are unrelated "to the federal interest in particular national projects or programs." [. . .] Finally, we have noted that other constitutional provisions may provide an independent bar to the conditional grant of federal funds.[179]

The condition hinted at was that the conditions imposed not be so extreme as to become coercive.[180]

Of these four conditions, only the second has any effect on structuring spending power. For it is just a clear statement rule, that functions here just as any clear statement rule. The fourth condition adds nothing to what the Constitution already requires—for of course, Congress may not pass a law disregarding "an independent bar" to a grant of federal funds. The first and the third conditions are in principle limits, but in practice can be no limit at all. The reason is the same as the reason that the fifth condition—that the conditions cannot be too extreme—cannot in practice be any limit at all. All three fail as limits because to apply them would be to violate the Frankfurter constraint. That would apply most clearly to the first rule, for there is no feasible way the Court could strike a statute as without the "general welfare" without the Court returning to the days of *Lochner*.[181] The Court acknowledges as much in announcing the rule. So too could the Court not apply the third or fifth condition. Whether a limitation on federal spending is "related" is just the same question the Court asks in the Necessary and Proper Clause context. There, as here, judgments about "relation" could not be made in a sufficiently predictable way to avoid seeming political.

---

[179] *South Dakota*, 483 US at 207–08 (citations omitted).

[180] Id at 211.

[181] The point is not just that these are matters of degree. All of law is a matter of degree. The point is that these are matters of degree in a context where drawing a line through these matters of degree will appear political. Drawing a line will not always appear political. But where it does, the Frankfurter constraint requires restraint.

What these considerations strongly suggest is that the political costs, or the rhetorical burden, of applying this rule to limit federal spending conditions would be extremely high, and consequently, as predicted, the number of times the rule has been applied to limit federal spending programs low—never. What the rule of Chief Justice Rehnquist barely hides is the judgment that there is nothing the Court *can* do to limit conditions on federal spending, even if there is something the Court *should* do.

Justice O'Connor, however, offered a rule that would certainly limit federal spending, motivated by a desire to preserve state autonomy, but pursuing this objective indirectly. She proposed a test that forbade any conditions on spending grants that were beyond regulations on how the money would be spent.[182] A condition that said no money granted may be spent on X, Y, and Z would be constitutional; a condition that said this money is accepted on the condition that the state do X, Y, Z would not.

The advantage of this rule is solely its administrability. The line between "conditions on how the money is spent" and other conditions is relatively clear. But what is striking about the test is its artificiality. For there is nothing in the text of the spending clause that would suggest these limits on federal spending; nor is there anything in its history. What is striking also is the crudeness of the rule. For the rule would force the federal government to do indirectly what it was not allowed to do directly.

But "artificiality" and "crudeness" are criticisms of a rule only if a better rule is available, and because of the Frankfurter constraint, I am not sure that one is. That is, again it seems that this indirect way of enforcing federalism interests is more effective than the direct way outlined by Chief Justice Rehnquist. Chief Justice Rehnquist's test is more obviously related to the federalist interest in limiting spending, yet it works to effect no substantial limit at all; while Justice O'Connor's test seems only accidentally related to the federalist interest, but would succeed in practice in substantially advancing federalism interests. Again, the difference here reflects an institutional constraint of the Court, but one which the Court cannot well ignore.

---

[182] *South Dakota*, 483 US at 215–17 (O'Connor dissenting).

COMMANDEERING

My third example is as specific a rule as the spending rule, but perhaps less significant, if only because the kind of "invasion" at issue is less prevalent.[183] This is the rule against "commandeering" given to us in *New York v United States.*[184]

At issue in *New York v United States* was a federal program designed to deal with the problem of nuclear waste. Among its many provisions was one set of requirements that constituted the "commandeering" that the Court held unconstitutional. In these regulations, Congress required that states either enact certain regulations, or take title to that state's nuclear waste. That the federal government couldn't force the states to take title seemed to flow from the principles of the first *New York v United States:* To force states to take title to this property of negative value would be in essence to tax the states; the first *New York* clearly indicated that a discriminatory tax against the states would be unconstitutional.[185]

What about simply requiring them to enact certain regulations? Well it is clear that the federal government would have the power to require private organizations to enact similar regulations, for the regulations here clearly affected interstate commerce. But what made these requirements problematic was that they were applied to the states. "[B]y directly compelling [states] to enact and enforce a federal regulatory program,"[186] the federal government was "commandeering" the states in the exercise of their sovereign power. This, the Court held, was unconstitutional.

Now again there is much to wonder about here. For why, one might ask, is there any real problem with much of what the federal government might require through commandeering?[187] Certainly there are plenty of cases where the commandeering the federal government achieves is really quite insignificant to any federalism interest. Why then a rule that cuts so crudely?

---

[183] Compare below at note 187.

[184] 112 S Ct 2408 (*New York II*).

[185] See *NYI*, 326 US at 575–76.

[186] Id at 2428.

[187] In some areas there has been a problem. The best example is in air pollution regulation, see David P. Currie, *Air Pollution: Federal Law and Analysis* §§ 2.40, 2.46 (Callaghan, 1991). See also Norman Dorsen, *The National No-Fault Motor Vehicle Insurance Act: A Problem in Federalism,* 49 NYU L Rev 45, 61–62 (1974).

But obviously the reason again links to the limitations on the Court's power to distinguish. For here again, Justice O'Connor, as she did with the spending rule, offers a rule that is both under- and overinclusive, which does not directly seem to advance federalism interests, but which can, because of its simplicity, be applied by the Courts to advance federalism values. Once again, she has offered a second-best rule because of the constraints making impossible any first-best rule.

THE LESSONS FROM THESE LIMITS

What federalism needs, as Justice O'Connor describes, is for the "Court to enforce affirmative limits on federal regulation of the States to complement the judicially crafted expansion of the interstate commerce power."[188] But for the slight flip in passivity, this, I think, captures well the problem a federalist-focused court faces. For it is not that the commerce power has grown because of the "craft" of the Court; it has grown because of the integration of a national economy, the craft of the Court notwithstanding. And it is not that the Court can simply "enforce" affirmative limits on federal regulation—such limits simply don't exist out there to be found; they must, instead, themselves be "crafted." What federalism requires is for the Court to craft, to construct, to make-up, limits on regulative authority, both state and federal, so as to check the growth in the commerce power, to the extent that growth has set the original balance askew. The task again is the same as that undertaken by the Court in the context of individual rights, where in the name of a founding vision of liberty, the (Warren) Court imposed affirmative limits on governmental power to reconstruct a space of individual liberty.

But in crafting these tools, the Court is constrained by its own institutional design. It is constrained first, I have argued, by what I have called the Frankfurter constraint: That in engaging in this practice of constructing, the Court cannot adopt a rule that, in context, appears to be political. This constraint, I have argued, explains well much of the change in the tools that the Court has indeed crafted. For what the change in these tools in part at least reflects is a sensitivity to the rhetorical burden of any particular

---

[188] *Garcia*, 469 US at 587 (O'Connor dissenting).

rule. As that rhetorical burden has increased, the Court has substituted other less burdensome tools.

At least when such substitutes are available. For a second lesson from the account so far is that sometimes such tools are not available. Sometimes the context has changed such that any effort at limiting the power of the government, in the name of fidelity or anything else, will be perceived as political. This at least was my account of the changes at the New Deal. In that context at least, regardless of the truth of the matter, the Court could not credibly constrain Congress without undermining its own institutional authority.

But times like the New Deal—and cases like *Casey*—are the exception. And to say that there are general classes of tools that are no longer available for translating federalism is not to say that no tools exist. My aim in this last part has been to argue that, indeed, such tools do exist; that they succeed to the extent that they can be enforced by a court without great rhetorical cost; and that there are at least three examples of these tools to consider.

What unites these second-best rules is that they have the effect of advancing the interests of federalism without requiring the Court to define those values in a way that is inevitably contestable. They are, therefore, ways of preserving fidelity while minimizing the institutional cost to the Court.

There should be more. But what limits this conservative effort at fidelity is a misplaced conservatism in the tools chosen by the Court. None of these second-best tools can be said to be derived from the text of the Constitution; each is plainly constructed and imposed upon a constitutional text in the name of a deeper fidelity with the Constitutional structure. Yet it is just this constructivism that this conservative Court seems wont to do. Rather than creatively adapting second-best tools to the end of fidelity, the Court more often than not adopts a tool that, while closer to the constitutional text, turns out to be self-defeating in application. Rather than strategic, the Court is plodding.

This presents, I suggest, an odd paradox. What the lessons of federalism's successes, and failures, teach is that fidelity requires a certain radicalness. That to be faithful to the constitutional structure, the Court must be willing to be unfaithful to the constitutional text. Yet this nominal infidelity this Court can't commit, thus committing it, I suggest, to an infidelity more fundamental.

It seems unable, that is, to adopt workable tools where those tools seem far removed from the constitutional text, and thus seems trapped in adopting textually supported rules that will, over time, prove unworkable.

As Applied to Lopez

The point is well made in *Lopez*. Alfonso Lopez was a student at Edison High School in San Antonio, Texas. On March 10, 1992, he showed up at school with a gun. He was arrested, and charged under Texas law. The next day, under a statute that made it a federal crime to possess a gun within 1,000 feet of a school, he was prosecuted by federal authorities as well. State charges were then dismissed.[189]

In the district and appeals courts, Lopez argued that the statute was beyond Congress's power. Surprisingly, the Court of Appeals for the Fifth Circuit agreed.[190] The court held the statute unconstitutional, as beyond Congress's power under the Commerce Clause.

And so too did the Supreme Court. In an opinion written by Chief Justice Rehnquist, the Court reiterated what had been a mere article of faith for some time—that Congress's power was not unlimited—but for the first time in more than half a century, the Court evinced that faith by striking down the statute.

Rehnquist's opinion was short and to the point. Commerce Clause jurisprudence has distinguished three kinds of regulations of Commerce:

> First, Congress may regulate the use of the channels of interstate commerce. . . . Second, Congress is empowered to regulate and protect the instrumentalities of interstate commerce, or persons or things in interstate commerce, even though the threat may come only from intrastate activities. . . . Finally, Congress's commerce authority includes the power to regulate those activities having a substantial relation to interstate commerce, . . . , *i.e.*, those activities that substantially affect interstate commerce.[191]

---

[189] *Leading Cases*, 109 Harv L Rev 111, 111–12 (1995).

[190] *United States v Lopez*, 2 F3d 1342, 1367–68 (5th Cir 1993).

[191] *Lopez*, 115 S Ct at 1629–30 (citations omitted).

Because there was no showing, or requirement of a showing, that this gun had traveled in interstate commerce, Congress could reach it only if it could be shown that the "activity" "regulated" had a "substantial relation to interstate commerce" or "substantially affect[ed]" interstate commerce. As the Court wrote,

> Section 922(q) is a criminal statute that by its terms has nothing to do with "commerce" or any sort of economic enterprise, however broadly one might define those terms. Section 922(q) is not an essential part of a larger regulation of economic activity, in which the regulatory scheme could be undercut unless the intrastate activity were regulated. It cannot, therefore, be sustained under our cases upholding regulations of activities that arise out of or are connected with a commercial transaction, which viewed in the aggregate, substantially affects interstate commerce.[192]

What captured the Chief Justice's opinion was an argument that is quite familiar. This is the *reductio:* Ours is a government of enumerated powers. Enumeration presumes that something is unenumerated. Therefore, any argument that entails that there is nothing the government can't regulate is an argument inconsistent with enumeration. Neither the dissent nor the government in *Lopez* could articulate any principle that would limit Congress's power under the Commerce Clause. The presupposition of enumeration was therefore violated. As the Court worried,

> Under the theories that the Government presents in support of §922(q), it is difficult to perceive any limitation on federal power, even in areas such as criminal law enforcement or education where States historically have been sovereign. Thus, if we were to accept the Government's arguments, we are hard-pressed to posit any activity by an individual that Congress is without power to regulate.[193]

So much should be common ground. Granted, in an economy such as our own, every activity "affects" interstate commerce, in the sense that "[m]otion at the outer rim is communicated perceptibly . . . to recording instruments at the center."[194] In an economy such

---

[192] Id at 1630–31.

[193] Id at 1632. See also id at 1628 (identifying the reason for the earlier restraints as the fear of this *reductio*); id at 1642 (Thomas concurring) (raising the fear that the power would include the power to regulate "marriage, littering, or cruelty to animals").

[194] *Schechter Poultry*, 295 US at 554 (Cardozo concurring).

as this, there is no limit to be found in the nature of the "effect." Granted also that if Congress exercised this power to its fullest, it would obliterate any space left for exclusive state legislation. Therefore, it follows, if a space is to be preserved, the power must be limited. With this much of the opinion, I do not believe anyone can fairly disagree.

The question is simply who should draw the limits: Congress or the Court. No doubt foxes don't guard hen houses well, and likewise, Congress may not be the ideal guardian of states' rights. But the question is not who is *ideal*; the question is who is *best*. The Court would be best if it could construct tools that would limit Congress's power without running afoul of the Frankfurter constraint. But whether the Court can construct such tools is the question to be answered. The answer is not a given.[195]

In my view, the tools that Chief Justice Rehnquist has provided in *Lopez* will run afoul of the Frankfurter constraint.[196] They will violate the Frankfurter constraint for the same reason that tools in *National League of Cities* run afoul of the Frankfurter constraint. This is not because any set of tools would similarly fail—indeed, at the end of this essay I will suggest limits that would not. But it is because the limits that *Lopez* sets are not stable, and that unless restructured, will invite a new Justice Blackmun, embarrassed by the mess that *Lopez* has created, to write the next *Garcia*. We are Sisyphus; the cycle has begun again.

This is indeed unfortunate. For by once again giving us a tool that attempts to track what federalism was *really* meant to protect, the Court has given us a tool that will really protect nothing.

---

[195] There is of course a long tradition that views judgments about such matters of "discretion" as resting with Congress, checked by the people alone. Frankfurter, of course, is a leader in this school, Frankfurter, *The Commerce Clause* at 41 (cited in note 30), but the genealogy of this view reaches back to *McCulloch*, and gets echoed in cases throughout our history. See, for example, *McCray v United States*, 195 US 27, 55–56 (1904).

[196] To endorse, as I have here, a place for the "Frankfurter constraint" in any theory about interpretive fidelity is not to endorse the extent to which the principle was carried by Frankfurter himself. Frankfurter's application of the rule often seemed to turn on whether there was an absolutely determinate result possible, rather than on whether indeterminacy would be viewed as political. Thus, in the apportionment cases, he objected to federal court involvement because mathematical certainty would not be possible. See *Baker v Carr*, 369 US 186, 266 (1962) (Frankfurter dissenting). But whether certainty is possible or not is not the question; the question is whether any uncertainty would be viewed as political. Whether it has is an open question; but whether it has is not simply a function of the uncertainty.

There is a realism in the Court's method. But we must be realistic about this realism if this effort at fidelity is to succeed: Realist limits can never effect effective judicial limits on governmental power, or at least the naive realism revealed here cannot. If limits are to be found, they must be made. And if they are to be made, they will be made only with the tools of a sophisticated formalism. What the neo-formalist realizes is that formalism is not an ontology; formalism is a tool.[197] And the lesson of realism should be that it is the only tool with which legal policy can be effected by a court against the will of a legislature.

In what follows, then, I want to sketch just why the tools that Rehnquist has given us will fail, and then very briefly I will outline the kinds of tools that might not.

THE INVISIBLE NECESSARY AND PROPER CLAUSE

The question the Court asks in *Lopez* is whether the statute is constitutional "under [Congress's] commerce power"[198]—whether the *"commerce authority"*[199] reaches this far. The Court concludes that it does not. But it never continues with what is ordinarily the next question in any power inquiry—whether the exercise of this power is nonetheless "necessary and proper" to the exercise of some congressional power, here the commerce power. For even if Congress's "commerce authority" does not reach this activity, it has long been understood that Congress's legislative authority may reach beyond the particular enumerated powers—to, that is, un-enumerated powers—so long as that Necessary and Proper authority is used "to effectuate other policies within the express powers."[200]

The source of this authority, of course, is *McCulloch v Maryland*,[201] a case decided six years before *Gibbons*, upholding the constitutionality of Congress's Second Bank of the United States.

---

[197] This again is Schauer's point. See Schauer, *Formalism*, 99 Yale LJ 509 (cited in note 137).

[198] *Lopez*, 115 S Ct at 1629.

[199] Id.

[200] Gardbaum, 79 Cornell L Rev at 781 (cited in note 112).

[201] *McCulloch*, 17 US (4 Wheat) 316.

Congress had no expressly enumerated power to incorporate a bank; nonetheless, held the Court, it did have the authority by virtue of the Necessary and Proper Clause. Founding a bank was just a means; and the Necessary and Proper Clause granted Congress the "discretion" to select the "means by which the powers" the Constitution confers on it "are to be carried into execution."[202] As Marshall wrote, practically copying Hamilton's earlier argument to President Washington,[203]

> Let the end be legitimate, let it be within the scope of the Constitution, and all means which are appropriate, which are plainly adapted to that end, which are not prohibited, but consist with the letter and spirit of the Constitution, are constitutional.[204]

Now of course the Court in *McCulloch* didn't tell us which end it thought the bank a necessary means to; Marshall suggested a number of possible ends, but never resolved really which the Court thought this statute served. Nonetheless, what is important is that *McCulloch* itself established, and later cases consistently agreed,[205] that Congress's power is not at an end once the end of an enumerated power is reached; always left for consideration is whether the activity being regulated can nonetheless be regulated under the Necessary and Proper power. Following this inquiry was the practice of the Court for much of the century and a half after *McCulloch*

---

[202] Id at 421.

[203] As Hamilton described Congress's power, what is constitutional or not,

is the *end* to which the measure relates as a *mean*. If the end be clearly comprehended within any of the specified powers, and if the measure have an obvious relation to that end and is not forbidden by any particular provision of the constitution—it may safely be deemed to come within the compass of national authority.

Randall, *Thomas Jefferson* at 506–07 (emphasis in original) (cited in note 11).

[204] *McCulloch*, 17 US (4 Wheat) at 421.

[205] *Gibbons* too supports this view. As I indicated above, the negative implication of the third part of Congress's power is best understood as referring to the Necessary and Proper power. Again, as Marshall indicated there, federal power would extend to objects wholly internal if they "concern" more than one state. But this is just the Necessary and Proper analysis of *McCulloch*. And thus again, the question of Congress's power is whether the power derives from the commerce power directly (that which reaches more than one state) or from the Necessary and Proper Clause (where regulation is "necessary" for the purpose "of executing some other power"). See note and text accompanying note 33.

was decided, in both commerce cases[206] and other powers cases as well.[207]

The practice comes to an end, for a brief period of time, during the first efforts of the Court to limit Congress's commerce power. For there too the Court simply ignored the Necessary and Proper Clause. The beginning was *Knight*, where again the Court determined the scope of the Sherman Act by considering the meaning of "commerce" alone, and concluded that "manufacturing" was not "commerce" so did not fall within the scope of the Act.

In the context of the Sherman Act, this narrow view may well have been proper—for again, the Sherman Act has no "necessary and proper" language. But outside the Sherman Act, it makes no sense. Even if the "Commerce Clause" does not reach "manufac-

---

[206] See, for example, *United States v Coombs*, 37 US (12 Pet) 72, 77 (1838) (actions which "interfere[ ] with, obstruct[ ], or prevent" commerce though not themselves on water, and hence not within Congress's admiralty power, "may be punished by Congress under its general authority to make all laws necessary and proper"); *United States v Dewitt*, 76 US 41, 44 (1869) (Congress's power does not reach "internal trade and business of the separate States; except, indeed, as a necessary and proper means for carrying into execution" another power of Congress); *Railroad Commn. of Wisconsin v Chicago, Burlington & Quincy R.R. Co.*, 257 US 563, 588 (1922) (regulation of intrastate railroad rates permissible when "incidental to the regulation of interstate commerce and necessary to its efficiency"); *Jones & Laughlin*, 301 US at 36–37 (power to regulate commerce "is the power to enact 'all appropriate legislation' for 'its protection and advancement' ") (citations omitted); *Darby*, 312 US at 121 (Congress may use "means reasonably adapted to the attainment of the permitted end, even though they involve control of intrastate activities"); *Wickard*, 317 US at 121; *Katzenbach*, 379 US at 302, quoting *United States v Wrightwood Dairy Co.*, 315 US 110, 119 (1942) (Congress's power "extends to those activities intrastate which so affect interstate commerce, or the exertion of the power of Congress over it, as to make regulation of them appropriate means to the attainment of a legitimate end"); *Heart of Atlanta*, 379 US at 275 (Black concurring) ("Congress . . . has power under the Commerce Clause and the Necessary and Proper Clause to bar racial discrimination in the Heart of Atlanta Motel and Ollie's Barbecue."). See also Currie, *The Constitution in the Supreme Court, 1789–1888* at 430 n 6 (cited in note 46) ("Congress had authority under the necessary and proper clause to protect interstate or foreign commerce by persons not themselves engaged in commerce."); Note, *Power of Congress to Regulate Intrastate Rates*, 14 Colum L Rev 583, 585 (1914) (questioning whether the Court means the power to reach internal commerce to flow from "the 'necessary and proper' clause, superadded to the Commerce Clause"); Charles E. Carpenter and Robert Charles Mardian, *When Is Commerce Interstate?* 22 S Cal L Rev 406, 406 (1949) ("However, it must not be forgotten that, even if this line of demarcation [between inter- and intrastate commerce] is clearly established . . . the control of Congress may still prevail because of the relation which the intrastate matter regulated bears to interstate commerce.").

[207] A favorite example is the power to construct a monument to the Battle of Gettysburg, upheld unanimously by the Court in *United States v Gettysburg Elec. Ry.*, 160 US 668, 681 (1896), held to be necessary and proper to, "inter alia, the power to raise armies, essentially because it would instill feelings of patriotism that would make better soldiers." Currie, *The Constitution in the Supreme Court, 1888–1986* at 24 n 117 (cited in note 46). See also id at 100.

turing" since "manufacturing" is not "commerce," there is still the question whether regulating manufacturing is necessary and proper to the regulating of commerce. This question, crucial to a complete analysis of Congress's power, never gets asked in these early cases limiting Congress's power under the Commerce Clause. Instead, as in *Lopez*, the Court limited its view to "commerce authority" alone: As the Court said in *Carter Coal*, "the validity of [Congress's] act depends upon whether it is a regulation of interstate commerce" and therefore that "the nature and extent of the power conferred upon Congress by the Commerce Clause becomes the determinative question."[208]

There are passages in some of the opinions in *Lopez* that makes it seem as if the Court simply forgot the Clause.[209] But I do not believe the Clause was forgotten either here, nor in the first cycle of these Commerce cases. The Clause is ignored, not forgotten; it is ignored because to consider it would be to make impossible any limit on Congress's power. For if the Court analyzed this exercise of power under the Necessary and Proper Clause, then there would have been no way to limit Congress's power without running afoul of the Frankfurter constraint.[210]

We can see this by briefly considering three narrower ways that the Necessary and Proper Clause could be interpreted. Each, I will argue, would either fail to limit Congress's power, or run afoul of the Frankfurter constraint. The first would be to require a tighter fit between ends and means when regulating in the Commerce sphere. This, in effect, is what *Lopez* does, though not under the Necessary and Proper Clause. It requires that the claim that something "affect" interstate commerce be made more plain than Congress did; and that the effect will not be so easily implied, at least

---

[208] *Carter Coal*, 298 US at 297.

[209] Justice Thomas, while referring once to the Necessary and Proper power, then apparently ignores it, resting his analysis on the meaning of the word "commerce" at the founding, and upon the meaning given the Commerce Clause by *Gibbons*. See, for example, *Lopez*, 115 S Ct at 1647 (Thomas concurring). Says Justice Thomas, "The Commerce Clause does not state that Congress may "regulate matters that substantially affect commerce . . . ." Id at 1644. True, but again, the Constitution *does* say that Congress may regulate means which are "necessary and proper" to regulating commerce, which matters "that substantially affect commerce" plainly are.

[210] Even in a fairly formal legal culture such as France, the determination of what is a "necessity" is viewed as political. See Alec Stone, *The Birth of Judicial Politics in France: The Constitutional Council in Comparative Perspective* 154 (Oxford, 1992).

where the activity involved is deemed "non-commercial." But the problem with this is just the problem Marshall saw in *McCulloch*: That the Court is not in the position to weigh these interests, to test the degree of necessity needed, and that its efforts here could not help but become inconsistent. What repeated litigation about the tightness of the means/end relationship would produce is just the inconsistency that the Frankfurter constraint enjoins.

A second technique is suggested by Gary Lawson and Patricia Granger. This would focus not so much on the "necessity" of a particular regulation, or again, the tightness of the fit between means and ends. Instead, this approach would focus on the "propriety" of any means selected.[211] So understood, a regulation would not be permitted under the Necessary and Proper Clause if it was a regulation with an improper purpose.

While this approach is doctrinally well executed, as others have suggested, it is not clear what it adds to the existing regime. For the approach is essentially formal; one needs to have a conception of "propriety" that would then govern whether a regulation was proper or not. That technique could look either to the end to be regulated, or the means used to regulate. If it is the former, then the test collapses into the purpose test; if it is the latter, then the question is how the Court determines what means are "proper." Should it look just to the what the framers would have thought "proper,"[212] or may "proper," like "cruel," "draw its meaning from the evolving standards of decency that mark the progress of a maturing society."[213] If it is the former, then it faces all the problems that the historical tests of the tax immunity cases and the *National League of Cities* cases faced above; if it is the latter, then in articulating this evolution, the Court would be describing contestable values that would expose it to the charge of violating the Frankfurter constraint.

The final technique is Marshall's in *McCulloch* itself. It asks

---

[211] Gary Lawson and Patricia B. Granger, *The "Proper" Scope of Federal Power: A Jurisdictional Interpretation of the Sweeping Clause*, 43 Duke L J 267, 333 (1993).

[212] Id ("An originalist, for example, would ask whether a fully informed public in 1789 would have regarded a particular distribution of governmental power as an 'improper' departure from sound separation of powers principles. Whatever the content of that doctrine may be, however, it is textually incorporated into the Constitution through the Sweeping Clause.").

[213] *Trop v Dulles*, 356 US 86, 101 (1958) (interpreting the Eighth Amendment).

whether the exercise of Congress's Necessary and Proper power is really just a pretext for invading forbidden domains.[214] While some have applied this pretext test to Congress's power generally,[215] in my view, the best reading of Marshall's opinion in *McCulloch* is to see it as a test to limit the necessary and proper power in particular, and not Congress's power generally. So understood, when Congress regulates directly under an enumerated power, its power is "whole," and the Court has no power to limit it because of a view that it has been exercised for an improper purpose.[216] On the other hand, when Congress regulates according to the Necessary and Proper Clause, either because of the textual requirement of "propriety" or because of the need to assure that this clause not become the demise of Congress's limited power, the Court should assure that the invocation of this clause not be for improper ends.[217]

But again, making the Court the police of propriety makes the Court the target of Frankfurter's complaint. The problem is the same as in the other two techniques. In each there is the gap that will sweep in the tensions with the Frankfurter constraint. To judge these matters of degree would be to judge matters seen as inherently policy driven. This is not to say that there is something conceptually impossible about requiring the Court to engage in such an inquiry. Indeed, the Court has done this before.[218] But what undermines this as a technique is the same thing that undermined other "purpose" techniques before: The difficulty of establishing an improper purpose means that the technique is just an effective way to ratify, rather than check, the power of Congress. The rhetorical burden of claiming pretext, given the multiplicity of reasons any legislation is passed, and given the basic questions about what intent means here anyway, means this technique too would likely fail effectively to constrain.

The only choice left open to the Court then was to dissemble;

---

[214] *McCulloch*, 17 US (4 Wheat) at 423.

[215] *Lottery Case*, 188 US at 372 (Fuller dissenting).

[216] See, for example, *McCray*, 195 US at 54–55.

[217] See, for example, *Carter Coal*, 298 US at 317–19 (Hughes concurring).

[218] See, for example, *Dewitt*, 76 US at 44 (1869) ("This consequence is too remote and too uncertain to warrant us in saying that the prohibition is an appropriate and plainly adapted means for carrying into execution the power of laying and collecting taxes.").

to ignore the clause as a way of limiting the reach of the commerce power. If this is a tool, no doubt it is an administrable one. But as a tool for limiting Congress's commerce power, it would also be incomplete. Thus *Lopez*'s second tool, which I discuss in the section below.

COMMERCIAL EFFECTS

The omission of the Necessary and Proper Clause is a necessary move to isolate the commerce question from a more general authority supporting Congress's power. But it alone does not do the work of the opinion. The battle in the future will be over the second tool in the *Lopez* set: the limitation of Congress's "affects interstate commerce" power in contexts where the activities regulated are not commercial.

One should say at the start that the scope and nature of this limitation are not at all clear from the opinion. The Court did not say absolutely that only commercial activities can be reached by the "affects" branch of Congress's "commerce authority" (the third part of Congress's "commerce authority"—that part reaching objects that "substantially affect" interstate commerce). It only indicated that it would be harder to so reach it. But how much harder? What more would be necessary before the Court will allow Congress to reach an activity, not itself commercial, but which affects interstate commerce? The safest reading might be that where the activity is not commercial, then the "aggregation principle" (that allows otherwise insignificant activities to be aggregated into an activity affecting interstate commerce) will not apply.[219] So understood, *Lopez* could be read as a limitation on *Wickard*, limiting *Wickard* to cases where the regulated activity is commercial.[220]

In my view, however, this hole in the opinion is of little real significance. Indeed, we could imagine it being filled with something like a clear statement rule, simply requiring Congress to make clear the links it imagines its statute to draw upon. Far more

---

[219] Compare Robert L. Stern, *That Commerce Which Concerns More States Than One*, 47 Harv L Rev 1335, 1364 n 125 (1934) (describing the necessity of the aggregation doctrine).

[220] See *Wickard v Filburn*, 317 US 111 (1942). This would be consistent with the facts in *Wickard*, though if one adopted Justice Thomas's view of commerce (excluding agriculture), it would not. See *Lopez*, 115 S Ct at 1643 ("As one would expect, the term 'commerce' was used in contradistinction to productive activities such as manufacturing and agriculture." (Thomas concurring)).

significant than this tiny hole is how this commercial/noncommercial distinction will be drawn.

We can best see the problem by focusing on two sorts of characterization problems that will no doubt plague *Lopez* litigation. The first is to characterize the activity that is being regulated. *Lopez* presents the problem adequately enough. If one says that the activity is "possessing a gun near school," then that is certainly not a "commercial" activity—at least that is so when one "injects" the word with a modern meaning. For us, at least, commerce is about making money, even though it is not so clear it had the same meaning for the framers.[221]

But if one defines the activity that narrowly, then it is unclear how, for example, the Civil Rights Act of 1964 gets upheld. For there, one could have defined the activity as "discriminating" and then asked whether discriminating is "commercial or not." Certainly the discriminating has an effect on economic activities, even if the discriminating itself is not commercial. So too, the possession of a gun near schools has an effect on commercial activities— the need to hire more guards, the effect on teachers' pay, etc.— even if the possession itself is not commercial.

The characterization problem is rendered even more plain in a case decided under *Lopez* involving the federal arson statute.[222] The facts in the case clearly established that the criminal act at issue— burning a house—was done for the purpose of defrauding an insurance company, as no doubt most arsons are. Yet Chief Judge Wallace of the Ninth Circuit held that this statute could not reach this case. Even though the statute had a jurisdictional requirement—requiring the government prove that the "residence was 'used in' or 'used in an activity affecting' interstate commerce"— the Ninth Circuit found the connection proven was not significant enough to invoke federal jurisdiction.

In one sense the case makes sense, especially under the market

---

[221] Consider, for example, Shakespeare's usage in Hamlet, Act 3, Scene 1, Ophelia, "Could beauty, my lord, have better commerce than with honesty?" I do not intend, however, to start down the Crosskey road, attempting an account of the meaning of "commerce" at the founding to compete with the quite different meaning Justice Thomas has provided. See Currie, *The Constitution in the Supreme Court, 1789–1888* at 170 n 86 (cited in note 46) (describing Crosskey's views). That two so fundamentally different views of the meaning of the term could be supportable, however, suggests something of the trouble of this particular form of "originalism."

[222] *United States v Pappadopoulos*, 64 F3d 522 (9th Cir 1995).

test for interstate commerce power sketched above.[223] The government had argued that the use of natural gas showed that the house "affected" interstate commerce, since the natural gas was part of interstate commerce. The court held this was not enough, since the link was not "substantial." But from the other side, this was arson for the purpose of insurance fraud. Insurance markets are clearly interstate. Thus if the activity is arson for the purposes of insurance fraud, federal jurisdiction would seem to follow.

The point is this: Not that a line couldn't be drawn, but that the activity of drawing it, across the full range of cases, will be extremely difficult. As lower courts ask the *Lopez* question in a range of cases, the characterization problem will mean that there may well be a large number of conflicts for the Court to resolve. And without any clear principle to resolve them, their resolution will most likely seem to fall afoul the Frankfurter constraint.

But a second characterization problem is more significant. Even if one could easily define the activity being regulated, what is it that determines whether the activity is "commercial" or not?

The opinion offers us nothing in the nature of the activity to look for. Indeed, the Court quite directly concedes that "depending on the level of generality, any activity can be looked upon as commercial."[224] So then what will determine whether the Court chooses to look upon an activity as commercial or not? What is the principle that will separate "commercial" from "commercial," given that "any activity can be looked upon as commercial."

It is here that we begin to see what underlies the opinion, and here that we should feel a certain déjà vu. For throughout the opinion, again, what drives the Court is the notion that if this can be regulated, then anything can, where the "anything" that is most feared is a very particular set of objects: "family law (including marriage, divorce, and child custody)," "a school's curriculum," "every aspect of local schools." What unites this list is what grounded the concurring opinion of Justice Kennedy—that these were activities of "traditional state concern."[225] What is drawing this line between "commercial" and "non-commercial but capable of being viewed as commercial" is simply the old line drawn and

---

[223] See above at note 28.

[224] *Lopez*, 115 S Ct at 1633.

[225] Id at 1638, citing *New York II*, 112 S Ct at 2417–22.

undermined in *National League of Cities*, namely, the line focusing on objects of traditional state concern.

This is an understandable line to draw; it is an understandable distinction to grasp. When first conceived, it has a certain plausibility that one could be forgiven for imagining, at least initially, could support a constitutional distinction.

But it is too late in this game to forgive the Court for this move. For over and over, in a wide range of federalism contexts, just this line has proved itself Maginot.[226] There is no thing out there called "tradition" that lower courts can look to to sort out just what objects of regulation should be federal and which local. And because there is nothing out there to guide the courts, courts will be guided to different conclusions. As these differences percolate, and thrust themselves on the Court to resolve, the results cannot help but seem, as they were before *Garcia*, inconsistent. There is no doubt that the possession of a small amount of marijuana will be "seen to be" commercial, and national, and plainly within the scope of the commerce power, while the possession of a gun is not. But at some point conflicts like this will not be sustainable; the rhetorical burden will be too great. And once again, the Court will be forced into a retreat.

USABLE TOOLS

What the Court's opinion does then is in two parts: It first shifts the focus of the power inquiry away from the unlimitable Necessary and Proper Clause, to the more manageable "commerce" inquiry; it then uses this more narrow question about commerce to construct a test that limits that regulation of commerce. While the first part of the test is manageable enough, the second returns us to a hopeless inquiry about the nature of "commercial," an inquiry I want to suggest, that will cross the line of the Frankfurter constraint.[227]

---

[226] Justice Fried makes the same point at Fried, 109 Harv L Rev at 44–45 (cited in note 29).

[227] And to the extent that it does not violate the Frankfurter constraint, we might wonder about whether it will have any significant effect. The signals are that it won't. Compare the decision issued just days after *Lopez, United States v Robertson*, 115 S Ct 1732 (1995) (per curiam), where the Court held that so long as even a minimal amount of commerce occurred across state lines, that was sufficient to bring it within the interstate commerce power. Only intrastate activities said to have an effect on interstate commerce have been subjected to this limiting interpretation. A similar conclusion can be drawn from *Allied-Bruce Terminix Cos. v Dobson*, 115 S Ct 834 (1995), where the Court allowed federal com-

My aim in this last part is to suggest tools that might have helped. I offer them here more to suggest the kind of radicalness that conservatism, or fidelity, requires. For the problem with the rule of *Lopez* is that it is far too timid, and by being timid it cannot protect itself against being undermined over time. What is needed is something less direct, but more manageable.

Here are four examples, each more artificial than the tools used by the Court, but each, I suggest, also more stable than the tools selected by the Court. I do not intend to defend the examples at any length; I offer them only as suggestive—but suggestive of the kind of enterprise that the Court must engage if its enterprise of translation is to succeed.

Clear statement of economic effect. The simplest rule parallels *Gregory*.[228] It simply requires that when regulating in an area of primarily intrastate economic activity, Congress make plain the economic effect that it estimates a statute will have on interstate commerce. The Court thus requires proof that Congress considered whether the issues legislated about are truly national. To be effective, the requirement needs to do very little more than signal that in the process of enacting the statute a proper showing had been made; ex post rationalizations would not suffice.

Now this tool will be criticized as an invasion on the legislative sphere. This it is. But any clear statement requirement is just such an invasion, though a far smaller invasion than an absolute limit. If the Court can say that certain areas cannot be regulated by Congress, I don't understand why it can't say that those areas can be regulated, but only if Congress shows that it has considered just why.

The value of a clear statement rule is its simplicity, and that its indirect effect, on both sides of that balance, would be to increase consideration of federalism interests. It is a tool, therefore, that can increase this consideration within the Frankfurter constraint.

In the context of the Commerce Clause, however, one might wonder about the effectiveness of this rule. *Lopez* itself raises this question: After the court of appeals had struck the statute in *Lopez*,

---

merce power to reach a local termite-protection plan bought by an Alabama homeowner from a multistate termite-control company. See the discussion of these cases, and a more general account of *Lopez*'s limited effect, in Deborah Jones Merritt, *Commerce!*, 94 Mich L Rev 674, 728–38 (1995). Compare Fried, 109 Harv L Rev at 41–45 (cited in note 29).

[228] 501 US 452 (1991).

but before the Supreme Court had a chance to rule on it, Congress passed "findings" for insertion into the statute.[229] Because it will always be easy simply to state the existence of some connection, one might wonder whether the statute would have any regulative effect at all.

The argument that a slight burden is no burden is not, in my view, a fair argument. More importantly, we can observe that in the related context of Eleventh Amendment jurisprudence, the slight burden has had some effect.[230] Whether it is enough of an effect goes to the question whether other tools should be used as well. Some of those might be as follows.

Self-imposed limits. An often forgotten part of *Miranda* was the Court's offer of compromise: The Court's offer that the states could evade the requirements imposed by the Court if they simply enacted a better system to protect the constitutional right at issue.[231] Oddly, no state has taken up the challenge.[232] But that is no reason why the Court couldn't make the same offer to Congress in the Commerce Clause context. In the context of commerce regulation, the Court could say to Congress that it will strike statutes regulating primarily intrastate activities, so long as Congress does not adopt some other regime for measuring the significance of an interstate effect. If Congress does establish such a regime—for example, an agency like the CBO, established for the purpose of tracking interstate effects—and if Congress limited its regulation to activities that affected only a specified level of interstate effects, then the Court could defer to the judgments of both the agency and Congress.

This was the strategy of the NLRB for limiting its jurisdiction under the NLRA. The NLRB announced guidelines for its jurisdiction that were tied to its view about industries that actually had a "substantial" effect on interstate commerce. While it believed

---

[229] *Lopez*, 115 S Ct 1632 n 4.

[230] See the discussion of William Eskridge in *Dynamic Statutory Interpretation* at 285–94 (cited in note 18).

[231] *Miranda v Arizona*, 384 US 436, 490 (1966) ("Congress and the States are free to develop their own safeguards for the privilege, so long as they are fully as effective as those described above in informing accused persons of their right of silence. . . .").

[232] The federal government has, but its lead has been ignored. See Title II of the Omnibus Crime Control and Safe Streets Act of 1968, 18 USC 3501 (1988), discussed in Craig Goldblatt, *Harmless Error as Constitutional Common Law: Congress's Power to Reverse Arizona v Fulminante*, 60 U Chi L Rev 985, 990 n 27 (1993).

these guidelines below a constitutional minimum, the agency restrained itself from exceeding the limits of the guidelines,[233] in part simply to signal that it was taking the limitations seriously.

In a similar way, the Court could shift to Congress the duty of defining "substantial" in a principled way, and defer to its judgment when it had established the mechanism for so measuring it. Such a mechanism might include primary jurisdiction in a commerce court that measures the significance of a regulation and its effect on commerce. But whatever the test, the aim would be to give Congress an inducement to limit its jurisdiction along principled lines. And it would create this incentive through the use of a rule that simply examined whether a mechanism to induce consideration had been adopted. This sort of monitoring the Court is quite capable of doing; and with this sort of monitoring, the Court could effect greater consideration of federalism interests.

Allowing opt-out. The third technique is perhaps more extreme, yet it too would induce greater respect for federalism interests without requiring the impossible of the Court. We can approach the idea indirectly by asking, What exactly was the state interest trampled by the federal government in *Lopez*? Was any state actually impaired in the exercise of its autonomy by this rule? Was there really a state that wanted to permit gun possession within 1,000 feet of a school, but which was disallowed by Congress's statute?[234]

To ask the question is to raise what is perhaps the oddest part of the *Lopez* debate. For it is not at all clear what state interest is being interfered with by *this* federalization of state criminal law. Indeed, such federalization gives plenty of benefits to the states.[235]

---

[233] See Bernard D. Meltzer and Stanley D. Henderson, *Labor Law: Cases, Materials and Problems* 699–700 (Little, Brown, 3d ed 1985) ("In 1950, the Board, in order to conserve its resources and to reduce the confusion of litigants and its own staff, began to publish 'jurisdictional yardsticks,' which prescribed various monetary minima for the exercise of jurisdiction. These yardsticks were revised in 1954 and again in 1958, with a view to expanding the Board's effective jurisdiction and, concomitantly, reducing the no-man's-land in which state authority was inoperative even though the Board declined to act."); NLRB, *Twenty-Third Annual Report of the National Labor Relations Board for the Fiscal Year Ended June 30, 1958* 8–9 (US GPO, 1959) (setting jurisdictional standards); NLRB, *Twenty-Fifth Annual Report of the National Labor Relations Board for the Fiscal Year Ended June 30, 1960* 19–20 (US GPO, 1961).

[234] Forty-two states, including Texas, have criminal penalties for the possession of firearms in and around schools. See *Leading Cases*, 109 Harv L Rev at 112 n 6 (cited in note 189).

[235] As examples of federal statutes that don't hurt state interests, see *Brooks v United States*, 267 US 432 (1925) (banning interstate transportation of stolen motor vehicles).

Federal prisons now hold many criminals that would otherwise burden state prisons. Federal prosecution removes many criminals from backlogged state proceedings. And federal enforcement supplements state enforcement. If the FBI's fingerprint lab is not an invasion on state autonomy, just why is the statute in *Lopez?* What is it taking from state control that states would really want to have?

What these questions might suggest is that there is a distinction between federal statutes that are true conflicts with state interests, and federal statutes that are not. Or alternatively, it might suggest that the invasions of some federal statutes are harmless, while others are not. One might then imagine a regime that tried to distinguish the harmless from the rest, and that allowed the federal invasion where the effect on states interests was harmless.

Sorting such interests directly would be a clear violation of the Frankfurter constraint. For to identify which conflicts were really conflicts would require the Court to identify which exercises of state autonomy were true, or necessary, or desired, as distinguished from which were not. But to do this would require the Court to embrace a normative conception of the proper domains of regulation, far too contestable for the Court to make any doctrine stand upon.

Thus the question then becomes whether an indirect sorting is possible. Why not this: The Court could say that it will presumptively uphold any federal statute that allows for a state opt-out provision. If a state passes a statute opting out from a federal law, then that law would not be enforced within that state. But if a state did not opt out, this would be good evidence (not great but good) that the statute did not invade a substantial interest of the state.

Thus, we could imagine some statutes where states would truly like to experiment—for example, drug laws. Some states may very much want to experiment with limited legalization as a way to lesson the secondary effects of the drug trade. And in those cases, we could imagine states passing opt-out statutes to allow such experimentation. But I doubt that any state would pass the "permit children to carry guns within 1,000 feet of schools" law, or a pro-arson law. For here again, no state interest is undermined by this federal law.

Now of course, "no state interest" is not quite right. There is an autonomy interest that is lost whenever the federal government crosses into state legislative domains. Moreover, we might think the framers' design was to force states to legislate in a broad domain, to keep local government vital.[236] On this view, the mere consent to federal regulation should not be enough. What the opt-out regime allows is the acquiescence of states in legislative judgments by the federal government, rather than forcing the states to act on their own. And one might well say, this shifts the original balance, and that rather than allow this shift, the Court should act to force the states to be free.

It should, I would agree, if there were a way that it could. But what federalism must face is something conservatives in other contexts are quite quick to assert: that there is only so much that a court can do. What a court must do is adopt usable tools to a fidelity end. These tools will be different from the framers' tools, no doubt. But so what. To say that the tools cannot be different is to say that the fidelity game is off. That would certainly be better than this cycle of remembering, and forgetting.

Jurisdiction stripping. One final tool might mark out the boundary of the extreme, but it follows from the considerations that we first encountered when discussing the source of the Frankfurter constraint. This is the idea of stripping jurisdiction over Commerce Clause claims from lower federal courts, and vesting it in one court, a commerce court, to pursue a more subtle and complex strategy for limiting Congress.[237]

Two thoughts might suggest this somewhat counterintuitive technique, both following from what should be an obvious point about Supreme Court control over congressional jurisdiction—namely, that such control needs to be exercised selectively, and rarely. The first is a direct application of the capacity point made above.[238] The problem with any complex or artificial rule for limiting congressional jurisdiction is that it cannot be reliably applied by the federal courts. Federal courts applying the rule will inevitably be drawn into conflict; and because the boundaries drawn by the Supreme Court are inevitably artificial—in the sense that to

---

[236] This was Tocqueville's view. See Tocqueville, *Democracy in America* at 158–70 (cited in note 1).

[237] In principle, it would be better to vest the jurisdiction in the Supreme Court, but the limits on original jurisdiction would preclude this. See *Marbury v Madison*, 5 US (1 Cranch) 137 (1803).

[238] See notes and text accompanying notes 136–43.

follow them requires a common understanding that this legal culture cannot rely upon existing—the Court, as in *Garcia*, will be
forced to confront the awkward conflicts the lower courts yield.
Moreover, because these cases raise questions about the application
of federal law, they are not cases where conflict can be ignored.
Conflicts raised here must be resolved by the Supreme Court.

The second thought is a bit more strategic. It might be that
given this inevitable conflict, the best strategy to limit Congress's
exercise of jurisdiction is a strategy that simply induces Congress
to consider the scope of its jurisdiction when legislating. The best
way for the Court to do this might be through the "bolt out of
the blue"[239] technique—a somewhat random and not fully clear
act by the Court striking down a statute of Congress that seems to
go "too far." Such a test, while protective of federalism interests,
obviously doesn't generalize, and hence can't be followed by lower
courts. But the very fact that it might be applied would induce
Congress into a more reflective mode of legislating. Then subsequently, the Court could uphold the statute when convinced that
interests were properly accounted.

The problem with following this second strategy, given the present diffusion of jurisdiction, is lower courts. While one court
might adequately limit a "gone too far" rule, it would be difficult
for lower courts consistently to apply just such a rule. In the present structure, any rule such as the "gone too far" rule that the
Supreme Court would announce is likely to be used by a lower
court, and hence inconsistently used by the lower courts, with the
consequence again that the Court may be forced to consider cases
it would be better for it to avoid.

Both thoughts lead to the suggestion that Congress merely strip
from the lower courts the power to address the constitutionality
of a federal statute under the commerce power, leaving that determination to one court alone, or alternatively, to one court (a commerce court) with very limited Supreme Court review. By so limiting jurisdiction, then, that court could articulate and apply rules
with less fear that the rules would get out of hand. It could therefore develop a richer and more effective set of rules for con-

---

[239] This is David Currie's view of much of the early limitations imposed by the Fuller
and White Courts. See Currie, *The Constitution in the Supreme Court, 1888–1986* at 101
(cited in note 46).

straining federal legislative jurisdiction. Hence by so limiting jurisdiction, the richness and power of judicial review in a post-realist
legal culture could be increased.

The justification for such a limitation should be plain enough.
What drives it is simply the practical cost of having federal statutes
struck in a piecemeal way. What the Court would be doing would
be balancing the interests of individuals to have local courts determine this constitutional question, against the state interests that
an effective rule to protect state autonomy be enforced. If the
choice is between a regime (the pre-*Lopez* regime perhaps) that
gave every court the power to strike an act of Congress, but under
a test that made every statute constitutional, and a rule that effectively limited the power to strike laws of Congress to the Supreme
Court, but under a test that was more restrictive and more protective of state autonomy interests, the latter result would dominate
the former regime.

What these four rules have in common is that each has a predictable effect (advancing interests of state autonomy); each can
be implemented at minimal judicial cost (since they don't require
judgments that fall afoul the Frankfurter constraint); and each
therefore helps translate federalism. What they also have in common is that they have as much relation to the text of the Constitution as the *Miranda* rule has to the text of the Constitution. They
are plainly made up, in the sense of not deriving from the text of
the Constitution.

But if federalism in particular, and translation in general, is to
succeed, we must get over this obsession about what is "made up."
We have no choice, if fidelity is our aim, but to make up limits that
better translate founding commitments. For the plain language of
our Constitution today abstracted from the context of the founding
yields a Constitution quite inconsistent with the vision of the framers. A plain reading of the Constitution's text yields federal power
far beyond what they imagined, and government power generally
far beyond what they imagined. Textualism gives us a far more
statist Constitution than the framers gave us. And if our commitment to fidelity is genuine and general, then what we need is a
technique, in both the individual and states' rights contexts, that
can properly restrict a framing balance.

The balance can't be restruck directly. The system can't depend
upon the Court to make judgments that cannot help but appear,

in context, political. Thus what these four rules do, and what many of the rules of the Warren Court do as well, is give us indirect ways to pursue a target that the courts can't pursue directly. These tools are made up; but the end to which they are directed is quite genuine.

CONCLUSION

There was a time when the limits of federalism were provided by the context within which federalism disputes were fought, just as there was a time when the crude technology of searching provided effective limits on the scope of government's power to invade individual privacy. Both contexts provided part of the support to an important substantive value enshrined in the constitutional text.

Both contexts changed. The question in each then became whether the Court would take steps to supplement what the context used to provide; whether it will take steps to provide through affirmative limits on governmental power what before was provided by implicit limits. In both cases, the question is whether when contexts render gaps in the original constitutional design, the Court will act to remedy these gaps.

My argument in this essay has been, first, that this has been precisely the practice of the Court in the context of federalism: That its aim has been to provide through implied limits on federal and state power something of a correction to assure a balance between both. This practice I have called translation, and I have traced something of its history.

But I have also suggested that this practice is constrained by a fundamental requirement that has been constant in the history of judicial review—the need for the Court, in differing ways, to avoid actions that appear, in context, political. What the Court must do is find limits on governmental power in the name of fidelity, subject to this constraint on its constructive role.

While *Lopez* is properly within this tradition, I have argued that it has not fully realized this limit. For just as Chief Justice Rehnquist did before in *National League*, *Lopez* launches a practice of limitation that will be unstable. The lines *Lopez* draws will not cut up the world of federal law in a predictable or usable manner. And as the inconsistencies increase, the feasibility of continuing this rule will be undermined.

A better set of limitations would have been more creative. As I have argued, the Court will never succeed in its efforts at construction unless it acknowledges the dynamic of construction. Only when it acknowledges the creative in the effort of translation will it begin to think more strategically, and successfully, about how federalism values are to be advanced. I have suggested four different rules here that may be more successful at advancing federalism's interest, subject to the constraint of the Frankfurter constraint. There are no doubt others. The only doubt is whether the Court's commitment to fidelity is strong enough to allow it to see them.

LISA HEINZERLING

THE COMMERCIAL CONSTITUTION

At least the Commerce Clause gives the Justices steady work. Indeed, few constitutional principles give the Court as regular or as easy business as the rule that state and local governments may not discriminate against interstate commerce. Once the Court finds that a law facially discriminates against interstate commerce, the law is as good as finished.[1] The Court does formally ask whether the government has shown that it has no evenhanded way of serving a valid interest. But this version of strict scrutiny indeed appears "strict in theory, but fatal in fact":[2] the modern Court has upheld only one law in the face of it.[3]

The Court's nondiscrimination principle has enjoyed remarkable support, both on and off the Court. Decisions applying this principle generally have provoked little disagreement on the part of individual Justices,[4] and legal scholars have overwhelmingly ap-

Lisa Heinzerling is Associate Professor of Law, Georgetown University Law Center.

AUTHOR'S NOTE: I am grateful to Peter Byrne, Steven Goldberg, Vicki Jackson, Milton Regan, Louis Michael Seidman, Girardeau Spann, Jane Stromseth, and Mark Tushnet for helpful comments. James Oleske provided excellent research assistance.

[1] For recent examples, see *Wyoming v Oklahoma*, 502 US 437 (1992); *Chemical Waste Management v Hunt*, 504 US 334 (1992); *Fort Gratiot Sanitary Landfill v Michigan Department of Natural Resources*, 504 US 353 (1992); *Oregon Waste Systems v Department of Environmental Quality*, 114 S Ct 1345 (1994); *C & A Carbone v Town of Clarkstown*, 114 S Ct 1677 (1994); *West Lynn Creamery v Healy*, 114 S Ct 2205 (1994). For an earlier, influential exposition, see *Philadelphia v New Jersey*, 437 US 617 (1978).

[2] Compare *Adarand Constructors v Pena*, 115 S Ct 2097, 2117 (1995) (in context of race-based classifications, plurality "wish[es] to dispel the notion that strict scrutiny is 'strict in theory, but fatal in fact' "), quoting *Fullilove v Klutznick*, 448 US 448, 519 (1980) (Marshall concurring in judgment).

[3] *Maine v Taylor*, 477 US 131 (1986) (upholding ban on importation of out-of-state baitfish).

[4] The main exception is Chief Justice Rehnquist, who has dissented in all of the recent cases invalidating laws found to discriminate against interstate commerce. *Wyoming v Okla-*

proved it.[5] To the extent that some scholars have disagreed with the Court's interpretation of the Commerce Clause as a limitation on the power of states and local governments, most have saved their fire for the Court's analysis of nondiscriminatory laws found to impose, unwittingly, undue burdens on interstate commerce.[6] And those who have disagreed with applying the nondiscrimination principle under the rubric of the Commerce Clause have managed to find the very same nondiscrimination principle in a separate, perhaps conveniently enlarged, constitutional provision.[7]

This unusual consensus cannot be attributed to the clarity of the constitutional text, nor to the force of history. As for the constitutional text, the Commerce Clause is perhaps most famous for what it does not say. It does not condemn state or local laws that burden, or even discriminate against, interstate commerce. And it does not give the Supreme Court the authority to regulate interstate commerce. It gives this authority only to Congress.[8] As a result, it took the Court itself some time to sort out what the grant of power to Congress meant for the power of the states,[9] and even

---

homa, supra note 1 at 461; *Chemical Waste Management*, supra note 1 at 349; *Fort Gratiot Sanitary Landfill*, supra note 1 at 368; *Oregon Waste Systems*, supra note 1 at 1355; *Carbone*, supra note 1 at 1692; *West Lynn Creamery*, supra note 1 at 2221.

[5] See, e.g., Mark Tushnet, *Rethinking the Dormant Commerce Clause*, 1979 Wis L Rev 125; Julian N. Eule, *Laying the Dormant Commerce Clause to Rest*, 91 Yale L J 425, 462 n 202 (1982); Donald H. Regan, *The Supreme Court and State Protectionism: Making Sense of the Dormant Commerce Clause*, 84 Mich L Rev 1091, 1093 (1986); Daniel A. Farber, *State Regulation and the Dormant Commerce Clause*, 3 Const Comm 395, 396 (1986); Michael P. Healy, *The Preemption of State Hazardous and Solid Waste Regulations: The Dormant Commerce Clause Awakens Once More*, 43 J Urban & Contemp L 177, 187 (1993).

[6] See sources cited in preceding note. Two rare exceptions to the statement in the text are Lino A. Graglia, *The Supreme Court and the American Common Market*, in A. Dan Tarlock, ed, *Regulation, Federalism, and Interstate Commerce* (1981) (absence of textual or historical support for invalidation of state laws under Commerce Clause fatal to Court's current doctrine), and Richard D. Friedman, *Putting the Dormancy Doctrine Out of Its Misery*, 12 Cardozo L Rev 1745 (1991) (arguing that Congress or federal agencies, not the courts, should determine whether state laws unjustifiably discriminate against, or unduly interfere with, interstate commerce).

[7] The favorite alternative site for the nondiscrimination principle is the Privileges and Immunities Clause—expanded to apply to corporations. See, e.g., Martin H. Redish and Shane V. Nugent, *The Dormant Commerce Clause and the Constitutional Balance of Federalism*, 1987 Duke L J 569, 606–12; Mark P. Gergen, *The Selfish State and the Market*, 66 Tex L Rev 1097, 1117–18 (1988); Eule, supra note 5 at 446–55.

[8] "The Congress shall have Power . . . [t]o regulate Commerce . . . among the several States." Art I, § 8, cl 3.

[9] For a concise history, see Tushnet, supra note 5 at 126–30, 150–53; see also David P. Currie, *The Constitution in the Supreme Court: The First Hundred Years* 171–83, 222–36 (1985).

those scholars who are quite enthusiastic about the Court's current approach find themselves almost apologizing for the silence of the relevant text on this issue.[10] As for history, judicial opinions and academic commentary frequently cite the unhappy experience with discriminatory trade barriers among the states under the Articles of Confederation as a principal motivation for calling the Constitutional Convention, and as evidence that the Court is right to undo such barriers today.[11] In fact, however, historical accounts of the events preceding and accompanying the adoption of the Commerce Clause point in different directions.[12]

These brief observations do not, of course, conclusively establish or refute the pedigree of the nondiscrimination principle as a matter of constitutional text or history. They do, however, demonstrate that the matter is complicated and ambiguous enough that these common tools of constitutional interpretation cannot explain the enthusiasm with which the nondiscrimination principle has been embraced.[13]

The widespread endorsement of a judicially enforceable rule that state and local governments may not discriminate against interstate commerce appears, instead, to arise from the widespread perception that this rule is a very good idea. Though almost every-

---

[10] See, e.g., Richard B. Collins, *Economic Union as a Constitutional Value*, 63 NYU L Rev 43, 51–52 (1988). Some argue that it is too late in the day to credit the formalist objection, based on the absence of clear constitutional text, to the Court's long-standing interpretation of the Commerce Clause as implicitly limiting the power of states. Daniel A. Farber and Robert E. Hudec, *Free Trade and the Regulatory State: A GATT's-Eye View of the Dormant Commerce Clause*, 47 Vand L Rev 1401, 1408 (1994).

[11] See, e.g., *H P Hood & Sons v DuMond*, 336 US 525, 533 (1949); *Hughes v Oklahoma*, 441 US 322, 325–26 (1979); *West Lynn Creamery*, supra note 1 at 2211 n 9; *Oklahoma Tax Comm'n v Jefferson Lines*, 115 S Ct 1331, 1336 (1995); Eule, supra note 5 at 430.

[12] Regarding the history prior to the adoption of the Commerce Clause, compare Edmund W. Kitch, *Regulation and the American Common Market*, in A. Dan Tarlock, ed, *Regulation, Federalism, and Interstate Commerce* 15–19 (1981) (history of trade barriers under Articles of Confederation has been exaggerated) and Charles L. Black, Jr., *Perspectives on the American Common Market*, in A. Dan Tarlock, ed, *Regulation, Federalism, and Interstate Commerce* 61–62 (1981) with, e.g., *Hughes v Oklahoma*, supra note 11 at 325–26 ("economic Balkanization . . . had plagued relations among the Colonies and later among the States under the Articles of Confederation"). Regarding the history of the adoption of the Clause, compare Redish and Nugent, supra note 7 at 586–87 n 109 (interpreting letter written by James Madison to indicate that Commerce Clause was intended as grant of power to Congress, not as a grant of power to the Court to invalidate state and local laws interfering with commerce), with *West Lynn Creamery*, supra note 1 at 2211 n 9 (citing same letter from Madison as support for Court's authority to strike down laws that discriminate against interstate commerce). For general discussion, see Collins, supra note 10 at 52–55, 57–58.

[13] For a fuller discussion of this idea, see Friedman, supra note 6 at 1747–53.

one seems to agree that the nondiscrimination principle serves an important purpose, there is some disagreement about precisely what that purpose is. The three standard candidates—each of which has been endorsed at various points by the Supreme Court and each of which enjoys substantial scholarly support—are economic efficiency, representation reinforcement, and national unity. I will argue that the Court's nondiscrimination principle serves none of these objectives.

Three cases decided during the 1993 Term, all invalidating state or local laws found to discriminate against interstate commerce, illustrate my point. Each decision showcases at least one of the standard rationales for the nondiscrimination principle, although the goal of economic efficiency has begun to play the dominant role in the Court's analysis. However, as I will explain, the Court's rationales do not fit its results.

The Court's nondiscrimination principle does not promote economic efficiency in individual cases (or if it does, it does so only sporadically and fortuitously), because the Court does not even attempt a serious accounting of the benefits and costs of laws that discriminate against interstate commerce. The Court dismisses as illegitimate the benefits to in-staters that derive from discriminating against interstate commerce *because* it is interstate commerce, and assumes costs to out-of-staters based on the mere fact of such discrimination. By starting from the assumption that discrimination against interstate commerce is inappropriate, the Court pretermits a responsible analysis of whether the benefits of a specific discriminatory law are worth its costs. Yet the Court also labors under institutional constraints—such as limited fact-gathering and one-law-at-a-time review—that impede its ability to perform a more reliable individualized cost-benefit analysis, had it the inclination to do so.

The Court's formalist approach might nevertheless be justified if it achieves efficiency across the run of cases, despite a failure to do so in isolated instances. This raises the question whether there is reason to believe that laws that discriminate against interstate commerce are, as a group, more likely than not to be inefficient. At this point, the efficiency-based rationale for the nondiscrimination principle blends into the process-based representation-reinforcement rationale. The process-based justification for the nondiscrimination principle seeks to protect underrepresented outsiders from the exploitation of represented insiders.[14] From the perspective of efficiency, this justification might support a rigid rule against discrimination because when costs are exported rather than internalized, there may be good reason to believe they will consistently exceed benefits. Discrimination is, however, a poor indicator of actual burdens on outsiders; a discriminatory tax on out-of-state goods, for example, may ultimately burden in-state consumers more than out-of-state businesses. Thus it is wrong to equate discrimination with wholesale externalization of costs. Moreover, the Court has so enlarged the concept of "discrimination" that it now embraces a law shown to harm no one except those inside the jurisdiction that enacted it,[15] substantially weakening the case for judicial intervention on behalf of underrepresented groups. In addition, the groups thought to be underrepresented in the political process—nonvoters from other states—may often turn out to be influential lobbyists, campaign contributors, and political organizers, which also undermines the need for judicial intervention on their behalf. In short, the process-based theory fails to justify an unbending rule against discrimination as a means either to promote efficiency or to combat political underrepresentation.

Finally, the nondiscrimination principle does not ensure that state and local governments will eschew preferences for those within their jurisdiction, and view their relevant community as the nation, rather than the state or county or town. For this purpose, the nondiscrimination principle is both too small and too big. It is too small because it does not, as currently conceived, disapprove all preferences for inside commerce at the expense of outside commerce.[16] State and local governments may favor their own citizens when they participate in the market; they *must* refrain from considering impacts on noncitizens in some regulatory settings; and they (probably) may favor their own citizens in distributing subsidies

---

[14] This is a version of the representation-reinforcement theory of judicial review suggested by Justice Harlan Stone in *United States v Carolene Products Co.*, 304 US 144, 152 n 4 (1938).

[15] See Section II.B.

[16] The Court now appears to view limits on out-of-town or out-of-county articles of commerce as suspiciously as limits on out-of-state commerce. *Carbone*, supra note 1 (invalidating limits on out-of-town waste processors); *Fort Gratiot Sanitary Landfill*, supra note 1 (invalidating limits on waste generated outside county). For this reason, my discussion pertains to discrimination at each of these levels (town, county, state), and I often refer to the protected articles of commerce as "outside" commerce—meaning they originate outside the jurisdiction attempting to regulate them.

from general tax revenues. Each of these practices reinforces the perception that the relevant community is not the nation, but the state or county or town, and thus undermines the national unity the nondiscrimination principle supposedly celebrates. If the purpose of the nondiscrimination principle is to forbid a certain kind of governmental classification (one based on outsider status), the nondiscrimination principle is also too big. A similar kind of purpose lies at the heart of the Equal Protection Clause, and yet there, unlike in the Commerce Clause setting, the Court looks to see whether the plaintiff has suffered a personal injury as a result of a discriminatory governmental classification.[17] No explanation has emerged as to why the Commerce Clause's nondiscrimination norm should relax this standing requirement.

Thus the nondiscrimination principle fails to serve two of the purposes asserted in favor of it, economic efficiency and representation reinforcement. Moreover, the Court's embrace of the protectionist impulse in some settings, and its casual treatment of injury, cannot be explained by a desire to promote national unity through the disapproval of preferences for inside commerce. What, then, does explain the nondiscrimination principle?

The answer is that the Court's nondiscrimination principle promotes a certain vision of the proper role of government. The Court's concept of discrimination embodies a preference for markets over regulation, and its view of what counts as "regulation" rests on undefended assumptions—reminiscent of the *Lochner* period, when forced departures from the free market as shaped by common-law entitlements were constitutionally suspect but the common-law entitlements were not—about what counts as government action and what as inaction. Since these substantive preferences are unarticulated in the Court's cases, the Court has not even attempted to justify its decisions as a matter of substantive due process. Because such a justification likely would sound the same themes—economic efficiency, representation reinforcement, and national unity—as the Court has developed under the Commerce Clause, and because these justifications have proved so inadequate in that context, I conclude that the Court would be unable to justify the nondiscrimination principle as a matter of substantive due process.

---

[17] *United States v Hays*, 115 S Ct 2431, 2436 (1995).

Thus the nondiscrimination principle not only is not compelled by the Court's text or history, it also does not serve the purposes that have been asserted to justify it. This should be enough to convince both originalists and nonoriginalists alike that the nondiscrimination principle ought to be abandoned, and that decisions about the proper scope of state and local regulation ought to be left where they would lie in the absence of some reason for judicial intervention—in the state and local political branches. To put the point directly: the Supreme Court should stop invalidating state and local laws that explicitly discriminate against interstate commerce—including such classic barriers to trade as tariffs and embargoes.

I. Discrimination

Last spring, for the first time in almost 60 years, the Supreme Court held that a federal law exceeded the scope of power granted Congress under the Commerce Clause.[18] While this ruling attracted a great deal of attention, another controversial part of the Court's Commerce Clause jurisprudence has been quietly developing for more than 100 years under the so-called "dormant" Commerce Clause. The dormant or "negative" aspect of the Commerce Clause denies states and local governments "the power unjustifiably to discriminate against or burden the interstate flow of articles of commerce."[19] When the Court finds that a state or local law facially discriminates against interstate commerce, it requires the government to show that it could not have achieved the same, legitimate ends with a nondiscriminatory law.[20] The Court approaches nondiscriminatory laws affecting commerce very differently. It considers their benefits and burdens, and asks whether the benefits are so fleeting or illusory that they signal a protectionist purpose.[21] Undoubtedly as a consequence of this more forgiving

---

[18] *United States v Lopez*, 115 S Ct 1624 (1995).

[19] *Oregon Waste Systems*, supra note 1 at 1349.

[20] See, e.g., *New Energy Co. of Indiana v Limbach*, 486 US 269, 278 (1988).

[21] For the most famous formulation of the Court's standard, see *Pike v Bruce Church*, 397 US 137, 142 (1970), whose ultimate progenitor was *Southern Pacific v Arizona*, 325 US 761 (1945).

test, many laws subject to this balancing analysis have survived the Court's review.[22]

In its 1993 Term, the Supreme Court struck down three different state and local laws under the Commerce Clause. In each case, the Court's work began and ended with the Court's determination that the law in question discriminated against interstate commerce. And each case brought the Court another step closer to the principle that *any* state or local tampering with the free operation of commercial markets is "discrimination" barred by the Commerce Clause.

In *Oregon Waste Systems v Department of Environmental Quality,*[23] the Court considered an Oregon law calling for a "surcharge" on imported solid waste—solid waste disposed of within, but generated outside, Oregon's borders. The state's environmental agency had set the disposal fee for out-of-state waste at $2.25 per ton, based on its calculation of the costs to Oregon of disposing of out-of-state waste "not otherwise paid for" under other state laws. This was $1.40 higher than the state's fee for the disposal of solid waste generated inside Oregon.[24]

Writing for the Court, Justice Thomas had no trouble finding Oregon's surcharge to be discriminatory. To reach this conclusion, it was enough to report that the "statutory determinant" of the disposal fee to be charged for a given ton of waste ($2.25 or $.85) was the waste's state of origin.[25]

In deciding that the law was facially discriminatory—and thus almost inevitably doomed[26]—the Court deemed irrelevant both its purpose and its actual effect.[27] As to the law's effect, the Court

---

[22] For a catalog of the recent cases, and an argument that the Court has lately been more apt to uphold nondiscriminatory state and local laws that burden interstate commerce, see Amy M. Petragnani, *The Dormant Commerce Clause: On Its Last Leg,* 57 Albany L Rev 1215 (1994).

[23] 114 S Ct 1345 (1994).

[24] Id at 1348 & n 2.

[25] Id at 1350.

[26] The Court observed: "The State's burden of justification is so heavy that 'facial discrimination by itself may be a fatal defect.' " Id at 1351, quoting *Hughes v Oklahoma,* supra note 11 at 337.

[27] 114 S Ct at 1350 ("the purpose of, or justification for, a law has no bearing on whether it is facially discriminatory"); id at n 4 ("the degree of a differential burden or charge on interstate commerce 'is of no relevance to the determination whether a State has discriminated against interstate commerce,' " quoting *Wyoming v Oklahoma,* supra note 1 at 455).

noted only that the plaintiffs were involved in transporting or disposing of out-of-state waste. It did not ask whether the surcharge had hurt the plaintiffs' business, or whether it had generally reduced interstate shipments of waste.[28] By Chief Justice Rehnquist's estimate in his dissenting opinion, the effect of the surcharge was an increased cost of approximately 14 cents per week for the average nonresident.[29] Even this cost was uncertain: Oregon did not require landfill operators to charge the costs of the surcharge to out-of-state waste generators, but left them free to spread the costs of the surcharge among all generators, inside and outside Oregon, as long as they remitted the appropriate payment to the state.[30]

Because it held Oregon's surcharge to be discriminatory, the Court required the state to show that the surcharge served a legitimate purpose that could not be served by an evenhanded fee.[31] Oregon might have attempted to show, the Court suggested, that the costs of disposing of out-of-state waste were higher than those for in-state waste, or that out-of-state waste was more dangerous than in-state waste. The state had attempted neither showing.[32]

To this point, *Oregon Waste Systems* was a reprise of the Court's decision two Terms before in *Chemical Waste Management v Hunt*.[33] There, the Court invalidated an Alabama hazardous waste law that, like Oregon's scheme for household waste, charged almost three times more for the disposal of out-of-state hazardous waste than for hazardous waste generated within Alabama.[34] The difference between the two cases is that in *Oregon Waste Systems*, the state explicitly set out to defend its law on the basis of administrative findings that the surcharge for out-of-state waste reflected real costs to Oregon, which Oregon citizens paid through general taxes. It argued, in other words, that its surcharge was a valid

---

[28] 114 S Ct at 1349.

[29] Id at 1355 & n 2 (Rehnquist dissenting).

[30] *Gilliam County v Department of Environmental Quality*, 114 Ore App 369, 383 n 17 (1992).

[31] 114 S Ct at 1351.

[32] Id.

[33] 504 US 334 (1992).

[34] Id at 338–39. The Court found that Alabama's surcharge discriminated against out-of-state waste, and that nondiscriminatory alternatives—including an evenhanded cap on all hazardous waste disposed of within the state—were available to satisfy the state's asserted goal of reducing the volume of hazardous waste buried there. Id at 342–46.

"compensatory tax"—a tax on out-of-state commerce designed to compensate for a "substantially equivalent" intrastate tax.[35]

This new argument did not help Oregon. The Court dispatched Oregon's claim by observing that Oregon's surcharge on out-of-state waste was not matched by any tax on a "substantially equivalent" in-state event. For one thing, Oregon imposed no discrete $2.25 fee on disposal of in-state waste, which might have served as the substantial equivalent of the surcharge on imported waste.[36] Moreover, its general taxation of in-state enterprises, in particular its income tax, was not directed at an event substantially equivalent to waste disposal. Especially persuasive to the Court was the fact that in-state shippers of out-of-state waste paid *both* the disposal surcharge and general taxes, a fact which, the Court held, "refute[d] respondents' argument that the respective taxable events are substantially equivalent."[37] The Court hinted that the only compensatory tax it would recognize today is a use tax on goods purchased out of state, compensating for a sales tax on goods purchased in the state.[38] It was worried that "permitting discriminatory taxes on interstate commerce to compensate for charges purportedly included in general forms of intrastate taxation 'would allow a state to tax interstate commerce more heavily than in-state commerce anytime the entities involved in interstate commerce happened to use facilities supported by general state tax funds.' "[39]

Because the Court found that generating income and disposing of waste were not substantially equivalent events, it was irrelevant whether Oregon's income tax imposed "an intrastate burden roughly equivalent to the out-of-state surcharge."[40] Indeed, the Court did not question the state environmental agency's conclusion that the $2.25 charge reflected the costs to Oregon (including tax credits and other public subsidies)[41] of disposing of out-of-state waste.

---

[35] 114 S Ct at 1351–52. Alabama had not pressed this argument in the Supreme Court in *Chemical Waste Management*. 504 US at 346 n 9.

[36] 114 S Ct at 1352–53.

[37] Id at 1353.

[38] Id.

[39] Id at 1353 n 8, quoting *Government Suppliers Consolidating Services v Bayh*, 975 F2d 1267, 1284 (7th Cir 1992).

[40] 114 S Ct at 1353.

[41] Id at 1355 n 1 (Rehnquist dissenting).

Finally, the Court distinguished Oregon's surcharge from other types of local favoritism previously approved by the Court, such as a state's preference for its own citizens when it participates in a commercial market.[42] The Court observed: "The Commerce Clause does not prohibit all state action designed to give its residents an advantage in the marketplace, but only action of that description *in connection with the State's regulation of interstate commerce*."[43] The Court thought it "plain[ ]" that Oregon's surcharge was "regulation."[44]

Perhaps because it found its analytical work so easy, the Court did not explain what purpose it believed it served by invalidating Oregon's law. Although the Court began its discussion with the ritual reference to the "economic Balkanization" that "had plagued relations among the Colonies and later among the States under the Articles of Confederation,"[45] and the ritual quotation of Justice Jackson's opinion for the Court in *H P Hood & Sons v Du Mond,* announcing that "our economic unit is the Nation,"[46] these passages do not reveal what is bad about economic Balkanization, or good about economic unity. Other recent opinions disapproving facial discrimination against interstate commerce are similarly unilluminating.[47]

Chief Justice Rehnquist's dissent, joined only by Justice Black-

---

[42] The Court has upheld state restrictions on interstate commerce—even facially discriminatory ones—where it has concluded that the government is acting as a "market participant" rather than as a "market regulator." *White v Massachusetts Council of Construction Employees,* 460 US 204 (1983); *Reeves v Stake,* 447 US 429 (1980); *Hughes v Alexandria Scrap,* 426 US 794 (1976). The market-participant doctrine has inspired a good deal of academic commentary. See, e.g., Jonathan D. Varat, *State "Citizenship" and Interstate Equality,* 48 U Chi L Rev 487 (1981); Dan T. Coenen, *Untangling the Market-Participant Exception to the Dormant Commerce Clause,* 88 Mich L Rev 395 (1989); Benjamin C. Bair, *The Dormant Commerce Clause and State-Mandated Public Preference Laws in Public Contracting: Developing a More Substantive Application of the Market-Participant Exception,* 93 Mich L Rev 2408 (1995).

[43] 114 S Ct at 1354 n 9, quoting *New Energy Co.,* supra note 20 at 278 (emphasis in original).

[44] 114 S Ct at 1354 n 9 (contrasting Oregon's surcharge with participation by a state in a commercial market, which the Court suggests is not "regulation").

[45] Id at 1349, quoting *Hughes v Oklahoma,* supra note 11 at 325–26.

[46] "This principle that our economic unit is the Nation, which alone has the gamut of powers necessary to control of the economy, . . . has as its corollary that the states are not separable economic units." 114 S Ct at 1349, quoting *H P Hood & Sons v Du Mond,* supra note 11 at 537–38.

[47] In *Philadelphia,* supra note 1 at 626–27, *Chemical Waste Management,* supra note 1 at 339–40, and *Fort Gratiot Sanitary Landfill,* supra note 1 at 359, 363, the Court condemned "economic protectionism" without explaining why it was bad.

mun,[48] followed themes developed in Rehnquist's dissenting opinions in earlier, similar cases.[49] Emphasizing the difficulty of finding safe disposal sites for this country's solid waste, Rehnquist asserted that "[t]he availability of safe landfill disposal sites in Oregon did not occur by chance" but rather was the result of a complex regulatory scheme relating to waste generation and disposal.[50] Thus, he thought landfill space in Oregon had " 'some indicia of a good publicly produced and owned in which a State may favor its own citizens in times of shortage.' "[51] Moreover, he asserted, the Court's decision perverted the Commerce Clause by giving Oregon's neighbors "a competitive advantage against their Oregon counterparts as they can now produce solid waste with reckless abandon and avoid paying concomitant state taxes to develop new landfills and clean up retired landfill sites."[52]

The second Commerce Clause case of the 1993 Term was *C & A Carbone v Town of Clarkstown*.[53] At issue in that case was a flow-control ordinance regulating the export of solid waste by requiring all solid waste in the town of Clarkstown to be processed at a transfer station designated by the town. The town had commissioned a private contractor to construct the transfer station and to operate it for five years. The town would then buy it for one dollar. The facility was financed by means of the flow-control measure challenged before the Supreme Court. By requiring all solid waste in the town to be processed at this transfer station, the town guaranteed that the contractor would receive the amount of waste, and thus the amount of revenue, necessary to cover the cost of the project.[54]

The Court again had no difficulty concluding that Clarkstown's flow-control ordinance was discriminatory. For the Court, Justice Kennedy wrote that the ordinance discriminated with respect to "the service of processing and disposing of" solid waste because

---

[48] 114 S Ct at 1355.

[49] *Philadelphia*, supra note 1 at 629–33; *Chemical Waste Management*, supra note 1 at 349–52; *Fort Gratiot Sanitary Landfill*, supra note 1 at 368–73.

[50] 114 S Ct at 1356.

[51] Id, quoting *Sporhase v Nebraska*, 458 US 941, 957 (1982).

[52] 114 S Ct at 1357.

[53] Id at 1677 (1994).

[54] Id at 1680.

"it allow[ed] only the favored operator to process waste that [was] within the limits of the town"[55] and thus "deprive[d] out-of-state businesses of access to a local market."[56] The Court thought it immaterial that Clarkstown's ordinance made no distinction between waste generated within Clarkstown and waste generated elsewhere, nor even between out-of-town processing facilities and local facilities other than the transfer station. The flow-control ordinance was, the Court concluded, just another "local processing requirement" like those invalidated in previous cases, the "essential vice" of which was that it "bar[red] the import of the processing service."[57]

For the Court, the fact that the flow-control ordinance favored a single local business, rather than all businesses within the town, only made the protectionism here "more acute": unlike processing requirements that at least allowed all businesses located in the local area to compete on equal terms, "[t]he flow control ordinance at issue here squelches competition in the waste-processing service altogether, leaving no room for investment from outside."[58]

Having found the ordinance discriminatory, the Court looked for nondiscriminatory ways of achieving the town's legitimate goals. By the Court's lights, satisfactory nondiscriminatory alternatives included achievement of the town's environmental goals through regulations applicable to all waste-processing facilities within the town,[59] and achievement of its financial goals through general taxes or municipal bonds.[60] The Court also hinted that at least one of the town's proferred interests was illegitimate: Clarkstown may not, it said, "justify the flow control ordinance as a way to steer solid waste away from out-of-town disposal sites that it might deem harmful to the environment. To do so would extend the town's police power beyond its jurisdictional bounds. States and localities may not attach restrictions to exports or imports in order to control commerce in other states."[61]

---

[55] Id at 1682.

[56] Id at 1681.

[57] Id at 1682–83 (citing cases).

[58] Id at 1683.

[59] Id.

[60] Id at 1684.

[61] Id at 1683.

In *Carbone*, the Court signaled its purpose more clearly than it had in *Oregon Waste Systems*. It began by identifying the "central rationale" of the rule against discrimination to be to prevent "laws that would excite those jealousies and retaliatory measures the Constitution was designed to prevent,"[62] suggesting, perhaps, that its purpose in striking down laws like the Clarkstown ordinance is to achieve national unity. After this one appearance, however, national unity dropped from the picture. In its place stood the free market. The Court's fixation on the anticompetitive aspects of the Clarkstown ordinance—such as its "squelch[ing]" of competition in waste processing[63]—evinces a desire to protect market competition. And its narrowing, indeed obliteration, of the geographic boundary within which such "squelching" may occur—so that a single waste processing facility in a single town falls outside that boundary—manifests an intent to protect competition even if the effect of anticompetitive regulation on *interstate* commerce is attenuated, or even hypothetical.

The main opinion in *Carbone* failed to draw the lopsided majority typical of previous cases involving waste disposal and the Commerce Clause.[64] Justice O'Connor concurred only in the judgment. In her view, Clarkstown's ordinance did not discriminate against interstate commerce because it did not treat local economic interests as a group more favorably than out-of-town interests. "Rather, the garbage sorting monopoly is achieved at the expense of all competitors, be they local or nonlocal."[65] She believed that such a burden on local interests ensures that the local government's " 'own political processes will serve as a check against unduly burdensome regulations.' "[66] In the end, however, Justice O'Connor voted to strike down the ordinance because she concluded it unduly interfered with interstate commerce.[67]

In a dissent joined by Chief Justice Rehnquist and Justice Black-

---

[62] Id at 1682.

[63] Id at 1683.

[64] The votes in previous cases were: *Philadelphia*, supra note 1 at 618 (7–2); *Chemical Waste Management*, supra note 1 at 335 (8–1); *Fort Gratiot*, supra note 1 at 354 (7–2); *Oregon Waste Systems*, supra note 1 at 1347–48 (7–2).

[65] 114 S Ct at 1689.

[66] Id, quoting *Raymond Motor Transportation v Rice*, 434 US 429, 444 n 18 (1978).

[67] 114 S Ct at 1689–91. Justice O'Connor thus invoked the "undue burden" line of Commerce Clause cases, see text at notes 20–21, which is not the focus of this article.

mun, Justice Souter thought it decisive that Clarkstown's ordinance did not distinguish between local and nonlocal waste processors, but instead excluded *both* in favor of one firm.[68] Indeed, Souter stressed, the record lacked any evidence that out-of-town businesses had been harmed by the ordinance.[69] The plaintiff in the case, a recycling center which apparently sought to avoid the transfer station's fee by shipping its waste directly to other states,[70] was located in Clarkstown.[71]

The ordinance was certainly anticompetitive, Souter conceded, but "the bar to monopolies . . . arises from a statutory, not a constitutional, mandate. No more than the Fourteenth Amendment, the Commerce Clause 'does not enact Mr. Herbert Spencer's Social Statics . . . [or] embody a particular economic theory, whether of paternalism . . . or of *laissez faire.*'"[72] Moreover, given its special contractual arrangements with the town, the favored transfer station was "essentially a municipal facility . . . perform[ing] a municipal function that tradition as well as state and federal law recognize as the domain of local government."[73] If the Court continued to assert the states' " 'special and specific position in our constitutional system,' "[74] and its effect on the scope of Congress's authority under the Commerce Clause, then, Souter concluded, "surely this Court's dormant Commerce Clause jurisprudence must itself see that favoring state-sponsored facilities differs from discriminating among private economic actors."[75]

In *West Lynn Creamery v Healy*,[76] the last in the trio of Com-

---

[68] Id at 1692.

[69] Id at 1700.

[70] The plaintiff had, in violation of the flow-control ordinance, shipped waste from Clarkstown to Indiana, Illinois, West Virginia, and Florida. Id at 1681.

[71] Id at 1680–81. Although the Court asserted that the flow-control ordinance left "no room for investment from outside," id at 1683, the record apparently did not indicate whether local or nonlocal investors owned the private firm that built the transfer station for Clarkstown. Id at 1696 n 7 (Souter dissenting).

[72] Id at 1699, quoting *Lochner v New York*, 198 US 45, 75 (1905) (Holmes dissenting).

[73] 114 S Ct at 1696–97.

[74] Id at 1697, quoting *Garcia v San Antonio Metropolitan Transit Authority*, 469 US 528, 556 (1985).

[75] 114 S Ct at 1697–98. Justice Souter's argument calls to mind (but does not rely on) the cases in which the Court has upheld state restrictions on interstate commerce where the government is acting as a "market participant." See cases cited in note 42.

[76] 114 S Ct 2205 (1994).

merce Clause cases of the 1993 Term, the Court considered a Massachusetts pricing order that taxed all milk dealers (in-state and out-of-state) doing business in Massachusetts and distributed the proceeds to in-state dairy farmers. In recent years, Massachusetts dairy farmers had lost a good deal of market share to lower-cost producers from other states because the federally established minimum price for raw milk no longer covered their costs.[77] Through its tax and subsidy scheme, the state hoped to save its ailing dairy industry by helping it to compete with lower-cost producers from other states.

In an opinion by Justice Stevens, the Court found the pricing order invalid for this very reason: "Its avowed purpose and its undisputed effect are to enable higher cost Massachusetts dairy farmers to compete with lower cost dairy farmers in other States."[78] By "neutraliz[ing] the advantage possessed by lower cost out-of-state producers," the order had the same effect as a tariff,[79] which the Court described as "the paradigmatic example of a law discriminating against interstate commerce."[80]

The Court brushed aside the state's argument that the order was valid because each piece of it—an evenhanded tax on all milk dealers doing business in Massachusetts, and a subsidy for the state's dairy farmers—was valid. While the Court pointedly refused to express general approval of subsidies for in-state business,[81] it also observed that a subsidy funded from general revenues "ordinarily imposes no burden on interstate commerce, but merely assists local business," whereas the pricing order burdened interstate commerce by taxing it.[82] In any event, the Court deemed the state's two-part tax and subsidy program "more dangerous to interstate commerce than either part alone."[83] This was because "[w]hen a nondiscriminatory tax is coupled with a subsidy to one of the groups hurt by the tax, a state's political processes can no

[77] Id at 2209.

[78] Id at 2212.

[79] Id at 2213.

[80] Id at 2211.

[81] Id at 2214 n 15 ("We have never squarely confronted the constitutionality of subsidies, and we need not do so now.").

[82] Id at 2214.

[83] Id at 2215.

longer be relied upon to prevent legislative abuse, because one of the in-state interests which would otherwise lobby against the tax has been mollified by the subsidy."[84] The Court noted that consumers were "unlikely to organize effectively to oppose the pricing order" because the price increase caused by the order was too small to be distinguished from ordinary price fluctuations.[85] In addition, even if insiders (Massachusetts consumers) were the ones who would end up paying higher prices for milk as a result of the order, the order was nevertheless invalid because it diverted market share toward Massachusetts dairy producers and away from producers in other states.[86]

Concurring in the judgment, Justice Scalia (joined by Justice Thomas) complained that the Court's opinion reflected "a broad expansion of current law"[87] insofar as it suggested that "every state law which obstructs a national market violates the Commerce Clause."[88] This broad principle, Scalia asserted, "calls into question a wide variety of state laws that have hitherto been thought permissible," such as state subsidies funded from general state revenues, and evenhanded regulation that happens to burden out-of-state firms more than in-state ones.[89]

West Lynn Creamery follows the same normative path the Court started down in *Carbone*. To be sure, the Court's discussion of the political process leading to Massachusetts' pricing order—in particular, the "mollifi[cation]" of in-state dairy farmers by the sub-

---

[84] Id.

[85] Id at 2215 n 18. In dissent, Chief Justice Rehnquist (joined by Justice Blackmun) objected: "Analysis of interest group participation in the political process may serve many useful purposes, but serving as a basis for interpreting the dormant Commerce Clause is not one of them." 114 S Ct at 2222.

[86] Id at 2217.

[87] Id at 2218.

[88] Id at 2219.

[89] Id. As he had in the past (e.g., *Itel Containers Int'l Corp. v Huddleston*, 113 S Ct 1095, 1107 & nn 1, 2 (1993) (Scalia concurring in judgment)), Justice Scalia announced that he would vote to invalidate a state law under the Commerce Clause only if it facially discriminated against interstate commerce or was "indistinguishable from a type of law previously held unconstitutional by the Court." 114 S Ct at 2220. Scalia thus had only to decide whether Massachusetts' tax and subsidy scheme was more like a nondiscriminatory tax that exempts in-state firms (previously held unconstitutional) or more like a subsidy for in-state firms funded from general revenues (never before held unconstitutional). Concluding that the pricing order was more like the former than the latter, he voted to invalidate it. Id at 2220–21.

sidy[90]—brings up a third rationale for the nondiscrimination principle: discrimination against interstate commerce is illegitimate because out-of-staters did not participate in the political process that produced it. The political participation (or nonparticipation) of *in-state* groups is thought relevant because the in-staters who are harmed may serve as proxies for the injured out-of-staters who may not vote; they act, in the Court's words, as a "powerful safeguard against legislative abuse."[91] But the virtues of the free market again lie at the heart of the Court's opinion. By "distorting . . . the geography of production," and "neutralizing the advantage possessed by lower cost out-of-state producers,"[92] the Massachusetts pricing order sinned against the dominant modern rationale for free trade: economic efficiency. Given its prominence in the Court's most recent cases, I begin my discussion of the purposes of the nondiscrimination principle with this rationale.

II. Economics

"The paradigmatic example of a law discriminating against interstate commerce," *West Lynn Creamery* informs us, "is the protective tariff or customs duty." Tariffs are unconstitutional, the Court continues, "because of their distorting effects on the geography of production": a tariff "artificially encourag[es] in-state production even when the same goods could be produced at lower cost in other States."[93]

This is the classic economic argument for free trade. Indeed, the Court's objection to "distorting effects on the geography of production" is strikingly similar to Judge Posner's explanation, in *Economic Analysis of Law*, of why state-imposed burdens on commerce may be inefficient: "[T]axes that discriminate against importers . . . distort[ ] the optimum geographical distribution of enterprise. Production that could be carried on more efficiently in State A will be carried on in B instead if B's tax on imports from A exceeds the cost advantage of producers in A."[94] Free trade, in

---

[90] 114 S Ct at 2215.

[91] *Minnesota v Clover Leaf Creamery*, 449 US 456, 573 n 17 (1981).

[92] Id at 2211, 2212.

[93] Id at 2211.

[94] Richard A. Posner, *Economic Analysis of Law* 638 (4th ed 1992).

contrast, exploits the benefits of specialization by guaranteeing each state (or nation) a market for the goods it is best at producing. Even if one state outshines all others in producing every good, and thus has an absolute advantage in producing everything, free trade still benefits all states (the theory goes) by encouraging the less efficient states to produce the goods they are least inefficient at producing. The more efficient states then spend their time producing the goods they are most efficient at producing.[95]

With its focus on efficiency, the economic justification for the nondiscrimination principle invites close attention to the benefits and costs of laws that discriminate against interstate commerce. One might therefore expect a Supreme Court committed to the economic account of free trade—as *West Lynn Creamery* suggests the current Court is—to undertake a careful examination of the actual effects of a discriminatory law before pronouncing it inefficient and unconstitutional. After all, the hallmark of a responsible cost-benefit analysis is a sober weighing of all benefits and costs.[96] In deciding whether laws that it has deemed discriminatory are constitutional, however, the Supreme Court eschews careful analysis in favor of a rigid rule that disregards benefits and fabricates costs in the service of a normative principle unrelated to the goal of efficiency.

A. BENEFITS

In reviewing laws held to discriminate against interstate products or services, the Court insists that the government offer "some reason, *apart from their origin*, to treat [such items] differently."[97] The government may not, in other words, justify differential treatment of an outside (out-of-state, out-of-town, or out-of-county) article of commerce by reference to its outsider status. As I explain below, however, disallowing outsider status as a basis for government action blocks the consideration of many benefits that an impartial cost-benefit analysis would take into account.

---

[95] This is the idea of "comparative advantage." For the seminal discussion, see David Ricardo, *The Principles of Political Economy and Taxation* 81–93 (J. M. Dent & Sons ed 1948). For critical analysis, see Herman E. Daly and John B. Cobb, Jr., *For the Common Good* 209–18 (2d ed 1994).

[96] For general discussion, see Edith Stokey and Richard Zeckhauser, *A Primer for Policy Analysis* 134–36 (1978).

[97] *Philadelphia*, supra note 1 at 627 (emphasis added).

The benefits of discriminating against outside commerce *on account of* its outsider status are perhaps most vivid in the environmental context. Here, the very concept of the "risk" appropriate for regulatory treatment may depend on the place in which a given risk originates.

Experts and laypeople tend to look at different things when they assess risk. In measuring "riskiness," experts in risk assessment tend to focus on statistical risk of physical harm—the probability of dying or of falling ill. Laypeople, on the other hand, also care about whether the risk is voluntarily or involuntarily imposed, whether its effects are catastrophic or diffuse, whether it is distributed equitably or inequitably in the population, and so forth.[98] These common attitudes help to explain why a person may be uneasy about nuclear power even as she calmly submits to a chest X-ray.[99] A basic issue in environmental policy today is whether the "risk" that is an appropriate object of regulation encompasses only statistical risk of physical harm, or also includes qualitative, non-physical attributes such as voluntariness and equity.[100]

Several of the attributes that make laypeople fear some activities or substances more than others (even if they pose the same statistical risk of physical harm) are intertwined with outsider status. The example of waste disposal helps to illustrate the point. The likelihood of public opposition to a new waste disposal facility stems in large part from the sense of "intrusion" a community feels on account of the facility. The depth of this sense of intrusion depends in part on the presence of coercion: where the community has no opportunity to reject a proposed facility (as where the Supreme Court interprets the Commerce Clause to limit its ability

---

[98] There is a large literature on this phenomenon. For general discussion, see Paul Slovic, *Perception of Risk*, 236 Science 280 (April 17, 1987); Lola L. Lopes, *Risk Perception and the Perceived Public*, in Daniel W. Bromley and Kathleen Segerson, eds, *The Social Response to Environmental Risk: Policy Formulation in an Age of Uncertainty* 62–67 (1992); Stephen Breyer, *Breaking the Vicious Circle* 33 (1993); Lisa Heinzerling, *Political Science*, 62 U Chi L Rev 449, 470–72 (1995).

[99] For a study using regression techniques to identify the major explanatory variables for the risk perceptions reported by laypeople in a series of classic studies, see Robin Gregory and Robert Mendelsohn, *Perceived Risk, Dread, and Benefits*, 13 Risk Analysis 259 (1993).

[100] For general discussion, and an argument that some qualitative attributes of risk should be taken into account in shaping regulation, see Richard H. Pildes and Cass R. Sunstein, *Reinventing the Regulatory State*, 62 U Chi L Rev 1, 48–64 (1995).

to do so), the community's perception of risk, and its opposition to the facility, almost inevitably will increase.[101]

A second factor increasing the feeling of intrusion—and the likelihood and intensity of public opposition—is the importation of waste from other places. State and local governments' continued willingness to enact restrictions on out-of-state waste, in the face of the Supreme Court's uniformly negative treatment of such laws, testifies to this phenomenon.[102] A corollary of the hostility to importation is that the sense of intrusion and the perception of risk decrease when waste is disposed of at its place of origin. Most hazardous waste disposal in this country occurs at the place where it is generated,[103] and engenders little public opposition from the surrounding communities.[104] There are at least two reasons why such disposal might be viewed more favorably than disposal of waste imported from elsewhere. It creates local jobs—more jobs than off-site disposal creates.[105] And it is perceived as more equitable than off-site disposal; the community is taking care of its own, but only its own, waste.[106]

Both of these factors, coercion and importation, are linked to outsider status. When a community must accept waste from other places, coercion—with its accompanying sense of intrusion and heightened fear—is clearly present.[107] And, obviously, the status of waste as an "import" is perfectly correlated with its place of origin, or outsider status. Forcing a community to accept waste imported

---

[101] Michael B. Gerrard, *Fear and Loathing in the Siting of Hazardous and Radioactive Waste Facilities: A Comprehensive Approach to a Misperceived Crisis*, 68 Tulane L Rev 1047, 1141–42 (1994) (footnotes omitted).

[102] Id at 1142. For an analysis of the distribution of the burden of solid waste disposal among the states, and an argument that the unevenness of that distribution would justify Congressional authorization for the states to enter into regulation compacts to address solid waste disposal, see Kirsten Engel, *Reconsidering the National Market in Solid Waste: Trade-offs in Equity, Efficiency, Environmental Protection, and State Autonomy*, 73 NC L Rev 1482 (1995).

[103] Office of Solid Waste and Emergency Response, US EPA, Pub No EPA530-R-94-039c, *National Biennial RCRA Hazardous Waste Report: National Analysis* 2–13 (1994) (97 percent of hazardous waste in United States managed on-site in 1991).

[104] Gerrard, supra note 101 at 1146–48.

[105] Id at 1146–47.

[106] Id at 1148.

[107] Coercion may also be present, of course, if an inside company opens a waste disposal facility against the community's wishes.

from elsewhere thus imposes real costs on the community: increased fear, a loss of autonomy, and a denial of equity. Accordingly, eliminating these costs by excluding outside waste from a community, or by allowing a community a choice in the matter, is a benefit of discrimination against outside waste.

This is a benefit the Supreme Court ignores when it requires a reason, "apart from their origin,"[108] for treating outside articles of commerce differently from inside ones. In its cases involving waste disposal and the Commerce Clause, the Court has suggested that a state may treat waste generated out-of-state differently from waste generated in-state only if out-of-state waste is more dangerous, or more costly to handle, than in-state waste.[109] And it has implied that, to justify differential treatment, out-of-state waste must be *physically different* from in-state waste.[110] "Dangerousness" and "cost" do not, in other words, include the qualitative attributes of risk. Thus, in a major public policy debate pitting expert risk assessors against lay citizens, the Court has sided with the experts.

One might argue that the Court is justified in ignoring the benefits of discrimination against outside waste because they do not derive from a *rational* reaction to the problem of waste disposal. Impartial cost-benefit analysis does not, however, pick and choose among costs and benefits and consider only those reflecting preferences deemed "rational." Indeed, economic analysis is famous for attending to costs and benefits many would dismiss as irrational, or even morally objectionable. The economic analysis of racial discrimination, which takes into account the "taste for discrimination" that goes unsatisfied if nondiscrimination laws are in place, is perhaps the most dramatic example here.[111] Precisely because it countenances an agnostic consideration of all costs and benefits,

---

[108] *Philadelphia*, supra note 1 at 627.

[109] See text at note 32; see also *Philadelphia*, supra note 1 at 629; *Chemical Waste Management*, supra note 1 at 343–44.

[110] In the one case in which it has allowed differential treatment of out-of-state commerce, the Court relied heavily on a finding that the out-of-state commerce at issue was physically different from its in-state counterpart. Maine had banned the importation of out-of-state baitfish, and the trial court had found that out-of-state baitfish harbored a parasite not found in Maine baitfish. *Maine v Taylor*, supra note 3 at 151, 152–52. See also *Chemical Waste Management*, supra note 1 at 348, quoting *Philadelphia*, supra note 1 at 629 (out-of-state waste must be more "inherently harmful" than in-state waste to justify differential treatment).

[111] Gary S. Becker, *The Economics of Discrimination* (2d ed 1971).

some have argued that cost-benefit analysis is not appropriate for all settings.[112] But if efficiency is to be the Court's touchstone, then the fear and loathing that accompanies the importation of waste must be accounted for in a cost-benefit analysis of laws discriminating against outside waste.

The shortcomings of the Court's truncated cost-benefit analysis are not limited to the environmental context. Consider the simple tariff on imported goods, the Court's "paradigmatic example" of impermissible discrimination against commerce.[113] One might wonder why any government would impose a tariff, given that its citizens will likely pay for it in higher prices.[114] The most obvious purpose for a tariff is to protect local industry, allowing it to raise its prices or to compete with lower-cost foreign competition.[115] Why protect local industry? Saving jobs,[116] tax revenues,[117] even a way of life,[118] may be behind such a decision.[119] Autonomy and self-

---

[112] See, e.g., Mark Sagoff, *The Economy of the Earth: Philosophy, Law, and the Environment* (1988).

[113] *West Lynn Creamery*, supra note 1 at 2211.

[114] For a study estimating the costs of U.S. trade protection policies to U.S. consumers, see Gary Clyde Hufbauer and Kimberly Ann Elliott, *Measuring the Costs of Protection in the United States* (Institute for Int'l Economics 1994).

[115] William J. Baumol and Alan S. Blinder, *Economics: Principles and Policy* 722–24 (2d ed 1982).

[116] Id at 723–24.

[117] Not only do the tariffs themselves make money for the government, but local businesses pay property and income taxes that are lost if the businesses move to another jurisdiction.

[118] Jack Michel has defended New York's law limiting entry into the dairy industry in areas adequately served by existing business, invalidated by the Supreme Court in *H P Hood & Sons v DuMond*, 336 US 525 (1949), as an attempt to preserve a rural, decentralized way of life, in which local communities retain control over production processes. See Jack Michel, *Hood v DuMond: A Study of the Supreme Court and the Ideology of Capitalism*, 134 U Pa L Rev 657 (1986). In general, preserving the American farmer's way of life has played a prominent role in government support for local agriculture. See, e.g., W. David Slawson, *The Right to Protection from Air Pollution*, 59 S Cal L Rev 672, 774 (1986); Thomas J. Schoenbaum, *Agricultural Trade Wars: A Threat to the Gatt and Global Free Trade*, 24 St Mary's L J 1165, 1178 (1993). See also Herman E. Daly, *The Perils of Free Trade*, Sci Am 50, 51 (Nov 1993) ("Uruguay is enriched by having a symphony orchestra of its own, even though it would be cost-effective to import better symphony concerts in exchange for wool, mutton, beef and leather.").

Of course, free trade itself might define a way of life. I merely suggest that, for some communities, the local way of life depends on a kind of isolationism.

[119] It is also possible that local industry has managed to get protective legislation passed against the interests of local consumers because the potential benefits to industry are concentrated (thus increasing the likelihood and effectiveness of its political participation), whereas the potential costs to consumers are diffuse (decreasing their political participation). See, e.g., Tushnet, supra note 5 at 133.

sufficiency may figure prominently here as well. Outside commercial interests are likely "very far removed from the life of the community that is affected significantly by their decisions," and thus "[y]our life and your community can be disrupted by decisions and events over which you have no control, no vote, no voice."[120] And, once a local economy has specialized in response to the demands of free trade, it "trades freely, but [it] is no longer free not to trade."[121] Of a regime of free trade, then, one might ask, "In what sense is it free?"[122]

Preserving the jobs, revenue, culture, and autonomy of a place—be it a town, a county, or a state—is a benefit, at least for that community, of protective tariffs. This is another benefit the Court ignores in reflexively invalidating laws that discriminate against outside commerce. Indeed, the Court not only ignores this benefit, it condemns it.[123]

So far I have been discussing benefits to insiders. Laws regulating commerce may also benefit outsiders. Again, an example from the environmental context illustrates the point. A powerful movement in environmental policy today is the effort to achieve an appropriate level of pollution control by forcing the price of a commodity to reflect its environmental costs.[124] As one part of this trend, many states now consider the environmental consequences of electricity production in selecting new energy resources. In choosing between a new conservation program and a new coal-

---

[120] Herman E. Daly, *From Adjustment to Sustainable Development: The Obstacle of Free Trade*, 15 Loyola LA Intl & Comp L J 33, 39 (1992).

[121] Daly and Cobb, supra note 95 at 228. Interestingly, the court responsible for adjudicating trade disputes in the European Community sustained Wallonia's emergency ban on importation of nonhazardous waste partly because it promoted self-sufficiency. Richard B. Stewart, *International Trade and the Environment: Lessons from the Federal Experience*, 49 Wash & Lee L Rev 1329, 1339 n 31 (1992); Michael D. Diederich, Jr., *Does Garbage Have Standing? Democracy, Flow Control and a Principled Constitutional Approach to Municipal Solid Waste Management*, 11 Pace Envir L Rev 157, 202–03 (1993).

[122] Daly and Cobb, supra note 95 at 228.

[123] *West Lynn Creamery*, supra note 1 at 2217: "Preservation of local industry by protecting it from the rigors of interstate competition is the hallmark of the economic protectionism that the Commerce Clause prohibits." See also *Alliance for Clean Coal v Miller*, 44 F3d 591, 598 (1995) (Cudahy concurring) (social cost of providing compensation to in-staters unemployed as a result of free trade "is an externality that the states may not recognize since the Commerce Clause effectively precludes consideration of local economic damage as a legitimate reason to handicap interstate commerce").

[124] For general discussion, see Lisa Heinzerling, *Selling Pollution, Forcing Democracy*, 14 Stan Envir L J 300 (1995).

fired power plant, for example, the public utility commissions in these states would consider not only the development and operating costs of these alternatives, but also the costs associated with their environmental impacts.[125] Most important for present purposes, these states often do not distinguish between in-state and out-of-state (or even global) environmental impacts in calculating the social cost of a new energy resource.[126] This approach is in line with basic economic analysis: an environmental harm that occurs in another state is just as much a cost of a new energy resource as one that falls within the regulating state. Indeed, this is the central insight of the analysis of externalities: costs are not to be discounted or ignored just because somebody else is picking up the tab.[127]

"Getting the price right" through the consideration of impacts on outsiders is another benefit the Supreme Court ignores in reviewing laws affecting outside commerce. Recall that in *Carbone*, the Court suggested that it would have been illegitimate for the town of Clarkstown to have enacted a flow-control measure for the purpose of steering its residents' garbage away from outside disposal sites especially harmful to the environment.[128] Benefits to

---

[125] For general discussion and criticism, see Bernard S. Black and Richard J. Pierce, Jr., *The Choice Between Markets and Central Planning in Regulating the U.S. Electricity Industry*, 93 Colum L Rev 1339, 1398–1430 (1993).

[126] See, e.g., Arizona Corporation Commission, *Report of the Externalities Task Force*, Docket No U-0000-92-035 at 18 (Dec 1992); *Re Rulemaking Regarding Resource Planning Changes Pursuant to 5P497*, 119 Pub Util Rep 4th 259, 267; *Re Biennial Resource Plan: Update Following the California Energy Commission's Seventh Electricity Report*, 124 Pub Util Rep 4th 181 (Cal Pub Util Comm'n 1991).

[127] For general discussion, see William J. Baumol and Wallace E. Oates, *Economics, Environmental Policy, and the Quality of Life* (1979). For an argument that it is illegitimate for one government to enact trade restrictions because it has a moral objection to participating in the environmental degradation of other places, see Stewart, supra note 121 at 1360–61; Jagdish Bhagwati, *The Case for Free Trade*, Sci Am 42, 46–48 (Nov 1993).

[128] See text at note 60. See also *Edgar v MITE*, 457 US 624, 644 (1982) ("While protecting local investors is plainly a legitimate state objective, the State has no legitimate interest in protecting non-resident shareholders. Insofar as the Indiana law burdens out-of-state transactions, there is nothing to be weighed in the balance."). One reviewer has explained the result in *Carbone* solely on the ground of "the Court's dissatisfaction with Clarkstown's attempt to control activity beyond its borders," in order to distinguish the case from those (previously upheld by the Court) in which a state or local government has granted a monopoly or exclusive franchise to a local business. *Leading Cases*, 108 Harv L Rev 139, 158 (1994).

Clarkstown may have had a selfish rather than altruistic reason for wanting to ensure the safe disposal of its waste in other places: avoiding liability for cleanup of the out-of-town disposal sites under the Comprehensive Environmental Response, Compensation, and Liability Act. Laura Gabrysch, *Case Note: Flow Control Ordinances That Require Disposal of*

outsiders, in other words, just do not count in the Court's calculus.[129] It is hard, again, to see how this approach comports with the goal of economic efficiency.

It may be that protecting local people and firms through a tariff or other barrier to trade also harms outsiders. I turn next to a discussion of the costs of discriminatory laws, and later, in Sections III and IV, to a discussion of whether there might be other reasons, apart from economic efficiency, for forbidding state and local governments to base their decisions on the outsider status of articles of commerce. For now, my point is that a proper cost-benefit analysis takes benefits as well as costs into account, and that the Court has given no reason—from the perspective of efficiency—for renouncing the benefits of discrimination against outside commerce.[130]

B. COSTS

Whereas the Court dismisses the potential benefits of laws that discriminate against commerce, it simply assumes their costs. After a conclusory reference to the plaintiff's stake in the controversy, the Court typically says no more about the actual negative effects of the discriminatory laws it condemns. Once it finds discrimination, the Court does not ask what the concrete effect of that discrimination might be on outside commerce, or indeed whether there is any.

All of the cases from the 1993 Term proceeded in this fashion. In *Oregon Waste Systems*, the Court described the plaintiffs' interest in the lawsuit thus: "Oregon Waste owns and operates a solid waste landfill in Gilliam County [another plaintiff in the case], at which it accepts for final disposal solid waste generated in Oregon and in other States." Columbia Resource Company, another plain-

---

Trash at a Designated Facility Violate the Dormant Commerce Clause, 26 St Mary's L J 563, 596 n 119 (1995).

[129] Compare Farber, supra note 5 at 398 & n 25 (in reviewing nondiscriminatory laws burdening interstate commerce, Court ignores benefits to outsiders); Stewart, supra note 121 at 1336 n 18 (benefits to outsiders "should presumably be included" in Court's assessment of burdens and benefits of nondiscriminatory laws).

[130] Compare Friedman, supra note 6 at 1754–55 (describing potential benefits of discriminatory treatment of outside commerce, including avoiding free rider problems where states choose to finance certain activities such as higher education and nurturing infant industry, and concluding that Congress, not the court, should decide whether these benefits are worth their costs).

tiff, "pursuant to a 20-year contract with Clark County, in neighboring Washington State, transports solid waste via barge from Clark County to a landfill in Morrow County, Oregon."[131] This oblique discussion of injury is the Court's sole reference to the effects of the Oregon surcharge on interstate commerce. Nowhere do we learn whether the interstate business of Oregon Waste or of Columbia Resource Company decreased as a consequence of the surcharge.

Economic theory might posit that the interstate business of companies that dispose of or ship interstate waste will decrease when the price of disposing of interstate waste increases. But real-world events might have intervened against this predicted result in this case. For one thing, it is not even clear that shippers of interstate waste paid more for waste disposal due to Oregon's surcharge than did shippers of intrastate waste. Recall that Oregon law did not require landfill operators to charge out-of-state waste shippers more than in-state shippers, but required only that they remit the appropriate payment, based on their share of in-state and out-of-state waste, to the state environmental agency.[132] The Court does not say whether the Oregon landfills in question passed on the costs of the surcharge solely to shippers of out-of-state waste, or whether they instead spread the costs of the state's charges for in-state and out-of-state waste evenly among their customers. In the latter case, of course, shippers of interstate waste were not disadvantaged, as compared to shippers of in-state waste, by the surcharge, even if overall demand for waste disposal decreased due to the cost increase (though we do not know whether it did). Even if the entire surcharge was passed on to shippers of interstate waste, the low cost of the surcharge to the average out-of-state household[133] may have been insufficient to induce changes in behavior (such as decreased waste generation) that would have reduced the plaintiffs' interstate business. And, even if Oregon's surcharge did reduce the generation of interstate waste, one must still ask whether the benefits of this reduction exceeded its costs. It is by now well known that Americans produce an extraordinary amount of household waste, and that we do so in large part because

---

[131] 114 S Ct at 1349.

[132] See text at note 30.

[133] See text at note 29.

we are not forced to internalize the full costs of this behavior.[134] A reduction in interstate shipments of waste due to a reduction in waste generation—due to greater internalization of costs—may thus produce benefits exceeding its costs. In short, the Court not only failed to uncover a causal link between Oregon's surcharge and injury to the plaintiffs; it failed to uncover any injury to plaintiffs at all, whatever the cause.[135]

The Court was equally casual about injury and causation in its earlier decision in *Chemical Waste Management v Hunt.*[136] There, the Court merely observed that the plaintiff owned and operated a large hazardous waste landfill in Alabama,[137] and that the state's hazardous waste law "has plainly discouraged the full operation of" the plaintiff's facility, citing evidence that, between 1989 and 1991 (the law took effect in 1990), the volume of waste buried at the landfill declined by approximately 500,000 tons.[138] Omitted from the Court's brief discussion is any reference to the contemporaneous nationwide decline in landfill demand, attributed in part to the economic recession.[139] Also missing is any mention of the fact that the *percentage* of waste coming from out-of-state had remained the same after the surcharge was imposed.[140] These facts

---

[134] See, e.g., Peter S. Menell, *Beyond the Throwaway Society: An Incentive Approach to Regulating Municipal Solid Waste*, 17 Ecol L Rev 655, 657–58 (1990).

[135] For an argument that the Court's famous decision in *H P Hood & Sons v DuMond*, 336 US 525 (1949), likewise relied on an unproven economic model, see Michel, supra note 118 at 683–86.

[136] 504 US 334 (1992).

[137] Id at 337.

[138] Id at 342 n 4. The Court did not cite a source for its figures, but the 1989 figure, at least, may be wrong by a substantial factor. The U.S. Environmental Protection Agency estimates that the amount of hazardous waste buried at plaintiff's landfill in 1989 was approximately 400,000 tons less than the Court's figure for that year. Office of Solid Waste and Emergency Response, US EPA, Pub No EPA530-R-92-027, *National Biennial RCRA Hazardous Waste Report*, 2–33 (1993) (reporting that in 1989, Emelle facility managed 360,463 tons of hazardous waste). The Court thus appears to have overestimated the decrease in disposal of hazardous waste at plaintiff's landfill between 1989 and 1991 by about five times.

[139] For discussion of this decline, see, e.g., Office of Solid Waste Management and Emergency Response, US EPA, Pub No EPA530-R-94-039c, *National Biennial RCRA Hazardous Waste Report: Executive Summary* ES-2 (1994); Gerrard, supra note 101 at 1059; Amicus Brief of the National Governor's Association in Support of the Respondents in *Chemical Waste Management v Hunt* 4–5 n 3 (US S Ct 91–471) (Apr 9 1992).

[140] Brief for the Respondents in *Chemical Waste Management v Hunt* 2 n 1 (US S Ct 91–471) (Apr 9 1992).

imply that something other than the discriminatory surcharge may have been responsible for plaintiff's reduced business, but the Court did not investigate this possibility.[141]

Carbone is much the same. Plaintiffs in that case operated a recycling center in Clarkstown handling both in-town and out-of-town waste.[142] Although Carbone attempted to evade the transfer station's tipping fee by clandestinely shipping waste from Clarkstown to other states,[143] nothing in the Supreme Court's opinion indicated that Carbone's interstate business would have suffered if Carbone could not have avoided Clarkstown's tipping fee. For the Court, it was enough to observe that, "[b]y requiring Carbone to send the nonrecyclable portion of this waste to the Route 303 transfer station at an additional cost, the flow control ordinance drives up the cost for out-of-state interests to dispose of their solid waste," and that it "deprives out-of-state businesses of access to a local market."[144] The ordinance, of course, drove up disposal costs for Clarkstown interests, too. And there was no evidence that increased costs at Carbone's facility led to increased costs even for out-of-staters who had used that facility in the past; perhaps they were able to shift their business to a different facility with no increase in cost[145] or to painlessly reduce their generation of waste.[146] Finally, the record did not identify any existing out-

---

[141] Compare Tushnet, supra note 5 at 142–43 (in cases involving nondiscriminatory burdens on interstate commerce, the Court's "sole focus has been on the increased cost of shipping or production, which has an indeterminate relation to reduced consumption of interstate goods").

[142] 114 S Ct at 1680–81.

[143] See text at note 70.

[144] 114 S Ct at 1681.

[145] Economic theory might predict that costs to outsiders using Carbone's facility would increase when Carbone's costs increased even if they could shift their business elsewhere, on the assumption that the outsiders were using the facility because it was the lowest-cost provider. However, such an assumption is often unrealistic, as where, for example, the market in question is captured by a monopoly such as a criminal syndicate. This appears true of at least some portions of the New Jersey and New York waste business. See George Anastasia, *FBI Tapes Provide Information Overflow on Mob*, The Record, Northern NJ at N4 (July 31, 1994) (discussing FBI investigation providing "details about the mob's multimillion-dollar control of the waste-hauling and trash disposal industry" in the New York–New Jersey area); Jeff Bailey, *In a Tussle Over Trash, 2 Haulers Could Win Ruling Costly to Towns*, Wall Street J A10 (Feb 28, 1994) (discussing speculations that partners in the Carbone facility in Clarkstown have mob ties).

[146] See text at notes 134–35.

of-state firms that were interested in competing for the business Clarkstown had withdrawn from the market.[147] For all we know, there were no such firms.

The situation in *West Lynn Creamery* was somewhat more complicated, but the relevant injury to the plaintiffs was equally obscure. Both plaintiffs were milk dealers licensed to do business in Massachusetts.[148] As milk dealers, they were both required to pay the premium called for by the challenged pricing order.[149] *All* milk dealers—whether they purchased raw milk from in-state or out-of-state producers—were required to make the same payment to the state. In effect, for Massachusetts milk dealers, the Massachusetts pricing order merely raised the price they were required to pay in order to transact in a given quantity of milk.

There are two injuries that Massachusetts dealers might have suffered as a consequence of this arrangement. First, if the premium payment increased the price of milk in Massachusetts, Massachusetts' overall demand for milk might decline and the dealers' business suffer. But there was no indication that milk dealers' business *outside* Massachusetts would likewise decline, nor was there even any evidence that milk dealers' business inside Massachusetts did in fact decline. In any case, such a decline in demand would be due to the evenhanded premium imposed on milk dealers, not the discriminatory distribution of the subsidy to Massachusetts milk producers. A second possible injury would be to dealers who had previously captured a larger share of the milk market by doing business mostly with out-of-state milk producers, rather than with their higher-cost, in-state counterparts. These dealers might cease to enjoy as large a competitive advantage because the subsidy would allow in-state producers to be more competitive. Such an injury would arise solely because of the subsidy to in-state dairy producers.[150]

In any event, the Court discussed neither of these potential injuries to the plaintiff milk dealers. Its sole focus was on the pricing order's potential impact on out-of-state *producers*, whose injury, if

---

[147] 114 S Ct at 1700 (Souter dissenting).

[148] Id at 2209.

[149] Id at 2210 & n 4.

[150] Again, however, there was no evidence that this had occurred.

any, would result from the subsidy to in-state producers.[151] Yet no out-of-state producers were before the Court.[152]

In each of these cases, the Court failed to link the alleged discrimination against interstate commerce with any proven injury to interstate commerce, or even to the parties to the cases. At most, the cases show injury only to the insiders responsible for the laws. While a thoroughgoing cost-benefit analysis would no doubt include injury to insiders as a cost of discriminatory laws, this would require the Court to second guess elected representatives' judgments about what is good and bad for their own citizens.[153] It would also expand the reach of the nondiscrimination principle beyond the protection of outside commerce, to include protection of *all* commerce, inside and outside.[154] By assuming the existence of costs to outsiders, the Court has avoided explicitly deciding whether insiders, too, ought to be protected by the Commerce Clause.

C. COST-BENEFIT AND THE SUPREME COURT

I have argued that the Supreme Court does a poor job of evaluating the benefits and costs of individual laws that discriminate against interstate commerce. It ignores benefits that an impartial efficiency analysis would take into account, and assumes costs on the basis of thin or nonexistent evidence. Thus it is impossible to conclude that in any given case the Court has promoted efficiency by invalidating a discriminatory law.

Even if the Court undertook a more careful analysis of the costs and benefits of each discriminatory law, however, there are good reasons to doubt that the Court would thereby ensure that the benefits of discrimination outweighed its costs. For one thing, responsible cost-benefit analysis depends on good information. But the Court has no investigative capacity of its own, and its review is limited to the facts and issues self-interested parties choose to

---

[151] Id at 2212, 2213, 2217.

[152] For a discussion of the Court's unusually lax approach to standing in Commerce Clause cases, see Section IV.B.

[153] See Stewart, supra note 121 at 1336.

[154] In Section V, I argue that this is indeed what the Court has done.

bring before it.[155] Thus the Court may lack a substantial amount of information essential to an objective weighing of costs and benefits.[156]

Furthermore, the Court's review is sporadic and reactive, and takes place one law at a time.[157] Each law the Court reviews may be only one piece of a more complicated picture, including discriminatory measures taken by other states. Disturbing just one piece, even if its costs outweigh its benefits when viewed in isolation, may upset one state's efforts to counteract another state's discrimination, and thus preserve rather than destroy a discriminatory regime.[158] In such circumstances, a second-best solution might be to allow one state to counteract another state's discrimination by engaging in discriminatory conduct of its own.[159]

---

[155] Ernest J. Brown, *The Open Economy: Justice Frankfurter and the Position of the Judiciary*, 67 Yale L J 219, 221 (1957); Friedman, supra note 6 at 1759 (Court's factfinding abilities compare unfavorably with those of administrative agencies). For an argument that the goal of achieving efficiency in individual Commerce Clause cases must be tempered by concerns about administrability, see Gergen, supra note 7 at 1110, 1115–16.

[156] See, e.g., Thomas K. Anson and P. M. Schenkkan, *Federalism, the Dormant Commerce Clause, and State-Owned Resources*, 59 Tex L Rev 71, 82–83 (1980); Tushnet, supra note 5 at 156 (inquiry into industry structure required by balancing test for nondiscriminatory laws is "far removed from the ordinary business of the Supreme Court"); but see Eule, supra note 5 at 442 (Court is accustomed to, and reasonably good at, balancing opposing interests).

[157] *McCarroll v Dixie Greyhound Lines*, 309 US 176, 188–89 (1940) (Black dissenting) ("Spasmodic and unrelated instances of litigation cannot afford an adequate basis for the creation of integrated national rules which alone can afford that full protection for interstate commerce intended by the Constitution.").

[158] This is somewhat akin to the problem faced by the Court in cases involving nondiscriminatory laws alleged to violate the Commerce Clause because they, in combination with other state laws, impose inconsistent obligations on interstate commerce. See, e.g., *Bibb v Navajo Freight Lines*, 359 US 520 (1959) (invalidating Illinois statute requiring curved mudflaps on trucks, which conflicted with other states' requirements of straight mud flaps). An important question raised by such cases is why the state statute being challenged, rather than the others with which that statute is in tension, must be the one to yield when the laws are inconsistent with each other. See Geoffrey R. Stone, Louis M. Seidman, Cass R. Sunstein, and Mark V. Tushnet, *Constitutional Law* 347–48 (2d ed 1991). For an argument that the Court should uphold discriminatory state and local laws that burden interstate commerce only if the laws of other states are taken into account, see Richard B. Collins, *Justice Scalia and the Elusive Idea of Discrimination Against Interstate Commerce*, 20 NM L Rev 555 (1990) (distinguishing "independent" discrimination (which burdens interstate commerce even if no other state or local laws are considered) from "dependent" discrimination (which burdens interstate commerce only if effects of other laws are considered)).

[159] For a similar point with respect to the Court's review of nondiscriminatory state and local laws, see Anson and Schenkkan, supra note 156 at 83 n 53; for an argument that states should not be able to restrict the importation of goods subsidized by other states, see Collins, supra note 10 at 105–06. On the theory of the second best, see generally 1 Alfred E. Kahn, *The Economics of Regulation: Principles and Institutions* 195–99 (1970).

The Court would say that the remedy for another state's discrimination is a lawsuit based on the Commerce Clause, not more discrimination in return.[160] But not all discrimination against outside commerce will be subject to the same searching judicial review, if any. For example, a state might subsidize its own industry in order to protect it from outside competition. It might fail to enact strict environmental or workplace safety laws because it wants to encourage in-state industry to stay in-state. Or it might fail to encourage the development of new waste disposal facilities, by declining to provide tax breaks or other incentives, in order to protect its citizens from the adverse consequences of such facilities. Each of these actions is "discriminatory" in the sense that it is undertaken for the purpose of benefiting insiders, and occurs to the detriment of outsiders. Moreover, the costs of each may outweigh the overall benefits.[161] However, a judicial remedy for such inefficient acts of discrimination may not exist. Not only has the Court traditionally treated subsidies for in-state firms more leniently than conventional regulation;[162] it also likely would refuse to overturn a state's failure to enact a stringent environmental program, or to encourage a domestic waste-processing industry, because it would probably not regard this conduct as the "regulation" of interstate commerce.[163] Indeed, the Court might not regard such failures to act as raising any constitutional problem at all, on the ground that they do not constitute state action.[164] A

---

[160] *A & P Tea Co. v Cottrell*, 424 US 366 (1976).

[161] For a concise restatement of the familiar argument that states acting to promote their own interests—or failing to act for the same reason—may produce overall welfare losses for the nation, see Evan H. Caminker, *State Sovereignty and Subordinacy: May Congress Commandeer State Officers to Implement Federal Law?* 95 Colum L Rev 1001, 1012 (1995).

[162] For a discussion of possible justifications for a distinction between subsidies and other kinds of protectionism, and of whether the Court's decision in *West Lynn Creamery*, supra note 1, reflects a shift in the Court's position, see Section IV.A.

[163] See text at note 43 supra. See also Section IV.A.

[164] A strong reluctance to review government failures to act runs through the Court's constitutional cases. See, e.g., *DeShaney v Winnebago County Dept of Social Services*, 489 US 189, 196 (1989) (in refusing to hold a state responsible for failure to protect a child from his father, whom the state knew to be abusive, Court explained, "the Due Process clauses generally confer no affirmative right to government aid"); *Flagg Bros v Brooks*, 436 US 149, 166 (1978) (in rejecting due process claim, Court explains, "the crux of respondent's complaint is not that the State *has* acted, but that it has *refused* to act") (emphasis in original); *Adickes v S H Kress & Co.*, 398 US 144, 230 (1970) ("our cases have never explicitly held that state inaction alone in the face of purely private discrimination constitutes a denial of Equal Protection"); Stone et al, supra note 158 at 1610 (while first noting that "many equal protection cases can be characterized as involving state inaction," the authors go on to

state faced with discrimination in the form of subsidies or nonregulation may thus be unable to respond with either retaliatory legislation or a viable lawsuit.[165] The Court's one-law-at-a-time invalidation of discriminatory laws, combined with its substantive responses to failures to act and subsidies, thus may serve only to restore the states to a position of imbalance and inefficiency.[166]

Finally, no matter how diligently the Court might attempt to pursue an objective analysis of costs and benefits, such analysis—and certainly the ultimate conclusion as to whether costs exceed benefits—would inevitably entail choices about values. Consider the moral and social choices involved in deciding whether the benefits of local autonomy and self-reliance outweigh the costs of higher consumer prices.[167] At this point it becomes appropriate to consider whether the politically unaccountable Supreme Court should be the institution to make these choices for us.[168]

For reasons like these, numerous legal scholars have called for an end to the Court's practice of balancing the burdens and bene-

---

concede that, "[o]f course, the state's failure to act in these situations is embedded in a context where the state is also acting").

In *SDDS v South Dakota*, 47 F3d 263 (8th Cir 1995), the court overturned a state referendum vetoing legislative approval for a new solid waste disposal facility on the ground that the referendum campaign was tainted by hostility to out-of-state waste. In essence, the plaintiffs challenged the state's *failure* to site their disposal facility. Presumably because the voters had "acted" by overturning legislative approval for the facility, however, the parties defending the referendum did not rely on the action/inaction distinction.

[165] Compare Tushnet, supra note 5 at 154: "[T]he courts can be summoned with respect to every single *regulation* by anyone adversely affected. Thus, one can expect that nearly every burdensome *regulation* will be the subject of judicial attention" (emphasis added).

[166] In considering only the one state or local law before it, the Court also ignores the lessons of game theory, which may contemplate strategic failures to act on the part of state and local governments. For an application of game-theoretic concepts to a number of legal problems, see Douglas G. Baird, Robert H. Gertner, and Randal C. Picker, *Game Theory and the Law* (1994).

[167] Without reducing the value of these interests to a common metric—such as dollars—it is hard to see how the Court can decide whether benefits exceed burdens. As Justice Scalia has observed, it is "like judging whether a particular line is longer than a particular rock is heavy." *Bendix Autolite Corp v Midwesco Enterprises*, 486 US 888, 897 (1988) (Scalia concurring). Yet expressing such interests as local autonomy and self-reliance in dollars is both controversial and complex. For general discussion, see Cass R. Sunstein, *Incommensurability and Valuation in Law*, 92 Mich L Rev 779 (1994).

[168] This is a prominent theme in many critiques of the Court's review of nondiscriminatory burdens on commerce. See, e.g., Anson and Schenkkan, supra note 156 at 83; Eule, supra note 5 at 441, 469 n 236; Healy, supra note 5 at 206; *Southern Pacific Co. v Arizona*, 325 US 761, 784, 794–95 (1945) (Black dissenting). Congress may, of course, override the Court's judgments in this area by exercising its own authority to regulate commerce, and thus Congress rather than the Court could have the last word. *Prudential Ins. Co. v Benjamin*, 328 US 408 (1946). For further discussion, see text at notes 265–69.

fits of nondiscriminatory state and local laws, and invalidating these laws when their burdens outweigh their benefits.[169] These scholars likely would regard it as a step in the wrong direction for the Court to undertake a case-by-case evaluation of the costs and benefits of discriminatory laws, the kind of analysis outlined in the preceding pages. Given the difficulties I have just described with this evaluation, this is a fair point. The question remains whether the Court's formalist approach to discriminatory laws—an approach which condemns discriminatory laws without attention to individual circumstances—performs any better, or is any more worthy of retention, than the case-by-case balancing these scholars have so forcefully criticized.[170]

The Court's formalist approach might be justified if it gets it right in most cases, even if it occasionally leads to mistakes. From the perspective of efficiency, this would mean that if the costs of laws that discriminate against outside commerce usually exceed their benefits, the Court would be justified in striking them all down if the costs of ferreting out the efficient from the inefficient would outweigh the benefits of preserving the occasional discriminatory-but-efficient law.[171] The argument in favor of an unbending rule against discrimination thus depends on the idea that in most cases the costs of discriminatory laws exceed their benefits.[172] In the next section, I discuss a prominent theory as to why this might be true.

III. POLITICS

The political process leading to the enactment of laws that discriminate against outside commerce is an important theme of

---

[169] See, e.g., Eule, supra note 5; Redish and Nugent, supra note 7; Farber, supra note 5.

[170] Obviously, the options available to the Court include not only formalism and case-by-case analysis, but also abandonment of the nondiscrimination principle altogether. I advocate the latter position. See Section V.

[171] For an economic account of the choice between narrowly drawn rules and broad standards, see Posner, supra note 94 at 542–47; see also id at 549–52 (discussing costs of error in civil cases). For a jurisprudential account (and criticism) of the arguments in favor of a formalist approach to the Commerce Clause, see Mark Tushnet, *Scalia and the Dormant Commerce Clause: A Foolish Formalism?* 12 Cardozo L Rev 1717, 1732–39 (1991).

[172] Some authors defend the Court's formalism on grounds other than efficiency. Some believe, for example, that laws that discriminate against interstate commerce are more likely to stem from an impermissible motive—protecting insiders at the expense of outsiders—and thus warrant especially demanding review. See, e.g., Cass R. Sunstein, *Naked Preferences and the Constitution*, 84 Colum L Rev 1689, 1706–07 (1984); Eule, supra note 5 at 461–62; see also text at note 193. I discuss this idea in Section IV.

the Court's decisions[173] and of academic commentary on the Commerce Clause.[174] An unforgiving approach to laws that discriminate against outside commerce is appropriate, according to this perspective, because discriminatory laws concentrate their benefits on insiders (represented in the local legislature) and their costs on outsiders (unrepresented in the local legislature).[175]

The idea behind process-based concerns is that, in enacting laws that discriminate against outside commerce, insiders have taken the opportunity to export the costs of their benefits to outsiders.[176] The disciplining effect of the internalization of costs—forcing those who enjoy benefits to think hard about whether they're worth their costs—is absent when costs are exported. Thus, where process fails, efficiency may suffer as well: the outside costs of discriminatory laws will at least sometimes exceed their inside benefits.[177] In this way, the process-based rationale for the nondiscrimination principle is closely allied with the efficiency-based rationale.[178] Indeed, some have observed that economic efficiency is important under the Commerce Clause only because outsiders may be harmed by a state or local government's restrictions on interstate commerce.[179]

---

[173] Justice Harlan Stone broke this ground for the Court. See *South Carolina State Highway Dept v Barnwell Bros*, 303 US 177, 184 n 2 (1938) ("when the regulation is of such a character that its burden falls principally upon those without the state, legislative action is not likely to be subjected to those political restraints which are normally exerted on legislation"); Herbert Wechsler, *Mr. Justice Stone and the Constitution*, in *Principles, Politics, and Fundamental Law: Selected Essays* 114–21 (1961).

[174] See Tushnet, supra note 5; Eule, supra note 5; Farber, supra note 5; William N. Eskridge, Jr., and John Ferejohn, *The Elastic Commerce Clause: A Political Theory of American Federalism*, 47 Vand L Rev 1355 (1994).

[175] First suggested by Justice Stone, see note 14 supra, the representation-reinforcement theory of judicial review was elaborated by John Hart Ely in *Democracy and Distrust* (1980). Simply stated, the idea is that "decisions of the political branches should be respected unless there is reason to believe that some interest is systematically underrepresented in the political process." Tushnet, supra note 5 at 128.

[176] See, e.g., Anson and Schenkkan, supra note 156 at 82 n 48 (economic protectionism shifts costs to underrepresented interests, that is, "the state is attempting to externalize some costs").

[177] Eule, supra note 5 at 445–46; Gergen, supra note 7 at 1109; Eskridge and Ferejohn, supra note 174 at 1363–64.

[178] See Tushnet, supra note 5 at 129 n 14 (process-based theory "can be viewed as a political application of the economists' theory of externalities: because a legislative body may underestimate the burdens that its proposals place on people who do not participate in its selection, the resulting statutes may be inefficient").

[179] Farber and Hudec, supra note 10 at 1404–07.

This analysis does not tell us whether, *in most cases,* outside costs will exceed inside benefits. Discriminatory treatment of inside and outside commerce does not dictate where costs and benefits will ultimately fall; the "magic words" of discrimination,[180] without more, do not tell us who is hurt and who helped by a barrier to trade.[181] Indeed, the Court's "paradigmatic example" of unlawful discrimination—a tariff—primarily imposes costs on inside consumers who must pay higher prices. As for the affected firms, there is no reason to believe that the costs for outside firms (decreased demand for their products) systematically exceed their benefits to inside firms. Moreover, once the concept of "discrimination" is expanded to include laws that have not been shown to harm anyone but insiders (as in *Oregon Waste Systems* and *Carbone*), the "cost-exporting" argument in favor of formalism collapses altogether.[182]

The process-based rationale also fails to take account of the conduct of outsiders that may have led to the insiders' discriminatory treatment of outside commerce. As noted above,[183] states and local governments may export costs to outsiders through inaction as well as action. Some laws that discriminate against outside commerce may simply be attempts to undo the harms done by other states' inaction—inaction in which outsiders were also underrepresented. There thus may be a lack of representation on both sides. Although "national supervision" may indeed be "designed to guarantee that the external costs of *regulation* are considered by local legislatures,"[184] this supervision does not at present guarantee that the external costs of *non*regulation are so considered.

Telling "insiders" from "outsiders" is also trickier business than proponents of the process-based theory have let on. The theory's premise has been that insiders are residents (voters) within the reg-

---

[180] Tushnet, *Scalia and the Dormant Commerce Clause,* supra note 171 at 1730.

[181] See Collins, supra note 10 at 68–72.

[182] Mark Tushnet has argued that insiders may need process-based protection, too, if they are at "a systematic disadvantage in legislative combat against organized groups" as a result of collective action problems. Tushnet, supra note 5 at 133, 148–49. He finds the source of this protection in substantive due process. Id at 148–49. See also Lea Brilmayer, *Carolene, Conflicts, and the Fate of the "Inside-Outsider,"* 134 U Pa L Rev 1291, 1308–10 (1986) (criticizing process theorists' preoccupation with discriminatory laws and suggesting that process theory would also justify heightened scrutiny of facially neutral laws).

[183] See text at notes 161–66.

[184] Tushnet, supra note 5 at 143 (emphasis added).

ulating jurisdiction, and outsiders are nonresidents (nonvoters).[185] But voting is only one means of political participation. Nonresidents, especially the large companies that are the primary plaintiffs in Commerce Clause litigation,[186] may participate by lobbying elected representatives and contributing to their campaigns, and by lobbying and organizing the voters themselves.[187] Indeed, these are the only means by which even *inside* firms may influence the political process, since corporations do not vote.[188] Thus laws that discriminate on their face against outside commerce may in fact discriminate only against "insiders," properly defined to include those having an influence over the political process.[189]

The process-based rationale also fails to recognize that insiders and outsiders may have different interests *because* they are insiders and outsiders, and not just because the burdens or benefits of a given regulation fall more heavily on one group than another. The Court thinks it significant, for example, when inside consumers share with outsiders the burden of a barrier to trade, because it believes this makes it more likely that the insiders will adequately protect the outsiders.[190] This assumes that the consumers are not

---

[185] Ely, supra note 175 at 82–85 (discussing Privileges and Immunities Clause).

[186] *Dennis v Higgins*, 498 US 439, 464 (1991) (Kennedy dissenting) ("typical dormant Commerce Clause plaintiff[s]" are "major corporations or industry associations").

[187] Mark Tushnet, *Darkness on the Edge of Town: The Contributions of John Hart Ely to Constitutional Theory*, 89 Yale L J 1037, 1055 (1980); Farber, supra note 5 at 404; Collins, supra note 10 at 69; see also Richard A. Posner, *Democracy and Distrust Revisited*, 77 Va L J 641, 648 (1991) ("Voting power is, moreover, only one element of political power; others include money, education, age, membership in or good access to a constitutionally protected class, and membership in a politically effective interest group.").

[188] It is also worth noting that a firm's state of incorporation has little, if any, relation to the state in which its shareholders or management vote. Thus, an apparently "outside" firm may in fact have many partisans within the regulating state.

[189] One might also describe outsiders as those who "have no ability to attract the attention of" insiders. *City of Cleburne v Cleburne Living Center*, 473 US 432, 445 (1985) (refusing to recognize mentally retarded persons as quasi-suspect class because they are not politically powerless). Note that explicit discrimination—because it is explicit, and thus easy to detect—may be especially good at attracting the attention of outsiders who may influence the political process. Explicit discrimination may thus invite the political participation (in the form of lobbying, campaign contributions, and organizing by affected nonresidents) that lies at the heart of the process-based rationale. For an argument, from another context, that explicit legislative directives invite more political participation than implicit ones, see Bruce A. Ackerman and William T. Hassler, *Clean Coal/Dirty Air* 47–48, 55–56 (1981).

[190] See, e.g., *West Lynn Creamery*, supra note 1 at 2215; Tushnet, supra note 5 at 135–36.

also workers whose jobs are protected by the barrier, or families of those workers, or members of the community in which the jobs are located.[191] It assumes that the consumers will place their own interest in lower prices over their community's interest in preserving jobs, tax revenues, or a way of life. But this, again, is just to abstract from the benefits of discrimination against outside commerce, on the assumption that classification based on outsider status is illegitimate.[192]

In sum, whatever the merits of process-based concerns on a case-by-case basis, they do not justify the Court's unbending rule against discrimination, whether one's concern with political process stems from a desire to promote economic efficiency or from a desire to improve political representation.[193] Yet, as discussed above, the Court is also unlikely to be very good at case-by-case analysis of the burdens and benefits of discriminatory laws.[194]

Perhaps the explanation for the process theorists' continued enthusiasm for the nondiscrimination principle is that they are not looking for disproportionate burdens on outsiders so much as they are on the lookout for discriminatory purpose. Indeed, some process theorists have suggested that the nondiscrimination rule is justified because discriminatory laws evince an *intent* to benefit inside commerce at the expense of outside commerce.[195] The process-based rationale, in other words, ultimately falls back on the idea that purposeful discrimination against interstate commerce—

---

[191] That people may belong to more than one group (consumers and workers, women and the poor, etc.) makes their classification as "insiders" or "outsiders" problematic. On the difficulty of defining "we" and "they," see Tushnet, *Darkness on the Edge of Town*, supra note 187 at 1052–53.

[192] Laurence Tribe has made a similar point in the equal protection context. Laurence H. Tribe, *The Puzzling Persistence of Process-Based Constitutional Theories*, 89 Yale L J 1063, 1075 (1980) ("Views about the 'differentness' of groups generally . . . may reflect an interacting set of judgments about activities or options or roles, expressed sometimes harmoniously and sometimes dialectically by *both* 'we' and 'they.' If so, the conclusion that a legislative classification reveals prejudicial stereotypes must, at bottom, spring from *a disagreement with the judgments that lie behind the stereotype* . . . ").

[193] Julian Eule agrees that even a facially discriminatory statute does not warrant a "per se" rule of invalidity, but would want the state to prove a compelling state interest in order to justify such a law. Eule, supra note 5 at 461–62.

[194] See Section II.C.

[195] Tushnet, supra note 5 at 131–32, 141; see also Tushnet, *Scalia and the Dormant Commerce Clause*, supra note 171 at 1742 n 104; Eule, supra note 5 at 457 (discriminatory purpose illegitimate).

regardless of the incidence of burdens and benefits—is illegitimate. But this leaves the question, What is wrong with such an intent?[196] In the end, the process-based rationale for the nondiscrimination principle fails for much the same reason that the efficiency rationale fails. In presuming the illegitimacy of purposeful discrimination, the process-based rationale—like the Court's cost-benefit analysis of discriminatory laws—rests on an undefended background principle that states and local governments ought not treat outside commerce differently from inside commerce because it is outside commerce. I next explore whether this kind of principle justifies the Court's rule against discrimination.

IV. Community

The Court's unforgiving principle of nondiscrimination seems to depend on the assumption that discrimination against outsiders cannot be good and is always bad. From this perspective, the Commerce Clause serves a function much like the Equal Protection Clause—that of disapproving certain reasons for government action.[197] The idea would be that such classifications draw

---

[196] Richard Friedman has criticized this emphasis on discriminatory purpose: "[I]n terms of what best serves national policy, a purpose test aims in the wrong direction. If the purpose of a state law and the impact of the law on interstate commerce diverge, it is the impact on commerce that should be determinative. A state law intended to discriminate against interstate commerce but ineffectual in achieving that end will not do much harm, while an innocent but obstructive law should not stand." Friedman, supra note 6 at 1759. Compare Daniel R. Ortiz, *Pursuing a Perfect Politics: The Allure and Failure of Process Theory*, 77 Va L Rev 721, 731 (1991) (criticizing process-based theory as applied to equal protection cases: "discrimination by itself does not warrant granting special solicitude to a particular group. . . . The question must be whether the difference in treatment is justified.").

[197] On one occasion the Court relied on the Equal Protection Clause in disapproving a preference for inside commerce, but has since stepped away from that decision. In *Metropolitan Life Insurance v Ward*, 470 US 869, 880 (1985), the Court invoked the Equal Protection Clause in striking down an Alabama statute imposing higher taxes on out-of-state insurance companies than in-state insurance companies, concluding that "promotion of domestic business within a State, by discrimination against foreign corporations that wish to compete by doing business there, is not a legitimate state purpose." Later that year, the Court upheld, against equal protection challenges, Massachusetts and Connecticut laws favoring regional banks over banks from other states. *Northeast Bancorp v Board of Governors*, 472 US 159 (1985). *Ward* was distinguished on the rather dubious ground that the Massachusetts and Connecticut laws favored out-of-state as well as in-state interests. Id at 177. In the ten years since it was decided, *Ward* has not been applied by the Supreme Court to invalidate any other state law.

Given my negative views of the Court's review of discriminatory state and local laws under the Commerce Clause, I do not suggest that the Court simply continue the same kind of review under a different constitutional heading, such as equal protection or privileges and immunities. For a different perspective, see Philip Weinberg, *Congress, the Courts, and Solid Waste Transport: Good Fences Don't Always Make Good Neighbors*, 25 Envir L Rev 57 (1995)

the relevant community too narrowly by considering the interests only of those within a state or county or town, reflecting inadequate respect for the principle that we are supposed to be united, as one nation.[198]

As I will discuss, however, this theory creates two puzzles. First, where subsidies and other public resources are at stake, the Court has approved distinctions between insiders and outsiders.[199] However, since public subsidies may have the same adverse effects on outsiders as conventional barriers to trade (such as tariffs), and since both can set off a cycle of interstate retaliation, the goal of national unity does not appear to explain why distinctions between insiders and outsiders are lawful in one context but not in another. Second, the Court's treatment of discrimination against outsiders as an injury in itself, without regard to the actual consequences for outsiders, sharply contrasts with its close inspection for injury in other settings. Even in equal protection cases, where the relevant injury stems from the government's inappropriate preference for one group over another, the Court has considered whether the plaintiff was personally injured by the challenged preference. The Court's inattention to injury in the Commerce Clause setting therefore cannot be explained by reference to the goal of promoting national community through the disapproval of distinctions between insiders and outsiders. These two puzzles suggest that the goal of national unity cannot fully explain the Court's Commerce Clause cases.

A. SUBSIDIES

The Court does not consistently condemn state and local protectionism. In some contexts, it has embraced the protectionist impulse. Where the Court has found, for example, that a state is acting as a "market participant" in its activities affecting com-

---

(arguing that Congressional statutes authorizing discriminatory state and local legislation are invalid under Equal Protection Clause even if they are valid under the Commerce Clause); see also sources cited in note 7 supra (proposing that judicial review of discriminatory state and local laws proceed under Privileges and Immunities Clause).

[198] See, e.g., Sunstein, *Naked Preferences*, supra note 172 at 1706; Tushnet, *Scalia and the Dormant Commerce Clause*, supra note 171 at 1731 n 67; see also Douglas Laycock, *Taking Constitutions Seriously: A Theory of Judicial Review*, 59 Tex L Rev 343, 362 (1981) (discussing Privileges and Immunities Clause).

[199] See Section II.B for a discussion of whether the Court's decision in *West Lynn Creamery* reflects a change in the Court's approach to subsidies favoring insiders.

merce, rather than as a "market regulator," it has upheld the state's actions. *Hughes v Alexandria Scrap*[200] is a leading case here. In order to encourage the scrap processing of old, unusable cars, Maryland paid a bounty to scrap processors. The bounty applied only to cars licensed in Maryland, and the law's most onerous documentation requirements applied to out-of-state, but not in-state, processors.[201] In upholding the law, the Court declared: "Nothing in the purposes animating the Commerce Clause prohibits a State, in the absence of congressional action, from participating in the market and exercising the right to favor its own citizens over others."[202]

Other examples of protectionism leap to mind. The benefits of public institutions such as schools, universities, and libraries, as well as social benefits such as welfare and unemployment compensation, have all, traditionally and uncontroversially, been distributed according to place of residency.[203] The only dispute has so far been whether the government has impermissibly narrowed the class of residents who may enjoy these benefits.[204] No one has suggested, for example, that in order to invite residents to use its public library free of charge, a town must extend the same invitation to nonresidents, or that a state that chooses to provide unemployment benefits to its citizens must provide them to noncitizens, too.[205] And in *Hughes v Alexandria Scrap*, no one questioned Mary-

---

[200] 426 US 794 (1976).

[201] Id at 800–01.

[202] Id at 810. See also cases cited in note 42 supra; cf *South-Central Timber Development v Wunnicke*, 467 US 82 (1984) (invalidating, as impermissible attempt to control downstream market in which state was not a participant, Alaska's requirement that successful bidder for state-owned timber process the timber in Alaska before exporting it).

[203] *Martinez v Bynum*, 461 US 321, 328 (1983) (a "bona fide residence requirement" is one that is "appropriately defined and uniformly applied [and which] furthers the substantial state interest in assuring that services provided for its residents are enjoyed only by its residents"); *County of Westchester v Koch*, 438 NYS 2d 951 (1981) (upholding New York City's policy of giving resident senior citizens a discount for bus fares); *American Commuters Assn v Levitt*, 279 F Supp 40 (SDNY 1967) (upholding numerous benefits granted on basis of residency, including use of the public schools, qualification for scholarships, and discounts for fishing licenses).

[204] For decisions striking down statutes because, by considering duration of residency, they impermissibly narrowed the class of residents receiving a government benefit, see *Attorney General of New York v Soto-Lopez*, 476 US 898 (1986); *Hooper v Bernalillo County Assessor*, 472 US 612 (1985); *Zobel v Williams*, 495 US 55 (1982); *Shapiro v Thompson*, 394 US 618 (1969).

[205] The economic case for free trade is often accompanied by a call for public assistance for the people who will be harmed by changed patterns of production. See, e.g., Baumol & Blinder, supra note 115 at 723–24. There is no suggestion, however, that the government

land's limitation of its bounty to *Maryland*-licensed cars—presumably because this "would threaten the validity of all local and state programs designed to subsidize or otherwise encourage local business at the expense of foreign competition."[206] It is a staple of government at all levels to attend to the needs of its citizens and to ignore the needs of outsiders. Indeed, it does not seem an overstatement to say the very idea of a town or a county or a state, even a nation, would become incoherent if these units of government were not allowed to distinguish between insiders and outsiders in distributing government resources and setting regulatory priorities.

Perhaps for this reason, the Court sometimes *requires* states and local governments to maintain a dichotomy between insiders and outsiders. Recall that in *Carbone*, the Court said that it would have been illegitimate for the town of Clarkstown to have enacted its ordinance in order to steer its residents' garbage away from outside disposal sites especially harmful to the environment.[207] A state or local government that takes into account the environmental consequences of its actions for its *own* citizens thus may not, at the same time, consider the environmental impacts it causes for outsiders. In a sense, then, *Carbone* requires states and local governments to discriminate against outsiders by excluding consequences to outsiders from consideration in government decisions.

It is thus wrong to suggest that the Commerce Clause condemns all distinctions based on outsider status.[208] How does one tell the distinctions that are lawful from those that are not? The Court has suggested that distinctions based on outsider status are lawful when they do not involve the "regulation" of interstate commerce.[209] This, in turn, raises another question: How is what the

providing assistance to its unemployed citizens must also provide it to the citizens of other governments.

[206] Kitch, supra note 12 at 32.

[207] See text at note 61.

[208] Even Donald Regan, whose influential article on this topic famously defends the view that the Commerce Clause prohibits laws based on protectionist motives, concedes that a protectionist purpose is acceptable so long as the state or local government's "scheme is not analogous in form to the traditional instruments of protection" such as tariffs and embargoes. Regan, supra note 5 at 1201.

[209] See text at note 43; see also *New Energy Co.*, supra note 20 at 278 (a direct cash subsidy to in-state producers of ethanol assumed to be constitutional because the Commerce Clause prohibited "only action . . . *in connection with the State's regulation of interstate commerce*") (emphasis in original).

Court regards as "regulation" different from other governmental conduct that makes distinctions based on outsider status?[210]

Sometimes the distinction between protectionist "regulation" and protectionist "subsidies" is defended by asserting that outsiders foot the bill for the former while insiders must pay for the latter. Subsidies thus ensure representation of the adversely affected interests in a way that "regulation" does not.[211] However, this simple assumption about who pays the ultimate costs of subsidies and conventional regulation will be wrong in many cases; recall the example of the tariff.[212] Recognizing this, Mark Gergen has suggested that the real distinction between subsidies and other forms of protectionism is that subsidies more clearly "signal" their costs to the state, which is important "because the hope that a state will correct inefficient measures when the cost is borne internally wanes when that cost is hidden."[213] Gergen concedes, however, that the constitutional status of this argument is unclear, since the distinction he describes would "in effect protect the citi-

---

[210] The language of the Commerce Clause does not answer this question. To be sure, the Clause applies only to the "regulation" of interstate commerce, but it does not define this term. See note 8 supra. For an argument that the text of the Commerce Clause, by encompassing only "regulation," supports the market-participant doctrine, see Coenen, supra note 42 at 436–37.

[211] See, e.g., Anson and Schenkkan, supra note 156 at 90 (state's discriminatory distribution of state-owned resources different from discriminatory regulation of private resources because when the state owns a resource, it makes the redistributive decision based on represented interests; thus distribution of state-owned resources should be treated differently for Commerce Clause purposes even if economic effects of such distribution and regulation of private resources are the same); Saul Levmore, *Interstate Exploitation and Judicial Intervention,* 69 Va L Rev 563, 573, 584–85 (1983) (discriminatory taxes are impermissible "exploitation," whereas discriminatory subsidies are permissible "interference" with commerce; fact that state must pay for subsidies means political process will disfavor them, or at least state will think hard before enacting them); see also Healy, supra note 5 (distinguishing *Fort Gratiot,* supra note 1, from *Chemical Waste Management,* supra note 1, on ground that Michigan but not Alabama had launched a comprehensive waste disposal program which created the landfill resource at issue); Eskridge and Ferejohn, supra note 174 at 1367–68 (distinguishing state "allocative and developmental policies" from "redistributive policies" on the ground that benefits and costs of former "fall largely within the jurisdiction. The policies are executed and financed by the people whose welfare is directly affected, and therefore democratic incentives are well-placed to ensure relatively efficient results."). But see Regan, supra note 5 at 1196 ("straightforward production subsidy for local producers . . . [i]n principle, should probably be forbidden" because if subsidy were "carefully calibrated," it could greatly benefit local producers with very little local expense, and thus "the expense of providing this benefit to locals would not be an effective constraint").

[212] See text at note 114. See also Gergen, supra note 7 at 1136 (costs of subsidies also fall on outside "communities that lose industry to a neighbor's enticements or by foreign producers that face a decline in price and market share").

[213] Gergen, supra note 7 at 1111–12; see also Coenen, supra note 42 at 435 n 242, 479.

zens of the state whose actions are being challenged, rather than outsiders."[214] The protection afforded by this argument would thus range beyond interstate commerce, to encompass a generalized preference for economic efficiency[215]—a task perhaps better suited for substantive due process than for the Commerce Clause.[216]

In any event, the idea that discriminatory subsidies are valid because insiders pay for them, and discriminatory "regulation" invalid because they do not, does not survive the Court's decision in *Oregon Waste Systems*. Recall that the Court refused even to consider whether Oregon's surcharge matched real costs imposed on insiders who paid general taxes.[217] It was irrelevant, in other words, whether insiders were paying a disproportionate share of the bill for the disposal of outsiders' waste. The Court's formalist approach to determining the "substantial equivalence" of the taxable events suggests that the Court did not care where burdens and benefits would fall in the absence of the surcharge. It was more concerned about the complexity of determining whether outsiders were being appropriately charged for their waste disposal,[218] and about the possibility that accepting Oregon's argument would mean states could always charge an additional fee for outsiders' use of state-funded services,[219] than it was about the possibility that insiders would, if Oregon's surcharge fell, end up subsidizing outsiders' waste disposal. Since the Court was unconcerned about the incidence of burdens and benefits when insiders were arguably bearing the brunt of the burdens, it may not, without arbitrariness, turn around and rely on the incidence of burdens and benefits in defending a distinction between "regulation" and "subsidies."

The Court has also tried to distinguish subsidies from "regulation" by positing a distinction between "burdens" on commerce

---

[214] Id at 1112.

[215] For examples of such reasoning, see Regan, supra note 5 at 1194 ("The very fact that spending programs involve spending and are therefore relatively expensive as a way of securing local benefit makes them less likely to proliferate than measures like tariffs. They are therefore less likely to damage the economy seriously in the aggregate, if they damage it at all."); Gergen, supra note 7 at 1136 (some assert that subsidies are preferable to other forms of protectionism because they benefit industry more by, for example, discouraging redistributive programs and decreasing the size of government).

[216] Tushnet, supra note 5 at 147–50. I return to this point in Section V.

[217] See text at notes 40–41.

[218] *Oregon Waste Systems*, supra note 1 at 1353.

[219] See text at note 39.

and "benefits" in the form of subsidies.[220] This distinction, elsewhere ridiculed by the Court,[221] merely states rather than explains
the Court's conclusion.[222] A subsidy may drive outside competitors
out of business just as surely as a tariff,[223] and may invite a cycle
of "retaliatory" subsidies as destructive to the ideal of national
unity, and to the efficient allocation of resources, as a series of
retaliatory embargoes.[224] The message of a subsidy for local people
or firms is clear: we want to protect you because you are our own.
It is difficult to see how this message fits more comfortably with

---

[220] *West Lynn Creamery,* supra note 1 at 2214. See also Coenen, supra note 42 at 422
(distinguishing states' discriminatory taxes and regulation from discriminatory buying and
selling decisions on the ground that the former "compels private action" whereas the latter
merely involves the state in "controlling and distributing its own resources").

[221] *Lucas v South Carolina Coastal Council,* 112 US 2886, 2899 (1992) ("the distinction
between regulation that 'prevents harmful use' and that which 'confers benefits' is difficult,
if not impossible, to discern on an objective, value-free basis"). See also *Tyler Pipe Industries
v Washington State Dept. of Revenue,* 483 US 232, 263 (1987) (Scalia concurring and dissenting) (distinguishing between regulations of commerce and police power regulations,
"while perhaps a textually possible construction . . . , is a most unlikely one," as it is "more
interesting as a metaphysical exercise than useful as a practical technique for marking out
the powers of separate sovereigns"). But see *Rust v Sullivan,* 500 US 173, 192–93 (1991)
(distinguishing between imposing a burden and failing to provide a benefit).

[222] The same goes for Donald Regan's attempt to distinguish measures funded by the
state from "mere regulation" on the ground that "state spending programs are less coercive
than regulatory programs or taxes with similar purposes," Regan, supra note 5 at 1194,
since Regan provides no reasoned basis for distinguishing coercive measures from noncoercive ones.

[223] See, e.g., Coenen, supra note 42 at 478 (the "key effect on interstate commerce of
subsidies and tariffs are the same: both forms of state intervention steer business to local
producers at the expense of more efficient out-of-state competitors"); Environmental Law
Institute, *Sustainable Environmental Law: Integrating Natural Resource and Pollution Abatement
Law from Resources to Recovery* 805 (Celia Campbell-Mohn, Barry Breen, and J. William
Futrell eds, 1993) (subsidies to coal industry are among the "many economic and institutional obstacles" standing in the way of a transition to renewable energy resources because
they artificially lower the price of serving energy needs with coal). To the same effect, see
Collins, supra note 10 at 98; Gergen, supra note 7 at 1134–35.

[224] Donald Regan has argued that measures funded from state revenues "are less likely
to produce resentment and retaliation" than "mere regulation or the positive imposition
of a tax." Regan, supra note 5 at 1194; see also Coenen, supra note 42 at 480 (discriminatory
tax exemptions more likely to inspire retaliation than subsidies). Regan's claim about retaliation is belied by the innumerable accounts of dueling subsidies offered by states and local
governments. A tiny sampling of such competing subsidies is described in Daniel Souther-
land, *Solarex Can't Resist Va.'s Subsidies,* Washington Post F1 (June 7, 1995), and David
Segal, *Md. Loses Another Firm to Virginia,* Washington Post F1 (July 1, 1995). Regan's belief
that measures funded from state revenues produce less resentment than "mere regulation"
is tied to his assertion that "it just seems obvious that when states distribute benefits they
can prefer their own citizens." Regan, supra note 5 at 1194; see also Gergen, supra note
6 at 1114, 1137 (tradition justifies upholding subsidies). I return to the question whether
there is something "obvious" or natural about the distinction between subsidies and "mere
regulation" in Section V.

the ideal of national unity than the message sent by a tariff having the same economic effect as the subsidy.[225]

Insofar as it casts doubt on the validity of the discriminatory distribution of subsidies to local firms, *West Lynn Creamery* raises the possibility that this whole discussion is beside the point. On its strongest reading, this decision has resolved the tension between the Court's nondiscrimination principle and its embrace of some discriminatory public programs by holding that such programs are, after all, unlawful.

Subsidies (in the form of both cash grants and in-kind distributions of public resources) that discriminate between insiders and outsiders bring with them all of the effects that the Court condemned in *West Lynn Creamery*. They "artificially encourag[e] instate production even when the same goods could be produced at lower cost in other States," "distort[ ] . . . the geography of production," "neutraliz[e] the advantage possessed by lower cost out-of-state producers," and "divert market share" to inside firms.[226] Even so, in *West Lynn Creamery* the Court took pains to distinguish "a pure subsidy funded out of general revenue" from the tax and subsidy scheme developed by Massachusetts. The former "ordinarily imposes no burden on interstate commerce, but merely assists local business," whereas the latter burdened interstate commerce by taxing it.[227] Likewise, the Court noted, "it is undisputed that States may try to attract business by creating an environment conducive to economic activity, as by maintaining good roads, sound public education, or low taxes."[228] The Court's basic objec-

---

[225] See Gergen, supra note 7 at 1137 n 207 (outsiders likely see little difference between a job training program subsidized by the government for the benefit of insiders, and a discriminatory hiring preference for insiders).

[226] *West Lynn Creamery*, supra note 1 at 2211, 2212, 2217.

[227] Id at 2214; see also id at 2218 n 21 (distinguishing between state's power to protect its citizens from dangers of interstate commerce and its lack of power to burden interstate commerce for the state's economic advantage). In *Fireside Nissan v Fanning*, 30 F3d 206 (1st Cir 1994), the court relied on the burden/benefit distinction in upholding a Rhode Island law giving Rhode Island, but not Massachusetts, automobile dealers located within 20 miles of a proposed new dealership an opportunity to protest approval of the new dealership by the state's Department of Transportation. The court explained that the " 'advantage in the marketplace' " bestowed by the challenged law was not one " 'in connection with the state's regulation of interstate commerce,' " because it did not "relate to the price of the automobiles being sold, the taxes paid for them, or the costs and conditions of selling them." Id at 216, quoting *New Energy Co.*, supra note 20 at 278.

[228] 114 S Ct at 2214 n 15.

tion to Massachusetts' pricing order was not that it drew a line between insiders and outsiders—subsidies funded from general revenues, and investments intended to lure business to one state and away from another, do the same—but that it funded the subsidy by taxing out-of-state firms in the same industry as the recipients of the subsidy.

Thus *West Lynn Creamery* does not solve the puzzle I described at the beginning of this section, but complicates it. There is yet another curious aspect of the Commerce Clause decisions, and that is their approach to the issue of standing.

B. STANDING

In *Lujan v Defenders of Wildlife*,[229] the Court reaffirmed and arguably tightened[230] the requirement that, in order to have standing to sue, a plaintiff prove that she has suffered an "injury in fact." For this, she must show that she herself "is among the injured,"[231] and that the injury she complains of is "actual or imminent."[232]

In *Lujan*, the plaintiffs challenged a Department of Interior regulation declining to apply the protections of the Endangered Species Act to overseas projects assisted by the federal government.[233] Plaintiffs had previously traveled to other countries where they had either seen or had tried to see the species allegedly endangered by federally assisted projects. In affidavits, both swore that they intended, one day, to visit these places again in order to see these species.[234] The Court held these " 'some day' intentions" insufficient to show "actual or imminent" injury.[235]

Contrast this with the Court's approach under the Commerce Clause. As explained in Part II.B above, in this context the Court either fails to look closely for any injury whatsoever, to the plaintiff or anyone else (as in *Oregon Waste Systems* and *Chemical Waste*

---

[229] 504 US 555 (1992).

[230] See Cass R. Sunstein, *What's Standing After Lujan? Of Citizen Suits, "Injuries," and Article III*, 91 Mich L Rev 163, 202–05 (1992).

[231] 504 US at 563, quoting *Sierra Club v Morton*, 405 US 727, 734–35 (1972).

[232] Id at 560. In addition, the plaintiff must prove that her injury was caused by the conduct she challenges and that her injury can be redressed by judicial action. Id.

[233] Id at 558.

[234] Id at 563.

[235] Id at 564.

Management), or hypothesizes *some* injury from the challenged discrimination (to outside waste processors in *Carbone*, and to outside dairy farms in *West Lynn Creamery*), indifferent to whether this injury has been suffered by any party before the Court.[236]

Although it has not tried to do so, perhaps the Court could explain the apparent difference in approach between *Lujan* and its Commerce Clause cases by characterizing the injury relevant for Commerce Clause purposes as an *opportunity* to compete for market share without regard to one's location or the location of one's patrons. This is the move the Court made in explaining how a white-owned firm could challenge an affirmative action program giving a preference to minority-owned businesses in government contracts even though the firm did not show that it would have gotten a contract but for the program.[237] The Court explained: "When the government erects a barrier that makes it more difficult for members of one group to obtain a benefit than it is for members of another group, a member of the former group seeking to challenge the barrier need not allege that he would have obtained the benefit but for the barrier in order to establish standing. The 'injury in fact' in an equal protection case of this variety is the denial of equal treatment resulting from the imposition of the

---

[236] The Court seldom even mentions standing in Commerce Clause cases. For the rare exceptions, see *Boston Stock Exchange v State Tax Comm'n*, 429 US 318, 321 n 3 (1977) (stock exchanges had standing to challenge New York's discriminatory tax in part because "they are asserting their right under the Commerce Clause to engage in interstate commerce free of discriminatory taxes on their busines" and "[t]hus, they are arguably within the zone of interest to be protected . . . by the . . . constitutional guarantee in question"); *Hunt v Washington Apple Advertising Comm'n*, 432 US 333, 343–45 (1977) (Washington agency responsible for promoting state's apple industry had standing to challenge North Carolina law that injured the industry agency was charged to protect); *Wyoming v Oklahoma*, supra note 1. Justice Scalia dissented in *Wyoming v Oklahoma*, arguing that Wyoming had no standing to challenge an Oklahoma statute requiring that 10 percent of coal burned in power plants in Oklahoma be in-state coal. Although Wyoming had alleged that it was injured by a reduction of coal sales to Oklahoma that had decreased revenue from severance taxes, it had failed to show that the loss of Oklahoma sales was not made up for by sales to other parties. Scalia also concluded that Wyoming was not within "zone of interests" protected by the Commerce Clause because its interest in collecting severance tax on coal was "antithetical" to the purposes of this provision, id at 470–71, and because granting standing to Wyoming would invite litigation: "if a State has a litigable interest in the taxes that would have been paid upon an unconstitutionally obstructed sale, there is no reasonable basis for saying that a company salesman does not have a litigable interest in the commissions that would have been paid, or a union in the wages that would have been earned." Id at 472.

[237] *Northeastern Florida Chapter of the Associated General Contractors v Jacksonville*, 113 S Ct 2297 (1993). For a discussion anticipating this move, see Sunstein, *What's Standing After Lujan?* supra note 230 at 203–04.

barrier, not the ultimate inability to obtain the benefit."[238] The Court might make a similar argument with respect to the Commerce Clause: the purpose of the Clause is to allow equality of competition as between in-state and out-of-state firms, and thus in such cases it matters only whether an out-of-state firm's opportunity to compete on an equal basis with in-state firms has been impaired, not whether the out-of-state firm's business has actually suffered economic injury, such as a decline in sales, due to a discriminatory law.[239]

Yet this leaves *West Lynn Creamery* and *Carbone* unexplained. In *West Lynn Creamery*, it was not the plaintiffs, but unnamed and unknown parties not before the Court, who had arguably been denied an opportunity to compete on account of their outside status. Even under the expansive view of standing the Court has adopted for equal protection cases involving racial discrimination,[240] the Court has required that the plaintiffs be among the injured parties.[241] And it has required this personal injury even though it has recognized that the harms from classifications based on race include the generalized harms of stigmatization and racial hostility.[242] Thus, in the equal protection context at least, simply

---

[238] 113 S Ct at 2303. To establish standing to challenge a set-aside program, therefore, a party "need only demonstrate that it is able and ready to bid on contracts and that a discriminatory policy prevents it from doing so on an equal basis." Id. Compare *Adarand Constructors*, supra note 2 at 2105 (white-owned firm had standing to challenge program giving preference to disadvantaged firms in highway contracts because state agency was "likely" to let highway contracts subject to program, plaintiff was "very likely" to bid for those contracts, and would "often" compete for the contracts with disadvantaged businesses granted a preference under the program).

[239] The Seventh Circuit used this kind of argument to explain why a trade association representing western coal mining and transportation companies had standing to challenge an Illinois statute encouraging the state's electric utilities to comply with the Clean Air Act by installing scrubbers rather than by burning lower-sulfur—predominantly Western—coal, even though these firms had not identified any actual business opportunities lost as a result of the law. *Alliance for Clean Coal v Miller*, 44 F3d 591, 594 (7th Cir 1995). For discussion of the problem of characterizing injury for standing purposes, see Cass R. Sunstein, *Standing Injuries*, 1993 Supreme Court Review 37.

[240] For an argument that the Court's results on standing vary according to the race of the plaintiffs (and thus white plaintiffs in affirmative-action cases fare better on the standing issue than do black plaintiffs in discrimination cases), see Girardeau A. Spann, *Color-Coded Standing*, 80 Cornell L Rev (1995).

[241] See *United States v Hays*, supra note 17 at 2435 (nonresidents of district allegedly reapportioned on basis of race have no standing to challenge reapportionment because they were not " 'personally denied equal treatment' " by the reapportionment, quoting *Heckler v Mathews*, 465 US 728, 740 (1984)).

[242] *United States v Hays*, supra note 17 at 2436.

living in a world that tolerates racial classifications—though they may stigmatize and encourage racial hostility—is insufficient injury to confer standing. In the commercial context, on the other hand, the Court appears to believe that discrimination "in the air," without a showing of actual injury to the plaintiffs, is enough.[243]

In *Carbone*, it was not an interstate firm, but a business located in the same community as the protected firm, that was injured. If the injury protected by the Commerce Clause is the opportunity of *interstate* firms to compete on equal terms with intrastate firms, then no one before the Court in *Carbone* was injured in the relevant sense. Only if the relevant injury is the denial of the opportunity to compete, period, was Carbone possibly injured.[244] But this would, again, enlarge the domain of the Commerce Clause, to encompass virtually all anticompetitive regulation.

The tension between the Commerce Clause cases and the standing cases highlights a possibility that has been hovering at the edges of this entire discussion. To reconcile *Carbone* with the standing cases, one must conclude that not only must outside firms have the opportunity to compete with inside ones, but *all* firms must have this chance—in which case the central purpose of the Commerce Clause is transformed from preventing discrimination against interstate commerce into preventing interference with commerce. In the next section, I will argue that this is the true purpose the Court's nondiscrimination principle aims to serve.

V. NONREGULATION

I have suggested that two of the purposes that the Commerce Clause is supposedly designed to achieve—economic efficiency and representation reinforcement—both take as their premise that discrimination against outside commerce is illegiti-

---

[243] There is even doubt as to whether out-of-state producers, protected by the Court in *West Lynn Creamery* despite their absence from the case, were injured in a constitutionally relevant sense by Massachusetts' pricing order. In a mirror image of *West Lynn Creamery*, these producers challenged the Commonwealth's pricing order. Faced with evidence that neither their sales volume nor the price these producers could command in Massachusetts had changed since the pricing order, the First Circuit nevertheless granted them standing based on "standard principles of 'supply and demand' " which would predict injury to the producers as a result of the pricing order. *Adams v Watson*, 10 F3d 915, 923 (1st Cir 1993).

[244] But see qualifications noted in text at note 143, regarding whether Carbone suffered such an injury.

mate, and thus cannot without circularity be used to defend the nondiscrimination principle. As for the idea that this principle derives instead from a desire to preserve national unity through the disapproval of classifications based on outside status, this founders on the Court's occasional endorsement of the protectionist impulse and on its failure to explain why, in this context alone, discrimination, without more, is an injury worthy of the Court's attention.[245] Because the legislative judgments of state and local governments should be allowed to stand unless the Court has given a reason for interfering with them, and because the Court's interference with state and local laws that discriminate against outside commerce has been justified on the ground that it serves important purposes, the failure to serve these purposes means the state and local laws in question ought to stand.[246]

There is more. The Court's approaches to subsidies and standing, in particular, suggest that there is something else driving the Commerce Clause cases besides economic efficiency, representation reinforcement, and national unity. The true purpose served by the nondiscrimination principle can be identified by taking a closer look at how the Court defines discrimination against, and regulation of, interstate commerce. Rather than promoting economic efficiency, representation reinforcement, and national unity, the Court's concepts of discrimination and regulation suggest a return to *Lochner*-style assumptions about the natural and proper

---

[245] One might argue that the nondiscrimination principle can be justified as the best way to promote these three goals in the aggregate, even if it does an imperfect job of promoting each goal considered alone. I have sought to show, however, that the rule against discrimination produces results that are at best random with respect to economic efficiency and representation reinforcement; aggregating negative results does not, of course, produce a positive sum. Moreover, the nondiscrimination principle serves the goal of national unity incompletely by disapproving only certain kinds of discrimination against outside commerce. This, in turn, might be justified as a compromise between national unity and a fourth goal, that of leaving some room for local decision making. See Stone et al, supra note 158 at 310. As I will explain, however, the way the Court has chosen to distinguish permissible from impermissible discrimination, and to strike the balance between national and local decision making, reflects *Lochner*-era understandings about the proper role of government.

[246] I do not suggest that state and local governments, or even Congress, will be better than the Court at promoting the three goals I have described. These are the purposes the Supreme Court has invoked to justify its invalidation of legislative judgments; they are not purposes the political branches must pursue in enacting legislation. See, e.g., *Williamson v Lee Optical Co.*, 348 US 483, 488 (1955) (state law need not comport with any particular economic theory to be upheld); *Prudential Ins. Co. v Benjamin*, 328 US 408 (1946) (Congress may allow states to enact laws that discriminate against interstate commerce).

role of government. Thus, the nondiscrimination principle is doomed not only by its failure to achieve its stated objectives, but by its promotion of an unstated, outdated view about government's appropriate boundaries. Again, I use the Court's most recent cases to frame the discussion.

In *Oregon Waste Systems*, the Court refused to deem Oregon's surcharge a compensatory tax—and thus concluded the surcharge constituted impermissible discrimination—partly out of a fear that doing so would allow states to charge more for outsiders' use of any state-funded resources and infrastructure.[247] The implication is that the states ought not be allowed to impose a complicated series of surcharges on outside commerce. This reasoning has nothing to do with discrimination in the usual sense. The concern was not that the surcharges states would impose would be unreasonable or exploitative in relation to taxes and charges on insiders, but that they would intervene too deeply in the functioning of the market.[248]

Carbone travels even farther in this direction. "Discrimination" here came to encompass a local ordinance shown to harm no one but insiders—and which at the very worst harmed insiders as much as outsiders—because the ordinance "squelch[ed] competition" in the local waste processing industry.[249] The Court does not explain how Clarkstown's law can be distinguished from the innumerable, long-standing laws that accomplish the same thing by granting an exclusive franchise or monopoly to one firm. Taken at its word, *Carbone* suggests that even traditional electric utility regulation—which grants an exclusive franchise to a utility company in return for an obligation to serve customers at a fair price—is discrimination inconsistent with the Commerce Clause.[250] Again, therefore, discrimination has more to do with potential interference with

---

[247] See text at note 39.

[248] Compare Gergen, supra note 7 at 1132–33 (states should not be allowed to close their highways, police protection, and courts to outsiders, "because these public services are essential to the market itself").

[249] *Carbone*, supra note 1 at 1700 (Souter dissenting).

[250] The Court has thus put a large thumb on the scales in favor of the trend toward deregulation of the electric utility industry. For discussions of this trend, and the states' mixed responses to it, see any recent copy of the industry trade journal, *Public Utilities Fortnightly*.

markets than it does with differential treatment of interstate commerce.[251]

Carbone's condemnation of the Clarkstown ordinance for its "squelching" of competition in Clarkstown's waste processing business recalls *Lochner*-era themes.[252] *Carbone* appears to assume that firms are constitutionally entitled to some minimum level of free competition. Since the Clarkstown ordinance applied to in-town and out-of-state waste processors alike, this level could not be derived from the principle that local governments may not treat outside commerce less favorably than inside commerce. Instead, it again appears to flow from a judgment about what governmental activities are normal or proper. Clarkstown had improperly refused to allow the market—rather than the town—to decide where its waste would be processed.

Finally, in *West Lynn Creamery*, the Court worried that the kind of "abuse" that can usually be prevented if insiders are harmed as well as outsiders was not prevented in that case because in-state dairy producers were "mollifi[ed]" by the subsidy.[253] But what was the source of this "abuse"? It was not the discriminatory subsidy, since this was what allowed the abuse to occur. Instead, the premium imposed on Massachusetts milk dealers appears to be the legislative abuse the Court was seeking to prevent. But this premium did not discriminate against anyone. Its only effect was to raise the price of, and thus perhaps lower the demand for, milk in Massachusetts.[254] In this case as well, discrimination thus came to embrace regulations that might shrink the size of the commer-

---

[251] For similar assessments of *Carbone*, see William N. Eskridge and Philip Frickey, *The Supreme Court 1993 Term: Foreword: Law as Equilibrium*, 108 Harv L Rev 26, 51 (1994); *Leading Cases*, supra note 128 at 149, 153; Gabrysch, supra note 128. For a pre-*Carbone* argument that flow-control measures do not regulate interstate commerce because they prevent waste from ever becoming an article of interstate commerce, see Diederich, *Does Garbage Have Standing?* supra note 121.

[252] Justice Souter (see text at note 72) and several commentators (see note 251 supra) have also noted a resemblance between *Carbone* and *Lochner*, although not between *Lochner* and the other discrimination cases under the Commerce Clause. In addition, Mark Tushnet has noted the similarity of the Court's balancing analysis for *non*discriminatory laws to substantive due process. See Tushnet, supra note 5 at 142, 144–45; see also Patrick C. McGinley, *Trashing the Constitution: Judicial Activism, the Dormant Commerce Clause, and the Federalism Mantra*, 71 Or L Rev 409, 436–37 (1992) (comparing Court's dormant Commerce Clause review generally to *Lochner*-era substantive due process, but using examples suggesting discussion pertains to Court's review of nondiscriminatory laws).

[253] 114 S Ct at 2215.

[254] Id.

cial market, even without singling out interstate commerce for unfavorable treatment.

The concept of injury in the Commerce Clause cases has a similar tendency. Discrimination itself—with whatever speculative consequences it may have for existent or nonexistent, inside or outside, firms—appears sufficient injury to invoke the jurisdiction of the federal courts. The relevant injury for Commerce Clause purposes thus is not an actual, discrminatory injury to individual people and firms, but an apparent restraint on the free operation of the market.

Moreover, the Court's distinction between "burdens" on interstate commerce in the form of "regulation" and "benefits" in the form of subsidies assumes there is an objective baseline from which to measure what counts as a benefit and what as a burden.[255] Such a baseline does not derive from a differential economic effect on outside commerce; as explained above, tariffs, subsidies from general revenues, and subsidies from dedicated funds all can have the same economic effect on outside commerce. Rather, the implicit benchmark separating benefits from burdens harks back to *Lochner*-era understandings about government's proper role. Just as drawing the line between state action and inaction entails, not "a search for whether the state has 'acted,' but instead an examination of whether it has deviated from functions that are perceived as normal and desirable,"[256] so, too, distinguishing benefits from burdens depends on an assessment of which actions are "natural" or "obvious"[257] for states to undertake, and which unnatural or nonobvious.[258] And, as with the state action doctrine,[259] the state

---

[255] See Cass R. Sunstein, *Lochner's Legacy*, 87 Colum L Rev 873, 876 (1987) ("The notion of subsidy is of course incoherent without a baseline from which to make a measurement.").

[256] Id at 887; see also Louis Michael Seidman, *Public Principle and Private Choice: The Uneasy Case for a Boundary Maintenance Theory of Constitutional Law*, 96 Yale L J 1006, 1016–18 (1987). For a defense of subsidies based partly on the action-inaction distinction, see Gergen, supra note 7 at 1137.

[257] Regan, supra note 5 at 1194.

[258] Some defenders of the subsidy/regulation distinction have admitted that, because subsidies will tend to increase output whereas regulation will tend to decrease it, a happy consequence of this distinction is the enlargement of the commercial market. See text at note 215 supra; Levmore, supra note 211 at 572. Others defend free trade generally on the ground that it limits governmental power. See Jean-Luc Migue, *Federalism and Free Trade* 15, Hobart Paper 122 (Institute for Economic Affairs 1993) ("Free trade . . . contributes to solving the problem of the monopolistic state by limiting the power of government.").

[259] Sunstein, *Lochner's Legacy*, supra note 255 at 887.

conduct apparently regarded as unnatural under the Commerce Clause—conventional regulation such as taxes, prohibitions, or the like—is that which interferes with common-law entitlements such as freedom of contract. A failure to grant a subsidy to an outside firm, in contrast to a restriction on doing business with inside consumers, denies the outside firm no common-law interest.[260]

Lochner-era understandings also appear in the Court's limited concept of a "subsidy." One of the insights of the New Deal period was that a *failure* to have regulation may subsidize industry as much as an outright cash grant. In upholding a minimum wage law for women (and rejecting *Lochner*), the Court observed: "The exploitation of a class of workers who are in an unequal position with respect to bargaining power and are thus relatively defenceless against the denial of a living wage . . . casts a direct burden for their support upon the community. . . . The community is not bound to provide what is in effect a subsidy for unconscionable employers."[261] In its Commerce Clause cases, however, the Court seems to have forgotten this idea. In *Oregon Waste Systems*, it refused to examine whether disposers of out-of-state waste were paying their fair share of the state's costs of disposal.[262] And in all of the waste disposal cases, the Court failed to consider whether the invalidation of state and local laws restricting disposal of outside waste in effect subsidized the production of such waste.[263]

These examples suggest that the Commerce Clause cases aim toward the preservation and enlargement of the commercial market, undisturbed by regulation interfering with common law rights. This is not necessarily their actual effect; the Court's willingness to hypothesize injuries upon a finding of discrimination prevents

---

[260] The implicit assumption that state or local action interfering with common-law entitlements is especially suspect may explain the dearth of cases challenging nondiscriminatory state common-law rules as undue burdens on interstate commerce. Perhaps there is a recognition that the Court does not view common-law rules as the "regulation" of interstate commerce. Compare *American Airlines v Wolens*, 115 S Ct 817, 824–26 (1995) (common-law contract remedy is not preempted by the Airline Deregulation Act as an " 'enact[ment] or enforce[ment] [of] any law, rule, regulation, standard, or other provision having the force and effect of law' ").

[261] Sunstein, *Lochner's Legacy* (cited in note 255), at 876, quoting *West Coast Hotel v Parrish*, 300 US 379, 399 (1937).

[262] See text at notes 40–41.

[263] In emphasizing that states should be allowed to take care of their own, but only their own, waste disposal problems, Chief Justice Rehnquist's dissents make a similar point. See text at notes 48–52.

any certainty that the Court is preventing a constriction of actual market operations. Thus, it is not clear that the Court's doctrine achieves even this, unstated purpose. This aimlessness alone would justify overthrowing the Court's nondiscrimination principle.

More fundamentally, the aspiration of carving out a space for market relations free from government involvement cannot be fulfilled, for the market itself is "the product of a set of legal choices defined in terms of common law categories."[264] Thus the conclusion that one state of affairs involves state action and another inaction, or one imposes burdens and another confers benefits, is really a decision that some kinds of governmental interference are preferable to others. This decision relies on contestable moral and empirical judgments about the kind of economic system we should have—the kinds of judgments on which *Lochner* gave the Supreme Court the last word.

Simply crying *"Lochner!"* does not by itself, of course, show that the Court should abandon the nondiscrimination principle.[265] One might argue, first of all, that *Lochner*-style adjudication is less problematic in the Commerce Clause context than in the due process context because Congress has the power to reverse the Court's Commerce Clause decisions.[266] Thus, in this context—unlike in *Lochner* itself—the Court's decisions do not finally bind the political branches to the Court's own economic and political theory. Rather, the decisions shift to state and local governments the burden of obtaining permission from Congress to enact the regulations of interstate commerce that they desire; put another way, state and local governments bear the "burden of overcoming congressional inertia."[267] But why must they bear this burden? The standard answer is that where Congress is silent as to state and local governments' authority to place burdens on interstate commerce, it should be presumed that Congress either disapproved such burdens, or would have done so if it had thought about it.[268]

---

[264] Stone et al, supra note 158 at 802.

[265] *Lochner* still claims adherents. Perhaps its most forceful contemporary defender is Richard Epstein. See Richard A. Epstein, *Takings: Private Property and the Law of Eminent Domain* 5 (1985).

[266] *Prudential Ins. Co. v Benjamin*, 328 US 408 (1946).

[267] Stone et al, supra note 158 at 274.

[268] Noel T. Dowling, *Interstate Commerce and State Power*, 27 Va L Rev 1, 19–28 (1940).

I am with those, however, who hear only silence in Congress's silence—or perhaps even an intent to leave matters where they stand.[269]

More fundamentally, to say that the Commerce Clause cases are different from *Lochner* because they merely impose a burden of enacting corrective legislation ignores the fact that *Lochner* itself purported only to increase the burden of enacting legislation: "Statutes of the nature of that under review . . . are not saved from condemnation by the claim that they are passed in the exercise of the police power and upon the subject of the health of the individual whose rights are interfered with, unless there be some fair ground, reasonable in and of itself, to say that there is material danger to the public health or to the health of the employees, if the hours of labor are not curtailed."[270]

Another argument against abandoning the nondiscrimination principle as a holdover from the *Lochner* period points in the opposite direction from the one just described. Because the principle's resemblance to *Lochner* stems in large measure from the Court's embrace of protectionism in some settings—such as subsidies and state-sponsored market activities—one might argue that rather than discarding the nondiscrimination principle, the Court should enlarge it to condemn *all* state and local distinctions based on outside status. But this would spell the end of state and local governments as entities separate from the national government. They exist as separate levels of government precisely because they may make distinctions between insiders and outsiders; indeed, as noted above,[271] the very concept of a state or local government becomes incoherent if a state or community may not draw a line at its bor-

---

[269] See Robert A. Sedler, *The Negative Commerce Clause as a Restriction on State Regulation and Taxation: An Analysis in Terms of Constitutional Structure*, 31 Wayne L Rev 885, 980–82 (1985); Redish and Nugent, supra note 7 at 588–90; Anson and Schennkan, supra note 156 at 85 n 59.

[270] *Lochner v New York*, 198 US 45, 61 (1905); see also id at 62 ("In our judgment it is not possible in fact to discover the connection between the number of hours a baker may work in the bakery and the healthful quality of the bread made by the workman. The connection, if any exists, is too shadowy and thin to build any argument for the interference of the legislature."); id at 64 ("It is manifest to us that the limitation of the hours of labor as provided for in this section of the statute . . . has no such direct relation to and no such substantial effect upon the health of the employee, as to justify us in regarding the section as really a health law.").

[271] See text at notes 206–07.

ders and treat those inside the line differently from those outside it.[272]

A final possibility is that the Court could forthrightly justify the nondiscrimination principle as a matter of economic substantive due process in this context, even though it has otherwise rejected this doctrine. Significantly, however, in undertaking such a justification the Court likely would be forced back upon the very explanations it has used to justify the nondiscrimination principle under the Commerce Clause. The Court might invoke economic efficiency[273] or representation reinforcement[274] in order to justify more searching due process review of discriminatory laws. Or it might seek to establish a "fundamental right" to commercial competition that is free from distinctions between commerce inside and outside the regulating jurisdiction. These are the only explanations the Court has developed, over a period of more than 100 years, for the nondiscrimination principle. As I have explained, they fail to support the Court's invalidation of discriminatory laws under the Commerce Clause. No more do they justify overturning discriminatory laws under the heading of economic substantive due process.

VI. Conclusion

I have argued that the nondiscrimination principle serves none of the objectives commonly cited in favor of it—neither economic efficiency, representation reinforcement, nor national unity. Indeed, I have illustrated a number of ways in which the Court's approach works against these objectives.

Where, as here, the dominant justification for invalidating state and local legislation is that this practice serves important purposes, purposelessness alone would warrant reconsideration of the Court's doctrine. Nonetheless, the nondiscrimination principle is imperiled not only by what it does not achieve, but by what it does: a mandated preference for markets over regulation, where

---

[272] Compare *Reeves v Stake*, supra note 42 at 442 (state residents are "those . . . whom the State was created to serve").

[273] For an argument that a proper role of substantive due process is to promote economic efficiency, see Tushnet, supra note 5 at 142–50.

[274] *United States v Carolene Products Co.*, 304 US 144, 152 n 4 (1938).

"regulation" is identified by an interference with the market as shaped by common-law entitlements. Thus the nondiscrimination principle is not an unassuming rule designed to rein in outlaw state and local governments, but a *Lochner*-style incursion on their legislative autonomy.

The cases applying the nondiscrimination principle to invalidate the political judgments of state and local governments are not the only examples of the current Court's usurpation of the legislative function. Some have also seen a repetition of *Lochner*'s mistakes in the Court's recent decisions on takings,[275] standing,[276] and the scope of Congressional power under the Commerce Clause.[277] With *Lochner* everywhere, it is perhaps not surprising that it should appear even in such a seemingly mundane and uncontroversial setting as the Court's review of laws that discriminate against interstate commerce. What is more surprising is that its presence there has gone largely unremarked.

---

[275] *Dolan v City of Tigard*, 114 S Ct 2309, 2326–29 (1994) (Stevens dissenting).

[276] Sunstein, *What's Standing After Lujan?* supra note 230 at 236 (referring to "*Lujan*'s odd adventure in substantive due process").

[277] *United States v Lopez*, 115 S Ct 1624, 1651 (1995) (Stevens dissenting); id at 1651–54 (Souter dissenting).

RICHARD D. FRIEDMAN

PRIOR STATEMENTS OF A WITNESS: A NETTLESOME CORNER OF THE HEARSAY THICKET

In *Tome v United States*,[1] for the fifth time in eight years, the Supreme Court decided a case presenting the problem of how a child's allegations of sexual abuse should be presented in court.[2] Often the child who charges that an adult abused her is unable to testify at trial, or at least unable to testify effectively under standard procedures. These cases therefore raise intriguing and difficult questions related to the rule against hearsay and to an accused's right under the Sixth Amendment to confront the witnesses against him.

One would hardly guess that, however, from the rather arid debate in *Tome*, which focused on a seemingly technical question concerning the interpretation of a provision in the hearsay portion of the Federal Rules of Evidence. In this article, I will examine both that question and some of the broader issues surrounding it. I will use *Tome* as a vehicle to explore what I believe is the impoverished state of the law concerning the admissibility of prior statements of a witness. This state, I will argue, is attributable in part to the Court's longstanding unwillingness to recognize that a party

Richard D. Friedman is Professor of Law, University of Michigan Law School.

AUTHOR'S NOTE: Many thanks to Roger Park for his comments—characteristically perceptive and constructive—on an early draft, and to Mike Thomas for high-quality, high-speed research assistance.

[1] 115 S Ct 696 (1995).

[2] See also *Coy v Iowa*, 487 US 1012 (1987); *Idaho v Wright*, 497 US 805 (1990); *Maryland v Craig*, 497 US 836 (1990); *White v Illinois*, 502 US 346 (1992).

may be substantially hindered in attempting to examine a witness with respect to a prior statement the truth of which the witness no longer affirms. A complete solution to the problem, however, would require a dramatic restructuring of the law of hearsay and confrontation, a prospect that I will touch on only briefly in the conclusion to this article.

I. The Tome Case: Facts and Opinions

As in other cases of alleged child sexual abuse, the transcript in *Tome* makes heartbreaking reading; one way or the other, something horrible has happened.

Matthew and Beverly Tome divorced in September 1988. They had a daughter, then approximately three years and three months old, decorously referred to by the Court as A.T. The parents were awarded joint custody, with Matthew having primary physical custody. During most of the time of concern, he lived on the Navajo Indian Reservation in New Mexico and Beverly lived in Colorado. In August 1990, Beverly, remarried and surnamed Padilla, presented Colorado authorities with allegations that Tome had sexually molested A.T. Tome was charged with sexual abuse of a child in violation of several federal statutes, the superseding indictment specifying four separate types of improper contact.[3] The conduct allegedly commenced in about June 1989, when A.T. turned four.[4]

Tome's trial, in the U.S. District Court for the District of New Mexico, did not begin until February 1992. A.T.—by then approximately six years, eight months old—was the Government's first witness. After she was questioned extensively about her ability to distinguish truth from a lie, the court allowed her to testify.[5] Her testimony on direct examination consisted largely of one- and two-word answers to leading questions, assisted by the use of dolls.

---

[3] They were contact between the penis and the vulva; contact between the mouth and the penis; contact between the mouth and the vulva; improper penetration of the genital opening by hand and finger. Transcript (T) 760–61. See 18 USC § 2246(2), formerly § 2245(2), defining "sexual act" to include these types of conduct. The conduct alleged was in violation of 18 USC § 1153, making a federal offense of certain crimes committed by an Indian "within Indian country," and of 18 USC § 2241(c), which criminalizes knowing engagement in a "sexual act" with a child under twelve "in the special maritime and territorial jurisdiction of the United States or in a Federal prison."

[4] Joint Appendix (JA) 2.

[5] Transcript (T) 69–80.

A.T. testified, in effect, that on one occasion Tome removed their clothes, got on top of her, and put his "private place" where she went "potty" and in her mouth.[6] After this happened, she said, she went to the bathroom and wiped blood off herself.[7] Extracting her testimony was a slow process, apparently painful all around; the prosecutor explained, outside the hearing of the jury, that A.T. was "very frightened" of Matthew Tome.[8]

The defense cross-examined A.T. for a total of about an hour and a quarter,[9] first on a Monday afternoon and then again on the Wednesday morning. Much of the examination concerned various

---

[6]

Q: Did daddy take your clothes off, yes or no?
A: Yes.
Q: Okay. Did daddy take his clothes off?
A: Yes.

* * *

Q: What did you do with your legs? What did you do?
A: I crossed it.
Q: . . . Did daddy do anything?
A: Yes.
Q: And what did daddy do? Go ahead.
A: He got on top of me.
Q: . . . Did he do something?
A: Yes.
Q: Was it good something or bad something?
A: Bad.
Q: It was bad. Did it hurt or did it feel good?
A: Hurt.

* * *

Q: . . . Did he put his private place any place on you?
A: Yes.

* * *

Q: Where did daddy place his private place, just point, point to me. Point to where you are looking right now . . .
Q: What do you call this place? What is that place on you? Do you have a name for that?
A: No.
Q: You don't call it anything? Do you go potty there?
A: Yes.
Q: Okay. And Andrea, where did your daddy place his private thing, anywhere else? And point to me if he did, where. Point to my body wherever he put it. Where? Is that my mouth you are pointing at? Say yes or no.
A: Yes.
Q: All right. Did he put his private thing in your mouth?
A: Yes.

T 88–89, 90, 92–93, quoted in part in Petitioner's Brief.

[7] T 93–94.

[8] T 91.

[9] T 166.

background issues, such as reasons why A.T. might prefer to live with her mother in Colorado rather than with her father in New Mexico. This line of questioning was clearly intended to support a contention that A.T. had fabricated the allegation of abuse, perhaps at the instigation of her mother, in order to secure a change in her custody arrangement.

In the first session, A.T. gave immediate answers, some in relatively detailed sentences. When A.T. resumed testifying on Wednesday, however, matters were far more strained. Sometimes she answered only after a long interval, estimated by the trial judge to run as much as 45 or 50 seconds, and in the end she provided no audible or discernible responses even to some very simple questions.[10] During a recess, the judge noted for the record that

> the witness seemed to be losing concentration. She would look up to the ceiling, would look to the back of the courtroom, she would look over my head, would not in instances face counsel who is inquiring of her.
> She twisted and turned, stretched a little bit sometimes. At other times she would put her hand to her mouth and clasp her lips with her hand. We have a very difficult situation here.[11]

After A.T. completed her testimony, the Government was allowed to present testimony of several prior statements by A.T. concerning the alleged abuse. It was the admissibility of these statements that created the issue that the Supreme Court chose to review, so it is worth examining them in detail.

Lisa Rocha, a friend of Padilla, testified to a conversation that occurred when she was baby-sitting A.T. on August 22, 1990—more than a year after the alleged molestation. At this time, A.T. was concluding a summer in her mother's custody; Padilla was continuing to seek primary custody, but she evidently expected to return A.T. to Tome,[12] and the next day she was to bring A.T. to New Mexico for a hearing that had been scheduled for August 24.[13] Rocha testified that A.T. said spontaneously, "Please don't

---

[10] T 125–62. In a few cases, the difficulty may have been attributable to defense counsel's failure to phrase the question in a way the girl was likely to understand, see T 141, 145, but, as the court indicated, this was not the principal problem. T 147.

[11] T 147–48, 3 F3d at 348 n 4.

[12] T 230.

[13] T 393, 401–04. In fact, the hearing had been rescheduled for August 22, T 533, so Padilla missed it. T 537–38.

let my mom take [me] back to my father." When Rocha asked her why, the girl responded, "Because I don't want to go back." Pressed further, A.T. said, "Because my father gets drunk and he thinks I'm his wife."[14]

According to Rocha, she told Padilla about this conversation only after Padilla returned from New Mexico, still with A.T.,[15] on August 26. After Padilla's unsuccessful effort the next day to get more information from A.T., Rocha questioned A.T. again.[16] This time, according to Rocha, A.T. told her that her father "does nasties" to her, and elaborated by saying that (apparently on one occasion) he dragged her through the house by her arms, took her clothes off, forced her legs open, and lay on top of her, which gave her a sharp pain near her stomach. When she cried for her mother, her father told her, "Your mother's a bitch." Furthermore, A.T. related that when she wiped herself the tissue was bloody.[17]

After this conversation, Padilla reported the allegation to the police.[18] Kae Ecklebarger, a Child Protection Service caseworker assigned to the case, testified that on August 29, 1990, Padilla and Rocha informed her of the allegation and that she then interviewed A.T.[19] Ecklebarger asked A.T. if she knew why she was there, and A.T. said it was because of what "Matthew" had done to her. A.T. said that she could remember one time particularly clearly. Her father had told her to remove her clothes, and when she refused he took off her panties, put her on the floor, and "put his balls" in her. Using anatomically correct dolls, A.T. simulated intercourse, and also told Ecklebarger that Tome had kissed her all over her body, including the vaginal area. Ecklebarger also testified that A.T. told her that her father asked her to touch his penis and that she refused. A.T. told once more about wiping herself with a tissue and finding blood, and added that she had shown it to her

---

[14] JA 11–12, T 218–19.

[15] Apparently on the advice of counsel Padilla returned to Colorado after she missed the hearing, T 404, 447; eventually, after the charges of abuse were made, she was awarded physical custody. T 541–43, 640.

[16] T 220–22. Padilla was listening from an adjoining room and was able to confirm Rocha's testimony only in small part. T 239, 408, JA 20.

[17] JA 12, T 222–23.

[18] Rocha suggested to Padilla that if Padilla made a report to the police she would not have to return A.T. T 450, 451.

[19] T 340.

grandmother and aunt, Tome's mother and sister.[20] A.T. said that he had engaged in this conduct "every single day" for a time before stopping.[21]

Ecklebarger referred the case to Karen Kuper, a pediatrician.[22] Dr. Kuper testified that she interviewed A.T. with Padilla present and that when she asked whether anyone had ever touched her in a way that hurt or was scary A.T. answered, "Just my dad." With the help of anatomical dolls, A.T. said that Tome had touched her vaginal area and put his fingers and his "thing" inside her there.[23]

Another pediatrician, Laura Reich, testified that she examined A.T. on September 21, 1990, for a rash that was apparently unrelated to sexual abuse. During the examination, she asked A.T. if anybody had touched her in her vaginal area and A.T. responded that her father had put his "thing" in her.[24] A third pediatrician, Jean Spiegel, who was an expert in child sexual abuse, examined A.T. on September 3, 1991, about two years after the alleged abuse. Dr. Spiegel testified that A.T. told her, in response to direct questions, that Tome had touched her breasts, her "front privates," and "her bottom where her poop comes out."[25]

The pediatricians each testified to physical evidence suggesting sexual abuse; Reich spoke most strongly, concluding that A.T. "had definitely had penile penetration in her vaginal area."[26] Tome testified in his own defense, denying that he had abused his daughter.[27] His mother and sister also testified for him, denying that A.T. had ever shown them a bloody tissue,[28] and several witnesses testified as to his good character.[29] He was not permitted to introduce evidence that he had passed a polygraph test denying that he had abused A.T.[30] The jury returned a verdict of guilty, with an-

---

[20] JA 16–19, T 317–20.

[21] JA 19, T 326.

[22] T 341.

[23] JA 15, T 255–56.

[24] JA 16, T 290, 292, 298.

[25] JA 20, T 509.

[26] T 294. See also T 259–62 (Kuper), 472–73 (Spiegel).

[27] T 642.

[28] T 607 (sister), 620, 622 (mother).

[29] T 655, 660–61, 665, 671.

[30] Record on Appeal, 10 Cir, vol 1, at 5–17.

swers to special interrogatories finding that he committed the four types of illicit acts charged,[31] and the court imposed a sentence of 12 years' imprisonment.

The U.S. Court of Appeals for the Tenth Circuit affirmed the judgment of conviction. The principal issue was the admissibility of A.T.'s out-of-court statements. The Court of Appeals held that all of the statements were admissible under Federal Rules of Evidence 801(d)(1)(B),[32] which provides:

> (d) *Statements which are not hearsay.*—A statement is not hearsay if—
> (1) Prior statement by witness.—The declarant testifies at the trial or hearing and is subject to cross-examination concerning the statement, and the statement is . . . (B) consistent with the declarant's testimony and is offered to rebut an express or implied charge against the declarant of recent fabrication or improper influence or motive . . . .

The court held that A.T. had been adequately subjected to cross-examination (for purposes of both the evidentiary rule and the confrontation clause), notwithstanding her unresponsiveness to some questions, and that Tome had made at least an implicit charge that she fabricated her testimony out of a preference to live with her mother. Tome argued, however, that the Rule could apply only to statements made before the alleged motive to fabricate arose; in this case, he contended, A.T. had made the statements *after* the motive, her desire to live with her mother, had arisen.

Several Courts of Appeals had indeed held that the Rule incorporates a "premotive" requirement.[33] But in *Tome* the Tenth Circuit aligned itself with those Courts of Appeals that had refused to recognize the requirement.[34] It conceded "that prior consistent statements made after a strong motive to lie has arisen may evi-

---

[31] These are listed in note 3.

[32] This was the principal basis on which the trial court had held the prior statements admissible, though it also held some of them admissible on alternative grounds, such as the hearsay exception for statements made for purposes of medical diagnosis or treatment, Rule 803(4).

[33] See, for example, *United States v Henderson*, 717 F2d 135, 138 (4th Cir 1983); *United States v Bowman*, 798 F2d 333, 338 (8th Cir 1986). The decisions adopting this view had, at least for the most part, done so quite casually. See note 108.

[34] See, for example, *United States v Montague*, 958 F2d 1094, 1096–99 (DC Cir 1992); *United States v Pendas-Martinez*, 845 F2d 938, 942 n 6 (11th Cir 1988).

dence only that the declarant is a consistent liar."[35] Nonetheless, it declined to find an absolute requirement that the statement precede the motive; rather, it regarded the determinative factor to be "whether a statement has probative value apart from its repetition."[36]

However useful that standard may be, the Court of Appeals' application of it—later to find favor by four members of the Supreme Court[37]—was remarkably slipshod: The court's discussion centered on the conclusory declaration that it did not find persuasive Tome's underlying argument that an improper motive led to the testimony. Apart from a reference to the apparent spontaneity of A.T.'s initial statement to Rocha, however, the Court of Appeals did not explain how the prior statements made Tome's argument *less* persuasive.[38]

The Supreme Court granted certiorari limited to the single question of whether Rule 801(d)(1)(B) incorporates a "premotive" requirement. By a five-four vote, the Court held that it does. Hence, the judgment of the Court of Appeals was reversed and the case remanded.

Justice Kennedy wrote the prevailing opinion, most of which was for a majority of the Court.[39] In his view, under the common

---

[35] 3 F3d at 350.

[36] Id.

[37] 115 S Ct at 710 (Breyer, J, dissenting, joined by Rehnquist, CJ, and O'Connor and Thomas, JJ).

[38] Applying this analysis to the present case, we conclude that the district court properly admitted evidence of A.T.'s prior consistent statements under Rule 801(d)(1)(B). The record reveals that A.T. spontaneously made her initial allegation of abuse to her baby-sitter. On cross-examination, Tome implied that A.T. fabricated the allegations about her father because she wanted to live with her mother. Although this argument does present some motive to lie, we do not believe that it is a particularly strong one. Moreover, Tome's contention would require us to believe that A.T.'s statements were the result of a calculated scheme to deceive. Yet Tome has presented no evidence that the five-year-old A.T. possessed the ability to appreciate the causal relationships inherent in the conception and implementation of such a scheme. Under these circumstances, we believe that A.T.'s consistent statements do carry probative force apart from mere repetition. We therefore find no abuse of discretion in admitting these prior consistent statements.

3 F3d at 351 (footnotes, citations omitted).

[39] Justices Stevens, Souter, and Ginsburg joined fully in the opinion. Justice Scalia concurred in the judgment and in all but one part of the opinion. He did not concur in Part IIB of the opinion, addressing the Advisory Committee Notes to the Federal Rules, because in his view that Part gave undue weight to the Notes, not merely treating them as a re-

law rule prevailing before adoption of the Federal Rules of Evidence in 1975, a statement previously made by a witness and consistent with the witness's testimony could be introduced to rebut a charge that the witness's testimony was a product of recent fabrication or improper influence or motive—but only "if the statement had been made before the alleged fabrication, influence, or motive came into being."[40] The Federal Rules left this premotive requirement unchanged, according to the Court, but expanded the purposes for which evidence satisfying it could be admitted. Ordinarily, a prior statement by a witness, like out-of-court statements generally, is hearsay, under both the common law and the Federal Rules, when offered to prove the truth of a matter asserted in the statement. Rule 801(d)(1), however, excludes from the definition of hearsay—and so exempts from the rule against hearsay—three categories of prior statements by a declarant who becomes a witness at trial. One of those categories, stated in subdivision (B), is for consistent statements offered to rebut a charge of fabrication or improper influence or motive. Thus, the Court concluded that the premotive requirement was simply carried over to the new, substantive use of the evidence.[41]

Justice Breyer dissented, joined by Chief Justice Rehnquist and Justices O'Connor and Thomas. Writing his first opinion on the Court, Justice Breyer went to some pain to emphasize that Rule 801(d)(1)(B) does not itself establish the premotive requirement: The Rule merely accords nonhearsay treatment to certain statements that could already be admissible for rehabilitation, and whether the statement was made before or after the motive arose appeared to have no bearing on the applicability of hearsay policy.[42] The key question, rather, was one of relevance—that is, whether a prior statement consistent with the witness's trial testimony might have sufficient probative value to warrant admissibility in rebutting a charge of recent fabrication even though the statement was made after the motive to fabricate arose. And the dissenters concluded that the common law statement of a premotive re-

---

spected and ordinarily persuasive source of scholarly commentary but according them authority in disclosing the purpose of the drafters. 115 S Ct at 706.

[40] 115 S Ct at 700.

[41] Id at 703–04.

[42] Id at 707–08. Justice Breyer's attempt to read a hearsay policy into the Rule is discussed briefly below in note 86 and the accompanying text.

quirement did not compel the Court to give an absolute negative answer to that question.

In most circumstances, the dissenters acknowledged, a postmotive statement would not have significant probative value in rebutting a charge of recent fabrication based on an improper motive.[43] But this, they contended, was not uniformly true; thus, some pre-Rules courts, albeit a minority, did recognize that the premotive requirement was not absolute.[44] The general tendency toward liberality in the admissibility of evidence reflected by the Rules, and the absence of any language in the Rules establishing such a requirement, weighed against incorporating the requirement into the Rules.[45]

In this case, the Court of Appeals, applying an approach similar to that advocated by the dissenting Justices, had "decided that A.T.'s prior consistent statements were probative on the question of whether her story as a witness reflected a motive to lie." This was a "factbound conclusion" that the dissenters found "no reason to reevaluate."[46] Hence, they would have affirmed the judgment of the Court of Appeals.

* * *

Behind the narrow problem resolved by *Tome* lurk significant issues that escaped analysis by either the Court or the dissent. First is the basis for the traditional doctrine, significantly modified but not abrogated by the Federal Rules of Evidence, that prior statements of a witness are hearsay. This doctrine was crucial to the case, for if there were no presumptive hearsay obstacle to the admissibility of A.T.'s prior statements, there would have been no need to explore whether the statements fit within the exemption provided by Rule 801(d)(1)(B). The Court did treat the statements as hearsay, but it did not explain why that might be sensible; to the contrary, it rather conclusorily suggested doubt about the persuasiveness of the traditional doctrine. In doing so, it implicitly followed a line of cases in which the Court has treated cross-examination as adequate notwithstanding that the prior state-

---

[43] Id at 710.

[44] Id at 708.

[45] Id at 709.

[46] Id at 710.

ment includes propositions that the witness did not assert in her testimony. In Part II, I will challenge this treatment.

In Part III, I will focus on what are generally referred to as prior consistent statements, the subject of Rule 801(d)(1)(B). In *Tome*, the Court interpreted that Rule as making admissible for substantive purposes prior consistent statements that otherwise would be admissible only for rehabilitation of the witness's credibility—but it failed to articulate the distinction between these two grounds of admissibility. Without examining whether there is any substance to this distinction, it is difficult to appreciate fully what was at stake in *Tome*. I will argue that the distinction is an important one when the prior statement includes assertions that the current testimony does not.

With this grounding, in Part IV I will narrow the focus further and analyze, within the framework of current law, the particular issue resolved by the Court. I will conclude that the rationale underlying Rule 801(d)(1)(B) would be better served without an absolute premotive requirement. In Part V, I show how the Rule ought to be applied in a case like *Tome*. Finally, in Part VI I conclude with some hints as to how the case might be decided in a radically different framework that would be sensitive to two factors that appear to have had no impact on the Court's analysis: The opponent of the evidence was a criminal defendant whose confrontation rights might have been at peril, and the witness was a child.

II. The Hindrance Issue: Examining a Witness on Assertions She No Longer Affirms

The basic definition of hearsay contained in Federal Rules of Evidence 801(c) follows traditional lines:

> " 'Hearsay' is a statement, *other than one made by the declarant while testifying at the trial or hearing*, offered in evidence to prove the truth of the matter asserted."[47]

But why should the definition extend to prior statements made by a witness? That is, why does the italicized passage not read something like *"other than one made by a person who testifies subject to cross-examination at the current trial or hearing"*?

---

[47] Emphasis added.

Rule 801(d)(1) and the accompanying commentary by the Advisory Committee that drafted the Federal Rules give an intriguing indication of the complexity and difficulty of this question. Rule 801(d)(1) leaves the traditional doctrine standing, but modifies it by withdrawing from the definition of hearsay a statement that was made previously by a witness who is subject to cross-examination at the current trial or hearing and that satisfies one of three sets of conditions: The statement (*a*) was made under certain restrictive conditions and is inconsistent with the witness's current testimony, (*b*) is consistent with the current testimony, and the opponent of the evidence has opened the door by suggesting "recent fabrication or improper influence or motive," or (*c*) is "one of identification of a person made after perceiving the person."

The Advisory Committee Note, however, does not help to explain why the Rules failed to create a broader rule classifying as nonhearsay all prior statements of a witness now subject to cross-examination. Although the Note presents arguments against maintaining hearsay treatment for such statements, the only consideration presented by the Committee in favor of hearsay treatment is its "unwillingness to countenance the general use of prior prepared statements as substantive evidence." But, though a rule against "prior prepared statements" easily could have been drafted,[48] the Committee did not propose such a Rule, nor did Congress enact one.[49] Moreover, the Committee confused matters by saying, "If

---

[48] Something like this might have done reasonably well:

> (*d*) *Statements which are not hearsay.*—A statement is not hearsay if
> (1) *Prior statement by witness.* The declarant testifies at the trial or hearing and is subject to cross-examination concerning the statement, unless the statement was prepared (A) for the declarant by another person, or (B) in anticipation of litigation.

[49] On the one hand, some prepared statements are exempted by the Rule. There is nothing in subdivisions (B) or (C) preventing them from applying to prepared statements. Subdivision (A), relating to prior inconsistent statements, does not, at least for the most part, cover prepared statements, because it applies only to statements made in a "proceeding" or deposition; this limitation was not included in the rule as proposed by the Advisory Committee, however.

On the other hand, many prior statements that are not prepared fall outside the Rule:

(1) Only statements falling within one of the three subdivisions are exempt. (As originally enacted, the Rule only had two subdivisions; subdivision (C), for statements of identification, was removed from the draft presented to Congress, but added back in by subsequent legislation.)

(2) Prior inconsistent statements, even though not prepared, do not satisfy the exemption under the Rule as enacted unless they were given both "under oath subject to the penalty of perjury" and "at a trial, hearing, or other proceeding, or in a deposition."

the witness admits on the stand that he made the statement and that it was true, he adopts the statement and there is no hearsay problem."[50] This pronouncement conflicts with traditional law[51] and with the text of Rule 801(d)(1) itself, which contains no such provision.[52]

Despite the decades-long trend against the traditional rule, prior statements made by a witness often do present serious concerns of the type generally associated with the rule against hearsay. These include the inability of the jury to observe the witness's demeanor in making the statement in question[53] and, in most cases,

---

(3) Prior consistent statements do not satisfy the exemption unless the opponent has opened the door by raising a charge of fabrication or improper influence or motive.

[50] Notes to Rule 801(d).

[51] See *Goings v United States*, 377 F2d 753, 761 (8th Cir 1967) (with respect to a statement supposedly used to refresh the witness's recollection and adopted by him: "even if the witness adopts the prior statement . . . [i]t is still a hearsay statement suggested to the witness rather than his own statement given under oath in court").

[52] That the witness adopts the prior statement does not in itself appear to make the statement exempt under Rule 801(d)(1) from the rule against hearsay. The prior statement may be admissible to give content to the current testimony, but that is a different matter: A jury adhering to this distinction (which is not necessarily a sensible one) could properly rely on the witness's memory as of the time of the testimony, but not the fresher memory as of the time of the statement.

[53] Learned Hand, in a passage quoted approvingly by McCormick and paraphrased approvingly by the Advisory Committee to the Federal Rules of Evidence, said:

> If, from all that the jury see of the witness, they conclude that what he says now is not the truth, but what he said before, they are none the less deciding from what they see and hear of that person and in court. There is no mythical necessity that the case must be decided only in accordance with the truth of words uttered under oath in court.

DiCarlo v United States, 6 F2d 364, 368 (2d Cir 1925), quoted in John William Strong, gen ed, 2 *McCormick on Evidence* § 251, at 118 (West, 4th ed 1992), and paraphrased in Adv Com Note to Fed R Evid 801(d)(1).

But this argument fails. To the extent that demeanor is important, see generally Olin Guy Wellborn III, *Demeanor*, 76 Cornell L Rev 1075 (1991) (arguing that the value of demeanor evidence is far less than usually thought), it is the demeanor of the witness in making the statement, and in answering questions about the statement and the events or conditions it describes, that is significant. Unless the witness was videotaped when making the statement, the factfinder is likely to be virtually unable to assess her demeanor in doing so.

Consider the situation addressed by Hand, in which the prosecution wishes to prove proposition X, but a recalcitrant witness testifies to Not-X and the prosecution then offers evidence of a prior statement made by the witness asserting X. Defendant's counsel has a sound argument:

> If the witness testified falsely to X, my cross-examination might have created demeanor clues—sweating, eye-shifting, nail-biting—that would have been strong indications of lying. There is no reason to suppose that the witness' truthful testimony of Not-X will yield similarly strong signals of truthtelling—or indeed that there *are* similarly strong signals. Such opportunity as I have had to *bolster* a friendly witness does not replace the opportunity I need to *confront* a hostile witness.

the absence of an oath when the declarant made the prior statement.[54] But the most important of these concerns is that, if the
witness's trial testimony does not affirm the truth of all material

---

In another situation, which occurred in *Tome*, the witness testifies at trial to X and the
prior statement is of X AND Y. Plainly, the in-court testimony cannot provide demeanor
evidence with respect to Y. (If the prior statement is only of X, then the demeanor problem
may be trivial—but so too may be the probative value of the prior statement.)

Moreover, if—as the argument in this part of the article suggests is often the case—the
opponent's ability to examine the witness with respect to the prior statement and the underlying events or conditions is hindered, the probative value of the witness's demeanor in
responding to such examination, as well as in making the statement itself, is also plainly
diminished.

[54] The Advisory Committee belittled this concern:

> So far as concerns the oath, [1] its mere presence has never been regarded as
> sufficient to remove a statement from the hearsay category, and [2] it receives
> much less emphasis than cross-examination as a truth-compelling device. While
> strong expressions are found to the effect that no conviction can be had or impor-
> tant right taken away on the basis of statements not made under fear of prosecu-
> tion for perjury, Bridges v. Wixon, 326 U.S. 135, 65 S.Ct. 1443, 89 L.Ed. 21103
> (1945), [3] the fact is that, of the many common-law exceptions to the hearsay
> rule, only that for reported testimony has required the statement to have been
> made under oath.

The assertions I have labeled [1], [2], and [3] are each true, but none of them proves
very much.

[1] Of course, the presence of the oath has never been regarded as *sufficient* to remove
from the hearsay category an out-of-court statement that has not been subjected to cross-
examination, but the *absence* of an oath is important: Modern systems still require witnesses
to take an oath or make an equivalent affirmation of obligation to testify truthfully. See,
for example, Fed R Evid 603.

[2] The oath may not be as effective as cross-examination in compelling the truth, but
there is good reason to believe that it reduces the incidence of false statement: A witness
is likely to speak more carefully, and with a greater sense of moral responsibility, if she
has "declare[d] that [she] will testify truthfully, by oath or affirmation administered in a
form calculated to awaken the witness' conscience and impress the witness' mind with the
duty to do so." Fed R Evid 603. Moreover, expressions such as those in *Bridges*, 326 US
at 153–54 (to allow a defendant "to be convicted on unsworn testimony of witnesses . . .
runs counter to the notions of fairness on which our legal system is founded"), suggest
that the value of the oath lies not only in the impact it has on the witness but also (at least
with respect to criminal prosecutions) in its very formality, in establishing an acceptable
setting for making statements with testimonial intent. The sense that accusing witnesses
are forced to take the matter of accusation with utmost seriousness may be important in
making criminal convictions acceptable; see generally Charles Nesson, *The Evidence or the
Event? On Judicial Proof and the Acceptability of Verdicts*, 98 Harv L Rev 1357 (1985) (emphasizing the importance of public acceptability of verdicts)—especially if the oath is *perceived*
to restrain false statement.

[3] A similar statement could be made with respect to cross-examination; that is, the
hearsay exemption for prior testimony is the only one that requires the declarant to have
been cross-examined. A more fruitful way of looking at the matter is this: If a statement
was made under oath and subject to a satisfactory opportunity for adverse examination, it
is exempted, as prior testimony, from the rule against hearsay if the defendant cannot testify
live at the present proceedings. See Fed R Evid 804(b)(1). All the other hearsay exemptions
address situations in which either or both of these conditions do not apply. Note also that
Rule 801(d)(1)(A), as eventually passed by Congress, does require an oath for prior inconsistent statements—but does *not* require cross-examination.

propositions asserted in the prior statement, the opponent's ability to cross-examine the witness with respect to those propositions is severely hindered as compared to what it would be if the witness had affirmed those propositions at trial. Such a hindrance is, of course, a substantial factor in determining whether the prior statement should be excluded, but it is not necessarily dispositive of that question. I shall discuss the hindrance here, and shall address the admissibility question briefly in Parts V and VI.

In discussing the hindrance question, and generally throughout this article, I will focus on the situation in which both the trial testimony of the witness and the prior statement of that witness are offered by a criminal prosecutor.[55] This is, of course, only one setting for the introduction of prior statements, but it is the setting of *Tome*, and it is one in which the hindrance problem may be quite stark.

At the outset, it is important to emphasize that the opponent is probably *not* substantially prejudiced in his ability to cross-examine the witness if she testifies to the entire substance of her prior statement: She can be cross-examined effectively with respect to whatever she said before, because she is also asserting it from the witness stand. At the same time, however, this congruence between the prior statement and the current testimony makes it doubtful, given the testimony, that there is any need for the prior statement. Of course, in some circumstances the timing of the prior statement may mean that the statement has significant probative value even given the current testimony. It may be that the prior statement was made before the emergence of some improper influence that might have deflected the witness from the truth.

---

[55] Thus, I am simplifying somewhat by speaking of cross-examination rather than adverse examination, and also by assuming that the opponent of the prior statement is the opponent of the party who put the witness on the stand.

It may be that the prior statement is offered against, rather than by, the party who called the witness to the stand; this sometimes happens if the prior statement is inconsistent with the current testimony. In such a case, the adverse examination would be on redirect. (Note that often the prior inconsistent statement is introduced by the party who put the witness on the stand because the witness's testimony has been less favorable than the prior statement to that party.)

Also, in some cases, like *Tome*, the prior statement is introduced, through another witness, after the declarant has left the stand. In such a case, under customary procedures, if the party opponent wanted to question the declarant about the prior statement he would usually have to recall her to the stand as his own witness. Alternatively, the party opponent might anticipate proof of the prior statements and present them to declarant while she is still on the stand. See text accompanying note 81.

And it may be that at trial the witness has a substantially weaker memory of the described event than she did when making the prior statement.

The problems are reversed when the prior statement asserts information that the current testimony does not. This disparity in content might arise in either of two basic ways. First, it might be that the prior statement is materially inconsistent with the witness's trial testimony, and so presumably introduced by the prosecution because that testimony disappointed it. Second, as in *Tome*, the trial testimony may be consistent in material respects with the prior statement, but less complete.[56] Whichever way it arises, the disparity in content makes it likely that the prior statement has significant probative value, even given the current testimony. But the same disparity may significantly hinder the opponent's ability to cross-examine.

This last suggestion seems to be in accordance with a declaration made by the Supreme Court thirty years ago, in *Douglas v Alabama*, that "effective confrontation" of a witness "was possible only if [the witness] affirmed the statement as his."[57] But it also conflicts squarely with the line taken by the Advisory Committee for the Federal Rules[58] and, consistently over the last quarter century, by the Court as well. In *California v Green*,[59] the Court held that a criminal defendant's opportunity to cross-examine the declarant of a statement is not rendered constitutionally inadequate by the fact that the declarant testifies at trial inconsistently with the prior statement.[60] The next year, in *Nelson v O'Neil*,[61] the Court went further, running over *Douglas* by holding

---

[56] A.T.'s prior statements included a wealth of information that was not conveyed by her trial testimony, which, for all the questions it took to secure, was rather skimpy in describing the alleged assault. Her prior statements, but not her trial testimony, included assertions (among others) that Tome's sexual assaults were repeated, and that he had kissed her all over, including her vaginal area, put his fingers in her vagina, touched her breasts and her bottom, asked her to touch his penis, and dragged her around the house.

[57] 380 US 415, 420 (1965). *Douglas* also said that the declarant "could not be cross-examined on a statement imputed to but not admitted by him." 380 US at 419.

[58] "Nor is it satisfactorily explained why cross-examination cannot be conducted subsequently with success." Note to Rule 801(d)(1). The Advisory Committee's view is analyzed further in notes 77–79 and accompanying text.

[59] 399 US 149 (1970).

[60] This was the holding of *Green*, even if it did not represent the actual facts of the case. The Court analyzed the case as if the witness testified inconsistently with the prior state-

that there was no constitutional problem, though the declarant not only testified inconsistently with the prior statement, but denied making it.[62] And seventeen years after *Nelson*, in *United States v Owens*,[63] the Court extended *Green* in another direction, holding that, under both the Confrontation Clause and Rule 801(d)(1), the opportunity to cross-examine is not rendered inadequate by the fact that at trial the witness no longer remembers the event described in the prior statement.

In effect, *Green*, *Nelson*, and *Owens* all concluded that cross-examination with respect to the prior statement was not only adequate, but hardly necessary. In the Court's view, because at trial the witness no longer asserts a proposition that she asserted in the prior statement, the opponent has essentially achieved the benefit of cross-examination with respect to that proposition.[64]

---

ment, and held that this did not render cross-examination constitutionally deficient. 399 US at 153–64. Only toward the end of the case did the Court seem to notice that in fact the witness claimed a failure of memory "and hence failed to give any current version of the more important events described in his earlier statement." Id at 168. The Court recognized that this factor raised an additional issue, and so remanded the case, id at 168–70; that issue was resolved in the *Owens* case, described below.

[61] 402 US 622 (1971).

[62] *Nelson* distinguished *Douglas* on the ground that, in *Douglas*, the declarant refused on the basis of the privilege against self-incrimination to answer any substantive questions.

In *Nelson*, defense counsel did not cross-examine the declarant at all. Contrary to the Court's implication, however, this does not suggest that the declarant's testimony left the defendant in a strong position; he was, after all, convicted. Rather, defense counsel presumably concluded that cross-examination of a witness who had just provided favorable testimony was unlikely to do much good.

[63] 484 US 554 (1988).

[64] In *Green*, 399 US at 159, the Court said:

   The most successful cross-examination at the time the prior statement was made could hardly hope to accomplish more than has already been accomplished by the fact that the witness is now telling a different, inconsistent story, and—in this case—one that is favorable to the defendant.

In *Nelson*, 402 US at 628–29, the Court said:

   Had Runnels in this case "affirmed the statement as his," the respondent would certainly have been in far worse straits than those in which he found himself when Runnels testified as he did. . . .

   The short of the matter is that, given a joint trial and a common defense, Runnels's testimony respecting his alleged out-of-court statement was more favorable to the respondent than any that cross-examination by counsel could possibly have produced, had Runnels "affirmed the statement as his."

And in *Owens*, 484 US at 561–62, the Court said:

   [L]imitations on the scope of examination by the trial court or assertions of privilege by the witness may undermine the process to such a degree that meaningful cross-examination within the intent of the Rule no longer exists. But that effect

For several reasons, I believe this analysis is misguided.

1. *Blunting the Tools.* Suppose the prosecution wishes to prove that the defendant, Dennis, was at a particular restaurant, The Scene, on a given night. If a witness, Whitney, testifies on direct examination, asserting proposition DENSCENE (that Dennis was at The Scene on the night in question) purportedly from her current memory, Dennis has an uncluttered opportunity to confront her. Through counsel, he might ask her questions that appear to have some relation to DENSCENE. For example, he might ask her whether GAILSCENE—the proposition that Gail, Dennis's girlfriend, was at The Scene at the same time—is true. If the witness does not in fact have a clear memory that DENSCENE is true, but she is eager to have the jury believe that it is, this question might put her in an awkward position. For all she knows, if she affirms GAILSCENE, Dennis might be able to show that GAILSCENE is false—perhaps there is a solid alibi for Gail—suggesting that the same testimonial failure that led to Whitney's inaccurate assertion of GAILSCENE might have led to her assertion of DENSCENE. And for all Whitney knows, if she denies GAILSCENE, Dennis might be able to demonstrate that it is highly unlikely that if DENSCENE is true GAILSCENE is false; perhaps Dennis and Gail are known to have been together earlier and later that night, and it seems highly implausible that Dennis would have dropped Gail off before going to The Scene and picked her up later. Finally, if she attempts to avoid the dilemma by denying ability to remember whether or not GAILSCENE is true, it might be that Dennis can demonstrate that it is highly unlikely that she would remember DENSCENE and not remember GAILSCENE; perhaps Gail was wearing a bright red dress, she and Whitney were good friends, and Dennis's presence at The Scene would likely have appeared utterly unremarkable to Whitney at the time, but Gail's presence was unusual.

Of course, Whitney might guess right when asked, "Was Gail there with Dennis?" She might assert what is in fact true, or at least what Dennis cannot effectively disprove. But Dennis has at least had the opportunity to lay the trap. If he lays enough of them,

---

is not produced by the witness' assertion of memory loss—which . . . is often the very result sought to be produced by cross-examination, and can be effective in destroying the force of the prior statement.

and Gail is not testifying truthfully in asserting her clear memory of DENSCENE, she is likely to fall into one of them.

The predicate for all this, though, is that Whitney asserts DENSCENE just before cross-examination. If Whitney *denies* DENSCENE on direct examination but her prior assertion of DENSCENE is admitted, cross-examination is unlikely to have the same effectiveness. Suppose the defense asks Whitney whether GAILSCENE is true and she denies it. Now, even if NOT-GAILSCENE, or the conjunctive proposition DEN-SCENE AND NOT-GAILSCENE, appears highly unlikely, the prosecution has a ready explanation—that the same testimonial failure that led to an *inaccurate* denial of GAILSCENE on cross led to an inaccurate denial of DENSCENE on direct. Similarly, if Whitney's prior statement of DENSCENE is admitted after she testifies on direct that she *cannot remember* whether or not DEN-SCENE is true, her testimony on cross that she cannot remember whether or not GAILSCENE is true will help Dennis little or not at all. If it does not already appear strange that Whitney remembered DENSCENE at the time of the earlier statement but not at trial, it will probably not appear strange that she does not remember GAILSCENE at trial. The prosecution is not put in the position of arguing that Whitney remembered the more forgettable and forgot the more memorable; a single "gauzy cloak" of forgetfulness[65] over the whole matter will provide a full explanation.

2. *Denial of the Possibility of Complete Nullification.* When a witness testifies on direct to ASSERTION, the best result the cross-examiner can hope to achieve is a repudiation of the direct testimony—a statement by the witness saying, in effect, "Although I just testified to ASSERTION on direct, I recognize now that I cannot affirm that it is true." This might occur if the witness follows along with the type of examination outlined above: "Gee, I have no idea whether or not CONSEQUENTIAL DETAIL is true, and I guess that if ASSERTION were true then I would know that CONSEQUENTIAL DETAIL is true, so I suppose I was mistaken in asserting ASSERTION." Nearly thirty years ago, in an extremely perceptive opinion in *Ruhala v Roby*,[66] the Supreme

---

[65] *California Retail Liquor Dealers Assn. v Midcal Aluminum, Inc.*, 445 US 97, 106 (1980) ("a gauzy cloak of state involvement over what is essentially a private price-fixing arrangement").

[66] 379 Mich 102, 124–28, 150 NW 2d 146, 156–58 (1967).

Court of Michigan showed how cross-examination might lead to this result. When this happens, as the *Ruhala* court pointed out, the witness's direct testimony of ASSERTION retains little probative value; it would almost certainly be struck and not allowed to support a verdict, at least if the witness did not again affirm ASSERTION on redirect.[67] Presumably the same result would obtain if the witness were allowed to testify on direct by adopting a prior statement in all its details, and then on cross repudiated it all: The recantation on cross of everything the witness had said on direct would mean that the "original recanted version no longer stands as substantive evidence."

But now suppose the starting point of the examination is that, although the witness once said ASSERTION, she says so no longer. The proponent will argue that the witness accurately stated ASSERTION at the earlier time and that some influence—failure of memory, perhaps, or bias—intervened to prevent her from stating ASSERTION at trial. If that argument is plausible, the prior statement retains probative value with respect to ASSERTION. And if for this reason the prior statement is admitted to prove ASSERTION, that means by definition that the opponent cannot hope to achieve the optimal result, nullification of a statement just made. "If I had been able to cross-examine immediately after the witness stated ASSERTION," the opponent can argue, "I might have secured a complete retraction that would have nullified the effectiveness of the current testimony. I can't do that now." Rather, the admissibility of the prior statement means that the jury is told, in effect, "You have two different versions before you, the prior statement and the current testimony. Consider them both and draw the best inference you can."[68]

Perhaps the lost opportunity to the cross-examiner seems trivial, the mere denial of a faint possibility of a "final triumphal flourish"

---

[67]

> When a cross-examiner on timely cross-examination *succeeds* in getting the witness to change his story, the integrity of the recantation is apparent, and *his original, recanted version no longer stands as substantive evidence.* If the only evidence of an essential fact in a lawsuit were a statement made from the witness stand which the witness himself completely recanted and repudiated before he left the witness stand, no one would seriously urge that a jury question had been made out.

379 Mich at 128, 150 NW2d at 158.

[68] The substantive admissibility of prior inconsistent statements was defended by McCormick on just this ground. Charles T. McCormick, *Evidence* § 39, at 75 (West 1954).

at the conclusion of cross-examination.[69] It is true, of course, that most witnesses do not make full recantations of assertions they have just made on direct. But the fact is that the witness *has* testified in a way at variance with the prior statement, failing to assert a proposition asserted in the prior statement; if the witness had made the assertion in direct testimony, and then disclaimed it on cross, the assertion would have been nullified.

3. *A Buffer Around the Statement.* The time gap between the prior statement and the trial testimony may provide a ready explanation for why the witness does not testify at trial to the substance of the statement. The witness may, for example, have suffered a memory loss because of trauma[70] or because of the more ordinary passage of time, she may have been intimidated into silence, or she may have been exposed to some bias-creating motive.[71] But showing such intervening influences is not generally to the advantage of the party opposing the proposition asserted in the prior statement.

To the contrary, it may be the proponent who wants to demonstrate these intervening influences.[72] If they tend to lead the declarant away from, rather than toward, the truth, they generally will tend to make more probable an account in which the events occurred as the proponent contends, the initial statement accurately reported the events, and then a testimonial failure occurred that prevented the witness from recounting the full substance of the earlier statement at trial.[73]

---

[69] Letter of Standing Committee on Rules of Practice and Procedure and Advisory Committee on Rules of Evidence to Sen. James O. Eastland, Chairman of Senate Committee on the Judiciary, May 22, 1974, quoted in Jack B. Weinstein, Margaret A. Berger, & Joseph M. McLaughlin, 4 *Weinstein's Evidence* 801–15 (Matthew Bender, 1995) (hereinafter "Joint Committee letter").

[70] That was quite clearly the situation in *Owens*, in which one Foster, the victim of the vicious battering with which Owens was charged, was unable at trial to identify his assailant, though he had previously made a statement identifying Owens.

[71] All these, except perhaps the last, are possible explanations of A.T.'s failure at trial to repeat the full substance of her earlier statements.

[72] It is thus laughable to think, as the Court suggested, that Owens "destroy[ed] the force" of Foster's statement by showing Foster's memory loss, or that he achieved "the very result sought to be produced" in his cross-examination of Foster, 484 US at 562; Owens was, after all, convicted largely on the basis of the statement.

[73] Thus, *McCormick on Evidence*, § 251, in a passage that originated with the second edition (Edward Cleary, gen ed, West, 1972), comments with respect to *State v Saporen*, 205 Minn 358, 285 NW 898 (1939), a case often cited in favor of the traditional view that prior statements of a witness are hearsay, that

Consider *Tome* itself. A.T. seemed to acknowledge at one point during her testimony that she made some of the prior statements, but the prosecutor did not ask her to affirm their truth to the extent that they went beyond her in-court testimony.[74] It seems unlikely that Tome would have been able effectively to cross-examine A.T. with respect to her prior statements.[75] Tome might, of course, be able to explore her lack of memory at the time of trial and her inability to testify articulately at trial. But this would not suggest that her previous articulations of sexual abuse, made in different circumstances a substantial time before, were concoctions of failed memory. Indeed, the *decay* of memory *in the period leading up to trial*, which Tome could easily demonstrate, has no obvious bearing on what he would want to show—that *in the period leading up to the statements* A.T., whether consciously or not, *fabricated* recollections. Rather, emphasizing A.T.'s inability to testify fully at trial would simply play into the prosecution's hands, given that the prior statements included information helpful to the prosecution and not affirmed by her trial testimony: It would make more likely a scenario in which the events occurred, she made the

---

the witness did change his story very substantially; rather than hardening, his testimony yielded to something between the giving of the statement and the time of testifying. This appears to be so in a very high proportion of the cases, and the circumstances most frequently suggest that the "something" which caused the change was an improper influence.

This is not really an argument that cross-examination of the declarant is adequate, or that the statement should not be considered hearsay. Rather, it is an argument that in the run of cases the prior statement should be deemed reliable. But surely this is too broad a generalization to support wholesale exemption of all prior statements from examination under the law of hearsay, especially when confrontation rights are at stake.

Indeed, in *Saporen* itself, the circumstances did not suggest that an improper influence had arisen between the time of the statement and the time of the testimony; on the contrary, the witness contended that he had made the prior statement, which was more favorable to the prosecution than was his current testimony, in response to threats. 205 Minn at 360, 285 NW at 900.

Interestingly, then, the Advisory Committee for the Federal Rules of Evidence, while defending a doctrine similar to that espoused by McCormick, took a far different approach to cases like *Saporen*. See notes 77–79 and accompanying text.

[74] T 158–59.

[75] Note that Rule 801(d)(1) requires that the witness be "subject to cross-examination concerning the statement," not " . . . concerning the subject matter of the statement." It would be possible to construe the two formulations so that the second one, but not the first, demands that the witness remember the subject matter of the statement, not merely the statement itself. On the other hand, arguably the first formulation but not the second demands that the opponent have an opportunity to examine the witness after the prior statement has been presented to the jury.

statements accurately describing them, and subsequently forgot them or became intimidated.

Sometimes at trial (not in *Tome*), the witness not only fails to confirm the entirety of the prior statement, but repudiates it and supplies a reason for making the statement notwithstanding its inaccuracy.[76] The drafters of the Federal Rules, arguing unsuccessfully in favor of a general exemption for prior inconsistent statements, contended that this result "is cross-examination beyond the dreams of avarice."[77] But that is plainly not so—as demonstrated by the convictions achieved in notable cases by prosecutors relying on prior accusatory statements repudiated from the witness stand by the accusers.[78] Indeed, this argument exposes a certain Janus-like quality in the arguments for the adequacy of later cross-examination. Is the point, as the drafters and the Supreme Court have contended, that the inconsistent testimony itself satisfies the need for cross-examination by exposing the weakness of the prior statement? Or is it the contrary point, advocated by the editors of *McCormick on Evidence*, that the prior statement is too valuable to lose because the inconsistency is likely attributable to a later-arising improper influence?[79]

Certainly the facts might appear to fit the McCormick portrayal—but this is not necessarily an argument for admissibility. The jury may be persuaded that the prior accusatory statement was the true one, and that the improper influence was brought to bear by the accused between the time of the prior statement and the time of trial, leading the witness not only to retract the prior statement but to concoct an explanation as to why she made that statement. Adverse examination of the witness at the time of trial, when she is making and explaining the repudiation, will plainly be of little avail in dispelling such a conclusion. The situation is much

---

[76] For example, in *Saporen*, the witness said that he had made the earlier statement in response to threats. In another such case, *People v Johnson*, 68 Cal 2d 646, 68 Cal Rptr 599, 441 P2d 111 (1968), rejected in *California v Green*, 399 US 149 (1970), the witnesses, the wife and daughter of the defendant, contended that previous personal interests of theirs had led them to accuse him falsely of sexual molestation. The Advisory Committee said that these cases, which argued for the inadequacy of the later cross-examination, "in fact demonstrate quite thorough exploration of the weaknesses and doubts attending the earlier statement." Note to Rule 801(d)(1).

[77] Joint Committee letter, cited in note 69.

[78] See *Saporen* and *Johnson*, discussed in note 76.

[79] See note 73.

as if there were two witnesses. One is in court, subject to examination, casting doubt on the prior statement, and so outwardly helping the accused, but in a suspicious manner wholly unpersuasive to the factfinder. The other, the one doing the damage, is not in court and is impervious to adverse examination.[80]

Put another way, cross-examination in this circumstance is somewhat like pushing on a string; the task cannot be done most effectively unless it meets resistance.

4. *Enhanced Cost and Risk. Tome* illustrates an additional obstacle that some opponents confront. Had A.T. testified on direct to the substance of the prior statements, then presumably Tome's counsel would not have foregone the opportunity in the course of her cross-examination, which followed immediately, to question A.T. about those assertions. But this was not the situation. A.T.'s prior statements were introduced through other witnesses after A.T. had left the stand; she herself gave conflicting and sometimes ambiguous testimony, on cross and redirect examination, as to whether she had even made the statements or remembered doing so.[81] Thus, to examine A.T. about the substance of the prior statements, which added considerable detail not in her testimony, counsel would have had to present those details to her. This she could have done in either of two basic ways. First, while A.T. was on the stand as the prosecution's witness, counsel could have anticipated the testimony of the other witnesses, reciting its substance to her—a move that would have been utterly self-defeating if

---

[80] As the *Ruhala* court suggested, the fact that the witness is no longer asserting the proposition at issue may force the opponent to treat her as more friendly than hostile. ("The would-be cross-examiner . . . is left with no choice but to become the witness's friend, protector and savior." 379 Mich at 125, 150 NW2d at 156.) And this means that "the real nature of cross-examination" is lost:

> Cross-examination presupposes a witness who affirms a thing being examined by a lawyer who would have him deny it, or a witness who denies a thing being examined by a lawyer who would have him affirm it. Cross-examination is in its essence an adversary proceeding. The extent to which the cross-examiner is able to shake the witness, or induce him to equivocate is the very measure of the cross-examiner's success.
>
> *** If [the witness] refuses to adopt his prior statement as true, there can be no adversary cross-examination upon it. If he refuses to affirm, no question can be put to him which would shake his own confidence in his affirmation.

379 Mich at 124, 150 NW2d at 156.

[81] T 152–53, 158–59.

Tome still hoped to keep any of that testimony away from the jury. Alternatively, counsel might have recalled A.T. to the stand after the other witnesses testified—a move that the jury might have regarded as desperate and overbearing—and reviewed that testimony. Either way, counsel would have had to give the prosecution's most vivid evidence an extra run-through in front of the jury. And if her examination of A.T. on these details fell flat, a very predictable prospect given A.T.'s performance on the stand, Tome would probably end up worse off than if she had never tried: The jury would likely have seen that, by presenting A.T. with the prior statements, counsel was going out of her way to dig her own hole, and failure to dig herself out might have been particularly damaging.

Not surprisingly, defense counsel, presumably reckoning that the risk outweighed the potential benefit, did not attempt to pursue the matter.

* * *

I do not mean to suggest that introduction of a prior statement made by a witness who no longer asserts all its substance necessarily leaves the party opponent in a helpless position; he is presumably better off than if a credible witness tells a convincing story that is impervious to cross-examination. Nor do I suggest that prior statements in this circumstance ought generally to be excluded; whether exclusion is appropriate does not depend exclusively on whether the opportunity for cross-examination is satisfactory. But what I have tried to show is that the opportunity for cross-examination is substantially hindered in this situation—and that the Supreme Court has failed since *Green* to recognize this.

The natural response to this problem, under the prevailing structure of the law, is to classify such prior statements as hearsay. *Within that structure*, the traditional classification of prior statements as hearsay makes more sense than was recognized by the Advisory Committee, which in large part retained it, or by the Supreme Court, which even in the extreme circumstances of *Owens* refused to recognize how the opportunity for effective cross-examination was hindered. But placing a statement within the basic definition of hearsay in Rule 801(c) is only the first step in determining whether it is excluded by the Rules as hearsay. I now turn to the exemption at issue in *Tome*.

III. Understanding the Rule on Prior "Consistent"
    Statements

Rule 801(d)(1)(B) exempts from the rule against hearsay a
prior statement by a declarant who is a witness at the trial or hearing, subject to cross-examination concerning the statement, if the
statement is "consistent with the declarant's testimony and is offered to rebut an express or implied charge against the declarant
of recent fabrication or improper influence or motive." The structure of the Rule has proved confusing. In two respects, thinking
about it might be simplified by replacing the first eight words in
this quotation by the word "admissible."

First, this change emphasizes the essential nature of the rule,
which some judges have misunderstood: *If* a prior statement is admissible on the limited ground stated in the Rule ("to rebut an
express or implied charge . . ."), then the rule against hearsay
should not bar admission of the statement to prove the truth of
a matter that it asserts.[82]

Second, consistency is a misleading standard. If a statement is
admissible for the described rebuttal purpose, then it should be
deemed consistent within the meaning of the Rule.[83] The prior

---

[82] The Advisory Committee Note stated this point rather clumsily: "Prior consistent
statements traditionally have been admissible to rebut charges of recent fabrication or improper influence or motive but not as substantive evidence. Under the rule they are substantive evidence." Adv Comm Note to Rule 801(d)(1)(B). But not *all* prior consistent statements are substantive evidence under the Rule, just as not all were traditionally admissible
for rebuttal purposes.

Some courts have been confused by the structure of the Rule because it appears to address
only a nonhearsay use of the prior statement. See, for example, *United States v Casoni*, 950
F2d 893, 905 (3d Cir 1991) (stating that "the rule is confusing" because if a statement is
offered to rebut a charge of recent fabrication "it is then not offered to prove the truth
of the matter asserted"). But placement of the Rule within the definition of hearsay seems
to make clear the framers' intention that *if* the prior statement is offered (or, in my view,
admissible) for the designated nonhearsay purpose, then the Rule also makes it exempt
from the rule against hearsay.

[83] Of course, mere logical consistency—that is, the absence of logical inconsistency—is
insufficient to invoke the rule. The statements "My father abused me" and "It is raining
today" are perfectly consistent, but the fact that the witness asserted one of them does not
suggest that she was telling the truth in asserting the other.

In *State v Collins*, 1989 Ohio App LEXIS 452, the court did attempt to find independent
meaning for the word "consistent" as used in Ohio Rule 801(d)(1)(B), which is identical
to the federal rule. Purporting to rely on a dictionary search, the court concluded that "the
concept of agreement" is the central core of the word's meaning in the rule, so that "statements to be consistent must be about the same subject matter" and "statements concerning
two differing subjects [such as, presumably, the abuse and rain statements presented just
above] are simply foreign to each other." But the court also said, after pointing out that
the prior statement in that case included matter foreign to the testimony, "Since the concept

statement may have the prescribed rebuttal effect if it contains precisely the same information as the current testimony, somewhat more (as in *Tome*) or less, or even if there are logical inconsistencies between the two.[84]

As emphasized by Justice Breyer's dissent, rebutting a "charge of recent fabrication or improper influence or motive" is not the only way in which a prior consistent statement may tend to rehabilitate a witness's testimony.[85] Why, then, was it the only form of rehabilitation mentioned by Rule 801(d)(1)(B)? Justice Breyer's attempt to develop a rationale is unpersuasive.[86] The most plausible explanation appears to be that this was just a careless bit of drafting. The intention of the drafters seems to have been that if a

---

of a prior consistent statement is primarily directed to rehabilitation of a witness charged with having fabricated his testimony, the testimony [of the prior statement] as admitted could not satisfy this purpose."

[84] *United States v Casoni*, 950 F2d 893, 896, 903 (3d Cir 1991) (holding that prior statements of witness "fall within Rule 801(d)(1)(B)'s definition of prior consistent statements because the rule does not require them to be consistent in every detail with [the witness's] testimony at trial"; the prior statements and the current testimony were indeed inconsistent in some details); *United States v Vest*, 842 F2d 1319, 1329 (1st Cir 1988) (holding prior statement "sufficiently close" to the testimony to be covered by the Rule, notwithstanding "the one inconsistency"; "a prior consistent statement need not be identical in every detail to the declarant's . . . testimony at trial").

Suppose Alfred testifies against Brenda, describing some wrongdoing that he says she committed. Brenda brings out that a year before trial Alfred developed a terrible grudge against Brenda when Brenda divorced Alfred's brother. Alfred or Charles might then testify against Brenda that several years before that, while family serenity reigned, Alfred had made a casual statement to Charles describing the wrongdoing; admissibility of the statement on this basis will not ordinarily be defeated on the ground that in the prior statement Alfred said the deed occurred on June 23 and in the current testimony he placed it on June 24.

[85] 115 S Ct at 707. Perhaps most importantly, a prior statement that reflects a significantly fresher memory than does the current testimony might help dispel the contention that the testimony is a product of faulty memory. The logic here is much the same as in the case of a premotive statement offered to rebut a charge of recent fabrication: A statement made before the alleged testimonial failure suggests strongly that the failure does not account for the testimony. Indeed, perhaps "fabrication" could be construed to reach the case of false testimony created by faulty memory—but that would be a stretch.

[86] He suggested that (1) jurors have trouble distinguishing between substantive and rehabilitative use of the type of statement covered by the Rule, (2) the Rule was a concession to this difficulty, and (3) "[i]f there was a reason why the drafters excluded from Rule 801(d)(1)(B)'s scope other kinds of prior consistent statements (used for rehabilitation), perhaps it was that the drafters concluded that those other statements caused jury confusion to a lesser degree." 115 S Ct at 707–08. The first proposition is unquestionably correct, but the third is, as Justice Breyer seemed to recognize, totally speculative; he suggested no reason to believe that it is true, and I doubt that there is. (The second proposition may be descriptively accurate, but as I show later in this part there are considerations not dependent on the effectiveness of a jury instruction that weigh in favor, within the prevailing structure of hearsay law, of maintaining the distinction between substantive and rehabilitative use.)

prior consistent statement is admissible for rehabilitation it should be admissible substantively—that is, to prove the truth of what it asserts—notwithstanding the rule against hearsay. The language used by the Rule describes the most *common*, but not the *exclusive*, situation in which a prior consistent statement might be admitted for rehabilitation.

Of course, this language, however careless, does limit the reach of the Rule. Only statements described by the Rule are exempted by it from the rule against hearsay. But the Rule should *not* be understood to state the bounds of the circumstances in which a prior statement consistent with a witness's testimony is admissible to support the credibility of the witness. The Rule would be oddly placed to set the bounds on rehabilitative use. It is in the Article dealing with the law of hearsay, and is expressly part of the definition of hearsay, not in the Article that deals with impeachment and support of witnesses. Moreover, it is clearly a rule designed to loosen an old restraint on admissibility, not to impose one. Unfortunately, some courts have interpreted the Rule to set the bounds of admissibility of prior consistent statements for rehabilitative as well as substantive purposes.[87] The issue was not posed by *Tome*, but some loose language in the majority opinion might suggest—unintentionally, I believe—that this was the Court's view.[88]

Why should, or should not, a prior consistent statement admissible for the rebuttal purpose described by the Rule (or for any other rebuttal purpose) also be admissible substantively—that is, to prove the truth of what it asserts? To ask this question brings into relief another perplexing question: What (if anything) is the

---

[87] See John William Strong, gen ed, 2 *McCormick on Evidence* § 251 nn 29–30 and accompanying text (West, 4th ed 1992) (collecting authorities going both ways).

[88] The Court seems to have spoken of Rule 801(d)(1)(B) as a rule of rebuttal testimony. See 115 S Ct at 702 ("if the drafters of Rule 801(d)(1)(B) intended to countenance rebuttal along that indirect inferential chain"), 705 ("The Rule permits the introduction of a declarant's out-of-court statements to rebut a charge of recent fabrication or improper influence or motive only when . . ."). On the other hand, the latter statement is prefaced by this statement: "Our holding is confined to the requirements for admission under Rule 801(d)(1)(B)." The Court's view seems to have been that the Rule implicitly (via the premotive requirement) limits the circumstances in which a prior statement might be admitted for the rebuttal purpose specified by the Rule itself, but not for other rebuttal purposes. Compare 115 S Ct at 707 (Breyer, J, dissenting: "The majority is correct in saying that there are different kinds of categories of prior consistent statements that can rehabilitate a witness in different ways . . . .").

difference between the two grounds of admissibility? I think the best answers to these questions, like the issue of the adequacy of cross-examination, depend very much on whether the prior statement introduces information not contained in the current testimony.

Consider first the situation in which the prior statement merely asserted a proposition, ACCUSATION, that is contained in the current testimony; according to the party opponent, some improper influence caused the witness to testify to ACCUSATION, but the prior statement, having been made (to keep matters simple) before the influence arose, suggests that this is not so. Even in this situation, there is an epistemological difference between admissibility of the prior statement only to rebut the charge of improper influence, on the one hand, and to prove the truth of the matter that the statement asserts, on the other—but it is a narrow and rather rickety one. Consider three mutually exclusive and exhaustive propositions:

> (1) Absent the intervention of the improper influence, the witness would not have testified to ACCUSATION at trial.
> (2) At the time of the prior statement, the witness believed ACCUSATION to be true [which makes ACCUSATION more likely true], and even absent the intervention of the improper influence she would have testified to ACCUSATION at trial.
> (3) At the time of the prior statement, the witness did not believe ACCUSATION to be true [which makes ACCUSATION less likely true], but even absent the intervention of the improper influence she would have testified to ACCUSATION at trial.

Admissibility only for the rebuttal purpose can be taken to mean that the jurors can use the prior statement to evaluate the probability of proposition (1) against propositions (2) and (3),[89] but not to evaluate the probability of proposition (2) against proposition (3).

---

[89] Even though the statement was made before the improper influence arose, it does not prove absolutely that the witness would have testified to ACCUSATION at the time of trial absent the influence. It could be that at the time of the statement the witness was subject to some other influence, not as strongly active at the time of trial, tending to lead her to state ACCUSATION. It could be, for example, that the witness states ACCUSATION at the earlier time, believing (whether accurately or not) that ACCUSATION is true, but by the time of trial has no recollection of ACCUSATION, and absent the improper influence would not testify as to it.

That this difference is logically coherent is perhaps the best that can be said for it. Even assuming a jury—or a court—can understand the distinction, adherence to it is improbable; neither is likely to cramp its reasoning so artificially.[90]

Perhaps more important, no good purpose is served by such a restriction. Recall from the last section that, if the substance of the prior statement is included in the current testimony, the party opponent is not genuinely hindered in cross-examination by the fact that the prior statement was made some time before the current testimony. If the prior statement is nevertheless to be excluded, the only sound reasons would be to induce the presentation of the witness's current testimony and, in light of that testimony, to avoid wasting time by presentation of evidence that has little incremental value. But the witness has given her current testimony, and even before the charge of improper influence is made the prior statement may have significant incremental value in that it reflects a substantially fresher memory than does the current testimony. Once the charge is made, the question is easy: The statement will be heard and considered by the jurors, at least for the rehabilitative purpose, and no time is saved by putting artificial shackles on them. Moreover, the party opponent, having suggested the intervention of an improper influence, is hardly in a position to complain if the jury is allowed to consider whether an earlier statement by the witness of ACCUSATION tends to make it more probable that the witness believed ACCUSATION when she asserted it, and therefore also that ACCUSATION is true. As the Advisory Committee said, "The prior statement is consistent with the testimony given on the stand, and, if the opposite party wishes to open the door for its admission in evidence, no sound reason is apparent why it should not be received generally."[91]

Indeed, in this situation, it appears that the only valid purpose

---

[90] Jack B. Weinstein and Margaret A. Berger, 4 *Weinstein's Evidence* ¶ 801(d)(1)(B)[01] (Matthew Bender, 1995), says that "as a practical matter, the jury in all probability would misunderstand or ignore a limiting instruction anyway, so there is no good reason for giving one."

I have two reactions to this statement. First, the problem does not reflect an inadequacy of jurors; the distinction I have drawn is paper thin, and I suspect that many judges as well would misunderstand and ignore it.

Second, as suggested below, limiting admissibility may be justified even assuming that a limiting instruction would not be effective.

[91] Note to Rule 801(d)(1)(B).

served by the distinction between rebuttal admissibility and sub-stantive admissibility is a door-keeping one. That is, assuming that the statement is inadmissible before the charge of improper influ-ence is made, the making of the charge opens the door to rebuttal admissibility, and so too a path that leads to substantive admissibil-ity. In this setting, Rule 801(d)(1)(B) reflects a sound judgment that the rule against hearsay ought not place any restriction on the use of the statement.

Now suppose that, while the current testimony is of GENERAL ACCUSATION, the prior statement asserted GENERAL AC-CUSATION AND DETAIL. In this setting, which resembles the one in *Tome*, there is what I will refer to as an overhang—the prior statement includes the proposition at issue but is more infor-mative than the current testimony. The overhang changes the situ-ation fundamentally in four respects.[92]

First, assuming the prior statement is admissible for both rebut-tal and substantive purposes with respect to GENERAL ACCU-SATION, there is a clear epistemological distinction between these uses of the statement and use with respect to DETAIL. The instruction, "You may consider the prior statement as tending to prove GENERAL ACCUSATION, but do not consider it with respect to DETAIL" is simple and quite clear; there is even the chance that the jury would obey it. It may be that the witness's assertion of DETAIL has some value in rebutting the contention of improper influence with respect to GENERAL ACCUSA-TION, but even if so the distinction remains clear: "You may con-sider the witness's prior assertion of DETAIL so far as it tends to prove that she would have testified to GENERAL ACCUSA-TION even had it not been for the intervention of the improper influence, but do not consider the statement as tending to prove that DETAIL is true."

Second, there is now a substantial consideration weighing in fa-vor of exclusion with respect to DETAIL, even assuming the state-ment is admitted to prove GENERAL ACCUSATION; as dis-cussed in Part II, the fact that the witness has not testified to DETAIL means that the party opponent may be severely hindered in his ability to cross-examine her.

---

[92] See generally *State v Collins*, 1989 Ohio App LEXIS 452 (holding that because the prior statement contained "an addition" to the current testimony it could not be considered a "consistent" statement within the Ohio rule, which is identical to the federal rule).

Third, more is at stake than the manner in which the jury uses the prior statement to prove a given proposition, and the court is in a position to protect those stakes without having to rely on an abstruse instruction. For example, it may be that DETAIL closely bears on an element of a crime and that, absent admissibility of the prior statement of DETAIL, there would be insufficient evidence of that element to go to the jury. (With respect to GENERAL ACCUSATION, by contrast, there is already the witness's testimony asserting GENERAL ACCUSATION.) *Tome* illustrates this situation. With respect to two of the acts charged and found by the jury, there would have been no substantial evidence had it not been for the prior statements.[93] As a consequence, a holding that the prior statement is inadmissible to prove DETAIL can be enforced by withholding that issue from the jury. The question whether the jury would adhere to an instruction drawing barely comprehensible distinctions is thus rendered moot.

Even if the prior statement of DETAIL would support the proof of material issues, but is not essential to sustain a jury verdict with respect to any of them, effective tools are at hand to ensure that the jury does not use the statement to prove DETAIL. Sometimes the nature of the statement allows severance, so that the proponent is allowed to prove that the witness asserted GENERAL ACCUSATION but not that she asserted DETAIL. And even where severance is not possible, another form of redaction might be appropriate, limiting and shaping what testimony may be given about the prior statement; in some cases, for example, the proponent's rebuttal needs might be satisfied by testimony that on a given date the witness made a statement indicating that she then believed GENERAL ACCUSATION to be true.[94] Furthermore, outright

---

[93] A.T. did not testify to contact between Tome's mouth and her vulva, or between Tome's fingers and her genitalia; the evidence supporting these findings was supplied by the prior statements reported by Ecklebarger and Kuper, respectively. See above notes 20, 23, and accompanying text; T 725 (prosecutor, in closing argument, referring to these statements as supporting findings of mouth-vulva and finger-genital contact). These statements were not necessary for the case as a whole to go to the jury, but the indictment specified four separate types of illicit acts, special interrogatories presented to the jury asked about the four, and the jury answered all four in the affirmative; it may be that Tome's sentence would have been lighter absent a jury finding of mouth-vulva and finger-genital contact. See generally 18 USC § 2246(2), formerly § 2245(2), listing the four types of conduct charged, among others, in the definition of "sexual act."

[94] Analogously, in rape cases most states allow the prosecution to present evidence, even before the complainant has been impeached, that she made a "fresh complaint"—that is, one soon after the incident—because the absence of such a complaint might appear suspi-

exclusion is also an available option: In some circumstances, the statement might have less value in supporting the witness's testimony of GENERAL ACCUSATION than prejudicial potential in tending to prove DETAIL through means made unsatisfactory by the hindrance on cross-examination.

Finally, the overhang deprives the door-opening argument of much of its force. At least where the proponent's rebuttal needs can indeed be protected by a severed statement or limited testimony about the statement, the fact that the party opponent suggested that testimony of GENERAL ACCUSATION was a product of improper influence should not give the proponent the ability to introduce a statement, not otherwise admissible, of DETAIL.

This analysis suggests a note of caution. In some cases, the court should ensure—by outright exclusion, severance of the statement, limitation of the testimony, or instruction—that the jury does not use the prior statement to prove propositions to which the witness has not testified. Nothing in Rule 801(d)(1)(B) precludes a ruling of limited admissibility in which the prior statement may be used only to prove (through both rebuttal and substantive use) the propositions asserted in the witness's current testimony. The Advisory Committee Note suggests that the drafters paid no attention to the overhang problem; they appear to have focused on the situation in which the witness reaffirms at trial the complete substance of the prior statement. There is no reason to suppose that they would be startled by an interpretation under which, if this condition does not hold, the Rule would apply only to the part of the prior statement that the witness does reaffirm.[95]

---

cious, but many jurisdictions limit the testimony that may be given on this basis to "a simple yes or no" in answer to the question "whether she made complaint that such an outrage had been perpetrated upon her." *Woods v State*, 233 Ind 320, 326, 119 NE2d 558, 562 (1954).

Where the statement is not practically severable, a court might present the opponent with a choice. For example, suppose the witness testifies at trial to a general proposition—such as "He was angry"—and the prior statement offered to rehabilitate her does not quite assert that proposition but instead asserts details from which the more general proposition might be inferred—"He was red and shaking." The court might rule: "I'm either going to admit Witness 2's testimony that Witness 1 said the accused was red and shaking, or if you prefer I'll allow Witness 2 to testify [or stronger yet: admit a stipulation] that Witness 1 made a statement indicating that she then believed the accused was angry. Choose your poison."

[95] Just the previous term, in *Williamson v United States*, 114 S Ct 2431 (1994), the Court itself demanded fine shaving of a statement for purposes of applying a hearsay exemption. *Williamson* held that the hearsay exception for declarations against interest, Rule 804(b)(3), incorporates a narrow meaning of "statement," as "a single declaration or remark," so that

In *Tome*, however, the Justices seem not to have questioned that if the statement was validly offered to rebut a charge of "recent fabrication or improper influence or motive" it would be admissible in its entirety.[96] The Court gave no suggestion that it would be troubled by the use of A.T.'s prior statements to sweep in a great deal of substance to which she did not testify. But, of course, the Court's holding was that Rule 801(d)(1)(B) does *not* remove the hearsay objection to her statements. It is conceivable that the Court was motivated by the overhang problem, but responded obliquely by constructing an absolute premotive requirement. I will turn now to the merits of that requirement.

IV. The Premotive Requirement

If a witness made a pretrial statement of ACCUSATION before an alleged improper influence arose, then ordinarily that statement will tend strongly—though not absolutely[97]—to prove that the witness's trial testimony of ACCUSATION was not a product of that influence. If, by contrast, the witness made the prior statement after the influence arose, it usually will have little or no probative value with respect to that question. Thus, many pre-Rules authorities indicated that a statement could rehabilitate a witness against a charge of improper motive only if the statement was made before the motive arose.

In some circumstances, however, there is reason to believe that, even though the prior statement was made after the improper influence allegedly arose, that influence had less impact on the witness when she made the prior statement than it did at trial. In such circumstances, as Justice Breyer argued in his *Tome* dissent, the prior statement might have significant probative value, notwithstanding its timing, to rebut the charge of improper influence.

One example is a grudge, or other improper influence, that builds over time.[98] If in its earlier, weaker form the influence did

---

the Rule "does not allow admission of nonself-inculpatory statements, even if they are made within broader narrative that is generally self-inculpatory." Id at 2431. Time will tell to what extent, if any, *Williamson* requires distinction among "We [understood to be Sam and the declarant] robbed a bank on Friday morning," "Sam and I robbed a bank on Friday morning," and "I robbed a bank on Friday morning. Sam helped."

[96] The Brief for the Petitioner did not challenge the point.

[97] See note 89 (explaining why the inference is not absolute).

[98] See *Tome*, 115 S Ct at 708 (Breyer, J, dissenting).

not seem as likely as later to cause the witness to fabricate a story, then it might have significant probative value in rebutting the charge of improper influence.[99]

Second, although the influence may have reached full strength by the time of the prior statement, the circumstances or manner in which the witness made the statement might suggest that the influence had little impact on her. Justice Breyer mentioned the possibility that "the postmotive statement was made spontaneously."[100] As the Court of Appeals suggested, this might have been the case in *Tome*, though this conclusion depends on a view of child psychology—on an assessment of the child's inability to concoct a plan of false statement or to recognize how it might advance her interests—that is not self-evidently true.[101]

Third, even assuming that the witness fully understood how a statement of ACCUSATION might advance her interests, it may have appeared unlikely to her that this would occur in the particular setting in which she made the statement. Suppose, for example, that the witness declared ACCUSATION to an intimate of hers, someone whose hearing a truthful statement of ACCUSATION would not hurt her and whose hearing a false statement of ACCUSATION would not help her. If the accused later contends that the witness's trial testimony of ACCUSATION is a product of a grudge, this prior statement should have rehabilitative value—even if it was made after the grudge arose.[102]

---

[99] The absolute premotive rule adopted by *Tome* can accommodate this situation, though not in an entirely satisfactory manner. The influence could be deemed not to have arisen for purposes of the premotive rule until such time as it appeared to achieve some level of strength, presumably enough to make it likely that given the influence the witness would declare ACCUSATION even without believing it. Put another way, the strength of the influence could be treated as a binary, rather than continuous, function.

[100] 115 S Ct at 708. Rule 803(2) would remove the hearsay bar to some, but not all, such statements. To satisfy that Rule, the statement must "relat[e] to a startling event or condition" and be "made while the declarant was under the stress of excitement caused by the event or condition."

[101] See note 38 (Court of Appeals doubting ability of A.T. to make statements as "the result of a calculated scheme to deceive").

[102] Thus, on some matters, an observer might have an incentive to lie to her boss or to a court but not to her husband.

Again, a court eager to admit this statement under Rule 801(d)(1)(B), and yet purport to adhere to an absolute premotive rule, might conclude that, although the grudge had arisen, the particular motive to lie—to accomplish harm to the party opponent by making a statement that would have operative force in litigation—had not. But, of course, this manipulation would weaken the premotive requirement.

Sometimes, then, when a witness testifies to a given proposition and the party opponent charges that she did so because of an improper influence, a prior statement by the witness of that proposition might help rebut the charge even though the statement was made after the influence arose. That does not indicate that all postmotive statements, or even all those with such rebuttal value, should be admitted—but it does cut sharply against an *absolute* exclusion of those statements from the exemption granted by Rule 801(d)(1)(B).

In *Tome*, the Court belittled the significance of the probative value of such statements in determining admissibility. Hearsay, it pointed out, is often relevant, but is nevertheless presumptively inadmissible.[103] The argument was a strange one for the Court to make, given that earlier in the opinion it had expressed doubts about whether the policies underlying the hearsay rule apply to the prior consistent statements of a witness at all[104]—and it made no attempt to argue that they do. Indeed, it could hardly do so without questioning the position it had taken in the *Green-Nelson-Owens* line that cross-examination is not hindered by the fact that a prior statement of the witness, rather than her current testimony, is at stake.

What other arguments support an absolute premotive requirement? The history of the Rule is not conclusive, though pre-Rules courts and commentators did frequently declare that only premotive statements could be admitted for rebuttal purposes. As pointed out by Justice Breyer, this view was not quite unanimous.[105] Perhaps more significantly, it appears that the premotive rule was perceived as simply a matter of relevance: A statement made after the motive arose could not be admitted to rehabilitate, because it had no rehabilitative value. Thus, *McCormick on Evidence*, in a passage most of which the Court quoted in *Tome*, declared that

> if the attacker has charged bias, interest, corrupt influence, contrivance to falsify, or want of capacity to observe or remember, the applicable principle is that the prior consistent state-

---

[103] 115 S Ct at 704.

[104] Id at 701.

[105] See id at 708 (Breyer, J, dissenting).

ment *has no relevancy to refute* the charge unless the consistent statement was made before the source of the bias, interest, influence or incapacity originated.[106]

Ordinarily, this argument is sound, but it does not apply where unusual circumstances, such as those described above, *do* give a postmotive statement significant rehabilitative value. The pre-Rules courts and commentators appear never to have squarely addressed the proposition that a postmotive statement could never be admitted for rehabilitative purposes *notwithstanding* such circumstances.[107] Neither, for that matter, have post-Rules decisions of the lower courts adopting a premotive requirement.[108]

Of course, arguably the Federal Rules, though extending the rule on prior consistent statements to substantive as well as rehabilitative admissibility, took the prevailing rule as it was usually articulated, and so incorporated the premotive requirement. Such a reading of history, however, gives an unfortunate freezing effect to the Rules. Before the Rules, I have suggested, a court attentive to the policies underlying evidentiary rules and not merely to casual statements of them should have been willing to consider whether a particular statement had rehabilitative value even though it was made after the improper motive arose. A post-Rules court should not be precluded from such consideration unless the intent of the drafters, or the language of the Rule itself, is very clear.

The drafters' commentary to Rule 801(d)(1)(B) is brief, clumsy,

---

[106] Edward Cleary, gen ed, *McCormick on Evidence* § 49, at 105 (West, 2d ed 1972) (emphasis added). This passage was essentially identical in the first edition, by Charles T. McCormick, § 49, p 108 (1954). See also John Henry Wigmore, 4 *Evidence* § 1128 at 268 (Little, Brown, 4th ed, James H. Chadbourn, rev, 1972), quoted in *Tome*, 115 S Ct at 700 ("A consistent statement, at a *time prior* to the fact said to indicate bias . . . will effectively explain away the existence of a force of the impeaching evidence" (emphasis in original)).

[107] At least those cited by the Court in *Tome* did not, nor have I found any that did.

[108] Some of these decisions have been very conclusory, with little or no discussion; see, for example, *United States v Henderson*, 717 F2d 135, 138 (4th Cir 1983). Others have been based on the propositions recited above, that a postmotive statement "is not relevant to the rebuttal of a charge of recent fabrication" because "mere repetition does not imply veracity." See, for example, *United States v Bowman*, 798 F2d 333, 338 (8th Cir 1986) (characterizing this as the reasoning of courts adopting premotive rule, and joining them); see also note 106 (McCormick, Wigmore). As with respect to the older cases, this reasoning—not so much a statement of an evidentiary rule as an exercise of logic about the most common type of postmotive statement—does not address the occasional circumstance in which a postmotive statement *does* have rehabilitative value.

and uninformative.[109] As for the text of the Rule, it certainly includes no explicit statement of a premotive requirement—such as "to rebut an express or implied charge against the declarant of fabrication or improper influence or motive *that arose after the statement was made.*" I do not believe the presence of the word "recent" before "fabrication" in the Rule can be taken to mandate such a requirement. Let us put aside the argument made by the Government in *Tome* that "recent" is meant only to modify "fabrication." Though the argument is not utterly implausible,[110] neither is it persuasive,[111] and Justice Breyer's formulation—that the statement must show "that the witness did not recently fabricate his testimony as a result of an improper influence or motive"[112]—seems useful. Even on this reading, however, "recent" is notoriously ambiguous. If taken literally, it seems to address the temporal relation of the fabrication, influence, or motive to the *trial*, not to the *statement.* Moreover, it seems clear that the word cannot be taken literally, in the dictionary sense of "occurring at a time immediately before the present."[113] Thus, "recent" should be given a construction that fits the rehabilitation idea underlying the Rule.

---

[109] See note 82.

[110] Note that, as the Government in effect argued, Brief for the United States at 23–24, "[recent fabrication] or [improper influence or motive]" reads more smoothly than "[recent] [fabrication or improper influence or motive]." Indeed, pre-Rules sources suggest that "recent" was attached to "fabrication" and not to "influence or motive." See M. C. Dransfield, Annotation, *Admissibility, for purpose of supporting impeached witness, of prior statements by him consistent with his testimony,* 75 ALR2d 909, 944 ("an examination of the later cases shows that the time of making the consistent statements that are sought to be used to support the credibility of the witness who has been impeached on the ground of having a motive to falsify, or having recently fabricated his testimony, has played an important part in their admissibility for such purposes").

[111] See Brief for Petitioner at 17 n 12. The "fabrication" seems to be a product of, rather than on the same plane with, the "improper influence or motive."

[112] 115 S Ct at 707. See also Annotation, cited in note 110, 75 ALR2d at 944 ("a fabrication of recent date").

[113] *American Heritage Dictionary* 1508 (Houghton, Mifflin, 3d ed 1992). See, for example, *People v Singer,* 300 NY 120, 124, 89 NE2d 710, 711 (1949) (rejecting an interpretation of "recent" as meaning "that the witness' statements at the trial must have been assailed as having been fabricated at some point just before the trial," and adopting "a relative, not an absolute meaning," under which the opponent "is charging the witness not with mistake or confusion, but with making up a false story well after the event. 'Recently fabricated' means the same thing as fabricated to meet the exigencies of the case." (citations omitted)); Judith A. Archer, Note, *Prior Consistent Statements: Temporal Admissibility Standard Under Federal Rule of Evidence 801(d)(1)(B),* 55 Ford L Rev 759, 768–69 (1987) ("The term 'recent' as used by FRE 801(d)(1)(B) indicates that the testimony was contrived at some point after the impeaching event, rather than proximate to its being given at trial.").

In my view, "arising recently enough that the prior statement retains substantial rebuttal value" satisfies this standard and does not distort the language. In most cases—but not in all—this construction would be equivalent to "arising after the statement was made."

V. Reconstructing Rule 801(d)(1)(B)

The arguments I have presented so far in this article suggest that—*assuming the prevailing structure of hearsay law*—Rule 801(d)(1)(B) and its state counterparts should take on this shape: First, the court should assess the rebuttal value of the prior statement. Rebuttal value requires both need to rebut the charge and effectiveness in doing so. Ordinarily, but not inevitably, a statement made after the alleged improper influence arose will not be effective in rebutting the charge that the witness's trial testimony is the product of the influence. Second, if the prior statement appears to have substantial rebuttal value, the court should consider factors weighing against admissibility of the statement. These include expenditure of time and, if the prior statement includes an overhang of assertions not included in the witness's trial testimony, the prejudice that this potentially creates, especially in hindering the party opponent's ability to cross-examine the witness with respect to those statements. If the negative factors are substantial, the court should consider excluding the statement, redacting the statement, or otherwise limiting the information that may be presented about it or the use that the jury may make of it.

How would this system work in *Tome?* If, as both the Court of Appeals[114] and the Supreme Court[115] believed, the charge of improper influence was a weak one, the need for rebuttal was correspondingly weak. The spontaneity of A.T.'s first statement, to her babysitter Rocha, might give that statement some rebuttal value, notwithstanding that the statement was made after the alleged influence arose. The subsequent pretrial statements, made after interrogation of A.T. began, have far less rebuttal value, and their

---

[114] 3 F3d at 351; see note 38.

[115] 115 S Ct at 705 ("a rather weak charge that A.T.'s testimony was a fabrication created so the child could remain with her mother").

incremental value would be less still if the first statement were admitted. Moreover, it was principally the subsequent statements that added information not contained in A.T.'s trial testimony. Though the first statement—"my father gets drunk and he thinks I'm his wife"—added some substance to the current testimony, this could easily be suppressed from Rocha's testimony.[116] Thus, the trial court could have decided to admit the first statement, in some form, but not the others. I do not mean to suggest that this outcome would be indubitably correct, only that it would be plausible, within the trial court's discretion.

But in *Tome* the Court perceived discretion itself as part of the problem. The Court cited the Advisory Committee's concern that making admissibility of hearsay depend entirely on a case-by-case evaluation of probative value would make it too discretionary and so too unpredictable.[117] The Committee's concern was valid, in my view, principally because the Court has not been able to enunciate a robust conception of the Confrontation Clause independent of ordinary hearsay law. Even accepting that validity, however, it seems for several reasons to have little bearing on this case.

First, the Committee's expressed concern was at a global level, invoked in opposition to the idea that the prevailing structure of doctrine, a presumptive exclusion of hearsay qualified by numerous exemptions, should be replaced by a system generally dependent on a balance of probative value and prejudicial potential.[118] But recognizing the dangers of such a wide-open system does not preclude allowing the trial courts a little bit of leeway so that they

---

[116] Moreover, in one respect the statement might significantly help Tome: A.T.'s statement that her father "thinks I'm his wife" suggests a level of sexual awareness that one might not expect in a girl of her age, making it far more plausible than otherwise might be supposed that she fabricated a story of sexual abuse.

[117] 115 S Ct at 704.

[118]

> Abandonment of the system of class exceptions in favor of individual treatment in the setting of the particular case, accompanied by procedural safeguards, has been impressively advocated. . . . The Advisory Committee has rejected this approach to hearsay as involving too great a measure of judicial discretion, minimizing the predictability of rulings, enhancing the difficulties of preparation for trial, adding a further element to the already overcomplicated congeries of pretrial procedures, and requiring substantially different rules for civil and criminal cases.

Advisory Committee's Introductory Note to Article VIII, quoted in part in *Tome*, 115 S Ct at 704.

can implement sensibly the narrow exemption provided by Rule 801(d)(1)(B). To quote Justice Cardozo, albeit far out of context, "Discretion [given the construction I suggest] is not unconfined and vagrant. It is canalized in banks that keep it from overflowing."[119]

Second, even with a premotive requirement attached, Rule 801(d)(1)(B) is dependent on an exercise of discretion. Recall that the predicate for application of the Rule, which allows use of the prior statement for a hearsay purpose, is that the statement is admissible for a rehabilitative purpose. But determining admissibility for that nonhearsay purpose is a discretionary matter. *Tome* characterized as "rather weak" the charge that A.T. had fabricated her testimony so that she could live with her mother, and it complained that "the Government was permitted to present a parade of sympathetic and credible witnesses who did no more than recount A.T.'s detailed out-of-court statements to them."[120] Now suppose A.T. had made all those statements at a time when, so far as she knew, a change of custody arrangements was not in the offing. Satisfaction of the premotive requirement might mean that the earlier statements more clearly rebut the fabrication charge— but that charge would be just as weak as in the actual case, meaning that the parade of witnesses would be, if anything, even less necessary and appropriate. Presumably the Court would not object to the trial court's exercise of discretion to admit only one prior statement in rebuttal. Allowing the trial court to discern rebuttal value even in some postmotive statements would prevent some cases from being decided by a shortcut rule, but it would not introduce discretion to a realm where it had been foreign.

Third, one aspect of discretion under the construction I suggest is concerned not with the premotive requirement but with the overhang problem—the danger that Rule 801(d)(1)(B) will automatically sweep into evidence prior accusatory statements that the witness did not assert in her trial testimony and as to which the accused has not had an adequate opportunity to cross-examine. If, within the present framework of hearsay law, the only way of preventing this is by an exercise of discretion, so be it.

---

[119] *Panama Refining Co v Ryan*, 293 US 388, 440 (1935) (dissenting opinion).

[120] 115 S Ct at 705.

Fourth, we can anticipate that trial courts' attempts to reach sensible results will continue to find an outlet; if *Tome*'s absolute premotive requirement precludes a candid exercise of discretion in applying the Rule, trial courts will tend to manipulate the scope of the requirement.[121] In some cases, it may be that the principal effect of *Tome* will not be to limit what trial courts do, but to prevent them from being frank in doing it.

Finally, *Tome* itself makes explicit that, if a statement fails the premotive requirement, it may nevertheless avoid the rule against hearsay by the most discretionary route of all, the residual exception provided in Rule 803(24); indeed, the Court expressly invited the Court of Appeals to consider whether A.T.'s prior statements should be admitted pursuant to that Rule.[122] Rule 803(24) and its virtually identical counterpart for unavailable declarants, Rule 804(b)(5), offer trial courts notoriously wide-open and virtually uncontrollable discretion to admit hearsay that does not fall within any categorical exception.[123] When all is said and done, the admissibility of a prior statement like those of A.T. will often depend in large part on whether the trial court believes it to be truthful.[124] *Tome*'s efforts to maintain bright-line rules in the hearsay realm may look increasingly unrealistic as trial courts continue to indulge themselves in the luxurious discretion provided by the residual exceptions.

---

[121] See notes 99, 102.

[122] 115 S Ct at 705.

[123] See, for example, 3 Stephen A. Saltzburg, Michael M. Martin, and Daniel J. Capra, *Federal Rules of Evidence Manual* 1447–48 (6th ed 1994); Myrna S. Raeder, *The Hearsay Rule at Work: Has It Been Abolished De Facto by Judicial Discretion*, 76 Minn L Rev 507 (1992).

[124] The trial judge held that A.T.'s August 22 statement to Rocha was admissible alternatively under Rule 803(24), but not her August 27 statements. He emphasized that the earlier statement was spontaneous, that it was made to ask an adult for help, and that it related to her current emotional state (though of course it narrated past facts). T 210–11.

On remand after the Supreme Court's decision, the Court of Appeals for the Tenth Circuit has decided that the statements made to Ecklebarger and Rocha did not satisfy the residual exception, principally because they were made too long after the events they described. *United States v Tome*, 61 F3d 1446, 1451–54 (10th Cir 1995); apparently the Government did not argue for the admissibility of the statements to Padilla. Id at 1454–55. The Court of Appeals held, however, that the statements to the three pediatricians were admissible under Rule 803(4), as having been made for purposes of medical treatment or diagnosis—even though A.T. presumably had no idea of the therapeutic or diagnostic value of some of the information she provided, especially that identifying her assailant. Id at 1449–51. This latter issue, which drew a sharp dissent from Judge Holloway, could plausibly bring the case back to the Supreme Court if Tome is found guilty on the retrial.

VI. Conclusion and Reflection

Tome deepens the ever-expanding thicket of hearsay law.[125] In my view, the question that the Court actually decided was a trivial one, and it gave an unduly rigid answer. The Court need not have granted certiorari, for there was no blazing conflict among the circuits. Courts rejecting a premotive requirement recognized that most often postmotive statements lack significant rehabilitative value. And courts articulating the requirement did not confront the issue of whether it really is an absolute one, to be imposed even on the unusual postmotive statement that does have such value, rather than merely a statement of the logic to be applied in the usual case. In adopting an absolutist rule, the Court was supposedly motivated by fear of judicial discretion—but it put its reliance on the most wide-open aspect of modern hearsay law, the residual exceptions. Moreover, the Court sowed potential confusion as to the nature of Rule 801(d)(1)(B). The Court's language (inadvertently, I think) seems to treat the Rule as one setting out the exclusive circumstances in which a prior consistent statement may be used to rehabilitate the testimony of a witness. Lower courts may infer from this that a statement that does not satisfy the Rule may not be used for rehabilitation.

Tome is frustrating because, while the issue actually decided by the Court was so narrow, the case itself highlights numerous broader issues that must be addressed if hearsay law is to be improved. The *Tome* Court cannot be faulted for failing to resolve issues not actually presented to it, or to write a dissertation on the law of hearsay. But it is fair game, I think, for commentary to point to issues that, given an ideal hearsay system, might have played a larger role in resolving the admissibility of A.T.'s prior statements.

In *Tome*, the Court showed no genuine recognition that, when a witness's prior statement is admitted into evidence but the witness's testimony on direct or redirect does not confirm all the substance of the statement, the opponent's opportunity to cross-examine is severely limited. Indeed, given *Green*, *Nelson*, and *Owens*, the Court felt no need to discuss the issue. The Court

---

[125] See John M. Maguire, *The Hearsay System: Around and Through the Thicket*, 14 Vand L Rev 741 (1961).

never even mentioned Tome's constitutional right of confrontation.

More broadly, the Court showed no awareness at all of what I have called the overhang situation, in which a prior statement offered to rehabilitate a witness's testimony contains significant information not contained in the testimony. Thus, the Court never addressed the possibility that a statement meeting this description should be analyzed any differently from one that asserts only propositions to which the witness has testified.

I believe that recognition of these issues is necessary if prior statements are to be addressed sensibly within the prevailing doctrine of hearsay law. But *Tome* also presents some factors that might be significant in an attempt to put the law of hearsay and confrontation into a fundamentally different framework.

First, Tome was a criminal defendant, and the prior statements offered against him accused him of a crime. The Court put no weight on these factors, which play no role in Rule 801(d)(1)(B). But it seems to me that they make the admissibility of hearsay suspect. In my view, the right to confront witnesses under the Sixth Amendment should not apply to all hearsay declarants. But if a declarant makes an accusatory statement, then ordinarily that statement should not be admitted into evidence unless the accused has had an opportunity to confront the declarant. A strong protection of the confrontation right not dependent on the manipulable bounds of hearsay law[126] would, I believe, make it possible to take a far more hospitable attitude toward hearsay when the confrontation right is *not* at stake.

Second, A.T., the declarant, was a young child, both when she made the statements and when she testified at trial. Perhaps her understanding and cognitive abilities were so undeveloped when she made the statements that, like a barking dog or a mechanical instrument, she should not be considered a "witness" within the meaning of the Confrontation Clause. Moreover, there is some suggestion in the record that A.T.'s difficulty in testifying was attributable to fear of Tome *and* that his wrongful conduct created

---

[126] The Supreme Court has defined the confrontation right so as to make it nearly congruent with the provisions of the Federal Rules of Evidence on hearsay. See, for example, *White v Illinois*, 502 US 346 (1992).

this fear.[127] If it could be shown to a high degree of confidence that *both* these propositions were true, then perhaps Tome should be held to have forfeited the right to object to admissibility of the prior statements.

The presentation of these thoughts here is obviously very sketchy, for it would take a series of other articles to explore them in depth. But I believe that focusing on this type of issue (Was the opportunity for cross-examination satisfactory? Is this the type of declaration, and declarant, to which the confrontation right should apply? Has the accused forfeited his right to object?) will lead to a far more satisfying style of analysis of hearsay issues than the mechanical approach reflected by *Tome*. If the law of hearsay is to be reshaped, as many besides me have contended it should be,[128] a change in the Rules will certainly be necessary. But so too will be a change in the law of confrontation. And in that respect, reform depends on the Supreme Court. Most broadly, it can attempt to define the confrontation right without relying on the perplexing categorizations of hearsay law. More narrowly, it should recognize that the mere fact that the declarant of a prior statement testifies at trial does not necessarily imply that the party opponent has had an adequate opportunity to cross-examine.

---

[127] T 91 (prosecutor saying A.T. is "very frightened" of Tome), 143 (A.T. saying she is afraid to go back to Tome), 162 (A.T. saying that she is afraid to live with him "[b]ecause he did something bad"), 681, 687 (guardian ad litem testifying that in 1991, after A.T. had been removed from Tome's custody, she was fearful of him and asked that visitation be stopped).

[128] See, for example, the articles and essays from the Minnesota Hearsay Reform Conference, 76 Minn L Rev 363–889 (1992).

KENT GREENAWALT

QUO VADIS: THE STATUS AND PROSPECTS OF "TESTS" UNDER THE RELIGION CLAUSES

I. Introduction: Recent Tests Under the Religion Clauses

As the 1994 term drew to a close, "tests" for the Religion Clauses were in nearly total disarray. Apart from cases of discrimination against religions, and disputes over church property, a student of the Supreme Court's jurisprudence could not formulate any general tests that a majority of the Justices clearly support. As exciting as this state of affairs is for those who welcome uncertainty and change, it is disquieting for lawyers and clients, for judges who must decide free exercise and establishment claims, and for Supreme Court Justices who aspire to stable principles of adjudication. In this essay, I provide a summary account of how the Court, with some "help" from Congress, has arrived at the present juncture, and I comment on possible lines of development.

For two decades up to 1990, adjudication under the Religion Clauses exhibited a remarkable, though fragile, stability. The Supreme Court had arrived at basic tests for both the Free Exercise and the Establishment Clauses. For free exercise cases, the basic standard was the compelling interest test: a law interfering with someone's exercise of religion could be applied against the person only if it served a compelling government interest that could not be achieved by a less restrictive means. For establishment cases,

Kent Greenawalt is University Professor, Columbia University.

Author's note: I've received very helpful comments from Vince Blasi, Michael Dorf, and my wife Elaine. Mark Hulbert provided perceptive, reliable, and speedy research assistance.

the basic standard was the threefold test of *Lemon v Kurtzman:*[1] a law was valid only if it was backed by a secular purpose, did not have a primary effect that promoted or inhibited religion, and did not unduly entangle the government with religion. For cases involving outright religious classifications, which give rise to both free exercise and establishment objections, the Court used the compelling interest test.

Those who possessed some familiarity with the Court's decisions realized that any statement of applicable tests obscured troubling complexities.

The Court demanded less in the way of justification to satisfy the free exercise compelling interest test than it required when it reviewed racial classifications and infringements on free speech. (However, when the Court discovered a religious classification, it treated it as "suspect" and demanded a high level of justification.[2]) In certain instances for which the test seemed relevant, the Court avoided applying it altogether, and in other instances it stated that claimants had not satisfied threshold requirements. Most scholars approved use of the compelling interest test, although they disagreed about desirable outcomes it should yield and about the appropriateness of the Court's techniques for evading the test.

The *Lemon* test for establishment cases was sharply challenged from within and without the Court. Each of the three strands was criticized as vague, ambiguous, and inappropriate. From time to time, the test did not seem crucial, and in one instance the Court explicitly disregarded it.[3] Major challenges stated that: (1) courts should not judge motives of legislators; (2) determining primary effects is too difficult; (3) a test condemning promotion of religion does not recognize permissible accommodations to religious exercise; (4) levels of supervision designed to avoid improper effects should not be treated as unacceptable entanglements; (5) the bar on undue entanglement has sometimes mistakenly included a separate focus on political divisiveness. Justice O'Connor proposed an "endorsement test" as an interpretation of the first two elements

---

[1] *Lemon v Kurtzman*, 403 US 602 (1971).

[2] *Larson v Valente*, 456 US 228 (1982). The compelling interest test was not said to apply when the form of religious classification was to achieve an acceptable accommodation to the religious needs of a group or groups.

[3] *Marsh v Chambers*, 463 US 783 (1983).

of *Lemon*. Under this test, adopted by the Court in one case,[4] judges inquire whether a reasonable person would take the challenged state action as endorsing a religion. Some Justices indicated that the core of a correct establishment standard is whether a law or practice would have a coercive effect on nonadherents. Some Justices proposed that the central question lies in how a challenged practice compares with practices accepted or rejected by the constitutional founders.

The various criticisms, interpretations, alternatives, and supplementary standards for the compelling interest and *Lemon* tests bear significantly on present prospects for adjudication under both Religion Clauses. To understand how this is so, we need initially to see how circumstances have changed in the last few years.

The Court startled religious clause scholars in 1990 when a majority of five declared that the compelling interest test did not apply to most free exercise cases.[5] With the leadership of some of these scholars and the forceful support of major religious organizations, Congress adopted a law that has reinstated the compelling interest test for federal and state cases.[6] The effect of that statute on the constitutional case law generates the main uncertainties about free exercise law.

The shift in establishment law has been more attenuated. In 1992, Justice Kennedy wrote a majority opinion forbidding school-sponsored prayers at public school graduation ceremonies.[7] It focused on coercion, but did not explicitly disavow the *Lemon* test and was joined by Justices who supported that test. A year later, Justice White, a steady opponent of results under *Lemon*, wrote a majority opinion employing its standards.[8] Answering Justice Scalia's ridicule of use of a test that a majority no longer supports, Justice White commented that *Lemon* had not been overruled and that this case "presents no occasion to do so."[9] In 1994 Justice O'Connor wrote that the Court should abandon the effort to for-

---

[4] *Allegheny County v ACLU*, 492 US 573 (1989).

[5] *Employment Division Oregon Dept. of Human Resources v Smith*, 494 US 872 (1990).

[6] Religious Freedom Restoration Act, 107 Stat 1488 (codified principally at 42 USC 2000bb (Supp V 1993)).

[7] *Lee v Weisman*, 505 US 577 (1992).

[8] *Lamb's Chapel v Center Moriches School Dist.*, 113 S Ct 2141 (1993).

[9] Id at 2148, n 7.

mulate a unified test for Establishment Clause litigation, recognizing that a test appropriate for one kind of problem may not be
appropriate for another.[10] By this point, four other Justices now
on the Court, Rehnquist, Kennedy, Scalia, and Thomas, had expressed their distaste for *Lemon*.

Two cases at the end of the 1994 term rang the death knell of
the *Lemon* test as an integrated whole. In the more significant decision, *Rosenberger v Rector and Visitors of the University of Virginia*,[11]
the Court held that if a state university authorizes payments from
its Student Activities Fund to printers that publish materials of a
broad range of student groups, it cannot decline to pay for publication of a magazine that urges commitment to a Christian life. The
posture of the constitutional issues was this. The organizers of the
magazine *Wide Awake* complained that the university's refusal of
funding violated the free speech principle that the state should not
discriminate among speech on the basis of content. The university interposed the Establishment Clause as a justification for its
content-based guidelines, under which funds were unavailable for
a religious activity, one which "primarily promotes or manifests a
particular belie[f] in or about a deity or an ultimate reality."[12] The
Court, by a 5–4 vote, accepted the claimant's free speech argument
and rejected the justification offered by the university.

One important aspect of the decision is the absence of reference
to *Lemon*. Justice Kennedy's majority opinion stresses that funding
of *Wide Awake* will allow religious advocacy to be treated equally
with other subjects of student concern. He emphasizes that no settled principle barring government funding of religion precludes
the payments. The opinion discusses some cases decided under the
"effects" strand of *Lemon*, but nowhere mentions the *Lemon* formulation about impermissible effects. Indicating that the Court's
approach, which requires no review of material, will involve less
official entanglement with religion than if the guidelines were
used, Justice Kennedy cites *Walz v Tax Commissioner*,[13] a pre-
Lemon decision sustaining tax exemptions for churches.

---

[10] *Board of Education of Kiryas Joel Village School Dist. v Grumet*, 114 S Ct 2481, 2499 (1994).

[11] 115 S Ct 2510 (1995).

[12] Id at 2515.

[13] 397 US 664 (1970), cited at 115 S Ct 2524. The cite is not offered directly but in a quote from *Widmar v Vincent*, 454 US 263 (1981).

Justice O'Connor, whose vote was crucial to make up a majority, wrote separately about the need to resolve in context a clash of the neutrality principle and the no funding principle.[14] She treats safeguards against any perception that the university endorses the magazine's religious perspective as significant, but she does not present "endorsement" as an overarching test. Instead, she repeats her observation that "experience proves that the Establishment Clause . . . cannot easily be reduced to a single test."[15]

Justice Souter's opinion for the four dissenters emphasizes the unacceptability of "direct funding of core religious activities by an arm of the State."[16] At one point, he indicates that a crucial issue is whether "the law is truly neutral with respect to religion (that is, whether the law either 'advance[s] [or] inhibit[s] religion', ...)";[17] but he does not offer the *Lemon* test as the correct way to approach the establishment question, sticking instead to the narrow preclusion of public funding. In sum, not a single Justice in *Rosenberger* relies on *Lemon* as a comprehensive standard for determining whether funding violates the Establishment Clause.

The other decision, *Capitol Square Review and Advisory Board v Pinette*,[18] involved a similar joinder of free speech and establishment claims. The Ku Klux Klan claimed a free speech right to place a cross on government property that was open to other free-standing structures of private groups; the government agency responsible for issuing permits urged that the Establishment Clause barred display of a religious symbol. Again, no Justice used the *Lemon* test as the standard of inquiry. The majority was composed of Justices adopting two different theories. Justice Scalia, joined in this part of his opinion by Chief Justice Rehnquist, Justice Kennedy, and Justice Thomas, maintained that so long as the government evenhandedly allows private speech on public property, possible perceptions of endorsement are irrelevant.[19] Justice O'Connor, joined by Justices Souter and Breyer, disagreed.[20] They

---

[14] 115 S Ct at 2525–28.

[15] Id at 2528 (quoting *Kiryas Joel*, 114 S Ct 2481, 2499).

[16] Id at 2533.

[17] Id at 2541 (quoting *Allegheny County v ACLU*, 492 US 573, 592).

[18] 115 S Ct 2440 (1995).

[19] Id at 2447–50. Justice Scalia writes slightingly of a "transferred endorsement" principle.

[20] Id at 2451–57.

asserted that if a reasonable, informed observer would perceive a government endorsement here, the display would be impermissible. But they concluded that, because such an observer would not perceive endorsement here, the display did not violate the Establishment Clause. Significantly, O'Connor's reiteration of the view that no single test suffices for establishment issues was embraced by Souter and Breyer.[21]

Justices Stevens and Ginsburg dissented. Justice Stevens, who has consistently favored a strong separation of church and state, adopted a version of an endorsement test, but one that leads to a finding of state endorsement much more easily than O'Connor's approach.[22] Justice Ginsburg's short dissent also makes endorsement central.[23] Because she neither joined Justice Stevens nor adopted Justice O'Connor's formulation about endorsement, one guesses that she has not yet resolved what version of that approach to use when different formulations may yield different results. *Pinette* shows that for *some issues* a majority of the Justices believe that endorsement is the crucial inquiry; but that majority is divided over how the test should be cast. Seven members of the present Court have now dissociated themselves from the *Lemon* test. No one defends *Lemon* as a whole in either *Rosenberger* or *Capitol Square*. Although the *Lemon* test has yet to be decisively rejected in a opinion of the Court, no Justice is likely to come forward and try to revive it.

Before discussing the present status of Religion Clause adjudication and its future prospects in more detail, I offer a few brief observations about constitutional tests. By a "constitutional test," I mean a standard of adjudication that is used by courts to determine whether a practice is constitutional or unconstitutional. The standard must be more than an enumeration of negative and positive factors; if the standard is satisfied, the outcome must be different from what it would be if the standard were unsatisfied. Although tests occasionally are merely conscious smokescreens or unconscious rationalizations for decisions reached on other bases, tests often reveal what judges regard as determinative; and the domi-

---

[21] Id at 2454.

[22] Id at 2464–73.

[23] Id at 2474–75.

nance of a test may lead judges to a result they would not otherwise reach.[24]

Identifying genuine adherence to a test is not always simple. Supreme Court Justices often join opinions, especially majority opinions, that employ basic standards they do not believe should be dominant. A Justice may conclude that failure under the opinion's standard condemns a practice, even though the Justice would prefer to concentrate on other elements.[25] Or the Justice is willing to use a prevailing test he or she would abandon when enough other Justices are ready to change direction.[26]

Challenges to constitutional tests may be based on "wrongness" or "indecisiveness." On the first score, a critic argues that adhering to all or part of a test produces legal results that are wrong, that the test focuses on the wrong factors (or on the right factors but in the wrong order or proportion). Under the heading of indecisiveness, a test may be attacked as too vague or ambiguous in its content, or as having terms that are too openended to give adequate guidance.[27]

Is there any alternative to using a "constitutional test"? As I have here defined tests, a court may do without one, measuring relevant factors against basic constitutional values but not offering any linguistic formula for its resolution.

II. FREE EXERCISE AND THE COMPELLING INTEREST TEST

The fate of free exercise claims and tests depends on how a majority of the Court relates their principles of constitutional

---

[24] This is most obviously true for judges in the hierarchy beneath the court that has established the test, but it also applies to Supreme Court Justices and judges on other courts that have adopted particular tests.

[25] Thus, the Justices who were willing to adopt Justice Kennedy's "coercion approach" to prayers at public school graduation did think that the indirect coercion rendered the prayers unconstitutional, even though concurring opinions show they would have found other elements more simply dispositive. They joined the Kennedy opinion in part because they wanted to have an opinion *of the Court,* and Justice Kennedy was disinclined to accept their theories.

[26] For these reasons, genuine allegiance to a test is shown most decisively when a Justice *says* that he or she adopts the test in a concurring or dissenting opinion. The adoption needs to be something more than: "Employing the Court's own approach to the case, its result is mistaken."

[27] However, some indecisiveness may be defended as a positive virtue. Whereas Justice Scalia is largely driven by a quest for standards that eliminate judicial discretion, Justice O'Connor has suggested that delicate judgments among conflicting principles in context are part of the heart of constitutional adjudication. See note 14. See also Frank I. Michel-

adjudication to an act of Congress that dictates a standard of decision for state and federal cases. Will the Court now employ a compelling interest test for free exercise claims and, if so, how will it apply that test?

A. BEFORE EMPLOYMENT DIVISION V SMITH

The Court first announced a compelling interest test for free exercise claims in *Sherbert v Verner*,[28] holding that a state may not refuse unemployment benefits to someone whose unwillingness to work on Saturday is motivated by religious convictions. Justice Brennan wrote that the state's law denying compensation could be applied only if "any incidental burden on the free exercise of appellant's religion may be justified by a compelling state interest in the regulation of a subject within the State's constitutional power to regulate. . . ."[29] The Court found no solid support for a worry that spurious claims might dilute the unemployment fund; even if that possibility existed, "it would plainly be incumbent upon the appellees to demonstrate that no alternative forms of regulation would combat such abuses without infringing First Amendment rights."[30]

The legal effect of this powerful language cannot be assessed solely by subsequent Supreme Court cases. Other courts sustained a variety of free exercise claims, and legislators granted statutory exemptions they believed might be constitutionally required. Nonetheless, apart from variations on the *Sherbert* problem, the Court upheld free exercise arguments only when the Amish asserted a constitutional right to withdraw their children from ordinary school after the eighth grade,[31] and when a Native American refused to use a social security number to receive welfare benefits.[32]

---

man, *The Supreme Court, 1985 Term—Foreword: Traces of Self Government*, 100 Harv L Rev 4, 33–36 (1986); Kathleen M. Sullivan, *The Supreme Court, 1991 Term—Foreword: The Justices of Rules and Standards*, 106 Harv L Rev 22 (1992).

[28] 374 US 398 (1963).

[29] Id at 403 (quoting *NAACP v Button*, 371 US 415, 438 (1963)).

[30] Id at 407.

[31] *Wisconsin v Yoder*, 406 US 205 (1972).

[32] *Bowen v Roy*, 476 US 693 (1986). See Stephen Pepper, *Taking the Free Exercise Clause Seriously*, 1986 BYU L Rev 299, 319–22. In *Jensen v Quaring*, 472 US 478 (1985) (per curiam), an equally divided Court affirmed an Eighth Circuit decision that the state could not insist that Mrs. Quaring have a driver's license with a photo. *Quaring v Peterson*, 728 F2d 1121 (8th Cir 1984). (Such affirmances have no precedential weight.)

The Court employed three strategies that explain why the compelling interest test failed to yield more victories for free exercise claims: (1) weak application, (2) evasion, and (3) threshold denial. Most straightforwardly, the Court accepted government interests of moderate strength as sufficiently compelling and did not look too hard at available alternatives.[33] The 1982 case of *United States v Lee*[34] reflects this approach. An Amish employer with Amish employees claimed a right not to pay their social security taxes. The Court understood that the Amish accept a religious responsibility to provide for their own elderly and needy within the community and are religiously opposed to participation in the national social security system. Congress has allowed self-employed Amish and members of other similar religious groups an exemption from social security taxes, but the exemption covers neither employers nor employees. The Court said that mandatory participation is indispensable to the fiscal vitality of the social security system, and that "it would be difficult to accommodate the comprehensive . . . system with myriad exceptions flowing from a wide variety of religious beliefs."[35] The Court urged that social security taxes could not be distinguished from general taxes and that people should not be able to avoid income taxes on religious grounds.

The Court is less than convincing. Social security taxes represent a kind of forced savings. Amish employees assert they draw from the fund kept for those who have paid social security taxes, and historical experience bears them out. If employers did not pay social security taxes when both they and their employees have religious objections *and* such employees rarely draw on public money, that result would not thwart any compelling interests the Court discusses. On the other hand, the Court might have worried that any exemption would encourage Amish employers to discriminate in hiring, and that some Amish employees will leave the faith and seek public funds. *Lee*'s result is defensible, but the Court's compelling interest test is hardly stringent and its treatment is casual.[36]

---

[33] Douglas Laycock, however, argues that the Court did not "water down" the compelling interest test in cases in which it applied it. Laycock, *RFRA, Congress, and the Ratchet*, 56 Mont L Rev 145, 149 (1995).

[34] 455 US 252 (1982).

[35] Id at 259–60.

[36] See Jesse Choper, *The Rise and Decline of the Constitutional Protection of Religious Liberty*, 70 U Neb L Rev 651, 663–65 (1991).

Goldman v Weinberger[37] was the most notable example of evasion, that is, not applying the test for kinds of situations its general terms would cover. The Air Force, with other branches of the armed forces, had a rule barring the wearing of headgear indoors. Dr. Goldman, a clinical psychologist, Orthodox Jew, and ordained rabbi, was ordered to stop wearing his yarmulke inside the hospital where he worked. For Goldman, wearing of the yarmulke was a form of religious observance. He had an indisputably sincere religious objection to application of the general rule. Three concurring Justices worried about possible discrimination against members of other religions who might wear less familiar headgear; but Justice Rehnquist's opinion for the Court emphasized that "our review of military regulations challenged on First Amendment grounds is far more deferential than constitutional review of similar laws or regulations designed for civilian society."[38] He noted that "[t]he considered professional judgment of the Air Force is that the traditional outfitting of personnel in standardized uniforms encourages the subordination of personal preferences and identities in favor of the overall group mission"[39] and he concluded that the military is "under no constitutional mandate to abandon their considered professional judgment" behind regulations that "reasonably and evenhandedly regulate dress. . . ."[40] One can imagine a court applying a compelling interest test with substantial deference to the military about the importance of an objective and the means of its accomplishment, but the Rehnquist opinion goes well beyond that. It surrenders any serious examination of either the overall need for the rule or of the risk of exceptions. The Court adopted the same approach for generally applicable rules within prisons.[41]

The Court's third strategy for not applying the compelling interest test has been threshold denial, based on a claimant's failure to establish some requisite needed to bring the test into play. The most significant case of this genre was *Lyng v Northwest Indian*

---

[37] 475 US 503 (1986).

[38] Id at 507.

[39] Id at 508.

[40] Id at 509–10.

[41] See *O'Lone v Estate of Shabazz*, 482 US 342 (1987).

Cemetery Protective Association.[42] The federal government proposed to develop federal land, and permit timber harvesting, in a manner that interfered with the privacy, silence, and undisturbed natural setting that some groups of Indians regarded as essential for worship at sacred sites. Justice O'Connor's opinion for the Court did not doubt that the logging and road building projects "could have devastating effects on traditional Indian religious practices."[43] Nevertheless, she said that the government's development of its own land was not the kind of activity that could "prohibit," even indirectly, anyone's exercise of religion. Because the First Amendment forbids Congress from "prohibiting" the free exercise of religion, it does not restrict such land development. In addition to this conceptual argument that the Indians had not shown a *relevant* burden, the Court expressed concern that the opposite approach would open courts up to all sorts of religious challenges to government decisions dealing with government property, requiring assessment of how central various features of religious practice are to those objecting to the government activities.[44] In dissent, Justice Brennan responded that claimants needed only to show that the land development raised a "substantial and realistic threat" to "central" aspects of their religion.[45] He strongly objected to the Court's view that coercion differs qualitatively for free exercise purposes from interferences with religious practice that land development can cause. The Native American plaintiffs did need to make a showing of centrality before the government had to satisfy a compelling interest test, but they "would be the arbiters of which practices are central to their faith, subject only to the normal requirement that their claims be genuine and sincere."[46]

B. EMPLOYMENT DIVISION V SMITH

In *Employment Division v Smith,*[47] Justice Scalia wrote the Court's opinion for himself and four other Justices. The heart of the case,

---

[42] 485 US 439 (1988). See also *Bowen v Roy*, 476 US 693 (1986), holding that the government's own internal use of social security numbers was not subject to a free exercise claim. See generally Ira C. Lupu, *Where Rights Begin: The Problem of Burdens on the Free Exercise of Religion*, 102 Harv L Rev 933 (1989).

[43] 485 US at 451.

[44] Id at 457–58.

[45] Id at 475.

[46] Id.

[47] 494 US 872 (1990).

as the Court considered it, was whether members of the Native American Church had a right to ingest peyote in worship services despite a state prohibition of the use of peyote. Some state courts had earlier noted that peyote formed the center of worship of the Native American Church and had decided that states lacked a compelling interest in barring this worship.[48] In *Smith*, the Court held that religious claimants have *no* special privileges in respect to laws of general application. If a reasonable law is neither directed against a religious practice nor discriminates among religious groups, it may be validly applied against people with religious objections. The state need not satisfy *any* test beyond the easy task of showing that the law is otherwise valid.

Justice Scalia wrote as if the decision represented no real change in the Court's approach to free exercise cases. To render that position remotely plausible, he had to explain *Wisconsin v Yoder*, in which the Amish claim to violate a valid school attendance law had been upheld. According to Justice Scalia, the critical feature of that case was that the free exercise claim had been *combined* with a parental claim to decide upon the education of children.

Smith sharply reduced the significance of the Free Exercise Clause. The Clause protected "the right to believe and profess whatever religious doctrine one desires,"[49] but the Free Speech Clause would safeguard these rights in any event.[50] The Clause protected other acts and abstentions if the government "sought to ban . . . [them] only when they are engaged in for religious reasons, or only because of the religious belief that they display."[51] Finally, the Clause might provide some undetermined protection when religious objectors also claimed parental rights, associational rights, free speech rights, or other constitutional rights. Although the Court said "it is easy to envision a case in which a challenge on

---

[48] See, e.g., *People v Woody*, 61 Cal 2d 716, 394 P2d 813, 40 Cal Rptr 69 (1964).

[49] 494 US at 877.

[50] It is *possible* that the protection of religious views would be greater in peripheral contexts than the protection of many other views themselves covered by the Free Speech Clause. Thus, the state *might* be barred from considering someone's religious opinions and associations in its own employment decisions or in awards of child custody, though it could consider other opinions and associations (such as virulent racist convictions or membership in the Ku Klux Klan). I touched on this issue in Greenawalt, *Religion as a Concept in Constitutional Law*, 72 Cal L Rev 753, 777 (1984), and am presently working on an article on religious and nonreligious associations that considers it.

[51] 494 US at 877.

freedom of association grounds would likewise be reinforced by Free Exercise Claims concerns,"[52] it did not bother to explain why claims about worship services were not relevantly about association. *Smith*, it said, did not present "a hybrid situation. . . ."[53]

Assessing the relevance of the "combination" or "hybrid" analysis in *Smith* is hard. Most scholars assume this language was a make-weight to "explain" *Yoder* that lacks enduring significance. In many cases, of course, free exercise claims have tracked free speech claims, but the free exercise claims were probably not necessary. Justice Scalia's implicit claim—that free exercise claims are a *necessary* component of some successful "hybrid" challenges but that claims of the same type can *never* succeed on their own—approaches, and possibly achieves, incomprehensibility. We may doubt that in future cases free exercise claims will be required for a result, though they could not conceivably be sufficient by themselves.[54]

In response to a subsequent challenge to a ban on killing animals for sacrifice, the Court held that the law was aimed specifically at religious practices and was unconstitutional.[55] Once having classified the law, the Court engaged in a compelling interest analysis, which it treated as genuinely strict scrutiny. For laws aimed at religious practice *or* discriminating explicitly among religions,[56] we can continue to expect a very stringent application of the compelling interest test.

C. THE RELIGIOUS FREEDOM RESTORATION ACT

After substantial lobbying by major religious organizations, a unanimous House of Representatives, by voice vote, and a nearly unanimous Senate[57] adopted the Religious Freedom Restoration Act in 1993.[58] The main operative part of the Act, Section 3, pro-

---

[52] Id at 882.

[53] Id.

[54] See *Kissinger v Board of Trustees of the Ohio Stat Univ.*, 5 F3d 177, 180 (6th Cir 1993). For brief accounts of some other cases discussing "hybrid" claims, see Choper (cited in note 36) at 681.

[55] *Church of Lukumi Babalu Aye v City of Hialeah*, 113 S Ct 2217 (1993).

[56] But see note 2 in respect to acceptable accommodations.

[57] See Douglas Laycock and Oliver S. Thomas, *Interpreting the Religious Freedom Restoration Act*, 73 Tex L Rev 209, 210–11 (1994).

[58] See note 6.

vides that "Government shall not substantially burden a person's exercise of religion even if the burden results from a rule of general applicability. . . . except that "Government may substantially burden a person's exercise of religion . . . if it demonstrates that application of the burden to the person (1) is in furtherance of a compelling governmental interest; and (2) is the least restrictive means of furthering that compelling governmental interest." "Government" specifically includes state and local, as well as federal, government. The "exercise of religion" is defined to mean "the exercise of religion under the First Amendment. . . ." Another section of the act, Section 7, provides that "Nothing in this Act shall be construed to affect, interpret or in any way address" the Establishment Clause, and, further, that any grants of government benefits and exemptions to the extent permissible under the Establishment Clause are not a violation of the act. Among the preliminary findings in the act are "that laws 'neutral' toward religion may burden religious exercise as surely as laws intended to interfere with religious exercise," that *Employment Division v Smith* "virtually eliminated the requirement that the government justify burdens on religious exercise imposed by laws neutral toward religion," and that "the compelling interest test as set forth in prior Federal court rulings is a workable test for striking sensible balances between religious liberty and competing prior governmental interests." Among the purposes of the act is "to restore the compelling interest test as set forth in" *Sherbert* and *Yoder*.

To understand what test the Supreme Court will apply in most free exercise cases, one must gauge how its members will relate the statute to the corpus of constitutional decisions. I suggest categorizing these relations into four possibilities: (1) statutory invalidity; (2) grudging application; (3) moderately protective standards, like those that existed in some years prior to *Smith*; (4) stronger protection of free exercise claims than has been given before.

If we ask, "How many Justices will have to accept the act in order for it to be practically effective?" the answer is *not* five. *Employment Division v Smith* is not yet a well-established constitutional precedent, and the division of Justices was as close as possible on its central doctrinal point. That doctrine, which drastically altered constitutional jurisprudence, has been overwhelmingly rejected by Congress. Justices who believe that *Smith* was mistaken or that its hostile reception justifies abandoning it[59] will feel free not to follow its constitutional standard. At least two Justices *do* apparently think the rule of *Smith* is mistaken,[60] and *some version* of the compelling interest test is the obvious alternative to apply in its place.

Other Justices, who accept *Smith* as authoritative *constitutional* doctrine, may also accept the Religious Freedom Restoration Act as a valid statute, which alters the standard courts should employ. A religious claimant can succeed in overturning *Smith's* standard of review by attaining a combination of five Justices who treat the act as valid *or* support overruling *Smith* on constitutional grounds.[61]

1. *Possible invalidity.* Is the Religious Freedom Restoration Act valid? It may be invalid as a whole, as it reaches state cases, or in specific applications. It may be invalid because it infringes upon individual rights, because it offends separation of powers, or because Congress lacks enumerated authority to enact it.

a) Individual rights. In purporting to vindicate free exercise claims, the statute might constitute an establishment of religion,[62] violate the free exercise rights of others, or infringe their rights

---

[59] As I discuss subsequently, a Justice may reasonably take Congress's view as influential about the desirable constitutional standard, independent of Congress's actual authority *to dictate* a different standard. See Daniel Conkle, *The Religious Freedom Restoration Act: The Constitutional Significance of an Unconstitutional Statute*, 56 Mont L Rev 39, 79–90 (1995).

[60] See *Church of the Lukumi Babalu Aye v City of Hialeah*, 113 S Ct at 2250 (Justice O'Connor joining Justice Blackmun in saying *Smith* was wrongly decided), at 2243–50 (Justice Souter expressing strong doubts about *Smith*). Justice Thomas joined the majority in *Church of the Lukumi Babalu Aye*, but has not had occasion to pass on the basic doctrinal approach of *Smith*. Justices Ginsberg and Breyer have yet to decide a free exercise case as members of the Supreme Court.

[61] Two further points follow. The version of the compelling interest test to be employed could be affected by whether a majority of five sustain the statute or is composed of some Justices relying on the statute and some on a direct constitutional test. The second point concerns a difference between the way the Supreme Court treats cases challenging the statute and the way other courts do. *Those courts* do (and should) regard themselves as bound to follow *Smith* as the appropriate constitutional standard. Thus, only if a majority of judges (or a single judge, sitting alone) accepts the statute as valid will a court apply the compelling interest test as a part of federal law. State courts may, I should add, interpret their own state constitutions as demanding a stricter standard of review than the one adopted in *Smith*, and a number of them have done so. See Angela C. Carmella, *State Constitutional Protection of Religious Exercise: An Emerging Post-Smith Jurisprudence*, 1993 BYU L Rev 275; Tracey Levy, *Rediscovering Rights: State Courts Reconsider the Free Exercise Clauses of Their Own Constitutions in the Wake of Employment Division v Smith*, 67 Temple L Rev 1017 (1994).

[62] I treat Establishment Clause rights as a species of individual rights, although the constitutional wrong of establishment need not be done to specific individuals.

to equal treatment as a matter of free speech or equal protection law. Any difficulties in these regards concern both federal and state applications.[63]

As first glance, the Establishment Clause problem might seem troublesome. The statute dictates substantial accommodation to religious exercise across a wide range of circumstances. In *Estate of Thornton v Caldor, Inc.*,[64] eight Justices agreed that a state's rigid statutory demand that employers accommodate sabbath observances of employees was impermissible. If a statute often demands accommodations to religion that constitute forbidden establishments, it will violate the Establishment Clause.

The concern about general invalidity turns out to be unthreatening.[65] On occasion, individual Justices have suggested that constitutional decisions requiring substantial accommodations to free exercise raise establishment worries, but typically these opinions have included comments that legislatures *may* accommodate if they choose to do so. Justice Scalia in *Employment Division v Smith* explicitly suggested that legislatures could constitutionally choose to afford a religious exemption from laws against using peyote.[66] The implication is that many accommodations are acceptable under the Establishment Clause. No Justice has ever proposed that employment of the compelling interest test as a general standard for free exercise cases itself violates the Establishment Clause.[67] Barring a huge shift in the law of the Religion Clauses, only *some* accommodations that the main section of the statute might require would violate the Establishment Clause.

The statute contains two internal devices to prevent *any* applications from violating the Establishment Clause. One is the specific

---

[63] According to prevailing "incorporation" doctrine, the First Amendment applies with the same force to state and federal governments, and the thrust of the Court's decisions is that in most respects the Due Process Clause of the Fifth Amendment imposes on the federal government the restrictions of the Equal Protection Clause.

[64] 472 US 703 (1985).

[65] *If* one advocated a radical alteration in the perceived relationship of the Free Exercise and Establishment Clauses, one might argue for general invalidity on this basis. See note 68.

[66] 494 US at 890.

[67] Justice Stevens has expressed concern that evaluation of the merits of various religious claims is a risk the Establishment Clause was meant to preclude. *United States v Lee*, 455 US 252, 263 n 2 (1982) (concurring opinion). See also *Goldman v Weinberger*, 475 US 503, 512 (1986) (concurring opinion).

provision that nothing in the act will be "construed to affect, interpret, or in any way address" the Establishment Clause. I take this provision to mean roughly this: "Do not refer to this statute to decide *how* the Establishment Clause should be interpreted, *and* do not apply the statute to violate the Establishment Clause." Suppose the main provision would apply to a claim, were it not for the Establishment Clause. One might say that the statute applies, but the Establishment Clause makes the application invalid. A preferable conceptualization, however, given the statutory language, is that the statute does not apply because of the safeguard provision.

The statute's compelling interest test itself yields the same effect. Suppose that a claimant seeks an accommodation that would violate the Establishment Clause. A state has a *compelling interest* in avoiding this unconstitutional situation.[68]

What I have said thus far about the Establishment Clause shows why possible free exercise, free speech, and equal protection objections are similarly ill-grounded. If granting the free exercise claims of one person would violate the free exercise rights of someone else, that action would also violate the Establishment Clause, since favoring of the first religion at the expense of the second would be a form of establishment. What of the possibility that some statutory applications might violate a principle of neutrality required by the rest of the First Amendment or the Equal Protection Clause? The Court *might* afford an exemption under the statute for religious claimants and announce that constitutional principle requires an extension to nonreligious claimants.[69] Suppose, instead,

---

[68] This does not *quite* dispose of concern that applications would violate the Establishment Clause. Suppose that the vast majority of accommodations apparently required by the act's main provision are barred by the Establishment Clause. In other words, only a small proportion of apparently required accommodations would be constitutionally permissible. One might then conclude that the whole statutory scheme, its effect on government action and the litigation it spawns, would violate the Establishment Clause. It could violate the Establishment Clause to force governments in many cases to demonstrate that they need not make accommodations because of that clause. This theory founders on the reality that, according to the heavily preponderant view (which I think is correct), *most* accommodations the statute would otherwise require would not violate the Establishment Clause. It is relevant in this regard that the statute does not require governments to force private enterprises to make accommodations, one kind of situation that has led the Court to interpose Establishment Clause objections.

[69] This is the position Justice Harlan took in *Welsh v United States*, 398 US 333, 357–58 (1970) (concurring opinion), about the claim of a nonreligious conscientious objector to receive an exemption from military service that Congress had given to religious objectors. In determining whether Congress would want the exemption extended to nonreligious

the Court concludes that the inequality should not be redressed in this way but that limiting an exemption to religious claimants would violate the Free Speech or the Equal Protection Clause. In that event, the government has a compelling interest in not granting the exemption.

Let us now consider two more subtle Establishment Clause concerns, the second of which shades into a problem of separation of powers. The first concern is that a general statute that provides exemptions for religious claimants represents a Congressional endorsement of religion.[70] A central theme of recent Establishment Clause jurisprudence is that government should endorse neither particular religions nor religion in general. Because the statute speaks of religious claims in general, perhaps it endorses religion as opposed to nonreligious outlooks.

The short response to this concern is that when state and federal courts have used the compelling interest test for free exercise claims, and when legislatures have adopted narrow accommodations granting religious exemptions, these have not been regarded as unconstitutional endorsements. A broader Congressional accommodation that employs the compelling interest test is not different in principle.

A deeper response must address the proper constitutional place of religious and nonreligious claims. If one believes that the appropriate posture is one of equal regard,[71] sameness of treatment for claims that are similar except in respect to a religious component, one may see this statute as favoring and endorsing religion. However, the text of the Free Exercise Clause and constitutional history suggest that some special protection of religious claims is warranted. And that approach can be defended without dependency on endorsement. In general, religious beliefs and practices place demands on people that are more intense, less subject to reasons that regulate civil society, more likely to generate conflicts with the state if not accommodated, than do nonreligious beliefs and

---

claimants or denied to religious ones, a court would (should) be influenced by the comparative numbers. For example, if the vast majority of claimants are predictably religious, the statutory scheme is better severed by an extension than by a denial to all claimants.

[70] See Christopher L. Eisgruber and Lawrence G. Sager, *Why the Religious Freedom Restoration Act Is Unconstitutional*, 69 NYU L Rev 437, 457–58, 472 (1994). See also Mark Tushnet, *The Emerging Principle of Accommodation (Dubitante)*, 76 Geo L J 1691, 1703 (1988).

[71] Eisgruber and Sager, note 70 supra, at 448–50.

practices.[72] Further, accommodation to those beliefs and practices may be appropriate because the Establishment Clause places particular limitations on assistance to religion that it does not extend to other beliefs and practices.[73] Thus, one can support accommodation to religious claims and the Religious Freedom Restoration Act without invoking the truth or superiority of religion, that is, without endorsing religion.

Another concern, expressed strongly in *Smith*, involves the appropriate function of courts. If courts find it impossible to sift out the power of religious claims and compare them against government interests in applying laws to everybody they cover,[74] imposing this task on courts may itself be unconstitutional. The point can be cast as an objection that when inadequately guided courts arbitrarily reward some religious claims and reject others, this amounts to an unacceptable establishment of religion. The concern is put more forcefully as involving separation of powers: legislatures may not impose on courts functions judges have decided they are unequipped to perform.[75] In either form, the argument for unconstitutionality is not persuasive. Under the direction of the Supreme Court, courts throughout the country employed the compelling interest test for free exercise cases for roughly twenty-seven years; some state courts continue to interpret their state constitutions as requiring that standard. Moreover, other areas of law require judgments of similar delicacy and difficulty.[76] Perhaps, as Justice Scalia keeps insisting, less open-ended and discretionary standards are more appropriate for courts. But it would constitute a startling reversal of modern constitutional law to declare that this well-established, long-standing formulation is so defective for

---

[72] See generally John H. Garvey, *Free Exercise and the Values of Religious Liberty*, 18 Conn L Rev 779 (1986); Stephen Pepper, *A Brief for the Free Exercise Clause*, 7 J Law & Religion 323, 346–52 (1989).

[73] See Christopher L. Eisgruber, *Madison's Wager: Religious Liberty in the Constitutional Order*, 89 Nw U L Rev 347, 348 (1995); Abner S. Greene, *The Political Balance of the Religion Clauses*, 102 Yale L J 1611 (1993).

[74] Eisgruber and Sager talk of the compelling interest test for free exercise cases as "unworkable," note 70 at 484, 451, 466.

[75] See Joanne C. Brant, *Taking the Supreme Court at Its Word: The Implications for RFRA and Separation of Powers*, 56 Mont L Rev 5 (1995).

[76] Compare Mary Ann Glendon and Raul F. Yanes, *Structural Free Exercise*, 90 Mich L Rev 477, 523 (1991); Ira C. Lupu, *The Trouble with Accommodation*, 60 Geo Wash L Rev 743, 759–60 (1992); Michael W. McConnell, *Free Exercise Revisionism and the Smith Decision*, 57 U Chi L Rev 1109, 1144 (1990), with Choper (cited in note 36) at 677–79.

free exercise cases that courts may not constitutionally use it, even when Congress directs them to do so.

b) Congressional power. Congressional power presents the most troublesome issue of constitutionality. Here we must distinguish between federal and state impingements on religious exercise. Congress definitely has the power to set standards of interpretation for review of actions by the federal government. It may, in effect, qualify the application of (past and future) federal statutes that are less generous to religious claimants than is the Religious Freedom Restoration Act.[77]

Does Congress have the authority to adopt a quasi-constitutional test for state and local infringements of free exercise rights? The hard question about the statute's validity is whether Congress's "power to enforce by appropriate legislation, the provisions" of the Fourteenth Amendment[78] includes the power to grant free exercise rights that the Supreme Court has declined to find.

Here we need to distinguish "ends-means," or remedial, extension from expansion of basic content. Without doubt, Congress can create rights not granted by the Fourteenth Amendment if these are needed to safeguard rights that are granted. If, for example, Congress believed that police often lie about consent to searches, Congress could adopt a law requiring written consent, even though the Fourth Amendment (made applicable to the states by the Fourteenth Amendment) does not directly require consent to be written.

How would such a theory work here? First, it might be argued that state legislatures frequently adopt ostensibly neutral laws with unconstitutional, but hidden, aims to harm unpopular religious groups, aims that would render the laws invalid if explicitly revealed in preambles. Since courts are unable to discover these aims in ordinary legal proceedings, Congress may forestall the success of this concealed unconstitutional behavior by granting direct protections against neutral laws.

To gauge the force of this defense of the Religious Freedom

---

[77] Although it *might* be argued that Congress wants a uniform standard for state and federal interferences with free exercise, and that, therefore, federal applications should not be upheld unless state applications are also valid, by far the better view is that the federal applications stand, whatever the conclusion about congressional power to determine standards for reviewing state laws.

[78] US Const, Amend XIV, § 5.

Restoration Act, one must measure the Act against the broad range of cases that it reaches. Without performing this exercise, I rather doubt that many cases can plausibly be covered by this sort of ends-means connection. To take the circumstances of *Employment Division v Smith*, state legislatures do not forbid use of peyote *in order to harm* religious groups (mostly Native American) that use peyote in worship. Douglas Laycock has suggested that an end-means justification can support the entire statute, even if the justification reaches only a small percentage of cases;[79] but I do not believe the justification can be stretched that far. If the great majority of applications of the act do not plausibly protect people against unconstitutional laws or state practices, the act cannot be sustained on that basis.[80]

A more complex and debatable version of the ends-means theory asserts that an objective of the Religion Clauses and the Equal Protection Clause is to assure that religions are treated equally.[81] Equal treatment is threatened by indifference and inattention as well as purposeful discrimination.[82] Legislators who would never impose burdens on dominant faiths may casually impose such burdens on fringe religions, either unaware of, or unconcerned about, this effect of a general law. Legislatures enacting prohibitions of use of alcohol always made exceptions for sacramental use of wine by Christians; legislatures enacting prohibitions of use of peyote have often failed to except sacramental use for Native American churches. The Court in *Smith* noted that "leaving accommodation to the political process will place at a relative disadvantage those

---

[79] He says, "Congress need not find that ninety, fifty or ten percent of the cases involve violations under the Supreme Court's definition. Even under a purely remedial theory, Congress need find only that there are enough such violations to justify congressional action." Laycock (cited in note 33) at 167.

[80] I do not pause to engage two questions about ends-means justification and general validity. If the percentage of instances supportable by an ends-means justification were very high, probably the statute would be valid even for the unusual instances when that justification seemed irrelevant. If the percentage of instances supportable by an ends-means justification were substantial (but not very high), that probably would be sufficient to preserve the law on its face as applied to state cases; *applications*, however, might be held invalid if neither ends-means nor any other valid justification were forthcoming for those circumstances.

[81] One might view this theory as a combination of modest expansion of basic content plus ends-means, since the Supreme Court has not held, and might not hold on its own, that inequality of consideration of the sort I describe violates the Constitution in any sense.

[82] To draw an analogy to criminal law concepts, one may treat indifference as like recklessness and inattention as like negligence.

religious practices that are not widely engaged in. . . ."[83] As Thomas Berg has suggested,[84] the Religious Freedom Restoration Act may enable minority religions to achieve through the judicial process what dominant religions obtain through the political process. *Perhaps* legislative failures to accord equal treatment to minority religions can be viewed either as unconstitutional, though not subject to correction through judicial enforcement of constitutional norms, *or* as at odds with basic constitutional values, though not strictly unconstitutional. In either event,[85] the Religious Freedom Restoration Act might supply a broad remedy for such failures.

This rationale would cover a high percentage of instances arising under the act[86] and would justify the entire act, if it is convincing. The difficulty lies in the premise that legislative indifference or inattention violates the Constitution, or comes close enough to bring the ends-means logic into play. To defend the premise, one would draw: from claims that the Constitution imposes broad obligations on legislators (e.g., to vote for constitutionally relevant reasons) that cannot effectively be enforced by courts; from extensive liability in the criminal law for recklessness and negligence; and from the rule that the Title VII restriction on discrimination may be violated (without proof of conscious discrimination) by use of tests that have a disproportionate impact and are not required by business necessity.[87] Opposed to the premise may be the standard view that conscious discrimination alone violates the Constitution; but this opposition is complete only if "conscious discrimination" is taken to mean a desire or aim to discriminate and not to include conscious indifference to unjustified comparative disadvantage. *Smith* appears to reject outright the premise that legislative indif-

---

[83] 494 US at 890.

[84] Thomas C. Berg, *What Hath Congress Wrought? An Interpretive Guide to the Religious Freedom Restoration Act*, 39 Vill L Rev 21-22 (1994). See also McConnell (cited in note 76) at 1132.

[85] The argument for validity is stronger, of course, if the "failures" are regarded as actually unconstitutional.

[86] Since members of dominant religions, and dominant churches, can also make claims under the act, this theory would not cover all situations.

[87] *Griggs v Duke Power*, 401 US 424 (1971). Jesse Choper provides an illuminating comparison of religious and racial discrimination in *Religion and Race Under the Constitution: Similarities and Differences*, 79 Cornell L Rev 49 (1994).

ference to minority religions is unconstitutional; it leaves minorities to the majoritarian political process. However, the language of the opinion in *Smith* focuses on the constitutional responsibilities of courts. The willingness of the Justices to assign minorities to an unsympathetic political process may be interpreted as not addressing the underlying constitutional responsibilities of legislators. Nevertheless, the tone of the *Smith* opinion offers less promise for this premise than it deserves. A sensitive view of what the Constitution covers should include at least self-conscious indifference to the plight to religious minorities.

For Justices who are not persuaded to accept this premise, the act will be valid against states only if another rationale supports it. The critical issue is whether Congress has some power to expand the content of constitutional rights the Court has declared. Put differently, once the Court has defined the content of Fourteenth Amendment rights, may Congress *define* those rights more broadly?

I have already mentioned one way the Court might accede to the approach of Congress. The Justices could say, in effect, "We resolved a difficult issue about free exercise in *Smith*. Congress has indicated its overwhelming opinion that our resolution was misconceived. We now reconsider the issue in light of our 'dialogue' with Congress. We find ourselves persuaded that our resolution was mistaken, and we adopt the compelling interest standard as the appropriate constitutional guide." On this approach, the Justices would give some deference to Congress, but would retain responsibility for appropriate principles of review. They would *not* apply a legislative standard of review at variance with one they could accept as constitutionally required. Congress appropriately indicates its views of the Court's constitutional holdings, and these views should carry some weight with the Justices. Let us suppose, however, that Justices who joined *Smith* are not persuaded to change their constitutional conclusions.

Does Congress have some independent authority to define the scope of rights under the Fourteenth Amendment? If one focuses on the ordinary linguistic significance of "power to enforce," this seems doubtful. Enforcing rights does not seem to imply authority to broaden the rights themselves. Nevertheless, a fairly strong argument supports such authority in Congress. When the Fourteenth Amendment was adopted, Congress was conceived as the branch of government to implement it. Those who approved the Amendment did not look to the Supreme Court that had decided *Dred Scott* as a major engine for achieving equality.[88] It may be reasonable to infer that Congress has the power to interpret rights in order to *expand* them beyond what the Court has concluded[89] the Constitution grants.

But if Congress may expand rights beyond what the Court has declared, may it also contract rights? Not necessarily. Most constitutional rights are countermajoritarian protections against legislatures. If it allows Congress to narrow rights, the Court accedes to majoritarian restrictions at the national level that it has rejected at the state level. When Congress "expands rights," the national legislature tells state legislatures they may not restrict individual behavior that the Court has left them free to control.

This fundamental difference between legislation expanding and limiting rights is straightforward, but does it matter? There are three, related answers. One answer starts from a tough-minded realism that federal powers under the Commerce and Spending Clauses already have been stretched so far that hardly any judicially enforceable protections of state authority against federal interference remain.[90] If that is so, we should not worry about minor additional erosions of state power brought about by generous congressional interpretations of the Fourteenth Amendment. The second answer is that the Fourteenth Amendment conceived a drastic shift of authority from states to Congress. The third answer rests on what are commonly called "the political safeguards of federalism."[91] Members of Congress are elected within states. When proposals are made to erode state authority in unacceptable ways, federal legislators will manifest their opposition. The states have a

---

[88] Laycock (cited in note 33) at 157–63.

[89] The basic issue of power is the same whether the Court has already taken a position or *would take* that position on the constitutional issue. I simplify in the text by talking of positions already taken.

[90] The Court did, however, decide in the last term that an asserted Commerce Clause justification was insufficient. *United States v Lopez*, 115 S Ct 1624 (1995).

[91] See William Cohen, *Congressional Power to Interpret Due Process and Equal Protection*, 27 Stan L Rev 603 (1975); Herbert Wechsler, *The Political Safeguards of Federalism*, in *Principles, Politics, and Fundamental Law* 49–82 (1961). It is sometimes suggested that Congress's ability to find facts also supports a "one-way rachet," but a special capacity to find facts might lead to limiting declared rights as well as expanding them.

political representation in Congress that minorities lack. Thus, the argument goes, the Court should accept Fourteenth Amendment enforcement legislation that impinges on state power.[92]

The Supreme Court has never resolved the precise issue of federal power that the Religious Freedom Restoration Act raises. The most important precedent is *Katzenbach v Morgan*.[93] The Court had earlier sustained against Fourteenth Amendment challenge a state requirement that voters be literate in English. Congress provided that no one who completes sixth grade in an "American-flag" school may be denied the right to vote because he or she is not literate in English, thus affording many Puerto Ricans a right to vote in New York despite the state's requirement of English literacy. Justice Brennan wrote that Section 5 of the Fourteenth Amendment grants Congress broad powers like those found in the Necessary and Proper Clause. The Court reasoned that voting may combat *other* forms of discrimination against Puerto Ricans—a version of the ends-means justification I have discussed.[94] The Court needed only "to perceive a basis upon which the Congress might resolve the conflict as it did."[95]

Justice Brennan continued that the result was the same if the legislation was aimed merely "at the elimination of an invidious discrimination in establishing voter qualifications." He referred to some possible factual conclusions by Congress, such as that voters might be adequately informed by Spanish-language newspapers, radio, and television. But he also spoke directly to the assessment of values that is central to constitutional adjudication. "Congress might have also questioned whether denial of a right deemed so precious and fundamental in our society was a necessary or appropriate means of encouraging persons to learn English, or of furthering the goal of an intelligent exercise of the franchise."[96] The prerogative to weigh competing considerations was Congress's;

---

[92] One rejoinder to this argument is that political representation may be unavailing if one or a few states want to order their affairs in a manner the other states dislike; but this rejoinder has no relevance here. The Religious Freedom Restoration Act received nearly unanimous support; it will affect legislative and executive decisions in all states, and was not directed at practices found in only a few states.

[93] 384 US 641 (1966).

[94] Id at 652–53.

[95] Id at 653.

[96] Id at 654.

"again, it is enough that we perceive a basis upon which Congress might predicate a judgment that the application of New York's English literacy requirement . . . constituted an invidious discrimination . . . ."[97] Directly addressing the possibility that the Court's resolution might allow Congress to restrict or dilute rights, Justice Brennan said that would not be enforcement: "§ 5 grants Congress no power to restrict, abrogate, or dilute these guarantees."[98]

Justice Harlan, joined by Justice Stewart, dissented.[99] He said Congress could undoubtedly pass remedial legislation, but the determination whether a constitutional command had been violated was for the courts, not Congress.

Katzenbach v Morgan clearly supports the Religious Freedom Restoration Act. One can reason that Congress decided after extensive testimony that the value of religious exercise necessitates a compelling interest standard. The Court can easily "perceive a basis" upon which Congress reached that conclusion. Moreover, *Katzenbach v Morgan* does not stand alone. In significant cases under both the Fourteenth and Thirteenth Amendments, the Court has acknowledged the authority of Congress to expand rights beyond those it has found or would find by itself.[100]

Still, it is far from certain that the Court will extend *Katzenbach v Morgan* and its successors to justify the new act. Distinctions are possible. First, factual judgments may have played a much larger role in adoption of the literacy statute, and other prior statutes, than in the new act, which mainly reveals disagreement with the Court's assessment of constitutional values. Second, the new act directs the courts to apply an open-ended standard involving difficult discretionary judgments across a wide range of circumstances;

---

[97] Id at 656.

[98] Id at 651.

[99] Id at 659–71. Insofar as the majority's opinion rested on possible factual conclusions Congress might have reached, Justice Harlan said these were unsupported by any legislative record.

[100] See, e.g., *Fitzpatrick v Bitzer*, 427 US 445 (1976); *Fullilove v Klutznick*, 448 US 448 (1980); *Jones v Alfred H. Mayer Co.*, 392 US 409 (1968). See generally Laurence Tribe, *American Constitutional Law* (2d ed, 1988), §§ 5–14; Archibald Cox, *Foreword: Constitutional Adjudication and the Promotion of Human Rights*, 80 Harv L Rev 91 (1966); Scott C. Idleman, *The Religious Freedom Restoration Act: Pushing the Limits of Legislative Power*, 73 Tex L Rev 247 (1994); Matt Pawa, *When the Supreme Court Restricts Constitutional Rights, Can Congress Save Us? An Examination of Section 5 of the Fourteenth Amendment*, 141 U Pa L Rev 1029 (1993). The authority is by no means all in one direction. These authors discuss cases and individual opinions that propose a more limited view of Congressional power.

the literacy law and others had dealt more precisely with narrower sets of circumstances. And third, the new act concerns the "incorporated" Free Exercise Clause rather than the flexible constitutional standard of equal protection.[101]

Any contention that federal power should be radically different for incorporated rights than for equal protection rights is not very forceful; the relationship of Congress to the Court should be parallel for all rights enforced by Congress under the Fourteenth Amendment. Further, guarantees of religious rights are *largely* guarantees for minorities, and may be justified as an aspect of equal protection. In principle, Congress should be able to direct courts to employ broad standards as well as more precise ones; and its authority to implement Fourteenth Amendment rights beyond what the Court has declared does not rest solely on some special fact-finding capacity. Thus, the most substantial argument for distinguishing *Morgan* and its successors is that the Religious Freedom Restoration Act rests on a disagreement with the Court, that Congress rejects the constitutional judgment of the Supreme Court outright, rather than building upon what the Court has decided.[102] Congress, the argument goes, has authority under the Fourteenth Amendment to cooperate with the Court in elaborating relevant norms,[103] but not to oppose its basic judgments about constitutional values.[104] However, some of the previous acts of Congress that have been sustained are not neatly categorized as cooperative. *Katzenbach v Morgan* followed a Court decision sustaining a literacy test; Congress said that such tests could not be applied in certain circumstances. In another case,[105] Congress protected equal treatment of women, although up to that point the Court had said that gender classifications needed to be supported

---

[101] However, in *Hutto v Finney*, 437 US 678 (1978), the Court upheld congressional authorization of attorneys fees in an Eighth Amendment civil rights suit, with Justice Rehnquist dissenting. The case is discussed in Pawa (cited in note 100) at 1095–96.

[102] Eisgruber and Sager (cited in note 70), at 445, talk of the statute as "at war with the Supreme Court's constitutional judgment."

[103] Samuel Estreicher, *Congressional Power and Constitutional Rights: Reflections on Proposed "Human Life" Legislation*, 68 Va L Rev 333, 427 (1982), talks of Congress's "ability to assist the Court in elaborating constitutional norms. . . ." as one basis for Congressional authority.

[104] Eisgruber and Sager (note 70 at 462) write, "Congress is not empowered . . . to command the Court to yield to congressional judgments about either the letter or the spirit of the Constitution's liberty-bearing provisions."

[105] *Fitzpatrick v Bitzer*, 427 US 445 (1976).

only by a rational basis. More important, the recent act does not fit unambiguously into the opposition mode. After all, the Supreme Court in *Smith* approved legislative accommodations and expressed some concern about the unequal treatment of religious minorities.[106] The Court's main concern was that judges could not sensibly apply the compelling interest standard. Legislative action mitigates that concern about the judicial function.[107] When both Congress and the President indicate they want courts to use a test, the risk is lessened that the judiciary will trespass on political functions. Finally, Congress has adopted a standard that the Supreme Court announced and purported to employ for more than twenty-five years and that four Justices accepted in *Smith*. The act hardly represents opposition to the Court's normative evaluations over time. Given all this, the act is in reasonable continuity with the Supreme Court's work. It is highly doubtful that cooperation, rather than opposition, should be a requisite of rights expansion under Section 5; in any event, this act is sufficiently cooperative to pass muster.

Although continuity with prior law and appropriate relations between Congress and the Court under the Fourteenth Amendment call for validation of the Religious Freedom Restoration Act as it applies to state laws and practices,[108] some Justices will be persuaded that the issue is importantly distinguishable from any resolved by prior cases, and others will adhere to the dissenters' stance in *Morgan* that the Court, not Congress, decides what actions violate the Fourteenth Amendment.[109] The fate of the act as it applies to state and local governments is decidedly uncertain.[110]

2. *What compelling interest test?* The Court might hold the new act valid, but give it a grudging application. One strategy for

---

[106] Moreover, it did not assert that its rule was *more consonant* with the language of the First Amendment and the history leading up to it than a constitutional rule requiring some accommodation to religious exercise. See McConnell (cited in note 76) at 1115–16.

[107] See Berg (cited in note 84) at 28.

[108] The principle that would extend *Morgan* to the Religious Freedom Restoration Act would also cover property rights. Suppose the Court renders a narrow interpretation of rights not to be deprived of property without due process. A Republican Congress might expand property rights. Such action might be supported under the Commerce Clause in any event, but an expansive view of Congress's power under the Fourteenth Amendment would also sustain such legislation.

[109] For cases supporting this view, see the treatise and articles cited in note 100.

[110] See Idleman (cited in note 100) at 304.

achieving this—declaring that religion should not be a permissible basis of categorization for benefits or burdens[111] and that accommodations to religious claims generally amount to impermissible establishments—would render the act ineffective, because governments would then have a compelling interest in not creating exemptions. This strategy is not open because the Court has supported wide legislative choice about when to make most accommodations to religious exercise.

A second strategy for narrow application arises out of the Court's argument in *Smith* of the ill wisdom and the difficulty for judicial review of the compelling interest test. In light of that difficulty, Justices might conclude they should defer generously to government assertions of compelling interest and least restrictive means, sustaining them unless irrational. A variation on this approach would be to find that few restrictions "substantially burden" the exercise of religion.

Neither variety of the second strategy has much appeal. The difficulty of applying a compelling interest test is hardly a justification for declining to apply it, in the guise of extreme deference to government claims. Congress evidently supposes that many restrictions do substantially burden religious exercise. Moreover, because *Smith* objects to any analysis of what is central to a religion or whether a burden on religion is significant, Justices who joined that opinion should be uncomfortable concluding that most sincere religious claims do not assert a substantial burden.[112]

Justices inclined to read the statute narrowly might emphasize all the doctrines prior to *Smith* that limited the import of the compelling interest test, taking the statutory commendation of the test "as set forth in prior Federal court rulings" as implicitly adopting those limiting doctrines. In this way, the Court could develop the law to give the statute relatively little force.[113]

---

[111] See Philip Kurland, *Of Church and State and the Supreme Court,* 29 U Chi L Rev 1 (1961); Steven G. Gey, *Why Is Religion Special? Reconsidering the Accommodation of Religion Under the Religion Clauses of the First Amendment,* 52 U Pitt L Rev 75 (1990); Mark Tushnet, *"Of Church and State and the Supreme Court": Kurland Revisited,* 1989 Supreme Court Review 373.

[112] They could, however, *consistently* say that "substantial burden" is a bad test for judges but one Congress has power to impose, *and* that the test happens to rule out most religious claims.

[113] For any assessment whether this may happen, it helps to recognize that of the five Justices who remain on the Court from the time of *Smith,* all except Justice O'Connor joined Justice Scalia's opinion (i.e., Scalia, Rehnquist, Stevens, Kennedy). Moreover, Justice

The serious issues of interpretation that the statute raises follow the lines of the three strategies the Court used prior to *Smith* to render the compelling interest test less exacting then it appeared. What, if anything, does the law do about weak application, evasion, and threshold denial?[114] I shall examine each of these, after a general comment about how the statute relates to the pre-*Smith* law.

The act's findings characterize "the compelling interest test as set forth in prior (to *Smith*) Federal court rulings" as "a workable test for striking sensible balances between religious liberty and competing governmental interests." One of the act's purposes is "to restore the compelling interest test as set forth" in *Sherbert* and *Yoder*. This statutory language transparently connects the statute to prior law. However, the juncture of the findings and purposes may be thought to raise this problem: *Sherbert* and *Yoder* represented the high-water mark of protection of religious liberty; subsequent cases reflected a serious weakening. Is the Court to apply the strong standard of the earlier cases or the weak standard of later cases? For what it is worth, the more specific purposes section should be given greater weight than the findings section;[115] but I believe this manner of conceiving the issue is itself somewhat misleading. What is most important is that the statute does not endorse particular pre-*Smith* results and reject others;[116] Congress has not decided just how stringent the standard of review should be. The language of *Sherbert* and *Yoder* sounds powerfully protective, but the results in those cases impinged on government interests only to a modest degree.[117] In no free exercise case has the

---

Thomas has so far voted with Justice Scalia in every Religion Clause case in which he has participated, although his concurring opinion in *Rosenberger* may indicate a favorable attitude toward accommodations of religion. *Rosenberger v Rector and Visitors of the University of Virginia*, 115 S Ct 2510, 2528–33 (1995). A majority ready to give the act a crabbed reading may be in hand.

[114] See Ira Lupu, *Of Time and the RFRA: A Lawyer's Guide to the Religious Freedom Restoration Act*, 56 Mont L Rev 171 (1995) (speaking of the "burdens," "enclaves," and "strict scrutiny" questions).

[115] See Laycock and Thomas (cited in note 57) at 224. The minority report in the House Committee commenting on different draft language said the law did not restore the law to the "high-water mark," House Comm on the Judiciary, Religious Freedom Restoration Act of 1993, HR Rep No 88, 103d Cong, 1st Sess 15 (1993), but that is an unreliable indication of the majority's aims.

[116] See Senate Committee on the Judiciary, Religious Freedom Restoration Act of 1993, S Rep No 111, 103 Cong, 1st Sess 6 (1993).

[117] *Sherbert* costs the government some money and administrative inconvenience; *Yoder*, covering a very small religious sect, has almost no practical impact on the larger society,

Supreme Court thwarted a substantial government interest.[118] Thus, the "high-water" mark of *Sherbert* and *Yoder* may be less high than the language of the opinions intimates. Courts should look at the whole course of decisions from *Sherbert* up to *Smith*, to give content to the statutory language, understanding that Congress meant to give significant protection to religious claimants.

I turn now to the three strategies, and the statutory response to them. Evasion (or avoidance) for military and prison cases is easiest. The operative language contains no exception for such cases. An exception for prisons was suggested and rejected.[119] The Senate Report indicates that none was intended.[120] The statute applies the compelling interest standard to military and prison cases. What it leaves open is whether some special degree of deference should be accorded military and prison authorities in defining compelling interests and determining how they should be satisfied.[121]

Congress's response to the strategy of threshold denial is less straightforward. The act grants protection only when government "substantially burden[s] a person's exercise of religion," that is, "the exercise of religion under the First Amendment. . . ."

The act definitely does not demand that people claim that challenged government restrictions force them to violate religious obligations.[122] It is sufficient that they have strong religious reasons for the behavior in which they want to engage. The language reflects a choice to protect more than outright conflicts between religious obligation and state coercion.[123]

---

although one might argue that state governments have a powerful interest in the full education of each child.

[118] Between *Sherbert* and *Yoder*, it rejected the free exercise claim of a selective conscientious objector, *Gillette v United States*, 401 US 437 (1971), although, in my judgment, granting the claim would not have posed a very serious threat to the draft system. See Greenawalt, *All or Nothing At All: The Defeat of Selective Conscientious Objection*, 1971 Supreme Court Review 31, 76.

[119] The process, including Attorney General Reno's opposition to an exception, is described briefly in Laycock and Thomas (cited in note 57) at 239–43.

[120] Sen Rep (cited in note 116) at 9–10.

[121] The Senate Report, id at 10, talks of courts continuing "to give due deference to the experience and expertise of prison and jail administrators. . . ." It contains similar language about military authorities. Id at § E, pp 11–12.

[122] Another point that is clear, although not perhaps from the language itself, is that the act protects churches and other religious institutions, as well as individuals. Laycock and Thomas (note 57) at 234–36. These organizations qualify as "persons" in legalese; even if they did not, a claim by an organization would constitute a claim by its individual members.

[123] See id at 231–34.

"Substantially burden" connotes some measure of magnitude. Does it also impose a threshold about the *kind* of burden that is involved? We can focus this question by considering the decision in *Lyng*. As noted earlier, the Court in *Lyng* said that the Indian tribes had not claimed a relevant infringement of religious exercise, because no coercion was involved. The new act does not *seem* to require direct or indirect coercion. If the land development in *Lyng* would have been devastating for the religious practices of some tribes, a possibility the Court concedes, their exercise of religion was substantially burdened. On the other hand, perhaps the term "substantially burden" and the reference to "the exercise of religion under the First Amendment" *implicitly* include the idea of a constitutionally relevant burden, thus effectively preserving threshold barriers of the *Lyng* variety. The statutory language, on balance, does not appear to incorporate a "coercion" threshold. The House and Senate Reports point in different directions on this issue.[124] The Court should proceed without any fixed assumption that claimants must establish coercion of a particular sort, but it should remain open to contentions that "substantially burden" may involve *some* thresholds.[125]

---

[124] The Senate Report (note 116) at 6, 9, says that the act does not affect the doctrine in *Lyng* that government development of land places no cognizable burden on religion. The House Report (note 115) at 6 says, "All government actions which have a substantial external impact on the practice of religion would be subject to the restrictions in this bill." The two reports are in accord on one of the issues posed by *Bowen v Roy*, 476 US 693 (1986); for the government to use a social security number for purely internal record keeping would not substantially burden religion. Douglas Laycock and Oliver Thomas take the two reports as accepting the approach of *Lyng*, the more general language of the House Report being responsive to the problem of autopsies. See Laycock and Thomas (cited in note 57) at 228–30. However, Justice Brennan's dissent in *Lyng* said that a religious claim met the threshold if the challenged action had "substantial external effects." 485 US at 470. The nearly identical language of the House Report falls much closer to the dissent than to the *Lyng* majority.

The subsequent proposal of legislation to protect sites of Native American worship on government land provides very slight support for the view that the Religious Freedom Restoration Act leaves *Lyng* intact. See Sen Rep S2269 on The Native American Cultural Protection and Free Exercise of Religion Act of 1994, 103d Cong, 2d Sess (1994).

How much does the legislative history count? If Justice Scalia treats the statute as valid, and follows his usual course of excluding internal deliberations in Congress from consideration, he *might* end up finding a law that more expansively rejects his approach to the Religion Clauses than do Justices who pay greater attention to legislative history. Overall, the legislative history is more favorable to the view that *Lyng* remains good law than is the statutory language. If one assigns great importance to the language and moderate weight to the legislative history, the proper approach in my view, the Court will not conclude that the law leaves *Lyng* untouched.

[125] For example, concerns about internal government record-keeping may fail. See note 124. As Ira Lupu showed in a 1989 article (cited in note 42), notions of necessary threshold burdens have not been very carefully refined. He then suggested an approach that concen-

A showing that a rule "substantially burdens" religious exercise obviously requires more than a trivial effect.[126] Suppose a church that plays music very loud and disturbs neighbors is told that ordinary nuisance law requires it to lower the volume. If it responds that music is an important part of its services and that the original volume *best* expresses its religious sensibility, but that the permitted volume is only slightly less desirable, the restriction would not constitute a substantial burden. On the other hand, suppose that a law forbidding drinking of alcohol makes no exception for wine during communion. The church responds that wine is important symbolically and for its physical effect, but not an absolute prerequisite for effective communion. Here the burden is substantial. Much more would be sacrificed by compliance than in the first case. An inquiry into substantial burden, like an inquiry into centrality, does require some appraisal of more or less important aspects of a religion. The flavor of the two phrases suggests that the hurdle for claimants showing a substantial burden on their religious exercise is somewhat lower than for a substantial threat to central aspects of their religion (Justice Brennan's approach in *Lyng*). Courts inquiring about substantial burden must make their assessment from the perspective of the sincere religious claimants; they need not (ordinarily) resolve disputes among adherents of the same religion.

What can one say about the statute's compelling interest test, with its crucial "least restrictive means" component?[127] I shall first

---

trates on whether an interference would violate some common law right, if committed by a private party, with further protection for "entitlements" (like unemployment compensation), and against discrimination. The claimants in *Lyng might* qualify under a common law approach on a theory of easement.

[126] Is "substantially burden" an inquiry into "centrality" by another name? Justice O'Connor apparently thinks not. She objected in *Lyng* to approaches that would require assessing centrality, yet in *Smith* she argued for a test of whether a burden is "constitutionally significant." Conceivably, she meant "constitutionally significant" to exclude *only* those burdens that fail to be of the relevant constitutional type, such as the burden in *Lyng;* but the phrase suggests a requirement of magnitude as well. Justice Scalia's opinion in *Smith* indicates that "constitutionally significant" *is* an inquiry about centrality by another name. Whatever may be true of O'Connor's phrase "constitutionally significant burden," the phrase "substantially burden" is definitely mainly one of magnitude.

[127] The *relation* between burden and government interest warrants brief mention. The test the act adopts involves two steps. The initial inquiry about "substantial burden" can apparently be decided without reference to the government's interest in imposing a burden. The inquiry about the government's interest and the means of its satisfaction can apparently be assessed without *further* consideration of the burden. Imagine that in two cases the government has equally strong interests and equally strong claims that no alternative means will suffice: in case 1, the burden on religion is *barely* substantial; in case 2, the burden is

ask if the test should be applied more rigorously than in the past and then address more specific proposals about content.

United States v Lee, in which the Court employed a less than stringent version of the compelling interest test and rejected the claim of Amish employers for an exemption from social security taxes, helps frame the general question. One can argue that the statute refers in its main operative language to the ordinary, highly stringent, compelling interest test, used most notably in racial classification and free speech cases. The language in the purposes section about *Sherbert* and *Yoder* may seem consonant with this line; those cases set forth a standard that sounds fairly stringent and yielded victories for religious claimants. Further support may be gleaned from *Church of Lukumi Babalu Aye*, in which the Court talked of the need for "interests of the highest order" and said that its compelling interest standard "really means what it says."[128]

This argument for a highly stringent test is not persuasive. The statute has in view the compelling interest test as it has been applied in the free exercise area. The law reflects no judgment that *when* the Supreme Court and other courts have applied the test and sustained government regulation, as they often have done, they have consistently done a faulty job. This conclusion that Congress did not mean to undo results like *Lee* is supported by a fundamental difference between most free exercise claims and the equal protection and free speech claims against which the government rarely satisfies the compelling interest test. For the latter, a court typically examines whether a law will be upheld despite a presumptively unconstitutional feature—a racial classification or regulation of the content of speech. For analogous cases of religious classification or discrimination against religion, like *Church of the Lukumi Babalu Aye*, the compelling interest test is also stringently applied. Typical free exercise claims are different; they involve assertions

---

very substantial. If a court responded precisely as the concepts instruct, the two cases would have identical results. This, however, is *not* how things actually work. Courts assess the strength of a government interest and the adequacy of alternative means in light of the burden imposed. If the burden is very great, courts will be more demanding in their appraisal of the government interest and the means it has chosen. See Berg (cited in note 84) at 51. It is a matter for debate whether a court should *try* to look at each side of the scale in succession (as the statutory language indicates), or should self-consciously see the issue as weighing each side against the other. Realism counsels that comparative weighing takes place, whatever judges say and self-consciously try to do.

[128] *Church of the Lukumi Babalu Aye v City of Hialeah*, 113 S Ct 2217, 2233 (1993).

that individuals should receive exemptions from generally valid laws. Courts, understandably worried about incentives to make false claims and about serious difficulties of administration, are unwilling to grant exemptions whenever a sincere religious claim of substantial interference is offered. The Court's approach in *Lee* to compelling interest is *too relaxed*, but judicial hesitancy to invalidate applications of statutes in free exercise cases is well grounded. The act does not import a compelling interest test as stringent as that used for other constitutional problems.[129]

What more can be said about the statute's test? For any compelling interest test, weight of interest and alternative means are more closely linked than appears at first glance.[130] When a court focuses on an important high-level interest, the issue comes down to available means; when a court focuses on a more particular interest a law serves, the issue is the strength of the interest.[131]

The Religious Freedom Restoration Act and its legislative history are clear that the government's interest is to be evaluated "at the margin." A court asks whether any compelling interest is served by applying the law against the religious claimant and others who are similarly situated.[132]

---

[129] It is relevant that when otherwise valid laws are claimed to interfere with an individual's freedom of expression, the Court has decided that a test less stringent than compelling interest should be used. *United States v O'Brien*, 391 US 367 (1968).

[130] See Berg (cited in note 84) at 40.

[131] Thus, one interest in *Goldman v Weinberger* was "discipline within the army," but it was extremely doubtful that complete uniformity of absence of headgear indoors was necessary to achieve that. If uniformity was itself cast as an interest, it was not compelling by itself. The crucial inquiry turns out to be whether complete uniformity in headgear is necessary for generally uniform appearance in light of the objectives behind generally uniform appearance.

[132] See, e.g., Laycock (cited in note 33) at 148–49. This inquiry can also be understood as one about less restrictive means: will the government's interest in having a law be adequately served if it is not applied to sincere religious objectors (a less restrictive means)? Scott Ideleman has observed that the less restrictive means component has never been firmly embedded in free exercise jurisprudence. See Ideleman (cited in note 100) at 280. If courts more seriously investigate the government's need to apply laws against religious claimants, the statutory test could become significantly protective, even if government interests of moderate force are treated as compelling. One important avenue of investigation is whether some *alternative* burden, like alternative civilian service for conscientious objectors, may be placed upon religious claimants, so that overall burdens are not too disproportionate. See Choper (cited in note 36) at 680. Exemptions for religious claimants alone do raise serious equal protection concern; see Geoffrey R. Stone, *Constitutionally Compelled Exemptions and the Free Exercise Clause*, 27 Wm & Mary L Rev 985, 987–89 (1986). These can be mitigated by alternative burdens. Indeed, the preferable approach, when feasible, is to permit anyone to opt for an exemption, but at the cost of an alternative burden that few would choose

Many suggestions have been offered on the slippery issue of what should make an interest sufficiently compelling for free exercise cases. Some proposals are negative. A government interest is not compelling (1) simply because the government says it is,[133] (2) if the interest is slight,[134] (3) if the interest involves only modest expense or administrative inconvenience,[135] (4) if the government has not protected the interest in other contexts,[136] (5) if claims of harm are purely speculative.[137] Although these proposals seem innocuous, some court decisions are hard to square with them.[138]

Can anything more positive be said about compelling interest in free exercise cases? As discussed earlier, the government has a compelling interest in avoiding constitutional violations. Thus, it need not grant an exemption that would strongly induce others to practice a religion, since such inducements violate the Establishment Clause.[139] Exemptions that many people would like to have for nonreligious reasons, as from paying taxes,[140] present the double problem of insincere claims and disproportionate burdens on those who do not receive the exemption. Courts and scholars agree exemptions should not be constitutionally required when the incentives to advance spurious self-interested claims are great.[141]

Scholars have offered some, more general positive formulations. Stephen Pepper has put it this way:[142] "[I]s there a real, tangible (palpable, concrete, measurable) non-speculative, non-trivial injury

---

unless they were deeply opposed to the standard requirement. See Kent Greenawalt, *Conflicts of Law and Morality* 327–28 (1987).

[133] See Michael Stokes Paulsen, *A RFRA Runs Through It: Religious Freedom and the US Code*, 56 Mont L Rev 249, 254 (1995).

[134] See Laycock and Thomas (cited in note 57) at 222–25.

[135] See Paulsen (cited in note 133) at 255.

[136] See Laycock and Thomas (cited in note 57) at 224, drawing from *Church of the Lukumi Babalu Aye.*

[137] See Berg (cited in note 84) at 34.

[138] A more controversial negative suggestion is that the government does not have a compelling interest in protecting adults from the consequences of their own religious beliefs and practices. See McConnell (cited in note 76) at 1145. The most troubling examples are practices that involve highly dangerous acts or even voluntary submission to death. In the near future, courts neither will nor should endorse the principle that the government can never protect people from grave harms that result from their religious choices.

[139] See Berg (cited in note 84) at 45.

[140] See generally Stone (cited in note 132).

[141] See, e.g., Laycock (cited in note 33) at 149; Berg (note 84) at 41–43.

[142] This test was suggested prior to the new act.

to a legitimate, substantial state interest."[143] Michael McConnell has proposed a more decisive test: that a law may be validly applied "only if it is the least restrictive means for (*a*) protecting the private rights of others, or (*b*) ensuring that the benefits and burdens of public life are equitably shared."[144] This formulation incorporates a principle that preventing harm to people because of their own religious choices is never a sufficient interest,[145] and it downgrades public interests that are not reducible to private rights or equitable sharing. We should expect that the courts will stick with more innocuous, vaguer language than this. What is critical is that judges both recognize that the free exercise test is sui generis, and take "compelling interest" and "least restrictive means" as serious hurdles.

III. Establishment Clause Prospects: The Shards of Lemon

Prospects for the Establishment Clause are both harder and easier to describe than prospects for the Free Exercise Clause. The doctrinal components of Establishment Clause litigation are now more amorphous, but in certain domains the results may be more predictable.[146]

A. CRITICAL PERSPECTIVES AND OTHER COURTS

As the introductory section indicates, *Lemon* has ceased to operate as a general Establishment Clause test. No sitting Justice has been committed over time to that test. Chief Justice Rehnquist and Justice Scalia have regularly attacked it and the separationist results it has yielded.[147] Justice Thomas has now placed himself squarely in their camp.[148] Justice Stevens, at the other end of the

---

[143] Stephen L. Pepper, *The Conundrum of the Free Exercise Clause—Some Reflections on Recent Cases*, 9 N Ky L Rev 265, 289 (1982). This formulation may be seen as the other side of the negative standards for what does not count as a compelling interest.

[144] Michael W. McConnell, *Taking Religion Seriously*, FIRST THINGS 30, 34 (May 1990).

[145] See note 138.

[146] Carl H. Esbeck provides an excellent view of how much is stable about adjudication under the Religion Clauses, *A Restatement of the Supreme Court's Law of Religious Freedom: Coherence, Conflict, or Chaos*, 70 Notre Dame L Rev 581 (1995).

[147] See, e.g., *Wallace v Jaffree*, 472 US 38, 91–114 (1985) (Rehnquist, J, dissenting); *Lee v Weisman*, 505 US 577, 631–46 (1992) (Scalia, J, dissenting, joined by Rehnquist, J).

[148] See, e.g., *Lee v Weisman*, id.

spectrum, has suggested that the *Lemon* test does not separate government from religion *enough*.[149] Justice Kennedy has favored an approach that focuses mainly on coercion.[150] Justice Souter's views fit comfortably with *Lemon*, and he has regretted the lack of respect for precedent;[151] but he has offered no full defense of *Lemon*. Justice O'Connor's emphasis on endorsement may be understood as either an interpretation or an alternative to the "purpose" and "effect" strands of the test.[152] She once followed the test, but with doubts about its cogency.[153] Joined by Justices Souter and Breyer in the last term, she has more recently asserted that the time has come to drop *Lemon* as a comprehensive test. In the present circumstances, no sensible Justice would endeavor to insist on the traditional version of *Lemon*, rather than focusing more narrowly on particular factors.

Where does this leave us? As far as immediate results are concerned, it leaves us with the judgments of Justices O'Connor and Kennedy. If these two Justices agree that a practice is constitutional, it will be upheld (because they will be joined by Rehnquist, Scalia, and Thomas). If either of them can be persuaded that the Establishment Clause has been violated, the practice will very probably not be upheld. (Conceivably, Justice Souter, Ginsburg, or Breyer will prove less "separationist" on some issue.) Justice Kennedy has emphasized "coercion," determining in *Lee v Weisman*[154] that even coercion that is indirect and less than grave may be impermissible. Justice O'Connor has often focused on endorsement. Although four other Justices agreed with Kennedy that the coercive elements of school-sponsored graduation prayers rendered them unconstitutional in *Lee*, a majority of Justices has never agreed that coercion lies at the heart of most Establishment Clause violations.[155] The status of Justice O'Connor's

---

[149] See, e.g., *Committee for Public Education v Regan*, 444 US 646, 671 (1980) (dissenting opinion).

[150] See, e.g., *Allegheny County v ACLU*, 492 US 573, 655–79 (1989) (Kennedy concurring in part and dissenting in part); *Lee v Weisman*, 505 US at 577 (1992).

[151] See *Lee v Weisman*, id at 609–31 (Souter, J, concurring).

[152] See *Lynch v Donnelly*, 465 US 668, 687–94 (1984), in which she proposes possible endorsement as being the crucial question under *Lemon*.

[153] See *Wallace v Jaffree*, 472 US 38, 68 (1985) (concurring opinion).

[154] 505 US 577 (1992).

[155] Chief Justice Rehnquist and Justice Scalia, however, joined Justice Kennedy's separate opinion in *Allegheny County v ACLU*, 492 US 573, 655–79 (1989); and the four dissenters in *Lee v Weisman* took possible coercion as their focus, 505 US at 632.

endorsement approach is different. A majority of Justices do agree that "endorsement" is the crucial inquiry for certain kinds of cases, but no majority agrees on the proper formulation of that test for at least some of these cases. Justice O'Connor emphasizes the relevance of endorsement in other settings for which most Justices assign it less importance.

How should other actors in the legal system respond to this morass? Federal and state courts face an uncommon problem of legal etiquette. Most Justices have now disavowed a previously prevailing test, but no majority opinion has explicitly cast it aside in favor of any alternative. Should judges continue to behave as if *Lemon* is in place? Prior to the end of the 1994 term, this seemed an appropriate stance, whatever additional analysis the judges might also have employed; but now that *Lemon* lacks *any* defenders on the Court, other judges would perform a shallow exercise were they to continue to apply its terms. They should recognize that the Supreme Court has definitely abandoned *Lemon*.

What courts and lawyers should do instead is focus on narrower principles relevant for particular circumstances, drawing these principles partly from the very Supreme Court cases decided under the *Lemon* test. The end of *Lemon* as such does not eliminate their significance as precedents, though it may shake the foundations of some of them. The Court's decidedly mixed signals leave other judges a greater freedom than usual to rely on principles they believe are sound; those who expect review and want to be affirmed will attend closely to Justices O'Connor and Kennedy.[156]

B. THE SHARDS OF LEMON

For twenty years, most establishment cases were decided under the threefold test of *Lemon v Kurtzman*.[157] Lemon has now been

---

[156] Lawyers will need to be as aware as they can be of how the relevant courts are likely to respond. "Awareness" is extremely difficult when lawyers are not yet aware which judges of a multi-member court will be assigned.

[157] 403 US 602 (1970). Application of the test did not determine *all* establishment issues. As I have said, the Court once explicitly refrained from using the standard, saying that legislatures might pay chaplains because the practice enjoyed long historical acceptance. *Marsh v Chambers*, 463 US 783 (1983). Other issues touching both free exercise and establishment were resolved primarily on other bases. The Court has regarded legislative classifications that favor some religions over others or discriminate against religious practices as presumptively unconstitutional, with the state bearing a heavy burden to show a compelling interest. See *Larson v Valente*, 456 US 228 (1982) (*also* declaring law invalid under *Lemon*); *Church of the Lukumi Babalu Aye v City of Hialeah*, 113 S Ct 2217 (1993). Disputes within church organizations were a major area in which the Court employed principles other than

abandoned. What difference does that make? The answer depends on how far the perceived infelicities of *Lemon* concerned wrongness rather than indecisiveness.[158]

One method of anticipating our Establishment Clause future is to examine the status of each of the three aspects of *Lemon*. On examination, it turns out that each of these is actually accepted in some form by every Justice; but the differences in what they regard as unconstitutional are striking.

1. *Entanglement.* All Justices agree that some connections of government and religious organizations are unconstitutional. The rule that courts cannot decide questions of religious doctrine can be understood as avoidance of one kind of entanglement. So also can the unchallenged principle that government constitutionally cannot delegate to religious organizations the power to make laws for the general public.[159]

Disagreement is over the kinds of "entanglements" that have been the basis for the Court's invalidation of laws. The Court's primary concern has been with administrative entanglement. In the pursuit of proper objectives, such as seeing that public funds do not advance religious objectives of parochial schools, state authorities may have to monitor the activities of religious organizations. The Court has held that when this oversight becomes too great, the Establishment Clause is violated.[160] The Court has regarded a second form of entanglement, "political divisiveness," as important in some instances. The concern here is that some issues, if left to the political process, will generate bitter religious divisions.[161] Allowing legislatures to decide how much money is to go to parochial schools would be divisive in this way; thus, such funding poses this second form of entanglement.

---

those of *Lemon,* declaring that courts cannot resolve matters of religious doctrine, e.g., *Presbyterian Church v Mary Elizabeth Blue Hull Memorial Presbyterian Church,* 393 US 440 (1969). Despite these pockets for which *Lemon* was not determining, it was the test for a wide range of establishment issues.

[158] Michael McConnell has written of "multipart tests that could be manipulated to reach almost any result," McConnell, *Accommodation of Religion: An Update and a Response to the Critics,* 60 Geo Wash L Rev 685 (1992); John Mansfield earlier complained of the "incantation of verbal formulae devoid of explanatory value." John H. Mansfield, *The Religion Clauses of the First Amendment and the Philosophy of the Constitution,* 72 Calif L Rev 846, 847 (1984).

[159] See, e.g., *Larkin v Grendel's Den,* 459 US 116 (1982); Esbeck (cited in note 146) at 605.

[160] E.g., *Aguilar v Felton,* 473 US 402 (1985).

[161] E.g., *Lemon v Kurtzman,* 403 US 602, 622–24 (1971).

Political divisiveness is different from close administrative supervision, and their union under the banner of "entanglement" is an accident of history. An issue can be highly divisive without involving administrative entanglement, and divisiveness need not accompany administrative entanglement. Political divisiveness has never figured very prominently, and some Justices have objected to the idea that people can make practices unconstitutional by raising political opposition to them.[162] The Court has said that a potential for political divisiveness is not, standing alone, a basis for holding a law invalid.[163] Although Justices will be influenced by apprehensions over this kind of divisiveness, and it stands as *a general reason* for restrictions on establishments, whether particular risks of political divisiveness should be an explicit justification for invalidating government action is at least doubtful.

Administrative entanglement is much more important. Some administrative interrelationships are so close that they should certainly be held unconstitutional, and all the Justices would probably find them so (though some might base invalidity on a ground different from entanglement).[164] Interestingly, Justices who hesitate to strike down a practice because of undue entanglement have occasionally offered *the lack of entanglement* as a ground why a practice is constitutionally acceptable. One reason the Court sustained tax exemptions for churches was that they involved less entanglement than would taxes;[165] and in *Rosenberger* the majority noted that enforcing of a guideline that forbade funding of religious activities would involve more entanglement than if religious activities were treated like other activities.[166]

The high-water mark of invalidation on entanglement grounds involved monitoring of public funds to be used for parochial school education. The Court treated oversight necessary to avoid an impermissible effect as undue entanglement, and dissenters com-

---

[162] E.g., *Lynch v Donnelly*, 465 US 668, 689 (1984) (concurring opinion of O'Connor, J).

[163] *Lynch v Donnelly*, 465 US 668, 683–84 (1984).

[164] Three Justices have expressed their dissatisfaction with the entanglement prong of *Lemon v Kurtzman*, 403 at 661–71 (1971) (White, Dissenting), and *Roemer v Maryland Public Words Bd.*, 426 US 736, 768–76 (1976); *Aguilar v Felton*, 473 at 430 (1985) (O'Connor, dissenting, joined by Rhenquist).

[165] *Walz v Tax Commission*, 397 US 664 (1970).

[166] *Rosenberger v Rector and Visitors of the University of Virginia*, 115 S Ct at 2465.

plained of a "Catch 22."[167] In the most controversial of these cases, *Aguilar v Felton*,[168] the Court held invalid a program in which ordinary public school personnel did remedial teaching within parochial school classrooms that lacked religious symbols. When the Court subsequently held invalid a law adopted to meet problems that decision generated,[169] four Justices indicated that *Aguilar* had been wrongly decided, and another, Justice Kennedy, said it "may have been erroneous."[170] Although most members of the Court continue to regard administrative entanglement as a possible source of invalidity, the combination of Justices who would not decide cases directly in terms of "entanglement," plus those who would allow *more latitude* in administrative supervision than do earlier decisions, is a majority. Greater entanglement will be allowed than in the past;[171] that is, it will take more to make entanglement excessive than when *Aguilar* was decided.

2. *Purpose*. Recent cases shed little light on the fate of *Lemon*'s first strand, the requirement of secular purpose. Partly because the Court has resolved that a significant secular purpose suffices, even if joined with an important religion purpose, that requirement has lacked a major impact. In most of the relatively few cases in which the court has been unable to find a secular purpose, an impermissible religious effect would have condemned the practice in any event.[172]

We can identify one straightforward disagreement and three complex problems arising out of the secular purpose requirement. The disagreement is over evidence of motivation not to be found in a statute's text. Every Justice seems to agree that a purpose an-

---

[167] E.g., *Aguilar v Felton*, 473 US 402, 420–21 (1985) (dissenting opinion of Rehnquist, J).

[168] 473 US 402 (1985). See, e.g., Glendon and Yanes (cited in note 76) at 514; Douglas Laycock, *Formal, Substantive, and Disaggregated Neutrality Toward Religion*, 39 DePaul L Rev 993, 1007–08 (1990).

[169] In *Bd of Ed of Kiryas Joel Village School Dist. v Grumet*, 114 S Ct 2481 (1994), the Court struck down New York's creation of a special school district for a community of religious Jews.

[170] Id at 2505 (concurring opinion).

[171] *Bowen v Kendrick*, 487 US 589 (1988), already represented a significant relaxation.

[172] In *Wallace v Jaffree*, 472 US 38 (1985), the Court did hold "moment of silence" legislation invalid because of a religious purpose, although a majority of the Justices indicated that they would sustain other statutes providing for moments of silence in public school. Id at 62 (concurring opinion of Powell, J); 67 (concurring opinion of O'Connor, J); and 83–113 (three dissenting Justices).

nounced in a preamble to promote acceptance of a particular religion would render a law invalid (whether or not a parallel secular purpose could be discerned).[173] Most Justices suppose that courts should examine legislative history to ascertain whether a dominant purpose is impermissible.[174] Justice Scalia would disregard evidence of the subjective motivation of legislators.[175] A related difference is that most Justices have engaged in a serious inquiry whether a purported nonreligious purpose is credible; Justice Scalia would be much more accepting of claimed secular purposes.[176]

What connections between religious understanding and legislative objectives shift a purpose from the permissible secular category to the impermissible religious one? One crucial issue concerns legislation that does not directly aid or promote a religion but makes no sense apart from a religious foundation. In *Bowers v Hardwick*,[177] which upheld legislation banning homosexual behavior among adults, the Court considered it irrelevant that the primary objection to such behavior was based on religious grounds. The Court determined that religious beliefs could appropriately underlie moral judgments on which legal prohibitions are founded. Four dissenters, invoking in passing the purpose strand of *Lemon*,[178] argued that such an underlying motivation was not adequate to sustain the law.

On the other hand, in *Edwards v Aguillard*,[179] the Court held that a law requiring any school that teaches evolution also to teach creationism was invalid because of its religious purpose. Justice Scalia strongly objected; he viewed the law as merely another instance in which religious motivation might have produced a law

---

[173] Some remarks Chief Justice Rehnquist made in *Wallace v Jaffree*, 472 US 108–09, may suggest he thinks no purpose requirement makes sense; but I strongly doubt he would accept an explicit aim to promote a particular religion.

[174] In *Wallace v Jaffree*, 472 US 38 (1985), the Court relied both on a comparison of the statute with its predecessor and on the words of legislative sponsors.

[175] E.g., *Edwards v Aguillard*, 482 US 578, 636–40 (1987) (dissenting opinion of Scalia, J). This position fits with Scalia's general attack on judicial reliance on subjective motivation and on legislative history.

[176] See id.

[177] 478 US 186 (1986).

[178] Id at 211. The dissenters cited *Stone v Graham*, 449 US 39 (1980), which relied on an impermissible purpose to hold invalid a posting of the Ten Commandments in the classrooms of a public school.

[179] *Edwards v Aguillard*, 482 US 578 (1987).

that imposes a nonreligious requirement—that schools teach alternative scientific theories. Without quite putting it this way, the
Court doubted that "creation science" is science. The Court's
main emphasis was that only religious belief produces belief in creation science and rejection of evolution, and that the teaching of
creation science is the indirect teaching of a religious point of
view.[180] The aim to promote such teaching and counter the teaching of evolution was thus a religious purpose.

If one looks at the results in *Bowers* and *Edwards*, one might
conclude that science-teaching requirements based on religious
judgments rest on an impermissible purpose, but that legal prohibitions may rest on moral judgments that rest in turn on religious
judgments. How can we explain this? Perhaps by a fundamental
difference between science and morality in our culture. When factual claims fall within the realm of science, and their only plausible
basis is religious, teaching the claimed facts as true, or as plausible
scientific hypotheses, seems to be a teaching of the underlying religious grounds, not science. When moral judgments squarely based
on religious beliefs are used as the basis for criminal enforcement
and moral teaching, the understanding may be different,[181] it being
assumed that morality is much less easy to disentangle from religion than is science, *and* that we lack agreed nonreligious methods
for resolving moral questions.

The two remaining major problems about purpose concern both
that strand of *Lemon* and the practically more important requirement that a law not have a primary effect of promoting religion.
One problem, permissible accommodations to religious exercise,
is partly terminological and partly substantive. Typical examples of
accommodations are legislation permitting members of the Native
American Church to use peyote in worship services and allowing

---

[180] Justice Brennan also suggested that creation science, with its claim that God created
human beings without any process of evolution from other animals, is directly a religious
doctrine. When "creation science" is reformulated as a theory of nonevolutionary generation, in a manner that does not explicitly introduce God, it may no longer be explicitly
religious; but most of the Court's basis for its conclusion would remain.

It is not clear what Justice Scalia would have thought *if* he had agreed that at that stage
of the litigation—before defenders of the law had had a chance to present evidence of a
scientific basis for creation science—the Court should have concluded that only religious
belief could support belief in creation science.

[181] My own view is that insofar as the religious judgment produces a belief that behavior
is simply wrongful, apart from secular harms, the purpose should be regarded as impermissible. Kent Greenawalt, *Religious Convictions and Political Choice* 247–49 (1988).

the Amish to withdraw children from school at an early age. All Justices agree that some legislation of this sort is appropriate.

The terminological criticism of *Lemon* was that accommodation legislation demonstrates that religious purposes and effects are sometimes salutary; therefore, requirements of a secular purpose and no primary religious effect are misconceived. The response to this criticism took one of two forms: either permissible religious accommodation is a secular purpose and effect, or the needed purpose and effect under *Lemon* should be more precisely understood as secular *or* acceptable religious accommodation.[182] The second response is more straightforward, because religious accommodation is not a typical secular purpose. With the demise of *Lemon*, the Court can simply say that a law that works an appropriate accommodation is permissible, without having to "explain" either that accommodation is not a purpose and primary effect that advances religion or that some purposes and primary effects that advance religion are really all right.

The terminological confusion about accommodation, although it has contributed to undermining the *Lemon* test, has been shadow boxing for those who understood what was at stake. However awkward the terms of *Lemon*, Justices who adhered to the test never supposed it barred all permissible accommodation to religious exercise. The criticism of *Lemon* that connects to the substantive problem about accommodation is that the test provided no help for courts drawing the line between permissible accommodations and unacceptable purposes and effects. Rather, it created only an illusion of a genuine standard of decision. The accuracy of this criticism can best be gauged after one directly faces the crucial substantive issue of how to distinguish permissible accommodations from impermissible advancements of religion, under the Establishment and Free Exercise Clauses. I discuss that issue in a final part of the article.

The second general problem that embraces purpose and effect concerns what amounts to an unacceptable endorsement, an in-

---

[182] In *Corporation of Presiding Bishop v Amos*, Justice White's majority opinion characterizes a purpose to accommodate as secular, 483 US 327, 335 (1987); Justice O'Connor, concurring, proposes a reformulation of the purpose test, id at 2874. Jonathan E. Nuechterlein, *The Free Exercise Boundaries of Permissible Accommodation under the Establishment Clause*, 99 Yale L J 1127 (1990), suggests a distinction between secular respect for religious scruples, and advancing religion for religious reasons.

quiry that also survives into the post *Lemon* era. I shall also put that question aside for the moment.

3. *Effect of advancing religion.* The prong of *Lemon* that yielded the most invalidations was the requirement that a law or practice not have a primary effect of advancing or inhibiting religion. The future of Establishment Clause jurisprudence will depend largely on what kinds of effects are judged to be impermissible. The Court's decisions in the 1994 term indicate significant areas of continuity and discontinuity. Before examining these, I mention some other problems about impermissible effect.

One problem involves the inhibition of religion. No Supreme Court decision has actually relied on the theory that a law inhibiting religion is a violation of the Establishment Clause, but statements of the *Lemon* test were evenhanded: a law may not advance or inhibit religion as a primary effect. The difficulty does not concern inhibition of one or a few religions, which rightly may be viewed as establishing alternative religions. But suppose religion in general were inhibited. Would a law favoring atheism, agnosticism, or secularism be a law "respecting an establishment of religion"? Some have thought not, arguing that such a law, rather, would violate the Free Exercise Clause by "prohibiting," in a loose sense, the free exercise of religion.[183]

For two reasons this conceptual quandary has never seemed very important. First, everyone has assumed either that the Religion Clauses together require equal treatment of religious and atheist or antireligious positions (the prevailing Supreme Court approach for most issues) *or* that religious positions can be favored (the approach of some Justices and critics of the Court). Almost no one has argued that atheist positions may permissibly be favored. Thus, whether an inhibition of religion offends the Establishment Clause has had little practical bite.[184] Second, legislatures in the United States do not adopt laws that are designed to inhibit religion. Some

---

[183] See, e.g., Douglas Laycock, *Towards a General Theory of the Religion Clause: The Case of Church Labor Relations and the Right to Church Autonomy*, 81 Colum L Rev 1373, 1378–85 (1981). Such an inhibition might violate not only the Free Exercise Clause but also the Equal Protection Clause, and, if it involved communication, the Free Speech Clause. See also Kent Greenawalt, *Religion as a Concept in Constitutional Law*, 72 Calif L Rev 753, 754, n 52 (1984).

[184] But see Douglas Laycock, *A Survey of Religious Liberty in the United States*, 47 Ohio St L J 409, 450 (1986), pointing and that more people can sue if the Establishment Clause is violated.

language in the *Rosenberger* opinion may support the view that avoiding religious teaching in the public schools is, indeed, as critics of the Court's bible reading and prayer decisions have long claimed, a kind of inhibition of religion. The Court treats the state university's choice not to fund publications devoted to making religious claims as a form of *viewpoint* discrimination[185] (a rather implausible conclusion since positive religious and atheist claims were treated equally[186]). If the university was guilty of viewpoint discrimination, it is not much of an extension to say that the suppression of religious teaching in public schools is a form of viewpoint discrimination, one that inhibits religion. The consequences of such a judgment remain to be seen; but the possibility that the Court *might* so characterize the absence of religious teaching in public schools suggests that it could deem more laws (and constitutional principles) to "inhibit religion" than has previously been thought. In any event, repetitions in the *Lemon* formula do not settle that laws inhibiting religion violate the Establishment Clause. That issue has never been directly presented, and the abandonment of *Lemon* removes the formula that may have made coverage by the Clause appear a stable constitutional principle.

A second problem concerns the relationship between potentially impermissible religious effects and appropriate secular effects. Under *Lemon*, the Court effectively resolved that a substantial religious effect of the wrong kind renders a law invalid, even if a secular effect is of equal or greater magnitude.[187] One would not expect the Court explicitly to turn around on this. Even if the Court sustains some measures that were held invalid under *Lemon*, it will probably do so on the ground that the challenged effects are permissible, or slight and speculative, rather than because secular effects are more substantial than substantial and potentially unconstitutional religious effects.

The third problem concerns accommodation of religious exercise, which I treat in greater depth after considering the two major establishment cases of the 1994 term.

---

[185] *Rosenberger v Rector and Visitors of the University of Virginia*, 115 S Ct 2510, 2516–20 (1995).

[186] The conclusion *was plausible* insofar as publications could discuss practical social problems from perspectives other than religious and antireligious ones. My analysis of this aspect of the opinion is in Viewpoints from Olympus, to be published in a Spring issue of the Columbia Law Review.

[187] See, e.g., *Grand Rapids School District v Ball*, 473 US 373, 381–83 (1985).

C. CAPITOL SQUARE AND ENDORSEMENT

Each of the cases at the end of the 1994 term reveals something of broad significance about future Establishment Clause litigation. I first address the *Capitol Square* case,[188] and the place of endorsement analysis for symbolic speech in public places and more broadly.

Capitol Square is not a typical establishment case in which a government connection to religious speech is claimed to amount to a constitutional violation. Rather, the board administering access to public property adjacent to the state capitol argued that it should be able to exclude religious speech, a large cross, because allowing the cross would constitute an establishment. This twist does not affect the significance of the case. Its use of endorsement analysis represents a vital thread of continuity. But the Justices fail to build stable principles even for those circumstances in which endorsement is the crucial inquiry. The nagging questions can be summed up as: (1) How many Justices support endorsement as the crucial inquiry? (2) Whose perceptions of endorsement count? and (3) What degree of endorsement is unconstitutional?

The first question is more straightforward than its answer. How many Justices now believe that an inquiry about perceived endorsement is central for cases of public symbolic speech and for other cases? We know from *Capitol Square* that four Justices did not think possible perceptions of endorsement mattered, so long as the government treated private "speakers" in a neutral, evenhanded way.[189] Five Justices considered endorsement *in some form* to be critical. Justice Scalia's opinion for the four Justices distinguished government allowance of private speech in a public forum from symbolic speech by the government itself. Thus, a reading of *Capitol Square* suggests that all Justices agree that endorsement is the proper inquiry if the government itself erects a crèche, cross, or menorah on its property. That may be deceptive. Three of the four Justices who joined the Scalia opinion once *resisted* endorsement analysis even for those cases.[190] They may or may not follow

---

[188] *Capitol Square Review and Advisory Board v Pinette*, 115 S Ct 2440 (1995).

[189] Id at 2447–50 (opinion of Scalia, J).

[190] See *Allegheny County v ACLU*, 492 US 573, 655–67 (1989) (Kennedy, J, dissenting, joined by Rehnquist, J, and Scalia, J). One would guess that if these three rejected an endorsement approach, so also would Justice Thomas.

precedent and accept an endorsement test for cases of government speech. Justice O'Connor's opinions have concentrated on endorsement in a much broader range of circumstances; how much weight other Justices give it in those circumstances is still uncertain.[191]

The central substantive question, "whose perceptions of endorsement?" has plagued the test from its inception. Originally proposing endorsement analysis in *Lynch v Donnelly*, a case involving a crèche placed among secular symbols at Christmas, Justice O'Connor has consistently maintained that the fundamental concern is that the government not send "a message to nonadherents that they are outsiders, not full members of the political community, and an accompanying message to adherents that they are insiders, favored members of the political community."[192] Should the inquiry about endorsement be about subjective reaction or objective evaluation? Should it focus on minorities or majorities?

Some problems with a subjective test are obvious.[193] First, if the test is to be applied by courts, including appellate courts, how are judges to ascertain people's reactions? Second, assuming that the most sensitive person will not determine the outcome, what percentage of "endorsement" reactions would be constitutionally significant? Third, are reactions of people in individual localities or people more generally to control?[194] Fourth, once one recognizes that most Jews might react differently to a crèche from most Christians, do the reactions of members of the minorities count more than the reactions of members of the majority?

With these difficulties, Justice O'Connor's opting for an objective approach, one that asks how a reasonable person would respond, is hardly surprising. A reasonable-person approach does

---

[191] A number of majority opinions have treated endorsement as a relevant factor. E.g., *Grand Rapids School Dist. v Ball*, 473 US 373, 389 (1985).

[192] 465 US 668, 688 (1984) (concurring opinion). Among scholars who have been supportive of Justice O'Connor's approach are Donald L. Beschle, *The Conservative as Liberal: The Religion Clauses, Liberal Neutrality, and the Approach of Justice O'Connor*, 62 Notre Dame L Rev 151 (1987); Arnold H. Loewy, *Rethinking Government Neutrality Towards Religion Under the Establishment Clause: The Untapped Potential of Justice O'Connor's Insight*, 64 NC L Rev 1049 (1986).

[193] See, e.g., Steven D. Smith, *Symbols, Perceptions, and Doctrinal Illusions: Establishment Neutrality and the "No Endorsement" Test*, 86 Mich L Rev 266, 291–92 (1987).

[194] If the focus were on individual communities, common sense would suggest that the matter would be one of fact, with very limited appellate review.

not itself eliminate the minority-majority worry—one can certainly imagine that a reasonable Jew might react differently from a reasonable Christian—but Justice O'Connor has conceived a reasonable-person standard that is not just some weighted sum of reasonable members of minorities and majorities. The overall trend in her opinions has been to pack more awareness of relevant factors into the reasonable person. In *Wallace v Jaffree* (the moment-of-silence case), she asked how the law would be perceived by "an objective observer acquainted with the text, legislative history, and implementation of the statute,"[195] and went on to say that the objective observer "is acquainted with the Free Exercise Clause and the values it promotes."[196] In *Capitol Square*, she said that "the reasonable observer in the endorsement inquiry must be deemed aware of the history and context of the community and forum in which the religious display appears."[197]

Justice O'Connor sets her position against one that would render religious speech invalid if *some* actual individuals or *some* reasonable individuals might perceive an endorsement. She does not, however, squarely face an evident implication of her approach. Most people who pass by a centrally located public space in a large city probably will *not be aware* of the history of the community and forum to the degree O'Connor assumes for her reasonable person. Thus, it is entirely possible that *most actual people*, even most people who would be reasonable in every other respect, might perceive an endorsement when Justice O'Connor's reasonable person, aware that the square is open equally to all private displays, would not. O'Connor's approach, joined by Justices Souter and Breyer, is defensible; but it is at some remove from the question whether many real people will feel excluded because they perceive government support of a religion that is not theirs.[198]

Justice Stevens also asks about the standpoint of a "reasonable observer" in *Capitol Square*, but he says, "It is especially important to take account of the perspective of a reasonable observer who

---

[195] 472 US 38, 76 (1985).

[196] Id at 83.

[197] 115 S Ct at 2455.

[198] William P. Marshall has argued that whether people feel offended should not be a standard for establishment cases, *The Concept of Offensiveness in Establishment and Free Exercise Jurisprudence*, 66 Ind L J 351 (1991).

may not share the particular religious belief [a symbol] expresses."[199] He rejects the idea that the reasonable person need be
aware of all the history of the forum, and asserts further that previous displays on the capitol square, such as a United Way display,
did reflect a kind of endorsement. His overall perspective is indicated by his comment that "when a statue or some other free
standing, silent, unattended, immoveable structure—regardless of
its particular message—appears on the lawn of the Capitol building, the reasonable observer must identify the State either as the
messenger, or, at the very least, as one who has endorsed the
message."[200]

Justice Ginsburg's brief opinion suggests that without a plainly
visible sign informing the public that the government did not endorse the message of the Klan's cross, the government was unac-
ceptably coupled with religion. Citing with a "cf." an article that
is absolutist in its rejection of religious symbols on government
property,[201] Justice Ginsburg does not indicate just how she will
approach inquiries about endorsement. Whether a majority will
settle on a single approach to endorsement is unclear, but Justice
O'Connor's approach is situated in the middle.[202] For the time being, her approach will determine results for cases in which most
Justices take endorsement as the central inquiry.

No approach to endorsement is without serious difficulties, but
I believe Justice O'Connor's formulation in *Capitol Square* takes
the test too far from its underlying justification.[203] In making this
criticism, I distinguish effects in public symbolic speech cases like
Lynch and *Capitol Square*, in which the test arose and has been
most securely rooted, from some other possible inquiries about
endorsement. In *Wallace v Jaffree*,[204] most of the public would have

---

[199] Id at 2466. See also Norman Dorsen, *The Religion Clauses and Nonbelievers*, 25 Wm &
Mary L Rev 863, 868 (1986).

[200] Id at 2467.

[201] Id at 2475, citing Kathleen M. Sullivan, *Religion and Liberal Democracy*, 59 U Chi L
Rev 195 (1992).

[202] More precisely, with Justices Souter and Breyer, she represents a plurality between
Justices who will find impermissible endorsement more easily (Stevens and probably Ginsburg) and Justices who think endorsement is all right or will be more hesitant to find it.

[203] See Kenneth L. Karst, *The First Amendment, the Politics of Religion and the Symbols of
Government*, 27 Harv CR-CL L Rev 503, 516 (1992).

[204] 472 US 38 (1985).

been unaware how the existing moment-of-silence statute compared with its predecessor and what reasons its sponsors offered for change. Asking whether the legislature has endorsed prayer may be a method a court uses to understand the legislature's aims. If endorsement is a useful concept for that endeavor, a highly objective standard that imputes substantial knowledge may be appropriate; the Court wants to develop its own perspective, not assess how ordinary people respond. However, when a court considers the effect of symbolic speech on government property, people's actual reactions are of primary importance.[205] The point is to avoid feelings of exclusion and dominance.[206] The difficulties of a subjective inquiry make a test formulated in terms of a reasonable person appropriate, but the reasonable person should have only an ordinary amount of knowledge of the law and of the history of symbols in public places. Further, since feelings of exclusion among members of minorities are so important, and since the majority (Christians) take cultural dominance so much for granted that they may not perceive endorsement of their position,[207] judges should attend especially to how reasonable members of minorities may react. For cases in which actual reactions are the vital concern, Justices should not impute to "reasonable people" a knowledge of legal and political matters that far exceeds that of ordinary people.[208]

Yet another problem about endorsement remains: "What *amounts* to endorsement?" This problem was implicit when a menorah was on public property, and it was exposed more sharply in the New York state legislature's creation of a special school district so that a small Orthodox Jewish community could get the benefit of public education for handicapped children.[209] No one would

---

[205] Probably the same conclusion holds when a court addresses *effects* of other connections of government to religion.

[206] Steven Smith (cited in note 193), at 306–09, doubts that endorsement ties closely to the political standing of citizens; but I agree with Kenneth Karst (note 203), at 518–19, that status within the political community in a broader sense is what matters.

[207] When I was a child and we gathered around a tree in our public school to sing Christmas carols, it did not occur to me that this was anything other than natural. Compare Sandy Levinson's reactions in Levinson, *Some Reflections on Multiculturalism, "Equal Concern and Respect," and the Establishment Clause of the First Amendment*, 27 U Richmond L Rev 989, 991 (1993).

[208] I disagree with Justice O'Connor's conclusions about the absence of endorsement in both *Lynch* and *Capitol Square;* but my criticism of her endorsement formulation in the latter case is not dependent on that. It is, of course, true that imputing a lot of knowledge to the observer may make a finding of no endorsement more plausible.

[209] *Board of Education of Kiryas Joel Village School Dist. v Grumet,* 114 S Ct 2481 (1994).

suppose that the state legislature was endorsing this Orthodox group as having the *right* religious view, but one might think it was recognizing the group as meritorious in the way in which much of society recognizes the Amish as meritorious. If *that message* is conveyed fairly strongly, is that endorsement or something less than endorsement? There is, of course, a wide range of positive messages that might be conveyed by legislative choice and perceived by reasonable observers; it is not simple to say which of these amount to inappropriate endorsement.[210]

Perhaps the key should be comparative. If a minority group is implicitly recognized as having some particular merit, but the legislature is neither embracing its position nor clearly holding it up as superior to some other group, probably no endorsement should be found. If, however, people would perceive that the group was being labeled as superior, or closer to the truth, than some other highly relevant group, that should constitute endorsement, even if no one supposes the group's position is being accepted as true. Thus, for example, it might constitute endorsement of Orthodox Judaism over Reform Judaism if portrayals of modern Jews in public school textbooks consistently showed men wearing yarmulkes.

D. ROSENBERGER AND PUBLIC FUNDING

The *Rosenberger* case[211] is important for many reasons. It reveals a good deal about how the Court will treat various principles and prior cases now that it has abandoned *Lemon*. Justice Kennedy implicitly adopts, and Justice O'Connor explicitly presents, an alternative to adjudication according to tests. Finally, the decision and opinions shake the foundations of what has been the most important area of Establishment Clause law—public aid to private religious schools. I set that prior law briefly, before examining the opinions.

The prevailing assumption in cases involving public financial support of religious schools and other institutions has been that government cannot support religious teaching and other religious activities. This has meant most obviously that the government

---

[210] See Smith (cited in note 193) at 276–77.

[211] *Rosenberger v Rector and Visitors of the University of Virginia*, 115 S Ct 2510 (1995).

cannot finance religious worship and religious teaching in themselves.[212]

The rule against public payments for religious teaching has proved even more restrictive. Suppose that for each student religious schools annually provide $3,000 of secular education. Some scholars have suggested states ought to be able to give undifferentiated grants of up to $3,000 per student to these schools.[213] The Court has decisively rejected that argument on the ground that such money would inevitably and impermissibly aid religious functions of the school as well as secular ones. Some cases have sustained assistance to students, which the students have chosen to spend at religious institutions, but the balance has been tipped by Justices who have considered such indirect aid as different in principle from direct grants. The only direct grants to religious schools that have been permitted have been directed to secular functions in a manner that does not also assist religious activities.[214] Even this avenue of aid has been sharply limited by the Court's rule of no "undue entanglement," under which supervision to assure that money does not go to religious teaching must not involve too much administrative entanglement.

In *Rosenberger*, the dissenters argued that giving an equal financial benefit to a religious activity was impermissible because it would violate the Establishment Clause. The university financed publication of various student journals, but it excluded activities that "primarily promot[ed] or manifest[ed] a particular belie[f] in or about a deity or an ultimate reality." By considerable ingenuity, the Court categorized the exclusion as viewpoint discrimination. The university interposed the Establishment Clause as a compelling interest in not financing the publication of religious (and antireligious) points of view.[215] From at least one perspective, this

---

[212] When tax exemptions were attacked as unconstitutional, the Court responded that exemptions were not grants and enjoyed long historical acceptance, *Walz v Tax Commission*, 397 US 664 (1970); it did not intimate that grants with the same economic effect would be all right.

[213] See, e.g., Jesse H. Choper, *The Establishment Clause and Aid to Parochial Schools*, 56 S Cal L Rev 260 (1968). See also Choper, *Securing Religious Liberty* 174–88 (1995). Various possible theories about aid are summarized succinctly in Laycock (note 184) at 443–46.

[214] Of course, if a necessary secular function is paid for by someone else, money otherwise necessary for that may end up going to a religious function.

[215] However, it did not press this argument before the Supreme Court. 115 S Ct at 2520–21.

seemed a *stronger* argument that establishment would be involved than has sufficed to defeat most school aid—here the university would be financing publication of evangelism, not some secular activity that happened to be connected to a religious organization.

Justices Kennedy and O'Connor mention various factors that differentiate funding of a student religious publication from tax support of the religious activities of churches.[216] Wide Awake Productions, which published the journal at issue, was not itself a religious organization; the government program would be neutral toward religion if publications of all kinds were funded; no endorsement would be implied; funding money is derived from a student fee, not general taxes; students with a conscientious objection to use of their fees for political or religious messages (unlike ordinary taxpayers) might have a constitutional right not to pay; direct payments go to the printer, not to the organization sponsoring a publication.

Evaluation of *Rosenberger* turns on the Court's conclusion about viewpoint discrimination and on whether the factors that distinguish the Virginia program from use of taxes to support churches make a constitutional difference. The university's exclusion is not accurately characterized as viewpoint discrimination. The Court might more persuasively have reasoned that the university's exclusion, though not mainly viewpoint discrimination, should be treated as presumptively unconstitutional because it indirectly disfavors religion and demands complex administrative determinations about religion; but I believe that argument also should have failed.[217] On the establishment issue, each of the factors by itself is not very significant. Whether in combination they make a crucial constitutional difference is more debatable, though I find more persuasive the dissenters' position that, despite all the variations from use of ordinary taxes to support religious activities, the funding of Wide Awake should be regarded as unconstitutional.

My primary interest here, however, is in the adjudicative strategy of *Rosenberger* and its future implications. Neither Justice Kennedy nor Justice O'Connor state anything that counts as a "*test.*" The neutrality principle dominates. The Court's strongest argu-

---

[216] 115 S Ct at 2522–24 (opinion of the Court); id at 2526–28 (opinion of O'Connor, J).

[217] See note 186.

ment runs from the cases requiring that religious groups be able to use facilities on an equal basis with other groups. Justice Kennedy reasons that physical facilities require payment for upkeep, that computer facilities are not different in principle from meeting rooms, that paying printers is not different in principle from allowing groups to use computer facilities. The "no funding" principle stands in the wings as a competitor, the Court explaining why that does not render the payments unconstitutional. The "neutrality" and "no funding" principles are not tests because the opinions provide no standard for settling a conflict between the two. Justice O'Connor, at least, is self-conscious about this. She not only rejects a Grand Unified Theory, as she puts it, she does not offer any explicit formula for resolving cases within this discrete domain. For the foreseeable future, we can expect the Court to follow this pattern in some cases, relying in others on some narrow test, such as the one about endorsement.

What does *Rosenberger* presage for aid to religious organizations? In *Bowen v Kendrick*,[218] the Court upheld federal funding for religious organizations among groups giving instruction in family planning, concluding that the funds were for a proper secular purpose and that government supervision need not be unduly entangling. Does *Rosenberger* signal a huge further step—that direct aid for religious activities is now permissible? That depends. Government funding going to churches, as churches, and not to other private associations definitely remains unconstitutional. Suppose, however, that private associations are all treated similarly. Recent literature in political science, particularly the writings of Robert Putnam,[219] suggests that liberal democracy is healthiest when private associations flourish. The private associations in which Americans are most active are religious ones. In order to encourage civic participation, the government might fund all private associations, allowing them to use funds to promote their own purposes. Churches would receive support as one kind of private association, using funds they receive for church purposes. In *Rosenberger*, Jus-

---

[218] 487 US 589 (1988). Many scholars have believed that *Bowen* may evidence a shift in favor of aid to parochial schools. See, e.g., Jesse H. Choper, *Separation of Church and State: "New" Directions by the "New" Supreme Court*, 34 J Church & State 363, 368–70 (1992); Ira C. Lupu (cited in note 76) at 765–66.

[219] See, e.g., Robert D. Putnam, *Bowling Alone: America's Declining Social Capital*, 6 J Democracy 65 (1995). See also Glendon and Yanes (cited in note 76) at 501.

tice Thomas indicates that he believes funding religious organizations neutrally with other groups is constitutionally acceptable.[220] That no other Justice joined his opinion probably indicates that none is now willing to commit to that position. Justice O'Connor's opinion, full of reservations about deciding conflicts of principle in context and about the special nature of the university fee and its program of support, shows she would reject funding church activities from tax revenues. Justice Kennedy's opinion for the Court is also contextual and qualified.[221]

When we join *Rosenberger* to the opinions in *Kiryas Joel* of the previous term, we can be sure that a relaxation of limits on aid to parochial education is in store. One would expect the five Justices who accepted financing of religious speech in universities to look favorably on assistance directed to the secular functions of religious schools, along with other private schools. A Court on which most Justices have expressed disagreement with *Aguilar* will worry less than the Court once did both about potential religious effects and about administrative supervision.

Finally, given *Rosenberger* and cases in which students receiving money for specialized purposes, such as education for the blind,[222] have been allowed to choose religious institutions, I predict that what are called "voucher programs" for school education will be sustained, even if a significant percentage of institutions in which parents use vouchers are religious.[223] In a typical voucher program, parents would be given credits to pay for schools of their choice. This element of voluntarism supports constitutionality. Since the vast majority of private schools are religious, most voucher money going to private schools would go to religious schools. That element has been thought to render voucher programs vulnerable, but both the emphasis on neutrality in *Rosenberger* and the disquiet with *Aguilar* point toward acceptance of a voucher program that implements parental choice and treats all private schools equally.

---

[220] 115 S Ct at 2528–33. The opinion is primarily focussed on Madison's position.

[221] Of course, some Justices may have accepted qualifications they do not regard as significant in order to achieve a majority opinion.

[222] *Witters v Washington Dept. of Services for the Blind*, 474 US 481 (1988).

[223] When I wrote about that subject some years ago, the prospects struck me as much more uncertain. Greenawalt, *Voucher Plans and Sectarian Schools: The Constitutional Problem*, in *Parents, Teachers, and Children* (Institute for Contemporary Studies (1977)).

IV. Accommodation and Discrimination

Here I draw the threads together about the central problem of accommodation in Religion Clause adjudication, asking what limits the Establishment Clause sets on accommodations that are required by the Free Exercise Clause or are permissibly granted by legislatures. One aspect of this problem is what treatment needs to be given others who are similarly situated in crucial respects.

A typical legislative choice to accommodate was made by Congress's decision to adopt a law allowing Orthodox Jewish military personnel to wear headgear indoors despite general military regulations to the contrary.[224] Most legislative accommodations involve exemptions from laws or the conferral of government benefits, but another form of legislative accommodation requires private actors to make concessions to religious claims.[225] The Religious Freedom Restoration Act is a quasi-constitutional legislative act that sets up a compelling interest standard as a general principle of accommodation for laws and government practices.

At present, the legal situation is this. Except for unemployment compensation claims and (a very suspicious category of) hybrids,[226] no accommodation is constitutionally required under the Free Exercise Clause. A fairly wide range exists for legislative accommodations, and these may sometimes restrict the behavior of private actors. The Religious Freedom Restoration Act constitutes a broad principle of accommodation against the federal government and, if valid, against state and local governments as well. Federal and state legislatures are free to make *some* further specific accommodations,[227] and state courts may interpret state constitutions to go

---

[224] See, responding to *Goldman v Weinberger*, 475 US 503 (1986), National Defense Authorization Act for Fiscal Year 1988 and 1989, Pub L No 100–180 §508, 101 Stat 1019, 1086–87 (codified at 100 USC § 774 (1988)). See also, Sullivan, *The Congressional Response to Goldman v Weinberger*, 121 Military L Rev 125 (1988).

[225] See, e.g., Title VII of the Civil Rights Act of 1964, 42 USC § 2000e(j) (1988). Michael McConnell (cited in note 158), at 712 (1992), suggests that language in some recent opinions indicates that such coercion of private actors cannot constitute appropriate accommodation. I am doubtful that the language he cites should be so understood, and in any event, agree with him that some action of this sort should and would be accepted as legitimate.

[226] As the first part of the article explains, *Employment Division v Smith*, 494 US 872 (1990), leaves these as the only sorts of situations in which a free exercise claim for an exemption will succeed.

[227] If, for example, the Religious Freedom Restoration Act does not protect Native American worship sites from development of federal land, Congress could explicitly provide such protection.

beyond the federal law.[228] Whether an accommodation is claimed to be constitutionally required or is chosen by a legislature, the Establishment Clause restricts what is constitutionally permissible.

Although many Establishment Clause cases are about possible accommodation in one form or another, not all are of this type. Because neither *Capitol Square* nor *Rosenberger* concerns special concessions to religious needs,[229] neither provides much guidance when such concessions are permitted. Older cases, however, afford a tolerable idea of the Court's direction.

A. DISCRIMINATION

Before I address core principles governing permissible accommodation, I consider a perplexing problem that haunts this subject: discrimination. If a special concession is made to some religious claims, others may suffer in comparison. It clarifies analysis to recognize that at least four different groups may be put at a disadvantage: (1) similar religious claimants, (2) similar nonreligious claimants, (3) persons who would *like* to perform the same act or get the same benefit, (4) persons who may bear the burden of the granted exemption or benefit in a different way.[230] For example, an exemption from military service might be limited to members of pacifist groups, thus treating less favorably other religious pacifists; it might be limited to religious conscientious objectors, treating less favorably nonreligious conscientious objectors; it might be limited to conscientious objectors, treating less favorably all those who would prefer to avoid military service for other reasons. Any exemption might harm the broader public if military defense is compromised.

I concentrate initially on the first two kinds of discrimination,

---

[228] The Religious Freedom Restoration Act may not require what the state constitution does because (1) the act is interpreted not to do so, or (2) it is held invalid as it applies to state and local governments.

[229] McConnell (cited in note 158), at 686, apparently has a somewhat broader notion of accommodation, covering circumstances "when the government has extended benefits or services to parallel secular concerns. . . ." If the only reason why religious persons or groups might not get a benefit is because they are religious and they nonetheless receive the benefit, I do not consider the extension to be an accommodation. If people get a benefit for various secular reasons (such as ill health), and are then given it for a specifically religious reason (religious conscience), while other secular reasons remain unavailing, that is a form of accommodation.

[230] See generally Laycock (cited in note 184) at 431–32.

discrimination among religious persons and discrimination between religious persons and otherwise similar nonreligious persons. If a kind of discrimination is constitutionally forbidden, it
does not necessarily follow that accommodation is forbidden. One
possibility is that accommodation *may* be made to members of one
group; members of another group might then acquire a constitutional right to the same treatment.[231] Ordinarily, when a classification is *among* religions, as in *Larson v Valente*,[232] in which one religious group received less favorable tax regulation than others, the
Court applies a stringent compelling interest test. Should the approach be different if an accommodation for the favored group is
constitutionally required or granted by a legislature? Let us suppose that the second group wants and needs an exemption as much
as the favored group, but the state's interest in denying the exemption to the second group is stronger than its interest in denying
it to the favored group. This could happen, for example, if a group
whose beliefs and practices are like those of the Amish has no history of successful community care for members and a high rate
of departure of young people. Under the ordinary free exercise
compelling interest test, this group might lose; should it win because the Amish have an exemption and any religious differentiation must meet the more stringent compelling interest test? The
court has never faced such a case. The Amish exemption *should*
affect the other group's claim in a positive way. The government
needs more powerful reasons to deny an exemption if others receive it, though the test should be less stringent than the strict
scrutiny compelling interest test.[233] One relevant factor should be
whether the unfavored group actually suffers in some way because
the benefit goes to the favored group.

When the state can favor religious groups and persons over nonreligious ones is more controversial. Three dissenting Justices regarded that as an appropriate accommodation in *Welsh v United
States*;[234] Justice Harlan believed the differentiation was unconstitu-

---

[231] See, e.g., McConnell (cited in note 158) at 708.

[232] 456 US 228 (1982).

[233] I discussed this problem in Greenawalt, *Religion as a Concept in Constitutional Law*, 72
Cal L Rev 753, 799–800 (1984). I then found a distinction between constitutionally required
accommodations and those granted by legislative choice more relevant than I do now.

[234] 398 US 333, at 369 (White, J, dissenting) (1970).

tional;[235] and the four Justices in the plurality tortured the statutory language to avoid the constitutional issue.[236] Justice Harlan's answer seems right for conscientious objectors: with an individualized screening process for all claimants, no sufficient reason exists for denying exemptions to nonreligious persons conscientiously opposed to participation in war. Imagine, however, an exemption given to persons who use peyote as a sacrament in worship. Constitutional principle should not require that the exemption be extended to those who use peyote as the center of nonreligious meetings.[237] To do so would require courts to make impossible judgments between groups that have deep beliefs about the virtues of peyote and those that merely enjoy use, between groups that are genuinely unified and those whose only connecting thread is a wish to evade restrictions on personal use of peyote. In brief, the religious clauses yield no rigid general rule about distinctions between religions and nonreligious; some distinctions of this kind should be accepted, others rejected.

Although the usual remedy for unacceptable discrimination is to put the complaining group in the same position as the favored group, an alternative is to withhold (or invalidate) any benefits for the favored group. Complex variations on this latter possibility have seemed relevant to some members of the Court in two modern free exercise and establishment cases. They have regarded the *potential* for discrimination as a reason not to grant a free exercise claim and to conclude that a statute violated the Establishment Clause.

The free exercise claim was Dr. Goldman's argument that he should be allowed to wear his yarmulke indoors.[238] Concurring Justices pointed out that if Dr. Goldman succeeded, members of other religious groups, such as Sikhs with Turbans, and Rastafarians with dreadlocks, might demand similar treatment, and their claims would raise more serious problems.[239] Justice Brennan's dissent argued that such claims could be reviewed when they arose

---

[235] 398 US at 357–58 (Harlan, J, concurring).

[236] 398 US 333.

[237] I assume that peyote is sufficiently attractive as a drug for recreational use to raise the problems I discuss.

[238] *Goldman v Weinberger*, 475 US 503 (1986).

[239] Id at 510–13 (Stevens, J, concurring, joined by White, J, and Powell, J).

under appropriate standards, regarding health, degree of disturbance, etc.[240] Justice Brennan also pointed out that the Air Force's
existing standards, which allowed the wearing of some kinds of
jewelry, and of items that were out of sight, effectively favored
Christians, because they allowed items that Christians tend to
wear. And, of course, Sikh officers would have no greater privileges
if Dr. Goldman's claim were denied than if his claim succeeded
and their subsequent claim failed; they would not be allowed to
wear turbans in either event.[241]

Is there anything to the worry of the concurring Justices? Part
of what troubled them is that two groups might conceivably be
treated differently, when the only difference between them was the
degree to which what they would wear would be startling or out
of the ordinary. Better treatment for the more "familiar" group
would reinforce conventional attitudes. Although the existing regulations implicitly did that to some extent (favoring Christians),
their terms did not require direct judgments about social acceptance of dress. The idea that courts might make such judgments
when applying free exercise rights is troubling. But the problem's
factual formulation in *Goldman* was flimsy. The Justices did not
know if significant numbers of members of other religious groups
had dress requirements at odds with military regulations *and* similar to the Jewish yarmulke except in the degree of disturbance they
might cause. (If only a few such persons could be identified, their
claims might be granted without much overall effect.[242]) In context,
this reason to deny Dr. Goldman's claims was weak; were it much
more powerful, it might constitute an interest sufficiently compelling for the government to deny a free exercise claim, or become
a separate ingredient of the constitutional analysis.

The Establishment Clause use of potential discrimination was
more puzzling. In *Kiryas Joel*, some Justices asserted that one reason to treat a legislative accommodation to the needs of an Orthodox Jewish sect as an establishment was because the legislature

---

[240] Id at 513–24.

[241] *If* Sikhs were in competition with Orthodox Jews for religious allegiance, they could
be put at a disadvantage by the benefit given to Orthodox Jews. I assume few people are
choosing between being a Sikh and an Orthodox Jew.

[242] It is no doubt conceivable that if a right to wear turbans were established, more Sikhs
would sign up for the American armed forces.

might not benefit similar groups in the same way.[243] Failing a showing that other similar groups existed, and given the possibility that any that arose could make a strong *constitutional* claim for equal treatment,[244] this was a weak basis to regard the legislative action as impermissible.

B. STANDARDS OF ACCOMMODATION

I now turn to the core question of what kinds of accommodations are permissible. Many accommodations, like that in *Yoder*, involve exemptions from ordinary requirements; others confer a positive benefit, as when the government pays for chaplains because military service removes personnel from their ordinary religious life.[245]

The most fundamental line regarding accommodation is between the permissible lifting of burdens on religious exercise and an impermissible promoting of religion.[246] Insofar as *Lemon*'s terms helped at all to draw the constitutional line, its language about government not promoting or advancing religion was the key. The government cannot encourage people to join one religious group, or religious groups in general; it cannot aim to enhance the stature of one religious group vis-à-vis others.

Another important consideration is whether an accommodation places a disproportionate burden on others who would like the same benefit and do not receive it or who pay the cost of an accommodation.[247] *Estate of Thornton v Caldor, Inc.*[248] provides an apt example. Connecticut required employers to allow employees a day off on their sabbath. Most employees would prefer not to work

---

[243] *Board of Education of Kiryas Joel Village v Grumet*, 114 S Ct 2481, 2491–92 (opinion of the Court), 2497–98 (O'Connor, J, concurring) (1994).

[244] The Justices expressed concern that if the legislature failed to grant a similar school district to a like group, judicial relief would be unavailable.

[245] See Lupu (cited in note 76) at 749–50; McConnell (note 158) at 686.

[246] See, e.g., *Texas Monthly, Inc. v Bullock*, 489 US 1 (plurality opinion of Brennan, J) (1989); McConnell (cited in note 158) at 696–702.

[247] *Texas Monthly v Bullock*, 489 US at 14–15 (plurality opinion of Brennan, J), discussed in McConnell (cited in note 158) at 702–03. Not all accommodations involve a cost to others. For example, members of a religious group might, at their own risk, be relieved from safety requirements that affect only themselves.

[248] 472 US 703 (1985).

on Saturday and Sunday.[249] If employers accede to sabbath observance, employees with seniority who want those days off will end
up working on Saturday or Sunday. Further, when employers cannot conveniently shift personnel around, the cost of accommodating sabbath days off will fall on them. The Court decided that the
rigid requirement to recognize sabbath observance imposed too
great a burden on others, and thus violated the Establishment
Clause.

Permissible accommodations are more comfortably distinguished from impermissible promotions if judges can conceptual-
ize differences rather than relying on matters of degree. Unfortunately, the notion of disproportionate burden is one of degree.
Given the aim of accommodating religious exercise, minor impositions on employers and other employees may be acceptable,[250] although the major impositions of the Connecticut law rendered it
unconstitutional.

The distinction between lifting burdens and promoting religion
is partly one of conceptual differentiation, but it also can depend
on judgments of degree. One must be able to discern some burden
on religion[251] from which an accommodation provides relief, and
according to a decision that held invalid tax relief limited to religious publications, the "burden" cannot be mere susceptibility to
costs imposed on all those engaged in similar activities.[252] A relevant burden must affect the religious claimants who obtain relief
in a way it does not affect most others.

What constitutes a "lifting of a burden" can often be highly
controversial. Is direct general aid to parochial schools, including
aid to religious objectives, a permissible accommodation? The
Court has always said "no," on the basis that such aid has an impermissible effect of promoting religion. Much depends on how

---

[249] I am passing over the point that personal preference might slide toward conscientious
nonreligious belief: "I believe it is a matter of my obligation as a parent not to work on
days of the week when my children are home from school."

[250] Federal law (see note 225) requires employers to make "reasonable accommodations"
to religious practices that do not cause undue hardship; the Supreme Court has considered
rather modest hardships to be "undue." See *TWA v Hardison*, 432 US 63 (1977). (I worked
on an amicus curiae brief arguing that the statute was constitutional and the desired accommodation reasonable.)

[251] Ordinary costs inherent in maintaining an organization and meeting competition do
not qualify as burdens.

[252] *Texas Monthly, Inc. v Bullock*, 489 US 1 (1989).

one views the public schools. If one thinks children have merely a privilege to attend nonpublic schools, the Court's analysis on this point sounds right, but suppose one thinks parents have a fundamental liberty to send children to religious schools *if* their religious consciences so guide them.[253] Since these parents pay school taxes, one may believe the state should *compensate* them for having to support schools they cannot (in conscience) use, *by assisting* the education they must use. On this view, aid to parochial schools does not look so different from *Yoder*.[254] No easy categorization of impermissible promotion versus permissible compensation resolves this problem; a deeper analysis is required.[255]

For many other problems, matters of degree are highly relevant to whether a burden is being lifted or religion is being promoted. Work exemptions for sabbath observance, again, yield an illustration.[256] Let us suppose that church (or equivalent) membership either is necessary to get the benefit of the state law or considerably strengthens one's claim to want a day off for the sabbath. If the employment benefits of sabbath observance are slight, few will join a religion to acquire them, but matters may be different if the law assures a day off. A new employee who has had a Christian upbringing and continues to have Christian beliefs, but is not a member of a church, may be tempted to join a church if she has a job with a retail outlet that requires most junior employees to work on Saturday and Sunday. She knows that churches do not take attendance and that no state agency will check how she spends most Sundays; even if she attends church *occasionally*, she will have most Sundays free for recreation. The benefit of an assured weekend day off may encourage people to join churches, synagogues, etc., although this modest and unintended effect of promotion should probably not be enough to render the law invalid.

The *Amos* case[257] suggests another way in which degree could

---

[253] See Michael W. McConnell, *The Selective Funding Problem: Abortions and Religious Schools*, 104 Harv L Rev 989 (1991); Levinson (cited in note 207) at 998–1007.

[254] Interestingly, this rationale might indicate that legislatures could aid religious schools without aiding nonreligious private schools.

[255] I believe that such aid should not be viewed as a permissible accommodation.

[256] One defense of the result in *Estate of Thornton* has been that the extreme inattention to the interests of employers and other employees demonstrates that the legislature's ambition was to promote religion rather than lift a burden. See Nuechterlein (cited in note 182) at 1141–43.

[257] *Corporation of the Presiding Bishop v Amos*, 483 US 327 (1987).

be important. The Court unanimously decided that Congress had made an acceptable accommodation in allowing religious organizations to discriminate with respect to all jobs in nonprofit endeavors.[258] Suppose a church organization is the main employer in a community. Its power to discriminate on religious grounds, if exercised, would strongly bolster its ability to win ostensible adherence from employees and prospective employees. Essentially the same kind of concession might seem to move from being a desirable accommodation to a forbidden religious promotion if the degree of assistance were large enough.[259]

The demise of *Lemon* may enhance awareness that easy categorical analysis fails to resolve many issues about accommodation, but that awareness does not by itself yield novel techniques for drawing necessary lines. The work of the Court over the past years suggests that the Justices may be fairly stingy about what accommodations are required under a general standard like the Religious Freedom Restoration Act; but they will not decide that many accommodations legislatures grant are precluded by the Establishment Clause.

V. CONCLUSION

If we step back from narrower doctrinal issues, how can we understand the Supreme Court's present position with respect to the Religion Clauses? It helps to enumerate five basic positions,[260] and one related free speech approach. (1) The Court might be strong on establishment and weak on free exercise, forbidding funding and other benefits for religious organizations, declaring that no exemptions for religious individuals and groups are required by the Free Exercise Clause and that few are permitted.

---

[258] Justice White's majority opinion treated it as dispositive that the statute merely *allowed* religious organizations to discriminate. Since the statute exempted these organizations from a requirement that applied to everyone else, the majority's ground understated severely the government's responsibility for the discrimination. The concurring Justices differed on the point. They perceived a genuine conflict of free exercise claims: the church organization's claim to autonomy and the individual employee's freedom to make his own religious judgment.

[259] Probably a proper constitutional analysis would accept the application of a statute if its effect in most communities would not involve such substantial assistance.

[260] Ira Lupu (cited in note 76), at 780, outlines four of these positions. See also Choper (note 218) at 363–65; Glendon and Yanes (note 76) at 477–78; Suzanna Sherry, *Lee v Weisman: Paradox Redux*, 1992 Supreme Court Review 123, 129.

Justice Stevens is close to this view. (2) The opposite approach would be for the Court to be strong on free exercise and weak on establishment, requiring and allowing many benefits to religious claimants, rarely finding that assistance amounted to an establishment. No one on the modern court has adopted this stance. (3) The Court could (at least try to) be strong on both establishment and free exercise, holding much assistance to be forbidden and many exemptions to be required. This position leaves little to legislative discretion, because the special treatment religious groups seek would usually be demanded by free exercise or precluded by establishment.[261] This position faces the greatest difficulty in drawing the line between those two categories, because almost everything amounts to required accommodation or impermissible promotion. Although Justices Brennan and Marshall joined opinions rejecting free exercise claims, they came closer to this basic position than other modern Justices. (4) The Court could be weak on both establishment and free exercise, rejecting claims of both sorts. This position, taken by Chief Justice Rehnquist, Justice Scalia, and probably Justice Thomas, leaves a great deal to legislative discretion. For those who believe that the Religion Clauses are countermajoritarian and that courts should be actively involved in marking out the limits of treatment of religious persons and groups, this surrender to legislatures is a serious drawback.[262] (5) The Court could interpret the Religion Clauses as mandating equality of treatment for the religious and the nonreligious. Justice O'Connor's emphasis on endorsement as a crucial establishment standard points in this direction, though she also thinks that some exemptions are constitutionally required[263] and that a "no funding" principle precludes using tax dollars for most religious activities.

The related free speech approach is the principle of "no content discrimination." When that comes into play, as it did in both *Capitol Square* and *Rosenberger*, it demands an "equal treatment" outcome unless "no-establishment" values support excluding religious

---

[261] See Lupu (cited in note 76) at 780.

[262] See, e.g., Glendon and Yanes (cited in note 76) at 530–31; Karst (note 203) at 511.

[263] Of course, some exemptions for minorities may be seen as necessary to put them on an equal footing with dominant groups whose interests are better respected by legislatures. See generally Laycock (cited in note 168) on different versions of neutrality.

speech, or free exercise values warrant giving it special benefits.[264] The principle of "no content discrimination" fits well with the equal treatment approach to the Religion Clauses, and both reflect the modern emphasis on equality in constitutional adjudication. But the free speech principle also works comfortably with other Religion Clause positions. Justice Scalia has been one of its strongest proponents.[265] When the principle is relevant, it restricts choice by the political branches. Thus, although Justice Scalia's basic position on the Religion Clauses leaves great latitude to legislative and executive judgment, he found the administrative choices in both of last term's cases to be unconstitutional. A rigorous application of the free speech principle can similarly affect outcomes under the other basic positions I have sketched.

Both *Employment Division v Smith* and the abandonment of *Lemon* represent, in part, a movement away from robust interpretations of the two Religion Clauses, under which religion must be treated as special (either in receiving exemptions or in not receiving aid), and toward principles of equal treatment and legislative discretion. If I am right about the prospects for school aid, this movement will be cashed out in approval of much more extensive financial assistance to private religious schools than has previously been accepted. For some other significant areas, the shift in doctrinal focus and overall position will have much less practical effect. One of those areas is symbolic speech on government property. At least for the time being, the endorsement inquiry, which took hold in the latter years of *Lemon*'s rule, continues to prevail. *Lee v Weisman* shows that a majority of the Court has no inclination to revisit the still controversial subjects of (vocal) school prayer and devotional bible reading. If an invocation and benediction at a single graduation ceremony involve unacceptable coercion and endorsement, daily devotions in the classroom undoubtedly do. The only avenue for overturning this branch of establishment law would be constitutional amendment.

For free exercise, as I have said, the issues are sharper. Congress has tried to implement its discretion, in the broadest way, to com-

---

[264] The former claim failed in *Capitol Square* and *Rosenberger*; the latter claim failed in *Texas Monthly, Inc. v Bullock*, 489 US 1 (1989).

[265] This is most powerfully exemplified by his opinion for the Court in *R.A.V. v City of St. Paul*, 505 US 377 (1992).

mand judicial attention to religious claimants. If it succeeds, courts will have to be sensitive to impingements on religious exercise, not as a matter of direct constitutional interpretation but in applying the Religious Freedom Restoration Act. Should the Court hold the act to be valid, the continuing task of delineating when possible accommodations to religious exercise violate the Establishment Clause will become more exigent. In that issue, more than any other, lies the heart of Religion Clause interpretation.

MICHAEL W. McCONNELL

ESTABLISHMENT AND TOLERATION IN EDMUND BURKE'S "CONSTITUTION OF FREEDOM"

The most memorable voices in American Founding–era debates over relations between church and state were raised in support of disestablishment and full and equal freedom of conscience. Statesmen such as James Madison and Thomas Jefferson, as well as evangelical leaders such as John Leland and Isaac Backus, made arguments against establishment and in favor of full and equal rights of religious conscience in terms of enduring principles of civil and religious liberty. Their words continue to inspire and guide our consideration of these weighty and contentious questions. There were, of course, other voices. Some patriotic and revered leaders, such as George Washington and Patrick Henry, thought full disestablishment a dangerous course for a republic in need of every support for public virtue. But their arguments have had little effect on the course of church-state affairs in the United States.

A parallel debate proceeded in Great Britain at the same time (the 1760s to the 1790s), but it took on a different character and reached a different conclusion. In those debates, the outstanding figure was Edmund Burke. Burke presents a profound alternative

William B. Graham Professor of Law, University of Chicago Law School.

AUTHOR'S NOTE: The author is grateful to Albert Alschuler, Thomas Berg, Gerard Bradley, Joseph Cropsey, David Currie, Stephen Gilles, Philip Hamburger, Gareth Jones, Elena Kagan, Dan Kahan, Ralph Lerner, Martin Marty, Mary McConnell, Daniel Ritchie, and Stephen Schulhofer for helpful comments on an earlier draft; to Jeffrey Seitzer for research assistance; and to the Morton C. Seeley Endowment Fund and the Arnold and Frieda Shure Research Fund for financial support during the preparation of this article.

to the American resolution of the church-state problem—but one equally grounded in liberal constitutionalism. At a time when the American constitutional principles of nonestablishment and free exercise are thought by many to be mired in a contradiction that the Supreme Court seems unable to resolve, it is instructive to see how Burke sought to reconcile the principles of establishment and toleration, and how he understood both to fit into the wider framework of his "constitution of freedom."[1]

Burke is best known for his views on representation, party politics, the French and American Revolutions, and the value of tradition. His contribution to the church-state question has received relatively little scholarly attention.[2] Yet establishment and toleration occupied Burke's attention throughout his forty years as a statesman and man of letters, and arguably were the most important elements in his understanding of British constitutionalism. His first published work, *A Vindication of Natural Society*,[3] was a satirical defense of revealed religion against the attacks of Lord Bolingbroke, and his last, the *Letters on a Regicide Peace*,[4] traced the enormities of the French Revolution to the aggressive atheism of the *philosophes*.

---

[1] The term "constitution of freedom" comes from Burke's great speech to his disgruntled constituents at Bristol, in which he defended his support for the Catholic Relief Act in the wake of the anti-Catholic Gordon riots. Edmund Burke, *Speech at Bristol, Previous to the Election* (Sept 6, 1780), in 2 *The Works of the Right Honorable Edmund Burke* 365, 416 (Little, Brown, 9th ed 1889) ("*Works*").

[2] To date, there has been no comprehensive study of Burke's principles in the field of religion and government. The most comprehensive study of Burke's political theology is Francis Canavan's *Edmund Burke: Prescription and Providence* (Carolina, 1987), but Canavan addresses the constitutional issues of toleration and establishment only in passing. A useful analysis of Burke's theory of establishment may be found in John MacCunn, *The Political Philosophy of Edmund Burke* 122–43 (Arnold, 1913), reprinted as *Religion and Politics* in Daniel E. Ritchie, ed, *Edmund Burke: Appraisals and Applications* 183 (Transaction, 1990). As this article went to press, Norman Ravitch published an instructive essay, *Far Short of Bigotry: Edmund Burke on Church Establishment and Confessional States*, 10 J Church and State 365 (1995). Ursula Henriques devotes a chapter of her *Religious Toleration in England 1787–1833* 99–135 (Toronto, 1961) to Burke's role in the development of British church-state doctrine, as does J. C. D. Clark, *English Society 1688–1832* 247–58 (Cambridge, 1985), but neither attempts to reconcile Burke's twin principles of toleration and establishment. Clark, indeed, treats Burke as an unreconstructed "champion of the Anglican aristocratic-monarchical regime," dismissing his advocacy of a broad toleration as evidence of an "early radicalism" abandoned by the mature Burke. Id at 250. As will become clear, I think this interpretation is untenable.

[3] Edmund Burke, *A Vindication of Natural Society* (1756), in 1 *Works* 1.

[4] Edmund Burke, *Three Letters to a Member of Parliament on the Proposals for Peace with the Regicide Directory of France* (1796–97), in 5 *Works* 231 ("*Letters on a Regicide Peace*");

Burke offers a sharp contrast to the Americans. Whatever the differences among the various American approaches to church-state issues, all stress the dangers and incapacities of government and the primacy of individual conscience, and most see problems in the inherent divisiveness of religion. Burke had a more benign view of government, a more institutional view of religious experience, and a greater awareness of the potential of organized religion to serve as a corrective to extremism and abuse of power.

Most striking is the difference over church-state separation. While Americans disagree over such issues as the conduct of the public schools, the participation of religious groups in government-funded programs, and the accommodation of religious minorities, almost every school of thought in America now adheres to one version or another of church-state "separation."[5] Burke, by contrast, maintained that "in a Christian commonwealth the Church and the State are one and the same thing, being different integral parts of the same whole."[6] The established church, he said, is "the foundation of [the] whole constitution."[7]

At the same time, Burke was in the forefront of efforts to achieve a broader toleration for Roman Catholics and other Dissenters from the established church. He stated that "[i]f ever there was anything to which, from reason, nature, habit, and principle, I am totally averse, it is persecution for conscientious difference in opinion."[8] This was not just talk. For the cause of toleration, Burke suffered frequent political calumny, lost his seat in Parliament, and was even threatened by a mob of anti-Catholic rioters. The cause of toleration inspired some of his most moving oratory and some of his most persistent and persuasive correspondence.

Are these twin attachments—to toleration and to establishment—incompatible? From the American perspective, it would seem so, and scholars have attributed these positions to different

---

Edmund Burke, *Fourth Letter on the Proposals for Peace with the Regicide Directory of France* (1795–97), in 6 *Works* 1.

[5] See Carl H. Esbeck, *Five Views of Church-State Relations in Contemporary American Thought,* 1986 BYU L Rev 371; Steven D. Smith, *Separation and the "Secular": Reconstructing the Disestablishment Decision,* 67 Tex L Rev 955 (1989).

[6] Edmund Burke, *Speech on the Petition of the Unitarians* (May 11, 1792), in 7 *Works* 39, 43.

[7] Edmund Burke, *Reflections on the Revolution in France* 87 (Hackett, 1987) (J. G. A. Pocock, ed) (originally published 1790) ("*Reflections*").

[8] Edmund Burke, *Speech on the Acts of Uniformity* (Feb 6, 1772), in 7 *Works* 1, 10.

periods of Burke's career.[9] But Burke did not see it that way. For him the establishment was not an instrument of intolerance or oppression, but of moderation, restraint, and even toleration. "Zealous as I am for the principle of an establishment," he proclaimed in his *Speech on a Bill for the Relief of Protestant Dissenters*, "so just an abhorrence do I conceive against whatever may shake it. I know nothing but the supposed necessity of persecution that can make an establishment disgusting. I would have toleration a part of establishment, as a principle favorable to Christianity, and as a part of Christianity."[10] Indeed, he considered the religious establishment not antithetical to, but an integral part of, England's system of civil liberty—much as he saw the monarchy and the nobility as integral to England's system of political liberty.

His instincts were confirmed when the revolutionaries in France simultaneously disestablished the Church and persecuted religious believers, and when the persecution of Catholics in Ireland drove that essentially conservative nation into Jacobinesque rebellion. He perceived that both establishment and toleration were obstacles to revolutionary tyranny, and that both were necessary elements of England's balanced constitution.

It is Burke's understanding of the symbiosis between establishment and toleration—so antithetical to the disestablishmentarianism of America—that most interests me here. Where it is helpful, I will compare Burke's ideas to doctrines and controversies in the American treatment of church and state; but this should not be taken to imply that Burke's ideas should—or even could—be transported to these shores. For Burke, moral and constitutional questions are always contextual, not to be governed by "abstractions and universals."[11] He advocated keeping the established church only "in the degree it exists, and in no greater,"[12] and based his support in large part on the dispositions and attachments of the people of England. The English obviously differ in these respects from the more diverse and sectarian Americans. On Burkean

---

[9] See Clark, *English Society* at 250 (cited in note 2).

[10] Edmund Burke, *Speech on a Bill for the Relief of Protestant Dissenters* (Mar 17, 1773), in 7 *Works* 21, 25.

[11] Burke, *Speech on the Petition of the Unitarians* (May 11, 1792), in 7 *Works* 39, 41. See also Edmund Burke, *An Appeal from the New to the Old Whigs* (1791), in 4 *Works* 57, 109.

[12] Burke, *Reflections* at 80.

principles, America could not have an established church. Burke's analysis of the issues nonetheless may help us to appreciate the complexities—even the paradoxes—of these difficult issues.

I. Burke, the Man and the Statesman

A. burke's religious background and beliefs

Burke was born in 1729 in Ireland of Catholic stock, at a time when the Penal Laws kept the Catholic majority in submission to the Protestant minority, called the "Ascendancy." Burke's mother, a nominal convert to the established church, was a practicing Catholic; Burke's beloved wife, Jane, was the same. Burke's father, a lawyer, converted to Anglicanism as a young man, seven years before Edmund's birth, apparently to enable him to practice his profession, which was at that time closed to Catholics.[13] Edmund himself never had to face that wrenching choice between his faith and his civil liberty, for he was baptized and raised in the (Anglican) Church of Ireland. He attended a rural Catholic school as a boy, a Quaker school in his youth, and institutions of the established church (Trinity College, Dublin, followed by the Inns of Court) for higher education. As an adult, Burke came to epitomize and to champion the English nation, the Anglican Church, and the Whig Party—the party of the Protestant settlement in 1688. That was his public face. But through his ties to the despised race of Irish Catholics, Burke had personal experience of religious persecution. His most recent biographer, Conor Cruise O'Brien, speculates that Burke's commitment to Catholic emancipation in Ireland (as well as his fight "against abuse of power in America, in India, and, at the end, above all, in France") was inspired by "the humiliating discovery of his father's having conformed, out of fear" and "the realisation that his own achievement would be based on the consequences of that act of conforming."[14]

There is little doubt that Burke was a committed and devout Christian. His editor J. G. A. Pocock calls him "the pious Burke,"[15]

---

[13] It is not certain that the "Richard Burke" who converted to Anglicanism in 1722 was the same Richard Burke who was Edmund's father, but the evidence, which is presented in Conor Cruise O'Brien, *The Great Melody: A Thematic Biography and Commented Anthology of Edmund Burke* 3–6 (Chicago, 1992) ("*The Great Melody*"), seems compelling.

[14] Id at 13–14.

[15] J. G. A. Pocock, *Editor's Introduction*, in Burke, *Reflections* at vii, xviii.

and O'Brien says he was a "devout Christian."[16] Burke fervently believed that "atheism is against, not only our reason, but our instincts,"[17] and his speeches and writings are filled with references to the divine order and judgment. In a letter to his fourteen-year-old son, Richard, who was studying in France, Burke urged him to keep himself "constantly" in the presence of God. "Remember [h]im first, and last, and midst."[18]

Although suspected of secret Catholicism for most of his life (political cartoons usually depicted Burke in the robes of a Jesuit, and at critical junctures in his political career Burke's enemies accused him of being a Jesuit and a Jacobite[19]), most evidence suggests that he loyally adhered to the Anglican faith adopted, however opportunistically, by his father.[20] He faithfully attended Anglican services, he regularly took sacraments from Anglican priests, his library was filled with orthodox Anglican theological works, and his writings on the role of church and providence in the life of the nation were deeply imbued with Anglican theology. In the *Reflections on the Revolution in France*, he declared: "We [the English] are Protestants, not from indifference, but from zeal."[21]

But Burke's faith was not at all sectarian. In his own words, to a friend: "I am attached to Christianity at large; much from conviction; more from affection."[22] In this letter—his most explicit

---

[16] O'Brien, *The Great Melody* at 588 (cited in note 13). Similarly, Burke's nineteenth-century biographer, Thomas MacKnight, described him as "sincerely attached to the principles of the Christian religion." Thomas MacKnight, 3 *History of the Life and Times of Edmund Burke* 164 (London, 1860) ("*Life and Times*"). Accord MacCunn, *Political Philosophy of Burke* at 187 (cited in note 2) (calling Burke "[r]everently religious"). The most comprehensive study of Burke's theology is in Canavan (cited in note 2). It places him in the mainstream of the Anglican tradition, with influences from high Medieval Catholic thought. Some scholars, however, suggest that Burke was a hidden skeptic. See, for example, Harvey Mansfield, Jr., *Burke on Christianity*, 9 *Studies in Burke and His Time* 864 (1968).

[17] Burke, *Reflections* at 80.

[18] *Letter from Edmund Burke to Richard Burke, Jr. and Thomas King* (Feb 4, 1773), in 2 *The Correspondence of Edmund Burke* 419, 421 (Chicago, 1960) ("*Correspondence*").

[19] Id at 50; MacKnight, 1 *Life and Times* 202–03, 422–23 (cited in note 16).

[20] See Canavan, *Burke: Prescription and Providence* at 71–74, 79–81 (cited in note 2). There have been rumors that Burke converted to Catholicism at the time of his marriage, O'Brien, *The Great Melody* at 37–38 (cited in note 13), and that he sought last rites as a Catholic on his deathbed, id at 590. There is no concrete evidence in support of these supposed conversions (which, if they had occurred, would have been kept closely secret), and in public life Burke conducted himself as a faithful member of the Church of England.

[21] Burke, *Reflections* at 79–80.

[22] *Letter from Edmund Burke to an Unknown Person* (Jan 20, 1791), in 6 *Correspondence* 214, 215.

discussion of denominational affiliation—he explained his adherence to the Anglican church in terms utterly devoid of spiritual, emotional, theological, or intellectual conviction:

> I have been baptised and educated in the Church of England; and have seen no cause to abandon that communion. When I do, I shall act upon my conviction or my mistake. I think that Church harmonises with our civil constitution, with the frame and fashion of our Society, and with the general Temper of the people. I think it is better calculated, all circumstances considerd [sic], for keeping peace amongst the different sects, and of affording to them a reasonable protection, than any other System. Being something in a middle, it is better disposed to moderate.[23]

This suggests a certain skepticism on Burke's part that individual religious conscience is able to grasp religious truth, which on many points "Providence" has "left obscure."[24] For the most part, Burke is content to accept religious doctrine that "seems to me to come best recommended by authority."[25] Indeed, Burke suggests that interpretation of scripture by the unaided efforts of the individual believer is likely to lead to "dangerous fanaticism."[26] This did not mean that Burke was willing to countenance persecution or repression of individual religious conscience; but, unlike the evangelical supporters of religious liberty in America, he thought that spiritual truth and harmony would be more likely achieved through authority and tradition than through individual conscience and scripture. This emphasizes the essential Englishness of Burke's position: a constitutional arrangement based on these premises could hardly flourish in a country, like newly independent America, inhabited by the spiritual descendants of Luther and Calvin.

Burke was especially concerned to minimize the differences between Anglicanism and the faith of his fathers (and mother, and wife, and cousins). "The Catholics of Ireland," he claimed, "have the whole of our *positive* religion: our difference is only a negation

---

[23] Id.

[24] Burke, *Speech on a Bill for the Relief of Protestant Dissenters* (Mar 17, 1773), in 7 *Works* 21, 29.

[25] Burke, id at 28.

[26] Burke, *Speech on the Acts of Uniformity* (Feb 6, 1772), in 7 *Works* 3, 19. See also Ravitch (cited in note 2), at 373.

of certain tenets of theirs."[27] Indeed, in the *Reflections*, Burke made the remarkable claim: "So tenacious are we [the English] of the old ecclesiastical modes and fashions of institution that very little alteration has been made in them since the fourteenth or fifteenth century. . . ."[28] Considering the doctrinal and ecclesiological tergiversations that the English church had undergone during that period, Burke's observation evinces an uncommonly powerful desire to obliterate the differences between the Catholic and Anglican communions. This ecumenical spirit, always present in Burke, became even more powerful after the Revolution in France, when militant atheism became a challenge to all religion. He wrote in 1795 that "[a]ll the principal religions in Europe stand upon one common bottom. The support that the whole or the favored parts may have in the secret dispensations of Providence it is impossible to tell. . . ."[29]

Some hints of Burke's personal theology can be gleaned from his letters and public statements. These sources convey an impression that Burke understood religion almost exclusively as a source of a moral code, of hope and consolation on earth, and of rewards and punishments in the life to come. In his private notebook, Burke wrote that "The Principle of Religion is that God attends to our Actions to reward and punish them."[30] Notably lacking in Burke's extensive speeches and writings about religion is any reference to the central tenet of mainstream Christianity: the vicarious atonement of Jesus Christ and redemption through faith in Him.[31]

---

[27] Edmund Burke, *Letter on the Affairs of Ireland* (1797), in 6 *Works* 413, 425 (italics in original).

[28] Burke, *Reflections* at 87.

[29] *Letter from Edmund Burke to William Smith, Esq., on the Subject of Catholic Emancipation* (Jan 29, 1795), in 6 *Works* 361, 368. See also *Letter from Edmund Burke to Richard Burke, Esq. on Protestant Ascendancy in Ireland* (1793), in 6 *Works* 385, 400 ("I do not pretend to take pride in an extravagant attachment to any sect."). Significantly, Burke participated in Presbyterian worship services at the time of his investiture as Lord Rector of Glasgow University—evincing an ecumenism rare for his day. MacKnight, 3 *Life and Times* at 76 (cited in note 16).

[30] Edmund Burke, *Religion of No Efficacy, Considered as a State Engine*, in H. H. F. Somerset, ed, *A Notebook of Edmund Burke* 67 (Cambridge, 1957) ("*Notebook*"). The *Notebook* was apparently written between 1750 and 1756, but not published. Compare Burke, *Reflections* at 140 ("The body of all true religion consists, to be sure, in obedience to the will of the Sovereign of the world, in a confidence in his declarations, and in imitation of his perfections. The rest is our own.").

[31] In his *Notebook*, Burke articulates a theology of works righteousness that is decidedly unorthodox from a Protestant point of view. "[O]ur Performance of our Duty here," he writes, "must make our fate afterwards." Somerset, *Notebook* at 72 (cited in note 30).

Indeed, Burke never mentions Christ (though he frequently mentions God), and he rarely quotes the Bible.[32] On the other hand, Burke did not move in the direction of rational religion, so attractive to many of his contemporaries. That would be the religious equivalent of the metaphysics and abstraction that he so deplored in politics. He was critical of clergy who, "shamed and frightened at the Imputation of Enthusiasm, endeavour to cover Religion under the Shield of Reason, which will have some force with their Adversaries."[33] Instead, Burke adhered to fundamentals of the faith, and was willing to "take that which seems to me to come best recommended by authority."[34]

B. BURKE'S EARLY EXPERIENCE IN IRELAND

Toleration was Burke's central preoccupation in his first public office. In 1759, he was appointed private secretary to William Gerard Hamilton, who served as Chief Secretary for Ireland from 1761 to 1764. In that capacity (officially powerless but in practice influential), Burke embarked upon a detailed study of the Penal Laws—the laws for the suppression of Roman Catholicism in Ireland—and began what was to be a lifelong campaign for reform. Writing in 1795, Burke recalled that he had begun to work against the Penal Laws in Ireland "four or five and thirty years ago" and that he had been "ever since, of the same opinion on the justice and policy of the whole and of every part of the penal system."[35]

The Irish Penal Laws in Burke's day were harsh and oppressive. Burke claimed that they were worse than "any scheme of religious persecution now existing in any other country in Europe, or which has prevailed in any time or nation with which history has made

---

[32] A rare exception is his quotation of *Matthew* 18:22–23, in a rebuke to certain Protestant dissenting clergy who opposed the extension of toleration to a wider category of Dissenters. Burke, *Speech on a Bill for the Relief of Protestant Dissenters* (Mar 17, 1773), in 7 *Works* 21, 30. In the *Reflections* he quotes passages from *Ecclesiasticus*, while carefully and explicitly maintaining agnosticism about the canonicity of the book. Burke, *Reflections* at 43 n 10.

[33] Burke, *Religion of No Efficacy, Considered as a State Engine*, in Somerset, *Notebook* at 67 (cited in note 30).

[34] Burke, *Speech on a Bill for the Relief of Protestant Dissenters* (Mar 17, 1773), in 7 *Works* 21, 28.

[35] *Second Letter from Edmund Burke to Sir Hercules Langrishe on the Catholic Question* (May 26, 1795), in 6 *Works* 375, 383–84.

us acquainted."[36] All monks, friars, and priests not then actually in parishes were banished from the kingdom under Queen Anne, on penalty of death if they should return, with rewards for apprehending them and penalties for harboring them. "As all the priests then in being and registered are long since dead," Burke commented, "and as these laws are made perpetual, every Popish priest is liable to the law."[37] In addition, the Catholic people of Ireland were subjected to severe civil disabilities, among them: denial of the vote; exclusion from public office, military service, higher education, and the practice of law (even as a clerk); denial of the right to bear arms even in self defense; susceptibility to search without warrant; denial of the right to buy or lease real property for any period exceeding thirty-one years; denial of the right to devise property by will or by primogeniture; insecurity of property (if children of Catholic property owners converted, they could seize their parents' property and leave only the life estate); destruction of parental rights in the event a Catholic's spouse converted; and prohibition of teaching. Any child who was educated in a Catholic school in another country was stripped for life of any right to legal capacity or property ownership, and so were the persons who sent or maintained them, unless the child abjured the Catholic faith within six months of return. Enforcement of these restrictions was by trial before Protestant magistrates and juries, often with the burden of proof shifted to the Catholic defendant.[38]

By Burke's day, anti-popery laws were little enforced in England and Scotland. Blackstone, an apologist for the Penal Laws, observed that they "are seldom exerted to their utmost rigour: and, indeed if they were, it would be very difficult to excuse them."[39] They inflicted more indignity than actual hardship. But in Ireland, the Penal Laws were not anachronisms. Although enforced with less severity than in the previous century, the laws continued to serve the political and economic interests of the dominant Protes-

---

[36] Edmund Burke, *Tract Relative to the Laws against Popery in Ireland* (circa 1761), in 6 *Works* 299, 318 ("*Tract on the Popery Laws*").

[37] Id at 317.

[38] See id at 302–17. The Irish Penal Laws and various Catholic Relief Acts of the period are reproduced in excerpted form as appendices to Thomas H. D. Mahoney, *Edmund Burke and Ireland* 325–42 (Harvard, 1960) ("*Burke and Ireland*").

[39] William Blackstone, IV *Blackstone's Commentaries on the Laws of England* 57 (Callaghan, 3d rev ed 1884).

tant minority, which had exclusive control of Irish Parliament, administration, court, and juries. The Protestant Ascendancy was not willing to give up its tools of legal domination without a struggle.[40]

It was during this period that Burke wrote (but never published) his *Tract Relative to the Laws Against Popery in Ireland*.[41] In the *Tract*, he argued that the Penal Laws were both unjust ("these politics are rotten and hollow at bottom, as all that are founded upon any however minute a degree of positive injustice must ever be"[42]) and ineffective as an instrument for the spread of the Protestant religion. "Ireland, after almost a century of persecution, is at this hour full of penalties and full of Papists. . . . We found the people heretics and idolaters; we have, by way of improving their condition, rendered them slaves and beggars: they remain in all the misfortune of their old errors, and all the superadded misery of their recent punishment."[43]

Burke's sympathy for the oppressed, even then, could not be divorced from his essentially conservative theory of government, which in later life would cause Burke to oppose the designs of revolutionaries and innovators with the same vigor that he opposed the tyranny in Ireland. All power—whether monarchical or democratic—must be restrained by the enduring truths of what Burke called "original justice,"[44] which reveals itself only slowly, with experience, over time. Accordingly, the persecution of Catholics in Ireland held for Burke a peculiar horror. Whether erroneous or not, Catholicism in Ireland drew its strength from long-standing practice and belief—precisely the same prop that supports and constrains legitimate government. Thus, he warned the English that "you punish them [the Catholics of Ireland] for acting upon a principle which of all others is perhaps the most necessary for preserving society, an implicit admiration and adherence to the establishments of their forefathers."[45]

---

[40] See *First Letter from Edmund Burke to Sir Hercules Langrishe* (Jan 3, 1792), in 4 *Works* 241, 252–53. This was even more true in the 1760s, when Burke first addressed the issue.

[41] Published in 6 *Works* 299. Unfortunately, all that survives is a substantial fragment, some of which is taken from a rough draft.

[42] Id at 337.

[43] Id at 334, 341.

[44] Id at 323.

[45] Id at 337.

Those scholars who purport to see a fundamental shift in Burke's principles—from a liberal, tolerant, whiggish beginning to a conservative, establishmentarian, tory conclusion[46]—have given insufficient attention to this early *Tract*, in which he grounded his argument for liberal reform in the same principles that later would inspire his essays decrying the Revolution in France. "It would be hard to point out any error more truly subversive of all the order and beauty, of all the peace and happiness of human society," Burke wrote in the *Tract*, "than the position, that any body of men have a right to make what laws they please."[47] Later, he would deploy the same argument in his attack on the French Revolution: "Neither the few nor the many have a right to act merely by their will."[48] In Ireland as in France, Burke invoked age-old experience both for the preservation of society and as the means of resistance to arbitrary government.

Despite his work on the Penal Laws and the general liberality of Hamilton's administration in Ireland, little progress toward toleration was made during Burke's tenure in office. The Penal Laws themselves were untouched. Much of Burke's attention was devoted to a defensive reaction to what were called the "Whiteboy" disturbances (after the participants' practice of wearing white shirts over their clothes, to distinguish one another at night). These uprisings, which Burke attributed to economic deprivations, were blamed by Protestant landlords on Jacobite and French sedition and used as an excuse to crack down on Irish Catholic dissent. A number of suspected Whiteboys were hanged by local authorities. When the administration refused to treat the Whiteboy disturbances as sectarian or political in nature, Protestant gentry were angered, and the cause of systemic reform rendered impossible.[49]

Burke made one other modest attempt toward toleration. In the first public position of his career, he won support from the Privy

---

[46] See Clark, *English Society* at 250 (cited in note 2). This charge of inconsistency had frequently been leveled against Burke by his critics, including Thomas Paine, Mary Wollstonecraft, and (later) Charles James Fox, and was answered by him in *An Appeal from the New to the Old Whigs* (1791), in 4 *Works* 57, 92 et seq.

[47] Burke, *Tract on the Popery Laws* (circa 1761), in 6 *Works* 299, 322. Compare Burke, *Reflections* at 82–86; Burke, *An Appeal from the New to the Old Whigs* (1791), in 4 *Works* 57, 120–21.

[48] Burke, *An Appeal from the New to the Old Whigs* (1791), in 4 *Works* 57, 162.

[49] See O'Brien, *The Great Melody* at 44–46 (cited in note 13). Burke later described these events in his *First Letter to Sir Hercules Langrishe* (Jan 3, 1792), in 4 *Works* 241, 254–55.

Council to allow six regiments of Catholic Irish to be formed to defend England's ally, Portugal, at Portuguese expense. It was thought that this would help to dispel the persistent suspicion that the Catholic majority were disloyal to Britain, and serve as a bridge toward enlargement of civil capacities. But even this small step was defeated in the Irish Parliament, because of fears that arming the Catholics could prove dangerous.[50]

Nothing more was to be accomplished. Hamilton was dismissed from his Irish post in 1764. With him, Burke returned to England. The following year the two men had a falling out, caused—at least in part—by differences over the Catholic question (as well as over money). Burke thought Hamilton insufficiently energetic in his efforts on behalf of Catholic emancipation. Hamilton, for his part, called Burke "a Jew and a Jesuit."[51]

C. BURKE'S EARLY PARLIAMENTARY CAREER

Burke soon acquired a more lasting and satisfactory patron, through whom he entered Parliament and rose to become one of its most influential figures. In July of 1765, he became private secretary to the Second Marquess of Rockingham, the leader of the most prominent faction of the Whig Party, who was then forming a government.[52] Later that year, Burke was elected to Parliament from Wendover, a pocket borough belonging to a Rockingham ally. Unfortunately for Burke, the Rockingham government fell the next year, its one significant achievement being repeal of the Stamp Act. For the next sixteen years Burke was but a member of the opposition. His talents, however, were such that, despite his inauspicious background as an Irishman and suspected Catholic, Burke became a formidable power in English politics, generally regarded as the intellectual leader and spokesman of the Rockingham Whigs.

Early in his career, Burke was forced to confront one of the

---

[50] For an account of this episode, see Mahoney, *Burke and Ireland* at 14–15 (cited in note 38).

[51] O'Brien, *The Great Melody* at 47–48 (cited in note 13).

[52] Burke's appointment was almost forestalled by the circulation of rumors that he was a Catholic and a Jesuit. Rockingham approached Burke to ask about the rumors, and Burke's response must have been satisfactory. Id at 48–49; Carl B. Cone, *Burke and the Nature of Politics: The Age of the American Revolution* 71–72 (Kentucky, 1957).

most vexing and persistent issues of eighteenth-century politics: the rights of Protestant Dissenters. In theory, "penal laws" punished the open practice (though never mere belief) of religion outside the Church of England, "disability laws" (notably the Test Act and the Corporation Act) excluded Dissenters from public (and some forms of private) office, and the "Act of Uniformity" prescribed Thirty-Nine Articles of Faith to which all clergy were required to subscribe.[53] Since the Glorious Revolution in 1688, however, Protestant Dissenters had enjoyed a significant degree of toleration. Under the Act of Toleration, enacted in the first year of the reign of William and Mary, the penalties of certain of the penal acts would not apply to Protestant Dissenters, and Protestant dissenting clergy were permitted to conduct religious worship services provided they adhered to 36 and part of one other of the Thirty-Nine Articles (omitting those that related to church governance and infant baptism).

The Act of Toleration was celebrated as a cornerstone of Protestant liberty, but we should not forget its limitations. As a formal matter, it lifted penalties only, leaving the legal requirements of conformity theoretically in place, and it extended only to trinitarian Protestants (primarily Presbyterians, Independents, and Baptists), thus excluding not only Catholics, Jews, and other non-Christians, but also the increasingly visible "Rational Dissenters": deists, Socinians, Arians, and Unitarians of various sorts who criticized orthodox Christianity as irrational, unscientific, and oppressive.[54] Moreover, the Act of Toleration did not affect the Test and Corporation Acts, which limited public and corporate office to those who participated in the Anglican sacrament. Repeated efforts were made between 1727 and 1739 to repeal the Test and Corporation Acts, but these were unsuccessful—though annual Indemnity Acts were passed after 1727 to suspend the penalty of the Test Laws, and the practice of "occasional conformity" enabled Dissenters to evade the laws by occasional, insincere participation

---

[53] See Blackstone, 4 *Blackstone's Commentaries* at 53–58 (cited in note 39). These restrictions help to explain the structure of the provisions of the United States Constitution relating to religion. The Free Exercise Clause prohibits enactment of laws similar to the Penal Laws; the Test Oath Clause of Article VI prohibits disability laws; and the Establishment Clause prohibits laws similar to the Act of Uniformity.

[54] See generally Michael R. Watts, *The Dissenters: From the Reformation to the French Revolution* 371–82, 464–78 (Clarendon, 1978).

in the Anglican sacrament. As a result of these measures (as well as informal nonenforcement), the penal and disability laws had far less practical consequence than their formal provisions would suggest. Burke called the Test Act "hardly anything more than a dead letter."[55] Dissenters were elected to municipal corporate office and even to Parliament, and it was not unusual for clergy within the Anglican Church to question some of the doctrinal tenets of the Thirty-Nine Articles. Nontrinitarian churches were generally able to conduct services without legal molestation.[56]

The Dissenters pursued a two-course strategy of urging greater "comprehension" within the established church (meaning relaxation and liberalization of the liturgical and doctrinal requirements specified by the Act of Uniformity) and greater toleration of Dissenters outside the church. In these efforts, they generally received the warm support of the Whigs and the opposition of the High Church and Tory parties. Burke, however, treated these two proposed lines of reform as different in principle. In his treatment of two proposals in 1772 and 1773 we can see the foundation of his understanding of the relation between establishment and toleration.

In 1772, some 250 Anglican clergymen signed a petition (called the "Feathers Tavern" petition) asking Parliament to abolish the requirement of subscription to the Thirty-Nine Articles of Faith of the Church of England, and replace it with a simple affirmation of the Bible as the source of divine truth.[57] The petition was supported by most of Burke's friends and allies in the Whig Party,[58] who saw it as a step toward a more tolerant and rational church. To their surprise, Burke spoke against the petition. He began by distancing himself from the High Church position, and from what

---

[55] *First Letter from Edmund Burke to Sir Hercules Langrishe* (Jan 3, 1792), in 4 *Works* 241, 264.

[56] See generally Henriques, *Religious Toleration* at 5–17 (cited in note 2); Clark, *English Society* at 316 (cited in note 2).

[57] The petition also sought similar relief on behalf of students of civil law and medicine at Oxford and Cambridge, who had to subscribe to the Articles in order to receive their degrees. Both sides in the parliamentary debate agreed on the justice of this aspect of the measure. When it came up for separate consideration the next year, however, Burke was out of the country, and the measure was defeated. Cone, *Burke and the Nature of Politics* at 219 n 22 (cited in note 52).

[58] See *Letter from Edmund Burke to the Countess of Huntingdon* (ante Feb 6, 1772), in 2 *Correspondence* 298, 299.

he considered to be erroneous grounds for opposition to the petition. He explained that "[i]f ever there was anything to which, from reason, nature, habit, and principle, I am totally averse, it is persecution for conscientious difference of opinion."[59] But, he said, the petition "does not concern toleration, but establishment"— the right of the people of England to maintain a church in accordance with their own theological principles.[60] Those who "do not like the Establishment . . . have free liberty to assemble a congregation of their own."[61] It is an essential right of any church, however, to determine its doctrines and require conformity from its clergy; in this respect the Church of England enjoys the rights of any church or voluntary society. "If you will have religion publicly practised and publicly taught," he noted, "you must have a power to say what that religion will be which you will protect and encourage."[62] If you allow the clergy "the power of taxing the people of England for the maintenance of their private opinions," he said, "you take away the liberty of the elector, which is the people, that is, the state."[63] The complaint, therefore, he said derisively, "is not toleration of diversity in opinion, but that diversity in opinion is not rewarded by bishoprics, rectories, and collegiate stalls."[64] The bill was defeated, and subsequently a significant body of Anglican clergy resigned their livings and joined the ranks of the Rational Dissenters.

The following year, a group of dissenting clergy sought repeal of the requirement that they adhere to any part of the Thirty-Nine Articles. This requirement was not generally enforced, and some members argued that it was therefore no serious grievance, but should be maintained as an essentially symbolic reminder of the exclusive character of the establishment. The repeal legislation easily passed the House of Commons, but, with royal intervention, was defeated in the House of Lords.

[59] Burke, *Speech on the Acts of Uniformity* (Feb 6, 1772), in 7 *Works* 3, 10.

[60] Id at 15.

[61] Id at 12. In this, Burke was expressing his opinion, rather than accurately stating the law. Technically, all clergy were required to subscribe to the Thirty-Nine Articles (or at least to the subset specified in the Act of Toleration). Burke supported efforts to repeal this limitation.

[62] Id at 16.

[63] Id at 12, 16.

[64] Id at 15.

On this occasion, Burke supported the Dissenters, making what might seem to be the obvious distinction between the right to preach and the right to preach as a clergyman of the Church of England. At the time, most observers regarded this as a reversal of position, because for most the battle lines were drawn between supporters of the establishment and advocates of theological change. For Burke the two positions were entirely consistent.

Burke addressed his remarks to an "honorable gentleman" who had argued that "establishing toleration by law is an attack on Christianity."[65] Burke, by contrast, was "persuaded that toleration, so far from being an attack upon Christianity, becomes the best and surest support that possibly can be given it."[66] "I may be mistaken, but I take toleration to be a part of religion."[67] Burke did not base his argument so much on the importance of individual conscience, but on the value of religion—even of dissenting religion. "Do not promote diversity," he said, but "when you have it, bear it; have as many sorts of religion as you find in your country; there is a reasonable worship in them all."[68] The real struggle, he argued, is not among the various religions, but between religion and atheism.

One thing had changed between the two petitions: Burke had gone to France and spent a month in the salons of Paris, where he became acquainted with the disturbingly atheistic ideas of the *philosophes*. In all likelihood, this is the background for Burke's surprisingly harsh denunciations of atheists as "outlaws of the constitution" and a "confederacy of the powers of darkness," who are "endeavoring to shake all the works of God established in order and beauty."[69] This may seem overwrought; Burke himself said "[p]erhaps I am carried too far."[70] But his experience in France solidified Burke's determination to create, through toleration, what he called "an alliance offensive and defensive"[71] of all religions against the threat of unbelief and its political manifestations.

---

[65] Burke, *Speech on a Bill for the Relief of Protestant Dissenters* (Mar 17, 1773), in 7 *Works* 21, 24.

[66] Id at 25.

[67] Id at 33.

[68] Id at 36.

[69] Id at 36, 37.

[70] Id at 37.

[71] Id.

The theory that Burke's early career was tolerant and liberal, and his later career conservative and establishmentarian,[72] or that his attitude toward radical Dissent soured when the Dissenters deserted Burke's Whig faction in favor of Pitt in the elections of 1784,[73] are difficult to sustain in light of these speeches in 1772 and 1773. At this point, Burke was at the center of Whig politics and a friend to Fox; his political relations with Dissenters were warm;[74] and the French Revolution was more than fifteen years in the future. This was Burke's most "liberal" period—if Burke's career can be divided between "liberal" and "conservative" periods. Yet even at this time, we see Burke as a staunch defender of the establishment, as a believer in ecclesiastical authority rather than individualistic conscience, and as an opponent of atheism. As his worst fears about the consequences of a politicized atheism came true in France in later years, the emotional temperature of Burke's "conservative" side undoubtedly increased, but the substance of his later arguments in the *Reflections* was plainly adumbrated in his treatment of the petitions of the Protestant Dissenters in 1772 and 1773.

D. CATHOLIC EMANCIPATION, THE GORDON RIOTS, AND DEFEAT IN BRISTOL

Burke's rising stature as a politician enabled him to run successfully for Parliament from the second city of the realm, the port of Bristol. In that capacity, Burke returned to his lifelong project of mitigating the anti-popery laws. In 1778, Burke induced Sir George Savile, a Protestant of aristocratic family with large land holdings in Ireland, to introduce legislation repealing the Penal Act of 1699, an act of "ludicrous cruelty" (according to Burke),[75] which outlawed performance of the Catholic mass and Catholic education, and which deprived Catholics of the right to bequeath property. Lord John Cavendish introduced a second bill authorizing the Irish Parliament to pass similar relief for the Catholics of that land. Although Burke was undoubtedly the prime mover of

---

[72] See note 16 and accompanying text.

[73] See Henriques, *Religious Toleration* at 117 (cited in note 2).

[74] Leading Dissenters praised Burke in 1772 for "magnificent efforts" in their behalf. Cone, *Burke and the Nature of Politics* at 224 (cited in note 52).

[75] Burke, *Speech at Bristol, Previous to the Election* (Sept 6, 1780), in 2 *Works* 365, 409.

these measures behind the scenes, he neither made the motions nor spoke in favor of the bills on the floor of the House, largely because of widespread insinuations that he was too close to the Catholic cause. The bills were enacted, and the Irish Parliament followed suit with a somewhat more limited bill of relief, which Burke later described as a "first faint sketch of toleration, which did little more than disclose a principle and mark out a disposition."[76]

Burke was widely given the credit in Ireland for passage of these measures, and it is reported that the King was influenced to sign by an "Address and Petition to the Throne" Burke had drafted some fourteen years before, which was preserved and presented to the monarch.[77] Burke himself attributed the change in opinion that enabled passage of the bills to the crisis precipitated by the American Revolution, which made it imperative that all the subjects of Britain be conciliated and united.[78]

The next step was introduction of a similar measure for Catholic emancipation in Scotland. This, however, was blocked by the fierce opposition of an organization called the Protestant Association, led by the fanatical Lord George Gordon. Gordon, a strange figure who later converted to Judaism and eventually died insane, led a mob of some 60,000 people to Parliament to present a petition demanding repeal of the English Relief Act. The mob, which one historian has called "unparalleled in the history of parliament," forced entering members of the Lords and Commons to wear blue cockades and shout "No Popery!," violently attacking those who resisted (including such luminaries as the Archbishop of York, the Bishop of Lincoln, the Duke of Northumberland, and Lord Chief Justice Mansfield).[79] There ensued a week of riots during which Catholic churches were looted and burned, homes and other property destroyed, many members of Parliament roughed up, and Burke's home, family, and person threatened. As many as 450 lives may have been lost.[80] Burke later described the scene at Parliament

---

[76] Id at 403–04.

[77] See Mahoney, *Burke and Ireland* at 69–74 (cited in note 38); MacKnight, 2 *Life and Times* at 236–46 (cited in note 16).

[78] Burke, *Speech at Bristol, Previous to the Election* (Sept 6, 1780), in 2 *Works* 365, 400–04.

[79] Mahoney, *Burke and Ireland* at 93–94 (cited in note 38).

[80] See Stanley Ayling, *Edmund Burke: His Life and Opinions* 97 (St. Martin's, 1988). See also Cone, *Burke and the Nature of Politics* at 350–52 (cited in note 52).

to his Bristol constituents, stating: "I do not wish to go over the horrid scene that was afterwards acted. Would to God it could be expunged forever from the annals of this country!"[81]

Despite urgings by his friends to leave the city, Burke repeatedly ventured among the mob, announcing his identity and his support for the Relief Act.[82] Inside Parliament, he unstintingly opposed repeal of the Act. As he described it:

> In this audacious tumult, . . . I, who had exerted myself very little on the quiet passing of the bill, thought it necessary then to come forward. I was not alone; but . . . I may and will value myself so far, that, yielding in abilities to many, I yielded in zeal to none. With warmth and with vigor, and animated with a just and natural indignation, I called forth every faculty that I possessed, and I directed it in every way in which I could possibly employ it. I labored night and day. I labored in Parliament; I labored out of Parliament. If, therefore, the resolution of the House of Commons, refusing to commit this act of unmatched turpitude, be a crime, I am guilty among the foremost.[83]

Burke prevailed and the Act survived, but the King and the government privately made clear that they would not support any further reform of the Penal Laws, for fear of future violence.[84] Indeed, the House of Commons passed (though the Lords rejected) a bill offered by Sir George Savile as a sop to the Protestant Association, which would restrain the "Papists, or persons professing the Popish religion, from teaching, or taking upon themselves the education or government of the children of Protestants."[85] Burke took a spirited part in debate against the bill, defending Catholic education and the rights of parents to direct the education of their offspring. This foreshadowed the U.S. Supreme Court's (1925) holding in *Pierce v Society of Sisters*.[86]

Burke found himself in political trouble with his Bristol constituents, who were not pleased with his activities in favor of Irish

---

[81] Burke, *Speech at Bristol, Previous to the Election* (Sept 6, 1780), in 2 *Works* 365, 410.

[82] Mahoney, *Burke and Ireland* at 95 (cited in note 38); MacKnight, 2 *Life and Times* at 366 (cited in note 16); Cone, *Burke and the Nature of Politics* at 351 (cited in note 52).

[83] Burke, *Speech at Bristol, Previous to the Election* (Sept 6, 1780), in 2 *Works* 365, 412–13.

[84] Mahoney, *Burke and Ireland* at 96 (cited in note 38).

[85] Id at 98–99.

[86] 268 US 510 (1925).

trade, in opposition to life imprisonment for debt, or in support of the American colonists—and most of all, who were distressed by his role in passage of the Catholic Relief Act. Burke delivered an impassioned speech defending his role in the Act, and the propriety of religious toleration. Despite his constituents' disapproval, he declared that he "never was less sorry for any action of my life."[87] "I could do nothing but what I have done on this subject," he told them, "without confounding the whole train of my ideas and disturbing the whole order of my life."[88] He explained that this was an issue on which he was compelled to follow his conscience rather than the wishes of his constituents. "No man carries further than I do the policy of making government pleasing to the people," he said, "[b]ut the widest range of this politic complaisance is confined within the limits of justice. . . . I never will act the tyrant for their amusement."[89]

Burke paid the price of electoral rejection. Thenceforth he served in Parliament in the less exalted role of member for a pocket borough.

E. BURKE'S LATER CAREER, THE REVOLUTION IN FRANCE, AND DISASTER IN IRELAND

The next decade was for Burke a time of frenetic activity, great achievement, and political disappointment. The Rockingham Whigs came to power (briefly) with the collapse of the war effort against the Americans in 1782. Though formally only a junior minister, Burke played a significant role in forcing peace on a reluctant George III, and won passage of his "economical reform." After only a few months, however, Rockingham died and Burke went into opposition, returning to power (again briefly) the following year. During this period, Burke began his crusade against corruption and colonial exploitation in India—an effort that brought about the defeat of his political party. The India effort occupied Burke's attention (in the form of prosecuting the impeachment of Warren Hastings, Governor-General of Bengal) for more than half a decade: a tiring, thankless, and ultimately fruitless task.

---

[87] Burke, *Speech at Bristol, Previous to the Election* (Sept 6, 1780), in 2 *Works* 365, 419.

[88] Id at 388.

[89] Id at 421.

All the while, Burke pursued his efforts for the toleration of Catholics in Ireland. One of the more dubious achievements of the Rockingham Administration was passage of legislation restoring power to the Irish Parliament.[90] The principal arena for reform of the Irish Penal Laws thus shifted to Ireland. In some ways, this made reform more difficult, because Catholics were excluded from Parliament as both electors and members.

Burke corresponded actively with members of the Irish Parliament as well as leaders in the movement for reform. Many of these letters were published and served as public advocacy. Among these, Burke's *Letter to a Peer of Ireland* (Lord Kenmare, then head of the Catholic Association) in 1782,[91] and *First Letter to Sir Hercules Langrishe* (a member of the Irish Parliament and moderate advocate of reform) in 1792,[92] are classics, and contributed significantly to the passage of reform legislation in those years. The 1782 Act removed restrictions on purchasing, inheriting, and bequeathing land and legitimated most of the priestly functions of parish priests. The 1792 Act opened the practice of law to Catholics, lifted the ban on religious intermarriage, permitted Catholic schools, and allowed foreign education of Catholic children.

In 1790, in recognition of Burke's guiding role, the Catholic Committee of Ireland hired his son, Richard, as its agent for the campaign for enfranchisement and other reform. As the chairman of the Committee observed, "The many obligations we are under to the Zeal and brilliant Abilities of the Father inspire us with the strongest reliance on the Son for his most strenuous exertions and able assistance in our behalf."[93] Burke wrote an interesting series of letters to his son in that capacity, discussing the circumstances in Ireland and the reasons for further reform. These offer insight both into the complicated political dynamics of the Irish question, and also into Burke's own principles of political prudence and reform. The overriding problem in Ireland, as perceived by Burke, was that the intransigence of the Protestant authorities was driving

---

[90] Burke opposed this measure, at least when it was first proposed, apparently because it would strengthen the hand of the Protestant Ascendancy. Later, after Irish leaders promised support for Catholic emancipation, Burke muted and perhaps abandoned his opposition. O'Brien, *The Great Melody* at 197–201, 243–45 (cited in note 13).

[91] Published in 4 *Works* 217.

[92] Published in 4 *Works* 241.

[93] Quoted in Mahoney, *Burke and Ireland* at 162 (cited in note 38).

the Catholics to violence, as well as to an association with the revolutionary principles emanating from France. He attempted a compromise based on preservation of the existing civil structure of the Irish nation, accompanied by Catholic emancipation and enfranchisement. Fearing the effects of violence, Burke urged on the Irish people a strategy of "still, discontented, passive obedience" in lieu of a "giddy unsupported resistance."[94]

Largely as a result of the efforts of Burke and his son, the British government pressured the Irish Parliament to enact a third Catholic Relief Act in 1793, extending to qualified Catholic citizens the rights to vote, to serve on juries, to hold military commissions, and to obtain university degrees, provided they took an oath that, among other things, denied the infallibility of the Pope and abjured any intention to disturb the established church.[95] Catholics remained excluded from Parliament and other high offices of Irish government, and the hostility between the Protestant government and the Catholic majority continued to fester.

During the same period, Protestant Dissent reemerged as an issue in Parliament, through a series of petitions for repeal of the Corporation and Test Acts. For Burke, this was not precisely an issue of toleration. Even as regards the Catholics of Ireland, Burke accepted the well-established distinction between the right to practice one's religion and even to vote, and the right to hold high political office.[96] Restrictions on officeholding had long been a constitutional device by which Parliament could restrict the power of untrustworthy monarchs to appoint officials who were not committed to the principles of the Protestant settlement of 1688. On the other hand, the form of the Test Act was particularly obnoxious: to require officeholders to take Anglican communion was, as Burke said, "a bad and insufficient test for the end it was meant to accomplish."[97] He called it "an abuse of the sacramental rite."[98]

Burke found it difficult to make up his mind. As of 1780, he

---

[94] Quoted in id at 202.

[95] Id at 211–16.

[96] See Burke, *Tract on the Popery Laws* (circa 1761), in 6 *Works* 299, 311; *First Letter from Edmund Burke to Sir Hercules Langrishe* (Jan 3, 1792), in 4 *Works* 241, 252–53.

[97] Edmund Burke, *Speech on Repeal of the Test and Corporation Acts* (Mar 2, 1790), in 28 *Parliamentary History of England* 432, 441 (T. C. Hansard, 1816) ("*Parliamentary History*").

[98] Id.

was prepared to support repeal of the Test and Corporation Acts.[99] But he perceived that the character of Dissent was changing. Rather than representing a difference of conscience, Burke believed that the organized forces of Dissent had been transformed into a *"political* faction," for the specific purpose of subverting the constitution of church and state, and destroying the Church of England.[100]

Moreover, Burke's views on the church-state issue were profoundly influenced by the events then unfolding in France. Among the first actions of the new revolutionary authorities were the disestablishment of the church, the seizure of its property, and harassment of its faithful clergy. It was not long before the church was actively persecuted and a "Temple of Reason" erected on the altar of Notre Dame. Even before the Terror, at a time when liberal politicians and preachers in England still hailed the revolution as a triumph of liberty, Burke responded with his most famous work, *Reflections on the Revolution in France*, denouncing the Revolution and warning of parallel movements in England. Burke, together with Hume, was the first to perceive that principles of Enlightenment, democratization, modernization, defeudalization, and human rights could, if unconstrained, produce a regime of tyranny and religious persecution. The *Reflections* contained his great defense of the established institutions of the English constitution: "We are resolved," he declared, "to keep an established church, an established monarchy, an established aristocracy, and an established democracy, each in the degree it exists, and in no greater."[101] Burke's counter-revolutionary fervor precipitated a painful break in 1791 with his friend and protege and the leader of his political party, Charles James Fox, who continued to support the Revolution. After this, Burke (ironically, the great defender of party loyalty) was a man without a party.

As the French Revolution came to dominate Burke's attention, he became less accommodating toward those radical Protestants who, he believed, were the vanguard of Jacobinism in the British

---

[99] He so stated publicly a decade later. Id at 442. See also *Letter from Edmund Burke to Edmund S. Pery* (July 18, 1778), in 6 *Works* 197, 202.

[100] Burke, *Speech on the Petition of the Unitarians* (May 11, 1792), 7 *Works* 39, 47 (emphasis in original).

[101] Burke, *Reflections* at 80.

Isles. He had learned from the French experience that "rationalist" critics of the church were capable of acts of antireligious fanaticism, and he was shocked when ostensibly liberal English Dissenters were enthusiastic—rather than horrified—about the events in France. Accordingly, he absented himself from the House when proposals for repeal of the Test and Corporation Acts came to the floor in 1787 and 1789,[102] and he moved into active opposition in debates in 1790 and 1792.[103] He explained in a letter to Richard Bright, a prominent Dissenter and a neighbor at Beaconsfield, that he had previously been willing to overlook "many things which appeard to me, perhaps not so commendable in the Conduct of those who seemd to lead [the Dissenters]" because he had thought them "animated with a serious, humane, hatred of Tyranny, oppression, and corruption in all persons in power."[104] But he had "found by experience" that they were "of a direct contrary Character"—that they were attempting to draw England into an imitation of the French Revolution, which would be "highly dangerous to the constitution and the prosperity of this Country."[105]

It is common for modern scholars to dismiss Burke's position on the Test and Corporation Acts as an abandonment of "the principle of religious toleration,"[106] but Burke understood the question of eligibility for political office as raising issues of politics and power rather than conscience. Thus, while he "professed himself

---

[102] In a letter, Burke wrote that if he were able to attend the vote on the bill in 1789, he would "certainly" vote for it, "in conformity to my known principles." *Letter from Edmund Burke to Richard Bright* (May 8–9, 1789), in 5 *Correspondence* 470. But in view of Burke's exhausting labors on the Hastings impeachment, his ill health, and the Dissenters' betrayal of the Whigs in the election of 1784, Burke stated that he would not engage in "Activity" in support of the bill, and that he would, in all likelihood, not attend the Parliamentary session. Id.

[103] See Burke, *Speech on Repeal of the Test and Corporation Acts* (Mar 2, 1790), in 28 *Parliamentary History* 432, 440–41. See also Burke, *Speech on the Petition of the Unitarians* (May 11, 1792), in 7 *Works* 39, 49–50.

[104] *Letter from Edmund Burke to Richard Bright* (Feb 18, 1790), in 6 *Correspondence* 82, 83.

[105] Id.

[106] See L. G. Mitchell, *Introduction*, to 8 *Writings and Speeches of Edmund Burke* 8 (Clarendon, 1989). Mitchell's further statement that, for Burke, "[r]eligious dissent of all kinds acquired a demonic character," id, suggests a misunderstanding of Burke. If anything, the French Revolution solidified Burke's disposition toward toleration of what he called all "serious religion." See Burke, *Speech on a Bill for the Relief of Protestant Dissenters* (Mar 17, 1773), in 7 *Works* 21, 37. See also discussion in text at notes 65–74. Burke's fear and distaste was reserved for atheists and those radical Dissenters whose emphasis was on attacking revealed and established religion rather than on any affirmative teaching of their own.

ready to grant relief from oppression to all men," he was "unwilling to grant power, because power once possessed was generally abused."[107] His argument was straightforward: the established Church of England is an essential element of the constitution ("a great national benefit, a great public blessing"[108]); prominent Dissenters have declared their intention to destroy and persecute the church; it is only their lack of access to political power that prevents them from achieving their announced objectives; the Test and Corporation Acts are thus necessary to protect the constitution, the establishment, and the Church. The "question," therefore "is, whether you should keep them within the bounds of toleration, or subject yourself to their persecution."[109] It is easy to say, in retrospect, that Burke's fears on this subject were exaggerated, but this was the world's first confrontation with revolutionary internationalism, and the rest of Europe was being swept into its vortex. Even so, Burke did not propose to add any new limitations or penalties on those he deemed so dangerous: he urged only that the occasion was not ripe for the lifting of political incapacities that already existed.

The form of the Test Act, however, remained problematic. Burke proposed replacement of the sacramental test with a formal promise not to "attempt to subvert the constitution of the church of England, as the same is now by law established."[110] Nothing came of this compromise suggestion.

In his continued efforts on behalf of Catholic emancipation, Burke the reformer became increasingly indistinguishable from Burke the conservative. While the intransigence of the Protestant authorities was driving many Irish Catholics into the arms of Jacobinism and rebellion, Burke maintained that the best and most effective arguments on their behalf came not from the new doctrines of the Rights of Man but from ancient principles of the English constitutional system. In his *First Letter to Sir Hercules Langrishe*, he explained why toleration for Catholics was consistent with the

---

[107] Burke, *Speech on Repeal of the Test and Corporation Acts* (Mar 2, 1790), in 28 *Parliamentary History* 432, 441.

[108] Burke, *Speech on the Petition of the Unitarians* (May 11, 1792), in 7 *Works* 39, 56.

[109] Id at 48.

[110] Burke, *Speech on Repeal of the Test and Corporation Acts* (Mar 2, 1790), in 28 *Parliamentary History* 432, 441 n *.

fundamental laws, going back to Magna Charta.[111] In an "essay" written for Henry Dundas, the Home Secretary, Burke argued that the denial of the franchise to Irish Catholics was a comparatively recent and deplorable innovation. The extension of a new right is "very dangerous," Burke wrote, since it could lead to unforeseen consequences; but restoration of the capacity to enjoy an old right is "extremely safe." He was careful to dissociate his appeal for enfranchisement of the Catholics of Ireland from any claim based on "speculative right" or "general principles of liberty, or as a conclusion from any given premise, either of natural or even of constitutional right." The French Declaration of the Rights of Man had exposed the dangers of arguments of that sort. Rather, the Catholic majority should be given the vote as "a protection, and a requisite security" which they lacked for the exercise of legal right.[112] This, Burke maintained, would strengthen the state, because "a greater number of persons will be interested in conservation" of the constitution. "[I]f the experience of mankind is to be credited, a seasonable extension of rights is the best expedient for the conservation of them. Every right, every privilege, every immunity, every distinction known in the world, and which has been preserved throughout the fluctuations of time and circumstance, has been so preserved."[113] The key words here —"conservation" and "preservation"—demonstrate the conservative character of Burke's argument, in which he sought to conserve and protect the ancient liberties of Irishmen and Englishmen against the "fluctuations of time and circumstance."

Despite the hostile reaction of his former political allies to the *Reflections* and the cool reception of his ideas by Pitt, Burke continued to write furious polemics against the Revolution in France. He gained credibility and political support as the terrible events bore out his predictions. He sought to discredit Fox as leader of the Whigs[114] and to persuade Pitt to commit to war against revolu-

---

[111] *First Letter from Edmund Burke to Sir Hercules Langrishe* (Jan 3, 1792), in 4 *Works* 241, 257–70.

[112] *Letter from Edmund Burke to Henry Dundas*, quoted in Mahoney, *Burke and Ireland* 207–09 (cited in note 38).

[113] Id at 208.

[114] This was the main purpose of Burke's *Observations on the Conduct of the Minority* (1793), in 5 *Works* 1.

tionary France.[115] He warned that ideological movements in Britain, especially among Rational Dissenters, were parallel to those that had brought about the Revolution in France, and that from "the same beginnings" might come "the very same effects."[116] Without the support of a political party, Burke became a party unto himself: a mighty, even obsessive force for counter-revolution. As Sir Gilbert Elliot wrote in 1793: "Burke is in himself a sort of *power* in the State. It is even not too much to say that he is a sort of *power* in Europe, though totally without any of those means, or the smallest share in them, which give or maintain power in other men."[117] These efforts eventually bore fruit. In 1793, England entered the war against France. In 1794, the Whig Party split. The larger faction, led by the Duke of Portland, who was friendly to Burke, joined with Pitt (and against Fox) in a coalition to prosecute war against France. This coalition marks the beginning of the modern Conservative Party.

In that same summer, Burke retired from Parliament. But not from public life. With his caustic *Letters on a Regicide Peace*,[118] he inveighed against proposals for a premature end to the war. On a happier note, with the entry of the Portland Whigs into government, hopes were raised for a complete Catholic emancipation in Ireland. Burke's friend and political patron, Rockingham's nephew Earl Fitzwilliam, was named Lord Lieutenant of Ireland. He immediately set about a thorough program of reform, in active consultation with Burke. Comprehensive reform legislation was introduced in the Irish Parliament, and a half million signatures were reportedly gathered in support. Within a few months of Fitzwilliam's arrival, however, the King announced his strong opposition to the emancipation plans, and the government instructed Fitzwilliam to use his "Zeal & Influence" to prevent any further proceeding on the emancipation bill.[119] Within a few weeks, Fitzwilliam

---

[115] See Edmund Burke, *Thoughts on French Affairs* (Dec, 1791), in 4 *Works* 313.

[116] Burke, *Speech on the Petition of the Unitarians* (May 11, 1792), in 7 *Works* 39, 50. See also Burke, *Speech on Repeal of the Test and Corporation Acts* (Mar 2, 1790), in 28 *Parliamentary History* 432, 440–41.

[117] *Letter from Sir Gilbert Elliot to Lady Elliot* (May 2, 1793), in 2 *Life and Letters of the First Earl of Minto* 137–38 (Countess of Minto ed, 1874), quoted in L. G. Mitchell, *Introduction*, in 8 *Writings and Speeches of Edmund Burke* 44.

[118] Burke, *Letters on a Regicide Peace* (1796–97), in 5 *Works* 231; Burke, *Fourth Letter on the Proposals for Peace with the Regicide Directory of France* (1795–97), in 6 *Works* 1.

[119] See Mahoney, *Burke and Ireland* at 250 (cited in note 38).

had been dismissed. According to Burke's Irish sources, the country was "now on the brink of a civil war."[120] Burke himself wrote to Fitzwilliam that "My heart is almost broken."[121]

No more was accomplished toward toleration in Burke's lifetime, and Ireland descended into an era of violence. Burke died in 1797, at a time when the armies of France were overrunning Europe. He was buried with the rites of the Anglican Church.

II. Burke's Defense of the Established Church

On what grounds did Burke defend the established church, and how was this connected to his advocacy of toleration? Nowhere does Burke set forth the argument in theoretical terms; it must be pieced together from speeches and essays addressing the particular political issues of the day.

The established church "is the first of our prejudices," he says in the *Reflections*, but he quickly adds that it is "not a prejudice destitute of reason, but involving in it profound and extensive wisdom."[122] As we shall see, Burke's establishment is different, both in purpose and in character, from the prototypical established church.

A. THE ROLE OF THE ESTABLISHMENT IN BURKE'S CONSTITUTION

Burke did not rest his defense of the established Church of England on any claim of its spiritual or theological superiority. "It is not morally true," he said, "that we are bound to establish in every country that form of religion which in *our* minds is most agreeable to truth, and conduces most to the eternal happiness of mankind."[123] Indeed, it may be said that his defense of the established church rested on no *theological* claim whatsoever. Rather, the argument was political and constitutional. This is evident, in part, from the fact that the argument appears in its fullest form in his *Reflections on the Revolution in France*, where the established church

---

[120] *Letter from Reverend Thomas Hussey to Edmund Burke* (Feb 26, 1787), in 8 *Correspondence* 162, 162.

[121] *Letter from Edmund Burke to Earl Fitzwilliam* (circa Feb 26, 1795), in 8 *Correspondence* 161, 162.

[122] Burke, *Reflections* at 80.

[123] Burke, *Speech on the Petition of the Unitarians* (May 11, 1792), in 7 *Works* 39, 42 (emphasis in original).

is presented as a means of upholding constitutional government and staving off revolution—and where revolution, for its part, is characterized as having the extirpation of religion as its principal object.[124] The question Burke addresses, then, is not how an establishment can contribute to the salvation of souls or the spiritual health of the nation, but how it can contribute to the stability of civil society.

The purpose of the establishment, Burke explains, is the "consecration of the state." By this he does not mean that the state is holy or exempt from criticism. On the contrary, it means that those who hold power in the state are "infused" with the "sublime principle[]" that "they should not look to the paltry pelf of the moment nor to the temporary and transient praise of the vulgar, but to a solid, permanent existence in the permanent part of their nature. . . ."[125] Government must be viewed as a "holy function"—not in the sense that it is above criticism, but in the sense that it must conform, in "virtue and wisdom," to principles higher than itself.[126] The established church thus stands as a reminder that those in power "act in trust, and that they are to account for their conduct in that trust to the one great Master, Author, and Founder of society."[127] It is a moral check on the abuse of power.

It is the democratic element in the English constitution, according to Burke, that most needs this kind of check. Princes are inherently more constrained because they must constantly win the support and approbation of others. "[W]here popular authority is absolute and unrestrained," however, "the people have an infinitely greater, because a far better founded, confidence in their own power." It is of "infinite importance," therefore, that the people "should not be suffered to imagine that their will, any more than that of kings, is the standard of right and wrong."[128] "When they are habitually convinced that no evil can be acceptable . . . to him whose essence is good, [the people] will be better able to extirpate out of the minds of all magistrates, civil, ecclesiastical, or

---

[124] See Burke, *Reflections* at 80–90.

[125] Id at 81.

[126] Id at 83.

[127] Id at 81.

[128] Id at 82.

military, anything that bears the least resemblance to a proud and lawless domination."[129]

In particular, the function of the establishment is to ensure continuity with the established traditions of the society. By "taking ground on that religious system of which we are now in possession," Burke explained, "we continue to act on the early received and uniformly continued sense of mankind."[130] Religion makes us aware that the civil order is but a part of the timeless moral order ordained by the universal sovereign, and not the mere choice of passing majorities.[131] Associate the state with the church, and the people will not be so ready as they otherwise might be to "chang[e] the state as often, and as much, and in as many ways as there are floating fancies or fashions."[132] To avoid

> the evils of inconstancy and versatility, ten thousand times worse than those of obstinacy and the blindest prejudice, we have consecrated the state, that no man should approach to look into its defects or corruptions but with due caution, that he should never dream of beginning its reformation by its subversion, that he should approach to the faults of the state as to the wounds of a father, with pious awe and trembling solicitude.[133]

The established church is a bulwark against hasty and incautious change.

This constitutional function explains why Burke insisted that the church must have a privileged role in the public sphere. She must "exalt her mitred front in courts and parliaments."[134] To reduce the church to one among many private, voluntary associations would deprive it of the grandeur and public authority needed to "show to the haughty potentates of the world . . . that a free, a generous, an informed nation honors the high magistrates of its church; that it will not suffer the insolence of wealth and titles,

---

[129] Id at 83.

[130] Id at 80.

[131] Id at 85. Burke returns to this theme in *An Appeal from the New to the Old Whigs* (1791), in 4 *Works* 57, 165–73.

[132] Burke, *Reflections* at 83.

[133] Id at 84.

[134] Id at 90.

or any other species of proud pretension, to look down with scorn upon what they looked up to with reverence."[135] A purely private church would not, in Burke's estimation, perform its desired constitutional role of reminding the wielders of political power that their exercise of that power is limited by higher Authority.

Even on Burke's own premises, these would not be adequate arguments for establishing religion in America. He insisted that in these matters a "good statesman" will be guided by "circumstances"—"a knowledge of [the people's] opinions, prejudices, habits, and all the circumstances that diversify and color life."[136] He recognized that when an attempt is made to impose an established church contrary to the "genius and desires" of the nation (giving Scotland at the time of Charles I as an example, but surely thinking of Ireland in his own time), such a "usurpation" will "excite[ ] a most mutinous spirit in that country."[137] As a practical constitutional prescription, Burke's combination of toleration and establishment is suited only to countries in which a single religious tradition is both numerically dominant and closely tied to the national culture and aspirations of the people. In such a case, complete disestablishment may not be possible without a degree of anticlericalism or hostility toward religion. Establishment *cum* toleration may be the best practicable arrangement.

Burke may therefore speak more directly to some of the emerging democracies of Eastern Europe, or to the nations of Latin America, than to the United States. Even in 1789, the United States was a place of such extensive religious diversity, with such regional variations in historical religious attachment, that a national religious establishment was out of the question. Even those who supported establishment in their own states agreed that there could be no establishment at the national level. In less than fifty years after the founding, even state establishments became untenable. As Burke predicted, where the established church did not reflect the opinions of the great majority of the people, it produced "mutiny" rather than "virtue and wisdom." Burke himself would

---

[135] Id. In this passage, Burke evinces the same respect mixed with disdain for aristocratic pomp and privilege that he later reveals in his *Letter to a Noble Lord* (1796), in 5 *Works* 171.

[136] Burke, *Speech on the Petition of the Unitarians* (May 11, 1792), in 7 *Works* 39, 45.

[137] Burke, *Speech on the Acts of Uniformity* (Feb 6, 1772), in 7 *Works* 3, 8.

not have advocated an establishment of religion in such a nation as the United States.

But that does not mean the United States can do without what Burke called "consecration." In an odd way, the Constitution of the United States performs much the same role that the established church performed in Burke's vision. The remedy against hasty and incautious change is the written constitution. As Madison stated in *The Federalist* No. 44:

> The sober people of America are weary of the fluctuating policy which has directed the public councils. They have seen with regret and indignation that sudden changes and legislative interferences, in cases affecting personal rights, become jobs in the hands of enterprising and influential speculators, and snares to the more industrious and less informed part of the community. . . . They very rightly infer, therefore, that some thorough reform is wanting, which will . . . give a regular course to the business of society.[138]

The Constitution is our bulwark against change—our guarantee that passing majorities, inflamed by "floating fancies or fashions," will not "destroy the entire fabric." And the Constitution itself is protected by a quasi-religious status in the popular mind.[139]

Moreover, rather than an established church, it is our First Amendment that most plainly serves as a reminder that legitimate government is limited by the immutable principles of a higher Authority. I have observed in another place that our Free Exercise Clause stands as a recognition that even the democratic will of the people is subordinate, in principle, to the commands of God as perceived in the individual conscience, and that in such a nation, with such a commitment, totalitarian tyranny is a philosophical impossibility.[140] As Madison put the point:

> Before any man can be considered as a member of Civil Society, he must be considered as a subject of the Governor of the Universe: And if a member of Civil Society, who enters into

---

[138] Federalist 44 (Madison) in Clinton Rossiter, ed, *The Federalist Papers* 280, 282–83 (Mentor, 1961).

[139] See Max Lerner, *Constitution and Court as Symbols*, 46 Yale L J 1290, 1294–95 (1937); Sanford Levinson, *"The Constitution" in American Civil Religion*, 1979 Supreme Court Review 123, 123–24.

[140] Michael W. McConnell, *The Origins and Historical Understanding of Free Exercise of Religion*, 103 Harv L Rev 1409, 1516 (1990).

any subordinate Association, must always do it with a reservation of his duty to the general authority; much more must every
man who becomes a member of any particular Civil Society, do
it with a saving of his allegiance to the Universal Sovereign.[141]

Religion—the recognition of an authority higher than the state—
is thus central to the constraint of governmental power in both
Burke's England and Madison's America, though Burke accom-
plishes this by incorporating the spiritual authority into the constitution of the state while Madison does so by placing the conscience
of the individual above the civil authority. The two systems may
appear to be opposites, but the true opposite of both is the totalitarian system first introduced in France, where the state, embody-
ing the "general will," is the highest authority and both established
church and individual conscience are subjugated to it.

Burke's view of establishment illuminates his disagreement with
social contract theory, and thus with the more radical idea that
the people have the right, at any time, to alter or abolish their
form of government and to institute one more to their liking.[142]
God—not the people—is the ultimate "institutor and author and
protector of civil society."[143] God willed the state, and His will is
"the law of laws and the sovereign of sovereigns."[144] In a famous
passage of the *Reflections* seemingly addressed to Locke, Burke conceded that "Society is indeed a contract"—but that it "ought not
to be considered as nothing better than a partnership agreement
in a trade of pepper and coffee, calico, or tobacco, or some other
such low concern, to be taken up for a little temporary interest,
and to be dissolved by the fancy of the parties." It must be "looked
on with other reverence." It is "a partnership not only between
those who are living, but between those who are living, those who
are dead, and those who are to be born." The authority of the
sovereign—even the people—is constrained by the immutable order ordained by God. "Each contract of each particular state is

---

[141] James Madison, *Memorial and Remonstrance against Religious Assessments*, reprinted as
an appendix to *Everson v Board of Education*, 330 US 1, 64 (1947) (Rutledge dissenting).

[142] See Burke, *An Appeal from the New to the Old Whigs* (1791), in 4 *Works* 57, 120–21,
161–63, 183.

[143] Burke, *Reflections* at 86.

[144] Id.

but a clause in the great primeval contract of eternal society . . . according to a fixed compact sanctioned by the inviolable oath which holds all physical and all moral natures, each in their appointed place." This divine law, he wrote, is not subject to the "will" of the people, who "are bound to submit their will to that law." Thus, it is in a case of "the first and supreme necessity only, a necessity that is not chosen but chooses," that a people have the right to dissolve the bands of society.[145] The established church, in Burke's view, is nothing more than "our recognition of a seigniory paramount"[146]—a recognition, like that in the American Pledge of Allegiance, that the nation is "under God" and therefore limited and constrained in its use of power.

Thus, far from augmenting the authority of the sovereign, the established church in Burke's vision is a means of limiting power.

It is noteworthy that Burke's assessment of the effect of the establishment in England was shared by his philosophical *bête noire*, Jean-Jacques Rousseau—though Rousseau deplored what Burke celebrated. According to Rousseau, "the Kings of England have made themselves heads of the Church, . . . but this title has made them less its masters than its ministers; they have gained not so much the right to change it, as the power to maintain it."[147] Thus he concludes, to his disgust, that "[t]here are [ ] two powers, two Sovereigns, in England. . . ."[148] To Rousseau, unlike Burke, this division of authority between church and state is "clearly bad," because "all institutions that set man in contradiction to himself are worthless."[149] The point of a civil religion, to Rousseau, is to "unite[ ] the divine cult with love of the laws" and to "mak[e] country the object of the citizens' adoration."[150] To Burke it is to remind both the rulers and the people of the limitations of the law and the obligations of the nation to a higher and more permanent order.

---

[145] Id at 84–85.

[146] Id at 86.

[147] Jean Jacques Rousseau, *The Social Contract* 132 (E. P. Dutton, 1950) (G. D. H. Cole, trans).

[148] Id at 133.

[149] Id at 134.

[150] Id.

B. POLITICS AND RELIGION

The proper role of religion in the civil order was moral and constitutional, according to Burke, rather than political. He did not wish to see the church become involved in day-to-day politics or in political agitation on particular issues. He had no respect for what he called "political theologians and theological politicians."[151] "[P]olitics and the pulpit are terms that have little agreement," he said. "The cause of civil liberty and civil government gains as little as that of religion by this confusion of duties. . . . Surely the church is a place where one day's truce ought to be allowed to the dissensions and animosities of mankind."[152] Burke observed that preachers who enter the political realm frequently are "[w]holly unacquainted with the world in which they are so fond of meddling, and inexperienced in all its affairs on which they pronounce with so much confidence." The result, he said, is that "they have nothing of politics but the passions they excite."[153] This promotes the worst sort of ideological politics. On the other hand, he criticized those who, on the basis of "but superficial studies in the natural history of the human mind have been taught to look on religious opinions as the only cause of enthusiastic zeal and sectarian propagation."[154] There is "no doctrine whatever," he warned, "that is not capable of the very same effect."[155] Indeed, while recognizing that "[r]eligion is among the most powerful causes of enthusiasm,"[156] Burke more often treated religion as a source of restraint, stability, and order, and found the antireligious zealotry of the revolutionaries far more frightening.

These positions may be driven more by Burke's view of politics than Burke's view of religion, for to him politics was a matter of prudence, caution, and experience; reliance on principles and abstractions, divorced from "circumstances," is likely to produce op-

---

[151] Burke, *Reflections* at 10.

[152] Id at 10–11. See also Burke, *Speech on the Repeal of the Test and Corporation Acts* (Mar 2, 1790), in 28 *Parliamentary History* 432, 439 ("[H]e agreed with his right hon. friend that the church and the pulpit ought to be kept pure and undefiled, and that politics should not be adverted to in either. With equal propriety might theological discussions, he said, be taken up in that House, and questions solely religious be debated there.").

[153] Burke, *Reflections* at 11.

[154] Burke, *Letters on a Regicide Peace* (1796–97), in 5 *Works* 231, 361.

[155] Id.

[156] Id.

pression and folly.[157] A religiously informed politics is, by its nature, a principled politics: one in which statesmen will be distracted from the real world of the possible by aspirations of the ideal. As an explicit opponent of utopian politics, it is natural that Burke would resist the force of religion, as he did any other form of politics driven by ideological principle. By the same token, it is only natural that those who are engaged in the politics of social and moral reform will find the language of religion a powerful means for awakening national consciousness, and will disdain Burke's politics of prudential judgment and incremental change as an excuse for the status quo.

In his disdain for mixing "politics and the pulpit," Burke also revealed something of his understanding of the proper function of religion in human affairs: not as a set of prescriptions for government, but as a call to reflection and an antidote to politics based on intellectual pride or self-interest. To borrow language from social critic Christopher Lasch, religion is not "a set of comprehensive and unambiguous answers to ethical questions," but rather "encourag[es] believers at every step to question their own motives."[158] "The very essence of religion," according to Lasch, is a "spiritual discipline against self-righteousness."[159] This echoes Burke's claim that religion is necessary to counteract the "arrogance, and selfopinion," as well as the "lust of selfish will," of those who hold political power.[160]

In modern controversies over the legitimacy of expressly religious argument in the formation of public policy,[161] both sides might therefore draw support from Burke. On the one hand, Burke criticized efforts to draw specific public policy prescriptions from religion and to use instrumentalities of the church for political organizing. He would likely see the growth of religious political lobbies—whether of so-called "religious right," liberal "social gospel," or radical "liberation theology"—as a dangerous (though

---

[157] Burke, *Speech on the Petition of the Unitarians* (May 11, 1792), in 7 *Works* 39, 41.

[158] Christopher Lasch, *The Revolt of the Elites and the Betrayal of Democracy* 243, 16 (Norton, 1995).

[159] Id at 16.

[160] Burke, *Reflections* at 82, 83.

[161] See, for example, Kent Greenawalt, *Private Consciences and Public Reasons* (Oxford, 1995); Stephen L. Carter, *The Culture of Disbelief* (Basic Books, 1993).

hardly novel[162]) aspect of politics, as well as a divisive development within the church. On the other hand, Burke would be unlikely to agree with the theory—formerly espoused by the Supreme Court—that political division along religious lines is uniquely divisive, and hence that measures supported by religious groups are for that reason constitutionally questionable.[163] Religious politics are objectionable as a species of ideological politics, not because of any special issues of "church and state."

C. THE INDEPENDENCE OF THE ESTABLISHED CHURCH IN BURKE'S CONSTITUTION

Perhaps the most unusual feature of Burke's conception of the established church is that it must enjoy a large measure of independence from the government. This is unusual because with government support for religion usually comes government control; indeed, England had a long-standing practice (with the theological label of "Erastianism") of subordination of the church to the state.[164] This enables the state to use the church as a subsidiary instrument of social control and national unity. This is found, in its most extreme form, in Hobbes.[165] Burke, however, insisted (ahistorically) that the people of England have "made their church, like their king and their nobility, independent."[166] This independence is essential if the establishment is to perform its constitutional function, he explained, for "[r]eligion, to have any force on men's understandings, indeed to exist at all, must be supposed paramount to laws, and independent for its substance upon any human institution."[167] Moreover, it is essential that churches other than the established church be free to govern themselves: "Never

---

[162] See *McDaniel v Paty*, 435 US 618, 641 n 25 (1978) (Brennan concurring) ("[C]hurch and religious groups in the United States have long exerted powerful political pressures on state and national legislatures, on subjects as diverse as slavery, war, gambling, drinking, prostitution, marriage, and education.").

[163] *Lemon v Kurtzman*, 403 US 602, 622–23 (1971).

[164] See generally Weldon S. Crowley, *Erastianism in England to 1640*, 32 J Church & State 549 (1990).

[165] Thomas Hobbes, *Leviathan* ch 42–43 at 521–626 (Penguin, 1968) (originally published 1651) (C. B. Macpherson, ed).

[166] Burke, *Reflections* at 88.

[167] Burke, *Tract on the Popery Laws* (circa 1761), in 6 *Works* 299, 338.

were the members of one religious sect fit to appoint the pastors to another."[168]

Burke thought that a properly ordered state church should take its doctrinal bearings not from political determinations or theological theory, but from "the established opinions and prejudices of mankind."[169] The Anglican Church held its position in England by prescription; it was the embodiment of the religious experience of the English people over the centuries (as the Presbyterian Church was of the Scottish and the Roman Catholic of the Irish).[170] Burke's emphasis on prescription reflected the orthodox conviction that the truths of revelation are not open to revision by process of ordinary investigation and analysis: that the truths of religion must be eternal if they are to be recognized as truths. It was decidedly unorthodox, however, in locating authority not in biblical text (the Protestant view) or apostolic succession (the Catholic view), or even the government (the Erastian view), but in the slowly evolving opinions of the nation.

Recognition of prescriptive authority protects the church from rapid and improvident alteration and at the same time insulates it from the will of the sovereign. More particularly, prescription inhibits use of the church as an instrument of revolutionary tyranny. Although in theory Burke maintained that government has a "general superintending control over . . . the publicly propagated doctrines of men,"[171] he insisted that the conditions under which Parliament could properly exercise power over the doctrines of the Church of England were exceedingly rare. "As an independent church, professing fallibility, she has claimed a right of acting without the consent of any other; as a church, she claims, and has always exercised, a right of reforming whatever appeared amiss in her doctrine, her discipline, or her rites."[172] In support of this independence, Burke invoked the ancient medieval principle, devel-

---

[168] Edmund Burke, *Letter to a Peer of Ireland* (Feb 21, 1782), in 4 *Works* 217, 234.

[169] Burke, *Speech on the Petition of the Unitarians* (May 11, 1792), in 7 *Works* 39, 43.

[170] See *Letter from Edmund Burke to William Smith, Esq., on the Subject of Catholic Emancipation* (Jan 29, 1795), in 6 *Works* 361, 368; Burke, *Reflections* at 80. For Burke's famous defense of the principle of prescription in political affairs, see Edmund Burke, *Speech on a Motion for a Committee to Inquire into the State of the Representation of the Commons in Parliament* (May 7, 1782), in 7 *Works* 89, 94–97.

[171] Burke, *Speech on the Petition of the Unitarians* (May 11, 1792), in 7 *Works* 39, 41.

[172] Burke, *Speech on the Acts of Uniformity* (Feb 6, 1772), in 7 *Works* 3, 7.

oped in full form during the papacy of Gregory VII, of the "liberty of the Church."[173] The power of Parliament over the doctrines of the church is essentially declaratory rather than directive: to give legal force and recognition to doctrinal change arising from the institutional church itself or to correct "intolerable . . . abuse" recognized as such by the majority of the people, whose church it is.[174] It is better to tolerate "imperfection"—which will exist in all human institutions—than to use the power of the state to bring about frequent religious "alterations," which lead to "religious tumults and religious wars."[175]

Independence is attained in the English system by endowing the church with sufficient private property that it is dependent neither upon "the unsteady and precarious contribution of individuals" nor upon the vagaries of Parliamentary appropriation. "They [the English people] certainly never have suffered, and never will suffer, the fixed estate of the church to be converted into a pension, to depend on the treasury and to be delayed, withheld, or perhaps to be extinguished by fiscal difficulties. . . ."[176] As one dependent on the largesse of others would know, such fiscal difficulties "may sometimes be presented for political purposes."[177] If the clergy depended upon appropriations from the Parliament, rather than the security of earnings from the lands of the church, they would be subordinate to the civil authorities, and subject to their whim and control. Thus,

> [t]he people of England think that they have constitutional motives, as well as religious, against any project of turning their independent clergy into ecclesiastical pensioners of state. They tremble for their liberty, from the influence of a clergy depen-

---

[173] Id. On the "freedom of the church," see Harold J. Berman, *Law and Revolution: The Formation of the Western Legal Tradition* 88–99, 105 (Harvard, 1983).

[174] Burke, *Speech on the Acts of Uniformity* (Feb 6, 1772), in 7 *Works* 3, 10.

[175] Id at 10–11.

[176] Burke, *Reflections* at 88.

[177] Id. One might speculate that Burke's sensitivities on this score were heightened by his own experience. Early in his career, he resigned an official pension of £300 per year because it would have made him, in effect, a perpetual retainer to his then-employer, William Gerard Hamilton. Later in the same year, Burke unexpectedly inherited an estate of approximately the same value—an inheritance that secured his independence to the same extent that the earlier pension would have imperiled it. See MacKnight, 1 *Life and Times* at 177–83 (cited in note 16). Though no commentator has noted the connection, Burke's depiction of the situation of the church in the *Reflections* has a certain autobiographical flavor.

dent on the crown; they tremble for the public tranquillity from the disorders of a factious clergy, if it were made to depend upon any other than the crown.[178]

It was this aspect of the establishment—the independence of the church through its base of private property—that was the first major casualty of the Revolution in France.

It is therefore not so clear as it might at first appear that Burke's position was in opposition to that of the opponents of the proposed Virginia Assessment Bill in 1785. That bill would, in effect, have made clergy pensioners of the state. While Burke presumably would not have agreed with Madison and Jefferson in their argument that the assessment would violate the conscience of the taxpayer, he might well have agreed with their equally important argument that the assessment would undermine the independence and vitality of the church. A Baptist declaration against religious assessments observed that if the state provided a "Support for Preachers of the Gospel," this would give the state a "Right to *regulate* and *dictate to;* it may judge and determine *who* shall preach; *when* and *where* they shall preach; and *what* they must preach."[179] That was precisely what Burke wished to avoid; perhaps he would have suggested that the assessment be shelved in favor of endowing the churches with public lands—the approach taken by the federal government in the Northwest Ordinance.

It was, I think, the independence of the church rather than its financial needs that principally underlay Burke's refusal to leave the church solely to the voluntary support of its members, as in America. To be sure, Burke tended to assume that the motivation for cutting the church off from public support was hostility to its mission: "[t]hey who think religion of no importance to the state," he said, "have abandoned it to the conscience or caprice of the individual; they make no provision for it whatsoever, but leave every club to make, or not, a voluntary contribution towards its support, according to their fancies."[180] But as an economic proposition, it is debatable that public financial support is in the interest

---

[178] Burke, *Reflections* at 88.

[179] *Declaration of the Virginia Association of Baptists* (Dec 25, 1776), in Julian P. Boyd, ed, 1 *The Papers of Thomas Jefferson* 660, 661 (Princeton, 1950) (emphasis in original).

[180] *First Letter from Edmund Burke to Sir Hercules Langrishe* (Jan 3, 1792), in 4 *Works* 241, 257.

of the church. Adam Smith made the plausible economic argument that ministers of the gospel who "depend altogether for their subsistence upon the voluntary contributions of their hearers" were likely to be superior in "[t]heir exertion, their zeal and industry," to those who derive their support from a "fund to which the law of their country may entitle them," whether it be a "landed estate, a tythe or land tax, or [an] established salary or stipend."[181] Burke was a sophisticated student of economics, whose thinking paralleled and in some respects anticipated Smith's work.[182] If creation of incentives for "zeal and industry" were all there were to it, Burke likely would have been forced to agree with Smith. The problem, from Burke's perspective, was that a voluntary system renders the clergyman dependent on the popularity and regard of his parishioners. From the perspective of his episcopal ecclesiology, this is no better than dependence on the political authorities. In America, where most Protestants adhered to some form of congregational ecclesiology, they would naturally be less concerned with this consequence of voluntarism.

There is reason to believe that Burke's (and Rousseau's) portrayal of the independence of the Church of England during this period was greatly exaggerated. Appointment of church officers and control over church benefices could hardly fail to give the government effective control. One historian has commented that "at no other time [than the eighteenth century] was the influence of state over church so great. . . . The privileged clergy were an integral part of the extravagant patronage network which dictated how England was governed, and high office in the church was determined by political considerations."[183] Burke's failure to acknowledge this situation is particularly striking in light of his criticism of the King's use of favors and offices to dominate the Parliament.[184] The *Reflections* must be understood as Burke's portrayal

---

[181] Adam Smith, V *An Inquiry into the Nature and Causes of the Wealth of Nations* 740–41 (Random House, 1937) (originally published 1776). Madison adopted this argument in paragraph 7 of his *Memorial and Remonstrance,* reprinted as an appendix to *Everson,* 330 US at 63, 67–68 (Rutledge dissenting), and the experience of religious vitality in America would seem to bear out Smith's prediction. See Gary M. Anderson, *Mr. Smith and the Preachers: The Economics of Religion in "The Wealth of Nations,"* 96 J Pol Econ 1066 (1988).

[182] See Donald Barrington, *Edmund Burke as an Economist,* 21 Economica 252 (1954).

[183] Eric J. Evans, *The Contentious Tithe: The Tithe Problem and English Agriculture, 1750–1850* 2 (Routledge, 1976).

[184] See, for example, Edmund Burke, *Speech on the Plan for Economical Reform* (Feb 11, 1780), in 2 *Works* 265.

of the ideal type of the English constitution, often in romantic and exaggerated terms—not as a hardheaded analysis of the realities.

Burke's insistence on the independence of the church is one point in common with American constitutional principles. The Supreme Court has stated that "religious organizations . . . [have] power to decide for themselves, free from state interference, matters of church government as well as those of faith and doctrine."[185] But for Burke, church independence was a matter of "equitable discretion" rather than legal right.[186] He did not deny that Parliamentary interference with church doctrine would be "most legal," but argued only that it would be "unwise or unwarrantable."[187] From an American perspective, it seems dubious to suppose that an established church, dependent on the equitable discretion of the government, could ever have the degree of independence Burke deemed necessary.

D. TOLERATION, COERCION, AND ESTABLISHMENT

Burke presupposed that an established church could be tolerant and, for the most part, noncoercive. "I am persuaded that toleration, so far from being an attack upon Christianity, becomes the best and surest support that possibly can be given to it," Burke declared.[188] Burke's established church was one that had made peace with Roman Catholicism,[189] allowed persons of various doctrinal persuasion to "live quietly under the same roof,"[190] and had embraced toleration as "a part of Christianity."[191] In this, Burke

---

[185] *Kedroff v St. Nicholas Cathedral*, 344 US 94, 116 (1952).

[186] Burke, *Speech on the Petition of the Unitarians* (May 11, 1792), in 7 *Works* 39, 42.

[187] Id.

[188] Burke, *Speech on a Bill for the Relief of Protestant Dissenters* (Mar 17, 1773), in 7 *Works* 21, 25. There is some reason to doubt that the tolerant establishment in Britain was, in actuality, as tolerant as Burke suggested it could be. See Jonathan Bush, *"Include Me Out": Some Lessons of Religious Toleration in Britain*, 12 Cardozo L Rev 881 (1991). But then, it was not until the 1840s that Britain could be said to have adopted Burke's recommendation for extending toleration to Catholics and Jews. See Henriques, *Religious Toleration* at 4–5, 136–205 (cited in note 2).

[189] Burke, *Reflections* at 79 ("Violently condemning neither the Greek nor the Armenian, nor, since heats are subsided, the Roman system of religion, we prefer the Protestant . . . . ").

[190] Burke, *Speech on a Bill for the Relief of Protestant Dissenters* (Mar 17, 1773), in 7 *Works* 21, 29.

[191] Id at 25.

can be seen as the voice of the road not taken in America, for at the time of the adoption of the First Amendment, almost half the states had some form of established church, all of which attempted to combine official support for religion with broad toleration and respect for diversity of sects.[192] By the 1830s, this attempt had been abandoned, and disestablishmentarianism prevailed in every state, later becoming a principle of national constitutional law through the Fourteenth Amendment.[193] Most modern American commentators (myself included) tend to assume that a prohibition on establishments is necessary as a backstop for full freedom of religion (whether or not disestablishment serves other, more institutional, values). Burke challenges that assumption by linking establishment together with toleration. "Zealous as I am for the principle of an establishment," he said, "I would have toleration a part of establishment, as a principle favorable to Christianity, and as a part of Christianity."[194] This meant that the establishment could not use direct coercion against Dissenters with regard to matters of conscience. In this, Burke resembles modern American commentators (and jurists) who interpret the Establishment Clause as directed primarily, if not exclusively, at the evil of religious coercion.

In part, Burke's rejection of direct coercion as an instrument of the established church was connected to his general advocacy of toleration, which will be discussed in greater detail in the next section. He wrote that "[i]f ever there was anything to which, from reason, nature, habit, and principle, I am totally averse, it is persecution for conscientious difference in opinion."[195] Perhaps more importantly, however, Burke maintained that persecution could undermine—but could not effectually support—religion. If it is the purpose of the establishment to promote religion, he maintained, coercive means would be counterproductive. In the *Tract on the Popery Laws*, he denied

---

[192] See McConnell, 103 Harv L Rev at 1436–37, 1455–58 (cited in note 140). Burke's views bear a strong resemblance to those of Joseph Story. See Joseph Story, *Commentaries on the Constitution of the United States* § 988 at 700 (Carolina, 1987) (originally published 1833).

[193] See Kurt T. Lash, *The Second Adoption of the Establishment Clause: The Incorporation of the Nonestablishment Principle*, 28 Ariz St L J (forthcoming 1996).

[194] Burke, *Speech on a Bill for the Relief of Protestant Dissenters* (Mar 17, 1773), in 7 *Works* 21, 25.

[195] Burke, *Speech on the Acts of Uniformity* (Feb 6, 1772), in 7 *Works* 3, 10.

that it is in a man's moral power to change his religion whenever his convenience requires it. If he be beforehand satisfied
that your opinion is better than his, he will voluntarily come
over to you, and without compulsion, and then your law would
be unnecessary; but if he is not so convinced, he must know
it is his duty in this point to sacrifice his interest here to his
opinion of his eternal happiness, else he could have in reality
no religion at all.[196]

As Conor Cruise O'Brien has pointed out, this passage has a "poi-
gnant ring," in light of the probable fact that Burke's father was
one of those who betrayed his "duty" by sacrificing his "opinion
of his eternal happiness" to the necessitudes of legal practice—
and that Burke himself could pursue his political career only on
account of that betrayal.[197] Perhaps that is why, in a letter to his
son written thirty years after he wrote the *Tract,* Burke stated:

Strange it is, but so it is, that men, driven by force from their
habits in one mode of religion, have, by contrary habits, under
the same force, often quietly settled in another. They suborn
their reason to declare in favor of their necessity. Man and his
conscience cannot always be at war. If the first races have not
been able to make a pacification between the conscience and
the convenience, their descendants come generally to submit
to the violence of the laws, without violence to their minds.[198]

This, too, has an autobiographical ring, perhaps more authentic
than the first—and more realistic. It is hard to deny that government power, executed prudently and effectively, can have an influence on opinion. But this insight made Burke all the more opposed to religious persecution, such as he witnessed in Ireland.
The Penal Laws were not devised to encourage conversion to Anglicanism, Burke pointed out, but solely to encourage apostasy
from Catholicism. "What do the Irish statutes?" he asked. "They
do not make a conformity to the *established* religion, and to its
doctrines and practices, the condition of getting out of servitude.
No such thing. Let three millions of people but abandon all that
they and their ancestors have been taught to believe sacred, and
to forswear it publicly in terms the most degrading, scurrilous, and

---

[196] Burke, *Tract on the Popery Laws* (circa 1761), in 6 *Works* 299, 335.

[197] O'Brien, *The Great Melody* at 42–43 (cited in note 13).

[198] *Letter from Edmund Burke to Richard Burke, Esq. on Protestant Ascendancy in Ireland*
(1793), in 6 *Works* 285, 395.

indecent for men of integrity and virtue, and to abuse the whole of their former lives, and to slander the education they have received, and nothing more is required of them."[199] The "deeper evil," Burke perceived, was not persecution, but that the persecution was purely destructive.[200] The Protestant Ascendancy in Ireland had this in common with the atheist philosophers of France and the Radical Dissenters of England: in each case, the object is not to convert the people to a better and truer religion, but to destroy traditional religious faith and leave in its place only a "dreadful void."[201] He deemed it "madness and folly" to drive men "from any *positive* religion whatever into the irreligion of the times, and its sure concomitant principles of anarchy."[202]

Burke thus rejected coercion as a means of maintaining the establishment. This meant that government power over religion was limited; it could give support and encouragement to beliefs that already were widely held, but could not impose beliefs on an unwilling populace. "Religion," he said, "is not believed because the laws have established it, but it is established because the leading part of the community have previously believed it to be true."[203] He nonetheless recognized that "men must believe their religion upon some principle or other, whether of education, habit, theory, or authority."[204] One important means of supporting religion is through education. He noted that "[o]ur education is in a manner wholly in the hands of ecclesiastics, and in all stages from infancy to manhood." By this means, "we attach our gentlemen to the church."[205] Burke thus allowed government to use its prestige and its resources to promote religion, and to give special status to the church established by law, but not to punish those who refused to conform or to penalize those who sought spiritual sustenance in another denomination. "[T]oleration," he wrote, "does not exclude national preference, either as to modes, or opinions; and all

---

[199] Id at 396 (emphasis in original).

[200] Id at 393–94.

[201] Id at 395.

[202] Burke, *Letter on the Affairs of Ireland* (1797), in 6 *Works* 413, 426 (emphasis in original).

[203] Burke, *Tract on the Popery Laws* (circa 1761), in 6 *Works* 299, 338.

[204] *Letter from Edmund Burke to Richard Burke, Esq. on Protestant Ascendancy in Ireland* (1793), in 6 *Works* 385, 395.

[205] Burke, *Reflections* at 87.

the lawful and honest means which may be used for the support of that preference."[206]

While these forms of "preference" may be far less oppressive than overt persecution, however, it remains true that they involve coercion of a sort, especially the coercion of taxation, which has been at the forefront of American controversies over church and state. Burke's position on the coercive aspects of the establishment was less than satisfactory. The right of the church to compel payment of tithes, for example, was the most irksome and unpopular aspect of the establishment during this period, and did more to bring the church into conflict and disrepute with the ordinary people of England than any other.[207] The tithe was in effect a tax, typically a tenth, on agricultural production and sometimes on the fruits of commerce or labor, with numerous and chaotic exceptions resting on custom, precedent, statute, and case law. Far from uniting the people and fostering respect for the divine representatives on earth, the tithing system led to widespread public disaffection and an appearance (if not the reality) of clerical oppressiveness.[208] It could not have escaped Burke's attention that this system was inimical to his vision of the role of the church. His only direct comments on the tithe, in a letter to his son, evinced great sympathy for Irish farmers who resisted the exaction.[209] Burke presumably found it difficult to attack the tithing system outright, however, for in legal form the tithes were an appurtenance of real property, of ancient provenance, not much different in their legal standing than any other nonpossessory property interest.[210] Thus, in his defense of the establishment we may perceive a discreet silence about the tithe. Instead, he argued optimistically that a greater security of the real property of the church might render

---

[206] Letter from Edmund Burke to William Burgh (Feb 9, 1775), in 3 Correspondence 110, 112.

[207] See generally Evans, The Contentious Tithe (cited in note 183).

[208] It was also an inefficient and counterproductive tax, as it discouraged both the improvements of the landlord and the cultivation of the farmer, as Adam Smith pointed out. Smith, V The Wealth of Nations at 789. Given Burke's attention to issues of public economics, and general agreement with Smith on such matters, it is likely that he was aware of this critique.

[209] Letter from Edmund Burke to Richard Burke, Esq. on Protestant Ascendancy in Ireland (1793), in 6 Works 385, 399–400.

[210] Evans, The Contentious Tithe at 8–9, 17 (cited in note 183). About one-third of the rights to tithes were owned by private persons, most of them derived from the sale of monastic properties at the time of Henry VIII. Id at 12, 17.

the collection of tithes less vital: "I heartily wish to see the Church secure in such possessions as will not only enable her ministers to preach the Gospel with ease, but of such a kind as will enable them to preach it with its full effect, so that the pastor shall not have the inauspicious appearance of a tax-gatherer."[211] So, Burke "wished" for an alternative, but made no protest against the tithe.

As with the issue of religious participation in politics, various positions in the American controversy over the importance of "coercion" as an aspect of establishment[212] can draw some support from Burke. Those who hold that coercion is a necessary element in finding an unconstitutional establishment will agree with Burke's position that coercion, rather than endorsement or general support, is the evil to be avoided. Those who hold that noncoercive government action can constitute an establishment can point out that Burke's advocacy of a noncoercive establishment precisely proves their point. And still others can point to Burke's ambivalence about tithes and imprecision in the use of the term "coercion" to show that the very meaning of "coercion" is too uncertain to be a useful category for deciding whether there is impermissible government support of religion.

E. WHY BURKE AND THE AMERICANS REACHED DIFFERENT CONCLUSIONS ON THE RELATION BETWEEN CHURCH AND STATE

What accounts for the difference between Burke and the Americans regarding the separation of church and state? Differences in circumstances surely account for a large part of the difference. But there are reasons of a more theoretical nature, as well.

First, a central tenet of the American rights tradition (especially under the First Amendment) is what one commentator calls the "postulate of distrust."[213] As Jefferson wrote in the *Kentucky Resolutions:*

---

[211] Edmund Burke, *Speech on Dormant Claims of the Church* (Feb 17, 1772), in 7 *Works* 137, 142. Burke's optimism had some basis in fact: during the last half of the eighteenth century, there was a "decisive shift in the source of income of many of the better endowed clergy" from tithes to direct ownership of land. Evans, *The Contentious Tithe* at 8 (cited in note 183).

[212] See *Board of Education of Kiryas Joel v Grumet*, 114 S Ct 2481, 2499 (1994) (O'Connor concurring); *Lee v Weisman*, 505 US 577, 587, 592–97 (1992); *County of Allegheny v ACLU*, 492 US 573, 659–62 (1989) (Kennedy concurring in part).

[213] Richard A. Epstein, *Property, Speech, and the Politics of Distrust*, in Geoffrey R. Stone, Richard A. Epstein, and Cass R. Sunstein, eds, *The Bill of Rights in the Modern State* 41, 48 (Chicago, 1992).

[I]t would be a dangerous delusion were a confidence in the men of our choice to silence our fears for the safety of our rights; that confidence is every where the parent of despotism; free government is founded in jealousy, and not in confidence; it is jealousy, and not confidence, which prescribes limited constitutions to bind down those whom we are obliged to trust with power.[214]

On much the same logic, Madison, in his *Memorial and Remonstrance against Religious Assessments*, wrote that

it is proper to take alarm at the first experiment on our liberties. We hold this prudent jealousy to be the first duty of citizens, and one of [the] noblest characteristics of the late Revolution. The freemen of America did not wait till usurped power had strengthened itself by exercise, and entangled the question in precedents. They saw all the consequences in the principle, and they avoided the consequences by denying the principle.[215]

To Burke, such an attitude would seem pathological. It is not possible to achieve the beneficent purposes of government if the very potential for abuse is treated as a reason for withdrawal of confidence. "You can hardly state to me a case to which legislature is the most confessedly competent, in which, if the rules of benignity and prudence are not observed, the most mischievous and oppressive things may not be done."[216] There is no alternative to confidence. It is "a moral and virtuous discretion, and not any abstract theory of right, which keeps governments faithful to their ends."[217] Questions of abuse of power should be examined in light of context and circumstance—and not rigid and acontextual principles. He therefore insisted that toleration should be understood not as a matter of universal human rights, but as "a part of moral and political prudence."[218] Burke maintained that the government should pursue a broad policy of toleration, reserving to itself the authority to intervene in cases of genuine danger to the "peace,

---

[214] *Kentucky Resolutions* (Nov 10, 1798), in Philip B. Kurland and Ralph Lerner, 5 *The Founders' Constitution* 131, 133 (Chicago, 1987).

[215] Madison, *Memorial and Remonstrance*, reprinted as an appendix to *Everson*, 330 US at 65 (Rutledge dissenting).

[216] Burke, *Speech on the Petition of the Unitarians* (May 11, 1792), in 7 *Works* 39, 42.

[217] Id.

[218] *First Letter from Edmund Burke to Sir Hercules Langrishe* (Jan 3, 1792), in 4 *Works* 241, 258.

order, liberty, and . . . security" of society.[219] He judged claims for toleration on their individual merits, in light of "the peculiar and characteristic situation of a people," and his "knowledge of their opinions, prejudices, habits, and all the circumstances that diversify and color life."[220] He adhered to this approach not only with regard to the Unitarians, whom he distrusted, but with regard to the Irish Catholics, whom he did not. Thus, in arguing for representation of Catholics in the Irish Parliament, he insisted that "I do not put the thing on a question of right," that "the whole question comes before Parliament as a matter for its prudence," and that the issue was one of "discretion."[221]

Americans had no such reticence about framing issues in terms of rights. Despite wide disagreement on questions of establishment, there was seemingly universal consensus that liberty of conscience or the free exercise of religion was a natural and inalienable right.[222] Where Burke's approach was flexible and contextual, allowing a prudent discretion to government officials to evaluate the facts of the case, the Madisonian-Jeffersonian ideal was driven by articulated principle and a pervasive distrust of government. In this, Burke resembles certain Justices on the modern Supreme Court, who eschew the discovery or articulation of any general principles to guide decision making in the church-state area, in favor of contextual, fact-specific decision making.[223] This gives government and courts more latitude to adjust policies in light of

---

[219] Burke, *Speech on the Petition of the Unitarians* (May 11, 1792), in 7 *Works* 39, 44.

[220] Id at 45.

[221] *First Letter from Edmund Burke to Sir Hercules Langrishe* (Jan 3, 1792), in 4 *Works* 241, 292. Similarly, in an essay entitled *On the State of Ireland*, written for Secretary of State Henry Dundas, Burke wrote, speaking for the Catholic Committee:

> [T]he Roman Catholics ask a share in the privilege of election; not as a matter of speculative right, not upon general principles of liberty, or as a conclusion from any given premises, either of natural or even of constitutional right. They ask it as a protection, and a requisite security which they now have not, for the exercise of legal right. They ask it from a practical sense of the evils they feel by being excluded from it. It is necessary for the free enjoyment of their industry and property, to secure a fair dispensation of justice, both criminal and civil and to secure them that just estimation and importance, without which, in human tribunals, they cannot obtain it.

4 *Correspondence of the Right Honourable Edmund Burke* 65, 67 (F. & J. Kivington, 1844).

[222] See McConnell, 103 Harv L Rev at 1455–56 (cited in note 140).

[223] See *Rosenberger v Rector & Visitors, Univ Va*, 115 S Ct 2512, 2526 (1995) (O'Connor concurring).

circumstance, rather than to adopt determinate "principles" to cabin the discretion of court or legislature.

Second, Burke could not share the assumption, common among Americans, that there is a fundamental distinction between matters of spiritual and temporal concern. The ideal of "separation of church and state" presupposes that we can—in Locke's words—"distinguish exactly the business of civil government from that of religion."[224] This is reflected in Jefferson's metaphorical "Wall of Separation."

But what if we cannot? What if "civil government" and "religion" are both legitimately involved in many of the same things? Burke claimed that the government cannot be "remote and indifferent" to anything that has an effect on the "concerns of men."[225] At the same time, Burke described religion as "one great source of civilization amongst us" and as "the basis of civil society."[226] "If religion only related to the individual, and was a question between God and the conscience, it would not be wise, nor in my opinion equitable, for human authority to step in."[227] But, Burke wrote, "[i]t is the interest, and it is the duty, and because it is the interest and the duty, it is the right of government to attend much to opinions; because, as opinions soon combine with passions, even when they do not produce them, they have much influence on actions."[228] It is therefore impossible for the people as a whole to lay down as a "universal proposition" that "nothing relative to religion was your concern."[229]

At the time of the American Founding, it may have appeared that the limited peacekeeping functions of the state could be distinguished from the more elevated functions of the church. Whether that was an accurate perception even then may be debated, but as the modern state has expanded its attentions to more and more aspects of life, previously private and frequently religious, Burke's position more closely resembles the reality. What

---

[224] John Locke, *A Letter Concerning Toleration*, in 6 *The Works of John Locke* 5, 9 (Thomas Davison, 1823).

[225] Burke, *Speech on the Petition of the Unitarians* (May 11, 1792), in 7 *Works* 39, 43.

[226] Burke, *Reflections* at 80, 79.

[227] Burke, *Speech on the Petition of the Unitarians* (May 11, 1792), in 7 *Works* 39, 48.

[228] Id at 44.

[229] Id at 46.

belongs to the governmental side of the Wall, and what to the religious? Education? Public health? Domestic relations? Charity? Character building? Art? The just conduct of war? Modern commentators, in contrast to the Jeffersons and Madisons of the Founding, typically accept as necessary and inevitable that governments will intervene to mold the beliefs and attitudes of the people, on everything from smoking to gender bias.[230] No longer does it seem heterodoxical to say that government should "attend much to opinions." But if Burke is right and Locke is wrong—if it is *not* possible to "distinguish exactly the business of civil government from that of religion"—how can a constitutional principle based on "separation" of the religious and civil spheres be made to work?

The difference here lies not so much in Burke's conception of the established church, but in his broader conception of government. There is a close, but generally unrecognized, connection between the idea of the "Wall of Separation" and the idea of a radically limited government. Once government shakes off its limited role and concerns itself with the general welfare of the people, including their cultural and intellectual lives, it has leapt the "Wall" and entered the traditional sphere of religion. In contrast to many of our Founders, Burke had a more modern conception of the jurisdiction of the state, which did not permit him the easy answer of a "Wall of Separation." If the government is "a partnership in all science; a partnership in all art; a partnership in every virtue and in all perfection,"[231] then it necessarily will be conveying a collective teaching on science, art, virtue, and perfection (whether we label the teaching a "religion" or not). It follows not that an establishment is desirable, but that it is inescapable. *Some* sort of opinions necessarily will guide the state in its "superintending control over . . . the publicly propagated doctrines of men."[232] If the Jeffersonian-Madisonian ideal of the limited state is abandoned as naive or outmoded, then the serious questions become how to protect against arbitrary or tyrannical use of this power and how to respect the legitimate rights of those who dis-

---

[230] See, for example, Lawrence Lessig, *The Regulation of Social Meaning*, 62 U Chi L Rev 943 (1995).

[231] Burke, *Reflections* at 85.

[232] *Speech on the Petition of the Unitarians* (May 11, 1792), 7 *Works* 42.

agree with the official orthodoxy. Burke's prescription—to limit governmental power by encouraging it to adhere to teachings broadly accepted by the public, preserved through diffuse institutions largely independent of the central state, to restrict it to noncoercive means, and to give broad toleration to dissenters—could possibly be the least dangerous alternative.

III. TOLERATION

As has already been seen, Burke supported establishment but had a commitment to toleration that was equally strong if not stronger. This was an atypical stance for his day. At risk of oversimplification, the positions on establishment and toleration at that time may be divided into three camps.[233] First were the evangelical separationists—a position that barely existed in Britain at this time, but was highly influential in America. Evangelical separationists in America, led by the Baptists, opposed the establishment both because they deemed it erroneous on theological grounds and because they thought government support rendered the clergy subservient to the state; and they supported the widest possible toleration or free exercise in matters of religion because they considered religion to be the central and most important activity of life. Second were the secularists—relatively rare in America, apart from Jefferson, but influential in England. Led by so-called "Rational Dissenters" like Richard Price and Joseph Priestly, they were superficially aligned with the evangelical separationists—both opposed the establishment—but the secularists sought to reduce the role of revealed religion in public life and generally believed that scientific ideas should supplant the superstition and nonrationalistic religion of the past. While the evangelical separationists stressed that religion is too sacred to be subject to human interference, the secularists maintained that religion is—or should be—irrelevant to the state. Third were the establishmentarians, such as Lord North and William Blackstone. By Burke's day, it was *de rigueur* to recognize a degree of toleration as part of the establishment; but this toleration was typically grudging, and held to a nar-

---

[233] These positions are set forth in greater detail and nuance in Henriques, *Religious Toleration* (cited in note 2).

row compass. In actual disputes over the extension of toleration, the establishmentarians were almost invariably opposed.[234]

A. TOLERATION OF CATHOLICS AND NON-CHRISTIANS

It should be noted that adherents of none of these positions had much enthusiasm for toleration of Roman Catholics, the most burning religious issue of the era. To the evangelicals, Catholicism represented the gravest of theological error; to the secularists and Rational Dissenters, Catholicism was superstitious and unenlightened;[235] to the establishmentarians, the constitutional status of the Protestant religion was a central tenet of the Glorious Revolution. It was widely held that the Glorious Revolution of 1688—the political heritage of Burke's Whig Party—was a victory over Papism, and thus that the suppression of Catholicism was part of the fundamental constitutional fabric of the realm, at least as long as Catholics maintained their potentially subversive loyalty to a foreign power, the Pope in Rome.[236] Antipathy toward Papists was widespread, and was one of the few attitudes that evangelical separationists, secularists, and establishmentarians had in common.

The perennial argument against admission of Catholics to the rights of citizens was that they were disloyal to the British government—that because of either their lingering loyalties to the Stuart line or their allegiance to the Pope in Rome, they might be ex-

---

[234] See generally G. U. Bennett, *The Tory Crisis in Church and State 1688–1730* (1975). Opposition to the extension of toleration proceeded along two dimensions. First, establishmentarians were disposed to support toleration only for those whose ideas were reasonably close to the national consensus. Thus, dissenting clergy who affirmed thirty-six of the Thiry-Nine Articles were freely permitted to preach, while those who dissented more fundamentally were (at least in theory) not. This was the issue involved in Burke's *Speech on a Bill for the Relief of Protestant Dissenters* (Mar 17, 1773), in 7 *Works* 21. Second, tolerant establishmentarians generally supported extension of the protection of natural rights to Dissenters, but resisted extension of the equal benefits of government action. See Philip A. Hamburger, *Equality and Diversity: The Eighteenth-Century Debate about Equal Protection and Equal Civil Rights*, 1992 Supreme Court Review 295, 318–22.

[235] As late as 1787, Dissenters' propaganda excused the Test Act as a safeguard against Popery, and sought to show that no such safeguard was needed against Protestants. See Henriques, *Religious Toleration* at 91 (cited in note 2). Conor Cruise O'Brien has pointed out that Burke's fury at Richard Price was driven partly by the latter's anti-popery rhetoric. *Great Melody* at 395.

[236] See Henriques, *Religious Toleration* (cited in note 2) at 57, 77–79 (describing the Tory theory that the Corporation and Test Acts were "fundamental laws" of the Union). Burke summarizes this argument in his *First Letter to Sir Hercules Langrishe* (Jan 3, 1792), in 4 *Works* 241, 245, and refutes it, id at 257–70.

pected to side with the Catholic powers of Europe in conflict with
the King. As Blackstone argued:

> If once they [Papists] could be brought to renounce the su-
> premacy of the pope, they might quietly enjoy their seven sac-
> raments, their purgatory, and auricular confession; their wor-
> ship of reliques and images; nay even their transubstantiation.
> But while they acknowledge a foreign power, superior to the
> sovereignty of the kingdom, they cannot complain if the laws
> of that kingdom will not treat them upon the footing of good
> subjects.[237]

These suspicions were all the stronger with regard to the Catholics
of Ireland, who might, in addition to any disloyalty arising from
their Catholicism, be expected to chafe against their subordination
to the English and to the Protestant ruling class.

Burke strenuously sought to refute these claims. Burke referred
to the idea of the Pope as a dangerous foreign power as a "commo-
dious bugbear"—an idea that, if it "were clearly brought forth and
defined, [ ] would meet with nothing but scorn and derision."[238]
He pointed to recent events in England and Canada to prove that
the Catholic citizens had "cast off all foreign views and connections" and had resolved to "stand or fall with their country."[239]
He could not, of course, deny that the Catholics of Ireland were
restive under the current regime, but the "real cause" of the disorders in Ireland was not their Catholicism; it was their persecution.
The Irish Popery Laws

> divided the nation into two distinct bodies, without common
> interest, sympathy, or connection. One of these bodies was to
> possess *all* the franchises, *all* the property, *all* the education:
> the other was to be composed of drawers of water and cutters
> of turf for them. Are we to be astonished, when, by the efforts
> of so much violence in conquest, and so much policy in regula-
> tion, continued without intermission for near an hundred years,
> we had reduced them to a mob . . . ?[240]

---

[237] Blackstone, 4 *Blackstone's Commentaries* at 55 (cited in note 39).

[238] *First Letter from Edmund Burke to Sir Hercules Langrishe* (Jan 3, 1792), in 4 *Works* 241,
280–81.

[239] Burke, *Speech at Bristol, Previous to the Election* (Sept 6, 1780), in 2 *Works* 365, 400
(describing the outpouring of Catholic support for the Crown during the American Revolution). See also *First Letter from Edmund Burke to Sir Hercules Langrishe* (Jan 3, 1792), in 4
Works 241, 304 (describing the loyalty of Canadian Catholic citizens).

[240] *First Letter from Edmund Burke to Sir Hercules Langrishe* (Jan 3, 1792), in 4 *Works* 241,
246–47.

Although Burke's most passionate commitment to toleration involved the Catholics of Ireland, he extended the principle to other
Dissenters from the established church as well. He advocated toleration for all of what he called "serious religion." He explained that

> [e]ven the man who does not hold revelation, yet who wishes
> that it were proved to him, who observes a pious silence with
> regard to it, such a man, though not a Christian, is governed
> by religious principles. Let him be tolerated in this country.
> Let it be but a serious religion, natural or revealed, take what
> you can get. Cherish, blow up the slightest spark: one day it
> may be a pure and holy flame.[241]

Burke attacked the hypocrisy of those who condemned the persecution of Protestants in Catholic France but excused the persecution of Catholics in Ireland. How could they "persuade themselves
that what was bad policy in France can be good in Ireland, or that
what was intolerable injustice in an arbitrary monarch becomes . . .
an equitable procedure in a country professing to be governed by
law"?[242] To Burke it was absurd to maintain "that the names of
Protestant and Papist can make any change in the nature of essential justice."[243] "Toleration is good for all, or it is good for
none."[244]

In his *First Letter to Sir Hercules Langrishe*, Burke wrote that
"[t]oleration, being a part of moral and political prudence, ought
to be tender and large. A tolerant government ought not to be
too scrupulous in its investigations, but may bear without blame,
not only very ill-grounded doctrines, but even many things that
are positively vices."[245] In 1775, Burke stated his desire to give
"full civil protection," including freedom of worship and religious
education, to "Jews Mahometans and even pagans."[246] In this, he
was more than fifty years ahead of his day. To be sure, Burke (like
others of his era) was not above the occasional anti-Semitic re-

---

[241] Burke, *Speech on a Bill for the Relief of Protestant Dissenters* (Mar 17, 1773), in 7 *Works*
21, 37.

[242] Burke, *Tract on the Popery Laws* (circa 1761), in 6 *Works* 299, 329–330.

[243] Id at 329.

[244] Burke, *Speech on a Bill for the Relief of Protestant Dissenters* (Mar 17, 1773), in 7 *Works*
21, 29.

[245] Reprinted in 4 *Works* 241, 258.

[246] *Letter from Edmund Burke to William Burgh* (Feb 9, 1775), in 3 *Correspondence* 110,
112.

mark,[247] and he undertook no specific Parliamentary action to repeal the laws against Judaism in England. But in Parliament he declared that the Jews are a people whom it was the special object of humanity to protect rather than abuse,[248] and in a letter to a Catholic friend, Burke commended the Austrian Emperor's extension of toleration to the Jews and indicated his support for such a measure in England—while opining that the nation was not yet ready for it, and that it could not pass without ministerial support.[249]

Burke devoted more than a decade of his life to fighting oppression in India, through his attacks on the East India Company and his prosecution of Warren Hastings. His principal efforts involved civil oppression and economic exploitation of the Indian people, but he did not fail to recognize and resist religious oppression as well. In a letter to a prominent English Protestant dissenter, Burke described his efforts against Hastings as "endeavoring . . . to relieve twenty Millions of Dissenters from the Church of England, in Asia from real grievances, which God forbid any of the Dissenters in Europe [should suffer]."[250] He inveighed against the East India Company's "indignities to the Indian Priesthood."[251] He studied Halhed's code of Hindu law intently in preparation for his case against Warren Hastings and—according to Charles James Fox—"spoke of the piety of the Hindoos with admiration, and of their holy religion and sacred functions with an awe bordering on devotion."[252] In his opening speech against Hastings, Burke stated: "We must not think to force [Hindus] into the narrow circle of our ideas; we must extend ours to take in their system of opinions and rites."[253]

---

[247] See Burke, *Reflections* at 42 (ugly comparison of French revolutionaries to "Jew brokers").

[248] Edmund Burke, *Speech on a Motion Relating to the Seizure and Confiscation of Private Property in the Island of St. Eustatius* (May 14, 1781), in 22 *Parliamentary History* 218, 223–26.

[249] See Mahoney, *Burke and Ireland* at 113 (cited in note 38).

[250] *Letter from Edmund Burke to Richard Bright* (May 8–9, 1789), in 5 *Correspondence* 470, 470.

[251] Henry Richard Lord Holland, I *Memoirs of the Whig Party* 5–6 (Longman, Brown, 1852).

[252] Id at 6.

[253] Edmund Burke, *Speech in Opening the Impeachment of Warren Hastings* (Feb 15, 1788), in 9 *Works* 327, 379.

Burke was, however, ambivalent about new religions. "The only faint shadow of difficulty" with regard to religious toleration, he wrote in his first work on the subject, the *Tract on the Popery Laws*, "is concerning the introduction of new opinions."[254] While new opinions may have been "favorable to the cause of truth," according to Burke, "[e]xperience has shown" that they are not "always conducive to the peace of society." Not only are new religious sects typically prone to "tumultuous and disorderly zeal," but they also are "the cause of the bitterest dissensions in the commonwealth" on account of their resistance to the present establishment.[255] While Burke did not ultimately find this to be a sufficient basis for persecution, he could understand why it might persuade "a man of sense and of integrity."[256] Some thirty years later, Burke's suspicion and distaste for new religions—this time the Unitarian Society—had only increased: "Old religious factions are volcanoes burnt out; on the lava and ashes and squalid scoriæ of old eruptions grow the peaceful olive, the cheering vine, and the sustaining corn. . . . But when a new fire bursts out, a face of desolations comes on, not to be rectified in ages."[257] Therefore, he said, "when men come before us, and rise up like an exhalation from the ground, they come in a questionable shape," and we must "try whether their intents be wicked or charitable, whether they bring airs from heaven or blasts from hell."[258]

B. BURKE'S ARGUMENTS FOR TOLERATION

To some extent, Burke's arguments for toleration resembled those typically offered in enlightened circles. Persecution was cruel, ineffective, hypocritical, and bad for business.[259] In typical Enlightenment fashion, Burke argued that "[i]t is not permitted to us to sacrifice the temporal good of any body of men to our

---

[254] Burke, *Tract on the Popery Laws* (circa 1761), in 6 *Works* 299, 336.

[255] Id.

[256] Id at 336–37.

[257] Burke, *Speech on the Petition of the Unitarians* (May 11, 1792), in 7 *Works* 39, 46.

[258] Id.

[259] On the latter point, see Burke, *Speech at Bristol, Previous to the Election* (Sept 6, 1780), in 2 *Works* 365, 406 (making argument that Catholics were among the "best manufacturers" in England and might be forced to emigrate to Holland if the Penal Laws were not reformed).

own ideas of the truth and falsehood of any religious opinions."[260] Burke expressed these points with his usual panache, but the substance of the arguments is not much different from that in other reformers of his era. Certainly, experience showed that the persecution of Catholics in Ireland was ineffectual: "Ireland, after almost a century of persecution, is at this hour full of penalties and full of Papists."[261] The effect of the Penal Laws was not to persuade, convert, or uplift, but merely to injure. "We found the people heretics and idolaters; we have, by way of improving their condition, rendered them slaves and beggars: they remain in all the misfortune of their old errors, and all the superadded misery of their recent punishment."[262]

Burke's advocacy of toleration, however, was antithetical to the Enlightenment project of secularization of society. For many advocates of toleration, this was part of the effort to reduce the power of "superstition" and to confine religion to the merely private. Burke, by contrast, advocated toleration as a means of fostering religion and enlarging its role in public life. In this, Burke had something in common with the Baptist and other evangelical advocates of religious freedom who were so influential in the movements for disestablishment and free exercise in the American states. Burke was well aware that some persons advocated toleration out of "a cold apathy, or indeed rather a savage hatred, to all Religion, and an avowed contempt of all those points on which we [Christians] differ, and on those about which we agree."[263] Jefferson predicted that the rise of liberty of conscience would bring about the decline of orthodox Christianity and usher in an era of rational religion.[264] Burke, by contrast, wrote that general toleration would "encrease real Zeal, Christian fervour, and pious emulation" and that it would never "introduce indifference."[265]

---

[260] Letter from Edmund Burke to Richard Burke, Esq., on Protestant Ascendancy in Ireland (1793), in 6 Works 385, 394.

[261] Burke, Tract on the Popery Laws (circa 1761), in 6 Works 299, 334.

[262] Id at 341.

[263] Letter from Edmund Burke to Thomas Hussey, in 8 Correspondence 245, 246.

[264] See Letter from Thomas Jefferson to Dr. Benjamin Waterhouse (June 26, 1822), in Paul Leicester Ford, ed, 12 The Works of Thomas Jefferson 243 (Knickerbocker, 1905); Letter from Thomas Jefferson to James Smith (Dec 8, 1822), in Adrienne Koch and William Peden, eds, The Life and Selected Writings of Thomas Jefferson 703 (Random House, 1944).

[265] Letter from Edmund Burke to William Burgh (Feb 9, 1775), in 3 Correspondence 110, 112.

Burke's advocacy of toleration was never based on the view that religion is unimportant or injurious. He maintained that "the glorious and distinguishing prerogative of humanity [is] that of being a religious creature,"[266] and was contemptuous of those who tolerated because of indifference: "[t]hat those persons should tolerate all opinions, who think none to be of estimation, is a matter of small merit. Equal neglect is not impartial kindness."[267] Burke is not like Jefferson, who based his toleration on the proposition that "it does me no injury for my neighbour to say there are twenty gods, or no god. It neither picks my pocket nor breaks my leg."[268] True toleration, Burke said, is the toleration of those who "think the dogmas of religion, though in different degrees, are all of moment, and that amongst them there is, as amongst all things of value, a just ground of preference. They favor, and therefore they tolerate."[269]

In some ways, therefore, Burke sounded more American than Jefferson did. The American struggle for religious freedom was led by religious enthusiasts rather than religious rationalists. The United States never associated religious freedom with anticlericalism, as in France. The emphasis here was always more on freedom *of* religion than on freedom *from* religion. But Burke's advocacy of toleration was not based on the same principles as that of the evangelical separationists. For the most part, the advocates of that position were sectarians, firmly convinced of the correctness of their theological position and imbued with a zeal for spreading the gospel as they understood it. For them, toleration was based on the theological principle that the moving force in the formation of Christian faith must be the calling of God (in the Calvinist camp) or the free will of the believer (in the Arminian camp)— but not the hand of government.[270] By contrast, Burke's toleration was ecumenical in spirit, based on the intrinsic worth of all reli-

---

[266] Burke, *Speech on a Bill for the Relief of Protestant Dissenters* (Mar 17, 1773), in 7 *Works* 21, 35.

[267] Burke, *Reflections* at 132.

[268] Thomas Jefferson, *Notes on the State of Virginia* 159 (Norton, 1955) (originally published 1787).

[269] Burke, *Reflections* at 132.

[270] See, for example, Issac Backus, *An Appeal to the Public for Religious Liberty* (1773), in Ellis Sandoz, ed, *Political Sermons of the American Founding Era 1730–1805* 327 (Liberty, 1991).

gious positions. True toleration, according to Burke, is based on the conviction that the "serious religion[s], natural or revealed,"[271] all share a common faith in the sovereignty of God and the immutable principles of morality and justice. The English, Burke said, "would reverently and affectionately protect all religions because they love and venerate the great principle upon which they all agree, and the great object to which they are all directed."[272] "[H]ave as many sorts of religion as you find in your country; there is a reasonable worship in them all."[273] Arguments for toleration were based more on an ecumenical evaluation of the worth of religion than on the inherent and sacred primacy of conscience.

As the French Revolution unfolded, Burke became alarmed at the connection between what he called "fanatical atheism"[274] and the spread of Jacobinism, which he considered the greatest of all threats to the constitution, to liberty, order, and religion, and all the more convinced that revealed religion is a vital protection against totalitarianism. He could not, therefore, view religion as a purely private matter, bereft of political significance, as Enlightenment reformers were wont to do. Rather, he developed a theory in which toleration was part of a general strategy, together with establishment, to maintain the social and cultural preconditions for limited government.

C. BURKE'S DISAVOWAL OF TOLERATION TO ATHEISTS

Like John Locke before him,[275] Burke disavowed toleration of atheists. "They are never, never to be supported, never to be tolerated."[276] Atheism, he maintained, was "the most horrid and cruel blow that can be offered to civil society."[277] Of all Burke's positions, this is the one that seems most foreign to American princi-

---

[271] Burke, *Speech on a Bill for the Relief of Protestant Dissenters* (Mar 17, 1773), in 7 *Works* 21, 37.

[272] Burke, *Reflections* at 132.

[273] Burke, *Speech on a Bill for the Relief of Protestant Dissenters* (Mar 17, 1773), in 7 *Works* 21, 36.

[274] Burke, *Letters on a Regicide Peace* (1796–97), in 5 *Works* 231, 363.

[275] See John Locke, *A Letter Concerning Toleration*, in 6 *The Works of John Locke* 1, 46–47 (cited in note 224).

[276] Burke, *Speech on a Bill for the Relief of Protestant Dissenters* (Mar 17, 1773), in 7 *Works* 21, 36.

[277] Id.

ples, the least defensible, the least consistent with a liberal society. In one of the more sensible statements in *Everson v Board of Education*, the Court declared that the state "cannot exclude individual Catholics, Lutherans, Mohammedans, Baptists, Jews, Methodists, Non-believers, Presbyterians, or the members of any other faith, *because of their faith, or lack of it*, from receiving the benefits of public welfare legislation."[278] In our tradition, protection of freedom of religion includes freedom not to believe. How can Burke's intolerance toward atheists be understood?

First, it is worth noting that acceptance of atheism as within the principle of freedom of religion is a nineteenth-century development, even in this country. In his studies of the Founders' views on religious liberty, Professor Philip Kurland found "no evidence that they were equally concerned with freedom for irreligion. Quite to the contrary, they sought to protect man's relation to his god."[279] Indeed, members of Congress engaged in drafting and proposing the Bill of Rights stated that they hoped "the amendment would be made in such a way as to secure the rights of conscience, and a free exercise of the rights of religion, but not to patronise those who professed no religion at all,"[280] and during the course of deliberating over constitutional exemptions from compulsory militia service it was said that "I do not mean to deprive [those who are religiously scrupulous in this respect] of any indulgence the law affords; my design is to guard against those who are of no religion."[281] It was not until the middle of the nineteenth century that courts began to recognize atheists and nonbelievers as having rights of religious freedom.[282]

Second, Burke made clear that he did not, and could not, support measures against nonbelievers on religious grounds, but only if they behaved as a political faction, threatening violence to the constitution. The only legitimate basis for restraint upon religious freedom, he said, is that "the person dissenting does not dissent from the scruples of ill-informed conscience, but from a party

---

[278] *Everson*, 330 US at 16 (emphasis in original).

[279] Philip B. Kurland, *The Origins of the Religion Clauses of the Constitution*, 27 Wm & Mary L Rev 839, 856 (1986).

[280] 1 *Annals of Congress* 730 (Aug 15, 1789) (remarks of Representative Huntington).

[281] Id at 767 (Aug 20, 1789) (remarks of Representative Scott).

[282] See Lash, 28 Ariz St L J (forthcoming 1996) (cited in note 193).

ground of dissension, in order to raise a faction in the state."[283] On the floor of Parliament, Burke read from the "political catechism" of the Unitarians to show that it "contained no precept of religion whatsoever," but was "one continued invective against kings and bishops."[284] He claimed that the religious assemblies of the Unitarians had been "turned into places of exercise and discipline for politicks; and for the nourishment of a party which seems to have contention and power much more than Piety for its Object," and which "is proceeding systematically, to the destruction of this Constitution in some of its essential parts."[285] Indeed, it was Burke's belief that atheists, if they could only seize political power as they had in France, would "not leave to religion even a toleration."[286] The goal of "fanatical" atheism is the "utter extirpation of religion."[287] The closest modern analogy is not to toleration of atheists, but to recognition of the Communist Party—a faction that, if it could seize power, would extirpate the freedoms of others.

Third, we should recognize that Burke's intemperate rhetoric against toleration of atheists was not connected with any program of actual persecution. Atheists were excluded from certain public and corporate offices, but in this they were treated no worse than any other Dissenters from the Church of England. Indeed, in some respects, atheists were in a less disadvantaged position than religious Dissenters (other than so-called "Orthodox Dissenters" who fell within the ambit of the Act of Toleration), since the latter could be punished for public acts of worship or preaching. No such strictures applied to atheists, since they did not engage in worship.[288] Indeed, it is not clear that the rights of atheists were

---

[283] Burke, *Speech on a Bill for the Relief of Protestant Dissenters* (Mar 17, 1773), in 7 *Works* 21, 30.

[284] Burke, *Speech on Repeal of the Test and Corporation Acts* (Mar 2, 1790), in 28 *Parliamentary History* 432, 436–37.

[285] *Letter from Edmund Burke to Richard Bright* (Feb 18, 1790), in 6 *Correspondence* 82, 83–84.

[286] Burke, *Speech on a Bill for the Relief of Protestant Dissenters* (Mar 17, 1773), in 7 *Works* 21, 37. See also Burke, *Speech on the Petition of the Unitarians* (May 11, 1792), 7 *Works* 39, 48.

[287] Burke, *Letters on a Regicide Peace* (1796–97), in 5 *Works* 231, 361–64.

[288] Burke commented on the fact that non-orthodox Dissenters were treated less favorably than atheists in his *Speech on a Bill for the Relief of Protestant Dissenters* (Mar 17, 1773), in 7 *Works* 21, 33–35.

dramatically different in Britain than the United States, even to-day. While atheism is often recognized as a "religion," it is un-likely that atheists could claim that they have any duties or de-mands arising from their nonbelief (which is not to say that they do not have moral duties arising from some nonreligious philo-sophical source, but that is not the same thing as to say that these arise from their religious beliefs). According, it is unlikely that atheists would have occasion to assert free exercise rights. For the most part, the religious freedom interests of atheists are protected not as a matter of free exercise, but as an aspect of nonestablish-ment—and for Establishment Clause purposes it is irrelevant what the nature of the claimant's beliefs (or lack thereof) may be. Thus, in this country, as in Burke's England, atheists have no significant rights in their capacity as atheists.

But these observations only mitigate the significance of the dif-ference between Burke and the modern American posture toward toleration of atheists. We must consider, as well, his justification. Burke's principal argument was that toleration is a form of benefit to Dissenters on account of the belief that all *"positive* religion"[289] has a certain worth, on account of its recognition of enduring prin-ciples of right and justice. Atheism, being mere negation, lacks this quality, and indeed fosters a spirit of anarchy.[290] He did not con-sider intolerance toward atheism as intolerance toward a reli-gion—but toward a denial of religion. Thus, he could say: "At the same time that I would cut up the very root of atheism, I would respect all conscience,—all conscience that is really such."[291] By his premises, therefore, exclusion of atheists and nonbelievers from toleration was not based on hatred or prejudice, but on legitimate differences. If toleration is extended to dissenting believers out of a recognition that their affirmative belief contributes to the com-mon good by reinforcing the ties of immutable justice and moral-ity, then there is no reason to treat mere unbelief, mere "nega-tion," in the same way. It may well be that certain affirmative philosophical beliefs held by atheists have a status that should be recognized as tantamount to religion,[292] but bare atheism, without

---

[289] Burke, *Letter on the Affairs of Ireland* (1797), in 6 *Works* 413, 426 (emphasis in original).

[290] Id.

[291] Burke, *Speech on a Bill for the Relief of Protestant Dissenters* (Mar 17, 1773), in 7 *Works* 21, 36.

[292] As the Supreme Court suggested in *Welsh v United States*, 398 US 333 (1970).

more, does not promote the habits of mind and spirit that entitle "serious religion" to a heightened degree of respect.

IV. Conclusion: The Connection between Toleration and Establishment

The central preoccupation of Burke's political thought is with the restraint of power. As Conor Cruise O'Brien has emphasized in his recent biography, the animating theme—what he calls, after Yeats, the "Great Melody"—of Burke's career was his opposition to the abuse of power: in the American colonies, Ireland, France, and India.[293] In each of these situations, men in authority over others, but not restrained by the authority of the law, exercised essentially unlimited power, to the detriment of those in whose names they were supposed to govern. To others, even to Burke's usual political allies, these presented different questions altogether: Whigs typically sympathized with the oppression of the Indians or the Americans, but optimistically assumed that the unbridled power of the revolutionaries in France would be liberating. To Burke, the "malignancy" was the same:

> I think I can hardly overrate the malignity of the principles of Protestant ascendancy . . . as they affect these countries, and as they affect Asia,—or of Jacobinism, as they affect all Europe and the state of human society itself. The last is the greatest evil. But it readily combines with the others, and flows from them.[294]

Arbitrary power is the polar opposite of the constitution of freedom; legitimate government is more than the mere will of the sovereign. In a speech directed against the claim by Warren Hastings of "arbitrary power" over the people of India, Burke declaimed:

> [A]rbitrary power is a thing which neither any man can hold nor any man can give. No man can lawfully govern himself according to his own will; much less can one person be governed by the will of another. We are all born in subjection,— all born equally, high and low, governors and governed, in subjection to one great, immutable, preexistent law, prior to all

---

[293] O'Brien, *The Great Melody* at xxiii (cited in note 13).

[294] *Second Letter from Edmund Burke to Sir Hercules Langrishe on the Catholic Question* (May 26, 1795), in 6 *Works* 375, 379.

> our devices and prior to all our contrivances, paramount to all
> our ideas and all our sensations, antecedent to our very exis-
> tence, by which we are knit and connected in the eternal frame
> of the universe, out of which we cannot stir.[295]

In his *Appeal from the New to the Old Whigs*, Burke wrote: "Neither
the few nor the many have a right to act merely by their will, in
any matter connected with duty, trust, engagement, or obligation."[296] Thus, to Burke, "the important, but at the same time the
difficult problem to the true statesman," is to use "moral instruction" and "civil constitutions" to impose restraint on the immod-
erate exercise of power.[297]

Burke understood religion—the consciousness of that "great,
immutable, pre-existing law" to which he appealed in his speech
against Hastings—to be essential to the restraint of power. Without religion, "it is utterly impossible," according to Burke, that
those in power (whether monarchs, aristocrats, or the people)
should "empt[y] themselves of all the lust of selfish will."[298] Knowledge that God's will is superior to man's is the strongest security
against the possibility that the people might imagine that their will
"is the standard of right and wrong."[299] Thus, "[a]ll persons possessing any portion of power ought to be strongly and awfully im-
pressed with an idea that they act in trust, and that they are to
account for their conduct in that trust to the one great Master,
Author, and Founder of society."[300]

For most people within a society, the established church is the
best guarantor of this sensibility of restraint. The Church of England reflects and represents the long-standing beliefs of the major
part of the nation, and thus speaks with the authority of prescription. Such a religion, Burke maintained, is "well fitted to the frame
and pattern of your [the English] civil constitution"; it is a "barrier
against fanaticism, infidelity, and atheism"; it "furnishes support

---

[295] Edmund Burke, *Speech in Opening the Impeachment of Warren Hastings* (Feb 16, 1788),
in 9 *Works* 396, 455.

[296] Burke, *An Appeal from the New to the Old Whigs* (1791), in 4 *Works* 57, 162.

[297] Id at 163–64.

[298] Burke, *Reflections* at 83.

[299] Id at 82.

[300] Id at 81.

to the human mind in the afflictions and distresses of the world, consolation in sickness, pain, poverty, and death"; and it "dignifies our nature with the hope of immortality, leaves inquiry free, whilst it preserves an authority to teach, where authority only can teach."[301] "[T]his national Church Establishment is a great national benefit," he said, "a great public blessing."[302] Indeed, Burke maintained, the English people "do not consider their church establishment as convenient, but as essential to their state." It is "the foundation of their whole constitution."[303]

But there were some in England and many more in Ireland who, for reasons of conscience and conviction, adhered to a religious faith other than that established by law. They, too, deserved the support and encouragement of the law. Their articles of faith may contain error (as, indeed, the established church may contain error), but all religions impart some measure of the truth of the sovereignty of God and therefore the restraint of man. "Do not promote diversity," Burke thus advised, but "when you have it, bear it; have as many sorts of religion as you find in your country; there is a reasonable worship in them all."[304] Burke declared that he would "never call any religious opinions, which appear important to serious and pious minds, things of no consideration. . . . As long as men hold charity and justice to be essential integral parts of religion, there can be little danger from a strong attachment to particular tenets in faith."[305]

Moreover, any attempt to root out dissenting faiths and replace them with the established church is likely to prove not just unsuccessful, but counterproductive. It is easier to destroy faith than to replace it with another. This is what Burke saw to be the consequence of the persecution of Catholics in Ireland, where the Penal Laws were "partly leading, partly driving into Jacobinism that description of [the Irish] people whose religious principles, church

---

[301] Burke, *Speech on the Petition of the Unitarians* (May 11, 1792), in 7 *Works* 39, 57.

[302] Id at 56.

[303] Burke, *Reflections* at 87.

[304] Burke, *Speech on a Bill for the Relief of Protestant Dissenters* (Mar 17, 1773), in 7 *Works* 21, 36.

[305] *Letter from Edmund Burke to William Smith, Esq., on the Subject of Catholic Emancipation* (Jan 29, 1795), in 6 *Works* 361, 365.

polity, and habitual discipline might make them an invincible dike against that inundation."[306] This persecution, to Burke, is "madness and folly." There is no conceivable justification for "driving men . . . from any *positive* religion whatever into the irreligion of the times, and its sure concomitant principles of anarchy."[307]

In these circumstances, Burke maintained that differences among religions must take second seat to the more important conflict between religion and its detractors. "If ever the Church and the Constitution of England should fall in these islands," he wrote, "it is not Presbyterian discipline nor Popish hierarchy that will rise upon their ruins. . . . It is the new fanatical religion, now in the heat of its first ferment, of the Rights of Man, which rejects all establishments, all discipline, all ecclesiastical, and in truth all civil order, which will triumph. . . ."[308] It was therefore just as important to tolerate and protect conscientious members of other faiths as it was to support the established church. He responded to a member of Parliament who opposed extension of toleration to those whom Burke called "conscientious Dissenter[s]":[309]

> The honorable gentleman would have us fight this confederacy of the powers of darkness with the single arm of the Church of England,—would have us not only fight against infidelity, but fight at the same time with all the faith in the world except our own.[310]

The spread of Jacobinism—along with a rising spirit of rebellion—in Ireland gave Burke's advocacy against the Protestant Ascendancy a new urgency. Catholicism ought to be a force for stability and order, but persecution was turning Catholics into allies of revolution. He wrote to an Irish parliamentarian that "in Ireland particularly the Roman Catholic religion . . . ought to be cherished as a good, (though not as the most preferable good, if a choice

---

[306] *Second Letter from Edmund Burke to Sir Hercules Langrishe on the Catholic Question* (May 26, 1795), in 6 *Works* 375, 380–81.

[307] Burke, *Letter on the Affairs of Ireland* (1797), in 6 *Works* 413, 426 (emphasis in original).

[308] *Letter from Edmund Burke to Richard Burke, Esq. on Protestant Ascendancy in Ireland* (1793), in 6 *Works* 385, 398.

[309] Burke, *Speech on a Bill for the Relief of Protestant Dissenters* (Mar 17, 1773), in 7 *Works* 21, 35.

[310] Id at 37.

was now to be made,) and not tolerated as an inevitable evil." As matters stand, "the serious and earnest belief and practice of [Catholicism] by its professors forms . . . the most effectual barrier, if not the sole barrier, against Jacobinism."[311] But instead, as he wrote to another member of the (Protestant) Irish Parliament, the suppression of Catholicism is "driving the people in precisely the opposite direction."[312] He elaborated:

> You make a sad story of the Pope. *O seri studiorum!* It will not be difficult to get many called Catholics to laugh at this fundamental part of their religion. Never doubt it. You have succeeded in part, and you may succeed completely. But in the present state of men's minds and affairs, do not flatter yourselves that they will piously look to the head of our Church in the place of that Pope whom you make them forswear, and out of all reverence to whom you bully and rail and buffoon them. Perhaps you may succeed in the same manner with all the other tenets of doctrine and usages of discipline amongst the Catholics; but what security have you, that, in the temper and on the principles on which they have made this change, they will stop at the exact sticking-places you have marked in *your* articles? You have no security for anything, but that they will become what are called *Franco-Jacobins,* and reject the whole together.[313]

This was Burke's nightmare: the Protestant Ascendancy and the principles of the French Revolution, tyranny and anarchy, advancing hand-in-hand in Ireland, and nothing he could do seemed to make any difference.

In Burke's constitution of freedom, toleration and establishment were not inconsistent principles, but alternative strategies for attaining the same objective: to nurture and strengthen the religious sensibilities that are the best and most reliable source of moral restraint. Burke strove his entire life to uphold constitutional principles of balanced government and incremental change that would protect against the dangers of arbitrary power. But in the end, he

---

[311] *Letter from Edmund Burke to William Smith, Esq., on the Subject of Catholic Emancipation* (Jan 29, 1795), in 6 *Works* 361, 369.

[312] *Second Letter from Edmund Burke to Sir Hercules Langrishe on the Catholic Question* (May 26, 1795), in 6 *Works* 375, 380–81.

[313] Id at 381 (emphasis in original).

said, quoting Virgil's *Aeneid*, "[w]e have but this one appeal against irresistible power—

> If you have no respect for the human race and mortal arms,
> Yet beware the gods who remember right and wrong.[314]

---

[314] Burke, *An Appeal from the New to the Old Whigs* (1791), in 4 *Works* 57, 165. Burke quoted, of course, in Latin.